The life and letters of

John Brown

Liberator of Kansas, and martyr of Virginia

Editor:

F. B. Sanborn

Alpha Editions

This edition published in 2019

ISBN : 9789353604417

Design and Setting By
Alpha Editions
email - alphaedis@gmail.com

THE

LIFE AND LETTERS

OF

JOHN BROWN,

LIBERATOR OF KANSAS, AND MARTYR OF VIRGINIA.

EDITED BY F. B. SANBORN.

BOSTON:
ROBERTS BROTHERS.
1885.

University Press:

John Wilson and Son, Cambridge.

CONTENTS.

THE TOUCHSTONE.

A MAN there came, whence none could tell,
  Bearing a touchstone in his hand,
  And tested all things in the land
By its unerring spell.

A thousand transformations rose
  From fair to foul, from foul to fair;
  The golden crown he did not spare,
Nor scorn the beggar's clothes.

Of heirloom jewels prized so much,
  Were many changed to chips and clods;
  And even statues of the gods
Crumbled beneath its touch.

Then angrily the people cried,
  "The loss outweighs the profit far, —
  Our goods suffice us as they are,
We will not have them tried."

But since they could not so avail
  To check his unrelenting quest,
  They seized him, saying, "Let him test
How real is our jail!"

But though they slew him with the sword,
  And in the fire the touchstone burned,
  Its doings could not be o'erturned,
Its undoings restored.

And when to stop all future harm,
  They strewed its ashes to the breeze,
  They little guessed each grain of these
Conveyed the perfect charm.

                          WILLIAM ALLINGHAM.

INTRODUCTION.

I N that "History of Napoleon I." which he never lived to complete, Lanfrey says: "Do not misconstrue events; history is not a school of fatalism, but one long plea for the freedom of man." In this pleading chronicle there are few chapters more pathetic than the career of my old friend JOHN BROWN, which I long since undertook to set forth, though strangely delayed in completing my task. It was begun in those dismal years when the Southern oligarchy and their humble followers at the North still controlled our degraded politics; and it has been continued through all the vicissitudes, the anxieties, and the assured repose of subsequent years. More than once in those earlier days recurred to me that gloomy magniloquence of the Roman annalist, where Tacitus complains that the tyranny of Domitian had suppressed the unheralded renown of Agricola: "Patient sufferance we showed, no doubt. Our ancestors saw the extreme of license, but we of servility; for our inquisitors would permit us neither to hear nor to tell, — and we might have lost the use of memory along with free speech, if to forget had been no harder than to forego praise. Now at last the occasion has returned, and we speak out; . . . but few of us are left, survivors of others, and even of our old selves, so many years have passed over us in silence, bringing the young to old age, and the old to the very sunset of life." [1]

Since the printing of these pages began, four months ago, two of those who stood with us in the contest against slavery have died, — Dr. CABOT, of Boston, and the famous VICTOR HUGO ; and every year removes the actors and the witnesses of memorable deeds. I have therefore sought to preserve the record of one hero's life, in his own words (when I could), and in the contemporary evidence of those who saw and bore witness to what he did, — mingling myself with the account as little as possible, except for attestation and comment, when doubt might else arise. The plan was at first to print all the extant letters of BROWN, which I fancied would easily find place in a volume of four hundred pages ; but I have in my hands letters enough to fill another book, and have not been able to use them. Those selected, however, exhibit his life sufficiently ; it was straightforward and all of a piece, so that even the details which are here given may seem tedious to some readers. In a second volume, should I live to publish it, on " The Companions of John Brown," I may carry the story further, and complete the record of a remarkable episode in American history. I have aimed at accuracy, but of course have not always succeeded ; and have necessarily omitted much that other writers will supply. My intention has been to put the reader in possession of evidence which either verifies itself or can readily be verified

---

[1] Dedimus profecto grande patientiæ documentum ; et sicut vetus ætas vidit quid ultimum in libertate esset, ita nos quid in servitute, — adempto per inquisitiones etiam loquendi audiendique commercio. Memoriam quoque ipsam cum voce perdidissemus, si tam in nostra potestate esset oblivisci quam tacere. Nunc demum redit animus, . . . pauci, ut ita dixerim, non modo aliorum, sed etiam nostri superstites sumus, exemptis e media vita tot annis, quibus juvenes ad senectutem, senes prope ad ipsos ætatis terminos per silentiam venimus. — TACITUS, *Agricola*, ii.

by a little research. Holding the key to much that has heretofore been obscure or ill related, I have furnished the true connection between events and persons where, in some cases, this had escaped notice. I shall gladly receive any correction of mistakes, but shall not pay much regard to inferential and distorted statements which traverse my own clear recollections, — supported, as these often are, by written evidence which I have not here printed, but hold in reserve.

I could not have completed this task of nearly thirty years but for the constant and friendly aid of the family of JOHN BROWN, who have placed without reserve their papers in my hands. I have had also the co-operation of Colonel Higginson, Edwin Morton, Mrs. Stearns, Lewis Hayden, Thomas Thomas, and other friends among the living; and of the late Dr. Howe, Wendell Phillips, George L. Stearns, F. J. Merriam, Osborn Anderson, and many more, who are now dead. To all these, named and unnamed, I would here return my acknowledgments. Particularly, I must thank those gentlemen of Kansas, my college friend and brother journalist Mr. D. W. Wilder, and Mr. F. G. Adams of the Kansas Historical Society, who by their accurate knowledge of Kansas history and topography, and the free access they have given me to important papers, have made it possible for me to write the chapters that concern their State. I am also indebted to Mr. James Redpath, Mr. Richard Hinton, Mr. Frederick Douglass, Mr. W. S. Kennedy, and to many correspondents and admirers of JOHN BROWN whose names are mentioned in the pages that follow. I might include in this ·acknowledgment a few malicious slanderers and misjudging censors of BROWN, who by their publications have caused the whole truth to be more carefully searched out.

LIFE AND LETTERS OF JOHN BROWN.

CHAPTER I.

ANCESTRY AND CHILDHOOD.

WHEN a man of mark is to appear in the world and give a new turn to the affairs of men, there has always been preparation made for him. Even the weeds and vermin of the field have their heredity and evolution, — much more a predestined hero like John Brown, of Kansas and Virginia. His valor, his religion, his Saxon sense, his Calvinistic fanaticism, his tender and generous heart were inherited from a long line of English, Dutch, and American ancestors, — men and women neither famous nor powerful, nor rich, but devout, austere, and faithful; above all free, and resolved that others should be free like themselves.

No genealogist has yet traced the English forefathers of Peter Brown the carpenter, who came over in the "Mayflower," and landed at Plymouth with the other Pilgrims in December, 1620; but his presence in that famous band is evidence enough of his character, even if the deeds of his descendants had not borne witness to it. He drew his house-lot on Leyden Street in the little town, with Bradford, Standish, and Winslow, and like them soon migrated to Duxbury, at the head of Plymouth Bay, where his family dwelt after his early death, in 1633, not far from Standish's abode at the foot of "Captain's Hill." A brother of Peter, John Brown, a weaver (sometimes confounded with a more distinguished John, who became a magistrate), also lived at Duxbury, and took some care of his deceased brother's four children, — two sons and two daughters, — who survived him. Peter Brown was unmarried when he landed at Plymouth, but within the next thirteen years he was twice married, and died, — as we learn from unquestionable authority, the "History of Plymouth Plantation," left in manuscript by William Bradford, who succeeded Carver in 1621 as governor of the colony, and died in 1657. Writing about 1650, Bradford says : "Peter Brown married twice. By his first wife he had two children, who are living, and both of them married, and one of them hath two children; by his second wife he had two more. He died about sixteen years since." It is supposed that his first wife was named Martha, and that Mary and Priscilla Brown were her daughters, — the two who are mentioned by Bradford as married in 1650. In 1644 they were placed with their uncle John, and in due time received each £15, which their father had left them by will. The rest of Peter's small estate went to his second wife and her two sons, of whom the younger, born in 1632, at Duxbury, was the ancestor of the Kansas captain.[1] He was named Peter for his father, removed from Duxbury to Windsor in Connecticut between 1650 and 1658, and there married Mary, daughter of Jonathan Gillett, by whom he had thirteen children. He died at Windsor, March 9, 1692, leaving to his family an estate of £409. One of his children, John Brown, born at Windsor, Jan. 8, 1668, married Elizabeth Loomis in 1691, and had eleven children. Among these was John Brown (born in 1700, died in 1790), who was the father and the survivor of the Revolutionary Captain John Brown, of West Simsbury. He lived and died in Windsor, there married Mary Eggleston, and Captain John Brown just mentioned, the grandfather of our hero, was his

---

[1] It would be curious to trace the English ancestry of Captain Brown, which, some suppose, goes back to that stout-hearted John Brown of Henry VIII.'s time, who was one of the victims of Popish persecution in the early years of that king. Fox, in his "Book of Martyrs," tells the story of his martyrdom at the stake, in the early summer of 1511, at Ashford, where he dwelt ; and adds that his son, Richard Brown, was imprisoned for his faith in the latter days of Queen Mary, and would have been burned but for the proclaiming of Queen Elizabeth, in 1558.

oldest son, born Nov. 4, 1728. He married Hannah Owen,
of Welsh descent, in 1758, whose father was Elijah Owen, of
Windsor, and her first ancestor in this country John Owen,
a Welshman who married in Windsor in 1650, just before
young Peter Brown went thither from Duxbury. A few
years afterward an Amsterdam tailor, Peter Miles or Mills,
came to Connecticut from Holland, settled in Bloomfield
near Windsor, and became the ancestor of John Brown's
grandmother, Ruth Mills, of West Simsbury. Thus three
streams of nationality — English, Welsh, and Dutch — united
in New England to form the parentage of John Brown.
His forefathers were mostly farmers, and among them was
the proper New England proportion of ministers, deacons,
squires, and captains. Both his grandfathers were officers
in the Connecticut contingent to Washington's army, and
one of them, Captain John Brown, died in the service. It
is his gravestone which the pilgrim to his grandson's grave,
in the Adirondac woods, sees standing by the great rock
that marks the spot; and among the other inscriptions [1]
which there preserve the memory of his slaughtered descendants, that of the Revolutionary captain stands first.

Owen Brown, — "Squire Owen," — son of this captain,
and father of the Kansas captain, was named for his mother's

[1] These remarkable epitaphs, several of which were written by John
Brown, of Kansas, are as follows : —

In
Memory of
CAPT. JOHN BROWN,
who Died at
New York, Sept. yᵉ
3, 1775, in the 48
year of his age.

JOHN BROWN
Born May 9, 1800
Was executed at Charlestown
Va., Dec. 2, 1859.

In memory of
FREDERICK,
Son of John and Dianthe
BROWN,

Born Dec. 31, 1830, and
Murdered at Osawatomie,
Kansas, Aug. 30, 1856, ·
For his adherence to
the cause of freedom.

WATSON BROWN
Born Oct. 7, 1835, was wounded
at Harper's Ferry,
Oct. 17, and Died
Oct. 19, 1859.

OLIVER BROWN
Born May 9, 1839, was
Killed at Harper's Ferry
Oct. 17, 1859.

family, and was the earliest of these Browns who seems to
have left any written memoirs. He migrated from Connecticut to Ohio, among the first of those who settled on
the Western Reserve, early in the century, and when nearly
eighty years old, while living at Hudson, Ohio, wrote an
autobiography for his children's perusal, which gives some
characteristic details of the state of society where he lived,
and where his renowned son was born.

OWEN BROWN'S AUTOBIOGRAPHY.

"My life has been of little worth, mostly filled up with vanity.
I was born at West Simsbury (now Canton), Connecticut, Feb. 16,
1771. I have but little recollection of what took place until the years
'75 and '76. I remember the beginning of war, and some things that
took place in 1775; but only a little until '76, when my father went
into the army.[1] He was captain in the militia of Connecticut, and
died in New York, with the dysentery, a few weeks after leaving
home. My mother had ten children at the time of my father's death,
and one born soon after, making eleven of us all. The first five
were daughters, the oldest about eighteen;[2] the next three were
sons; then two daughters, and the youngest a son. The care and
support of this family fell mostly on my mother. The laboring men
were mostly in the army. She was one of the best of mothers;
active and sensible. She did all that could be expected of a mother;
yet for want of help we lost our crops, then our cattle, and so became
poor. I very well remember the dreadful hard winter of 1778–79.
The snow began to fall in November, when the water was very low
in the streams; and while the snow was very deep, one after another
of our hogs and sheep would get buried up, and we had to dig them
out. Wood could not be drawn with teams, and was brought on
men's shoulders, they going on snow-shoes until paths were made
hard enough to draw wood on hand-sleds. The snow was said to
be five feet deep in the woods. Milling of grain could not be had,
only by going a great distance; and our family were driven to the
necessity of pounding corn for food. We lost that winter almost
all of our cattle, hogs, and sheep, and were reduced very low by
the spring of 1779.

---

[1] He entered the army of Washington in the summer of 1776, and died
shortly before the battle of Long Island, in which his regiment took part.

[2] John Brown married Hannah Owen in 1758, and his eldest daughter
was but little more than seventeen at his death in 1776.

" I lived at home in 1782; this was a memorable year, as there was
a great revival of religion in the town of Canton. My mother and my
older sisters and brother John dated their hopes of salvation from
that summer's revival, under the ministry of the Rev. Edward Mills.
I cannot say as I was a subject of the work; but this I *can* say, that
I then began to hear preaching.[1] I can now recollect most, if not
all, of those I heard preach, and what their texts were. The change
in our family was great; family worship, set up by brother John,
was ever afterward continued. There was a revival of singing in
Canton, and our family became singers. Conference meetings were
kept up constantly, and singing meetings, — all of which brought
our family into a very good association, — a very great aid of restraining grace.

" About 1784 the Rev. Jeremiah Hallock [2] became the minister at
Canton. I used to live with him at different times, and received a
great deal of good instruction from him. About this time I began to
make shoes, and worked mostly winters at shoemaking, and at farming at home summers. In the winter of 1787 I took a trip into
Massachusetts, through Granville, Otis, and Blandford. In these
towns I worked at shoemaking over half of the winter. I was but a
bungling shoemaker, yet gave good satisfaction, was kindly treated
as a child, and got my pay well, in clothing and money. I then
went to Great Barrington, Sheffield, and Salisbury. Here I hired
out to a very good shoemaker, at about half price, with a view of
learning to be a better workman. I returned home in the spring of
1788 and worked on the farm through the summer. In 1789 I lived
at home, but in the fall I went to Norfolk, and worked at shoemaking
all winter, mostly around at houses, for families.

[1] He was then in his twelfth year; his brother John was, perhaps,
fifteen or sixteen. This brother was a faithful and honored deacon of
the church in New Hartford, Conn., for many years. Another brother,
Frederick, born Aug. 14, 1769, in Canton, Conn., represented the neighboring town of Colebrook in the State Legislature during the war of 1812,
but in 1816 removed to Wadsworth, Medina County, Ohio, and assisted in
founding that town. On the organization of the county, he was chosen
senior Associate Judge for fourteen years. During this term of office, the
Presiding Judge having a large circuit, most of the business in Wadsworth
came before Judge Brown, who gained a high reputation as a magistrate
and citizen. " He never spoke disparagingly of a neighbor, nor of any
other church than his own." Two of his sons were physicians of celebrity;
another a successful minister of the Gospel.

[2] The Hallock family were connected by marriage with the Browns, and
we shall find them mentioned hereafter, — John Brown having studied for
a while with the Rev. Moses Hallock.

"In the spring of 1791 we as a family were rising in the gain of property; we had good crops; our stock had increased, and we felt able to make a small purchase of land; our credits were good for the payment of debts. In all this, we must acknowledge the kind providence of God. Our former poverty had kept us out of the more loose and vain company, and we appeared to be noticed by the better class of people. There was a class of young men and ladies that were a little older than my brothers, who had rich parents that dressed their families in gay clothing, giving them plenty of money to spend, and good horses to ride. Oh, how enviable they appeared to me, while my brothers and sisters lacked all these things! Now, while I write, I am thinking what was the change of fifteen or twenty years with these smart young folks. I cannot think of more than one or two that became even common men of business, but a number of them did become poor drunkards, and three came to their end by suicide. God knows what is best.

"In the spring of 1790 I returned and hired out to the Rev. Jeremiah Hallock for six months. Here I had good instruction and good examples. I was under some conviction of sin, but whether I was pardoned or not, God only knows; this I know, I have not lived like a Christian.

"About this time I became more acquainted with Ruth Mills (daughter of the Rev. Gideon Mills), who was the choice of my affections ever after, although we were not married for more than two years. In March, 1793, we began to keep house; and here was the beginning of days with me. I think our good minister felt all the anxiety of a parent that we should begin right. He gave us good counsel, and, I have no doubt, with a praying spirit. And I will say, never had any person such an ascendancy over my conduct as my wife. This she had without the least appearance of usurpation or dictation; and if I have been respected in the world, I must ascribe it to her influence more than to any one thing. We began with very little property, but with industry and frugality, which gave us a comfortable support and a small increase. We took children to live with us very soon after we began to keep house. Our own first child was born at Canton, June 29, 1794, — a son, we called Salmon, a thrifty, forward child.

"We lived in Canton about two years, I working at shoemaking, tanning, and farming; we made butter and cheese on a small scale, and all our labors turned to good account; we were at peace with all our neighbors, and had great cause for thanksgiving. We were living in a rented house, and I felt called to build or move. I thought of the latter, and went directly to Norfolk, as I was there acquainted, and my wife had taught school there one summer. The people of

BIRTHPLACE OF JOHN BROWN.

TORRINGTON, CONN.

Norfolk encouraged me, and I bought a small farm with a house and barn on it. I then sold what little I had, and made a very sudden move to Norfolk. We found friends in deed and in need. I there set up shoemaking and tanning, employed a foreman, did a small good business, and gave good satisfaction. "Feb. 18, 1796, my little son Salmon died. This was a great trial to us. In the spring of 1796 my business was very much increased, but owing to sickness of wife and self, I could not get but a small part of the leather out in the fall. The people became somewhat dissatisfied with me, and things went hard that winter; but when spring returned, my leather came out well, and from that time I gave good satisfaction to the people, as far as I knew. July 5, 1798, my daughter Anna was born in Norfolk. Soon after this, my wife and I made a public profession of religion, which I have so poorly manifested in my life.

"In February, 1799, I had an opportunity to sell my place in Norfolk, which I did without any consultation of our neighbors, who thought they had some claim on my future services, as they had been very kind and helped; and they questioned whether I had not been hasty. But I went as hastily to Torrington and bought a place, although I had but little acquaintance there. I was quick on the move, and we found there good neighbors, and were somewhat prosperous in business. In 1800, May 9, John was born, one hundred years after his great grandfather; nothing else very uncommon. We lived in peace with all men, so far as I know. (I might have said the years of '98 and '99 were memorable years of revivals of religion in the churches of our town and the towns about us. Perhaps there has never been so general a revival since the days of Edwards and Whitfield.) April 30, 1802, my second son Salmon was born.

"In 1804 I made my first journey to Ohio. I left home on the 8th of August, came through Pennsylvania and saw many new things. Arrived in Hudson about the 1st of September; found the people very harmonious and middling prosperous, and mostly united in religious sentiments. I made a small purchase of land at the centre of Hudson, with the design of coming at a future day. I went to Austinburg, and was there taken sick, which proved to be the fever and ague; was there a month, very sick and homesick. I started for home against counsel, and had a very hard journey, — ague almost every day or night, — but arrived home on the 16th of October. I had the ague from time to time over one year; yet my determination to come to Ohio was so strong that I started with my family in company with Benjamin Whedon, Esq., and his family, on the 9th of June, 1805. We came with ox teams through Pennsylvania, and I found Mr. Whedon a very kind and helpful companion on the road.

"We arrived in Hudson on the 27th of July, and were received with many tokens of kindness. We did not come to a land of idleness; neither did I expect it. Our ways were as prosperous as we had reason to expect. I came with a determination to help build up, and be a help in the support of religion and civil order. We had some hardships to undergo, but they appear greater in history than they were in reality. I was often called to go into the woods to make division of lands, sometimes sixty or seventy miles from home, and be gone some weeks, sleeping on the ground, and that without serious injury.

"When we came to Ohio the Indians were more numerous than the white people, but were very friendly, and I believe were a benefit rather than an injury. In those days there were some that seemed disposed to quarrel with the Indians, but I never had those feelings. They brought us venison, turkeys, fish, and the like; sometimes they wanted bread or meal more than they could pay for at the time, but were always faithful to pay their debts. In September, 1806, there was a difficulty between two tribes: the tribe on the Cuyahoga River came to Hudson, and asked for assistance to build them a log-house that would be a kind of fort to shelter their women and children from the firearms of their enemy. Most of our men went with teams, and chopped, drew, and carried logs, and put up a house in one day, for which they appeared very grateful. They were our neighbors until 1812, but when the war commenced with the British, the Indians left these parts mostly, and rather against my wishes.

"In Hudson my business went on very well, and we were somewhat prosperous in most of our affairs. The company that we received being of the best kind, the missionaries of the gospel and leading men travelling through the country called on us, and I became acquainted with the business people and ministers in all parts of the Western Reserve, and some in Pennsylvania. In 1807 (Feb. 13) Frederick, my sixth child, was born. I do not think of anything else to notice but the common blessings of health, peace, and prosperity, for which I would ever acknowledge the goodness of God with thanksgiving. I had a very pleasant, orderly family, until Dec. 9, 1808, when all my earthly prospects seemed to be blasted. My beloved wife gave birth to an infant daughter who died in a few hours; as my wife expressed it, 'She had a short passage through time.' My wife followed a few hours after. These were days of affliction. I was left with five small children (six, including Levi Blakesly, my adopted son), the eldest but about ten and a half years old: The remembrance of this scene makes my heart bleed now. These were the first that were buried in the ground now occupied as a cemetery at the centre of Hudson. I kept my children mostly around me, and married my second wife, Sally Root, Nov. 8, 1809. Through all these changes I experienced much of the goodness of God in the enjoyment of health in myself and family, and general prosperity in my business. April 19, 1811, Sally Marian was born.

" In July, 1812, the war with England began ; and this war called loudly for action, liberality, and courage. This was the most active part of my life. We were then on the frontier, and the people were much alarmed, particularly after the surrender of General Hull at Detroit. Our cattle, horses, and provisions were all wanted. Sick soldiers were returning, and needed all the assistance that could be given them. There was great sickness in different camps, and the travel was mostly through Hudson, which brought sickness into our families. By the first of 1813 there was great mortality in Hudson. My family were sick, but we had no deaths. July 22, 1813, Watson Hughs, my seventh son was born ; he was a very thrifty, promising child. We were mostly under the smiles of a kind Providence. Florilla, my fourth daughter, was born May 19, 1816. From this time I had many calls from home, and was called to fill some places of trust which others were more capable of filling. I now believe it was an injury to my family for me to be away from them so much ; and here I would say that the care of our own families is the pleasantest and most useful business we can be in. Jeremiah Root, my eighth son, was born Nov. 8, 1819, and Edward, my ninth son, July 13, 1823.

" Nothing very uncommon in this period, save that there was a change in general business matters. Money became scarce, property fell, and that which I thought well bought would not bring its cost. I had made three or four large purchases in which I was a heavy loser. I can say the loss or gain of property in a short time appears of but little consequence ; they are momentary things, and will look very small in eternity. Job left us a good example. About this time my son Salmon was studying law at Pittsburgh. I had great anxiety and many fears on his account. Sept. 21, 1825, Martha, our fifth daughter, was born ; Sept. 18, 1826, she died from whooping-cough. Lucian, my tenth son, was born Sept. 18, 1829. Here I will say my earthly cares were too many for the good of my family and for my own comfort in religion. I look back upon my life with but little satisfaction, but must pray, ' Lord, forgive me for Christ's sake, or I must perish.' Jan. 29, 1832, my son Watson died, making a great breach in my family. He had not given evidence in health of being a Christian, but was in great anxiety of mind in his sickness ; we sometimes hope he died in Christ. Martha, my sixth daughter, was born June 18, 1832 ; and Sept. 6, 1833, Salmon, my third son, died in New Orleans with yellow fever. He was a lawyer, and editor of a French and English newspaper called the ' New Orleans Bee ; '

was of some note as a gentleman, but I never knew that he gave evidence of being a Christian. Aug. 11, 1840, my second wife died with consumption, which she had been declining under for a long time. I think she died a Christian. Here my old wounds were broken open anew, and I had great trials.

"Some little time before this there had been great speculation in village lots, and I had suffered my name to be used as security at the banks. My property was in jeopardy; I expected all to be lost. I had some to pity me, but very few to help me; so I learned that outward friendship and property are almost inseparably connected. There were many to inform me that I had brought my troubles upon myself. April, 1841, I was married to the Widow Lucy Hinsdale. My worldly burdens rather increased, but I bore them with much patience. April, 1843: about this time my family had so scattered — some by marriage and other ways — that I thought best to leave my favorite house and farm, and to build new at the centre of Hudson.

. . . I have great reason to mourn my unfaithfulness to my children. I have been much perplexed by the loss of property, and a long tedious lawsuit; while my health has been remarkably good for one of my age, and I have great reason for thanksgiving."

This artless narrative, written by Owen Brown at the age of seventy-eight, discloses his character, and sketches in some manner the conditions of life under which John Brown was born and bred. But another paper from the same hand shows how naturally the son inherited from his Connecticut ancestors his hatred of slavery. Owen Brown thus described, about 1850, some events of which he had been cognizant sixty or seventy years earlier : —

"I am an Abolitionist. I know we are not loved by many; I have no confession to make for being one, yet I wish to tell how long I have been one, and how I became so. I have no hatred to negroes. When a child four or five years old, one of our nearest neighbors had a slave that was brought from Guinea. In the year 1776 my father was called into the army at New York, and left his work undone. In August, our good neighbor Captain John Fast, of West Simsbury, let my mother have the labor of his slave to plough a few days. I used to go out into the field with this slave, — called Sam, — and he used to carry me on his back, and I fell in love with him. He worked but a few days, and went home sick with the pleurisy, and died very suddenly. When told that he would die, he said he should go to Guinea, and wanted victuals put up for the journey. As I recollect, this was the first funeral I ever attended in the days of my youth. There were but three or four slaves in West Simsbury. In the year 1790, when I lived with the Rev. Jeremiah Hallock, the Rev. Samuel Hopkins, D.D. came from Newport, and I heard him talking with Mr. Hallock about slavery in Rhode Island, and he denounced it as a great sin. I think in the same summer Mr. Hallock had sent to him a sermon or pamphlet-book, written by the Rev. Jonathan Edwards, then at New Haven. I read it, and it denounced slavery as a great sin. From this time I was antislavery, as much as I be now. In the year 1798 I lived in Norfolk. There was a Presbyterian or Congregational minister settled in Virginia at the beginning of the Revolutionary War, by the name of Thomson, who on account of the war came to North Canaan with slaves, and not knowing how long the war would last, he bought a small farm in North Canaan, and lived on it till the close of the war; he then moved back to Virginia, and left a family of blacks on the farm. About 1798 he came up to sell his farm and move back his slaves, as he called them. Some time before this, slavery had been abolished in Connecticut. Mr. Thomson had difficulty in getting away his slaves. One man would not go, and ran into the woods, and Mr. Thomson hired help to catch him. He was secreted among blacks that lived in a corner of Norfolk. Mr. Thomson preached for Mr. Robbins at Norfolk, assisted in the administration of the sacrament, etc. There were blacks who belonged to the church, that absented themselves. Mr. Thomson attended meetings, I think, three Sabbaths; preached about twice. The last Sabbath it was expected he would preach in the afternoon; but there were a number of the church members who were dissatisfied with his being asked to preach, and requested Deacon Samuels and Deacon Gaylord to go and ask Mr. Robbins not to have Mr. Thomson preach, as it was giving dissatisfaction. There was some excitement amongst the people, some in favor and some against Mr. Thomson; there was quite a debate, and large numbers to hear. Mr. Thomson said he should carry the woman and children, whether he could get the man or not. An old man asked him if he would part man and wife, contrary to their minds. He said: ' I married them myself, and did not enjoin obedience on the woman.' He was asked if he did not consider marriage to be an institution of God ; he said he did. He was again asked why he did not do it in conformity to God's word. He appeared checked, and only said it was the custom. He was told that the blacks were free by act of the Legislature of Connecticut; he replied that he belonged to another State, and that Connecticut had no control over his property. I think he did not get away his ' property,' as he called it. Ever since, I have been an Abolitionist; and I am so near the end of life I think I shall die an Abolitionist."

To these papers of his father should now be added John Brown's own account of his childhood and youth, written for Harry Stearns, a boy of thirteen. This is printed and punctuated exactly as Brown wrote it.

THE CHILDHOOD OF JOHN BROWN.

RED ROCK, IA., 15th July, 1859.
MR. HENRY L. STEARNS.

MY DEAR YOUNG FRIEND, — I have not forgotten my promise to write you ; but my constant care, & anxiety have obliged me to put it off a long time. I do not flatter myself that I *can* write anything which will very much interest you : but have concluded to send you a short story of a certain boy of my acquaintance : & for convenience & shortness of name, I will call him John. This story will be mainly a narration of follies and errors; which it is to be hoped *you may avoid ;* but there is one thing connected with it, which will be calculated to encourage any young person to persevering effort ; & that is the degree of success *in accomplishing his objects* which to a great degree marked the course of this boy throughout my entire acquaintance with him ; notwithstanding his moderate capacity; & still more moderate acquirements.

John was born May 9th, 1800, at Torrington, Litchfield Co. Connecticut; of poor but respectable parents: a deceudant on the side of his father of one of the company of the Mayflower who landed at Plymouth 1620. His mother was deceuded from a man who came at an early period to New England from Amsterdam, in Holland. Both his Father's and his Mother's Fathers served in the war of the revolution: His Father's Father ; died in a barn in New York while in the service ; in 1776.

I can not tell you of anything in the first Four years of John's life worth mentioning save that at that *early age* he was tempted by Three large Brass Pins belonging to a girl who lived in the family & *stole them.* In this he was detected by his Mother; & after having a full day to think of the wrong; received from her a thorough whipping. When he was Five years old his Father moved to Ohio ; then a wilderness filled with wild beasts, & Indians. During the long journey, which was performed in part or mostly with an *ox-team ;* he was called on by turns to assist a boy Five years older (who had been adopted by his Father & Mother) & learned to think he could accomplish *smart things* in driving the Cows; & riding the horses. Sometimes he met with Rattle Snakes which were very large ; & which some of the company generally managed to kill. After getting to Ohio in 1805 he was for some time rather afraid of the Indians, & of their Rifles; but this soon wore off: & he used to hang about them quite as much as was consistent with good manners ; & learned a trifle of their talk. His father learned to dress Deer Skins, & at 6 years old John was installed a young Buck Skin. He was perhaps rather observing as he ever after remembered the entire process of Deer Skin *dressing ;* so that he could at any time dress his own leather such as Squirel, Raccoon, Cat, Wolf and Dog Skins, and also learned to make Whip Lashes, which brought him some change at times, & was of considerable service in many ways. At Six years old he began to be a rambler in the wild new country finding birds and squirrels and sometimes a wild Turkey's nest. But about this period he was placed in the school of *adversity ;* which my young friend was a most necessary part of his early training. You may *laugh* when you come to read about it ; but these were *sore trials* to John: whose earthly treasures were very *few* & *small.* These were the beginning of a severe but *much needed course* of dicipline which he afterwards was to pass through ; & which it is to be hoped has learned him before this time that the Heavenly Father sees it best to take all the little things out of his hands which he has ever placed in them. When John was in his Sixth year a poor *Indian boy* gave him a Yellow Marble the first he had ever seen. This he thought a great deal of; & kept it a good while ; but at last *he lost it* beyond recovery. *It took years to heal the wound* & I *think* he cried at times about it. About Five months after this he caught a young Squirrel tearing off his tail in doing it ; & getting severely bitten at the same time himself. He however held on *to the little bob tail Squirrel ;* & finally got him perfectly tamed, so that he almost idolized his pet. *This too he lost ;* by its wandering away; or by getting killed ; & for a year or two John was *in mourning ;* and looking at all the Squirrels he could see to try & discover Bobtail, *if possible.* I must not neglect to tell you of a verry *bad & foolish* habbit to which John was somewhat addicted. I mean *telling lies ;* generally to screen himself from blame ; or from punishment. He could not well endure to be reproached ; & I now think had he been oftener encouraged to be entirely frank ; *by making frankness a kind of atonement* for some of his faults ; he would not have been so often guilty of this fault ; nor have been (in after life) obliged to struggle *so long* with *so mean* a habit.

John was *never quarelsome ;* but was *excessively* fond of the *hardest & roughest* kind of plays ; & could *never get enough* [of] them. Indeed when for a short time he was sometimes sent to School the opportunity it afforded to wrestle & Snow ball & run & jump & knock off old seedy Wool hats ; offered to him almost the only compensation for the confinement, & restraints of school. I need not tell you that with such a feeling & but little chance of going to school *at all:* he did not become much of a schollar. He would always choose to stay at home & work hard rather than be sent to school ; & during the warm season might generally be seen *barefooted & bareheaded:* with Buck skin Breeches suspended often with one leather strap over his shoulder but sometimes with Two. To be sent off through the wilderness alone to very considerable distances was particularly his delight ; & in this he was often indulged so that by the time he was Twelve years old he was sent off more than a Hundred Miles with companies of cattle; & he would have thought his character much injured had he been obliged to be helped in any such job. This was a boyish kind of feeling but characteristic however.

At Eight years old, John was left a Motherless boy which loss was complete & pearmanent for notwithstanding his Father again married to a sensible, intelligent, and on many accounts a very estimable woman; yet he never *adopted her in feeling ;* but continued to pine after his own Mother for years. This opperated very unfavourably uppon him ; as he was both naturally fond of females ; &, withall, extremely diffident; & deprived him of a suitable connecting link between the different sexes; the want of which might under some circumstances, have proved his ruin.

When the war broke out *with England,* his Father soon commenced furnishing the troops with beef cattle, the collecting & driving of which afforded him some opportunity for the chase (on foot) of wild steers & other cattle through the woods. During this war he had some chance to form his own boyish judgment of *men & measures:* & to become somewhat familiarly acquainted with some who have figured before the country since that time. The effect of what he saw during the war was to so far disgust him with Military affairs that he would neither train, *or drill ;* but paid fines ; & got along like a Quaker until his age finally has cleared him of Military duty.

During the war with England a circumstance occurred that in the end made him a most *determined Abolitionist:* & led him to declare, *or Swear: Eternal war* with Slavery. He was staying for a short time with a very gentlemanly landlord since a United States Marshall who held a slave boy near his own age very active, inteligent and good feeling ; & to whom John was under considerable obligation for numerous little acts of kindness. *The master* made a great pet of John: brought him to table with his first company; & friends; called their attention to every little smart thing he *said or did:* & to the fact of his being more than a hundred miles from home with a company of cattle alone ; while the *negro boy* (who was fully if not more than his equal) was badly clothed, poorly fed ; *& lodged in cold* *weather ; & beaten before his eyes with Iron Shovels or any other thing that came first to hand. This brought John to reflect on the wretched, hopeless condition, of *Fatherless & Motherless* slave *children :* for such children have neither Fathers or Mothers to protect, & provide for them. He sometimes would raise the question *is God their Father ?*

At the age of Ten years an old friend induced him to read a little history, & offered him the free use of a good library ; by; which he acquired some taste for reading : which formed the principle part of his early education : & diverted him in a great measure from bad company. He by this means grew to be verry fond of the company, & conversation of old & intelligent persons. He never attempted to dance in his life; nor did he ever learn to know *one* of a pack of *Cards* from *another*. He learned nothing of Grammer ; nor did he get at school so much knowledge of common Arithmetic as the Four ground rules. This will give you some general idea of the first Fifteen years of his life ; during which time he became very strong & large of his age & ambitious to perform the full labour of a man ; at almost any kind of hard work. By reading the lives of great, wise & good men their sayings, and writings; he grew to a dislike of vain & frivolous *conversation & persons;* & was often greatly obliged by the kind manner in which older & more inteligent persons treated him at their houses : & in conversation; which was a great relief on account of his extreme bashfulness.

He very early in life became ambitious to excel in doing anything he undertook to perform. This kind of feeling I would recommend to all young persons both *male & female:* as it will certainly tend to secure admission to the company of the more inteligent ; & better portion of every community. By all means endeavour to excel in some laudable pursuit.

I had like to have forgotten to tell you of one of John's misfortunes which set rather hard on him while a young boy. He had by some means *perhaps* by gift of his father become the owner of a little Ewe Lamb which did finely till it was about Two Thirds grown ; & then sickened & died. This brought another protracted *mourning season :* not that he felt the pecuniary loss so much : for that was never his disposition ; but so strong & earnest were his atachments.

John had been taught from earliest childhood to " fear God and keep his commandments ; " & though quite skeptical he had always by turns felt much serious doubt as to his future well being ; & about this time became to some extent a convert to Christianity & ever after a firm believer in the divine authenticity of the Bible. With this book he became very familiar, & possessed a most unusual memory of its entire contents.

Now some of the things I have been *telling of;* were just such as I would recommend to you : & I would like to know that you had selected these out ; & adopted them as part of your own plan of life ; & I wish you to have *some deffinite plan.* Many seem to have none ; & others never stick to any that they do form. This was not the case with John. He followed up with *tenacity* whatever he set about so long as it answered his general purpose: & hence he rarely failed in some good degree to effect the things he undertook. This was so much the case that he *habitually expected to succeed* in his undertakings. With this feeling *should be coupled ;* the consciousness that our plans are right in themselves.

During the period I have named, John had acquired a kind of ownership to certain animals of some little value but as he had come to understand that the *title of minors* might be a little imperfect : he had recourse to various means in order to secure a more *independent ;* & perfect right of property. One of those means was to exchange with his Father for something of far less value. Another was by trading with others persons for something his Father had never owned. Older persons have some times found difficulty with *titles.*

From Fifteen to Twenty years old, he spent most of his time working at the Tanner & Currier's trade keeping Bachelors hall ; & he officiating as Cook : & for most of the time as foreman of the establishment under his Father. During this period he found much trouble with some of the bad habits I have mentioned & with some that I have not told you off : his conscience urging him forward with great power in this matter : but his close attention to *business ;* & success in its management ; together with the way he got along with a company of men, & boys ; made him quite a favorite with the serious & more inteligent portion of older persons. This was so much the case ; & secured for him so many little notices from those he esteemed ; that his vanity was very much fed by it : & he came forward to manhood quite full of self-conceit ; & self-confident ; notwithstanding his *extreme* bashfulness. A younger brother [1] used sometimes to remind him of this : & to repeat to him *this expression* which you may somewhere find, " A King against whom there is no rising up." The habit so early formed of being obeyed rendered him in after life too much disposed to speak in an imperious or dictating way. From Fifteen years & upward he felt a good deal of anxiety to learn ; but could only read & studdy a little ; both for want of time ; & on account of inflammation of the eyes. He however managed by the help of books to make himself tolerably well acquainted with common arithmetic ; & Surveying ; which he practiced more or less after he was Twenty years old.

[1] This was Salmon, no doubt.

At a little past Twenty years led by his own inclination & *prompted also* by his Father, he married a *remarkably plain ;* but neat industrious & economical girl ; of excellent character ; earnest piety ; & good practical common sense ; about one year younger than himself. This woman by her mild, frank, & *more than all else :* by her very consistent conduct ; acquired & ever while she lived maintained a most powerful ; & good influence over him. Her plain but kind admonitions generally had the right effect ; without arousing his haughty obstinate temper. John began early in life to discover a great liking to fine Cattle, Horses, Sheep, & Swine ; & as soon as circumstances would enable him he began to be a practical *Shepherd : it being* a calling for which *in early life* he had a kind of *enthusiastic longing :* together with the idea that as a business it bid fair to afford him the means of carrying out his greatest or principal object. I have now given you a kind of general idea of the early life of this boy ; & if I believed it would be worth the trouble ; or afford much interest to any good feeling person : I might be tempted to tell you something of his course in after life ; or manhood. I do not say that I *will do it.*

You will discover that in using up my *half sheets to save paper ;* I have written Two pages, so that one does not follow the other as it should. I have no time to write it over ; & but for unavoidable hindrances in traveling I can hardly say when I should have written what I have. With an honest desire for your best good, I subscribe myself,

Your Friend,

J. Brown.

P. S. I had like to have forgotten to acknowledge your contribution in aid of the cause in which I serve. God Almighty *bless you ;* my son.

J. B.

This autobiography had its origin, as did so many other words and acts of John Brown in 1857–1859, in the hospitalities of one house in Massachusetts where the old hero was always welcome. Mr. George Luther Stearns, a wealthy merchant and manufacturer of Boston, but living in a beautiful villa at Medford, had invited Brown to Boston in December, 1856, when he came eastward from his first campaigns in Kansas. Brown accepted the invitation, and reached Boston a little after Christmas, 1856, meeting Mr. Stearns in the street and going with him to the rooms of the Massachusetts Kansas Committee, where I first met

2

him. The next Sunday, the first in January, 1857, Brown
went to the Boston Music Hall to hear Theodore Parker
preach, and there met Mrs. Stearns (a niece of Mrs. Child,
the graceful author of "Philothea"), who invited him to
her house in Medford. He spent there the second Sunday
in January, 1857, and made a deep impression on the oldest
son of the family, then in his thirteenth year, by the stories
he told of the sufferings of the pioneer families in Kansas.
Running to the next room, and bringing forth his hoard of
pocket-money, the boy thrust it into John Brown's hand,
saying, "Will you buy something, — a pair of shoes, or
something, — for one of those little Kansas children?"
and then adding, as the old man thanked him, "Captain
Brown, will you not write me, sometime, what sort of a
little boy you were?" Brown looked at him with surprise
and pleasure, and promised him to do so. In due time this
long letter reached Medford, addressed to Harry, but with a
short note to Mr. Stearns at the end of it. Mrs. Stearns,
who at once saw its value, treasured it carefully; and after
Brown's death she requested her friend Mr. Emerson to
make this autobiography part of a sketch of the hero which
he was urged to write. Mr. Emerson admired and praised
it, but was compelled to decline the task of writing Brown's
Life, as also did Henry Thoreau (who knew Brown well) and
Mrs. Child. Then Mrs. Stearns permitted Mr. Redpath to
print it in his biography, for the sake of bringing money to
supply the needs of the widow and children of Brown. It
has been since reprinted again and again from Mr. Redpath's book. I have made my copy from the original letter, and thus corrected some variations in the punctuation
and spelling, which had crept into the published copies.
Brown's writing was peculiar in these respects, and by no
means uniform; but his style everywhere shows the same
vigor and simplicity, and he had the art of Homer and
Herodotus to mingle the colloquial with the serious, without any loss of dignity or effect. He thought humbly of
his own composition, and would sometimes say, "I know
no more of grammar than one of that farmer's calves;"
but he had what is essential in all grammars, — the power
to make himself understood.

The house in which John Brown was born, as mentioned in this autobiography,[1] still stands in Torrington, Conn., in the western part of the town, three miles from Wolcottville, six from Litchfield, and ten from Winsted, on a by-road. It much resembles the old farm-house in Concord in which Thoreau was born, and the engraving of one might easily pass for that of the other. The log-house of Owen Brown, in Hudson, Ohio, stood on what is now the public square in that town; and in a little valley near by, not far from the railroad, was the tannery where John Brown learned his father's trade. His childhood was passed in Hudson and its vicinity in the manner above described. He read the Bible, the " Fables of Æsop," the " Life of Franklin," the hymns of Dr. Watts, " Pilgrim's Progress," and a few more books; but his school education was very scanty.

Although in order of time the following correspondence belongs in a later chapter, I introduce it here to show what were the relations throughout life of John Brown and his father. The latter lived till within four years of John Brown's execution, dying May 8, 1856, at the age of eighty-five. Only six weeks before his death he wrote as follows to his son in Kansas, — *verbatim et literatim :* —

Letter of Owen Brown to John Brown.

HUDSON (OHIO), March 27, '56.

DEAR SON JOHN, — I received yours of 13th on the 25th, and was very glad to larn that all your Famelys were so well, and that you had not been distourbed by the enemy. Your letters come very regular, and we look carfuly after them. I have been faithfull to answer

---

[1] It was after hearing this letter read that Miss Osgood, of Medford, remarked, " If Captain Brown had not been called, in the providence of God, to a very different work, what charming stories he could have written for young children ! " The original manuscript fills six pages of closely written letter-paper, without division into paragraphs. The contributions made by Harry Stearns and by others "in aid of the cause in which I serve," were given to help the oppressed pioneers of Kansas whom Brown was then defending. His father, Owen Brown, as a beef contractor, was with Hull's army at or just before the surrender at Detroit in 1812, accompanied by his son John. John, then twelve years old, circulated among the American soldiers and officers, and overheard many conversations in camp

them, not out of ambishon, but to keep one or more on the road all the time. My health at present is not so good; for three weeks past I am somewhat put to it to breathe, mostly nights, and sometimes feel as though death was at the dore. I feel as though God was very mersofull to keep such a great sinner on probation so long. I ask all of you to pray more earnestly for the salvation of my soul than for the life of my body, and that I may give myself and all I have up to Christ, and honer him by a sacrafise of all we have.

I think that the moovments of Congress will prevent an invasion of your rights ; they have voted to send to Kansas to investigate the situation [and] elections. I think of cliping from some papers some short Acts of Congress and incluse them in a private letters and send them to you. I think I shall have them very regular. I wrote Mr. Giddeons[1] [" Giddings " in John Brown's hand written over this name] about 3 weeks ago to send me the debats and Acts of Congress on the subjects of Kansas from time to time. He was at home then sick, but has now returned to Con [in John Brown's hand " Washington " is written in before " Con "] and the papers begin to come.

Friends are midling well as far as I know. I am now at Edward's ; it is rather a cold, stormy day. We have had a remarkable cold, snowe winter, and the snow is mostly on the ground now. We have 3 only plesent dayes this week, but have had no rain through the winter. I consider all of my Children at Kansas as one Famely, and hope you will take turns in writeing. They are midling well at Edward's, and wish to be remembered.

Your unfaithful Parent,

OWEN BROWN.

N. B. 28th. After writing the above, Edward had a paper from which we clipt the within.[2]   O. B.

concerning General Hull and his position. He saw much of General Cass, then a captain under Hull; and it is to him, no doubt, that allusion is made as one of those " who have figured before the country since that time." Long afterward (in 1857), he told me that he overheard such conversation from Cass, McArthur, and other officers as would have branded them as mutineers, if he could have reported it to the Washington authorities. He believed that Hull was forced into the false position which led to his surrender, by the ill-conduct of his subordinate officers.

[1] Owen Brown and most of his sons and grandsons when in Ohio were constituents of Joshua R. Giddings, the famous antislavery Congressman from the Western Reserve.

[2] This letter is addressed in the feeble handwriting of an old man to " John Brown, Osawatomie, K. T.," and is indorsed in his son's handwriting, " Owen Brown's Letter, March 27, 1856." The original is among

This was the last of many letters written to his son in the
forty years since 1817, when John first left home for long
absences.   A few of John Brown's replies have come into
my hands, chiefly of the years 1846–1849, of which the
following are specimens : —

John Brown to his Father.

SPRINGFIELD, MASS., 29th Oct., 1846.

DEAR FATHER, — Yours of the 22d, telling us of the death of
brother King, is received.   I must say, that, with all his imperfections
and faults, I certainly feel that if he has not been a very warm-
hearted, yet he has been a steady, friend, and on some accounts a
useful friend ; and I mourn his frailties and death sincerely.   You
say he expected to die, but do not say how he felt in regard to the
change as it drew near.   I have to confess my unfaithfulness to my
friend in regard to his most important interest.   I did not fail to write
you, as soon as I returned myself, from want of inclination, but because I thought it would please you quite as much to get a letter from
Jason.   We are getting along moderately with our business, but when
we shall be able to close it up will be difficult to say, for we still
continue to receive large quantities of wool.   Prices rather improve.
We expect to be ready to close up all the lots Jerry brought on in a
very few days.   Have contracted away the lowest he brought at
twenty-five cents per pound.   There is no doubt but we might make
the most advantageous exchanges of wool for any description of
woollen goods that are wanted in the country.   We shall probably
take hold of the business with a view to such exchanges another year.
if we continue the wool business.   We find no difficulty in disposing
of the very coarsest wools, now that we have learned better where to
sell them, and can turn them cash.   Please write often, and let us hear
how you all get along, and what you think proper to say to us.
                    Your affectionate son,
                                        JOHN BROWN.

SPRINGFIELD, MASS., 10th Dec., 1846.

DEAR FATHER, — Yours, dated 2d and 3d December, we received this evening.   It is perhaps needless for me to say that I am
always grateful for everything of that kind I receive from you, and

the Brown Papers in the library of the Kansas Historical Society at Topeka,
from whose invaluable collections I have drawn much material for this
work.

that I think I have your whole correspondence for nearly thirty years laid up to remember you by, — I mean, of course, what you have directed to me. I would further say, that I feel grateful to you, and my brother, for calling to see my dear afflicted wife and children in their calamity. It is a great comfort that *I can* in my imagination *see* my always kind and affectionate old father with them, while at the same time the responsibilities I have assumed constrain me to be absent, very contrary to my feeling (and it may be contrary to my duty, too; but trust not). I mean to return sometime in February, and should feel like one out of prison could I leave to-morrow. I hope you will visit my family as often as you *can* during my absence, and that you will write us often while here. We will endeavor, one of us, to reply promptly at least. We are getting along with our business slowly, but prudently, I trust, and as well as we could reasonably expect under all the circumstances; and so far as we can discover, we are in favor with this people, and also with the many we have had to do business with. I sent home a good supply of excellent cloth for pantaloons, from which you can have some if it suits you, and should arrive safe. If it does not, please write me without delay. Jason took the cloth with him (cost eighty-five cents per yard). I can bring more cloth of almost any kind when I return, should there be need.

When I think how very little influence I have even tried to use with my numerous acquaintances and friends, in turning their minds toward God and heaven, I feel justly condemned as a most wicked and slothful servant; and the more so, as I have very seldom had any one refuse to listen when I earnestly called him to hear. I sometimes have dreadful reflections about having fled to go down to Tarshish.

Affectionately yours,

JOHN BROWN.

SPRINGFIELD, MASS., April 2, 1847.

DEAR FATHER, — Your very kind as well as rational letter I received last evening. I trust I do in some measure realize that only a few, *a very few*, years will of necessity bring to me a literal accomplishment of the sayings of the Preacher. I am quite sensible of the truth of your remark, that my family are quite as well off as though we possessed millions. I hope we may not be left to a feeling of ingratitude, or greediness of gain; and I feel unconscious of a desire to become rich. I hope my motive for exerting myself is higher. I feel no inclination to move my family to Springfield on account of any change that I am itching for, and think it very doubtful whether I ever conclude on it as the best course. My only motive would be to have them with me, if I continue in my present business, *which I am by no means attached to.* I seem to get along middling well, and hope to return in a short time. Wrote Jeremiah some days since. I shall pay ten cents very cheerfully to hear that you are alive and well, at any time; and should not grudge to pay more for such kind and ever seasonable pointing me to the absolute vanity of this world's treasures, as well as the solemn future which is before me. It affords me great satisfaction to get a letter from you at this period of your life, so handsomely written, so well worded, and so exactly in point, both as to manner and (what is much more) matter. I intend to preserve it carefully.

Your affectionate son,

JOHN BROWN.

SPRINGFIELD, MASS., 1st Nov., 1847.

DEAR FATHER, — After some three or four days' delay on the road, we arrived here safe to-day about noon, and found all here well; but our hard hearts are never thankful as they should be. Always dependent and constantly receiving, we are ungrateful enough to be cast off, — if that were our only fault! Our business, so far as I can judge, has gone along middling well during my absence. Watson is not yet very stout, but is perhaps a little improved since I left. We shall all be anxious to hear from Lucian, and from you all, and how you got home from Austinburg, as soon and as often as we can.

Affectionately yours,

JOHN BROWN.

Mr. Hubbard has deeded his swamp farm to John Sherman. Has not sold his thirty-acre lot at Munroville, but has offered it for sale to William Hickox and Kelsey.

Yours,

J. B.

SPRINGFIELD, MASS., 2d Dec., 1847.

DEAR FATHER, — Yours of the 9th November was received a few days since, but I have delayed writing on two accounts since receiving it. One is the greater press of business, and increased anxiety on account of the sudden change in money matters; the other, that it is always hard for me to make out a letter without something to make it out of. We have been middling well since I returned, except John and Watson. John has had a short turn of fever, and Watson has seemed to have a number of complaints, but both are better now. Our business seems to be going on middling well, and will not probably be any the worse for the pinch in the money concerns. I trust that getting or losing money does not entirely engross our attention; but I am sensible that it occupies quite too large a share in it. To get a little property together to leave, as the world have done, is really a low mark to be firing at through life.

> " A nobler toil may I sustain,
> A nobler satisfaction gain."

You wrote us that Lucian seemed to decline. This is not unexpected; but we hope that a life still lengthened may not all be misspent, and that the little of duty to God and mankind it may yet be in his power to do may be done with his might, and that the Lord Jesus Christ will be the end of the law for righteousness, for that which must be left undone. This is the only hope for us *bankrupts*, as we may see at once if we will but look at our account. We hope to hear how you all are again soon.

Affectionately yours,

JOHN BROWN.

SPRINGFIELD, MASS., 16th Jan., 1848.

DEAR FATHER, — It is Sabbath evening; and as I have waited now a long time expecting a letter from you, I have concluded to wait no longer for you to write to me. I received the Hudson paper giving an account of the death of *another* of our family. I expected to get a letter from you, and so have been waiting ever since getting the paper. I never seemed to possess a faculty to console and comfort my friends in their grief; I am inclined, like the poor comforters of Job, to sit down in silence, lest in my miserable way I should only add to their grief. Another feeling that I have in your case, is an entire consciousness that I can bring before your mind no new source of consolation, nor mention any which, I trust, you have not long since made full proof of. I need not say that I know how to sympathize with you; for that you equally well understand. I will only utter one word of humble confidence, — " Though He slay me, yet will I trust in Him, and bless His name forever." We are all in health here, but have just been taking another lesson on the uncertainty of all we hold here. One week ago yesterday, Oliver found some root of the plant called hemlock, that he supposed was carrot, and eat some of it. In a few minutes he was taken with vomiting and dreadful convulsions, and soon became senseless. However, by resorting to the most powerful emetics he was recovered from it, like one raised from the dead, almost.

The country in this direction has been suffering one of the severest money pressures known for many years. The consequence to us has been, that some of those who have contracted for wool of us are as yet unable to pay for and take the wool as they agreed, and we are on that account unable to close our business. This, with some trouble and perplexity, is the greatest injury we have suffered by it. We have had no winter as yet scarcely, the weather to-day being almost as warm as summer. We want to hear how you all are very much, and all about how you get along. I hope to visit you in the spring. Farewell.

Your affectionate, unworthy son,

JOHN BROWN.

SPRINGFIELD, MASS., 5th Feb., 1849.

DEAR FATHER, — I write you at this time more because you said in your last that you "love letters more now than ever before," than on account of anything I have to write. We are here all middling well, except our youngest child, who has been quite feeble since last fall. Owen's arm seems to be improving slowly. We have been selling wool middling fast of late, on contract, at 1847 prices. We have in this part of the country the strongest proofs that the great majority have made gold their *hope*, their *only hope*. I think that almost every product of industry will soon become high, from the fact alone that such a vast number of those who have hitherto been *producers* will cease to be so, and hereafter, for a time at least, be only *consumers*. I am inclined to think that persons who are in debt, and who hold any property of value, are likely to have a most favorable time to get out of debt. Would it not *be well* to have the word go round *amongst all the Browns*, that they may get ready to sell off enough of something to pay all debts? I really wish that Oliver and Frederick[1] would take the hint, and when things get up (which I feel confident they will do), go at once to selling off and paying up. There is no way of making money so easy as by selling when every one wants to buy. It may cost us some little sacrifice of feeling at first, but would open *a new world almost*, if thoroughly done.

I have felt a good deal of anxiety about the injury you received on your way home; was glad to hear that you was in any measure comfortable. I did not intend to put off writing so long; but I always find it exceedingly hard work to write when I have nothing to communicate that is worth as much as the paper and postage. Your letters are not of so barren a character; so that we shall not expect *you* to pay the postage when you write, which we hope will be often.

Your affectionate but unworthy son,

JOHN BROWN.

[1] His brothers, or cousins ; not his sons.

These letters show upon what terms of affection and religious sympathy John Brown lived with his pious father, — a man everywhere respected. Colonel Perkins, of Akron, Ohio, who was the capitalist partner of John Brown in the wool business, and lost money thereby, had no great respect for his partner's prudence, but said : " His father had more brains than John Brown, and was a more prudent man." He was long a trustee of Oberlin College, and it was through him that John Brown was sent to Virginia in 1840, to survey the wild lands there which belonged to that college. John Brown, Jr., says : " My grandfather, Owen Brown, of Hudson, had no son for whom he entertained more sincere regard than for his son John. I was myself for years almost as one of my grandfather's family, and had the best means of knowing." His aunt, John Brown's half-sister, Mrs. Marian Hand, of Wellington, Ohio, now living, confirms this statement. She also furnishes me with some facts concerning her brother Salmon, for whom his father had " great anxiety and fears " while he was studying law at Pittsburg in 1824, and who, he says, " was of some note as a gentleman, but I never knew that he gave evidence of being a Christian."

It seems that Salmon Brown, after beginning to practise law, travelled far and wide over the United States, and particularly in the South, where he finally took up his residence at New Orleans, and became the editor of a newspaper, " The Bee," which was published both in French and English, and seems to have opposed the administration of Andrew Jackson. His career as a journalist was from 1830 to 1833, and he died at Thibodeauxville, or New Orleans, in the autumn of 1833. A letter from John Brown to his brother Frederick thus mentions Salmon's death, among other matters of smaller concern : —

RANDOLPH, PENN., Oct. 26, 1833.

DEAR BROTHER, — I arrived at home without any mishap on Saturday of the week I left you, and found all well.   I had received newspapers from Thibodeauxville during my absence, similar to those sent to father, but no letters respecting the death of our brother.   I believe I was to write father as soon as I returned, but I have

nothing further to write, and you can show him this.   I will immediately let him know what answer I get to the letter I shall send to
the South by this mail, respecting our dear brother.

I enclose fifteen dollars, and wish you to let me know that you receive it.   Destroy my note, and accept my thanks.   If you afford
my colt plenty of good pasture, hay, and salt, it is all I wish, unless
he should fall away badly or be sick.   Your's bore his journey well.
Please tell Milton Lusk that I wish to have him pay over the money
I left with him to Julian, without delay.

Affectionately yours,

JOHN BROWN.

P. S.   I want to be informed of any news respecting Salmon as
soon as any of you get any.

The three following letters are all that I have received
from the papers of Salmon Brown, who wrote a neat hand
and rather a diffuse, ceremonious style, at variance with the
direct, laconic manner of his father and brother, but who resembled them in the earnestness with which he pursued his
objects, and the serious affection he manifested for all his
family, and particularly for his father.

Salmon Brown to Owen Brown, Sr.

HUNTSVILLE, ALA., Feb. 28, 1829.

HONORED FATHER, — In order to avoid that circumlocution of
"compliments," which I have heard you mention as one of the de-
fects of my letters in general, it shall be the object of this to make
known to you, with the least preamble and in the fewest possible
number of words, all that a parent, kind and solicitous as you have
ever been, might desire to know in relation to the welfare of an absent child.   My health, thank God, has been uniformly good since I
was at Hudson last July.   From New York, if I mistake not, sometime in the month of September, I wrote you a letter, and inclosed
one of my printed circulars, by which I presumed you would be made
acquainted with the tour I had in contemplation, and the several
points to which letters might be directed in season to reach me.
This probably was not received till after your return from New
England, which circumstance sufficiently accounts for its not being
answered.   I have pursued almost literally the track indicated by the
circular alluded to, and still intend to persevere, till I have accomplished the entire journey.   My operations have been as successful as
heretofore, though I have experienced more delays than usual.   On

leaving this place, I shall proceed South, by the way of Tuscaloosa and Mobile, to New Orleans; but having business to transact at a great many intermediate places, I cannot determine with any degree of certainty when I shall reach there, or how early I shall be able to leave that place in the spring.

This, I am resolved, shall be my last tour in the United States, at least on the extensive scale I have practised for the last three years. I however still intend to execute the project which I disclosed to you last summer; and I cannot neglect the present opportunity to thank you for the very valuable hint which you suggested to me, in respect of availing myself of the facilities which my travels afford, to collect materials and information to be made use of hereafter in public lecturing. I have reflected much on the subject, and I am fully persuaded the business may be turned to a good practical account, in reference to my intended operations abroad. I am therefore applying myself to the subject in good earnest, both by extending my own personal observations as widely as possible, and by consulting any written authority which may throw light upon my object of research. But pray let this matter, as well as the other, rest for the present between ourselves *exclusively.*

I am exceedingly anxious to receive a letter from you. When shall I be gratified? On my arrival at New Orleans? I hope so. I also hope that you will not be sparing of the local news of your vicinity. I should like to know something of the results of your journey to the East. You doubtless heard of me among our family relations. I am obliged to leave off abruptly, and I will not delay sending this for the sake of filling out the sheet at another time. My love to all our family, and to my friends in general. Adieu.

SALMON BROWN.

ST. LOUIS, June 18, 1829.

HONORED FATHER, — Having ascended the river to this place, and being under the necessity of returning again to Natchez in order to close some unfinished business, I write to advise you of my intended movements. By the ordinary course of steamboat navigation I shall reach there (Natchez) in the course of five or six days, and my stay in that region will be as short as possible. It is my intention afterwards to proceed by the interior of Alabama to Florida, and thence through Georgia and the Carolinas to the North. I cannot at this time name with certainty any place where letters directed to my address would be received, though Tallahassee in Florida would seem to be the most eligible point; at all events, I hope you will write to me there. I left New Orleans without receiving any letters from you, which was a great disappointment. I however made arrangements by which I shall still get them, if any come on to that post-office. I have enjoyed good health and thus far a reasonable share of prosperity in the prosecution of my business, though delays have been more frequent than I anticipated, and of longer duration, which will be the means of detaining me all summer in the Southern country. I beg you will not permit yourself to be uneasy on account of my health. I shall avoid the low country on the sea-coast, and by confining myself to the high ground of the interior, I apprehend very little danger. Finally, go where I may, I am in the hands of the same kind Providence that has heretofore guided me safely through an infinity of perils. I have been preserved, no doubt, for some wise purpose. I hope it may be to accomplish some great good in the world ; if not, why should I desire to live ?

I am still occupied, heart and soul, with the scheme I have intimated to you before. It is the theme of my constant meditations, night and day ; and I am devoting all my leisure moments for its accomplishment. That the design is a good and laudable one, I have no doubt. This gives me confidence to expect great success.[1]

I cannot write more at this moment, but if I am prospered, you shall hear from me frequently. Adieu.

Your affectionate son,

SALMON BROWN.

LOUISVILLE, KY., Aug. 22, 1830.

HONORED FATHER, — I avail myself of the first moment of leisure on my arrival at this place to relieve you from the anxiety which I am conscious you have ere this begun to feel on my account. I could not have neglected writing so long had I anticipated the possibility of being detained so long at the South. One cause of delay after another prolonged the period of my departure from New Orleans till the latter part of July, and having to stop at several places on the river where I had business to look after, and the rivers being almost too low for steamboat navigation at this season, August has almost passed away before I could reach here. My health, thank God, has been uniformly good, and I am quite well at this time.

I am without news from any of my family or friends these several months past, which makes me exceedingly anxious about their welfare. I hope some of you will write instantly on receiving this, and

---

[1] It does not appear what this "laudable design" was, but it must have been, in part at least, of a public nature. At this time Salmon Brown was twenty-seven years old. He was the brother next in age to John, and was at school with him for a time in Connecticut.

direct to Wheeling, Virginia, where I expect to be in the course of three or four weeks. It is impossible for me to determine whether I can visit Hudson this fall or not. I am engaged about some political arrangements in opposition to the present unprincipled and corrupt Administration, to which I have become so committed as not to be master of my own time. The arrangements alluded to have for their object the best interests of our common country ; and believing that I may be instrumental in doing good in this way, I feel it to be my duty to exert my endeavors. I go from this place to Frankfort, thence to Lexington,[1] thence to Maysville, and thence to Wheeling. If it shall be possible for me to visit Hudson before I proceed to the eastward, I will do so.

An infirmity of my nerves, proceeding from an unknown cause, makes it difficult to write legibly. I have been conscious that this was growing on me for years, without being able to apply any remedy. I never lived so temperately as I have the year past. Pray present me to the recollection of my brothers and sisters, and to all my friends affectionately. Years do but increase and confirm the sense of filial duty and gratitude with which I remain

Your son,

SALMON BROWN.

---

[1] Henry Clay lived near Lexington, and it was doubtless in the interest of that statesman and his friends that young Brown undertook this crusade against the " unprincipled and corrupt administration " of General Jackson, who had been elected in 1828 and inaugurated in 1829, in spite of Clay, — defeating John Quincy Adams. I have not yet found copies of Brown's " New Orleans Bee," but doubtless the sting of this journal was directed against Jackson in the city which he rescued from British invasion.

CHAPTER II.

YOUTH AND EARLY MANHOOD.

JOHN BROWN'S childhood passed, like that of most boys in a new country, in the midst of active labor and rude sport, but with little advantage of schooling at home. Like all serious-minded lads of Puritan stock, however, he dreamed at one time of completing his education in a college, and then studying for the ministry. He "experienced religion," and joined the "Orthodox" or Congregational Church at Hudson in 1816. Soon after this he revisited Connecticut, and went to the town of Canton to consult a kinsman of his father, the Rev. Jeremiah Hallock, concerning his studies in divinity, — whose advice was that Owen Brown's son should fit for Amherst College (where his uncle, the Rev. Heman Humphrey, was soon to be President), and that his teacher should be the Rev. Moses Hallock, of Plainfield, in Massachusetts.[1] This school at Plainfield was famous for graduating ministers and missionaries, and the poet Bryant had been a student there a few years before, — Plainfield being next to Cummington, where Bryant was born, and not far from Amherst. No doubt the lad's hope was to fit himself at Plainfield and then enter at Amherst, working his way by his own efforts, as so many young men have since done. But he was at-

---

[1] John Brown seems to have been for a short time at the Morris Academy in Connecticut, in company with his younger brother Salmon, already mentioned. A story of the two brothers is told, how John, finding that Salmon had committed some school offence, for which the teacher had pardoned him, said to the teacher: "Mr. Vaill, if Salmon had done this thing at home, father would have punished him. I know he would expect you to punish him now for doing this, — and if you don't, I shall." That night, finding that Salmon was likely to escape punishment, John made good his word, — more in sorrow than in anger, — giving his brother a severe flogging.

tacked with inflammation of the eyes, which soon became
serious, so that he was forced to give up study, and go back
to his father's tan-yard in Hudson.   The time spent at the
Plainfield school was short, and there are few reminiscences
of him at that period.   In December, 1859, Heman Hallock,
the youngest son of the Rev. Moses Hallock, wrote to
his brother Gerard Hallock, then editor of the New York
"Journal of Commerce," as follows : —

"Your youngest brother does remember John Brown, who studied
at our house.   How long he lived there, or at what period, I do not
know.   I think it must have been at the time of my visits to Plainfield, when I was or had been at Amherst Academy, perhaps in
1819 or 1820.   I have the name 'John Brown' on my list of father's
students.   It is said that he was a relative of Uncle Jeremiah Hallock's wife, and that Uncle J. directed him to Plainfield.   He was a
tall, sedate, dignified young man, from twenty-two to twenty-five
years old.[1]   He had been a tanner, and relinquished a prosperous
business for the purpose of intellectual improvement.   He brought
with him a piece of sole-leather about a foot square, which he had
himself tanned, for seven years, to re-sole his boots.   He had also
a piece of sheep-skin which he had tanned, and of which he cut
some strips, about an eighth of an inch wide, for other students to
pull upon.   Father took one string, and winding it around his fingers said, with a triumphant turn of the eye and mouth, 'I shall
snap it.'   The very marked yet kind immovableness of the young
man's face, on seeing father's defeat, father's own look, and the
position of people and things in the old kitchen, somehow gave
me a fixed recollection of this little incident."

From theology, young Brown turned his attention to surveying ; and his text-book, "Flint's Survey," now owned by
his son John Brown, Jr., bears date at Hudson in 1820.   He
became a skilful surveyor ; but his chief occupation from
1819 for nearly twenty years was the tanning of leather,

___

[1] The maturity of John Brown's appearance at the age of nineteen is
shown by this remark : he could not have been twenty years old when studying at Plainfield.   My own date for this experience would be 1819 ; for Brown
was married to Dianthe Lusk, June 21, 1820.   He had previously been disappointed in love, and as he said in a letter written from Gerrit Smith's
house, Feb. 24, 1858, "felt for a number of years in earlier life a steady,
strong desire to die."   This letter will be found on a later page, in its due
connection.

which his father had taught him, and in which he had acquired much skill before 1820, as may be inferred from his autobiography. His log-house and tan-yard were a mile or more from his father's, and northwest of the village of Hudson. The home which was built under his direction in 1824 is a large wooden farm-house, standing in pleasant rural scenery ; and Hudson itself, which is one of the oldest villages in Northern Ohio, and for many years the seat of a small college, has the air of a thriving Connecticut town. When John Brown first occupied his cabin in 1819–20, he was unmarried, and his housekeeper was Mrs. Lusk, the widow of Amos Lusk, a Hudson farmer, and the mother of Brown's future wife. Her brother, Milton Lusk, who was living in 1882, gave me then some reminiscences of his brother-in-law, which may serve to complete the sketch drawn by Brown himself of his resolute, serious, and headstrong youth.

"I am now seventy-nine years old," said this kinsman of John Brown, "for I was born in 1803, my sister Dianthe in 1801, and Brown in 1800. I knew him from a boy, went to school with him, and remember well what a commanding disposition he always had. There was once a Democratic school and a Federal school in Hudson village, and the boys used to snow-ball each other. Brown and I were federalists, as our fathers, Squire Brown and Captain Lusk, were. One day the Democratic boys found a wet hollow in the battle-field of snow-balls, and began to throw wet balls, which were hard and hurt 'masterly.' John stood this for a while, — then he rushed alone upon the little Democrats, and drove them all before him into their schoolhouse. He did not seem to be angry, but there was such force and mastery in what he did, that everything gave way before him. He doted on being the head of the heap, and he was ; he doted on his ability to hit the mark. Dianthe, my sister, was not tall like my father (who fought at the siege of Sandusky and died in the spring of 1813), but about her mother's height ; she was plain, but attracted John Brown by her quiet, amiable disposition. She was my guiding-star, my guardian angel ; she sung beautifully, most always sacred hymns and tunes ; and she had a place in the woods, not far from the house, where she used to go alone to pray. She took me there sometimes to pray with me. She was a pleasant, cheerful person, but not funny ; she never said anything but what she meant. When mother and Dianthe were keeping house for John Brown at the old log-cabin where he had his tannery, I was working as a boy at Squire Hudson's in the village, and had no

3

time to go up and see my mother and sister except Sundays.[1] Brown
was an austere feller, and he did n't like that; one day he said to me,
'Milton, I wish you would not make your visits here on the Sabbath.' I said, 'John, I won't come Sunday, nor any other day,'
and I stayed away a long time. When Dianthe was married, I
would not go to the wedding. I did not get along very well with
him for some years; but when he was living in Pennsylvania, and I
had my controversy with the church in Hudson, he came and prayed
with me, and shed tears, and said perhaps I was nearer right than he
had thought. After my sister's death he said to John, his son, 'I
feel sure that your mother is now with me and influencing me.' He
was tasty in his dress, — about washing, bathing, brushing, etc.;
when he washed him, he pushed his hair back from his forehead."

John Brown, Jr., who was born at his father's first home
in Hudson, gives the following account of one of his first
recollections of that neighborhood: —

"Our house, on a lane which connects two main roads, was built
under father's direction in 1824, and still stands much as he built it,

[1] Hudson was named for a Connecticut farmer, David Hudson (born in
Goshen, 1758), commonly called "the Squire," who led the settlement
there in 1799, and whose daughter, Mrs. Harvey Baldwin, whom I saw
in 1878, was the first white child born in the town. Her father is
buried in the cemetery not far from the grave of Owen Brown, out of which
a young hemlock tree, twelve feet high, was growing when I visited it
in 1878. Squire Hudson gave the land in Hudson on which the Western Reserve College was built; he was a strict Calvinist, and an original
abolitionist, like Owen Brown. Mr. Elizur Wright, now of Boston,
formerly a schoolmate of John Brown, and afterwards a professor in the
college at Hudson, tells me that he met Squire Hudson, one day in September, 1831, coming from his post-office, and reading a newspaper he
had just received, which seemed to excite him very much as he read.
As Mr. Wright came within hearing, the old Calvinist was exclaiming,
"Thank God for that! I am glad of it. Thank God they have risen at
last!" Inquiring what the news was, Squire Hudson replied, "Why, the
slaves have risen down in Virginia, and are fighting for their freedom as
we did for ours. I pray God they may get it." This was the "Southampton massacre" of Aug. 23, 1831, in which Nat Turner, with six fellow-
slaves, raised a revolt in Southampton County, on the edge of the Dismal
Swamp in Virginia, and had killed more than fifty whites, without the loss
of a single follower, when his band was dispersed on the 25th of August.
Turner escaped arrest for eight weeks longer, but was captured Oct. 30,
1831, tried November 5, and hanged November 11, almost exactly twenty-
eight years before John Brown's execution, Dec. 2, 1859.

with the garden and orchard around it which he laid out. In the
rear of the house was then a wood, now gone, on a knoll leading
down to the brook which supplied the tan-pits. I was born in an
older log-house. When I was four or five years old, and probably no
later than 1825, there came one night a fugitive slave and his wife
to father's door, — sent, perhaps, by some townsman who knew John
Brown's compassion for such wayfarers, then but few. They were
the first colored people I had seen; and when the woman took me
up on her knee and kissed me, I ran away as quick as I could,
and rubbed my face ' to get the black off; ' for I thought she would
' crock ' me, like mother's kettle. Mother gave the poor creatures
some supper; but they thought themselves pursued, and were uneasy. Presently father heard the trampling of horses crossing a
bridge on one of the main roads, half a mile off; so he took his guests
out the back door and down into the swamp near the brook, to hide,
giving them arms to defend themselves, but returning to the house
to await the event. It proved a false alarm : the horsemen were
people of the neighborhood going to Hudson village. Father then
went out into the dark wood, — for it was night, — and had some
difficulty in finding his fugitives ; finally he was guided to the spot
by the sound of the man's heart throbbing for fear of capture. He
brought them into the house again, sheltered them awhile, and sent
them on their way."

At this time John Brown could not have been more than
twenty-six years old. The children of his first marriage
were born, married, and died as follows : —

John Brown, Jr., born July 25, 1821, at Hudson, Ohio ;
married Wealthy C. Hotchkiss, July, 1847.

Jason Brown, Jan. 19, 1823, at Hudson ; married Ellen
Sherbondy, July, 1847.

Owen Brown, Nov. 4, 1824, at Hudson (never married).

Frederick Brown (1), Jan. 9, 1827, at Richmond, Pa. ;
died March 31, 1831.

Ruth Brown, Feb. 18, 1829, at Richmond, Pa. ; married
Henry Thompson, Sept. 26, 1850.

Frederick Brown (2), Dec. 31, 1830, at Richmond, Pa. ;
murdered at Ossawatomie by Rev. Martin White, Aug. 30,
1856.

An infant son, Aug. 7, 1832 ; was buried with his mother
three days after his birth, at Richmond, Pa.

A letter of John Brown to his father, of which only a

portion is preserved, describes the death of his first wife in
the most touching manner. Her character has already been
given in the fragmentary autobiography, and in the recollections of her brother, Milton Lusk. She was descended
through her mother (Mary Adams, of West Stockbridge,
Mass., daughter of John Adams, an army contractor in the
Revolution) from the same ancestors as John Adams the
second President, and Samuel Adams the Revolutionary
patriot.[1] Of the seven children above-named, the four
eldest are still living (1885), — John and Owen at Put-in-
Bay Island, Ohio; and Jason and Ruth (who married a New
Hampshire farmer's son, Henry Thompson, at North Elba,
N. Y.) at Pasadena, Cal. I am indebted to all of them for
many details of their father's career, and many letters

[1] In December, 1867, John Brown, Jr., copied the following record from
the Lusk family Bible in the possession of Judge Stephen H. Pitkin, husband of his aunt Julia Lusk, by which it appears that Mary (Adams)
Lusk was five years older than her husband, and was a widow when Captain Lusk married her : —

Amos Lusk, born Thursday, March 6, 1773 ; Mary (Hull) Lusk (his
wife), born Sunday, May 15, 1768 ; Sophia Hull, born Wednesday, April
29, 1789 ; Laura Hull, born Thursday, Dec. 8, 1791 ; Minerva Lusk, born
Sunday, Oct. 18, 1795 ; Maria Lusk, born Sunday, June 27, 1797 ; Loring
Lusk, born Tuesday, June 3, 1799 ; Dianthe Lusk, born Monday, Jan. 12,
1801 ; Milton Adams Lusk, born Thursday, June 2, 1803 ; Julian H.
Lusk, born Monday, Sept. 16, 1805 ; Sophia H. Lusk, born Thursday,
July 28, 1808 ; Julia Lusk, born Saturday, Feb. 10, 1810 ; Edward Lusk,
born Tuesday, Dec. 31, 1811 ; Laura Hull, married Sept. 23, 1810 ; Amos
Lusk, died May 24, 1813 ; Dianthe Lusk Brown, died Aug. 10, 1832 ;
Mary Lusk, wife of Amos Lusk, died Jan. 20, 1843.

Captain Lusk removed to Ohio from East Bloomfield, N. Y., with his
family, then consisting of his wife and her six children (including Sophia
and Laura Hull by her first husband), in 1801. Several families, including his sister's (Mrs. Hannah Lindley), made up the emigrating party.
Buffalo was then a small village, and Ohio almost an unbroken wilderness.
On their journey, while stopping at a tavern, an incident occurred which
came near terminating the life of Dianthe Lusk, then a baby six weeks old.
While the mother was preparing food for their breakfast, the father, anxious to move on in the morning, proceeded to gather up the bedding, on
which, unperceived by him, the baby was lying. Pillows, blankets, etc.,
were thrown on the feather-bed, and quickly tied together with a rope, and
the whole hastily rolled downstairs. The mother, recollecting where she
had left her baby, gave the alarm, but by the time it could be uncovered
it was nearly lifeless.

which concern the family. Ruth, the only daughter of the
first marriage, gives me these incidents of her early recollections : —

"Father used to hold all his children, while they were little, at
night, and sing his favorite songs, one of which was, 'Blow ye the
trumpet, blow!' One evening after he had been singing to me, he
asked me how I would like to have some poor little black children
that were slaves (explaining to me the meaning of slaves) come and
live with us; and asked me if I would be willing to divide my food
and clothes with them. He made such an impression on my sympathies, that the first colored person I ever saw (it was a man I met on
the street in Meadville, Penn.,) I felt such pity for him that I wanted
to ask him if he did not want to come and live at our house. When
I was six or seven years old, a little incident took place in the church
at Franklin, Ohio (of which all the older part of our family were
members), which caused quite an excitement. Father hired a colored man and his wife to work for him, — he on the farm, and she in
the house. They were very respectable people, and we thought a
great deal of them. One Sunday the woman went to church, and
was seated near the door, or somewhere back. This aroused father's
indignation at once. He asked both of them to go the next Sunday;
they followed the family in, and he seated them in his pew. The
whole congregation were shocked; the minister looked angry; but I
remember father's firm, determined look. The whole church were
down on him then." She adds : " My brothers were so disgusted to
see such a mockery of religion that they left the church, and have
never belonged to another."

This daughter remembers when she was admitted to the
church, in Richmond, by baptism. She says : —

"The first recollection I have of father was being carried through
a piece of woods on Sunday, to attend a meeting held at a neighbor's
house. After we had been at the house a little while, father and
mother stood up and held us, while the minister put water on our
faces. After we sat down, father wiped my face with a brown silk
handkerchief with yellow spots on it in diamond shape. It seemed
beautiful to me, and I thought how good he was to wipe my face
with that pretty handkerchief. He showed a great deal of tenderness
in that and other ways. He sometimes seemed very stern and strict
with me; yet his tenderness made me forget that he was stern. He
told me, a few years before his death, to reason calmly with my children when they had done wrong, and in that way encourage them

to be truthful; and never to punish them, whatever they had done,
if they told the truth about it. Said he: 'If I had my life to live
over again, I should do very differently with my children. I meant
to do right, but I can see now where I failed.'

"Whenever he and I were alone, he never failed to give me the
best of advice, just such as a true and anxious mother would give a
daughter. He always seemed interested in my work, and would
come around and look at it, when I was sewing or knitting; and
when I was learning to spin he always praised me, if he saw that I
was improving. He used to say: 'Try to do whatever you do in the
very best possible manner.'"

Writing to Ruth when she was eighteen years old, her
father said : —

"I will just tell you what questions exercise my mind in regard to
an absent daughter, and I will arrange them somewhat in order as
I feel most their importance.

"What feelings and motives govern her? In what manner does
she spend her time? Who are her associates? How does she conduct in word and action? Is she improving generally? Is she provided for with such things as she needs, or is she in want? Does
she enjoy herself, or is she lonely and sad? Is she among real
friends, or is she disliked and despised?

"Such are some of the questions which arise in the mind of a certain
anxious father; and if you have a satisfactory answer to them in
your own mind, he can rest satisfied."

The testimony of all John Brown's children is the same
respecting his domestic life and his affection for them.
His daughter has perhaps related more particulars of his
home life, because she saw it more constantly, — having
seldom been separated from him until her marriage, except
by his long absences upon business, of which more will be
said hereafter. She thus describes his reading and his
family worship, as she remembers it: —

"My dear father's favorite books, of a historical character, were
'Rollin's Ancient History,' Josephus, Plutarch, 'Napoleon and
his Marshals,' and the Life of Oliver Cromwell. Of religious
books, Baxter's 'Saints' Rest' (in speaking of which at one time he
said he could not see how any person could read it through carefully
without becoming a Christian), the 'Pilgrim's Progress,' and Henry
'On Meekness.' But above all others, the Bible was his favorite
volume; and he had such a perfect knowledge of it, that when any

person was reading it, he would correct the least mistake. His favorite passages were these, as near as I can remember : —

" ' Remember them that are in bonds as bound with them.'

" ' Whoso stoppeth his ear at the cry of the poor, he also shall cry himself, but shall not be heard.'

" ' He that hath a bountiful eye shall be blessed; for he giveth his bread to the poor.'

" ' A good name is rather to be chosen than great riches, and loving favor rather than silver or gold.'

" ' Whoso mocketh the poor, reproacheth his Maker; and he that is glad at calamities, shall not be unpunished.'

" ' He that hath pity upon the poor lendeth to the Lord, and that which he hath given will He pay to him again.'

" ' Give to him that asketh of thee, and from him that would borrow of thee turn not thou away.'

" ' A righteous man regardeth the life of his beast; but the tender mercies of the wicked are cruel.'

" ' Withhold not good from them to whom it is due, when it is in the power of thine hand to do it.'

" ' Except the Lord build the house, they labor in vain that build it; except the Lord keepeth the city, the watchman walketh in vain.'

" ' I hate vain thoughts, but thy law do I love.'

" The last chapter of Ecclesiastes was a favorite one, and on Fast-days and Thanksgivings he used very often to read the fifty-eighth chapter of Isaiah.

" When he would come home at night, tired out with labor, he would, before going to bed, ask some of the family to read chapters (as was his usual course night and morning); and would almost always say, ' Read one of David's Psalms.'

" His favorite hymns (Watts's) were these : ' Blow ye the trumpet, blow !' ' Sweet is Thy word, my God, my King!' ' I 'll praise my Maker with my breath ;' ' Oh, happy is the man who hears !' ' Why should we start, and fear to die !' ' With songs and honors sounding loud ;' ' Ah, lovely appearance of death !' "

John Brown, Jr., says that the first time he ever saw his father *kneel* in prayer was when he communicated to the older children (about 1837) his purpose to make active war upon slavery, and then implored the blessing of God upon such an undertaking, and His pity for the oppressed slaves. The three sons entered into a solemn compact with their father to labor for emancipation ; and when, in 1838, and

subsequently, John the eldest son went from home to get
a better education, his father said "he had lost one of the
main spokes of his wheel." Owen Brown, like his son,
was fervent in prayer; and it was noticed that he, though
a sad stammerer in conversation, spoke much more clearly
in prayer.

There was always great tenderness and delicacy in John
Brown's conduct towards his family, notwithstanding the
natural austerity of his character. In childhood he governed them strictly, not sparing the rod; but no sooner
were they men and women than he ceased to command and
almost to request their obedience, but left it for them to be
persuaded in their own minds towards any course he wished
them to take. He very early imparted to them his own
fixed purposes in regard to slavery, and sought their co-
operation, which they readily gave. Ruth's reminiscences
show this, and so also does this curious letter, written and
franked by John Brown when he was postmaster, under
President Jackson, at Randolph, Pa.[1]

John Brown to his brother Frederick.

RANDOLPH, Nov. 21, 1834.

DEAR BROTHER, — As I have had only one letter from Hudson
since you left here, and that some weeks since, I begin to get uneasy
and apprehensive that all is not well. I had satisfied my mind about
it for some time, in expectation of seeing father here, but I begin to
give that up for the present. Since you left me I have been trying
to devise some means whereby I might do something in a practical
way for my poor fellow-men who are in bondage, and having fully
consulted the feelings of my wife and my three boys, we have agreed
to get at least one negro boy or youth, and bring him up as we do our
own, — viz., give him a good English education, learn him what we
can about the history of the world, about business, about general
subjects, and, above all, try to teach him the fear of God. We think
of three ways to obtain one : First, to try to get some Christian slaveholder to release one to us. Second, to get a free one if no one will
let us have one that is a slave. Third, if that does not succeed, we

---

[1] The town of Randolph in which it was written, and where John Brown
was appointed postmaster in the administration of John Quincy Adams,
seems to have included Richmond, which is now a separate town.

have all agreed to submit to considerable privation in order to buy one. This we are now using means in order to effect, in the confident expectation that God is about to bring them all out of the house of bondage.

I will just mention that when this subject was first introduced, Jason had gone to bed; but no sooner did he hear the thing hinted, than his warm heart kindled, and he turned out to have a part in the discussion of a subject of such exceeding interest. I have for years been trying to devise some way to get a school a-going here for blacks, and I think that on many accounts it would be a most favorable location. Children here would have no intercourse with vicious people of their own kind, nor with openly vicious persons of any kind. There would be no powerful opposition influence against such a thing; and should there be any, I believe the settlement might be so effected in future as to have almost the whole influence of the place in favor of such a school. Write me how you would like to join me, and try to get on from Hudson and thereabouts some first-rate abolitionist families with you. I do honestly believe that our united exertions alone might soon, with the good hand of our God upon us, effect it all.

This has been with me a favorite theme of reflection for years. I think that a place which might be in some measure settled with a view to such an object would be much more favorable to such an undertaking than would any such place as Hudson, with all its conflicting interests and feelings; and I do think such advantages ought to be afforded the young blacks, whether they are all to be immediately set free or not. Perhaps we might, under God, in that way do more towards breaking their yoke effectually than in any other. If the young blacks of our country could once become enlightened, it would most assuredly operate on slavery like firing powder confined in rock, and all slaveholders know it well. Witness their heaven-daring laws against teaching blacks. If once the Christians in the free States would set to work in earnest in teaching the blacks, the people of the slaveholding States would find themselves constitutionally driven to set about the work of emancipation immediately. The laws of this State are now such that the inhabitants of any township may raise by a tax in aid of the State school-fund any amount of money they may choose by a vote, for the purpose of common schools, which any child may have access to by application. If you will join me in this undertaking, I will make with you any arrangement of our temporal concerns that shall be fair. Our health is good, and our prospects about business rather brightening.

Affectionately yours,

JOHN BROWN.

Randolph is in Crawford County, Penn., and now contains
some two thousand inhabitants; but in 1834 it was very
thinly settled. John Brown was one of the chief persons
there; he managed a large tannery in the present township
of Richmond, and the school of the settlement had been at
one time kept for part of the year in his great log-house,
near the tan-yard. His proposition to his brother Frederick,[1] who then lived with or near his father in Hudson,
Ohio, was in effect to remove to Richmond, and take part
in a plan for settling colored families there, with a view to
their better education, before their race should be emancipated. At this time it was a penal offence in most of the
slave States to teach them to read, and practically it was so
in some free States. In the year preceding the date of this
letter, the State of Connecticut (in consequence of the admission by Miss Prudence Crandall of colored girls to her
private school in Canterbury) passed a law (May 24, 1833)
that no school should be established in any town in Connecticut for the education of colored persons from other towns,
"without the consent in writing, first obtained of a majority
of the civil authority, and the selectmen of the town."
Under this law Miss Crandall was arrested and sent to jail;
and during that year (1833) her house was set on fire, and
she was otherwise so persecuted by the people of Canterbury that she was forced to give up her school about a year
before the above letter of John Brown was written.

It was while Brown was living at Randolph (now Richmond) that he was married a second time, July 11, 1833,
to Mary Anne Day, daughter of Charles Day, of Whitehall,
N. Y., but then living at Troy, Penn. She survived him
twenty-five years, and died in San Francisco, in 1884.[2] Her
children were thirteen in number, of whom seven died in
early childhood; two were killed at Harper's Ferry, and
four, — Salmon, Anne, Sarah, and Ellen, — are still living

---

[1] This letter is thus addressed and post-marked : —

Randolph, Pa.   *Free.*

Nov. 22.   *J. Brown, P. M.*

Mr. FREDERICK BROWN,

HUDSON, PORTAGE Co., Ohio.

[2] February 29.

in California with their children and grandchildren. The
record of this whole family is as follows : —

CHILDREN OF JOHN BROWN AND HIS WIFE MARY.

Sarah Brown, born May 11, 1834, at Richmond, Pa. ; died
Sept. 23, 1843.

Watson Brown, born Oct. 7, 1835, at Franklin, Ohio;
married Isabella M. Thompson, September, 1856 ; killed at
Harper's Ferry, Oct. 19, 1859.

Salmon Brown, born Oct. 2, 1836, at Hudson, Ohio ; married Abbie C. Hinckley, Oct. 15, 1857.

Charles Brown, born Nov. 3, 1837, at Hudson, Ohio; died
Sept. 11, 1843.

Oliver Brown, born March 9, 1839, at Franklin, Ohio ;
married Martha E. Brewster, April 7, 1858 ; killed at Harper's Ferry, Oct. 17, 1859.

Peter Brown, born Dec. 7, 1840, at Hudson, Ohio ; died
Sept. 22, 1843.

Austin Brown, born Sept. 14, 1842, at Richfield, Ohio ;
died Sept. 27, 1843.

Anne Brown, born Dec. 23, 1843, at Richfield, Ohio.

Amelia Brown, born June 22, 1845, at Akron, Ohio; died
Oct. 30, 1846.

Sarah Brown, born Sept. 11, 1846, at Akron, Ohio.

Ellen Brown, born May 20, 1848, at Springfield, Mass. ;
died April 30, 1849.

Infant son, born April 26, 1852, at Akron, Ohio ; died May
17, 1852.

Ellen Brown, born Sept. 25, 1854, at Akron, Ohio.[1]

The loss of so many children in their early years was a
sore trial to John Brown, and is often mentioned in his
family letters. In their illness he was a devoted nurse, and

---

[1] It was at the house of this youngest daughter, Mrs. Ellen Fablinger,
of Saratoga, Cal., that the widow of John Brown spent the last years of her
life ; but she died in San Francisco, under the care of her daughter Sarah,
after a painful illness. Miss Sarah Brown resides in San Francisco ; Mrs.
Anne Brown Adams, in Rohnerville, Humboldt County; and Salmon
Brown, farther north, in the same county, where he keeps sheep, as his
father did in Ohio.

he had acquired much skill in the care of all invalids. Concerning the death of his first daughter Ellen, in April, 1849, Mrs. Thompson thus writes : —

" In the fall of 1848, father and mother, with our youngest sister, a babe of six months old, visited a brother of Mrs. Brown (Orson Day), who was then living at Whitehall, N. Y., — she stopping there with the child, while father went into the Adirondac wilderness to North Elba. He was charmed with the grand mountain scenery, and felt that he was needed there to encourage and help by his experience the few colored families who had already settled in the wilderness, and those who might move there the following spring. Here was an opportunity also to train some of the bravest of those men for the great work which had been his life-long study. He went back to Springfield much encouraged. While on their journey back the little babe took a violent cold that ended in quick consumption, and she died at the end of April, 1849. Father showed much tenderness in the care of the little sufferer. He spared no pains in doing all that medical skill could do for her, together with the tenderest care and nursing. The time that he could be at home was mostly spent in caring for her. He sat up nights to keep an even temperature in the room, and to relieve mother from the constant care which she had through the day. He used to walk with the child and sing to her so much that she soon learned his step. When she heard him coming up the steps to the door, she would reach out her hands and cry for him to take her. When his business at the wool store crowded him so much that he did not have time to take her, he would steal around through the wood-shed into the kitchen to eat his dinner, and not go into the dining-room, where she could see or hear him. I used to be charmed myself with his singing to her. He noticed a change in her one morning, and told us he thought she would not live through the day, and came home several times to see her. A little before noon he came home, and looked at her and said, ' She is almost gone.' She heard him speak, opened her eyes, and put up her little wasted hands with such a pleading look for him to take her that he lifted her from the cradle, with the pillows she was lying on, and carried her until she died. He was very calm, closed her eyes, folded her hands, and laid her in her cradle. When she was buried, father broke down completely, and sobbed like a child. It was very affecting to see him so overcome, when all the time before his great tender heart had tried to comfort our weary, sorrowing mother, and all of us."

It was not the temporal welfare and happiness of his children that lay nearest the heart of Brown : their spiritual interests, their religious state, were much more a care to him. His letters show this constantly; and in one written to his oldest daughter three years later (January, 1852), his anxiety finds expression in these words : —

" My attachments to this world have been very strong, and Divine Providence has been cutting me loose, one cord after another. Up to the present time, notwithstanding I have so much to remind me that all ties must soon be severed, I am still clinging, like those who have hardly taken a single lesson. I really hope some of my family may understand that this world is not the home of man, and act in accordance. Why may I not hope this of you ? When I look forward, as regards the religious prospects of my numerous family, — the most of them, — I am forced to say, and feel too, that I have *little, very little*, to cheer. That this should be so is, I perfectly well understand, the legitimate fruit of my own planting ; and that only increases my punishment. Some ten or twelve years ago I was cheered with the belief that my elder children had chosen the Lord to be their God, and I relied much on their influence and example in atoning for my deficiency and bad example with the younger children. But where are we now ? Several have gone where neither a good nor a bad example from me will better their condition or prospects, or make them worse. I will not dwell longer on this distressing subject, but only say that, so far as I have gone, it is from no disposition to reflect on any one but myself. I think I can clearly discover where I wandered from the road. How now to get on it with my family is beyond my ability to *see* or my courage to *hope*. God grant you *thorough* conversion from sin, and full purpose of heart to continue steadfast in his way, through the very short season you will have to pass."

The earlier letters of Brown to his elder children contain many remarks of this character ; and there is one long letter to his son John, mainly made up of Scripture texts arranged so as to bring forcibly to the young man's mind the Calvinistic theology, point by point, — its terrors as well as its promises. Here it is : —

AKRON, OHIO, Aug. 26, 1853.

DEAR SON JOHN, — Your letter of the 21st instant was received yesterday, and as I may be somewhat more lengthy than usual I begin my answer at once. The family have enjoyed as good health as usual since I wrote before, but my own health has been poor since

in May. Father has had a short turn of fever and ague; Jason and
Ellen have had a good deal of it, and were not very stout on Sunday
last. The wheat crop has been rather light in this quarter; first
crop of grass light; oats very poor; corn and potatoes promise well,
and frequent rains have given the late grass a fine start. There has
been some very fatal sickness about, but the season so far has been
middling healthy. Our sheep and cattle have done well; have raised
five hundred and fifty lambs, and expect about eighty cents per pound
for our wool. We shall be glad to have a visit from you about the
time of our county fair, but I do not yet know at what time it comes.
Got a letter from Henry dated the 16th of August; all there well.
Grain crops there very good. We are preparing (in our minds, at
least) to go back next spring. Mrs. Perkins was confined yesterday
with another boy, it being her eleventh child. The understanding
between the two families continues much as formerly, so far as I
know.

In Talmadge there has been for some time an unusual seriousness
and attention to future interests. In your letter you appear rather
disposed to sermonize; and how will it operate on you and Wealthy
if I should pattern after you a little, and also quote some from the
Bible? In choosing my texts, and in quoting from the Bible, I perhaps select the very portions which " another portion " of my family
hold are not to be wholly received as *true*. I forgot to say that my
younger sons (as is common in this " progressive age ") appear to
be a *little in advance* of my older, and have thrown off the *old
shackles* entirely; after THOROUGH AND CANDID investigation they
have discovered the Bible to be ALL a fiction ! Shall I add, that
a letter received from *you* some time since gave me little else than
pain and sorrow? " The righteous shall hold on his way; " " By
and by he is offended."

My object at this time is to recall your particular attention to the
fact that the earliest, as well as all other, writers of the Bible seem
to have been impressed with such ideas of the character of the religion
they taught, as led them to apprehend a want of steadfastness among
those who might profess to adhere to it (no matter what may have
been the motives of the different writers). Accordingly we find the
writer of the first five books putting into the mouth of his Moses expressions like the following, — and they all appear to dwell much on
the idea of two distinct classes among their reputed disciples; namely,
a genuine and a spurious class : —

" Lest there should be among you man, or woman, or family, or
tribe, whose heart turneth away this day from the Lord our God, to
serve the gods of these nations; lest there should be among you a
root that beareth gall and wormwood." " Then men shall say,

because they have forsaken the covenant of the Lord God of their fathers." "But if thine heart turn away so that thou wilt not hear, but shalt be *drawn away*, and worship other gods, and serve them." "Now therefore write ye this song for you, and teach it to the children of Israel; put it in their mouths, that this song may be a witness for me against the children of Israel." "For I know that after my death ye will utterly corrupt yourselves, and turn aside from the way which I have commanded you." "They have corrupted themselves, their spot is not the spot of his children." "Of the Rock that begat thee thou art unmindful, and hast forgotten God that formed thee." "Oh, that they were wise, that they understood this, that they would consider their *latter end !*"

The writer here makes his *Moses* to dwell on this point with a most remarkable solicitude, a most heart-moving earnestness. The writer of the next book makes his *Joshua* to plead with Israel with the same earnestness. "Choose you this day whom you will serve." "Ye are witnesses against yourselves that ye have chosen you the Lord, to serve him." The writer of the book called Judges uses strong language in regard to the same disposition in Israel to backslide : "And it came to pass when the judge was dead, that they returned and corrupted themselves more than their fathers; they ceased not from their own doings, nor from their stubborn way." The writer of the book Ruth makes Naomi say to Orpah, "Thy sister-in-law is gone back unto her people and unto her gods." The writer of the books called Samuel represents Saul as one of the same spurious class. Samuel is made to say to him, "Behold, to obey is better than sacrifice; and to hearken, than the fat of rams," — clearly intimating that all service that did not flow from an obedient spirit and an honest heart would be of no avail. He makes his Saul turn out faithless and treacherous in the end, and finally consult a woman "having a familiar spirit," near the close of his sad career. The same writer introduces Ahitophel as one whose counsel "was as if a man had inquired at the oracle of God ;" a writer of the Psalms makes David say of him, "We took sweet counsel together, and walked to the house of God in company ;" but he is left advising the son of David to incest publicly, and soon after hangs himself. The spot of those men seems not to be genuine.

One distinguishing mark of *unsoundness* with all the Old Testament writers was aversion to the character of the God whom Moses declares in his books, and by whose direction all the so-called prophets affirmed that they spoke and wrote. The writer of the books called Kings says of Solomon: "And the Lord was angry with Solomon, because his heart was turned away from the Lord God of Israel, which had appeared to him twice." The same writer makes

Elijah inquire of Israel: " How long halt ye between two opinions?
If the Lord be God, follow him; but if Baal, then follow him." He
makes Elijah pray thus: " Hear me, O Lord! hear me, that this
people may know that thou art the Lord God, and that thou hast
turned their heart back again." The same writer makes God say
to Elijah, " Yet I have left me seven thousand in Israel, all the
knees which have not bowed unto Baal, and every mouth which hath
not kissed him." The same writer makes John say, " Come with
me and see my zeal for the Lord; " but says of him afterward, " But
John took no heed to walk in the law of the Lord God of Israel with
all his heart." This writer also says of Josiah, " And like unto him
there was no king before him, that turned to the Lord with all his
heart and with all his *soul* and with all his *might*, according to all
the law of Moses; neither after him arose there any like him." The
writer of the book called Chronicles says of Judah, in a time of most
remarkable reformation: " And they sware unto the Lord with a
loud voice, and with shouting, and with trumpets, and with cornets;
And all Judah rejoiced at the oath, for they had sworn with all their
heart, and sought him with their whole desire, and he was found of
them, and the Lord gave them rest round about." Those who wrote
the books called Ezra and Nehemiah notice the same distinguishing
marks of character.

The writer of the book called Job, makes God to say of him:
" There is none like him in the earth; a perfect and an upright man,
one who feareth God and escheweth evil, and still he holdeth fast his
integrity." The same writer makes Eliphaz put to Job these questions, remarkable, but searching: " Is not this thy fear, thy confidence, thy hope, and the uprightness of thy ways?" This writer
makes his different characters call the unstable and unsound, hypo-
crites. Bildad says, " So are the paths of all that forget God, and
the hypocrite's hope shall perish. Whose hope shall be cut off, and
whose trust shall be a spider's web." Zophar says of the same class
of persons, " And their hope shall be as the giving up of the ghost."
Eliphaz says, " Let not him that is deceived trust in vanity, for
vanity shall be his recompense." Job says, " I know that my Redeemer liveth, whom I shall see for myself, and mine eyes behold,
and not another." Zophar says, " The triumphing of the wicked is
short, and the joy of the hypocrite but for a moment." Job is made
to inquire concerning those who deceive themselves (as though the
thing had come to be well understood in his day): " Will he delight himself in the Almighty? Will he always call upon God?"
One writer of the Psalms says of those who did not love Israel's God,
" Through the pride of his countenance he will not seek after God.
God is not in all his thoughts."

A writer of the Psalms, in view of the different feelings of men toward the God of the Bible, has this language : " With the merciful thou wilt show thyself merciful, with an upright man thou wilt show thyself upright, with the pure, thou wilt show thyself pure, and with the froward thou wilt show thyself froward." Again in the Psalms we read, " The *meek* shall eat and be satisfied, they shall praise the Lord that seek him." Again, " The *meek* will he guide in judgment, and the *meek* will he teach his way." " All the paths of the Lord are mercy and truth unto such as keep his covenant and testimonies." " The secret of the Lord is with them that fear him, and he will show them his covenant." " Oh, how great is thy goodness which thou hast laid up for them that fear thee, which thou hast wrought for them that trust in thee before the sons of men ! " " The angel of the Lord encampeth round about them that fear him, and delivereth them." " The Lord redeemeth the soul of his servants, and none of them that trust in him shall be desolate." " Though he fall, yet he shall not be utterly cast down, for the Lord upholdeth him with his hand." " The law of his God is in his heart ; none of his steps shall slide." " But the salvation of the righteous is of the Lord ; he is their strength in the time of trouble." " Mark the perfect man, and behold the upright, for the end of that man is peace." " The Lord will strengthen him upon the bed of languishing ; thou wilt make all his bed in his sickness." " Our heart is not turned back, neither have our steps declined from thy way." " They go from strength to strength ; every one of them in Zion appear before God." " Great peace have they that love thy law, and nothing shall offend them." " Then shall I not be ashamed when I have respect unto all thy commandments." " If I forget thee, O Jerusalem ! let my right hand forget her cunning." " The backslider in heart shall be filled with his own ways." " To the law and to the testimony ! if they speak not according to their word, it is because there is no light in them." " Thus saith the Lord, What iniquity have your fathers found in me that they are gone far from me, and have walked after vanity, and have become vain ? " " Turn, O back-sliding children, saith the Lord." " But they hearkened not, nor inclined their ear, but walked in the counsels and in the imaginations of their evil heart, and went backward and not forward." " Yea, the stork in the heaven knoweth her appointed times, and the turtle and the crane and the swallow observe the time of their coming, but my people know not the judgment of the Lord. " " The heart is deceitful above all things, and desperately wicked ; who can know it ? " " Thy prophets have seen vain and foolish things for thee, and they have not discovered thine iniquity." " They that observe lying vanities forsake their own mercy." " Then they shall answer, Because they

4

have forsaken the covenant of the Lord their God." " Forty years
long was I grieved with this generation, and said it is a people that
do err in their heart, and they have not known my ways." " But
they like men have transgressed the covenant ; there have they dealt
treacherously against me." " Many shall be purified and made white
and tried, but the wicked shall do wickedly ; and none of the wicked
shall understand, but the wise shall understand." " The preacher
sought to find out acceptable words, and that which was written was
upright, even words of truth." " That the generation to come might
know them, even the children which should be born, who should
arise and declare them to their children ; that they might set their
hope in God, and not forget the works of God, but keep his commandments ; and might not be as their fathers, a stubborn and rebellious generation ; a generation that set not their heart aright, and
whose spirit was not steadfast with God." " Who is wise and shall
understand these things ; prudent, and he shall know them ? For the
ways of the Lord are right, and the just shall walk in them ; but the
transgressor shall fall therein."

" Whosoever therefore shall confess me before men, him will I also
confess before my Father which is in Heaven." " And many false
prophets shall arise, and shall deceive many ; and because iniquity
shall abound, the love of many shall wax cold." " And blessed is he
whosoever shall not be offended in me." " They on the rock are
they which when they hear, receive the word with joy ; and these
have no root, and for a while believe, and in time of temptation fall
away." " From that time many of his disciples went back, and
walked no more with him." " He that rejecteth me, and receiveth
not my words, hath one that judgeth him : the word that I have
spoken, the same shall judge him at the last day." " Every branch
in me that beareth not fruit he taketh away." " But if our gospel
be hid, it is hid to them that are lost." " I marvel that ye are so
soon removed from him that called you into the grace of Christ,
unto another gospel." " Ye did run well : who did hinder you that
ye should not obey the truth ? " " Beware lest any man spoil you
through philosophy and vain deceit, after the tradition of men, after
the rudiments of the world, and not after Christ." " For now we
live, if ye stand fast in the Lord." " For the time will come when
they will not endure sound doctrine." " Therefore we ought to give
the more earnest heed to the things which we have heard, lest at any
time we should let them slip." " Let us therefore fear lest a promise
being left us of entering into his rest, any of you should seem to come
short of it." " And we desire that every one of you do show the
same diligence to the full assurance of hope unto the end ; that ye be
not slothful, but followers of them who through faith and patience

inherit the promises." "Now the just shall live by faith ; but if any man draw back, my soul shall have no pleasure in him." "And this I pray, that your love may abound yet more and more in knowledge and in all judgment, that ye may approve things that are excellent, that may be sincere and without offence till the day of Christ." "And make straight paths for your feet, lest that which is lame be turned out of the way, but let it rather be healed." "Looking diligently lest any man fail of the grace of God." "For it had been better for them not to have known the way of righteousness, than after they have known it to turn from the holy commandment delivered unto them." "Nevertheless I have somewhat against thee, because thou hast left thy first love. Remember therefore from whence thou art fallen, and repent." "Be watchful, and strengthen the things which remain and are ready to die, for I have not found thy works perfect before God." "He that overcometh, the same shall be clothed in white raiment; and I will not blot out his name out of the book of life, but I will confess his name before my Father, and before his angels." "Blessed is he that watcheth and keepeth his garments, lest he walk naked and they see his shame. Amen." "And I beseech you [children] to suffer the word of exhortation."

AKRON, OHIO, Sept. 23, 1853.

DEAR CHILDREN. — It is now nearly a month since I began on another page. Since writing before, father has seemed quite well, but Jason, Ellen, Owen, and Frederick have all had more or less of the ague. They were as well as usual, for them, yesterday. Others of the family are in usual health. I did mean that my letter should go off at once, but I have not become very stout, and have a great deal to look after, and have had many interruptions. We have done part of our sowing, and expect to get all our corn (of which we have a good crop) secure from frost this day. We shall be glad to see you here at the time of our county fair, which is to be on the twelfth and thirteenth of October.

I hope that through the infinite grace and mercy of God you may be brought to see the error of your ways, and be in earnest to turn many to righteousness, instead of leading astray ; and then you might prove a great blessing to Essex County, or to any place where your lot may fall. I do not feel "estranged from my children," but I cannot flatter them, nor "cry peace when there is no peace." My wife and Oliver expect to set out for Pennsylvania before long, and will probably call on you ; but probably not until after the fair. We have a nice lot of chickens fattening for you, when you come.

Your affectionate father,

JOHN BROWN.

The blending of spiritual and worldly considerations in
this apostolic epistle is characteristic. The kingdom of
heaven and the affairs of earth were closely associated in
John Brown's mind, as in Cromwell's. He could trust in
God and keep his powder dry. The explanation of his son's
indifference to the Calvinistic Church and its Bible-worship
is not wholly discreditable to the young man, however; and
since John Brown, Jr., has not only furnished me this letter, but has related the origin of his coldness towards the
churches, I will quote his words. He says : —

" About 1837 mother, Jason, Owen, and I joined the Congregational Church at Franklin, the Rev. Mr. Burritt pastor. Shortly
after the other societies, including Methodists and Episcopalians,
joined ours in an undertaking to hold a protracted meeting under
the special management of an Evangelist preacher from Cleveland,
named Avery. The house of the Congregationalists being the largest,
it was chosen as the place for this meeting. Invitations were sent
out to Church folks in adjoining towns to ' come up to the help of
the Lord against the mighty ; ' and soon the house was crowded, the
assembly occupying by invitation the pews of the church generally.
Preacher Avery gave us in succession four sermons from one text, —
' Cast ye up, cast ye up! Prepare ye the way of the Lord ; make
his paths straight!' Soon lukewarm Christians were heated up to a
melting condition, and there was a bright prospect of a good shower
of grace. There were at that time in Franklin a number of free
colored persons and some fugitive slaves. These became interested
and came to the meetings, but were given seats by themselves, where
the stove had stood, near the door, — not a good place for seeing
ministers or singers. Father noticed this, and when the next meeting (which was at evening) had fairly opened, he rose and called
attention to the fact, that, in seating the colored portion of the audience, a discrimination had been made, and said that he did not
believe God is ' a respecter of persons.' He then invited the colored
people to occupy his slip. The blacks accepted, and all of our family
took their vacated seats. This was a bomb-shell, and the Holy
Spirit in the hearts of Pastor Burritt and Deacon Beach at once
gave up his place to another tenant. Next day father received a call
from the Deacons to admonish him and ' labor ' with him ; but they
returned with new views of Christian duty. The blacks during the
remainder of that protracted meeting continued to occupy our slip,
and our family the seats around the stove. We soon after moved to
Hudson, and though living three miles away, became regular attend-

auts at the Congregational Church in the centre of the town.   In
about a year we received a letter from good Deacon Williams, informing us that our relations with the church in Franklin were ended
in accordance with a rule made by the church since we left, that 'any
member being absent a year without reporting him or herself to that
church should be cut off.' This was the first intimation we had of
the existence of the rule. Father, on reading the letter, became
white with anger. This was my first taste of the proslavery diabo-
lism that had intrenched itself in the Church, and I shed a few uncalled for tears over the matter, for instead I should have rejoiced in
my emancipation. From that date my theological shackles were a
good deal broken, and I have not worn them since (to speak of), —
not even for ornament." [1]

Milton Lusk, the uncle of the elder children of John
Brown, told me in 1882 that he first separated from the
Congregational Church in Hudson upon the issue of colonization for the colored people, although in his case there
were other grounds of difference.   His brother-in-law never
"came out" from the Church in the sense of the early abolitionists, although he censured the subservience of the clergy
and the laity to the prejudices of the people.   Brown's reverence for the Bible as a divine gift to man and a rule of life
never faltered, and his ancestral faith was declared as fer-
vently in his last days of glorious imprisonment as any of
the Christian martyrs avowed theirs.   But he grew more
tolerant of differences of opinion as he advanced in years,
and he found no fault with the religion of Theodore Parker,
though it was so unlike his own.

[1] A shorter account of this affair, as remembered by Ruth Thompson,
has already been given.

CHAPTER III.

JOHN BROWN AS A BUSINESS MAN.

THE letters of Brown to his father, already cited, show that he was diligent in his worldly calling. His vocations were various, as is customary with Americans of New England origin, — and with all his higher qualities, John Brown was a true Yankee. His autobiography shows how active and ambitious he was when a boy; and this activity never deserted him. His father had trained him to his own occupation, that of a tanner; but he was also a land-surveyor, lumber-dealer, postmaster, wool-grower, breeder and trainer of race-horses, stock-fancier, land speculator, farmer, orchardist, wool-factor, wool-sorter, and pioneer in a new country, like the Adirondac wilderness around Whiteface and Lake Placid. Emerson almost described him when he wrote in his "Self-Reliance" of that "sturdy lad from New Hampshire or Vermont, who in turn tries all the professions, — who *teams it, farms it,* peddles, keeps a school, preaches, edits a newspaper, goes to Congress, buys a township, and so forth, in successive years, and always like a cat falls on his feet." This man, says Emerson further, "walks abreast of his days, and feels no shame in not ' studying a profession; ' for he does not postpone his life, but lives already."

Following the advice of Franklin, who was one of Brown's oracles, he married young, as we have seen, so that his oldest son was but twenty-one years younger than himself. Having begun thus early to "give hostages of fortune," as Bacon says, John Brown devoted himself with diligence to his occupation, for the support of his young family. He was a tanner and land-surveyor at Hudson until 1825, when he moved to Richmond, near Meadville, in Pennsylvania, and there carried on the same vocations. He remained until 1835, then removed to Franklin Mills, Portage County,

Ohio, and there mingled speculation in land with his tanning. Upon this point, John Brown, Jr., says : " When
the Pennsylvania and Ohio canal was located through Franklin, father purchased the old Haymaker farm and divided
it into village lots. In the reverses and pecuniary disas-
ters of 1836–37, he made an assignment of all his property
for the benefit of his creditors. His farm in South Kent
(then Franklin), now covered by valuable residences and
shops, went with the rest. Those who visit Kent now
[1884] will see that father's business anticipations were
only a little in advance of the times." It was at a later
date that the sale of Brown's farms in Hudson was followed
by an adventure which has given occasion for some petty
scandal against him. This has been answered, and the
affair explained by his son John, as follows : " The farm
in question father lost by indorsing a note for a friend. It
was attached and sold by the sheriff at the county seat.
The only bidder against my father was an old neighbor,
hitherto regarded as a friend, who became the purchaser.
Father's lawyer advised him to 'hold the fort' for a time
at least, and endeavor to secure terms from the purchaser.
There was, as I remember, an old shot-gun in the house, but
it was not loaded nor pointed at any one. No sheriff came
on the premises ; no officer or posse was resisted ; no threat
of violence offered. The purchaser finally swore out a peace
warrant against father ; and within half an hour after our
arrest by a constable, he tore down that terrible old log
fort."

The bankruptcy of John Brown, to which he alludes in
several of his letters, and in connection with which he was
once imprisoned in the county jail at Akron, occurred in
1842, and the imprisonment was in consequence of this
affair of the Hudson farm. Among his creditors then was
the New England Woollen Company at Rockville in Connecticut, to whose agent he gave the following agreement,
with the letter annexed : —

RICHFIELD, Oct. 17, 1842.

Whereas I, John Brown, on or about the 15th day of June, A. D.
1839, received of the New England Company (through their agent,
George Kellogg, Esq.), the sum of twenty-eight hundred dollars for

the purchase of wool for said company, and imprudently pledged the same for my own benefit, and could not redeem it; and whereas I have been legally discharged from my obligations by the laws of the United States, — I hereby agree (in consideration of the great kindness and tenderness of said Company toward me in my calamity, and more particularly of the moral obligation I am under to render to all their due), to pay the same and the interest thereon, from time to time, as Divine Providence shall enable me to do. Witness my hand and seal.

JOHN BROWN.

RICHFIELD, SUMMIT COUNTY, OHIO, Oct. 17, 1842.

GEORGE KELLOGG, ESQ.

DEAR SIR, — I have just received information of my final discharge as a bankrupt in the District Court, and I ought to be grateful that no one of my creditors has made any opposition to such discharge being given. I shall now, if my life is continued, have an opportunity of proving the sincerity of my past professions, when legally free to act as I choose. I am sorry to say that in consequence of the unforeseen expense of getting the discharge, the loss of an ox, and the destitute condition in which a new surrender of my effects has placed me, with my numerous family, I fear this year must pass without my effecting in the way of payment what I have encouraged you to expect (notwithstanding I have been generally prosperous in my business for the season).

Respectfully your unworthy friend,

JOHN BROWN.

These papers show the real integrity of Brown in a transaction where he might have escaped the obligation which he thus assumed. He had not paid the whole of this debt at his death in 1859. In his will then made he bequeathed fifty dollars toward paying the claim, which the Company received and placed to his credit.

Another of Brown's creditors at a later period was Dwight Hopkins, formerly of Ohio, but lately of Montana, who followed him to Kansas in 1855–56 to collect some part of his debt. He found Brown, as the story goes, "in a little cabin with his toes out of his boots, and nothing but mush and milk on the table, — the old man tearfully regretting his lack of better entertainment." [1] Hopkins got his pay

[1] Letter of Hosea Paul, of Wabash, Ind., Jan. 17, 1875, from which some of the above statements are taken.

finally ; but that was not always the case with Brown's creditors, as we have seen, and shall see. He would seem to have been " a visionary man in business affairs, and of a restless, speculating disposition, not content with the plodding details of ordinary trade." As to his wool speculations, Colonel Simon Perkins, of Akron, when questioned by me in 1878 [1] about Brown's wool-growing and wool-dealing, replied, " The less you say about them the better." I answered that the more I knew, the better I should be able to say the less. He then said that Brown was a rough herdsman, though a good wool-sorter ; "in general terms, he was not a good shepherd, though a nice judge of the quality of wool." He used shepherd dogs, " because it was then the fashion to use them, as much for company as anything else; but they did more harm than good." He said he kept but one thousand five hundred sheep when Brown had charge of them, and that he could easily distinguish every sheep from every other, for " sheep look about as much alike as men do." " Brown took all the care and risk of the flock, and accounted to me at the end of the year, when we divided the profits ; he was here off and on for ten or twelve years. In the wool business at Springfield I furnished the capital ; Brown managed according to his own impulses : he would not listen to anybody, but did what he took into his head. He was solicitous to go into the business of selling wool, and I allowed him to do it ; but he had little judgment, always followed his own will, and lost much money. His father had more judgment and less will. I had no controversy with John Brown, for it would have done no good." " Do

---

[1] May 29, 1878, I visited the large farm of Colonel Perkins, lying just outside the city limits of Akron, in the township of Portage, where Brown herded sheep as late as 1854. Calling on Colonel Perkins a little before noon, I found him walking in his garden, a white-bearded man with a forbidding manner, who evidently grudged me the half-hour I asked of him to talk about Brown. He said he had letters of Brown ; but they were business letters, and not to be shown. He said he no longer kept sheep, because " it does not pay to keep them here, so near to the city ; " that his crops were wheat, fruit, vegetables, etc. I told him that I knew much of Brown's Virginia campaign, but little of his life as a sheep-farmer, and obtained the information given above.

you mean to connect me with that Virginia affair?" said Colonel Perkins. "I consider him and the men that helped him in that the biggest set of fools in the world." Evidently he had treated Brown more generously than he now spoke of him, and no doubt sympathized with him in his effort to help the wool-growers. Mr. T. B. Musgrave, of New York, who was then well acquainted with the wool-trade, has told me that the warehousing of wool at Springfield and elsewhere was a new feature introduced by Brown, in order to enhance prices in the interest of the farmers.

Brown went from Franklin to Hudson in 1839, having also lived at Hudson in 1836–37, and in 1840 for a time. In 1841 he kept the sheep of Captain Oviatt, a farmer and merchant of Richfield. After his reverses in 1837 he had taken up the romantic life of a shepherd, — that, as he says, "being a calling for which in early life he had a kind of enthusiastic longing." At the age of thirty-nine, when he entered fully upon this "calling," he also had, as he says, "the idea that as a business it bid fair to afford him the means of carrying out his greatest or principal object." This object was the liberation of the slaves; and the plan which he had formed for this was in substance the same in 1839 that it was twenty years later, when he put it in execution. "If he kept sheep," said Emerson, "it was with a royal mind; and if he traded in wool, he was a merchant-prince, not in the amount of wealth, but in the protection of the interests confided to him." A few of his letters at this period may be cited to show how he dealt with these interests, whether of animals or of men.

Letters of John Brown to his Children.

RICHFIELD, OHIO, July 24, 1843.

DEAR SON JOHN, — I well know how to appreciate the feelings of a young person among strangers, and at a distance from home; and no want of good feeling towards you, or interest in you, has been the reason why I have not written you before. I have been careful and troubled with so much serving, that I have in a great measure neglected the one thing needful, and pretty much stopped all correspondence with heaven. My worldly business has borne heavily, and still does; but we progress some, have our sheep sheared, and have

done something at our haying. Have our tanning business going on
in about the same proportion, — that is, we are pretty fairly behind
in business, and feel that I must nearly or quite give up one or other
of the branches, for want of regular troops on whom to depend. We
should like to know how you expect to dispose of your time hereafter,
and how you get along, what your studies are, and what difficulties
you meet. I would send you some money, but I have not yet received a dollar from any source since you left. I should not be so dry
of funds could I but overtake my work ; but all is well, — all is well.
Will you come home or not this fall ? I suppose there are some persons in Richfield who would be middling fond of seeing you back once
more, wherever you may be. I hope you may behave yourself wisely
in all things.

From your affectionate father,

JOHN BROWN.

RICHFIELD, Jan. 11, 1844.

DEAR SON JOHN, — Your letter, dated December 21, was received some days ago, but I have purposely delayed till now, in
order to comply with your request that I should write about everything. We are all in health ; amongst the number is a new sister,[1]
about three weeks old. I know of no one of our friends that is not in
comfortable health. I have just met with father ; he was with us a
few days since, and all were then well in Hudson. Our flock is well,
and we seem to be overtaking our business in the tannery. Divine
Providence seems to smile on our works at this time ; I hope we
shall not prove unthankful for any favor, nor forget the giver. (I
have gone to sleep a great many times while writing the above.)
The boys and Ruth are trying to improve some this winter, and are
effecting a little I think. I have lately entered into a copartnership
with Simon Perkins, Jr., of Akron, with a view to carry on the
sheep business extensively. He is to furnish all the feed and shelter
for wintering, as a set-off against our taking all the care of the flock.
All other expenses we are to share equally, and to divide the profits
equally. This arrangement will reduce our cash rents at least $250
yearly, and save our hiring help in haying. We expect to keep the
Captain Oviatt farm for pasturing, but my family will go into a very
good house belonging to Mr. Perkins, — say from a half a mile to a
mile out of Akron. I think this is the most comfortable and the most
favorable arrangement of my worldly concerns that I ever had, and
calculated to afford us more leisure for improvement, by day and by
night, than any other. I do hope that God has enabled us to make

---

[1] Anne Brown, now Mrs. Adams.

it in mercy to us, and not that he should send leanness into our souls. Our time will all be at our own command, except the care of the flock. We have nothing to do with providing for them in the winter excepting harvesting rutabagas and potatoes.

This, I think, will be considered no mean alliance for our family, and I most earnestly hope they will have wisdom given to make the most of it. It is certainly indorsing the poor bankrupt and his family, three of whom were but recently in Akron jail, in a manner quite unexpected, and proves that notwithstanding we have been a company of " Belted Knights," our industrious and steady endeavors to maintain our integrity and our character have not been wholly overlooked. Mr. Perkins is perfectly advised of our poverty, and the times that have passed over us. Perhaps you may think best to have some connection with this business. I do not know of ANY person in RICHFIELD that you would be likely to be fond of hearing from in particular, excepting one at Cleveland; and if hearing from ANY person prove to be a very up-stream business, I would advise not to worry at present. Will you let me know how it stands between you and all parties concerned?[1]

Your father,
JOHN BROWN.

To his wife he wrote thus at this period : —

SPRINGFIELD, MASS., March 7, 1844.

MY DEAR MARY, — It is once more Sabbath evening, and nothing so much accords with my feelings as to spend a portion of it in conversing with the partner of my choice, and the sharer of my poverty, trials, discredit, and sore afflictions, as well as of what comfort and seeming prosperity has fallen to my lot for quite a number of years. I would you should realize that, notwithstanding I am absent in body, I am very much of the time present in spirit. I do not forget the firm attachment of her who has remained my fast and faithful affectionate friend, when others said of me, " Now that he lieth, he shall rise up no more." . . . I now feel encouraged to believe that my absence will not be very long. After being so much away, it seems as if I knew pretty well how to appreciate the quiet of home. There is a peculiar music in the word which a half-year's absence in a distant country would enable you to understand. Millions there are who have no such thing to lay claim to. I feel considerable regret by turns that I have lived so many years, and have in reality done so

---

[1] The allusion at the close of this letter is to some affairs of the heart in which the young man then had an interest ; for love was no more a stranger to these Ohio shepherds than to those of Sicily.

little to increase the amount of human happiness. I often regret that
my manner is no more kind and affectionate to those I really love
and esteem; but I trust my friends will overlook my harsh, rough
ways, when I cease to be in their way as an occasion of pain and un-
happiness. In imagination I often see you in your room with Little
Chick and that strange Anna. You must say to her that father
means to come before long and kiss somebody. I will close by
saying that it is my growing resolution to endeavor to promote my
own happiness by doing what I can to render those about me more
so. If the large boys do wrong, call them alone into your room, and
expostulate with them kindly, and see if you cannot reach them by a
kind but powerful appeal to their honor. I do not claim that such
a theory accords very well with my practice; I frankly confess it does
not; but I want your face to shine, even if my own should be dark
and cloudy. You can let the family read this letter, and perhaps you
may not feel it a great burden to answer it, and let me hear all about
how you get along.

Affectionately yours,

JOHN BROWN.

CLEVELAND, June 22, 1844.

DEAR SON JOHN, — I received your letter some days ago, but was
so busy in preparing for my journey to Lowell (on which I now am)
that I could find no time to write before. We had been waiting for
news from you for some time, not knowing where you were, and were
all glad of your letter. I will give a little account of things since
you left. We moved to Akron about the 10th of April; get along
very pleasantly with our neighbors Perkins; find them very affable
and kind. Have had a good deal of loss amongst our sheep from
grub in the head. Have raised 560 lambs, and have 2,700 pounds
of wool; have been offered 56 cents per pound for one ton of it.
Jason spends most of his time in Richfield. Have not yet done
finishing leather, but shall probably get through in a few weeks
after my return. The general aspect of our worldly affairs is favorable. Hope we do not entirely forget God. I am extremely ignorant
at present of miscellaneous subjects. Have not been at Richfield for
some time, and have but a moment to write, on board a boat. I
enclose three dollars, and would more, but may be short of expense
money. May write you at Lowell or Boston ;[1] may return by you.

Your affectionate father,

JOHN BROWN.

[1] Mr. Amos A. Lawrence, of Boston, writes me (Feb. 25, 1885), "Brown
was the agent of our Firm to buy wool in Ohio, as early as 1843."

AKRON, Jan. 27, 1846.

DEAR SON JOHN, — I arrived at home December 2d ; had a fatiguing but I should think a prosperous journey, and brought with me a few choice sheep. Our wool sold by the sort, at from 24 cents to $1.20 per pound, just as we wash it on the sheep ; average, about the same as last year, perhaps a little better. Our flock have done remarkably this winter, and are in good condition and health. We have lost but three by disease since sometime in the fall. Our sales of sheep (mostly bucks) since August amount to about $640. Since my return, I have been troubled considerably with my eyes. They are better now. Your letter to Ruth is received, and she is preparing to go with you when you come out. I have a plan to lay before you for your operations after the first of June next, and hope you will not commit yourself for a longer time until you hear it. I think we have quite as much worldly prosperity as will be likely to be a real blessing to us. Fred is in Richfield for the present, with about 250 sheep and a dog under his command. He seems disposed to reading and some thought. Would like to have you write him there, or here perhaps would be better. Write often.

Affectionately your father,   JOHN BROWN.

RICHMOND, JEFFERSON COUNTY, OHIO, March 24, 1846.

DEAR SON, — I am out among the wool-growers, with a view to the next summer's operations. Left home about a week ago ; all were then in middling health except some very hard colds. I expect to be out some three or four weeks yet, and on that account do not know as I shall be able to hear from you and Ruth until I get home. Hope to hear from you then. Mr. Perkins came home a day or two after you left, full in the faith of our plan, having completed our arrangements. Our plan seems to meet with general favor. Jason and I have talked of a visit to Canada on our return next fall. We would like to know more about that country. We should be glad to hear something from George Delamater, and to know where he is, and what he really means to be. You may, if you think best, say so to him, and tell him we have not forgotten him. Our unexampled success in minor affairs might be a lesson to us of what unity and perseverance might do in things of some importance. If you learn of any considerable wool-dealers or wool-growers, you can use the circular, and more may be sent if best ; of that you can judge after a little inquiry. I may write you again before I go home. *Say to Ruth, to be all that to-day which she intends to be to-morrow.*

Your father,

JOHN BROWN.

The "circular" mentioned in the last letter is the following, first issued in 1846, and written by Brown : —

THE UNDERSIGNED, commission wool-merchants, wool-graders, and exporters, have completed arrangements for receiving wool of growers and holders, and for grading and selling the same for cash at its real value, when quality and condition are considered. Terms for storing, grading, and selling will be two cents per pound, and about one mill per pound additional for postage and insurance against loss by fire. These will cover all charges. Those consigning wool to us should pay particular attention to the marking of their sacks; near one end of each sack should be marked in plain characters, " From ——" (here give the owner's name in full, together with the No. and weight of each bale). On the side of each sack direct to Perkins & Brown, Springfield, Mass.

REFERENCES.

Persons wishing for information in regard to our responsibility, punctuality, etc., are referred to the following gentlemen : —

HON. JEREMIAH H. HALLOCK, Steubenville, Jefferson County, Ohio.

ADAM HELDENBRAND, Esq., Massillon, Stark County, Ohio.

JAMES W. WALLACE, Esq., Brandywine Mills, Summit County, Ohio.

MATTHEW MCKEEVER, Esq., West Middletown, Washington Co., Penn.

JOHN SMART, Esq., Darlington, Beaver County, Penn.

FRED'K BRANDT, Esq., Germano, Harrison County, Ohio.

BISHOP ALEXANDER CAMPBELL, Bethany College, Va.

J. D. & W. H. LADD, Richmond, Jefferson County, Ohio.

H. T. KIRTLAND, Esq., Poland, Trumbull County, Ohio.

JOHN R. JONES, Esq., Vernon. N. Y.

AUSTIN B. WEBSTER, Esq., Vernon, Oneida County, N. Y.

WILLIAM PATTERSON, Esq., Patterson's Mills, Washington County, Penn.

JAMES PATTERSON, Esq., Patterson's Mills, Washington County, Penn.

SAMUEL PATTERSON, Esq., Patterson's Mills, Washington County, Penn.

JESSE EDDINGTON, Esq., Steubenville, Jefferson County, Ohio.

PATTERSON & EWING, Burgettstown, Washington County, Penn.

WM. BROWNLEE, Esq.. Washington, Washington County, Penn.

FRED'K KINSMAN, Esq., Warren, Trumbull County, Ohio.

HEMAN OVIATT, Esq., Richfield, Summit County, Ohio.

VAN R. HUMPHREY, Esq., Hudson, Summit County, Ohio.

PERKINS & BROWN.

SPRINGFIELD, MASS., 1846.

In 1846, while in the midst of these occupations as a wool-grower and wool-dealer, John Brown came back to New England for a few years, and took up his abode at Springfield, in Massachusetts, not very far from the first

Connecticut home of his ancestors in Windsor. He went
there to reside as one of this firm of Perkins & Brown,
agents of the sheep-farmers and wool-merchants in Northern Ohio, Pennsylvania, New York, and Virginia, whose
interests then required an agency to stand between them
and the wool-manufacturers of New England, to whom they
sold their fleeces. The Ohio wool-growers fancied that
they were fleeced as well as their flocks in the transactions
they had with these manufacturers, who would buy wool
before it was graded, pay for it at the price of a low grade,
and then sort it so as to bring themselves a large profit. In
the contest which Brown carried on with them, these New
England manufacturers finally won, but, as he thought, by
bribing one of his subordinates. Concerning his business
life at Springfield, I have the following particulars and
anecdotes from Mr. E. C. Leonard, now of New Bedford,
who had an office in the same block with Brown, at Springfield, near the railroad station and the Massasoit House.
Mr. Leonard calls him, familiarly, " Uncle John," but not
from relationship.

" I first knew John Brown in the summer of 1847, when he rented
the upper part of John L. King's old warehouse by the railroad, and
I occupied the lower floor and cellar. He was busy with his men
sorting wool upstairs, and seldom stopped to say more than a short
pleasant word, in passing up or down through my store.

" Chester W. Chapin was building a block next south of the old
railroad office, and Uncle John had engaged one store and the lofts,
into which he moved early in 1848. In 1850 he was winding up
his wool business, and I engaged the room he occupied, and moved into the store while he still held the lofts. I was then more intimately
in contact with him, and learned more of his nature and opinions,
and then learned to respect him highly. His wool business was unsuccessful. I always understood that some time in 1845-46, the
wool-growers of Pennsylvania and Ohio, and perhaps of Illinois, had
a convention in some western city, among them Uncle John, who
then owned a flock of Saxony sheep with Mr. Perkins of Akron,
Ohio, said to be the finest and most perfect flock in the United States,
and worth about $20,000. At this convention Uncle John suggested
the plan of having an agent in Massachusetts to whom the growers
should send their wool, have it graded, and sold at a certain sum per
pound. The idea took, and to the surprise of Uncle John, they pitched

upon him as their agent.   I understood that he was finally persuaded
to take the agency with considerable difficulty, but at last consented,
and went into it with his usual energy.   The idea of the Association
was, that all their wool should go there, be graded, sold, and each
to share proportionally in the price, according to quality, fineness,
cleanliness, etc.   This was all very well the first year, when wool
advanced somewhat upon the opening market, and the growers
netted better prices than they had been in the habit of getting;
but it did not last.   Uncle John tried to carry out the idea impar-
tially, with all the rigor of theory and of his habits of thought.   But
those growers who had taken pains with the fineness, cleanliness,
etc., of their wool found they had to discount from the price it
brought on account of the carelessness of other growers, when the
general average was made up at the end of the season.   Those, too,
who had brought their wool to market early, and had it graded and
sold early at good prices, found there was a discount from the falling
of the market later in the season.   Besides, Uncle John was no
trader: he waited until his wools were graded, and then fixed a
price ; if this suited the manufacturers they took the fleeces ; if not,
they bought elsewhere, and Uncle John had to submit finally to a
much less price than he could have got.   Yet he was a scrupulously
honest and upright man, — hard and inflexible, but everybody had
just what belonged to him.   Brown was in a position to make a fortune, and a regular-bred merchant would have done so, — benefiting
the wool-growers and the manufacturers mutually.   But, as I said,
it was a failure."

How extensive this business became before it closed may
be seen by some calculations before me, in Brown's handwriting, but without any date of the year, — presumably,
however, before he went to Europe, in 1849.   These figures evidently represent the agent's transactions in one
year's business : —

Freight	$1,000.52
Insurance	140.76
Commissions	2,598.49
Postage	1.10
Cash	52,701.33
Interest to 7th Aug.	1,332.21
Sundries	110.07
Total paid,	$57,884.48
Total received,	49,902.67
	$7,981.81

This seems to indicate that Brown had advanced money on the wool stored in Springfield, and that the excess of his advances over the cash received and the expenses of the business had been nearly $8,000 at this time. The whole stock of wool covered by this account was nearly one hundred and thirty thousand pounds, and the average price received apparently less than forty cents a pound, — the different prices ranging from twenty-five to eighty-five cents a pound.

Frederick Douglass (once a Maryland fugitive, and since the Marshal of the United States at Washington, twenty years after Brown's death, but who knew him in 1847–48 as a radical abolitionist, very friendly to all men of color, and especially to fugitive slaves) describes Brown's way of life at Springfield as he then saw it. Douglass had called at his wool warehouse first, and finding *that* a substantial brick building on a prominent street, he inferred that the occupant must be a man of wealth. But the dwelling-house of the wool-merchant amazed him : —

" It was a small wooden building on a back street, in a neighborhood chiefly occupied by laboring men and mechanics ; respectable enough, to be sure, but not quite the place, I thought, where one would look for the residence of a flourishing and successful merchant. Plain as was the outside of the house, the inside was plainer. Its furniture would have satisfied a Spartan. It would take longer to tell what was not in this house than what was in it. There was an air of plainness about it which almost suggested destitution. My first meal passed under the misnomer of tea, though there was nothing suggestive of that meal as it is generally understood. It consisted of beef soup, cabbage, and potatoes, a meal such as a man might relish after following the plough all day. There were no servants, — the mother, daughters, and sons did the serving, and did it well. They were evidently used to it, and had no thought of any impropriety or degradation in being their own servants. It is said that a house in some measure reflects the character of its occupants ; this one certainly did. In it there were no disguises, no illusions, no make-believes ; everything implied stern truth, solid purpose, and rigid economy. . . . He fulfilled St. Paul's idea of the head of the family. His wife believed in him, and his children observed him with reverence. Whenever he spoke his words commanded earnest attention. His arguments, which I ventured at some points to oppose, seemed to convince all; his appeals touched all, and his will impressed all. Certainly, I never felt myself in the presence of a stronger religious influence than while in this man's house."

Douglass soon learned that his host was living in this Spartan way in order to save as much money as possible for his great enterprise of freeing the slaves; and this agrees with what we know from other sources. It was from James Forman probably that Mr. Redpath obtained the typical anecdote that Brown would not sell leather by the pound from his tannery until the last drop of moisture had been dried out of it, "lest he should sell his customers water instead of leather." The general testimony of his business associates is that of Heman Oviatt who knew him at Richfield, and who said in 1859: "Through life he has been distinguished for his integrity, and esteemed a very conscientious man by those who have known him."

It was to advance the price of wool that Brown visited Europe, hoping to open there a market for American wool, some lots of which he had previously forwarded to his agents, the Pickersgills, in London. As will be seen later, the price actually got at auction in England for the second grade of wool was less than thirty cents a pound, or far below the American average. Mr. Leonard happened to be an eyewitness to one of the instances in which Brown was grievously disappointed in his English speculation, and has thus described what took place. We must suppose the time to be after Brown's return from Europe. Mr. Musgrave, the Yorkshire manufacturer, established in Northampton, Mass., was the father of T. B. Musgrave of New York, already cited.

" A little incident occurred in 1850. Perkins & Brown's clip had come forward, and it was beautiful; the little compact Saxony fleeces were as nice as possible. Mr. Musgrave of the Northampton Woollen Mill, who was making shawls and broadcloths, wanted it, and offered Uncle John sixty cents a pound for it. 'No, I am going to send it to London.' Musgrave, who was a Yorkshire man, advised Brown not to do it, for American wool would not sell in London, — not being thought good. He tried hard to buy it, but without avail. Uncle John graded it himself, bought new sacking, and had it packed under his own eye. The bags were firm, round, hard, and true almost as if they had been turned out in a lathe, and away it went. Some little time after, long enough for the purpose, news came that it was sold in London, but the price was not stated. Musgrave came into my counting-room one forenoon all aglow, and said he wanted me to go with him, — he was going to have some fun. Then he went to the stairs and called Uncle John, and told him he wanted him to go over to the Hartford depot and see a lot of wool he had bought. So Uncle John put on his coat, and we started. When we arrived at the depot, and just as we were going into the freight-house, Musgrave says : ' Mr. Brune, I want you to tell me what you think of this lot of wull that stands me in just fifty-two cents a pund.' One glance at the bags was enough. Uncle John wheeled, and I can see him now as he ' put back' to the lofts, his brown coat-tails floating behind him, and the nervous strides fairly devouring the way. It was his own clip, for which Musgrave, some three months before, had offered him sixty cents a pound as it lay in the loft. It had been graded, new-bagged, shipped by steamer to London, sold, and reshipped, and was in Springfield at eight cents in the pound less than Musgrave offered.

"The last time I saw him was in 1851. He had some native wine that he had made, and he asked me to taste it, — I think from currants, native grapes, and the raspberry. The latter was very excellent, and when I told him of the great quantities of Franconia raspberries growing by the roadsides in the White Mountain region, he took down directions, and said he should try to go there the next season and make a quantity of wine."

So it seems he was a vintager as well as a shepherd; indeed, he sought perfection in all his undertakings, and was constantly improving the stock of cattle, the quality of orchards, grape-vines, etc., as his sons do still. In March, 1839, he drove a herd of cattle from Ohio to Connecticut, and in July brought back with him a few fine sheep, from which he bred his first flock in Richfield. He had made a previous journey to Connecticut the same year, in connection with his financial embarrassment, and in the course of it wrote the following letter to his wife : —

NEW HARTFORD, CONN., Jan. 23, 1839.

. . . I have felt distressed to get my business done and return, ever since I left home, but know of no way consistent with duty but to make thorough work of it while there is any hope. Things now look more favorable than they have, but I may still be disappointed.

We must all try to trust in Him who is very gracious and full of compassion and of almighty power; for those that do will not be made ashamed. Ezra the prophet prayed and afflicted himself before God, when himself and the Captivity were in a straight, and I have no doubt you will join with me under similar circumstances. Don't get discouraged, any of you, but hope in God, and try all to serve him with a perfect heart.

In 1840 he had returned to Hudson, where his father still lived, and there engaged largely in sheep-raising.[1] His partner at first was Captain Oviatt, of Richfield, a neighboring town; and in 1842 Brown had removed to Richfield, where he lived for two years, and where his daughter Anne was born. Here, too, he lost four children in less than three weeks, — Sarah, aged nine; Charles, almost six; Peter, not quite three; and Austin, a year old. Three of these were carried out of his house at one funeral, and were buried in the same grave, in September, 1843. In Springfield also, as we have seen, one of his children died under pathetic circumstances. Yet he looked back on his life in that city with pleasure.

[1] John Brown bred racing-horses in Franklin in 1836–37, from a horse called "Count Piper," and from another called "John McDonald." There was a race-course at Warren, Ohio, frequented by Kentuckians and others, the only racing-ground then in the Western Reserve. A certain Dr. Harmon owned or kept "Count Piper" and "John McDonald," from which Brown bred several colts; and young John, who gave me these facts, says that he "broke" a young McDonald at three or four years old, — perhaps in 1837–38. His father had no scruple about breeding race-horses at that time, but afterwards gave it up on principle. "He had no wish to breed merely draft-horses, but was always thinking of running with horses and of military operations." He wanted his sons to become familiar with swift horses, and to understand all about their management, and was himself a good rider, — not particularly graceful, his sons say, "but it was very hard to throw him." He "broke" racing-horses himself. At first, he argued that if he did not breed them, somebody else would; but his son John "convinced him that was the gamblers and the slaveholders argument, and he abandoned the business, and went into sheep-farming and tanning." This I heard from John and Owen Brown in 1882, when they were relating to me their adventures on horseback in Kansas, in which they owed their escape from their enemies to the speed of their horses and the training of the latter to leap fences, etc. Among the men who were associated with John Brown in business were Gilbert Hubbard (son of a ship chandler of Boston, and afterwards a chandler himself at Chicago), who was

While engaged in his Springfield agency, and wishing to
make a market for his wool, which he thought he could sell
in Europe to advantage, he went abroad in 1849, and traversed a part of England and the Continent, on business, but
also with an eye to his future campaigns against slavery.
He visited wool-markets and battle-fields, and took notice
of the tricks of trade and the manœuvres of armies with
equal interest. He was then noted among wool-dealers for
the delicacy of his touch in sorting the different qualities
and his skill in testing them when submitted to him. Give
him three samples of wool, — one grown in Ohio, another in
Vermont, and a third in Saxony, — and he would distinguish
them from each other in the dark, by his sense of touch.
Some Englishmen, during his sojourn abroad, put this power
to the test in an amusing manner. One evening, in company with several English wool-dealers, each of whom had
brought samples in his pocket, Brown was giving his opinion
as to the best use to which certain grades and qualities
should be put. One of the party very gravely drew a sample from his pocket, handed it to the Yankee farmer, and
asked him what he would do with such wool as that.
Brown took it, and had only to roll it between his fingers
to know that it had not the minute hooks by which the
fibres of wool are attached to each other. "Gentlemen,"
said he, "if you have any machinery in England that will
work up dog's hair, I advise you to put this into it." The
jocose Briton had sheared a poodle and brought the fleece
with him; but the laugh went against him when Brown
handed back his precious sample. His skill in trade was
not so great; and, as we saw, after trying the markets
of Europe, he finally sold his Liverpool consignments of
wool at a lower price than they would have brought in
Springfield.

connected with Brown at Hudson in sheep-raising, and afterwards with him
at Springfield in the wool business, and J. C. Fairchild, father of General
Lucius Fairchild, of Wisconsin, who was a partner with Brown in tanning
at Hudson, and afterwards lived at Cleveland. A young man named Forman, who became connected afterwards by marriage with the Fairchilds,
was brought up by Brown at Randolph, and was living in 1861 at Youngs-
ville, Penn.

A few letters of his from Europe are in existence, and will soon be given. The only other record of his European experiences is, perhaps, that noted down by me from conversations in 1857–59, in which he described what he chiefly noticed abroad, — the agricultural and military equipment of the countries visited, and the social condition of the people. He thought a standing army the greatest curse to a country, because it drained away the best of the young men, and left farming and the industrial arts to be managed by inferior persons. The German farming, he said, was bad husbandry, because the farmers there did not live on their land, but in villages, and so wasted the natural manures which ought to go back without diminution to the soil. He thought England the best cultivated country he had ever seen ; but as we were driving away one morning in 1859 from the country seat of Mr. John M. Forbes at Milton, near Boston, he told me that he had seen few houses of rich men in England so full of beauty and comfort as this, in which he had passed the night. He had followed the military career of Napoleon with great interest, and visited some of his battle-fields. We talked of such things while driving from Concord to Medford one Sunday in April, 1857. He then told me that he had kept the contest against slavery in mind while travelling on the Continent, and had made a special study of the European armies and battle-fields. He had examined Napoleon's positions, and assured me that the common military theory of strong places was unsound; that a ravine was in truth more defensible than a hill-top. So it is for an army of heroes, as Leonidas demonstrated at Thermopylæ; but for ordinary warfare, we may believe that Napoleon was right. Brown often witnessed the evolutions of the Austrian troops, and declared that they could always be defeated (as they have since been in Italy and elsewhere) by soldiers who should manœuvre more rapidly. The French soldiers he thought well drilled, but lacking individual prowess ; for that he gave the palm to our own countrymen.

John Brown sailed for England in August, 1849, and returned to Springfield in October. He wrote to his son as follows : —

LONDON, Aug. 29, 1849.

DEAR SON JOHN, — I reached Liverpool on Sabbath day, the 26th inst., and this place the 27th at evening, — a debtor to Grace for health and for a very pleasant and quick passage. Have called on the Messrs. Pickersgill, and find they have neither sold any wool nor offered any. They think that no time has been lost, and that a good sale can yet be expected. It is now the calculation to offer some of it at the monthly sale, September next, commencing a little before the middle of the month. I have had no time to examine any wools as yet, and can therefore express no opinion of my own in the matter. England is a fine country, so far as I have seen; but nothing so very wonderful has yet appeared to me. Their farming and stone-masonry are very good; cattle, generally more than middling good.[1] Horses, as seen at Liverpool and London, and through the fine country betwixt these places, will bear no comparison with those of our Northern States, as they average. I am here told that I must go to the Park to see the fine horses of England, and I suppose I must; for the streets of London and Liverpool do not exhibit half the display of fine horses as do those of our cities. But what I judge from more than anything is the numerous breeding mares and colts among the growers. Their hogs are generally good, and mutton-sheep are almost everywhere as fat as pork. Tell my friend Middleton and wife that England affords me plenty of roast beef and mutton of the first water, and done up in a style not to be exceeded. As I intend to write you very often I shall not be lengthy; shall probably add more to this sheet before I seal it. Since writing the above, I find that it will be my best way to set out at once for the Continent, and I expect to leave for Paris this evening. So farewell for this time, — now about four o'clock P. M.

Your affectionate father,

JOHN BROWN.

LONDON, Sept. 21, 1849.

DEAR SON JOHN, — I have nothing new to write excepting that I am still well, and that on Monday a lot of No. 2 wool was sold at the auction sale, at from twenty-six to twenty-nine cents per pound. This is a bad sale, and I have withdrawn all other wools from the

---

[1] Writing Sept. 30, 1850, to an inquiring correspondent, John Brown said : " None of my cattle are pure Devons, but a mixture of that and a particular favorite stock from Connecticut, — a cross of which I much prefer to any pure English cattle, after many years experience, of different breeds. I was several months in England last season, and saw no one stock on any farm that would average better than my own."

market, or public sales. Since the other wools have been withdrawn, I have discovered a much greater interest among the buyers, and I am in hopes to succeed better with the other wools ; but cannot say yet how it will prove on the whole. I have a great deal of stupid, obstinate prejudice to contend with, as well as conflicting interests, both in this country and from the United States. I can only say that I have exerted myself to the utmost, and that if I cannot effect a better sale of the other wools privately I shall start them back. I believe that not a pound of No. 2 wool was bought for the United States ; and I learn that the general feeling is now that it was quite undersold. About one hundred and fifty bales were sold. I regret that so many bales were put up; but it cannot be helped now, for after wool has been subjected to a London examination for public sale, it is very much injured for selling again. The agent of Thirion, Mailard, & Co., has been looking at them to-day, and seemed highly pleased ; said he had never seen superior wools, and that he would see me again. We have not yet talked about price.

I now think I shall begin to think of home quite in earnest at least in another fortnight, possibly sooner. I do not think the sale made a full test of the operation. Farewell.

Your affectionate father,

JOHN BROWN.

WESTPORT, N. Y., Nov. 9, 1849.

DEAR SON JOHN, — I reached home last week, and found all well, and the weather fine, which has been the case since you left Essex County. I expect to return to Springfield some day next week, but wish you would forward me (*without delay*) by letter directed to me at this place (Westport, Essex Co.), care of F. H. Cutting, a draft on New York for $250, payable to my order. Please let my wife know.

Your affectionate father,   JOHN BROWN.

John Brown landed in England, Sunday, Aug. 26, 1849, and was in Paris on the 29th and 30th of August. His journey through Germany must have been swift, for he was again in London, September 21 ; but he may have visited the Continent again in October, for he did not land in New York until the last week in October, and proceeded from there to Westport on his way to North Elba (where his family were then settled), as the short letter above printed shows. His wife, however, was then at a water-cure establishment in Northampton, while John was managing

the business in Springfield. The story of his settlement in
the wilderness of northern New York will be more fully
given hereafter. So far as his wool business was concerned,
this forest home afforded him a quiet retreat from the
annoyances which the failure of his mercantile enterprise
brought upon him. All through 1850 it was evident that
the result would be unfortunate, and it was feared his losses
might be large. Brown was anxious, not without reason,
lest his partner in Ohio, Simon Perkins, might blame him
for his peculiar and obstinate course in trying to force the
market, without success. The following letters show how
this affair turned : —

John Brown to his Family.

BURGETTSTOWN, PENN., April 12, 1850.

DEAR SON JOHN AND WIFE, — When at New York, on my way
here, I called at Messrs. Fowler & Wells's office, but you were
absent. Mr. Perkins has made me a visit here, and left for home
yesterday. All well at Essex when I left; all well at Akron when
he left, one week since. Our meeting together was one of the most
cordial and pleasant I ever experienced. He met a full history of
our difficulties and probable losses without a frown on his countenance, or one syllable of reflection ; but, on the contrary, with words
of comfort and encouragement. He is wholly averse to any separation of our business or interest, and gave me the fullest assurance of
his undiminished confidence and personal regard. He expresses
strong desire to have our flock of sheep remain undivided, to become
the joint possession of our families when we have gone off the stage.
Such a meeting I had not dared to expect, and I most heartily wish
each of my family could have shared in the comfort of it. Mr. Perkins has in the whole business, from first to last, set an example
worthy of a philosopher, or of a Christian. I am meeting with a
good deal of trouble from those to whom we have over-advanced, but
feel nerved to face any difficulty while God continues me such a
partner. Expect to be in New York within three or four weeks.
Your affectionate father,
JOHN BROWN.

AKRON, April 25, 1850.

DEAR SON JOHN AND WIFE, — I reached here well yesterday,
and found all well. Since I came I have seen your letter to Jason,
by which I am taken somewhat by surprise; but am exceedingly

gratified to learn that you have concluded to quit that city. I have
only to say at this moment, do suspend all further plans and movements until you can hear the result of a general consultation over
matters with Mr. Perkins, your grandfather, and Jason. I will just
say, in few words, that such is the effect here of the California fever,
that a *man* is becoming more precious than gold ; and I very much
want my family to take the legitimate and proper advantage of it.
Edward has got married and gone to California.

Your affectionate father,

JOHN BROWN.

WHITEHALL, N. Y., Nov. 4, 1850.

DEAR SON JOHN, — I was disappointed in not seeing you and
Wealthy [1] while in Ohio; and not till within a few days did I get to
know where to write you, as I have been on the move most of the
season. I should have written you while at Ravenna, but expected
every day to see you. We have trouble: Pickersgills, McDonald,
Jones, Warren, Burlington, and Patterson & Ewing, — these different claims amount to some forty thousand dollars, *and if lost* will
leave me *nice and flat.* This is in confidence. Mr. Perkins bears the
trouble a great deal better than I had feared. I have been trying to
collect, and am still trying. Have not yet effected a sale of our wool.
I expect to take some of the best of my cattle to Akron. Our crops
in Essex were very good this season, and expenses small. The family were well when last heard from. Am now on my way home.
Ruth was married in September, and I think has done well. I want
you to write me at Springfield all how you get along, and what you
are doing and intend to do, and what your prospects are. I have in
no way altered my plan of future operations since conversing with
you, and I found Mr. Perkins's views fully correspond with my own.
I have my head and hands quite full; so no more now.

Your affectionate father,

JOHN BROWN.

SPRINGFIELD, MASS., Dec. 4, 1850.

DEAR SONS JOHN, JASON, FREDERICK, AND DAUGHTERS, — I
this moment received the letter of John and Jason of the 29th November, and feel grateful not only to learn that you are all alive and
well, but also for almost everything your letters communicate. I am
much pleased with the reflection that you are all three once more together, and all engaged in the same calling that the old patriarchs
followed. I will say but one word more on that score, and that is

[1] The wife of John.

taken from their history : " See that ye fall not out by the way," and all will be exactly right in the end. I should think matters were brightening a little in this direction, in regard to our claims ; but I have not yet been able to get any of them to a final issue. I think, too, that the prospect for the fine-wool business rather improves. What burdens me most of all is the apprehension that Mr. Perkins expects of me in the way of bringing matters to a close what no living man can possibly bring about in a short time, and that he is getting out of patience and becoming distrustful. If I could be with him in all I do, or could possibly attend to all my cares, and give him full explanations by letter of all my movements, I should be greatly relieved. He is a most noble-spirited man, to whom I feel most deeply indebted ; and no amount of money would atone to my feelings for the loss of confidence and cordiality on his part. If my sons, who are so near him, conduct wisely and faithfully and kindly in what they have undertaken, they will, beyond the possibility of a doubt, secure to themselves a full reward, if they should not be the means of entirely relieving a father of his burdens.

I will once more repeat an idea I have often mentioned in regard to business life in general. A world of pleasure and of success is the sure and constant attendant upon *early rising*. It makes all the business of the day go off with a peculiar cheerfulness, while the effects of the contrary course are a great and constant draft upon one's vitality and good temper. When last at home in Essex, I spent every day but the first afternoon surveying or in tracing out old lost boundaries, about which I was very successful, working early and late, at two dollars per day. This was of the utmost service to both body and mind ; it exercised me to the full extent, and for the time being almost entirely divested my mind from its burdens. so that I returned to my task very greatly refreshed and invigorated.

John asks me about Essex. I will say that the family there were living upon the bread, milk, butter, pork, chickens, potatoes, turnips, carrots, etc., of their own raising, and the most of them abundant in quantity and superior in quality. I have nowhere seen such potatoes. Essex County so abounds in hay, grain, potatoes, and ruta-bagas, etc., that I find unexpected difficulty in selling for cash oats and some other things we have to spare. Last year it was exactly the reverse. The weather was charming up to the 15th November, when I left, and never before did the country seem to hold out so many things to entice me to stay on its soil. Nothing but a strong sense of duty, obligation, and propriety would keep me from laying my bones to rest there ; but I shall cheerfully endeavor to make that sense my guide, God always helping. It is a source of the utmost comfort to feel that I retain a warm place in the sympathies, affections, and confidence of my own most familiar acquaintance, *my family ;* and allow me to say that a man can hardly get into difficulties too big to be surmounted, if he has a firm foothold at home. *Remember that.*

I am glad Jason has made the sales he mentions, on many accounts. It will relieve his immediate money wants, a thing that made me somewhat unhappy, as I could not at once supply them. It will lessen his care and the need of being gone from home, perhaps to the injury somewhat of the flock that lies at the foundation, and possibly to the injury of Mr. Perkins's feelings on that account, in some measure. He will certainly have less to divide his attention. I had felt some worried about it, and I most heartily rejoice to hear it; for you may all rest assured that the old flock has been, and so long as we have anything to do with it will continue to be, the main root, either directly or indirectly. In a few short months it will afford another crop of wool.

I am sorry for John's trouble in his throat; I hope he will soon get relieved of that. I have some doubt about the cold-water prac- tice in cases of that kind, but do not suppose a resort to medicines of much account. Regular out-of-door labor I believe to be one of the best medicines of all that God has yet provided. As to Essex, I have no question at all. For stock-growing and dairy business, consider- ing its healthfulness, cheapness of price, and nearness to the two best markets in the Union (New York and Boston), I do not know where we could go to do better. I am much refreshed by your letters, and until you hear from me to the contrary, shall be glad to have you write me here often. Last night I was up till after midnight writing to Mr. Perkins, and perhaps used some expressions in my rather cloudy state of mind that I had better not have used. I mentioned to him that Jason understood that he disliked his management of the flock somewhat, and was worried about that and the poor hay he would have to feed out during the winter. I did not mean to write him anything offensive, and hope he will so understand me.

There is now a fine plank road completed from Westport to Eliza- bethtown. We have no hired person about the family in Essex. Henry Thompson is clearing up a piece of ground that the "colored brethren" chopped for me. He boards with the family; and, by the way, he gets Ruth out of bed so as to have breakfast before light, mornings.

I want to have you save or secure the first real prompt, fine-look- ing, black shepherd puppy whose ears stand erect, that you can get; I do not care about his training at all, further than to have him learn to come to you when bid, to sit down and lie down when told, or something in the way of play. Messrs. Cleveland & Titus, our lawyers in New York, are anxious to get one for a plaything;

and I am well satisfied, that, should I give them one as a matter of friendship, it would be more appreciated by them, and do more to secure their best services in our suit with Pickersgill, than would a hundred dollars paid them in the way of fees. I want Jason to obtain from Mr. Perkins, or anywhere he can get them, two good junk-bottles, have them thoroughly cleaned, and filled with the cherry wine, being very careful not to roil it up before filling the bottles, — providing good corks and filling them perfectly full. These I want him to pack safely in a very small strong box, which he can make, direct them to Perkins & Brown, Springfield, Mass., and send them by express. We can effect something to purpose by producing unadulterated domestic wines. They will command great prices.[1] It is again getting late at night; and I close by wishing every present as well as future good.

Your affectionate father,

JOHN BROWN.

SPRINGFIELD, MASS., Dec. 6, 1850.

DEAR SON JOHN, — Your kind letter is received. By same mail I also have one from Mr. Perkins in answer to one of mine, in which I did in no very indistinct way introduce some queries, not altogether unlike those your letter contained. Indeed, your letter throughout is so much like what has often passed through my own mind, that were I not a little sceptical yet, I should conclude you had access to some of the knocking spirits.[2] I shall not write you very long, as I mean

---

[1] This fixes the date of the anecdote told by Mr. Leonard concerning the wines which Brown had to exhibit ; it must have been after this time, and probably in 1851. John Brown, Jr., has been for many years cultivating the grape on an island in Lake Erie, and his brother Jason is now doing the same in Southern California. Their principles, however, forbid them to make wine.

[2] This was the period when the Fox family, at Rochester, N. Y., were astonishing the world with their knockings and the messages from another world which these were supposed to convey. John Brown, Jr., was inclined to believe in the reality of this "rat-hole revelation" (as Emerson described it to Henry Ward Beecher) ; but his father was sceptical. He talked with his son at the American House, Springfield, in 1848, concerning this matter, and told him that the Bible contains the whole revelation of God ; that since that canon was closed, "the book has been sealed." In his later years he was less confident of this ; and in 1859, when he last talked with John Brown, Jr., on the subject, he said he had received messages, as he believed, from Dianthe Lusk, which had directed his conduct in cases of perplexity. Milton Lusk has been a believer in "Spiritualism" for many years ; indeed, he is naturally heretical, and was excommunicated by the church in Hudson, in 1835.

to write again before many days. Mr. Perkins's letter, to which I just alluded, appears to be written in a very kind spirit; and so long as he is right-side up, I shall by no means despond; indeed, I think the fog clearing away from our matters a little. I certainly wish to understand, and I mean to understand, "how the land lies" before taking any important steps. You can assist me very much about being posted up; but you will be able to get hold of the right end exactly by having everything done up first-rate, and by becoming very familiar, and not by keeping distant. I most earnestly hope that should *I* lose caste, my family will at least prove themselves worthy of respect and confidence; and I am sure that my three sons in Akron can do a great job for themselves and for the family if they behave themselves wisely. Your letter so well expresses my own feelings, that were it not for *one expression* I would mail it with one I have just finished, to Mr. Perkins. Can you not all three effectually secure the name of good business men this winter? That you are considered honest *and rather intelligent* I have no doubt.

I do not believe the losses of our firm will in the end prove so very severe, if Mr. Perkins can only be kept resolute and patient in regard to matters. I have often made mistakes by being too hasty, and mean hereafter to "ponder well the path of my feet." I mean to pursue in all things such a course as is in reality wise, and as will in the end give to myself and family the least possible cause for regret. I believe Mr. Newton is properly authorized to take testimony. If so, I wish you to ascertain the fact and write me; if not, I want you to learn through Mr. Perkins who would be a suitable person for that business, as I expect before many weeks to want your testimony, and I want you to give me the name. I forgot to write to Mr. Perkins about it, and have sealed up my letter to him. I mentioned about your testimony, but forgot what I should have written.

Your affectionate father,

JOHN BROWN.

As may be inferred from these letters, the settlement of Perkins & Brown's affairs involved several lawsuits, some brought by them and some against them. These were tried in several places, — at New York, at Troy, and in one instance at Boston. The latter was tried before Caleb Cushing in the winter of 1852–53, and was one of the last cases heard by Judge Cushing before leaving his seat in the Supreme Court of Massachusetts to take his place in President Pierce's cabinet as attorney-general. The suit was brought

by the Burlington Mills Company of Vermont, represented
in Boston by Jacob Sleeper and others, against John Brown
and others, for a breach of contract in supplying wool to
these mills of certain grades; and the damages were laid at
sixty thousand dollars. It was pending for a long time, the
counsel against Brown being Rufus Choate and Francis B.
Hayes, and his own senior counsel being the eminent New
York lawyer, Joshua V. Spencer. It finally came to trial
in Boston, Jan. 14, 1853, and after several postponements
and the taking of much testimony it was settled, Feb. 3,
1853, by a compromise between the counsel, the anticipated
decision of the court being against Brown. About a year
later he won a similar suit in a New York court; and he
always believed that he should have won his Boston suit, if
the case had been tried on its merits. An appeal was taken
from the verdict in Brown's favor, at Troy, N. Y.; and
while this was pending, in the spring of 1854, he was at Vernon, near Utica, N. Y., assisting his counsel, Mr. Jenkins,
to prepare the case. A person in the law-office of his counsel tells this anecdote, to show how his love of liberty
interfered with his business : —

" The morning after the news of the Burns affair reached Vernon,
Brown went at his work immediately after breakfast; but in a few
minutes started up from his chair, walked rapidly across the room
several times, then suddenly turned to his counsel and said, ' I am
going to Boston.' ' Going to Boston! ' said the astonished lawyer;
' why do you want to go to Boston ? ' Old Brown continued walking
vigorously, and replied, ' Anthony Burns must be released, or I will
die in the attempt.' The counsel dropped his pen in consternation;
then he began to remonstrate: told him the suit had been in progress
a long time, and a verdict just gained; it was appealed from, and that
appeal must be answered in so many days, or the whole labor would
be lost; and no one was sufficiently familiar with the whole case
except himself. It took a long and earnest talk with old Brown to
persuade him to remain. His memory and acuteness in that long
and tedious lawsuit often astonished his counsel. While here he
wore an entire suit of snuff-colored cloth, the coat of a decidedly Qua-
kerish cut in collar and skirt. He wore no beard, and was a clean-
shaven, scrupulously neat, well dressed, quiet old gentleman. He
was, however, notably resolute in all that he did."

At this time Brown was fifty-four years old, but looked five years beyond his age; and this aged appearance was increased by his hardships in Kansas, so that he might have passed for seventy at his death in 1859.

The following letters relate to these lawsuits : —

STEUBENVILLE, OHIO, May 15, 1851.

DEAR SON JOHN, — I wrote you some days since, enclosing ten dollars, and requesting you to acknowledge it, and also to hold yourself in readiness to go to Pittsburgh when called upon ; since which I have not heard from you. I am now on my way to Akron; and as our causes at Pittsburgh have been continued until next fall, we shall not need you there until then. We have now no prospect of any trial until fall, except with Henry Warren; and we wish you to so arrange your business that you can leave for Troy upon a short notice. I also want you to keep me advised at Akron of your whereabouts, so that I may call upon you should I have time. I did expect to go to Hartford when I left home, but find I must alter my course. I was in Essex on Tuesday last. Left Ruth and husband well, and very comfortably situated. We seem to get along as pleasantly as I expected, so far ; can't say how long it will be so ; hope we may continue. I want you to write often and let us know how you get along. Had sad work among our Saxony ewes and lambs by dogs, Saturday night last : probably forty killed and wounded.

Your affectionate father,

JOHN BROWN.

CLEVELAND, Oct. 30, 1851.

DEAR SON JOHN, — I have just landed here from Buffalo, and expect to leave for Akron by next train. As soon as I learn at what time we shall want you at Pittsburgh I will let you know ; but I now suppose we shall want you there immediately, and wish you to hold yourself in constant readiness. Have heard nothing further from home or from Essex since we parted. Met Mr. Jenkins at Albany, and we came on together to Utica. He was pleased with the course we took at Lanesboro, and was in very good spirits ; says he learned through Brigham, while at Albany, that Warren's attorneys feel pretty well cornered up : [1] says we did right in not taking your deposition in Burlington case.

Your affectionate father,   JOHN BROWN.

[1] In a previous letter to his family, Brown says (Oct. 6, 1851) : "I have strong hopes of success finally in disposing of our business here [Troy], but it is exceedingly troublesome and expensive."

AKRON, OHIO, Dec. 1, 1851.

DEAR SON JOHN, — Yours, dated November 14, came on in season, but an increased amount of cares has prevented me from answering sooner. One serious difficulty has been with Frederick, who has been very wild again. He is again, however, to all appearance nearly recovered from it by the return to an abstemious course of living, — almost, if not quite, the only means used. He had gradually slid back into his old habit of indulgence in eating, the effect of which I consider as being now fully demonstrated. I now expect to set out for Troy on Wednesday of this week, at furthest; and if you do not see me at Vernon before the stage leaves on Thursday, I wish you to take it on that day, so as to meet me at Bennet's Temperance House in Buffalo. The going is too bad to go by private convey-ance, and I am yet at a loss how I can get through from Warren to Vernon with my trunk of books, etc. I intend to bring my watch with me. I have accomplished a good deal in the way of preparation for winter, but shall be obliged to leave a great deal un-done. If you do not find me at Buffalo (or before you get there), you may wait there not longer than till Saturday evening, and then take the cars for Troy. You will learn at Bennet's whether I am behind or not. If you have not funds sufficient to take you to Troy, you can probably borrow a little, to be refunded immediately when I see you, by Perkins & Brown.

Yours,   J. B.

NEW YORK, March 11, 1852.

SIMON PERKINS, ESQ.

DEAR SIR, — I called on Messrs. Cleveland & Titus to-day. Found Mr. Cleveland intended to charge us three hundred dollars as a bal-ance of accounts. I asked him for the principal items of his charge, which he promised to make up, and leave, directed to you, care of Messrs. Delano, Dunlevy, & Co., 39 Wall Street. He said he could not make it up without keeping me detained over night. As I could see no advantage to be derived from waiting, after hearing his expla-nation of the matter, I concluded not to wait. He says he drew an amended bill after drawing the first complaint, and that he gave more time to that than he did to the complaint. Since I left him I have thought this was not quite right, after the conversation we had with him together, and after our letter to them dated May 16, 1851. He said to me that if I was not satisfied with the charge it should be reduced. I did not tell him what I thought; but if I had thought of our letter at the time I should have asked him to refer to it, as I think he went contrary to his own advice, and also to our last instructions. If you call on him, I wish you would ask him to read

that letter to you. I think it can do no harm, and that he will probably abate something from his charge. I should not now, after
reflecting upon it, hesitate to say that I think he ought to do it (and
since looking up the copy of our letter to them). In haste,

Your friend,   JOHN BROWN.[1]

P. S. If you call on Cleveland & Titus, and can find room, I
would be glad to have you bring the papers in that case. I forgot
to ask for them.

Yours truly,   J. B.

The Boston trial was put off from time to time, — from
September, 1852, to November, and then to December. John
Brown wrote to his son John in September : " When our suit
comes on in November, we shall not need to detain you but
a few days, and the want of your testimony might work our
ruin. Write me on receipt of this." Nov. 20, 1852, he wrote
again, —

I parted with Frederick at Ravenna, on his way to your place ;
he has told you of the death of our Mr. Jenkins (of Vernon, N. Y., a
brother of Timothy Jenkins). We have employed Timothy Jenkins,
M. C., to finish up his business, and I am now on my way to assist
him to understand it, previous to having our trial with O. J. Richardson. We now expect our trial at Boston to come off sometime about
the middle of December, and hope to see the end of it before the
close. We hope the situation of your family is such, before this time,
that you are relieved in regard to the anxiety you have expressed, so
that you can leave at once, and go on when you get notice of the time.
I will send you funds for your expenses and the earliest possible information of the exact time when the trial will come on. All were well
at home and at Hudson this morning. I should wait and go on with
you, did not our Warren business require my immediate attention. I
suppose our Pittsburgh cause is decided before this ; but we had not
heard from it when I left. I will only add that you all have my most
earnest desire for your real welfare. Will you drop me a line (care
of A. B. Ely, Esq., Boston), on receipt of this, to let me hear how
you all do ?

Your affectionate father,   JOHN BROWN.

---

[1] On the same date (March 11, 1852), but from New Haven, Brown
writes to his family : " I received Henry's letter of the 3d at Troy, which
place I left yesterday in order to meet Mr. Perkins, who has come on here
on railroad business. I have at last got through trying our cause at Troy,
but have not yet got a decision. I think it will, without doubt, be in our
favor."

VERNON, ONEIDA COUNTY, N. Y., Dec. 8, 1852.

DEAR SON JOHN, — I have this moment got a line from Mr. Ely, saying our trial at Boston will not come on until the first week in January next. I give you this early notice, in hopes that it will relieve your mind in a measure, and that it will be more convenient for you to be absent at that time. I do not know whether I shall be able to go home again before that time or not. Will write you hereafter when to set out for Boston, and supply you with funds for expenses. My best wishes for you all.

AKRON, OHIO, Dec. 9, 1852.

DEAR SON JOHN, — I reached home last night, and found all well. I came by the Erie Railroad, and got along very well until I left Dunkirk. Fare from Dunkirk to Cleveland, $8.90 ; expenses from same to same, $4.02, and was two and a half entire days getting through, the roads being vastly worse than when we went out. Had I expected so hard and so expensive a trip, I should not have returned. I mean to go back by Pittsburgh and Philadelphia, there being on that route but twenty-eight miles of sleighing, from Troy to Hudson, and that on a good road. I intend to get back to Troy by the 17th if I can. Have not yet seen Mr. Perkins, to have any conversation with him of any account. Whatever you may do in the preparation of papers will be all well for the Burlington case. You will have saved a great amount of exposure, hardship, and expense by staying behind.

Your affectionate father,

JOHN BROWN.

VERGENNES, VERMONT, Dec. 22, 1852.

DEAR SON JOHN, — I have written Mr. Perkins to send you money for expenses, so that you may set out for Boston by the 21st January at furthest. I am too much used up about money to remit, or I should do so. I have written Mr. Perkins to come on himself by way of Vernon; but if he does not get on, or send you money in time, do not on any account delay setting out, if you have to borrow the money for a few days. The money will be sent, and if it does not reach you in time, Wealthy [1] can use it to pay, should you not have it on hand. Mr. Beebe has got home from Europe, which we think very fortunate. Mr. Harrington is here with me from Troy ; he has got his case against Warren affirmed during the last week. I hope this may prove a sickness to Warren about standing out against us.

[1] The wife of John Brown, Jr.

I am so much in haste, and have my mind so full, that I can think
of no more now, except that I stop at the Exchange Coffee House in
Boston. May God in mercy bless you all.

Your affectionate father,

JOHN BROWN.

This trial, so anxiously awaited and prepared for, went
against Brown, as has been said, and he withdrew from
trade and litigation, for which he was ill-fitted, to the life
of a shepherd and a pioneer once more. Profiting by his
experience, however, he gave this good advice to his son
John, who at one time was tempted to take up the business
of wool-buying : —

HUDSON, OHIO, May 20, 1851.

DEAR SON JOHN, — I learn by brother Jeremiah, who has just
returned, that you have engaged yourself to buy wool. I have no
objection to your doing so ; but an untiring anxiety for your welfare
naturally inclines me to remind you of some of the temptations to
which you may be exposed, as well as some of the difficulties you
may meet with. Wool-buyers *generally* accuse each other of being
unscrupulous liars; and in that *one* thing *perhaps* they are not so.
Again, there are but very few persons who need money, that can
wholly resist the temptation of feeling too rich, while handling any considerable amount of other people's money. They are also liable to
devote God's blessed Sabbath to conversation or contrivances for fur-
thering their schemes, if not to the examination and purchase of wool.
Now, I would not have you barter away your conscience or good name
for a commission. You will find that many will pile away their wool,
putting the best outside, and will be entirely unwilling you should
handle it all. I would at once leave such lots, unless that point is
yielded. I would have an *absolute* limit of prices on the different
grades. You can throw into different grades, pretty fast, a lot of wool,
so as to see pretty nearly whether it will average above or below the
grade you wish generally to buy. Do not let your anxiety to buy carry
you one inch beyond your judgment. Do not be influenced a particle
by what you hear others have offered. *Never make an absolute offer
to any one for his wool.* If persons will not set a price on it, which you
feel *confident* you are authorized to pay, you can *ask* them if they will
not take so much, without really making any bid. If you make bids,
some other buyer will follow you, and get the wool by offering a
trifle more. A very trifling difference will very often do as much
towards satisfying persons as would a greater one. You will gener-

ally buy to the best advantage where the wool is *generally* good and washed; you can buy to better advantage by finding a good stand, and there buying no more than you have the funds on hand to pay for. *Do not agree to pay money you have not on hand.* Remember that. Say who you are employed to buy for frankly if asked. The less you have to say about the why or wherefore the better, other than that you are limited. A book containing the grading of numerous lots of wool is with me at Akron, to which you can have access; it may be of service to you about knowing how different lots will average. Buy you a superior cow, one that you have milked yourself, and know to give a good quantity of milk, before getting a horse. The getting of a horse will get for you numerous absolute wants you would otherwise not have. All well. Shall want to know where to find you.

Your affectionate father,

JOHN BROWN.

We see here the homely, Franklin-like wisdom and Connecticut caution of the man. In his whole business life, though his judgment was often at fault, his uprightness was manifest. Though unfortunate, he was never unjust. He was industrious in whatever he undertook, fair and scrupulous in his business transactions, but with a touch of eccentricity, which showed itself particularly, his friends thought, in his deeds of charity. While living in Pennsylvania he declined to do military duty, and paid his fine rather than encourage war by learning the art, resolving, as Thoreau said in 1859, "that he would have nothing to do with any war unless it were a war for liberty." He caused the arrest of an offender there, who had done him no injury, but was a plague to the community; and while this man was in prison, Brown supplied his wants and supported his family until the trial, out of his own earnings. One of the apprentices in his tanyard at that time bears testimony to the singular probity of his life. "I have known him from boyhood through manhood," said Mr. Oviatt, of Richfield, "and he has always been distinguished for his truthfulness and integrity." Another Ohio acquaintance, who first knew him in 1836, says: "Soon after my removal to Akron, he became a client of mine, subsequently a resident of the township in which the town of Akron is situated, and during a portion of the time a member of a Bible-class taught by me. I always regarded him as a man of more than ordinary mental capacity, of very ardent and excitable temperament, of unblemished moral character; a kind neighbor, a good Christian, deeply imbued with religious feelings and sympathies. In a business point of view, his temperament led him into pecuniary difficulties, but I never knew his integrity questioned by any person whatsoever." Mr. Baldwin, of Hudson, son-in-law of that Squire Hudson for whom the town was named, said that he first knew John Brown in 1814, and always found him "of rigid integrity and ardent temperament," which describes him well. When he went to live in Springfield, he was for some years the client of the late Chief-Justice Chapman, who called him "a quiet and peaceable citizen and a religious man," and further said: "Mr. Brown's integrity was never doubted, and he was honorable in all his dealings, but peculiar in many of his notions, and adhering to them with great obstinacy." This was true, also, of the chief-justice, and is a New-England trait. But for Brown's "peculiar notions" and "great obstinacy," there would have been no occasion to write this biography.

John Brown, Jr., who was well acquainted with his father's business life from 1837 onward, has furnished me this statement bearing on several of the events in this period of his life: —

"The bankruptcy of 1842 had little to do with any speculation in wool, for at that time my father was not a wool-dealer on a large scale, but sold his own 'clip,' as other farmers did. His failure, as I now remember, was wholly owing to his purchase of *land* on credit, — including the Haymaker farm at Franklin, which he bought in connection with Seth Thompson of Hartford, Trumbull County, Ohio, and his individual purchase of three rather large adjoining farms in Hudson. When he bought those farms, the rise in value of his place in Franklin was such that good judges estimated his property worth fully twenty thousand dollars. He was then thought to be a man of excellent business judgment, and was chosen one of the Directors of a Bank at Cuyahoga Falls. The financial crash

came in 1837, and down came all of father's castles, and buried the
reputation he had achieved of possessing at least good common-sense
in respect to business matters. In his conversations with me in later
years respecting the mistakes he had made, I have heard him say
that ' these grew out of *one root, — doing business on credit.*'
' Where loans are amply secured,' he would say, 'the borrower,
not the lender, takes the risks, and all the contingencies incident to
business; while the accumulations of interest and the coming of
pay-day are as sure as death. Instead of being thoroughly imbued with the doctrine of *pay as you go,*' he said, ' I started out in
life with the idea that nothing could be done without capital, and
that a poor man *must* use his credit and borrow; and this pernicious
notion has been the rock on which I, as well as so many others,
have split. The practical effect of this false doctrine has been to
keep me like a toad under a harrow most of my business life. Running into debt includes so much of evil that I hope all my children
will shun it as they would a pestilence.'

" His imprisonment in the county jail had nothing to do with any
of his wool matters, but related entirely to the affair of ' the old log
fort.' The purchaser of the Hudson farm got out a warrant against
father, Jason, Owen, and me for breach of the peace, alleging
that he feared personal harm in his attempts at taking possession;
and, alleging further that he could not obtain justice in Hudson, he
swore out his warrant before a Justice in an adjoining township.
We made no resistance whatever to the service of the writ, and
appeared for examination before the Justice in that town, who was
plainly in full sympathy with the complainant; and after a brief
hearing he required us to enter into bonds for our appearance at the
county court in Akron. These we would not give; and next day
we went to jail. The sheriff, a friend of father, and who understood the merits of the case, went through the form of turning the
jail-key on us, then opened the door and gave us the liberty of the
town, putting us upon our honor not to leave it. We were then taken
to board at a nice private residence, at county expense, for three or
four days only, as it was just before the sitting of Court. On calling the case it was ' *nolled,*' and we returned home. This scheme of
the purchaser resulted in his getting possession of one of the fine
farms which father then owned in Hudson, and that too within half
an hour after our arrest. This is all there was in the matter of our
having once been in Akron Jail.

" In correction of what you told me Colonel Perkins said to dis-
parage my father's skill as a shepherd, his success in business,
etc., let me remark that the correspondence of Perkins & Brown, if
exhibited, would not confirm these statements. Since father had

become well known as a grower of the finest Saxony wool by the fine-wool growers of Pennsylvania and Ohio, and somewhat of Western Virginia, when these men all thought they were victimized by the manufacturers of fine wool, father was urged by these growers to undertake the work of grading their wool and selling it on commission, in hopes to obtain in this way fairer prices. Mr. Perkins not only 'allowed' father to undertake this, but entered heartily into the plan, which for a year or two was successful, until the manufacturers discovered that Perkins & Brown were receiving a large share of the really fine wool grown in this country, and that if they bought it they must pay a fairer price for it. This would greatly diminish the profits heretofore made by the manufacturers of these very fine wools ; and so this high-handed attempt, not to 'control,' as stated by Mr. Musgrave, but to *influence* the price somewhat ' in the interest of the farmers,' must be squelched. The manufacturers combined, and ' boycotted' these upstart dealers. From the quoted prices in the London market of grades of wool not equal, as father well knew, to the wool he had, he became satisfied that rather than take the prices which the combination would pay it would be better to send the wool abroad. The clique had long arms, and finally bought at low rates and brought back the wool he shipped to London ; and the farmers, most of whom had consented to the undertaking of sending it abroad, suffered great loss. Thus ended the wool business of Perkins & Brown."

CHAPTER IV.

PIONEER LIFE IN THE ADIRONDACS.

THE Brown family were born to be pioneers, and none of them more than our Kansas hero. His first American ancestor was a pioneer at Plymouth in 1620; the next generation were pioneers in Connecticut; and their descendants went from wilderness to wilderness until New England was fairly civilized. Then Owen Brown, of Torrington, took up the march again, and encamped in Ohio, where his famous son took the first lessons of a pioneer among the Indians of Cuyahoga and the Great Portage. This experience ended, and the attractions of civilization proving too weak for him, he pushed eastward into the woods of Pennsylvania, where we have seen him serving as postmaster, and planning a negro village for the education of that enslaved race.

What his way of life was at Richmond has been told by one of his neighbors, Mr. Delamater, who was born at Whitehall, N. Y., but remembers when Brown built there in 1826–27, and cleared up his small farm.[1] The houses of John Brown and of the elder Delamater were four miles apart; and in these was kept the school of the neighborhood, — at Brown's house in the winter, and at Delamater's in the summer. Both houses were of logs, with two large rooms on the ground floor, — one used as kitchen, dining-room, and living-room; and the other for the school, and as a sleeping-room. In family worship, which daily took place in the family room, Brown gave each person present some part to take, — himself leading in prayer. The post-office, of course, was kept in this log-cabin of Brown, and

---

[1] Brown owned five hundred acres of land heavily timbered with hemlock, the bark of which he used for tanning. Delamater's log-house was near the State Road, about eight miles east of Meadville.

the men who worked in his tannery boarded with him. It was here that his first wife died, and to this cabin he brought his second wife (who was related to the Delamaters) in 1833. Ruth and Frederick were born in this house, and John, Owen, and Jason received a part of their schooling there. Their father kept a record of their boyish sins, and on one occasion, at least, when they amounted to twenty in number, he allowed one blow of the rod for each fault; but only half the blows were given to the boy, who then took the rod and punished his father with just as many blows. This was an earlier example of Mr. Alcott's method of punishment in his Boston school.[1]

Among the childish recollections of the eldest son (who was born in a log-cabin near where his father built in 1824 a large frame house, which is still standing) are the following, which relate chiefly to Richmond, but date back to the Hudson tannery : —

" Father had a rule not to threaten one of his children. He commanded, and there was obedience. Up to this time (1824) I had not heard a threat. I was playing round where the timbers for the new house were being hewed, and occasionally I picked up the tools belonging to Mr. Herman Peck the carpenter, who spoke up sharp to me and said, ' John, put them down, or I'll cut your ears off!' Believing he would do so, I scrambled under the timbers which were laid up on logs to be hewed (and in my hurry I bumped the back of my head on most of them as I went), and ran off to the tannery, in a room of which we were temporarily living; for the log-house in which I was born had been torn down to give place to the new one. Besides the sharpest recollection of this, I have heard father mention,

---

[1] The family government of Brown was always strict, but with something humorous about it too. His son John relates that when he and George Delamater were playing one winter evening in the school-room, and were so noisy as to disturb the father who was sitting in the kitchen, Brown, after repeating several times, " Children, you make too much noise," all at once called out, " John and George, you may come here to me ! " When they came and stood one on each side of him, he said, " Boys, I think you need to hear the bell ring." Then taking out his clasp-knife and opening it, he held it by the blade and tapped his son John with the handle, smartly on the top of the head. This made his mirthful expression change so quickly that George burst out laughing. Thereupon Brown tapped George on the head, and John burst out laughing. After " ringing the bell " twice or three times in this way their mirth was changed to melancholy.

when speaking of the matter of threatening children, how greatly
alarmed I was on that occasion. I cannot say how old I was then, —
probably less than three, — yet my memory of the event is clear. I
don't know the year when we moved to Pennsylvania, though I remember the circumstances. Owen was then a baby.

"My first apprenticeship to the tanning business consisted of a three
years' course at grinding bark with a blind horse. This, after months
and years, became slightly monotonous. While the other children
were out at play in the sunshine, where the birds were singing, I
used to be tempted to let the old horse have a rather long rest, especially when father was absent from home; and I would then join the
others at their play. This subjected me to frequent admonitions and
to some corrections for ' eye-service,' as father termed it. I did not
fully appreciate the importance of a good supply of ground bark, and
on general principles I think my occupation was not well calculated
to promote a habit of faithful industry. The old blind horse, unless
ordered to stop, would, like Tennyson's Brook, ' go on forever,' and
thus keep up the appearance of business; but the creaking of the
hungry mill would betray my neglect, and then father, hearing this
from below, would come up and stealthily pounce upon me while at
a window looking upon outside attractions. He finally grew tired of
these frequent slight admonitions for my laziness and other short-
comings, and concluded to adopt with me a sort of book-account,
something like this: —

JOHN, DR.,
For disobeying mother . . . . 8 lashes
"   unfaithfulness at work 3   "
"   telling a lie 8   "

This account he showed to me from time to time. On a certain Sunday morning he invited me to accompany him from the house to the
tannery, saying that he had concluded it was time for a settlement.
We went into the upper or finishing room, and after a long and tear-
ful talk over my faults, he again showed me my account, which exhibited a fearful footing up of *debits*. I had no credits or off-sets,
and was of course bankrupt. I then paid about *one-third* of the
debt, reckoned in strokes from a nicely-prepared blue-beech switch,
laid on ' masterly.' Then, to my utter astonishment, father stripped
off his shirt, and, seating himself on a block, gave me the whip and
bade me ' lay it on ' to his bare back. I dared not refuse to obey,
but at first I did not strike hard. ' Harder!' he said ; ' harder,
harder!' until he *received the balance of the account.* Small drops of
blood showed on his back where the tip end of the tingling beech cut
through. Thus ended the account and settlement, which was also

my first practical illustration of the Doctrine of the Atonement. I was then too obtuse to perceive how Justice could be satisfied by inflicting penalty upon the back of the innocent instead of the guilty; but at that time I had not read the ponderous volumes of Jonathan Edwards's sermons which father owned."

Ruth Thompson, in her reminiscences of her father, says : —

"My mother, Dianthe Lusk Brown, died at Randolph, Pa., in August, 1832. The baptism of myself and my brother Fred must have been in the spring of 1832, when I was a little more than three years old, and while my own mother was living. The first housework that I remember is wiping some dishes for my new mother, perhaps when I was five years old. My father was married a second time to Mary Anne Day, July 11, 1833, and I continued to live at Randolph (now Richmond) until 1835, when we went back to Ohio, where my grandfather, Owen Brown, was living. While I was wiping the knives, at the time I mention, I cut my finger and was faint, so that father got some wine for me, and told me to drink it. The boys bothered me about that wine for a long time, but were very careful never to say anything about it before father, who was sometimes very stern and strict. He used to whip me quite often for telling lies, but I can't remember his ever punishing me but once when I thought I did n't deserve it, and then he looked at me so stern that I did n't dare to tell the truth. He had such a way of saying ' tut, tut!' if he saw the first sign of a lie in us, that he often frightened us children. When we were moving back from Pennsylvania to Ohio, father stopped at a house and asked for a pail of water and a cup to give us a drink ; but when he handed the cup of water to mother he said, with a queer, disgusted look, ' This pail has sore ears.'

"When I first began to go to school, I found a piece of calico one day behind one of the benches, — it was not large, but seemed quite a treasure to me, and I did not show it to any one until I got home. Father heard me then telling about it, and said, ' Don't you know what girl lost it ?' I told him I did not. ' Well, when you go to school to-morrow take it with you, and find out if you can who lost it. It is a trifling thing, but always remember that if you should lose anything *you* valued, no matter how small, you would want the person that found it to give it back to you.' The impression he made on me about that little piece of calico has never been forgotten. Before I had learned to write, the school-teacher wanted all the scholars to write a composition or read a piece. Father wanted me to read one of Æsop's fables, — I can't remember what

fable. Brother John said he would write it for me. ' No,' I said, ' I
had rather have one of the other boys write it, for if you do the whole
school will soon know I did not write it.' My father spoke up quickly
and said, ' Never appear to be what you are not, — honesty is the
best policy.' When I was telling something done by another girl
that I thought was wrong, he said, ' Who made you to differ ? ' He
showed a great deal of tenderness to me ; and one thing I always
noticed was my father's peculiar tenderness and devotion to his father.
In cold weather he always tucked the bedclothes around grandfather,
when he went to bed, and would get up in the night to ask him if he
slept warm, — always seeming so kind and loving to him that his
example was beautiful to see.   He used to tell us a story of a man
whose old father lived with him, and broke a plate while he was
eating ; and then his son concluded to make him a trough to eat out
of.   While he was digging the trough, his little boy asked him what
he was making.   ' I am making a trough for your grandfather to eat
out of.'   The little boy said, ' Father, shall I make a trough for you
to eat out of when you are old ? '   This set the man thinking, and he
concluded his father might still eat on a plate.   He often told us
when we were where old people were standing, always to offer them
a seat if we had one, and used to quote this verse, ' Thou shalt
rise up before the hoary head, and honor the face of the old man.'
While we were living at Hudson, an old man, leading an old white
ox, came to our house one rainy afternoon, asking for something to
eat and to stay over night.   Father and the older boys were gone
from home, and mother and we younger children were afraid of him,
— he acted so strangely, did not talk much, but looked down all
the time, and talked strangely when he said anything.   Mother gave
him something to eat, and told him there was a tavern a half mile
from there, where he could stay.   He went on, and we thought no
more about him.   The next Sunday father was talking to us about
how we should treat strangers, and read this passage from the Bible,
' Forget not to entertain strangers, for thereby some have entertained
angels unawares.'   Mother then told about the old man.   John said,
' I met that same old man as I was coming home from Franklin
about midnight, riding his old white ox ; it was raining and cold.'
When father heard that he said, ' Oh, dear ! no doubt he had no
money, and they turned him off at the tavern, and he could get no
place to stay, and was obliged to travel all night in the rain.'   He
seemed to feel really hurt about it.   When his children were ill
with scarlet fever, he took care of us himself, and if he saw persons
coming to the house, would go to the gate and meet them, not wishing them to come in, for fear of spreading the disease.   Some of his
friends blamed him very much for not calling in a physician, — but

he brought the whole family through nicely, and without any of the
terrible effects afterward, which many experience.   Right away he
became famous as a doctor, and those who blamed him most were
the first to call for him when they were taken with the same disease.
"As a shepherd, he showed the same watchful care over his sheep.
I remember one spring a great many of his sheep had a disease
called 'grub in the head,' and when the lambs came the ewes would
not own them. For two weeks he did not go to bed, but sat up or
slept an hour or two at a time in his chair, and then would take a
lantern, go out and catch the ewes, and hold them while the lambs
sucked. He would very often bring in a little dead-looking lamb,
and put it in warm water and rub it until it showed signs of life,
and then wrap it in a warm blanket, feed it warm milk with a tea-
spoon, and work over it with such tenderness that in a few hours it
would be capering around the room.   One Monday morning I had
just got my white clothes in a nice warm suds in the wash-tub, when
he came in bringing a little dead-looking lamb. There seemed to be
no sign of life about it. Said he, 'Take out your clothes quick, and
let me put this lamb in the water.' I felt a little vexed to be hindered
with my washing, and told him I did n't believe he could make it
live ; but in an hour or two he had it running around the room, and
calling loudly for its mother. The next year he came in from the
barn and said to me, 'Ruth, that lamb that I hindered you with
when you were washing, I have just sold for one hundred dollars.'
It was a pure-blooded Saxony lamb."

From Pennsylvania back to Ohio, in 1835–36, and from
Ohio to Massachusetts in 1845–46, were for the Brown
family a temporary recall from their frontier and pioneer
duty to the haunts of civilization ; and in this interval the
children of the second marriage were nearly all born, and
in part educated.   The older children also received some
education which the backwoods could not furnish ; and it
was seriously contemplated at one time to send John Brown,
Jr., to West Point, where he might receive a military education in the national school.   At Franklin in 1836 and during
the short period when the wool business at Springfield was
flourishing, John Brown had hopes of becoming a capitalist,
— not for the sake of giving himself an easier life, but to
educate his children better, and to lay up money with which
he could carry out his chosen purpose of setting the slaves
free.   This hope faded away, but the purpose remained fixed,

and was the occasion of his seeking once more the freedom
and the hardships of a backwoodsman. On the anniversary
of West India emancipation, August 1, 1846, Gerrit Smith,
the agrarian emancipationist of New York, had offered to
give one hundred thousand acres of his wild land in that
State to such colored families, fugitive slaves or citizens
of New York, as would occupy and cultivate them in
small farms. Two years later (April 8, 1848) when a
few of these families had established themselves in the
Adirondac wilderness, John Brown visited Mr. Smith at
Peterboro', New York, and proposed to take up land in
the same region for himself and his children, while at
the same time he would employ and direct the labor of
those colored backwoodsmen who had settled there. Mr.
Smith, who had inherited from his father landed property in more than fifty of the counties of New York, knew
very well when he made his princely offer that those who
might accept it would need all the encouragement and direction they could receive from men like Brown, for there
were many difficulties in the way of its acceptance by the
Southern fugitives and the free people of color in the
Northern cities. The Adirondac counties were then, much
more than now, a backwoods region, with few roads, schools,
or churches, and very few good farms. The great current
of summer and autumn travel, which now flows through it
every year, had scarcely begun to move; sportsmen from
New York and New England, and the agents of men interested in iron-mines and smelting-forges, were the chief
visitors. The life of a settler there was rough pioneer
work : the forest was to be cut down and the land burned
over; the family supplies must be produced mainly in the
household ; the men made their own sugar from the maple
woods, and the women spun and wove the garments from
the wool that grew on the backs of the farmers' sheep.
Winter lingers there for six months out of the twelve, and
neither wheat nor Indian corn will grow on these hillsides
in ordinary years. The crops are grass, rye, oats, potatoes,
and garden vegetables ; cows, and especially sheep, are the
wealth of the farmer ; and, as Colonel Higginson mentioned
in 1859, the widow of Oliver Brown, when he was killed at

Harper's Ferry, was considered not absolutely penniless, because her young husband had left her five sheep, valued at ten dollars. Such a region was less attractive to the negroes than Canada, for it was as cold, less secure from the slave-hunter, and gave little choice of those humble but well-paid employments, indispensable in towns, to which the colored race naturally resort. There was no opening in the woods of Essex for waiters, barbers, coachmen, washer-women, or the other occupations for which negroes had been trained.

In spite of these discouragements, at the date of Brown's first call at the hospitable home of Mr. Smith (where he was ever after a welcome visitor) a small colony of colored people had gone to North Elba in Essex County, to clear up the forest land, and were braving the hardships of the first year in the cold backwoods of Northern New York. Brown introduced himself to Mr. Smith, and made him this pro-posal : " I am something of a pioneer ; I grew up among the woods and wild Indians of Ohio, and am used to the climate and the way of life that your colony find so trying. I will take one of your farms myself, clear it up and plant it, and show my colored neighbors how such work should be done ; will give them work as I have occasion, look after them in all needful ways, and be a kind of father to them." His host knew the value of such services ; with his quick eye for the nobler traits of human nature, he saw the true character of Brown, and the arrangement was soon made. Brown purchased a farm or two, obtained the refusal of others, and in 1848–49, while still engaged in his wool busi-ness, he removed a part of his family from Springfield to North Elba, where they remained much of the time between 1849 and 1864, and where they lived when he was attacking slavery in Kansas, in Missouri, and in Virginia. Besides the other inducements which this rough and bleak region offered him, he considered it a good refuge for his wife and younger children, when he should go on his campaign ; a place where they would not only be safe and independent, but could live frugally, and both learn and practise those habits of thrifty industry which Brown thought indispen-sable in the training of children. When he went there, his

7

youngest son Oliver was ten years old, and his daughters
Anna and Sarah were six and three years old. Ellen, his
youngest child, was born afterwards.

Brown soon fell in love with the region thus chosen for
his home and burial-place. His romantic spirit, which in
early life made him long to be a shepherd, made him also
keenly alive to the attractions of the wild and sublime in
Nature. Had he been born among these mountains he could
not have felt their beauty more deeply. In the summer and
early autumn, for a few months, this wilderness is charming.
The mountains rise grand and beautiful on all sides; the
untamed forest clothes their slopes and fills up the plains
and valleys, save where the puny labors of men have here
and there rescued a bit of fertile land from its gloom. On
such spots the houses are built, and around them grow the
small cultivated crops that can endure the climate, while
the woods and meadows are full of wild fruits. Many of
the dwellings were then log-cabins; and in the whole township of North Elba there was scarcely a house worth a
thousand dollars, or one which was finished throughout.
Mrs. Brown's house, at my first visit, in 1857, had but two
plastered rooms, yet two families lived in it, — and at my
second visit, in February, 1860, two widowed women besides,
whose husbands were killed at Harper's Ferry. I slept on
both occasions in a little chamber partitioned off with a rude
framework, but not plastered, the walls only ornamented
with a few pictures (among them a portrait of Brown) ; and
in winter the snow sifted through the roof and fell upon the
bed. I arrived at nightfall, closely pursued from the shore
of Lake Champlain by a snowstorm, which murmured and
moaned about the chamber all night; and in the morning I
found a small snowdrift on my coverlet, and another on the
floor near the bed.[1] This house had been built by John
Brown about 1850, and the great rock beside which he lies
buried is but a few rods from its door. At that time, far
more than now, the wild raspberries and other fruits were

---

[1] The new-born babe of Oliver Brown (the captain's youngest son, who
had been killed at Harper's Ferry four months before) died in the house
that night, and the poor young mother did not long survive.

in abundance, the woods abounded in game, and the streams and lakes with fish. But the mode of life was rude and primitive, with no elegance, and little that we should call comfort, as will appear by the reminiscences of Mrs. Thompson, soon to be cited. The contrast between this region, in 1849, and the thriving towns of Massachusetts, like Springfield, was striking.

One of the first things that Brown did in this wilderness was to introduce his favorite breed of cattle, and to exhibit them for a prize at the annual cattle-show of Essex County, in September, 1850. They were a grade of Devons, and the first stock of the kind that had ever been seen at the county fair. The agricultural society, in its annual report for 1850, said: "The appearance upon the grounds of a number of very choice and beautiful Devons, from the herd of Mr. John Brown, residing in one of our most remote and secluded towns, attracted great attention, and added much to the interest of the fair. The interest and admiration they excited have attracted public attention to the subject, and have already resulted in the introduction of several choice animals into this region." The same result, on a much grander scale, was observed some years later, when John Brown exhibited specimens of a choicer and bigger breed of *men* than had been seen lately in Virginia or New England. "We have no doubt," added the Essex County farmers, "that this influence upon the character of our stock will be permanent and decisive."

Mrs. Ruth Thompson has given some anecdotes of the pioneer life at North Elba, whither she went at the age of twenty. She says : —

"Before moving to North Elba, father rented a farm, having a good barn on it, and a one-story house, which seemed very small for a family of nine. Father said, ' It is small ; but the main thing is, *all* keep good-natured.' He had bought some fine Devon cattle in Connecticut, near his birthplace ; these my brothers Owen, Watson, and Salmon drove to North Elba. At Westport he bought a span of good horses, and hired Thomas Jefferson (a colored man, who with his family were moving to North Elba from Troy) to drive them. He proved to be a careful and trusty man, and so father hired him as long as he stayed there, to be his teamster. Mr. Jefferson by his kind ways

soon won the confidence of us all. He drove so carefully over the
mountain roads that father thought he had been very fortunate in meeting him. The day we crossed the mountain from Keene was rainy
and dreary; but father kept our spirits up by pointing out something new and interesting all the way. We stopped occasionally to get
a cup of water from the sparkling streams, that were so clear we could
see the bottom covered with clean sand and beautiful white pebbles.
We never tired of looking at the mountain scenery, which seemed
awfully grand. Father wanted us to notice how fragrant the air was,
filled with the perfume of the spruce, hemlock, and balsams. The
little house of Mr. Flanders, which was to be our home, was the second house we came to after crossing the mountain from Keene. It
had one good-sized room below, which answered pretty well for
kitchen, dining-room, and parlor; also a pantry and two bedrooms;
and the chamber furnished space for four beds, — so that whenever 'a
stranger or wayfaring man' entered our gates, he was not turned
away. We all slept soundly; and the next morning the sun rose
bright, and made our little home quite cheerful. Before noon a
bright, pleasant colored boy came to our gate (or rather, our bars)
and inquired if John Brown lived there. 'Here is where he stays,'
was father's reply. The boy had been a slave in Virginia, and
was sold and sent to St. Augustine, Fla. From there he ran away,
and came to Springfield, where by his industry and good habits he
had acquired some property. Father hired him to help carry on
the farm, so there were ten of us in the little house; but Cyrus did
not take more than his share of the room, and was always good-
natured.

"As soon as father could go around among the colored families,
he employed Mrs. Reed, a widow, to be our housekeeper and cook;
for mother was very much out of health.

"While we were living in Springfield our house was plainly furnished, but very comfortably, all excepting the parlor. Mother and
I had often expressed a wish that the parlor might be furnished
too, and father encouraged us that it should be; but after he made
up his mind to go to North Elba he began to economize in many
ways. One day he called us older ones to him and said : ' I want
to plan with you a little ; and I want you all to express your minds.
I have a little money to spare; and now shall we use it to furnish
the parlor, or spend it to buy clothing for the colored people who may
need help in North Elba another year ? ' We all said, ' Save the
money.' He was never stingy in his family, but always provided
liberally for us, whenever he was able to do so. Frederick Douglass
has said in his last book, that John Brown economized so closely in
order to carry out his plans, that we did not have a cloth on the

table at meal-times. I think our good friend is mistaken ; for *I* never sat down to a meal at my father's table without a cloth. He was very particular about this. Father had been planning ever since a boy how he could help to liberate the slaves at the South, and never lost an opportunity to aid in every possible way those who were escaping from bondage. He saw in Mr. Smith's proposal an opening through which he thought he might carry out his cherished scheme. He knew that the colored people who might settle on those Adirondac lands were inexperienced. Most of them had lived in cities, and were unused to the hardships and privations they must necessarily undergo in making homes in that wild mountain region. Therefore, as soon as we had got fairly settled, father began to think what he could do to help the new colored settlers to begin work on their lands. The greater number of them were intelligent, industrious people, and glad to do the best they could ; but many of them had been cheated badly by a land-surveyor, who took advantage of their ignorance, and got them to settle on lands that did not correspond with the deeds Gerrit Smith had given them. Some of them began working on low land that was hard to cultivate ; and when they found they had been cheated they were discouraged, and many went back to their city homes. Father felt deeply over the way so many of them had been treated, and tried to encourage and help them in every way he could. He spent much of his time in surveying their land, running out their lines, and helping them to locate on land actually belonging to them ; and he also employed several of the colored men to cut the timber off a part of the farm where he now lies buried. He bought a quantity of provisions for them, and some cloth to be made up into garments.

"It was not long after we settled in North Elba that Mr. R. H. Dana, with Mr. Metcalf, of Eastern Massachusetts, and Mr. Aikens, of Westport, came to our house one morning, and asked for something to eat. They met father in the yard, and told him they had been lost in the woods, and had eaten nothing since the morning before. Father came in, and asked me if I could get breakfast for some men that had been out all night, and were very hungry. 'Certainly I can,' said I. They lay on the grass while I made preparations to cook something substantial for them, but they were so hungry they could not wait ; so they came in and said, ' Do not wait to cook anything ; just give us some bread and milk, for we are nearly starved.' I hurried some bread, butter, and milk on the table, and they ate as only hungry men can. I filled the milk-pitcher and bread-plate several times, until I was afraid they would hurt themselves ; and then I persuaded them to go upstairs and sleep a few hours until I could get them a cooked dinner, and they did so.

While they were resting on the beds upstairs, our excellent cook got dinner for them, — venison and some speckled brook-trout, with other things necessary to make a substantial dinner. After all was ready I called them, and the three came down and ate alone. They seemed to enjoy the dinner; but their appetites did not appear as keen as in the morning, when they ate the bread and milk. They paid us liberally for their meals, and thanked us kindly for our trouble; took their boots in their hands (for their feet were too much swollen to put them on), and bade us good-by. Their teamster had been sent for, and he took them to Mr. Osgood's, — as Mr. Dana mentions. We saw at once that they were gentlemen, despite their forlorn appearance; we were interested in their story, and were glad to entertain them."

Mr. Dana wrote an account of this adventure, which was printed in the "Atlantic Monthly" for July, 1871, and in which he thus describes the country as John Brown first saw it in 1848: —

"From Keene westward we began to meet signs of frontier life, — log-cabins, little clearings, bad roads overshadowed by forests, mountain torrents, and the refreshing odor of balsam firs and hemlocks. In the afternoon we came into the Indian Pass. This is a ravine or gorge, formed by two close and parallel walls of nearly perpendicular cliffs, thirteen hundred feet in height, and almost black in their hue. Before I had seen the Yosemite Valley these cliffs satisfied my ideal of steep mountain walls. From the highest level of the Pass flow two mountain torrents in opposite directions, — one the source of the Hudson, and so reaching the Atlantic; and the other the source of the Au Sable, which runs into Lake Champlain, and at last into the Gulf of St. Lawrence. . . . The Adirondac Mountains wave with woods, and are green with bushes to their summits; torrents break down into the valleys on all sides; lakes of various sizes and shapes glitter in the landscape, bordered by bending woods whose roots strike through the waters. There is none of that dreary barren grandeur that marks the White Mountains, although Tahawus [Mt. Marcy], the highest peak, is about fifty-four hundred feet high, only some six or seven hundred feet less than Mt. Washington. . . . From John Brown's small log-house, old White Face, the only exception to the uniform green and brown and black hues of the Adirondac hills, stood plain in view, rising at the head of Lake Placid, its white or pale-gray side caused, we were told, by a landslide; all about were the distant highest summits."

This was not the house that Brown built, and near
which he now lies buried, but the smaller one that he first
occupied. Of Brown's appearance and family arrangements
in June, 1849 (he was then forty-nine years old), Mr. Dana
says : —

" He was a tall, gaunt, dark-complexioned man, walking before his
wagon, having his theodolite and other surveyor's instruments with
him. He came forward and received us with kindness ; a grave,
serious man he seemed, with a marked countenance and a natural
dignity of manner, — that dignity which is unconscious, and comes
from a superior habit of mind. At table he said a solemn grace. I
observed that he called the two negroes by their surnames, with
the prefixes of Mr. and Mrs. He introduced us to them in due form,
— ' Mr. Dana, Mr. Jefferson,' etc. We found him well informed on
most subjects, especially in the natural sciences. He had books, and
evidently made a diligent use of them. He had confessedly the best
cattle and best farming utensils for miles round. He seemed to have
an unlimited family of children, from a cheerful, nice, healthy woman
of twenty or so [Ruth], and a full-sized, red-haired son [Owen],
through every grade of boy and girl, to a couple that could hardly
speak plain. Friday, June 29, we found them at breakfast in the
patriarchal style, — Mr. and Mrs. Brown, and their large family of
children, with the hired men and women, including three negroes,
all at the table together. Their meal was neat, substantial, and
wholesome."

Concerning the house in which Mr. Dana visited her
father, Mrs. Thompson says : —

" It stood near the schoolhouse, on the road to Keene and Westport,
from the grave by the great rock on father's own farm, and more than a
mile east from that spot. The Indian Pass, mentioned by Mr. Dana,
is a ' notch' between Mt. Marcy and Mt. McIntyre, a few miles south
of our cabin, while Mt. White Face was as many miles to the north.
The Au Sable River is the stream which drains these mountains, and
flows through North Elba in a winding course into Lake Champlain,
at Port Kent. Westport is the town on Lake Champlain, south of
the mouth of the Au Sable, from which travellers commonly start in
going into the Adirondac wilderness by Keene ; and it was through
this town that father usually went to and from North Elba. On one
of his trips home from Springfield, in the winter, he hired a man to
take him from Westport to Keene, but could not get any one to carry
him over the mountain to North Elba that afternoon. Being very

anxious to get home, he started from Keene on foot, carrying a heavy
satchel. Before he came within several miles of home, he got so
tired and lame that he had to sit down in the road. The snow was
very deep, and the road but little trodden. He got up again after
a while, went on as far as he could, and sat down once more. He
walked a long distance in that way, and at last lay down with fatigue
in the deep snow beside the path, and thought he should get chilled
there and die. While lying so, a man passed him on foot, but did
not notice him. Father guessed the man thought he was drunk, or
else did not see him. He lay there and rested a while, and then
started on again, though in great pain, and made out to reach the
first house, Robert Scott's. (This was afterwards a noted tavern
for sportsmen and travellers, and became known far and wide as
'Scott's.' It is now kept by Mr. Scott's kinsman Mr. Ames, and
is the nearest hotel to the 'John Brown Farm,' where father lies
buried.) Father rested at this house for some time, and then Mr.
Scott hitched his oxen to the sled, and brought him home to us.
Father could scarcely get into the house, he was so tired.

"I had in the mean time married Henry Thompson, of North Elba
(two of whose brothers were afterwards killed at Harper's Ferry),
and was living with my husband on his farm not far from where
father's grave now is. Father's lawsuits about his wool business
had brought him back from Ohio to Troy, N. Y., nearly a hundred
miles from North Elba; but hearing that the small-pox was in one
of the mountain towns not far from us, he made the long journey
into the wilderness, and came to our house early one morning (fearing
my husband had not been vaccinated, and so might get the small-
pox). We were much surprised to see him; and when he told us
what brought him back, I thought was there ever such love and
care as his! When any of the family were sick, he did not often trust
watchers to care for the sick one, but sat up himself, and was like a
tender mother. At one time he sat up every night for two weeks
while mother was sick, for fear he would oversleep if he went to bed,
and then the fire would go out, and she take cold. No one outside
of his own family can ever know the mingled strength and tenderness
of his character. Oh, what a loss his death seemed to us! Yet we
did not half know him until he was taken from us.

"He did not lose his interest in the colored people of North Elba,
and grieved over the sad fate of one of them, Mr. Henderson, who
was lost in the woods in the winter of 1852, and perished with the
cold. Mr. Henderson was an intelligent and good man, and was
very industrious, and father thought much of him. Before leaving
for Kansas in 1855, to help defend the Free State cause, and, if an
opportunity offered, to strike a blow at slavery, he removed his family

from Ohio back to the farm in North Elba.   On leaving us finally to
go to Kansas that summer, he said,' 'If it is so painful for us to part
with the hope of meeting again, how dreadful must be the feelings of
hundreds of poor slaves who are separated for life!' "

When John Brown, Jr., visited with his father at North
Elba in 1858, he thus described the place in a letter to his
brother : —

"From Keene we came by a new road, laid south of the old route
over the mountains. This new road is open for travel in the winter
months, as it leads by Long Pond, which is itself used as a road when
frozen over. The route is the most romantically grand and beautiful
that I ever saw in my life. I am fully convinced that North Elba is
the country for us to come to. Building materials of good quality
are very cheap; and I can purchase the wild lands having excellent
sugar orchards on them, of from two hundred to one thousand good
maple-trees, for about one dollar per acre. The land is easily cleared
by 'slashing' and burning, and by sowing on grass-seed can be converted into good pasture within a year. It is excellent for rye,
spring-wheat, oats, potatoes, carrots, turnips, etc., and in some places
hardy apples can be raised to advantage. I can get Mr. Dickson's
place (forty acres, with five or six improved, or at least cleared),
with a good log-house, a frame barn, 20 × 30 feet, for $150."

John Brown himself often declared his fondness for this
region, and it was by his express request that he was buried
on the hill-side, in view of Tahawus and White Face.   In
June, 1854, while living in Ohio, he thus wrote to his son
John : —

"My own conviction, after again visiting Essex County (as I did
week before last), is that no place (of which I know) offers so many
inducements to me, or any of my family, as that section; and I would
wish when you make a move that you go in that direction. I will
give my reasons at length when I have a little more time. Henry
and family are well, and appear satisfied that North Elba is about
the place after all. I never saw it look half so inviting before."

In an earlier letter he thus writes : —

NORTH ELBA, N. Y., Dec. 15, 1852.

DEAR SON JOHN, — I got here last night, and found all very comfortable and well, except Henry, who is troubled with a lame back,

something like rheumatism I presume. The weather has been very mild so far, and things appear to be progressing among our old neighbors ; so that I feel as much as ever disposed to regard this as my home, and I can think of no objection to your coming here to live when you can sell out well. A middling good saw-mill is now running a few rods down the river [1] from the large pine log we used to cross on, when we went to help Henry take care of his oats. The more I reflect on all the consequences likely to follow, the more I am disposed to encourage you to come here ; and I take into the account as well as I can the present and *future* welfare of yourself and family, and prospects of usefulness. Our trial at Boston is to come on by agreement on the 6th January. I shall write Mr. Perkins to send you money for expenses, so that you can get on to Boston by the 3d January. We shall want to look the papers over, and talk the business over beforehand. Ruth intends occupying the balance of the sheet. My best wishes for you all.

Your affectionate father,

JOHN BROWN.

The hardships of existence in a new country like North Elba fall heaviest on the women. Mrs. Brown had been an invalid before leaving Springfield, and she was long out of health in this forest home. To encourage her, as he frequently did, Brown had recourse to letters of sympathy and exhortation, mingled with prosaic details of the economy they must practise at North Elba. One or two of these letters will here be given, together with letters to Ruth and his other children.

John Brown to his Wife.

SPRINGFIELD, MASS., Nov. 28, 1850.

DEAR WIFE, — . . . Since leaving home I have thought that under all the circumstances of doubt attending the time of our removal, and the possibility that we may not remove at all, I had perhaps encouraged the boys to feed out the potatoes too freely. . . . I want to have them very careful to have no hay or straw wasted, but I would have them use enough straw for bedding the cattle to keep them from lying in the mire. I heard from Ohio a few days since ; all were then well. It now seems that the Fugitive Slave Law was to be the means of making more Abolitionists than all the lectures

---

[1] A branch of the Au Sable.

we have had for years. It really looks as if God had his hand on
this wickedness also. I of course keep encouraging my colored
friends to " trust in God, and keep their powder dry." I did so
to-day, at Thauksgiving meeting, publicly. . . . While here, and at
almost all places where I stop, I am treated with all kindness and
attention ; but it does not make home. I feel lonely and restless, no
matter how neat and comfortable my room and bed, nor how richly
loaded may be the table; they have few charms for me, away from
home. I can look back to our log-cabin at the centre of Richfield,
with a supper of porridge and johnny-cake, as a place of far more
interest to me than the " Massasoit "[1] of Springfield. But "there's
mercy in every place."

Jan. 17, 1851.

. . . I wrote Owen last week that if he had not the means on hand
to buy a little sugar, to write Mr. Cutting, of Westport, to send out
some. I conclude you have got your belt before this. I could not
manage to send the slates for the boys, as I intended, so they must
be provided for some other way. . . . Say to the little girls that I
will run home the first chance I get ; but I want to have them learn
to be a little more still. May God in his infinite mercy bless and
keep you all is the unceasing prayer of

Your affectionate husband,

JOHN BROWN.

To Henry Thompson.

NORTH HUDSON, N. Y., March 15, 1851.

I have drawn an order on you, payable in board of Mail-carrier,
horse-feed, or oats, in favor of Mr. Judd for $7.00, which you will
oblige me by paying in oats at forty cents per bushel, or in board as
above, whichever he may choose. When you can sell my stuff please
pay your father $2.00 for me. I also wish you to send on of my shin-
gles that Hiram Brown carried out, two thousand to Alva Holt, as
we settled about the oats on condition of my sending him two thousand. I wish you to open an account of debt and credit with me from
this time on, as I shall have a good many errands to trouble you
with. I wish you would notify Mr. Flanders by letter *at once* (if
Nash calls on you for the $3.00) to go ahead with the suit. Mr.
Kellogg told me he thought the Trustees would settle with me, were
he to write to them. We are getting along very well ; the boys are
still ahead, and Jack is with us. Mr. Blood talked of taking the
shingles before I sold the two thousand to Holt, and said he would

---

[1] A noted inn.

go and look at them, and give me $1.50 per thousand for them if he liked them. I wish to do the handsome thing by him about it. Would be glad to have you see him about it. My love *unceasing* to Ruth.

Affectionately yours,

JOHN BROWN.

TROY, N. Y., Oct. 6, 1851.

DEAR CHILDREN, — As I am still detained at this place, I improve a leisure moment to write you, as the only means of communicating with a part of my family in whose present and future interests I have an inexpressible concern. Words and actions are but feeble means of conveying an idea of what I always feel whenever my absent children come into mind ; so I will not enlarge on that head. . . .

I wish you to say to Mr. Epps [1] that if Mr. Hall does not soon take care of the boards that are fallen down about the house he built, I wish he and Mr. Dickson would go and take them away, as I paid for them, and am the rightful owner of them. I wish to have them confine themselves entirely to those of the roof and gable-ends. I mean to let Hall have them if he will occupy the building, or have any one do it on his account ; but I do not mean to have him let them lie year after year and rot, and do no one any good. I wish this to be attended to before the snow covers them up again.

ELIZABETHTOWN, Feb. 6, 1852.

DEAR HENRY, — Mr. Judd is wanting to buy a large quantity of oats, for which he is now paying one cent per pound, cash. He also wants to buy a supply for his teams that carry the mail to Saranac, for the next season. He says oats that have rye mixed with them will be worth as much by the pound for his own teams as those which have none. Thinking it might be of advantage to you to know of this, and perhaps to see him, I concluded to send you a line at any rate.

Affectionately yours,

JOHN BROWN.

To his Wife.

UTICA, N. Y., Dec. 27, 1852.

. . . I seem to be pretty much over the effects of the ague, except as to my sight, which is some impaired, and which will not probably ever become much better. I made a short visit to North Elba, and left them all well and very comfortable, one week ago to-day. . . . The colored families appear to be doing well, and to feel encouraged.

[1] One of his colored neighbors at North Elba.

They all send much love to you. They have constant preaching on the Sabbath ; and intelligence, morality, and religion appear to be all on the advance. Our old neighbors appear to wish us back. I can give no particular instructions to the boys, except to take the best care of everything, — not forgetting their own present and eternal good. If any young calves come that are nice ones, I want them to be well looked after, and if any very mean ones, I would have them killed at once. I am much pleased to get such a good account from the boys, and from Anne and Sarah.

To Henry and Ruth Thompson.

AKRON, April 6, 1853.

I have thought a good deal how to arrange as well as possible in regard to a home, should I live to go back to North Elba. I am a good deal at a loss how to divide the land so as to accommodate both families in the best way ; and I wish to call your attention to that matter, as you may perhaps be able to think of some way that will exactly suit all hands. I would be glad if Henry will send me his views freely in regard to the following questions, namely : Are you fond of the business or care of a sawmill ? Are there any springs on that part of the lot lying east of the river, so situated as to accommodate a family on that side ; or do you think there is a prospect of getting a good well where the strip is of some width, and the face such as would be convenient to build on ? Would you divide the land by the river, or by a line running east and west ? Will it be any damage to you if you defer building your house until we can hit on some plan of dividing the land, or at least for another year ? If I was sure of going back next spring I should want to get some logs peeled for a house, as I expect to be quite satisfied with a log-house for the rest of my days. Perhaps by looking over the land a little with a view to these things, you can devise a plan that will suit well. I do not mean to be hard to please ; but such is the situation of the lot, and so limited are my means, that I am quite at a loss. Will it be convenient to have the ground that is gone over on the east side of the river got into grass this season ? . . . I can think of but little to write that will be worth reading. Wishing you all present and future good, I remain,

Your affectionate father,

JOHN BROWN.

AKRON, OHIO, June 30, 1853.

DEAR CHILDREN, — Your very welcome letters were received last night. In regard to a house, I did not prefer a log one, only in view of the expense; and I would wish Henry to act according to his own best judgment in regard to it. If he builds a better house than I can pay for, we must so divide the land as to have him keep it. I would like to have a house to go into next spring, if it can be brought about comfortably. I ought to have expressed it more distinctly in better season, but forgot to do so. We are in comfortable health, so far as I know, except father, Jason, and Ellen, all of whom have had a run of ague. Father, when I saw him last, was very feeble; and I fear that in consequence of his great age he will never get strong again. It is some days since I went to see him. We are not through sheep-shearing or hoeing, and our grass is needing to be cut now. We have lately had very dry weather. . . . I am much rejoiced at the news of a religious kind in Ruth's letter; and would be still more rejoiced to learn that all the sects who bear the Christian name would have no more to do with that mother of all abominations, — man-stealing. I hope, unfit and unworthy as I am, to be allowed a membership in your little church before long; and I pray God to claim it as his own, and that he will most abundantly bless all in your place who love him in truth. " If any man love not his brother whom he *hath* seen, how can he love God whom he *hath not* seen?" I feel but little force about me for writing or any kind of business, but will try to write you more before long. Our State fair commences at Dayton the 20th of September, and will be held open four days.

Your affectionate father,

JOHN BROWN.

AKRON, April 14, 1854.

DEAR CHILDREN, — I did not get Ruth's letter, dated on the 1st instant, until the 12th, but was very glad to hear from you then, and to learn that you found things as well as you did. In fact, God never leaves us without the most abundant cause for gratitude; and let us try and have it in habitual exercise. We have had some complaints among several of us of late, but none of us have been very unwell. We had a most comfortable settlement of last year's business with Mr. Perkins, and division of stock. I had nine of the company calves, and he sold me four of the old for one hundred dollars, which I used to have. I have two young bull calves, — one a full blood, — which I think among the best I ever saw.

AKRON, Nov. 2, 1854.

DEAR CHILDREN, — I feel still pretty much determined to go back to North Elba; but expect Owen and Frederick will set out for Kansas on Monday next, with cattle belonging to John, Jason, and them-

selves, intending to winter somewhere in Illinois. I expect to set
out for Albany to-morrow, and for Connecticut after the 8th. I mean
to go and see you before I return, if my money for expenses will hold
out. Money is extremely scarce, and I have been some disappointed,
so that I do not now know as I shall be able to go and see you at
this time. Nothing but the want of means will prevent me, if life
and health are continued. Gerrit Smith wishes me to go back to
North Elba; from Douglass and Dr. McCune Smith I have not yet
heard. I shipped you a cask of pork containing 347 pounds clear
pork, on the 19th, directed to Henry Thompson, North Elba, Essex
Co., N. Y., care C. B. Hatch & Son, Westport. We are all in
usual health.

Your affectionate father,

JOHN BROWN.

This letter was preliminary to Brown's first expedition to
Kansas in 1855, in defence of the free settlers there, particularly his own sons.

While he was preparing for the further defence of Kansas
in 1857–58, and for his attack on slavery elsewhere, he
did not by any means forget or neglect the family at North
Elba, but busied himself in securing for them an addition
to the two farms in the wilderness on which his wife and
married daughter, Mrs. Thompson, were living. Several of
his Massachusetts friends, chief among whom were Mr.
George L. Stearns and Mr. Amos A. Lawrence, raised a
subscription of one thousand dollars to purchase one hundred and sixty acres of land for division in equal portions
between these farms. Mr. Stearns contributed $260 to this
fund, and Mr. Lawrence $310, — these two gentlemen hav-
ing made up the sum by which the original subscription fell
short of one thousand dollars. The connection of Mr. Lawrence with this transaction, and his personal acquaintance
with Brown in 1857,[1] were afterwards held to imply that he

[1] At this time neither Gerrit Smith nor Mr. Stearns nor myself had any
knowledge of Brown's scheme for a campaign in Virginia. The subscription paper was as follows : —

" The family of Captain John Brown, of Ossawatomie, have no means of
support, owing to the oppression to which he has been subjected in Kansas
Territory. It is proposed to put them (his wife and five children) in possession of the means of supporting themselves, so far as is possible for persons in their situation. The undersigned, therefore, will pay the following

had some knowledge of Brown's Virginia plans, which was not the case. The subscription thus raised was expended in completing the purchase of the tract in question, originally sold by Gerrit Smith to the brothers of Henry Thompson (Brown's son-in-law), but which had not been wholly paid for. In August, 1857, as the agent of Messrs. Stearns and Lawrence, I visited North Elba, examined the land, paid the Thompsons their stipulated price for improvements, and to Mr. Smith the remainder of the purchase money, took the necessary deeds, and transferred the property to Mrs. Brown and Mrs. Thompson, according to the terms arranged by Captain Brown in the preceding spring. I have before me as I write the pencil memorandum, in Gerrit Smith's

sums, provided one thousand dollars should be raised. With this sum a small farm can now be purchased in the neighborhood of their late residence in Essex County, New York.

May, '57. Paid. William R. Lawrence, Fifty dollars.

Paid. Amos A. Lawrence,
} one hundred dollars.
$235 more.
———
$335

Paid. George L. Stearns,
} Fifty dollars.
$235 more
———
$285

Paid. John E. Lodge, twenty-five dollars.
Paid. J. Carter Brown [by A. A. L.], one hundred dollars.
Paid. J. M. S. Williams, fifty dollars.
Paid. John Bertram [by M. S. W.], seventy-five dollars.
Paid. W. D. Pickman, fifty dollars.
Paid. R. P. Waters [by W. D. P.], ten dollars.
Paid. S. E. Peabody, ten dollars.
Paid. John H. Silsbee, ten dollars.
Paid. B. Silsbee, five dollars.
Paid. Cash, ten dollars.
Paid. Wendell Phillips, twenty-five dollars.
Paid. W. J. Rotch, ten dollars.
Paid. George L. Stearns, two hundred and thirty-five dollars.
Paid. A. A. Lawrence, two hundred and thirty-five dollars.

One thousand dollars in all.   July 27, 1857.

BOSTON, Nov. 5, 1857. John Bertram's subscription being $75, instead of $25, as I supposed, I have returned to Amos A. Lawrence twenty-five dollars, making his whole subscription, $310 ; my subscription, $260 ; all others, $430, — total, $1000.

(Signed)   GEORGE L. STEARNS."

familiar handwriting, showing this transaction. Here it
is : —

Draft of F. B. S.		$1000
Due Thompsons $574		
Due me on note 111.66		
" " on land 288.89	974.55	
		$25.45

This sum ($25.45) I handed to Mrs. Brown at North Elba,
Aug. 13, 1857.

A few days later I reported to Mr. Stearns as follows : —

" I wrote you from Buffalo, I think, telling you of the settling of
the business of Captain Brown with Mr. Smith ; since when I have
been in North Elba, and passed a night under his roof. There I
found Mrs. Brown, a tall, large woman, fit to be the mother of heroes,
as she is.   Her family are her two sons and three daughters, one of
them a child of three years.   One of the sons has been in Kansas ;
the other was to go with his father this summer, but I think his marriage, which took place in April, may have prevented it.   Owen is
now with his father, and both, I suppose, are in Kansas, for on the
17th of July they were beyond Iowa City with their teams.   I shall
have much to tell you about this visit.   The subscription could not
have been better bestowed, and the small balance, which I paid Mrs.
Brown, came very opportunely."

I had previously written to Brown, August 14, from Au
Sable Forks, to which he replied from Tabor, in Iowa, Aug.
27, 1857, as follows : —

MY DEAR FRIEND, — Your most welcome letter of the 14th inst.,
from Au Sable Forks, is received.   I cannot express the gratitude I
feel to all the kind friends who contributed towards paying for the
place at North Elba, after I had bought it, as I am thereby relieved
from a very great embarrassment both with Mr. Smith and the young
Thompsons, and also comforted with the feeling that my noble-hearted
wife and daughters will not be driven either to beg or become a burden to my poor boys, who have nothing but their hands to begin with.
I am under special obligation to you for going to look after them and
cheer them in their homely condition.   May God reward you all a
thousandfold!   No language I have can express the satisfaction it
affords me to feel that I have friends who will take the trouble to look
after them and know the real condition of my family, while I am " far
away," perhaps never to return.   I am still waiting here for *company*,

8

additional teams, and means of paying expenses, or to know that I can make a *diversion* in favor of our friends, in case they are involved again in trouble. Colonel Forbes has come on and has a small school at Tabor. I wrote you some days ago, giving a few particulars in regard to our movements; and I intend writing my friend Stearns, as soon as I have anything to tell him that is worth a stamp. Please say to him, that, *provided* I do not get into *such a speculation* as shall swallow up all the property I have been furnished with, I intend to keep it all safe, so that he may be remunerated in the end; but that I am wholly in the dark about it as yet, and that I cannot flatter him much now. Will direct where to write me when I know how to do so.

Very respectfully your friend,

N. H.

"N. H." stands for "Nelson Hawkins," one of the names by which Brown was known to his friends when in an enemy's country. Soon afterwards he did write to Mr. Stearns: "I have learned with gratitude what has been done to render my wife and children more comfortable. May God himself be the everlasting portion of all the contributors! This generous act has lifted a heavy load from my heart."

John Brown had returned to North Elba in April, 1857, after two years' absence; and it was on this visit that he carried with him the old tombstone of his grandfather, Captain John Brown, the Revolutionary soldier, from the burial place of his family in Canton, Conn. He caused the name of his son Frederick, who fell in Kansas, to be carved on this stone, with the date of his death, and placed it where he desired his own grave to be, — beside a huge rock on the hillside where his house stands, — giving directions that his own name and the date of his death should be inscribed there too, when he should fall, as he expected, in the conflict with slavery. That stone now marks his grave, and tells a story which more costly monuments and longer inscriptions could not so well declare. Beside him are buried, after a strange separation of many years, the bones of his son Watson, over which funeral services were performed on this hillside in October, 1882, in the presence of his mother, his wife, his two eldest brothers, and his sister Ruth. The wander-

ings of the father and the son have ceased, and they rest
together in this mountain-home of their affections, — these
pioneers of Liberty, their long march ended at last.[1]

[1] This pioneer instinct of the family has led the sons of John Brown into
many a new country, either for exploration or for settlement. All of them
at one time or another tried their fortune in Kansas ; the youngest surviving son, after the Civil War was decided, journeyed with his mother and
sisters across the great plains to California, where he is a sheep-farmer on
the ranges of Humboldt County. Others of the family have since gone to
Southern California ; while the two eldest sons established themselves
among the first on one of the charming vineyard islands of Lake Erie.
The oldest son, in 1875, while exploring the region about the Black Hills,
encountered Indians on the journey, who made some threats of attacking
"men with hats" if the United States should try to remove them from
their hunting-grounds as had been proposed ; but they were friendly to the
exploring party, and being told that this was the son of Captain Brown,
of Harper's Ferry, of whom, though wild Indians, they had heard the story,
they testified much respect for the son of such a brave. The whole Brown
family now live widely separated, and all are far away from their father's
grave among the Adirondac Mountains. Ruth, the oldest daughter, with
her husband Henry Thompson, is living with her children and grandchildren at Pasadena, Cal. ; Anne has long been married, and has a family of children ; Salmon has seven or eight children ; John, the eldest
brother, has two children, — so that the grandchildren of Captain Brown
already number about twenty. There is no danger of that family becoming
extinct, even though it lost so many members in the war with slavery.
Nor are the Browns likely to become enervated by too much contact with
luxury and the life of cities, for they follow the romantic impulse of their
father, and of Daniel Boone, and keep on the advancing edge of civilization,
— whereof they are pioneers, in more senses than one.

CHAPTER V.

PREPARATIONS FOR THE CONFLICT.

ALL this unwearied industry of John Brown in pioneer life, in the pursuit of wealth, in the establishment of his children, in the formation of acquaintance, and the maintenance of his family, was but preparatory, in his thought and in fact, to the fore-ordained and chosen task of his life, — the overthrow of American slavery. During the English war of 1812 he began to reflect, he says, "on the wretched, hopeless condition of fatherless and motherless slave children, sometimes raising the question, 'Is God their Father?' When this was answered in the Old Testament way, the boy in his teens declared and swore 'eternal war with slavery.'" He did not hasten forward towards the achievement of what he had undertaken, until the fulness of time had come, and he had furnished himself with such military and general knowledge as he deemed requisite. He kept it steadily before him for forty years, educated himself and his children for it, and made it as much a part of his household discipline as were his prayers at morning and evening. Emerson, indeed, in his speech at Salem in 1859, a month before Brown's death, fixes a much earlier date as the beginning of his enterprise against slavery in Virginia. "It was not a piece of spite or revenge, — a plot of two years or of twenty years, — but the keeping of an oath made to heaven and earth forty-seven years before. Forty-seven years at least, — though I incline to accept his own account of the matter at Charlestown, which makes the date a little older, when he said, 'This was all settled millions of years before the world was made.'" Mrs. Brown told me in 1860 that she had known his design and been pledged to aid it for more than twenty years; and John Brown himself had said in 1857, early in my acquaintance

with him, " I always told her that when the time came to
fight against slavery, that conflict would be the signal for
our separation.   She made up her mind to have me go long
before this ; and when I did go, she got ready bandages and
medicine for the wounded."

" For twenty years," he told Richard Hinton in 1858, " I
have never made any business arrangement which would
prevent me at any time answering the call of the Lord.   I
have kept my affairs in such condition that in two weeks
I could wind them up and be ready to obey that call ; permitting nothing to stand in the way of duty, — neither wife,
children, nor worldly goods.   Whenever the time should
come, I was ready ; that hour is very near at hand, and all
who are willing to *act* should be ready."

In 1820, at the time of the Missouri Compromise, when
his hostility to slavery took definite shape ; in 1837, when he
formed his plans for attacking slavery by force ; and even
in 1858, when he had organized an armed band to carry them
out, — his scheme would have seemed mere madness to most
persons.   But Brown had the spirit of his ancestors, the Pilgrim Fathers ; he entered upon his perilous undertaking with
deliberate resolution, after considering what was to be said for
and against it, as did the Pilgrims before they set forth from
Holland to colonize America.   William Bradford, their bravest leader and their historian, has recorded the arguments
for attempting the voyage to America in words which will
apply, with very little change, to the adventure undertaken
two centuries and a half later by Peter Brown's stalwart
descendant, the last of the Puritans.

" It was answered," says Bradford in his History, " that all great
and honourable actions are accompanied with great difficulties, and
must be both enterprised and overcome with answerable courages.   It
was granted the dangers were great, but not desperate ; the difficulties
were many, but not invincible.   For though there were manie of them
likely, yet they were not certain.   It might be sundrie of the things
feared might never befall; others, by provident care and the use of
good means, might in a great measure be prevented ; and all of them,
*through the help of God, by fortitude and patience, might either be borne
or overcome.*   True it was that such attempts were not to be made and
undertaken without good ground and reason ; not rashly or lightly as

many have done for curiosity or hope of gaine, etc. But their condition was not ordinarie; their ends were good and honourable; their calling lawfull and urgente; and therefore they might expecte the blessing of God in their proceeding. Yea, *though they should loose their lives in this action,* yet might they have comforte in the same, and endeavors would be honourable."

The world now sees how honorable the endeavors of Bradford, Standish, and John Brown were, and what momentous results have followed. " Christ died on the tree," said Carlyle to Emerson at Craigenputtock in August, 1833: "that built Dunscone kirk yonder; that brought you and me together." The sequence of events in John Brown's case was the same, and far more important, — since from the crucifixion at Jerusalem a light sprang forth that was reflected back without obstruction from the ugly gallows of Virginia. John Brown took up his cross and followed his Lord; and it was enough for this servant that he was as his Master.

Even from the statesman's point of view the enterprise was glorious, as the event has proved. John Quincy Adams was a statesman sufficiently prudent; yet when the Missouri Compromise was under fierce debate in Congress (Mr. Adams being then Secretary of State, and Mr. Calhoun Secretary of War, to James Monroe) he made this entry in his journal: —

" *Feb.* 24, 1820. I had some conversation with Calhoun on the slave-question pending in Congress. He said he did not think it would produce a dissolution of the Union, but if it should, the South would be compelled to form an alliance, offensive and defensive, with Great Britain. I said that would be returning to the colonial state. He said, ' Yes, pretty much; but it would be forced upon them.' . . . I pressed the conversation no further. But if the dissolution of the Union should result from the slave-question, it is as obvious as anything that can be foreseen of futurity, that *it must shortly afterwards be followed by the universal emancipation of the slaves;* . . . the destructive progress of emancipation, which, like all great religious and political reformations, is *terrible in its means, though happy and glorious in its end.* Slavery is the great and foul stain upon the North American Union, and it is a contemplation worthy of the most exalted soul whether its total abolition is or is not practicable; if practicable, by what means it may be effected, and if a choice of means be within the scope of the object, what means would accomplish it at the smallest cost of human sufferance ?   *A dissolution, at least temporary, of the Union as now constituted would be necessary ; and the dissolution must be upon a point involving the question of slavery, and no other.   The Union might then be reorganized on the fundamental principle of emancipation.*   This object is vast in its compass, awful in its prospects, sublime and beautiful in its issue. A life devoted to it would be nobly spent or sacrificed."

Such a life was that of John Brown.   He entered upon it when as a boy, "during the war with England," seven years before this colloquy of Adams with Calhoun, he saw his little black playmate starved and beaten, and with boyish ardor " swore eternal war with slavery." He ended it upon the gallows in Virginia, and men said he "died as a fool dieth." But the method that he devised for emancipation was that which, within five years from his death, the nation adopted and carried to a successful issue.   It was the method of force ; and it proceeded gradually, as Brown had foreseen that it must, from State to State, and without overthrowing the general government.   There was, however, what Adams had predicted, — a temporary dissolution of the Union, followed by " amendment and repeal," as Brown desired ; and then by that which Adams and Brown both had longed for, — a reorganization of the Union " on the fundamental question of emancipation." Thus, again, in human history, as so many times before, did the divine paradox reassert itself, and the stone which the builders rejected became the head of the corner.   Beside the Potomac, where the founder of our Republic lived and died, crowned with honors, it was decreed that the restorer of the Republic should also die by the hangman's hand.   The work that Washington and Jefferson left unfinished, Brown came to complete ; and Lincoln with his proclamations, Grant and Sherman with their armies, did little more than follow in the path that Brown had pointed out.   "Of all the men who were said to be my contemporaries," wrote a Concord poet, "it seemed to me that John Brown was the only one who had not died.   I meet him at every turn.   He is more alive than ever he was ; he is no longer working in secret ; he works in public, and in the clearest light that shines on this land."

This was Thoreau's verdict in 1860, before the great Civil
War had shown the world what Brown's true place was among
the successful champions of humanity. Fifteen years after
his death, when the American Republic had regained the
universal freedom of men, for which Jefferson formulated
its charter in 1776, and when the French Republic had re-
called Victor Hugo from his long and honorable exile, that
commanding genius of his century thus addressed the widow
of John Brown : [1] —

MADAM, — Several years have passed away since your noble husband completed the sacrifice of a life consecrated to the most generous
of all aims. The gallows on which he suffered called forth a cry of
universal indignation, which was the signal for securing the emancipation of a race till then disinherited. Honor be to him, and to
his worthy sons who were associated with him in his endeavors !
To the blessing with which the present age crowns their memory
shall be added that of future generations. These thoughts, Madam,

[1] This letter, written by Hugo, was signed also by the other members of
a French committee which presented to Mrs. Brown in 1874 a gold medal
in honor of her husband. Their names were Louis Blanc, Victor Schœlcher,
Patrice Larroque, Eugène Pelletan, Melvil-Bloncourt, Capron, Ch. L. Chas-
sin, Étienne Arago, Laurent-Pichat, and L. Gornes. The medal itself was
modelled by Wurder, of Brussels, bearing on one side a bearded head of
Brown, and on the reverse this inscription : " To the memory of John
Brown, judicially murdered at Charlestown, in Virginia, on the 2d of December, 1859 ; and in commemoration also of his sons and comrades who,
with him, became the victims of their devotion to the cause of negro emancipation." This medal (weighing nearly five ounces) was sent to Mrs.
Brown in California by her son John, who received it from William Lloyd
Garrison, to whom the French committee gave a bronze copy of the medal,
with the following letter : —

PARIS, Oct. 20, 1874.
Wm. Lloyd Garrison.

SIR, — We have received, through the hands of M. Victor Schœlcher, the letter by
which the son of John Brown informs you that the family will receive, with all due
appreciation, the gold medal struck in memory of the glorious death of his father. We
beg you, therefore, to be kind enough, in accordance with your generous offer, to charge
yourself with its delivery to the Brown family, together with the letter to Mrs. Brown
accompanying it. In thanking you for your kind intervention, we beg you to accept
the assurance of our high esteem ; and also a copy of the medal, in bronze, which is the
work (without remuneration) of a sympathizing artist. We have sent to the agency of
the house of Lebeau, who represent the line of steamers from Liverpool to Boston, the
box containing the gold medal addressed to the widow of John Brown, — expenses pre-
paid.

The Delegate CAPRON.
PATRICE LARROQUE, Secretary.

must assuredly tend greatly to alleviate your great sorrow. But you have sought a higher consolation for your grief, in the reflection that beyond the imperfect justice of man sits enthroned that Supreme Justice which will leave no good action unrewarded and no crime unpunished. We hope, also, that you may derive some comfort from this expression of our sympathy, as citizens of the French Republic, which would have reached you earlier but for the prolonged and cruel sufferings through which our unfortunate country has been forced to pass.

Though Brown drew this applause from the French Republicans for his generous martyrdom, nothing could be further from the Red Republican temper and from French impiety than were his temper and devout purpose. He was a Saxon follower of the French Calvin and the Mauritanian Augustine, as they were followers of the Hebrew Scriptures. John Brown was a Bible-worshipper, if ever any man was. He read and meditated on the Bible constantly ; in his will he bequeathed a Bible to each of his children and grand-children ; and he wrote to his family a few days before his execution, " I beseech you every one to make the Bible your daily and nightly study." Such was the man — of the best New England blood, of the stock of the Plymouth Pilgrims, and bred up like them " in the nurture and admonition of the Lord " — who was selected by God, and knew himself to be so chosen, to overthrow the bulwark of oppression in America. His prayers and meditations from childhood had been leading him towards this consecration of himself to a great work, and he had no dearer purpose in life than to fulfil the mission. He seems to have declared a definite plan of attacking slavery in one of its strongholds, by force, as early as 1839; and it was to obtain money for this enter-prise that he engaged in land-speculations and wool-mer-chandise for the next ten or twelve years. His ventures failed ; it was not destined that he should grow rich and be able to help the poor from his abundance; and he accepted the narrow path of poverty. While tending his flocks in Ohio, with his sons and daughters about him, he first com-municated to them his purpose of attacking slavery in arms. From that time forward, a period of more than twenty years, he devoted himself, not exclusively, but mainly, to the un-

dertaking in which he sacrificed his life. He looked on his
mercantile connections, on his acquaintance at home and his
travels abroad, as means to this great end; he came back
from Europe poor, but more in love than ever with American democracy, and more resolved that American slavery
should be destroyed. In his campaign against it he did not
contemplate insurrection, but partisan warfare, — at first on a
small scale, then more extensive; yet he did not shrink from
the extreme consequences of his theory. A man of peace
for more than fifty years of his life, he nevertheless understood that war had its uses, and that there were worse evils
than battles for a great principle. He more than once said
to me, and doubtless to others, "I believe in the Golden
Rule and the Declaration of Independence. I think they
both mean the same thing; and it is better that a whole
generation should pass off the face of the earth, — men,
women, and children, — by a violent death, than that one
jot of either should fail *in this country.* I mean exactly *so,*
sir." He also told me that " he had much considered the
matter, and had about concluded that forcible separation of
the connection between master and slave was necessary to
fit the blacks for self-government." First a soldier, then a
citizen, was his plan with the liberated slaves. "When they
stand like men, the nation will respect them," he said; " it
is necessary to teach them this." He looked forward, no
doubt, to years of conflict, in which the blacks, as in the later
years of the Civil War, should be formed into regiments
and brigades and be drilled in the whole art of war, — like
the black soldiers of Toussaint L'Ouverture and Dessalines,
in Hayti. But in his more inspired moments he foresaw a
speedier end to the combat which he began. Once he said,
" A few men in the right, and knowing they are right, can
overturn a mighty king. Fifty men, twenty men, in the
Alleghanies, could break slavery to pieces in two years."

The actual attempt of Brown in Virginia to break in
pieces this national idol of slavery was judged as madness by his countrymen at the moment, and even now, as
we look back on it, seems devoid of the elements which
would make success possible. But with God all things are
possible, — and success followed the noble madness of his

assault. That brief campaign, with its immediate frustra-
tion and its ultimate and speedy triumph, is now seen to
have been an omen of the divine purpose. It has already
become a part of the world's history and literature, — a new
chapter added to the record of heroism and self-devotion, a
new incident in the long romance which has been for three
hundred years the history of Virginia. It was little to the
honor of Virginia then; but so heavy has been the penalty
since visited on that State and her people, that we may omit
all censure upon what was done. God has judged between
them and John Brown; and His judgment, as always, will be
found not only just but merciful, since it has removed from
a brave and generous people the curse of human slavery. It
was for this result, and this alone, that Brown plotted and
fought, prayed and died; and even before his death he saw
that his prayers would be answered.

Although John Brown would have justified a slave insurrection, or indeed almost any means of destroying slavery,
he did not seek to incite general insurrection among the
Southern slaves. The venture in which he lost his life was
not an *insurrection* in any sense of the word, but an invasion
or foray, similar in its character to that which Garibaldi was
to make six months later in Sicily for the overthrow of the
infamous Bourbon tyranny there. The Italian hero succeeded, and became dictator of the island he had conquered;
the American hero failed for the moment, and was put to
death. But his soul went marching on; and millions of his
countrymen followed in his footsteps two years later, to
complete the campaign in which Brown had led the forlorn
hope. As usual, the forlorn hope was sacrificed, but by their
death the final victory was won.

While this servant and prophet of God was waiting for
the accepted time, he continued those efforts in behalf of
fugitive slaves which began so early. He was specially active in this after the enactment of Senator Mason's Fugitive
Slave Bill in 1850, — supported as it was by Webster, of
Massachusetts, and Clay, of Kentucky. Poor black men were
then hunted down at the instigation of rich white men, even
in Boston; and the courts of Massachusetts were disgraced
by the chains of Virginian slavery. Early in 1851, while

Brown was nominally a resident of the Adirondac woods,
he was at his old home in Springfield, and there formed an
organization among the colored people, many of whom were
refugees, to resist the capture of any fugitive slave, no matter by what authority. The letter of instructions given by
Brown at that time to his Springfield "Gileadites," as he
called them, deserves to be cited here, as an authentic document throwing light on the character and purposes of
Brown at that time, nearly nine years before his campaign
in Virginia. It is somewhat condensed from his manuscript:

WORDS OF ADVICE.

Branch of the United States League of Gileadites. Adopted Jan. 15, 1851,
as written and recommended by John Brown.

"UNION IS STRENGTH."

Nothing so charms the American people as personal bravery.
Witness the case of Cinques, of everlasting memory, on board the
"Amistad." The trial for life of one bold and to some extent successful
man, for defending his rights in good earnest, would arouse more sympathy throughout the nation than the accumulated wrongs and sufferings of more than three millions of our submissive colored population.
We need not mention the Greeks struggling against the oppressive
Turks, the Poles against Russia, nor the Hungarians against Austria
and Russia combined, to prove this. *No jury can be found in the
Northern States that would convict a man for defending his rights to
the last extremity. This is well understood by Southern Congressmen,
who insisted that the right of trial by jury should not be granted to
the fugitive.* Colored people have ten times the number of fast
friends among the whites than they suppose, and would have ten
times the number they now have were they but half as much in earnest to secure their dearest rights as they are to ape the follies and
extravagances of their white neighbors, and to indulge in idle show,
in ease, and in luxury. Just think of the money expended by individuals in your behalf in the past twenty years! Think of the number who have been mobbed and imprisoned on your account! Have
any of you seen the Branded Hand? Do you remember the names
of Lovejoy and Torrey?

Should one of your number be arrested, you must collect together
as quickly as possible, so as to outnumber your adversaries who are
taking an active part against you. Let no able-bodied man appear
on the ground unequipped, or with his weapons exposed to view:

let that be understood beforehand. Your plans must be known only to yourself, and with the understanding that all traitors must die, wherever caught and proven to be guilty. " Whosoever is fearful or afraid, let him return and part early from Mount Gilead " (Judges, vii. 3; Deut. xx. 8). Give all cowards an opportunity to show it on condition of holding their peace. *Do not delay one moment after you are ready : you will lose all your resolution if you do.* Let the first blow be the signal for all to engage ; and when engaged do not do your work by halves, but make clean work with your enemies, — and be sure you meddle not with any others. By going about your business quietly, you will get the job disposed of before the number that an uproar would bring together can collect ; and you will have the advantage of those who come out against you, for they will be wholly unprepared with either equipments or matured plans ; all with them will be confusion and terror. Your enemies will be slow to attack you after you have done up the work nicely; and if they should, they will have to encounter your white friends as well as you; for you may safely calculate on a division of the whites, and may by that means get to an honorable parley.

Be firm, determined, and cool; but let it be understood that you are not to be driven to desperation without making it an awful dear job to others as well as to you. Give them to know distinctly that those who live in wooden houses should not throw fire, and that you are just as able to suffer as your white neighbors. *After effecting a rescue, if you are assailed, go into the houses of your most prominent and influential white friends with your wives; and that will effectually fasten upon them the suspicion of being connected with you, and will compel them to make a common cause with you, whether they would otherwise live up to their profession or not. This would leave them no choice in the matter.* Some would doubtless prove themselves true of their own choice; others would flinch. That would be taking them at their own words. You may make a tumult in the court-room where a trial is going on, by burning gunpowder freely in paper packages, if you cannot think of any better way to create a momentary alarm, and might possibly give one or more of your enemies a hoist. But in such case the prisoner will need to take the hint at once, and bestir himself; and so should his friends improve the opportunity for a general rush.

A lasso might possibly be applied to a slave-catcher for once with good effect. Hold on to your weapons, and never be persuaded to leave them, part with them, or have them far away from you. *Stand by one another and by your friends, while a drop of blood remains ; and be hanged, if you must, but tell no tales out of school. Make no confession.*

Union is strength. Without some well-digested arrangements nothing to any good purpose is likely to be done, let the demand be never so great. Witness the case of Hamlet and Long in New York, when there was no well-defined plan of operations or suitable preparation beforehand.

The desired end may be effectually secured by the means proposed; namely, the enjoyment of our inalienable rights.

AGREEMENT.

As citizens of the United States of America, trusting in a just and merciful God, whose spirit and all-powerful aid we humbly implore, *we will ever be true to the flag of our beloved country, always acting under it.* We, whose names are hereunto affixed, do constitute ourselves a branch of the United States League of Gileadites. That we will provide ourselves at once with suitable implements, and will aid those who do not possess the means, if any such are disposed to join us. We invite every colored person whose heart is engaged in the performance of our business, whether male or female, old or young. The duty of the aged, infirm, and young members of the League shall be to give instant notice to all members in case of an attack upon any of our people. We agree to have no officers except a treasurer and secretary *pro tem.*, until after some trial of courage and talent of able-bodied members shall enable us to elect officers from those who shall have rendered the most important services. Nothing but wisdom and undaunted courage, efficiency, and general good conduct shall in any way influence us in electing our officers.

Then follows, in the original manuscript, a set of resolves, such as John Brown, with his methodical, forward-looking mind, was in the habit of drawing up whenever he organized any branch of his movement against slavery. This paper, which is sufficiently curious, reads as follows : —

Resolutions of the Springfield Branch of the United States League of Gileadites. Adopted 15th Jan., 1851.

1. *Resolved,* That we, whose names are affixed, do constitute ourselves a Branch of the United States League, under the above name.

2. *Resolved,* That all business of this Branch be conducted with the utmost quiet and good order; that we individually provide ourselves with suitable implements without delay ; and that we will sufficiently aid those who do not possess the means, if any such are disposed to join us.

3. *Resolved*, That a committee of one or more discreet, influential men be appointed to collect the names of all colored persons whose heart is engaged for the performance of our business, whether male or female, whether old or young.

4. *Resolved*, That the appropriate duty of all aged, infirm, female, or youthful members of this Branch is to give instant notice to all other members of any attack upon the rights of our people, first informing all able-bodied men of this League or Branch, and next, all well known friends of the colored people; and *that this information be confined to such alone*, that there may be as little excitement as possible, and no noise in the so doing.

5. *Resolved*, That a committee of one or more discreet persons be appointed to ascertain the condition of colored persons in regard to implements, and to instruct others in regard to their conduct in any emergency.

6. *Resolved*, That no other officer than a *treasurer*, with a president and secretary *pro tem.*, be appointed by this Branch, until after some trial of the courage and talents of able-bodied members shall enable a majority of the members to elect their officers from those who *shall have rendered the most important services.*

7. *Resolved*, That, trusting in a just and merciful God, whose *spirit* and *all-powerful aid* we humbly implore, we will most cheerfully and heartily support and obey such officers, when chosen as before; and that nothing but *wisdom, undaunted courage, efficiency*, and *general good conduct* shall in any degree influence our individual votes in case of such election.

8. *Resolved*, That a meeting of all members of this Branch shall be immediately called for the purpose of electing officers (to be chosen by ballot) after the first trial *shall have been made* of the qualifications of individual members for such command, as before mentioned.

9. *Resolved*, That as citizens of the United States of America we will ever be found true to the flag of our beloved country, always acting under it.[1]

[1] This is signed by the following members : —

B. C. Dowling.	Henry Johnson.	Henry Hector.
John Smith.	G. W. Holmes.	John Strong.
Reverdy Johnson.	C. A. Gazam.	Wm. Burns.
Samuel Chandler.	Eliza Green.	Wm. Gordon.
J. N. Howard.	Jane Fowler.	Joseph Addams.
Charles Rollins.	H. J. Jones.	Wm. Green.
Scipio Webb.	Ann Johnson.	Wm. H. Montague.
Charles Odell.	Cyrus Thomas.	Jane Wicks.
L. Wallace.	Henry Robinson.	James Madison.

And seventeen others.

This was not the only undertaking of the sort in which
John Brown lent his aid and advice to the fugitive slaves
and their free brethren of color at the North. For years
he labored quietly among them, seeking to bring them to
a better knowledge of their position, and to form habits
that would fit them for freedom ; and in this period he
wrote some curious papers. Among these are the following
chapters of an unfinished pamphlet called "Sambo's Mistakes," which he began to publish in an obscure Abolitionist
journal called " The Ramshorn," — with a distant allusion,
I suppose, to the downfall of Jericho at the blowing of the
Hebrew horns. The manuscript of these chapters is now in
the library of the Maryland Historical Society at Baltimore,
in the handwriting of John Brown, and reads thus : —

SAMBO'S MISTAKES.

I.

MESSRS. EDITORS, — Notwithstanding I may have committed a
few mistakes in the course of a long life, like others of my colored
brethren, yet you will perceive at a glance that I have always been
remarkable for a seasonable discovery of my errors and quick perception of the true course. I propose to give you a few illustrations in
this and the following chapters.

For instance, when I was a boy I learned to read ; but instead of
giving my attention to sacred and profane history, by which I might
have become acquainted with the true character of God and of man ;
learned the true course for individuals, societies, and nations to pursue ; stored my mind with an endless variety of rational and practical ideas ; profited by the experience of millions of others of all
ages ; fitted myself for the most important stations in life, and fortified my mind with the best and wisest resolutions, and noblest
sentiments and motives, — I have spent my whole life devouring
silly novels and other miserable trash, such as most newspapers of
the day and other popular writings are filled with ; thereby unfitting
myself for the realities of life, and acquiring a taste for nonsense and
low wit, so that I have no relish for sober truth, useful knowledge,
or practical wisdom. By this means I have passed through life
without profit to myself or others, a mere blank on which nothing worth perusing is written. But I can see in a twink where I
missed it.

Another error into which I fell in early life was the notion that
chewing and smoking tobacco would make a man of me, but little
inferior to some of the whites. The money I spent in this way
would, with the interest of it, have enabled me to have relieved a
great many sufferers, supplied me with a well-selected, interesting
library, and paid for a good farm for the support and comfort of my
old age ; whereas I have now neither books, clothing, the satisfaction of having benefited others, nor where to lay my hoary head.
But I can see in a moment where I missed it.

Another of the few errors of my life is, that I have joined the
Free Masons, Odd Fellows, Sons of Temperance, and a score of
other secret societies, instead of seeking the company of intelligent,
wise, and good men, from whom I might have learned much that
would be interesting, instructive, and useful ; and have in that way
squandered a great amount of most precious time, and money enough,
sometimes in a single year, which if I had then put the same out on
interest and kept it so, would have kept me always above board,
given me character and influence among men, or have enabled me
to pursue some respectable calling, so that I might employ others
to their benefit and improvement ; but, as it is, I have always been
poor, in debt, and now obliged to travel about in search of employment
as a hostler, shoe-black, and fiddler. But I retain all my quickness
of perception ; I can see readily where I missed it.

II.

Another error of my riper years has been, that when any meeting
of colored people has been called in order to consider of any important matter of general interest, I have been so eager to display my
spouting talents, and so tenacious of some trifling theory or other
that I have adopted, that I have generally lost all sight of the business in hand, consumed the time disputing about things of no moment, and thereby defeated entirely many important measures calculated to promote the general welfare ; but I am happy to say I can
see in a minute where I missed it.

Another small error of my life (for I never committed great blun-
ders) has been that I never would (for the sake of union in the
furtherance of the most vital interests of our race) yield any minor
point of difference. In this way I have always had to act with but
a few, or more frequently alone, and could accomplish nothing worth
living for ; but I have one comfort, I can see in a minute where I
missed it.

Another little fault which I have committed is, that if in anything
another man has failed of coming up to my standard, notwithstanding

that he might possess many of the most valuable traits, and be most
admirably adapted to fill some one important post, I would reject him
entirely, injure his influence, oppose his measures, and even glory
. in his defeats, while his intentions were good, and his plans well
laid. But I have the great satisfaction of being able to say, without
fear of contradiction, that I can see very quick where I missed it.

III.

Another small mistake which I have made is, that I could never
bring myself to practise any present self-denial, although my theories
have been excellent. For instance, I have bought expensive gay
clothing, nice canes, watches, safety-chains, finger-rings, breastpins,
and many other things of a like nature, thinking I might by that
means distinguish myself from the vulgar, as some of the better class
of whites do. I have always been of the foremost in getting up
expensive parties, and running after fashionable amusements; have
indulged my appetite freely whenever I had the means (and even
with borrowed means); have patronized the dealers in nuts, candy,
etc., freely, and have sometimes bought good suppers, and was
always a regular customer at livery stables. By these, and many
other means, I have been unable to benefit my suffering brethren,
and am now but poorly able to keep my own soul and body together;
but do not think me thoughtless or dull of apprehension, for I can
see at once where I missed it.

Another trifling error of my life has been, that I have always expected to secure the favor of the whites by tamely submitting to every
species of indignity, contempt, and wrong, instead of nobly resisting
their brutal aggressions from principle, and taking my place as a
man, and assuming the responsibilities of a man, a citizen, a husband,
a father, a brother, a neighbor, a friend, — as God requires of every
one (if his neighbor will allow him to do it); but I find that I get,
for all my submission, about the same reward that the Southern
slaveocrats render to the dough-faced statesmen of the North, for
being bribed and browbeat and fooled and cheated, as the Whigs and
Democrats love to be, and think themselves highly honored if they
may be allowed to lick up the spittle of a Southerner. I say I get
the same reward. But I am uncommon quick-sighted; I can see in
a minute where I missed it.

Another little blunder which I made is, that while I have always
been a most zealous Abolitionist, I have been constantly at war with
my friends about certain religious tenets. I was first a Presbyterian.
but I could never think of acting with my Quaker friends, for they
were the rankest heretics; and the Baptists would be in the water,

and the Methodists denied the doctrine of Election, etc. Of later
years, since becoming enlightened by Garrison, Abby Kelly, and
other really benevolent persons, I have been spending all my force
on my friends who love the Sabbath, and have felt that all was at
stake on that point; just as it has proved to be of late in France, in
the abolition of slavery in their colonies. Now I cannot doubt,
Messrs. Editors, notwithstanding I have been unsuccessful, that you
will allow me full credit for my peculiar quick-sightedness. I can see
in one second where I missed it.

This paper, dating before 1850, illustrates the points
of resemblance between Franklin and John Brown, — for
"Poor Richard" himself might have written these keen
and kindly sayings. Brown disliked the effort of writing,
which led him to shorten almost everything he wrote; so
that "Sambo's Mistakes" was one of his longest essays,
and perhaps the most satirical. He took little part in the
public debates on slavery, and when in the last year of his
life (1859), he was present for a day or two at the Antislavery meetings in Boston, he came out saying, "Talk! talk!
talk! — that will never set the slave free." His form of
activity was something that would operate, as he said in
his letter of 1834, "like powder confined in rock;" and
such was the effect of his own movements in Kansas and
in Virginia.

His daughter, Mrs. Thompson, thus speaks of his concern
for the fugitive slaves in the anxious season of 1850–51,
when the slaveholders, encouraged by the success of the
Clay and Webster Compromises, sought to insult and worry
the people of the North by reclaiming all runaway slaves
wherever they might be : —

"Father did not close up his wool business in Springfield when he
went to North Elba, and had to make several journeys back and forth
in 1849–50. He was at Springfield in January, 1851, soon after the
passage of the Fugitive Slave Law, and went round among his colored
friends there who had been fugitives, urging them to resist the law,
no matter by what authority it should be enforced. He told them to
arm themselves with revolvers, men and women, and not to be taken
alive. When he got to North Elba he told us about the Fugitive
Slave Law, and bade us resist any attempt that might be made to
take any fugitive from our town, regardless of fine or imprisonment.

Our faithful boy Cyrus was one of that class; and our feelings were
so roused that we would all have defended him, though the women
folks had resorted to hot water. Father at this time said, 'Their
cup of iniquity is almost full.' One evening as I was singing 'The
Slave Father Mourning for his Children,' containing these words, —

> 'Ye 're gone from me, my gentle ones,
> With all your shouts of mirth ;
> A silence is within my walls,
> A darkness round my hearth,' —

father got up and walked the floor, and before I could finish the
song, he said, 'O Ruth! don't sing any more; it is too sad!'"

This letter to Mrs. Brown relates to the same emergency : —

SPRINGFIELD, MASS., Jan. 17, 1851.

DEAR WIFE, — . . . Since the sending off to slavery of Long
from New York, I have improved my leisure hours quite busily with
colored people here, in advising them how to act. and in giving them
all the encouragement in my power. They very much need encouragement and advice ; and some of them are so alarmed that they tell
me they cannot sleep on account of either themselves or their wives
and children. I can only say I think I have been enabled to do
something to revive their broken spirits. I want all my family to
imagine themselves in the same dreadful condition. My only spare
time being taken up (often till late hours at night) in the way I
speak of, has prevented me from the gloomy homesick feelings
which had before so much oppressed me : not that I forget my
family at all.

Some of the advice thus given has already been copied :
more condensed suggestions are as follows : —

" Collect quietly, so as to outnumber the adversaries who are taking
an active part against you ; make clean work with all such, and be
sure you meddle not with any other. Do not delay one moment after
you have a fair majority of your own men over those who are actually
about the mischief. Let the collection of a fair majority be your signal to engage ; and when engaged do not do your business by halves.
When one of you engage, let all the others fall to work without noise
or confusion. Stand by one another and by your friends while a drop
of blood remains, and be hanged if you must, but tell no tales out of
school ; *make no confessions.* Hold on to your tools, and never be

scared or persuaded, by the world combined, to part with them, or to leave them away from you. Do not trust them with friend or foe. Always keep your families advised of the places where you may be found when absent from home."

Four or five years earlier than this, and soon after Brown's arrival in Springfield, he had begun to communicate his purpose of attacking slavery by force to the colored men whom he found to be worthy of trust. In 1846 there was living in Springfield (where he still resides) a fugitive slave from the Eastern Shore of Maryland, — Thomas Thomas by name, — whom Brown engaged to work for him as a porter in his wool warehouse. "How early shall I come to-morrow," said Thomas the day he was hired. "We begin work at seven," said Brown; "but I wish you would come round earlier, so that I can talk with you." Thomas therefore went to his employer's the next morning between five and six o'clock, found Brown waiting for him, and there received from him the outlines of his plan to liberate the slaves, and was invited to join in the enterprise, which he agreed to do. This was nine years before Brown went to Kansas, and two years before Sumner, Wilson, Adams, S. C. Phillips, Hoar, and their friends formed the Free Soil party of Massachusetts. Thomas was afterward sent by Brown to look up Madison Washington, the leader of the courageous slaves of the vessel "Creole," who was wanted as a leader among the colored recruits that were to join the band of liberators; but Washington, when found, proved to be an unfit person for such a task.

It is said that the first definite thought of the place where he should make his attack upon the slave system came to Brown while he was surveying lands for Oberlin College, in what is now West Virginia, in 1840. These lands were, in part at least, in the county of Jackson, which borders on Ohio, and is separated from that State by the Ohio River. It is west of the Alleghanies, and is not very mountainous; but in approaching or leaving it Brown had occasion to observe how useful those mountains would be to any band of men who were aiming at emancipation by force. "The mountains and swamps of the South," said Brown in Kansas,

" were intended by God as a refuge for the slave, and a defence against his master." That he cherished this purpose
when he wrote the following from West Virginia, nearly
twenty years before his foray at Harper's Ferry, is certain ;
and the thought that he had his great project in mind then,
gives an interest to the brief letter : —

To his Family.

RIPLEY, VA., April 27, 1840.

. . . I like the country as well as I expected, and its inhabitants
rather better ; and I have seen the spot where, if it be the will of
Providence, I hope one day to live with my family. . . . Were
the inhabitants as resolute and industrious as the Northern people,
and did they understand how to manage as well, they would become
rich ; but they are not generally so. They seem to have no idea of
improvement in their cattle, sheep, or hogs, nor to know the use of
enclosed pasture-fields for their stock, but spend a large portion
of their time in hunting for their cattle, sheep, and horses ; and the
same habit continues from father to son. . . . By comparing them
with the people of other parts of the country, I can see new and
abundant proof that knowledge is power. I think we might be very
useful to them on many accounts, were we so disposed. May God
in mercy keep us all, and enable us to get wisdom ; and with all our
getting or losing, to get understanding !

Affectionately yours,

JOHN BROWN.

Before John Brown went to the Adirondacs to look after
the colored people there, he seems to have had another
project of the same sort in view, in connection with these
Oberlin lands. The records of that Ohio college (where
white and colored students were educated together, before
any other such institution ventured to do so) show the following entries : —

" *April* 1, 1840. In the Prudential Committee, Brother John
Brown from Hudson being present, some negotiations were opened
in respect to our Virginia lands.

" *April* 3, 1840. A communication from Brother John Brown, of
Hudson, was presented and read by the Secretary, containing a proposition to visit, survey, and make the necessary investigation respecting boundaries, etc., of those lands, for one dollar per day, and
a moderate allowance for necessary expenses ; said paper frankly

expressing also his design of viewing the lands, as a preliminary step to locating his family upon them, should the opening prove a favorable one: whereupon, *Voted*, that said proposition be acceded to, and that a commission and needful outfit be furnished by the Secretary and Treasurer."

"*July* 14, 1840. The report of John Brown, respecting his agency to Virginia and examination of the Smith donation of land, was read by the Secretary and deferred."

"*Aug.* 11, 1840. *Voted*, that the Secretary address a letter to John Brown, of Hudson, in reference to the Virginia land agency."

In the records of the Board of Trustees, under date of Aug. 28, 1840, is the following minute: —

"*Voted*, that the Prudential Committee be authorized to perfect negotiations, and convey by deed to Brother John Brown, of Hudson, one thousand acres of our Virginia land on the conditions suggested in the correspondence which has already transpired between him and the committee."

There is nothing in the record of the subsequent action of the Prudential Committee or of the Trustees which goes to show that a deed was actually given to John Brown, or that the conditions were fulfilled by him.

Concerning the opening of this negotiation, I find this letter from an Oberlin official, Levi Burnell, to John Brown's father, Owen, who was a Trustee of the college: —

OBERLIN, April 3, 1840.

DEAR BROTHER BROWN, — I received your favor by your son John, and our committee have opened negotiations with him preliminary to his visiting our Virginia lands. We hope for a favorable issue, both for him and the institution. When he has thoroughly examined the papers and spent the necessary time upon the premises, we expect that he will know more than all of us about the matter; and I trust we shall feel disposed to offer liberal inducements for him and others to settle there, if that is best. Should he succeed in clearing up titles without difficulty or lawsuits, it would be easy, as it appears to me, to make provision for religious and school privileges, and by proper efforts, with the blessing of God, soon see that wilderness bud and blossom as the rose.

The main outlines of Brown's plan have been given by one of his Kansas company, Richard Realf, who heard him explain it in Canada in 1858, and who professed to have made this statement up from Brown's own words. It is evidently colored and exaggerated in many particulars by the imagination of the reporter, and at several points is contrary to what is otherwise known. But with these abatements, it may be taken as a general outline of what Brown actually said. This is Realf's report, which it needs a long breath to read, for its odd rhetoric : —

"John Brown stated that for twenty or thirty years the idea had possessed him like a passion of giving liberty to the slaves; that he made a journey to England, during which he made a tour upon the European continent, inspecting all fortifications, and especially all earthwork forts which he could find, with a view of applying the knowledge thus gained, with modifications and inventions of his own, to a mountain warfare in the United States. He stated that he had read all the books upon insurrectionary warfare that he could lay his hands on : the Roman warfare, the successful opposition of the Spanish chieftains during the period when Spain was a Roman province, — how with ten thousand men, divided and subdivided into small companies, acting simultaneously yet separately, they withstood the whole consolidated power of the Roman Empire through a number of years. In addition to this, he had become very familiar with the successful warfare waged by Schamyl,[1] the Circassian chief, against the Russians; he had posted himself in relation to the war of Toussaint L'Ouverture; he had become thoroughly acquainted with the wars in Hayti and the islands round about; and from all these things he had drawn the conclusion, — believing, as he stated there he did believe, and as we all (if I may judge from myself) believed, — that upon the first intimation of a plan formed for the liberation of the slaves, they would immediately rise all over the Southern States. He supposed that they would come into the mountains to join him,

[1] It is singular that while this Schamyl, the daring Lesghian chieftain, who, in alliance with the Circassians, had defied the Czar for twenty years, was visiting St. Petersburg as the honored guest of his foeman, John Brown at that very time was captured and executed by the American slaveholders. Schamyl was at once the warrior and the prophet of his race, and in the fastnesses of the Caucasus, where the Russians assailed him, he had worn out their armies by delays, ambuscades, and surprises. At last, after enormous losses of men and material by the Russians, they stormed his stronghold, and he surrendered in 1859. The same New York newspapers which contained the news of Brown's failure described the hospitable reception of Schamyl at the capital of Nicholas.

where he purposed to work, and that by flocking to his standard they would enable him (making the line of mountains which cuts diagonally through Maryland and Virginia, down through the Southern States into Tennessee and Alabama, the base of his operations) to act upon the plantations on the plains lying on each side of that range of mountains ; that we should be able to establish ourselves in the fastnesses. And if any hostile action were taken against us, either by the militia of the States or by the armies of the United States, we purposed to defeat first the militia, and next, if possible, the troops of the United States ; and then organize the free blacks under the provisional constitution, which would carve out for the locality of its jurisdiction all that mountainous region in which the blacks were to be established, in which they were to be taught the useful and mechanical arts, and all the business of life. Schools were also to be established, and so on. The negroes were to be his soldiers."

This was in fact the purpose of Brown, — to enlist a sufficient number of the slaves and the free negroes of the North as soldiers, without exciting a general insurrection, and then to establish his armed force where it could best annoy the slaveholders and make their property unsafe. He intended to officer his army with white and colored men, but to use the latter for soldiers chiefly. He had a higher opinion than most men at that time of the capacity of the negro as a soldier and a citizen, — an opinion since justified by events. I have often heard Brown dwell on this subject, and mention instances of his fitness to take care of himself ; saying, in his quaint way, " negroes behaved so much like *folks*, he almost thought they were so." He thought a forcible separation between master and slave might be necessary, in order to educate the slaves for self-government.

A part of Brown's preparation for the warfare in which he meant to engage was his Spartan mode of life and his self-denial in most matters of food, dress, amusement, and personal comfort. His daughter's testimony is clear on this point ; and all who knew him can recall instances of this self-denial. He followed strictly the sage's injunction, " At rich men's tables eat thou bread and pulse ; " and he was rather averse to accept the hospitality of those friends who lived luxuriously. He avoided the sumptuous hotels of

New York and other cities, and went by preference to plain
taverns where farmers and drovers were entertained. His
dress was neat but plain, and he wore the same garments a
long time, always from choice, and sometimes from necessity.
He never used tobacco in any form, and seldom drank wine
or spirits. When at home he drank milk or water. It was
not till a few years before his death that he drank tea or
coffee, and he took up this habit only from the desire to
give no trouble to others; for he found that in travelling it
sometimes annoyed good people to see their guest drink
water instead of tea. He never ate cheese or butter; and
said that as a boy, ten years old, he was once sent of an
errand where a lady gave him a piece of bread and butter;
he was so bashful that he did not dare tell her he never ate
butter, but as soon as he got out of the house he ran as fast
as he could for a long time, and then threw her gift out of
sight. He had great skill in providing for a company of
men, and could have maintained a force in the field at very
little cost. But his health was much affected in his later
years by malaria and other ills of advancing age, from which,
when he entered upon active service, he lost much time and
suffered great hardships.[1]

---

[1] Jason Brown, who remembers well the oath taken by himself and his
family when his father first made known to them his purpose of attacking
slavery by force, thinks the time was not 1837, but 1839. The place, he
says, was Franklin, and the time was "when the colored preacher Mr.
Fayette was at father's; and he (Mr. F.) and mother, John, Jason, and
Owen were sworn to secrecy, and to do all in their power to abolish slavery." Jason also thinks he cut the date of the year on a rock near the
swimming-place in Hudson which he and Owen used to frequent. Mrs.
Brown gave me the impression it was in 1838; but the exact date is
unimportant. The Oberlin College enterprise was connected with the successful effort made by Miss Martineau and others in England in December,
1839, to raise funds for the college in which education was given without
distinction of color or sex. See "Harriet Martineau's Autobiography,"
edited by Mrs. Chapman, vol. ii. pp. 345, 346.

CHAPTER VI.

FAMILY COUNSELS AND HOME LIFE.

ALTHOUGH he lived so actively in his business affairs, and planned so much public activity, yet a great part of John Brown's life was spent in the most quiet, humble, and domestic manner. Before entering, therefore, upon the startling record of his public career, let me disclose more fully his home life, and his affectionate, practical relations to all those who depended upon him; which can best be done by his family letters at different dates, before he sent his sons to Kansas or set forth to join them there.

To his Children.

HUDSON, Jan. 18, 1841.

DEAR SON JOHN, — Since I parted with you at Hudson some thoughts have passed through my mind which my intense anxiety for your welfare prompts me to communicate by writing. I think the situation in which you have been placed by Providence at this early period of your life will afford to yourself and others some little test of the sway you may be expected to exert over minds in after life, and I am glad, on the whole, to have you brought in some measure to the test in your youth. If you cannot now go into a disorderly country school and gain its confidence and esteem, and reduce it to good order, and waken up the energies and the very soul of every rational being in it, — yes, of every mean, ill-behaved, ill-governed boy and girl that compose it, and secure the good-will of the parents, — then how are you to stimulate asses to attempt a passage of the Alps? If you run with footmen and they should weary you, how should you contend with horses? If in the land of peace they have wearied you, then how will you do in the swelling of Jordan? Shall I answer the question myself? "If any man lack wisdom, let him ask of God, who giveth liberally and upbraideth not." Let me say to you again, love them all, and commend them and yourself to the God to whom Solomon sought in his youth, and he shall bring it to pass. You have heard me tell of dividing a school into two large spelling-classes, and of its effects; if you should think best, and can remember the process, you can try it. Let the grand reason, that one course is right and another wrong, be kept continually before your own mind and before your school.

From your affectionate father,

JOHN BROWN.

AKRON, May 23, 1845.

DEAR SON JOHN, — Yours of the 28th April we did not get very seasonably, as we have been very busy, and not at the post-office often. We are all obliged for your letter, and I hope thankful for any comfort or success that may attend you. If the days of mourning have indeed and in truth *ceased*, then I trust all is well, — all is well as it should be; and I have known fair days to follow after very foul weather. The great trouble is, we are apt to get too damp in a wet, foggy spell. We are all well but little Annie, who is afflicted with a singular eruption of the skin, and is withal quite unwell. We get along in our business as well as we ever have done, I think. We have some sheep, but not as many as for two seasons past. Matters seem to go well betwixt us and our friend Perkins, and for anything that I know of, our worldly prospects are as good as we can bear. I hope that entire leanness of soul may not attend any little success in business. I do not know as we have yet any new plans; when we have, we will let you hear. We are nearly through another yeaning time, and have lost but very few. Have not yet counted tails: think there may be about four hundred. Never had a finer or more thrifty lot. Expect to begin washing sheep next week. Have received our medals and diploma. They are splendid toys, and appear to be knock-down arguments among the sheep-growers who have seen them. All were well at Hudson a few days since. Father was here, and had just moved into the Huniston house out west. You did not say in your letter whether you ever conversed with him in regard to his plans for his old age, as was talked of when you were here and were helping pick sheep; should like to know if you did, etc. Cannot tell you much more now, except it be that we all appear to think a great deal more about this world than about the next, which proves that we are still very foolish. I leave room for some others of the family to write, if they will.

Affectionately yours,

JOHN BROWN

May 30, 1845.

DEAR SON, — We are at this time all well, but very busy preparing for shearing. Have had a most dreadful frost over night, and am afraid the wheat is all killed. There will be here no article of fruit. I trust you will perform your service with patient spirit, *doing with your might.* The children will write you hereafter.

Affectionately yours,

JOHN BROWN.

AKRON, OHIO, June 6, 1846.

DEAR SON AND DAUGHTER, — I wrote you some time since, enclosing five dollars; but neither of you have let me know whether you received it or not, nor how much you were in immediate want of. Two lines would have told me all, and that you were or were not well. I now enclose you ten dollars; and I want to hear from you without one moment's delay, or I cannot till I get to New England (possibly). Say to me how much you must have for your bills at Austinburg and expenses back to this place. I can calculate for John's expenses to Springfield from here, and will provide for that. I have some nice cloth for an entire suit, which I think I had better take for you (John) to Springfield, so that you can have it made up there if you have any want of clothes before winter. We have plenty of it on hand, and it will save paying out the money. We are getting a good pair of calfskin boots made for you. We intend to take on a good supply of nice well-made shirts, in order to save your paying there for such things more than is indispensable, and also to prevent your being delayed after you come back here with Ruth.

It is barely possible that Jason and I may come by way of Austinburg. We expect to start in a little more than a week from this. If I do not come by your place on my way, you may look for another letter before I start for the East. It may be that some of your bills can lie unpaid till I can sell some of our wool, and let you draw on Perkins & Brown at Springfield for the amount, instead of making a remittance by mail. Some of your merchants or other business men might be glad to get a small draft of that kind, payable at sight. Let me know all about matters. All are well here.

Affectionately yours,

JOHN BROWN.

The letter above printed was written to John and Ruth Brown, who were then at school, or taking lessons, in Austinburg, Ohio. Their father was about removing to Massachusetts.

To his Wife and Children.

SPRINGFIELD, Sept. 29, 1846.

DEAR MARY, — . . . Your letter dated the 20th was received last night, and afforded me a real though a mournful satisfaction. That you had received, or were to receive, a letter from either John or Jason I was in perfect ignorance of till you informed me; and I am glad to learn that, wholly uninfluenced by me, they have shown a disposition to afford you the comfort in your deep affliction which the nature of the case would admit of. Nothing is scarcely equal with me to the satisfaction of seeing that one portion of my remaining family are not disposed to exclude from their sympathies and their warm affections another portion. I accept it as one of the most grateful returns that can be made to me for any care or exertion on my part to promote either their present or their future well-being ; and while I am able to discover such a feeling, I feel assured that notwithstanding God has chastised us often and sore, yet he has not entirely withdrawn himself from us nor forsaken us utterly. The sudden and dreadful manner in which he has seen fit to call our dear little Kitty to take her leave of us is, I need not tell you how much, in my mind; but before Him I will bow my head in submission and hold my peace. . . . I have sailed over a somewhat stormy sea for nearly half a century, and have experienced enough to teach me thoroughly that I may most reasonably buckle up and be prepared for the tempest. Mary, let us try to maintain a cheerful self-command while we are tossing up and down ; and let our motto still be Action, Action, — as we have but one life to live.

Affectionately yours,

JOHN BROWN.

SPRINGFIELD, MASS., Jan 5, 1847.

DEAR DAUGHTER RUTH, — Yours dated the 20th and Jason's dated the 16th of December were both received in season, and were very grateful to our feelings, as we are anxious to hear from home often, and had become very uneasy before we got word from Jason. We are middling well, and very much perplexed with our work, accounts, and correspondence. We expect now to go home, if our lives and health are spared, next month, and we feel rejoiced that the time is so near when we hope to meet you all once more. Sometimes my imagination follows those of my family who have passed behind the scenes; and I would almost rejoice to be permitted to make them a personal visit. I have outlived nearly half of all my numerous family, and I ought to realize that in any event a large proportion of my journey is travelled over.

You say that you would like very much to have a letter from me, with as much good advice as I will give. Well, what do you suppose I feel most anxious for in regard to yourself and all at home ? Would you believe that I ever had any such care on my mind about them as we read that Job had about his family (not that I would ever think to compare myself with Job) ? Would you believe that the long story would be that ye *sin* not, that you form no foolish attachments, and that you be not a companion of fools?

Your affectionate father,

JOHN BROWN.

SPRINGFIELD, March 12, 1847.

DEAR SON JOHN, — Yours dated Feb. 27th I this day received. It was written about the same time I reached this place again. I am glad to learn that you are relieved in a good measure from another season of suffering. Hope you will make the right improvement of it. I have been here nearly two weeks. Have Captain Spencer, Freeman, the Hudsons, together with Schlessinger and Ramsden, all helping me again. Have turned about four thousand dollars' worth of wool into cash since I returned; shall probably make it up to seven thousand by the 16th. Sold Musgrave the James Wallace lot yesterday for fifty-eight cents all round. Hope to get pretty much through by the middle of April. Have paid your account for the " Cincinnati Weekly Herald and Philanthropist," together with two dollars for one year's subscription to " National Era," being in all three dollars. I should have directed to have the " National Era " sent you at Austinburg, but could not certainly know as you would be there to take it. You had better direct to have it sent to you there. I now intend to send Ruth on again soon after my return. Jason writes on the 3d that all are well at home. I feel better than when I left home, and send my health to all in and about Austinburg.

Yours affectionately,

JOHN BROWN.

SPRINGFIELD, MASS., April 12, 1847.

DEAR SON JOHN, — Yours of the 5th is just received. I was very glad to learn by it that you were then well. I had begun to feel anxious, not hearing for so long a time since you wrote, that you were unwell. My own health is middling good ; and I learn that all at home were well a few days since. I enclose ten dollars; and I must say that when you continue to make INDEFINITE applications for money, without giving me the least idea of the amount you need, after I have before complained of the same thing, — namely,

your not telling me frankly how much you need, — it makes me feel
injured. Suffice it to say that it always affords me the greatest
pleasure to assist you when I can; but if you want five, ten, twenty,
or fifty dollars, why not say so, and then let me help you so far as I
am able? It places me in an awkward fix. I am much more willing to send you all you actually need (if in my power), than to send
any when you do not tell what your wants require.

I do not *now* see how we could make the exchange Mr. Walker
proposes in regard to sheep, but should suppose it might be done to
his mind somewhere in our direction. I should think your brother
student might pay the postage of a letter ordering the " Era " to you
at Austinburg till the year expires. I have ten times as many papers
as I can read. Have got on middling well, since I wrote you, with
the wool-trade, and mean to return shortly, and send Ruth to Austinburg. Do not see how to take time to give you further particulars
now, having so much every hour to attend to. Write me on receipt
of this. Will send you a Steubenville report.

Affectionately your father,

JOHN BROWN.

P. S.   Had I sent you twenty dollars, you deprive me of the comfort of knowing that your wishes have been at all complied with.

AKRON, July 9, 1847.

DEAR SON JOHN, — I wrote you yesterday to urge your coming
here to keep up the family for a few months, as I knew of no way to
provide for Jason or Owen's board ; but that matter is all got over,
and the probability is that Jason will have a wife as soon as you.
We mean to have the business done up before we leave, so as to
have no breaking up of the family here. I would now say that if
you can get ready and meet us at Buffalo on the 14th or 15th, we
shall be glad to have you go on with us. I would be willing to
delay for a day or more in order to bring it about. It would seem as
though you might bring it about by that time, so early as to get here
on the 16th, as you wrote. As matters now stand, I feel very anxious to have you go on with us, — and partly on Frederick's account.
I sent you yesterday a certificate of deposit for fifty dollars, directed to
Vernon, care of Miss Wealthy Hotchkiss.[1]   Should it so happen that
you get to Buffalo before we do, wait for us at Bennett's Hotel ; or
we will wait for you awhile. Inquire for us at Bennett's, or of George
Palmer, Esq. If you get this in season, you may perhaps get to

---

[1] Soon to be Mrs. John Brown, Jr.

Buffalo before we can. Mary is still quite feeble. Frederick appears to be quite as well as when you left. Say to Ruth I remember her.

Affectionately yours,

JOHN BROWN.

SPRINGFIELD, Sept. 1, 1847.

DEAR DAUGHTER RUTH, — I have not heard from you since John left to come on here; and I can assure you it is not for want of interest in your welfare that I have so long delayed writing you. We got over the tedious job of moving as well as we could expect, and have both families comfortably fixed. Frederick has been under the treatment of one of the most celebrated physicians in Massachusetts, and for some part of the time has appeared to be as well as ever, but has not appeared so well for a few days past. Your mother is quite unwell with a bilious fever, and has been so for a day or two. We think she is doing well now, and hope she will get around soon. We have almost all of us complained more or less since we got on here. We have heard from Akron every few days since we came on. All were well there a short time since.

Our business here seems to go on middling well, and should nothing befall me I hope to see you about the last of this month or early next. John says he will write you soon. I supposed he had done so before this, until now. We are very busy, and suppose we are likely to be for the present. We expect you to write us how you get along, of course.

Affectionately yours,

JOHN BROWN.

VERNON, ONEIDA CO., N. Y., March 24, 1851.

DEAR SON JOHN, — I now enclose draft on New York for fifty dollars, which I think you can dispose of to some of the merchants for a premium at this time in the season. I shall pay you the balance as soon as I can; but it may be out of my power until after we sell our wool, which I think there is a prospect now of doing early. I hope to get through here so as to be on our way again to Ohio before the week closes, but want you and Jason both to hold on and take the best possible care of the flock until I do get on, at any rate. I wrote you last week that the family is on the road: the boys are driving on the cattle, and my wife and the little girls are at Oneida Depot, waiting for me to go on with them.[1]

Your affectionate father,

JOHN BROWN.

---

[1] The family were removing from North Elba to Akron, leaving Ruth and her husband, Henry Thompson, in the Adirondac woods.

To his Wife.

Boston, Mass., Dec. 22, 1851.

Dear Mary, — . . . There is an unusual amount of very interesting things happening in this and other countries at present, and no one can foresee what is yet to follow. The great excitement produced by the coming of Kossuth, and the last news of a new revolution in France, with the prospect that all Europe will soon again be in a blaze, seems to have taken all by surprise. I have only to say in regard to those things, I rejoice in them, from the full belief that God is carrying out his eternal purpose in them all. I hope the boys will be particularly careful to have no waste of feed of any kind, for I am strongly impressed with the idea that a long, severe winter is before us.

This letter shows how closely Brown attended to politics in Europe as well as in America, notwithstanding his laborious life and the urgency of his private affairs. The " new revolution in France " was the *coup d'état* of Louis Napoleon, which happened in this month of December, 1851. At the same time the Hungarian patriot Kossuth was exciting great enthusiasm in Massachusetts and the Northern States in general ; Charles Sumner was celebrating him in an eloquent speech at Washington ; Emerson at Concord was bidding him welcome to the historic battle-ground there; and Theodore Parker, in his Boston pulpit, was preaching in behalf of Hungarian independence. The friends of Brown, on whom he relied in later years, were singularly in accord with him in 1851, though neither Emerson nor Parker nor Sumner had then seen Brown. I was then a student at Exeter, preparing for Harvard College, and I remember the interest that Kossuth aroused there. An old lady with whom I sometimes took tea, and with whom in her youth Daniel Webster had taken tea when a student at Exeter fifty-five years before, used to divide the talk at her little round tea-table between anecdotes of Webster (whom she admired for his beauty and eloquence, but abhorred for his betrayal of the Northern cause) and eulogies of Kossuth, Sumner, Garrison, and the other friends of freedom in Europe and America. While Miss Betsey Clifford thus manifested her enthusiasm at the age of seventy, her young guest at the age of twenty was publishing verses addressed to Kossuth in praise and to Webster in censure of their public action. But the pithy comment of John Brown — "God is carrying out his eternal purpose in them all " — was as profitable an utterance as that of any scholar or statesman of that period. He belonged to the school of the prophets, though a herdsman like Amos the Hebrew and the Arabian seer. I have been able to find but few of Brown's letters in the years 1850–51, when the first general agitation against the aggression of Southern slaveholders took place in the North ; nor do his earlier letters contain much allusion to the antislavery crusade of Garrison, Gerrit Smith, Arthur Tappan, Wendell Phillips, and the other emancipationists. But he took the warmest interest in these discussions from the first, and like Garrison and his associates early declared against the colonizationists, who would send the free negroes away to Liberia. Milton Lusk, Brown's brother-in-law, already quoted, has given me some details of antislavery action at Hudson fifty years ago. At that time Rev. Henry R. Storrs, a devoted antislavery man, was at the head of the Western Reserve College in Hudson, and a communicant, if not pastor, of a Congregational church there. In that to which Mr. Lusk belonged it had been customary before 1835 to take up a collection occasionally for the cause of colonization, which was advocated from the pulpit by agents of the Colonization Society. On one of these occasions "Brother Lusk" was asked to take up the collection as usual, but refused. His pastor earnestly questioned him why; whereupon Milton Lusk showed the clergyman a speech or letter of Chief-Justice Marshall, in which colonization was advocated as a relief to the Virginia slaveholders, by removing the troublesome class of the free negroes from the State. "If that is genuine," argued Mr. Lusk, "then the slaveholders are asked to give money for colonization to protect slavery; while we are asked for money to remove slavery by colonization. If our contributions go into the same fund, I for one will never help to raise another dollar." The pastor could not deny the premises of his parishioner, and was forced to accept his conclusion ; but not long afterward Milton Lusk was ex-

communicated for various errors of opinion, among which
the colonization incident was not quite forgotten.[1]

TROY, N. Y., Jan. 23, 1852.

DEAR CHILDREN, — I returned here on the evening of the 19th
inst., having left Akron on the 14th, the date of your letter to John.
I was very glad to hear from you again in that way, not having received anything from you while at home. I left all in usual health,
and as comfortable as could be expected; but am afflicted with you
on account of your little boy. Hope to hear by return mail that you
are all well. As in this trouble you are only tasting of a cup I have
had to drink deeply, and very often, I need not tell you how fully I
can sympathize with you in your anxiety. . . .

How long we shall continue here is beyond our ability to foresee,
but think it very probable that if you write us by return mail we
shall get your letter. Something may possibly happen that may
enable us (or one of us) to go and see you, but do not look for us. I
should feel it a great privilege if I could. We seem to be getting
along well with our business so far, but progress miserably slow.
My journeys back and forth this winter have been very tedious. If
you find it difficult for you to pay for Douglass' paper, I wish you
would let me know, as I know I took liberty in ordering it continu-
ued. You have been very kind in helping me, and I do not mean
to make myself a burden.

Your affectionate father,

JOHN BROWN.

AKRON, OHIO, March 20, 1852.

DEAR CHILDREN, — I reached home on the 18th at evening, meeting with father on the way, who went home with me and left us
yesterday; he kept me so busied that I had no time to write you
yesterday. I found all in usual health but Frederick, who has one
of his poor turns again ; it is not severe, and we hope will not be so.
I now enclose the Flanders lease. You will discover that the bargain I had with him for the second year is simply an extension of the

_____

1 " 'I threw down Judge Marshall's speech and stamped on it,' said Milton Lusk. ' Why, Milton, what ails you ?' said my sister. I told her I
had got through raising money for colonization. I asked our minister if
our contributions here in Ohio went into the same chest with those from
Virginia, where men sold slaves and put a part of the purchase-money into
the contribution-box ? He said he supposed so. Then, I said, I could have
nothing to do with it."

time made on the back of it, except that for the last year I was to pay the taxes. Owen says he thinks the tooth fell out of the harrow while lying on a pile of sticks and old boards near the corner of the barn, between that and the house; and that if you do not find it among the rubbish, nor in the house or barn, — over the door from the barn into the back shed, — he cannot tell where it will be found. Expecting to hear from you again soon,

I remain your affectionate father,

JOHN BROWN.

AKRON, OHIO, May 14, 1852.

DEAR CHILDREN, — I have a great deal to write, and but very little time in which to do it. A letter was received from you, which Salmon put in his pocket before it had been opened, and lost it. This grieved me very much indeed ; I could hardly be reconciled to it. We have been having the measles, and now have the whooping-cough among the children very bad. Your mother was confined by the birth of the largest and strongest boy she ever had two weeks ago, and has got along well considering all our difficulties. The little one took the measles, and was very sick, and has now the whooping-cough so bad that we expect to lose him; we thought him dying for some time last night. Annie and Sarah cough badly; Oliver is getting over it. Our little one has dark hair and eyes like Watson's ; notwithstanding our large number, we are very anxious to retain him.

Jason and Owen have gone on to a large farm of Mr. Perkins over in Talmadge. Frederick is with us, and is pretty well. The family of Mr. Perkins have the whooping-cough, and have had the measles. They have another son, a few days older than ours. Our other friends are well, so far as we know. Father was with us, quite well, a few days ago. We have had so much rain that we could do but little towards spring crops. Have planted our potatoes. The grass is forward ; great prospect of apples and cherries, but no peaches scarcely. Have twelve of the finest calves I ever saw. Our Troy suit went in our favor, but not to the extent that it ought. I have bought out the interests of Jason and Owen in the lot we got of Mr. Smith, on which, I suppose, you are living before this. I can send you no more now than my earnest wishes for your good, and my request that as soon as you can you send me the substance of your last letter, with such additions as you may be able to make.

Your affectionate father,

JOHN BROWN.

AKRON, OHIO, July 20, 1852.

DEAR SON JOHN, — I wrote you a few days before the death of our infant son, saying we expected to lose him; since then we have some of us been sick constantly. The measles and whooping-cough went so hard with Sarah that we were quite anxious on her account, but were much more alarmed on account of my wife, who was taken with bleeding at the lungs two or three days after the death of her child. She was pretty much confined to her bed for some weeks, and suffered a good deal of pain, but is now much more comfortable, and able to be around. About the time she got about I was taken with fever and ague, and am unable to do much now, but have got the shakes stopped for the present. The almost constant wet weather put us back very much about our crops, and prevented our getting in much corn. What we have is promising. Our wheat is a very good quality, but the crop is quite moderate. Our grass is good, and we have a good deal secured. We shall probably finish harvesting wheat to-day. Potatoes promise well. Sheep and cattle are doing well; and I would most gladly be able to add that in wisdom and good morals we are all improving. The boys have done remarkably well about the work; I wish I could see them manifest an equal regard for their future well-being. Blindness has happened to us in that which is of most importance.

We are at a loss for a reason that we do not hear a word from you. The friends are well, so far as I know. Heard from Henry and Ruth a few days since.

Your affectionate father,

JOHN BROWN.

AKRON, OHIO, Aug. 6, 1852.

DEAR SON JOHN, — I had just written a short letter to you, directed and sealed it, when I got yours of the 1st instant. I am glad to hear from you again, and had been writing that I could not remember hearing anything from you since early last spring. I am pretty much laid up with the ague, and have been for more than a month. The family are about in their usual health. Your mother is not well, but is about the house at work. The other friends are well, so far as I know. After something of a drouth, the weather has become very unsteady; yet we have not had a great amount of rain. We get a little so often that we progress slowly with our haying, of which we have yet considerable to do; we have also some late oats to cut. Have our wheat secured. Our corn we had to plant over once; it now looks promising. The prospect for potatoes, since the rains have begun to come, is good. Our sheep and cattle are doing well; we think of taking some to Cleveland to show. Have not heard from Henry and Ruth since June 26, when they were well. Mr. Ely of Boston writes us that our trial there will come on about the 21st September, and that we must then be ready. He says Mr. Beebe had not returned from Europe July 24, but is expected this month. We want you without fail to have your business so arranged that you can go on and be there by that date, as we cannot do without you at all. We have not yet sold our wool. I hope your corn and oats will recover; ours that was blown down last year did in a good measure.

One word in regard to the religious belief of yourself, and the ideas of several of my children. My affections are too deep-rooted to be alienated from them; but " my gray hairs must go down in sorrow to the grave" unless the true God forgive their denial and rejection of him, and open their eyes. I am perfectly conscious that their eyes are blinded to the real truth, their minds prejudiced by hearts unreconciled to their Maker and Judge ; and that they have no right appreciation of his true character, nor of their own. " A deceived heart hath turned them aside." That God in infinite mercy, for Christ's sake, may grant to you and Wealthy, and to my other children, " eyes to see," is the most earnest and constant prayer of

Your affectionate father,

JOHN BROWN.

AKRON, OHIO, Aug. 10, 1852.

DEAR RUTH, — Your letter to mother and children is this day received. We are always glad to hear from you, and are much pleased with the numerous particulars your letters contain. I have had a return of the ague (rather severe), so that I am pretty much laid up, and not good for much anyway; am now using means to break it up again. Your mother is still more or less troubled with her difficulties, but is able to keep about and accomplish a good deal. The remainder of the family (and friends, so far as I know) are quite well. We are getting nearly through haying and harvest. Our hay crop is most abundant ; and we have lately had frequent little rains, which for the present relieves us from our fears of a terrible drouth. We are much rejoiced to learn that God in mercy has given you some precious showers. It is a great mercy to us that we frequently are made to understand most thoroughly our absolute dependence on a power quite above ourselves. How blessed are all whose hearts and conduct do not set them at variance with that power ! Why will not my family endeavor to secure *his* favor, and to effect in the *one only* way a perfect reconciliation ?

The cars have been running regularly from Akron to Cleveland since July 5, so that there is now steam conveyance from Akron to Westport. This is a great comfort, as it reduces the journey to such a trifling affair. We are making a little preparation for the Ohio State Fair at Cleveland, on 15th, 16th, 17th September next, and think we shall exhibit some cattle and sheep. Mr. and Mrs. Perkins have been away at New York for about three weeks. Mr. Perkins is away for a great part of the time. We are quite obliged to our friend Mrs. Dickson for remembering us; are glad she is with you, and hope you will do a little towards making her home with you happy on our account, as we very much respect her, and feel quite an interest in her welfare.

Our Oliver has been speculating for some months past in hogs. I think he will probably come out about even, and maybe get the interest of his money. Frederick manages the sheep mostly, and butchers mutton for the two families. Watson operates on the farm. Salmon is chief captain over the cows, calves, etc., and he has them all to shine. Jason and Owen appear to be getting along with their farming middling well. The prospect now is that the potato crop will be full middling good. Annie and Sarah go to school. Annie has become a very correct reader. Sarah goes singing about as easy as an old shoe. Edward still continues in California. Father is carrying on his little farming on his own hook still, and seems to succeed very well. I am much gratified to have him able to do so, and he seems to enjoy it quite as much as ever he did.[1] I have now written about all I can well think of for this time.

Your affectionate father,   JOHN BROWN.

AKRON, OHIO, Sept. 21, 1852.

DEAR SON JOHN, — I now enclose five dollars to pay you for the expense of your trip to Cleveland as near as I can. I would have given you more at Cleveland had I met with Mr. Perkins in season after you concluded to leave. We will hereafter arrange about your time so as to make that satisfactory. We drew three second premiums at the fair, but no first premium. Our bull — by far the most extraordinary animal we have — got no premium at all. We heard a very strong expression of dissatisfaction with the award on Devon bulls from numerous strangers, as well as from many good judges of our acquaintance, before we left the ground. We received a first premium on a yearling buck, and he was the meanest sheep of fourteen that we exhibited; we got no other premium on sheep.

---

[1] Owen Brown was now eighty-one years old. Edward was his youngest son. Sarah was John Brown's daughter, at this time six years old.

AKRON, OHIO, Sept. 24, 1852.

DEAR CHILDREN, — We received Ruth's letter of the 31st August a few days before our State fair at Cleveland, which came off on the 15th, 16th, and 17th instant. John and myself expected to go from there to Boston, and John came on to Cleveland for that purpose; but just then we learned that our trial would not come on until November next. I may leave to go on to Boston before November, but cannot say now. We got four premiums on cattle and sheep at the fair, — two of ten dollars each, one of fifteen dollars, and one of twenty-five dollars. The Perkinses were much pleased with the show of stock we had to make, but felt, as many others did, that great injustice was done in not giving us but one first premium, and that on our poorest buck exhibited. The premiums were paid in silver cups, goblets, etc., and are of little use, except for mere show. All the friends were well at the time of the fair, and a large portion of them on the show-ground, — father among the rest. It was supposed to be the greatest exhibition ever had in the Western States, far exceeding those of the State of New York; but a vast majority of those who were at much pains and cost to exhibit their stock and other things went away disappointed of any premiums. This is a mortifying reflection.

We are busy taking care of our potatoes and apples, and preparing to sow our grain. I have had no shake of ague for some time, but am not strong. The family are in usual health. Write again.

Your affectionate father,

JOHN BROWN.

To his Wife.

BOSTON, MASS., Jan. 16, 1853.

DEAR WIFE, — I have the satisfaction to say that we have at last got to trial, and I now hope that a little more than another week will terminate it. Up to this time our prospects appear favorable. . . . I have no word for the boys, except to say I am very glad to hear they are doing so well, and that every day increases my anxiety that they all will decide to be wise and good; and I close by saying that such is by far my most earnest wish for you all.

Your affectionate husband,

JOHN BROWN.

The Boston trial went badly, as we have seen in a former chapter, nor did the religious views of Brown's children ever square perfectly with his own. As years went forward he became less anxious on this point, and was more willing to leave the matter with Providence; but his own opinions never changed.

AKRON, OHIO, Feb. 21, 1853.

DEAR CHILDREN, — It was my intention, on parting with John at Conneaut, to have written you soon; but as Mr. Perkins (immediately on my return home) expressed a strong desire to have me continue with him at least for another year, I have deferred it, in hopes from day to day of being able to say to you on what terms I am to remain. His being absent almost the whole time has prevented our making any definite bargain as yet, although we have talked considerably about it. Our bargain will not probably vary much from this, — namely, he to furnish land, stock of all kinds, teams, and tools, pay taxes on lands, half the taxes on other property, and furnish half the salt ; I to furnish all the work, board the hands, pay half the taxes on personal property put in, half the interest on capital on stock, and half the insurance on same, and have half the proceeds of all grain and other crops raised, and of all the stock of cattle, sheep, hogs, etc. He seems so pleasant, and anxious to have me continue, that I cannot tear away from him. He is in quite as good spirits since he came home as I expected.

We are all in good health; so also was father and other Hudson friends a few days ago. Our sheep, cattle, etc., have done very well through the winter. Got a letter from Ruth a few days ago. All appears well with them. She writes that they have had quite a revival of religion there, and that Henry is one of the hopefully converted. My earnest and only wish is, that those seeming conversions may prove genuine, as I doubt not "there is joy over *one* sinner that repenteth." Will you write me ?

Your affectionate father,

JOHN BROWN.

AKRON, OHIO, Sept. 24, 1853.

DEAR CHILDREN, — We received Henry's letter of the 16th August in due time, and when it came I intended to reply at once ; but not being very stout, and having many things to look after, it has been put off until now. We were very glad of that letter, and of the information it gave of your health and prosperity, as well as your future calculations. We have some nice turkeys and chickens fattening, to be ready by the time you come on to Akron. Father and Jason were both here this morning. Father is quite well. Jason, Ellen, Owen, and Fred have all been having the ague more or less

since I wrote before. Other friends are in usual health, I believe.
We have done part of our sowing, got our fine crop of corn all secured against frosts yesterday, and are digging potatoes to-day. The
season has been thus far one of great temporal blessing; and I would
fain hope that the Spirit of God has not done striving in our hard
hearts. I sometimes feel encouraged to hope that my sons will give
up their miserable delusions and believe in God and in his Son our
Saviour. I think the family are more and more decided in favor of
returning to Essex, and seem all disposed to be making little preparations for it as we suppose the time draws near. Our county fair
comes off on the 12th and 13th October, but we suppose we can
hardly expect you so soon. Should be much pleased to have you
here then. . . .

AKRON, OHIO, Jan. 25, 1854.

DEAR CHILDREN, — I remember I engaged to write you so soon as
I had anything to tell worth the paper. I do not suppose the balance
will be great now. So far as I know, the friends here are about in
usual health, and are passing through the winter prosperously. My
wife is not in as good health as when you were here. Have not
heard from Hudson for some days. The loss of sheep has been merely
a nominal one with us. We have skinned two full-blood Devon
heifers, — from the effects of poison, as we suspect; for several of our
young cattle were taken sick about the same time. The others appear
to be nearly well.

This world is not yet freed from real malice or envy. It appears
to be well settled now that we go back to North Elba in the spring.
I have had a good-natured talk with Mr. Perkins about going away,
and both families are now preparing to carry out that plan. I do
not yet know what his intentions are about our compensation for the
last year.[1] Will write you when I do, as I want you to hold yourself
(John, I mean) in readiness to come out at once, should he decide to
give me a share of the stock, etc. Should that be the case, I intend
to let you have what will give you a little start in the way of red
cattle.

I learn, by your letters to others of the family, that you have pretty
much decided to call your boy John, and that in order to gratify the
feelings of his great-grandfather and grandfather. I will only now
say that I hope to be able sometime to convince you that I appreciate
the sacrifices you may make to accommodate our feelings. I noticed

---

[1] By referring to a previous letter of Feb. 21, 1853, it will be seen that
Mr. Perkins's mind had changed within the year. It has been intimated
that political opinions had something to do with this change.

your remark about the family settling near each other; to this I would say, I would like to have my posterity near enough to each other to be friendly, but would never wish them to be brought so in contact as to be near neighbors or to intermarry. I may possibly write you again very soon.

Your affectionate father,

JOHN BROWN.

AKRON, OHIO, Feb. 9, 1854.

DEAR SON JOHN, — I write by direction of Mr. Perkins to ask you to come out immediately to assist him, instead of Mr. Newton, in closing up my accounts. He has seen the above, and it is a thing of his own naming; so I want you, if possible, to come right away. He has told me he intends to give me one share, but would like to have the stock mostly. We are on excellent terms, so far as I know. All well except my wife, and I hope she will soon be better.

Your affectionate father,

JOHN BROWN.

AKRON, OHIO, Feb. 24, 1854.

DEAR SON JOHN, — Since writing you before, I have agreed to go on to the Ward place for one year, as I found I could not dispose of my stuff in time to go to North Elba without great sacrifice this spring. We expect to move the first of next week, and do not wish you to come on until we get more settled and write you again. As I am not going away immediately, there will be no particular hurry about the settlement I wrote about before. On reckoning up our expenses for the past year, we find we have been quite prosperous. I have sold my interest in the increase of sheep to Mr. Perkins for about $700, in hogs for $51, in wheat on the ground for $176. These will pay our expenses for the year past, and the next year's rent for the Ward place, Crinlen place, and Old Portage place. These places I get for one year in exchange for my interest in wheat on the ground; and it leaves me half the wool of last season (which is on hand yet), half the pork, corn, wheat, oats, hay, potatoes, and calves sixteen in number. If I could have sold my share of the wool, I might have gone to Essex this spring quite comfortably; but I have to pay Henry $100 before he leaves, and I cannot do that and have sufficient to move with until I can sell my wool. We are all middling well. Henry and Ruth intend to leave for home about the 15th March, and to go by your place if they can. We have great reason to be thankful that we have had so prosperous a year, and have terminated our connection with Mr. Perkins so comfortably and on such friendly terms, to all appearance. Perry Warren, to whom Henry Warren conveyed his property, was here a few days ago, feeling about for a compromise: did nothing, and left, to return again soon as *he* said. We think they are getting tired of the five years' war. I shall probably write you again before a great while.

Your affectionate father,

JOHN BROWN.

AKRON, OHIO, April 3, 1854.

DEAR SON JOHN, — We received your letter of the 24th March two or three days since, and one from Henry, dated 25th March, about the same time. They had got on well so far, but had to go by stage the balance of the way. Father got home well, and was with us over night Friday last. We have all been middling well of late, but very busy, having had the care of the whole concern at Mr. Perkins's place until Friday night. I had a most comfortable time settling last year's business, and dividing with Mr. Perkins, and have to say of his dealing with me that he has shown himself to be every inch a gentleman. I bring to my new home five of the red cows and ten calves; he to have $100 out of my share of the last year's wool, to make us even on last year's business; after dividing all crops, he paying me in hand $28.55, balance due me on all except four of the five cows. I am going now to work with a cheap team of two yoke oxen, on which I am indebted, till I can sell my wool, $89; $46 I have paid towards them. I would like to have all my children settle within a few miles of each other and of me, but I cannot take the responsibility of advising you to make any *forced* move to change your location. Thousands have to regret that they did not let middling "well alone." I should think you ought to get for your place another $125; and I think you may, if you are not too anxious. That would buy you considerable of a farm in Essex or elsewhere, and we may get the Homestead Law passed yet. It has been a question with me whether you would not do better to hire all your team work done than to have your little place overstocked possibly, after some trouble about buying them, paying taxes, insurance, and some expense for implements to use them with. If you get a little overstocked, everything will seem to do poorly. Frederick is very much better, but both he and Owen have been having the ague lately. They leave the Hill farm soon. I do not at this moment know of a good opening for you this way. One thing I do not fear to advise and even urge; and that is the habitual "fear of the Lord, which is the beginning of wisdom." Commending you all to his mercy, I remain

Your affectionate father,

JOHN BROWN.

AKRON, OHIO, Aug. 24, 1854.

DEAR CHILDREN, — I have just received Henry's letter of the
13th instant, and have much reason to be thankful for the good news
it brings. We are all in middling health, so far as I know, in this
quarter, although there is some sickness about us. Mother Brown,
of Hudson, was complaining some last week ; have not heard from
her since then. This part of the country is suffering the most dreadful drouth ever experienced during this nineteenth century. We
have been much more highly favored than most of our neighbors in
that we were enabled to secure a most excellent hay crop, whilst
many others did not get theirs saved in time, and lost it notwithstanding the dry weather. Our oats are no better than those of our
neighbors, but we have a few. We shall probably have some corn,
while others, to a great extent, will have none. Of garden vegetables
we have more than twenty poor families have in many cases. Of
fruit we shall have a comfortable supply, if our less favored neighbors do not take it all from us. We ought to be willing to divide.
Our cattle (of which we have thirty-three head) we are enabled to
keep in excellent condition, on the little feed that grows on the moist
grounds, and by feeding the stalks green that have failed of corn, —
and we have a good many of them. We have had two light frosts,
on August the 9th and 18th, but have had more extreme hot
weather in July and August than ever known before, — thermometer
often up to 98° in the shade, and was so yesterday ; it now stands
(eleven o'clock P. M.) at 93°.

I am thinking that it may be best for us to dispose of all the cattle
we want to sell, and of all our winter feed, and move a few choice
cattle to North Elba this fall, provided we can there buy hay and
other stuff considerably cheaper than we might sell our stuff for here,
and also provided we can get a comfortable house to winter in. I
want you to keep writing me often, as you can learn how hay, all
kinds of grain, and roots can be bought with you, so that I may be the
better able to judge. Our last year's pork proves to be a most perfect article, but I think not best to ship any until the weather gets a
little cooler. The price Mr. Washburn asks for his contract may not
be much out of the way, but there seems to be some difficulty about
a bargain yet. First, he wants to hang on all his stock, and I do not
know at present as I want any of them. I do not know what he has
on hand ; he may perhaps be able to get them off himself. Then,
again, I do not know as Mr. Smith[1] would give a deed of half the lot
before the whole purchase-money for the entire lot and interest are
paid. You may have further information than I have. Early in

---

[1] Gerrit Smith, who still owned much land at North Elba.

the season all kinds of cattle were high, scarce and ready cash; now, as the prospects are, I am entirely unable to make an estimate of what money I can realize on them, so as to be able to say just now how much money I can raise, provided those other impediments can be got over. I intend to turn all I consistently can into money, and as fast as I can, and would be glad to secure the purchase of Washburn, if it can be done consistently and without too much trouble. Write me again soon, and advise us far as you can about all these matters. We could probably sell all our produce at pretty high prices. How are cattle, horses, sheep, and hogs selling in your quarter?

Your affectionate father,

JOHN BROWN.

These family letters, full of repetitions, of petty concerns, of old-fashioned forms of expression, and with their whimsical mixture of important and unimportant affairs, have a value, in exhibiting the true character of John Brown, that more elaborate epistles, elegantly written with an eye to the public, could not possibly hold. Like the rude verses of Lucilius, they paint the whole life of the old man; but they were written, unlike the Roman verses, without the least thought of publication. The later letters of the series — written five years before he engaged in his Virginia campaign, which Colonel Perkins thought so foolish — point to the final separation between these two unequally yoked partners. They had worked together, each in his own way, for more than ten years; and they parted amicably, though with some after-thoughts which hindered them from ever uniting in sentiment again. At this time the sons of Brown were beginning to look towards Kansas as a place for their husbandry; and we shall see in the next chapter why its open territory attracted them.

CHAPTER VII.

KANSAS, THE SKIRMISH-GROUND OF THE CIVIL WAR.

THE State of Kansas, which gave John Brown his first
distinction, occupies territory with which the names of
other famous men are associated, though with none is it
more closely connected than with his. The first of Euro-
peans to visit Kansas was Vasquez de Coronado, a Spanish
captain, who in 1541–42 reached its southern and western
counties, coming up from Mexico in search of gold, silver,
and fabulous cities. He called the land "Quivira," and described it as "the best possible soil for all kinds of Spanish
productions, very strong and black, and well watered by
brooks, springs, and rivers;" but in reaching it from Mexico he marched nine hundred and fifty leagues, and traversed
"mighty plains and sandy heaths, smooth and wearisome,
and bare of wood." These plains he found "all the way
as full of crook-back oxen [buffaloes] as the mountain Serena
in Spain is full of sheep." At this very time De Soto was
discovering the river Mississippi; but neither he nor Father
Marquette, one hundred and thirty years later, set foot in
Kansas. La Salle, in 1687, might have crossed it, on his way
from Texas to Canada, if he had not fallen by the hand of
mutiny; but the first Frenchman to explore it was Dutisne,
in 1719, who, in travelling westward from the Osage River,
may have crossed the Pottawatomie near where John Brown
afterward labored and fought. It was then and long after a
part of the French king's broad colony of Louisiana, and as
such was ceded by Napoleon to Jefferson in 1802. Nearly
twenty years before this, in 1784, Jefferson had undertaken
to free the whole northwestern territory of the United States
from the curse of slavery, by what has since been known
as the Ordinance of 1787. As drawn by Jefferson in 1784,

this great charter of Western freedom provided that all new States to be carved out of the national domain should in their governments uphold republican forms, "and after the year 1800 of the Christian era there shall be neither slavery nor involuntary servitude in any of them." This was defeated by a single vote in Congress, much to Jefferson's disgust. In 1786 he said: "The voice of a single individual would have prevented this abominable crime [the introduction of slavery into new territory]. Heaven will not always be silent; the friends to the rights of human nature will in the end prevail." They did prevail in John Brown's time, and largely through his heroism; and in the conflict Kansas became the skirmish-line of our Civil War.

After the cession of Louisiana, which brought with it to the United States all the region then known as "the Missouri territory," including Kansas, the latter was again declared free soil by the Missouri Compromise of 1820;[1] for it was then enacted by Congress (March 6, 1820), when erecting Missouri into a State, —

"That in all that territory ceded by France to the United States, under the name of Louisiana, which lies north of 36° 30′ north latitude, not included within the limits of the State contemplated by this act, slavery and involuntary servitude, otherwise than in the punishment of crimes, shall be, and is hereby, forever prohibited."

It was in the face of this solemn declaration that the slaveholders of 1854–56 undertook to establish slavery by

[1] The Missouri Compromise — as Charles Sumner said in his great speech of May 19 and 20, 1856, "The Crime against Kansas" — was the work of slaveholders, who insisted that Missouri should come into the Union as a slave State, but for this concession were willing to give up all the Northern territory to freedom. Sumner says: "It was hailed by slaveholders as a victory. Charles Pinckney, of South Carolina, in an oft-quoted letter written at eight o'clock on the night of its passage, says: 'It is considered here by the slaveholding States as a great triumph.' At the North it was accepted as a defeat, and the friends of freedom everywhere throughout the country bowed their heads with mortification." The chief advocates of this compromise were William Pinkney, of Maryland, and Henry Clay, of Kentucky; among the chief advocates of excluding slavery from Missouri were Rufus King, then of New York, and Harrison Gray Otis, a nephew of the Revolutionary orator James Otis, of Massachusetts.

11

force and by fraud in Kansas. As a preliminary, they had carried through Congress, under the lead of Senator Douglas of Illinois, what was known as the "squatter sovereignty" clause of the Kansas-Nebraska bill, — leaving the people at each election to determine the existence of slavery for themselves. This plausible form of words covered a purpose on the part of the South to fasten slavery upon the new States, which Jefferson had striven to free from the possibility of such a misfortune; and when the prairies of Kansas were opened to settlement in 1854, this purpose became offensively manifest. Indeed, there could be no doubt why Douglas had introduced his bill, or what was the intention of the Democratic administration under Franklin Pierce of New Hampshire, and of the presidential candidates, including Douglas, who hoped to succeed Pierce in office. A new slave State was wanted, since California had excluded slavery, and there were one or two Northern Territories likely soon to come in as States with slavery also excluded. By this time the Southern slaveholders, abandoning the early doctrine of Washington, Jefferson, George Mason, Madison, and Marshall, and even the cautious ground that Clay and Pinckney held in 1820, were thirsting to extend the area of their detestable institution. They had annexed Texas and made war on Mexico for this purpose; and they were seeking to deprive Spain of Cuba, and conquer San Domingo, in order to re-establish slavery where it first cursed Spanish America, and to carry on the slave-trade openly once more. The prediction made by Taylor of New York, in opposing the Missouri Compromise, had been singularly verified. Taylor said to the slaveholders in 1820 : —

"On an implied power to acquire territory by treaty, you raise an implied right to erect it into States, and imply a compromise by which slavery is to be established and slaves represented in Congress. Is this just? Is it fair? Where will it end? . . . Your lust of acquiring is not yet satiated. You must have the Floridas. Your ambition rises. You covet Cuba, and obtain it; you stretch your arms to the other islands in the Gulf of Mexico, and they become yours. Are the millions of slaves inhabiting those countries to be incorporated into the Union and represented in Congress? Are the freemen of the old States to become the slaves of the representatives of foreign slaves?"

Such was, indeed, the dream of South Carolina and Mississippi and Louisiana; such the purpose of Jefferson Davis, Soulé of New Orleans, and Mason of Virginia, — a degenerate descendant of Washington's friend George Mason. "Manifest Destiny" was the watchword of these politicians, to whom the Northern Democrats — Pierce, Buchanan, Cass, and Douglas — basely submitted. As the discussion on Douglas's Kansas-Nebraska bill proceeded, it became evident, from the very nature of the case, that there was a purpose to force slavery into Kansas, the more southern Territory of the two. There would have been no need of repealing the Missouri Compromise except to carry out this purpose. It was also evident that the great mass of Northern and European emigration would turn away from Kansas if it became probable that slavery would enter there. "No single man or single family unwilling to enter a slave State would trust themselves, unsupported, in a Territory which would probably become one," said Edward Hale in 1854, speaking as the organ of the Massachusetts Emigrant Aid Company, which Eli Thayer, Dr. Howe, Richard Hildreth, and other antislavery men of Boston and Worcester had joined with Mr. Hale, then a clergyman of Worcester, to organize, but which in its management soon fell into the hands of men like Amos A. Lawrence, Judge Chapman of Springfield, and others who were not considered fanatical against slavery. Mr. Hale further said : [1] —

" Meanwhile a rapid emigration has been going on into the Territories, particularly into Kansas, quite independent of the Emigrant Aid Companies. During the close of the winter of 1853-54, it is said, large numbers of persons from Northwestern States collected in the towns on the eastern side of the Missouri, awaiting the opening of the Territories, that they might go in and stake out their locations. As the spring opened, a rapid current of emigration began. At first the Northern settlers went generally into Nebraska ; but so soon as it was known that determined and combined arrangements would be made to settle Kansas from the North, the natural attractions of that Territory began to exercise their influence, and the preponderance of emigration

[1] See "Kansas and Nebraska," by Edward E. Hale (Boston : Phillips, Sampson, & Co., 1854), — a very useful book at the time. The passage cited is at pp. 233, 234.

through the summer of 1854 has been into its borders. The Indian treaties were ratified only at the close of the session of the Senate; some of them not till the beginning of August. Settlement on the Indian lands was therefore, until that time, strictly illegal. But persons intending to emigrate, in many instances, made arrangements with the Indians, or, at the least, staked off the land on which they wished to settle, and made registry of the priority of their claim on the books of some ' Squatters' Association.' A large number of the residents of Western Missouri have in this manner passed over the line, and made claim to such sections as pleased them, intending, at some subsequent period, to make such improvements as will give them a right of pre-emption, when the lands are offered for sale, but for the present not residing in the new Territory."

Some of these last-named persons were actually intending to settle in Kansas; but most of them were either land-speculators or slavery-propagandists, who meant to make Kansas a slave State, whether they lived there or not. The acting Vice-President of the United States, David R. Atchison, of Western Missouri, whose name, along with that of President Pierce, is signed to the Kansas-Nebraska law (May 30, 1854), five months afterwards made a speech in the county of Platte, in which he said : —

" The people of Kansas in their first elections will decide the question whether or not slaveholders are to be excluded. Now, if a set of fanatics and demagogues a thousand miles off [meaning Messrs. Lawrence, Chapman, John Carter Brown, etc.] can afford to advance their money and exert every nerve to abolitionize Kansas and exclude the slaveholder, what is your duty, when you reside within one day's journey of the Territory, and when your peace, quiet, and property depend on your action? You can, without an exertion, send five hundred of your young men who will vote in favor of your institutions. Should each county in the State of Missouri only do its duty, the question will be decided quietly and peaceably at the ballot-box."

This was the advice of Vice-President Atchison, — much of the same character as if Senator Edmunds, of Vermont, who has honored the place that Atchison disgraced, should advise the citizens of Northern Vermont to march over into Canada and vote at the elections there. A Vermonter has now as much right to vote in Sherbrooke or Montreal as a

Missourian in 1854 had to vote in Leavenworth or Lawrence; and this was practically admitted by a confederate
of Atchison, General Stringfellow, of Missouri, who said
in 1855 : —

"To those who have qualms of conscience as to violating laws,
State or national, I say the time has come when such impositions
must be disregarded, since your rights and property are in danger.
And I advise you, one and all, to enter every election district in
Kansas in defiance of Reeder and his vile myrmidons, and vote at
the point of the bowie-knife and revolver. Neither give nor take
quarter : our cause demands it. It is enough that the slaveholding
interest wills it, from which there is no appeal."

They acted on this advice, as appears by another speech
of Atchison after the first invasion : —

"Well, what next? Why, an election for members of the Legislature to organize the Territory must be held. What did I advise
you to do then? Why, meet them on their own ground, and beat
them at their own game again; and, cold and inclement as the
weather was, I went over with a company of men. My object in
going was not to vote. I had no right to vote, unless I had dis-
franchised myself in Missouri. I was not within two miles of a
voting place. My object in going was not to vote, but to settle a
difficulty between two of our candidates. The Abolitionists of the
North said, and published it abroad, *that Atchison was there with
bowie-knife and revolver, — and, by God, 't was true! I never did
go into that Territory, I never intend to go into that Territory,
without being prepared for all such kind of cattle.*"

The whole South, and particularly South Carolina, Georgia, and Alabama, were urged to send men into Kansas, as
Atchison and Stringfellow urged the Missourians to go in, —
law or no law, — to secure the triumph of slavery. Stringfellow wrote to the "Montgomery Advertiser" (published
at the town in Alabama where the Southern Confederacy
first established its seat of government in 1861): "Not
only is it profitable for slaveholders to go to Kansas, but
politically it is all-important." A South Carolina youth,
Warren Wilkes by name, who commanded for a while an
armed force of Carolina and Georgia settlers in Kansas,

wrote to the "Charleston Mercury," of South Carolina, in the spring of 1856 : —

" By consent of parties, the present contest in Kansas is made the turning-point in the destinies of slavery and abolitionism. If the South triumphs, abolitionism will be defeated and shorn of its power for all time. If she is defeated, abolitionism will grow more insolent and aggressive, until the utter ruin of the South is consummated. If the South secures Kansas, she will extend slavery into all territory south of the fortieth parallel of north latitude, to the Rio Grande ; and this, of course, will secure for her pent-up institution of slavery an ample outlet, and restore her power in Congress. If the North secures Kansas, the power of the South in Congress will be gradually diminished, and the slave population will become valueless. All depends upon the action of the present moment."

To this reasoning men like John Brown assented, and were ready to join issue for the control of Kansas upon this ground alone. But Brown had another and quite different object in view ; he meant to attack slavery by force, in the States themselves, and to destroy it, as it was finally destroyed, by the weapons and influences of war.

What, then, was the slavery which South Carolina wished to establish in Kansas and all over the North, and upon what grounds was it advocated ? It is hard, at this distance of time and in the complete change of circumstances that the Civil War has produced, to show another person or make real to one's self the despotism which a few slaveholders exercised in 1856 over the rest of mankind in this country. Though a meagre minority in their own South, they absolutely controlled there not only four millions of slaves, but six millions of white people, nominally free, while they directed the policy and the opinions of more than half the free people of the non-slaveholding States. They dictated the nomination and secured the election of Pierce and afterward of Buchanan as President, — the most humble servants of the slave-power who ever held that office ; they had not only refused to terminate the slave-trade (as by treaty we were bound to assist in doing), but they had induced the. importation of a few cargoes of slaves into Carolina and Georgia ; they had not only broken down the Missouri

Compromise of 1820 (imposed by themselves on the unwilling North), but had done their best to extend slavery
over the new Territories of the nation, and to legalize its
existence in all the free States. Through the mouth of
Chief-Justice Taney, who simply uttered the decrees of the
slaveholding oligarchy, they were soon to make the Supreme
Court of the nation declare virtually, if not in set terms,
that four million Americans, of African descent, had practically "no rights which a white man was bound to respect;" and they were exerting themselves in advance in
every way to give effect to that foregone conclusion. The
Dred Scott decision was not made by Taney until 1857,
when it led at once to the execution of John Brown's long-
cherished purpose of striking a blow at slavery in its own
Virginian stronghold. That decision flashed into the minds
of Northern men the conviction which Brown held and John
Quincy Adams had long before formulated and expressed, —
that "the preservation, propagation, and perpetuation of
slavery was the vital and animating spirit of the National
Government." It was this conviction that led to the election of Abraham Lincoln in 1860, as it had led John Brown
and his small band of followers to assert freedom by force in
Kansas.

At the time when the young South Carolinian wrote the
words above-cited, his State was an oligarchy founded upon
negro slavery, and its State Constitution provided that a
citizen should not "be eligible to a seat in the House of Representatives unless legally seized and possessed in his own
right of a settled freehold estate of five hundred acres of
land and ten negroes." A few years earlier, Chancellor
Harper, of South Carolina, in an address before a Society
for the Advancement of Learning, at Charleston, made
these statements, which were cited by J. B. De Bow, a Louisiana writer, in 1852 : —

"The institution of slavery is a *principal cause of civilization*. It
is as much the order of nature that men should enslave each other as
that other animals should prey upon each other. The African slave-
trade has given the boon of existence to millions and millions in our
country who would otherwise never have enjoyed it. It is true that
the slave is driven to his labor by stripes. Such punishment would

be degrading to a free man, who had the thoughts and aspirations of
a freeman. In general, it is not degrading to a slave, nor is it felt to
be so. Odium has been cast upon our legislation, on account of its
forbidding the elements of education to be communicated to slaves.
But, in truth, what injury is done them by this? He who works
during the day with his hands does not read in intervals of leisure for
his amusement or the improvement of his mind. A knowledge of
reading, writing, and the elements of arithmetic is convenient and
important to the free laborer, but of what use would they be to the
slave? *Would you do a benefit to the horse or the ox by giving him a
cultivated understanding or fine feelings?* The law has not provided
for making the marriages of slaves indissoluble, nor could it do so.
It may perhaps be said that the chastity of wives is not protected by
law. It is true that the passions of the men of the superior caste
tempt and find gratification in the easy chastity of the female slave.
But she is not a less useful member of society than before. She has
done no great injury to herself or any other human being; *her off-
spring is not a burden, but an acquisition to her owner;* his support is
provided for, and he is brought up to usefulness. If the fruit of intercourse with a free man, his condition is perhaps raised somewhat
above that of his mother. I am asked, How can that institution be
tolerable, by which a large class of society is cut off from improvement and knowledge, to whom blows are not degrading, theft no
more than a fault, falsehood and the want of chastity almost venial;
and in which a husband or parent looks with comparative indifference
on that which to a freeman would be the dishonor of wife or child?
*But why not, if it produce the greatest aggregate of good? Sin and
ignorance are only evil because they lead to misery.*"

Except for these utterances of shame and guilt, the name
of Chancellor Harper is now forgotten. But the name of
JEFFERSON remains in honor, and rises higher with each
succeeding year which, by the lapse of time, converts him
from a statesman into a prophet. A hundred years ago
(May 10, 1785), the printers in Paris finished Jefferson's
"Notes on Virginia," which he at once sent to his most intimate friends and disciples in America, Madison and Monroe,
who afterwards succeeded him in the Presidency. In trans-
mitting the little book, he wrote to Madison: "I wish to
put it into the hands of the young men at the college, as
well on account of the political as physical parts; but there
are sentiments on some subjects which might be displeasing

to the country, perhaps to the Assembly, or to some who lead
it. I do not wish to be exposed to their censure, nor do I
know how far their influence, if exerted, *might effect a misapplication of law to such a publication, were it made.* If you
think it will give no offence, I will send a copy to each of
the students of William and Mary College, and some others
to my friends and to your disposal." [1] Being informed that
he might send them to his Virginia friends without risk
of censure, Jefferson did so. The eighteenth chapter, or
" Query," contains these often-quoted words, written at
Monticello in 1782 : —

" There must doubtless be an unhappy influence on the manners
of our people produced by the existence of slavery among us. The
whole commerce between master and slave is a perpetual exercise of
the most boisterous passions, the most unremitting despotism, on the
one part, and degrading submissions on the other. Our children see
this, and learn to imitate it; for man is an imitative animal. If a
parent could find no motive, either in his philanthropy or his self-love,
for restraining the intemperance of passion towards his slave, it should
always be a sufficient one that his child is present. But generally it
is not sufficient. The parent storms; the child looks on, catches the
lineaments of wrath, puts on the same airs in the circle of smaller
slaves, gives a loose rein to his worst passions, and thus nursed,
educated, and daily exercised in tyranny, cannot but be stamped by
it with odious peculiarities. The man must be a prodigy who can
retain his manners and morals undepraved by such circumstances.
And with what execration should that statesman be loaded who, permitting one half the citizens to trample on the rights of the other,
transforms those into despots and these into enemies, destroys the
morals of the one part and the *amor patriæ* of the other? For if a

[1] It appears by a letter from Monroe to Jefferson (New York, Jan. 19,
1786), that it was what he had said of the Indians of Virginia, rather than
his attack upon negro slavery, which Jefferson feared might not be well received in his native State, — he loved to call it his " country." Monroe
thanks Jefferson for the book, " which I have read with pleasure and improvement," and then says : " I should suppose the observations you have
made on the subjects you allude to *would have a very favorable effect,* since
no considerations would induce them but *a love for the rights of Indians and
for your country.*" It would seem that the passage concerning slavery gave
no offence, but the eloquent speech of Logan did ; and in 1797, while Jefferson was Vice-President, he felt compelled to give chapter and verse for
the incidents of that world-famous affair of Logan and Cresap.

slave can have a country in this world, it must be any other in preference to that in which he is born to live and labor for another; in
which he must lock up the faculties of his nature, contribute, as far
as depends on his individual endeavors, to the evanishment of the
human race, or entail his own miserable condition on the endless
generations proceeding from him.[1] With the morals of the people
their industry is also destroyed; for in a warm climate no man will
labor for himself who can make another labor for him. This is so
true, that of the proprietors of slaves a very small proportion indeed
are ever seen to labor. And can the liberties of a nation be deemed
secure when we have removed their only firm basis, — a conviction
in the minds of the people that these liberties are the gift of God,
that they are not to be violated without his wrath? Indeed, I tremble for my country [Virginia] when I reflect that God is just; that
His justice cannot sleep forever; that considering numbers, nature,
and natural means only, a revolution of the wheel of fortune is among
possible events; that it may become probable by supernatural interference. The Almighty has no attribute that can take sides with us
in such a contest."

After this generous outburst of indignation against what
he saw everywhere about him in Virginia, Jefferson added,
with that wise optimism which was so strong a feature in
his character: "I think a change already perceptible since
the origin of the present Revolution. The spirit of the master is abating; that of the slave is rising from the dust, his
condition is mollifying; the way, I hope, preparing under
the auspices of Heaven for a total emancipation; and that
this is disposed, in the order of events, to be *with the consent
of the masters rather than by their extirpation.*" This prediction was fulfilled within half a century from Jefferson's
death, though not in the way he had conceived, and not without that manifestation of God's awakened justice, at the
thought of which the true Virginian trembled for Virginia.
Kansas, a part of the vast region which Jefferson had wrested
from Spain and France and devoted to liberty, was to be the
first theatre of God's judgments; and John Brown, Jeffer-

---

[1] Sole estate his sire bequeathed
(Hapless sire to hapless son),
Was the wailing song he breathed,
And his chain when life was done.
EMERSON, *Voluntaries.*

son's most radical disciple, who went even beyond his master in devotion to freedom, was that servant of the Lord who most clearly comprehended and fulfilled the divine purpose, whether in Kansas or Virginia. This the heart of the people instinctively recognized from the first, and to this even his enemies have borne witness. One of the most garrulous of these enemies (though formerly professing to be Brown's friend), Charles Robinson of Kansas, wrote thus to a true friend of Brown, James Hanway, in February, 1878, concerning one of the Kansas hero's most debated deeds: "I never had much doubt that Captain Brown was the author of the blow at Pottawatomie, *for the reason that he was the only man who comprehended the situation and saw the absolute necessity of some such blow, and had the nerve to strike it.*"

The condition of affairs in Kansas when John Brown appeared there, in October, 1855, had become such that no milder measures than he adopted would meet the exigency. The advice given by Atchison and the leaders of the slave oligarchy all over the South had been followed, and had borne fruit accordingly. The first of many Territorial governors of Kansas, a Pennsylvania Democrat, Andrew H. Reeder by name, reached Leavenworth in October, 1854, and established his office temporarily there. He ordered an election for delegate to Congress, Nov. 29, 1854, at which hundreds of Missourians voted, casting, with other proslavery men, 2.258 votes for Whitfield, the proslavery candidate, out of 2,905 votes thrown. On the 28th of February, 1855, a census of the voters was completed by Governor Reeder, and the number declared to be 2,905, the whole number of inhabitants in eighteen election districts being then 8,501. The most important election, that for members of the Territorial Legislature, was appointed for March 30, 1855, at which time the genuine population could not have exceeded ten thousand, nor could there have been more than three thousand legal voters in Kansas. Yet the vote actually counted was 6,307, of which no less than 5,427 were for the proslavery candidates. Not less than four thousand of these were fraudulent votes. A writer, whose home was in Lawrence at the time, says that for some days before

the election crowds of men began to assemble at certain
rendezvous on the border counties of Missouri, — "rough,
brutal-looking men, of most nondescript appearance," but all
wearing the proslavery badge, — a white or blue ribbon.
Many Missourians who did not or could not join these voting
excursions gave money or provisions or lent their wagons to
help on the expedition. At St. Joseph, near the Missouri
border, Stringfellow made the speech already quoted, in
which he also said, according to the "Leavenworth Herald,"
a proslavery newspaper: "I tell you to mark every scoundrel among you that is the least tainted with free-soilism or
abolitionism, and exterminate him. Neither give nor take
quarter from the d——d rascals. I propose to mark them
in this house and on the present occasion, so you may crush
them out." This phrase, "Neither give nor take quarter,"
became the watchword of the Border Ruffians, as these invaders were fitly called. Provisions were sent before these
parties; and those intended for use at Lawrence were stored
in the house of one Lykins, for whose kinsman a county had
been named. The polls were also opened at his house. Some
of these Lawrence voters came in from Missouri the evening before election, pitched tents near Lawrence, and held a
meeting that night, in which Colonel Young, of Boone County,
Mo., declared "that more voters were here than would be
needed to carry the election," but that there was a scarcity
at Tecumseh, Bloomington, Hickory Point, and other places
eight, ten, and twelve miles distant. Volunteers came forward for those elections, and the next morning left Lawrence
to vote there. The village of Lawrence, then containing a
few hundred persons, was entered March 30, 1855, by about
a thousand men, under the command of Colonel Young
and of a distinguished Missourian, Claiborne F. Jackson.
They came in about a hundred wagons and on horseback,
with music and banners; armed with guns, pistols, rifles,
and bowie-knives. They brought also two cannon loaded
with musket balls, but had no occasion to use them, for
the Lawrence people submitted quietly to this outrage.
Colonel Young did not send off any of his armed volunteers
to other points until he was satisfied, as he said, that "the
citizens of Lawrence were not going to offer any resistance

to their voting." Mrs. Charles Robinson, who published a
volume about Kansas in 1856, says, what is confirmed by
the testimony taken by the Congressional Committee of
1856 : [1] —

"When this band of men were coming to Lawrence, they met Mr.
N. B. Blanton, formerly of Missouri, who had been appointed one of
the judges of election by Governor Reeder. Upon his saying that he
should feel bound, in executing the duties of his office, to demand the
oath as to residence in the Territory, they attempted, by bribes first,
and then with threats of hanging, to induce him to receive their votes
without the oath. Mr. Blanton not appearing on the election day,
a new judge, by name Robert A. Cummins, who claimed that a man
had a right to vote if he had been in the Territory but an hour, was
appointed in his place. The Missourians came to the polls from the
second ravine west of the town, where they were encamped in tents,
in parties of one hundred at a time. Before the voting commenced,
however, they said that 'if the judges appointed by the governor did
not allow them to vote, they would appoint judges who would.'
They did so in the case of Mr. Abbott, one of the judges, who had
become indignant, and resigned. The immediate occasion was Colonel Young's refusing to take the oath that he was a resident of Kansas. When asked by Mr. Abbott 'if he intended to make Kansas
his future home,' he replied that 'it was none of his business;' that
'if he was a resident there, he should ask no more.' Colonel Young
then mounted on the window-sill, telling the crowd 'he had voted,
and they could do the same.' He told the judges 'it was no use
swearing them, as they would all swear as he had done.' The other
judges deciding to receive such votes, Mr. Abbott resigned."

At other voting-places the judges of election were treated
with great indignity, and particularly at Bloomington, where
an "old soldier," John A. Wakefield, was one of the chief
citizens. Upon the refusal of the judges to resign, the mob
broke in the windows of the polling-place, and, presenting
pistols and guns, threatened to shoot them. A voice from
the outside cried, "Do not shoot them; there are proslavery
men in the house!" The two Free-State judges still refusing
to allow Missourians to vote, one Jones led on a party with
bowie-knives drawn and pistols cocked, telling the judges

[1] Of this committee John Sherman, now Senator from Ohio, was a
member.

"he would give them five minutes to resign or die." The
five minutes passed by. Jones said he "would give another
minute, but no more." The proslavery judge snatched up
the ballot-boxes, and, crying out "Hurrah for Missouri!"
ran into the crowd. The other judges, persuaded by their
friends, who thought them in imminent peril, passed out,
one of them putting the poll-books in his pocket. The Missouri mob pursued him, took the books away, and then
turned upon Wakefield, shouting, "Take him, dead or
alive!" What followed may be given in Wakefield's own
words : —

"I ran into the house and told Mr. Ramsay to give me his double-
barrelled shot-gun. The mob rode up, and I should think a dozen or
more presented their pistols at me. I drew up the gun at Jones, the
leader. We stood that way perhaps for a minute. A man professing to be my friend undertook to take the gun from me, saying, 'If
you shoot, we will all be killed : we can't fight this army.' My reply
was, to stand off, or I would shoot him — which he did. Then one
of my friends spoke in a very calm manner and said, 'Judge, you
had better surrender; we cannot fight this army without arms.' I
then said I must know the conditions; and remarked to the mob,
'Gentlemen, what do you want with me?' Some one said, 'We
want you to go back to the polls and state whether it was not you
that persuaded the judges to take away the poll-books.' I said I
could easily say no, for I could not get in hearing of the judges; but
if I could have, I should have done it. I said I would go back, but
go alone; I went back, and got upon a wagon and made them a
short speech. I told them I was an old soldier, and had fought
through two wars for the rights of my country, and I thought I had
a privilege there that day. I said they were in the wrong, — that
we were not the Abolitionists they represented us to be, but were
Free-State men; that they were abusing us unjustly, and that their
acts were contrary to organic law and the Constitution of the United
States. A man cried out, while I was speaking, several times,
'Shoot him! he's too saucy.' When I got through and got down
from the wagon, a man came up and told me he wanted to tie a white
ribbon in my button-hole, or 'the boys would kill me.' I first refused; but he insisted, and I let him do it; then I turned round and
cut it out with my knife. I then made an attempt to leave, when
they cried out, 'Stay with us and vote; we don't want you to leave.'
I thanked them, but told them they could have it to themselves
then, I should leave them; and I went."

There was something of Falstaff about this old Judge
Wakefield, whose house was afterward burned in some of
the raids of 1856, and of whom many anecdotes are told.
But neither he nor the other brave men who took part in
this election could do much against an invasion from Missouri in such overwhelming numbers. An English traveller,
Mr. Thomas H. Gladstone, distantly related to the English
premier, who visited Kansas in 1856, and has written a book
about it,[1] relates, on the authority of others, some incidents
of this fraudulent, or "bogus," election thus:—

"A Presbyterian clergyman, the Rev. Frederic Starr, who was an
eye-witness of the fraud and intimidation practised at Leavenworth
City, and has published a statement of this and preceding events,
describes a scene by no means rare on the occasion of this election.
'Some four days later,' he writes, 'I was on my horse returning from
Platte City to Weston, when four wagons came along, and on the
bottoms sat six men. A pole about five feet high stuck bolt upright
at the front of the wagon ; on its top stuck an inverted empty whiskey-
bottle ; across the stick at right angles was tied a bowie-knife ; a
black cambric flag, with a death's-head-and-bones daubed on it in
white paint, and a long streamer of beautiful glossy Missouri hemp,
floated from the pole ; there was a revolver lashed across the pole,
and a powder-horn hanging loosely by it. They bore the piratical
symbols of Missouri ruffians returning from Kansas.'"

A Missouri newspaper friendly to the Border Ruffians
said, soon after this affair:—

"From five to seven thousand men started from Missouri to attend
the election ; some to remove, but the most to return to their families, with an intention, if they liked the Territory, to make it their
permanent abode at the earliest moment practicable. But they intended to vote. The Missourians were, many of them, Douglas
County men. There were one hundred and fifty voters from this
county, one hundred and seventy-five from Howard, one hundred
from Cooper. Indeed, every county furnished its quota; and when
they set out it looked like an army. They were armed ; and as there
were no houses in the Territory, they carried tents. Their mission

---

[1] The Englishman in Kansas ; or, Squatter Life and Border Warfare.
By T. H. Gladstone, Esq., author of the "Letters from Kansas" in the
London Times. New York : Miller & Co., 1857. The book has 328
pages, and contains a clear statement of the Kansas question.

was a peaceable one, — to vote, and to drive down stakes for future
homes. After the election, some fifteen hundred of the voters sent a
committee to Mr. Reeder to ascertain if it was his purpose to ratify
the election. He said that it was, and that the majority must carry
the day. But it is not to be denied that the fifteen hundred, *appre-
hending that the governor might attempt to play the tyrant, — since
his conduct had already been insidious and unjust, — wore on their
hats bunches of hemp. They were resolved, if a tyrant attempted to
trample on the rights of a sovereign people, to hang him.*"

The Legislature chosen in the manner above described held
its sessions within a mile or two of the Missouri border, at
a place called the Shawnee Mission, but spent the time when
they were not in session at the Missouri town of Westport.
They unseated most of the few Free-State members who
were declared by Governor Reeder elected; but the most
distinguished member of the Council, or upper house, Martin
F. Conway (a Maryland lawyer, who afterward represented
Kansas in Congress), resigned his seat on the ground that
the whole election was illegal. Governor Reeder early notified both houses that he could not recognize their legality
or approve their legislation; but he was removed by the
subservient President Pierce, who dared not resist the dictates of the slaveholders; and the "bogus" Legislature
proceeded, in August and September, 1855, to the most extreme and infamous action in support of slavery. A resolution offered by J. H. Stringfellow was adopted in these
words : —

"*Be it resolved by the House of Representatives, the Council concur-
ring therein,* That it is the duty of the proslavery party, the Union-
loving men of Kansas Territory, to know but one issue, Slavery;
and that any party making, or attempting to make, any other is and
should be held as an ally of Abolitionism and Disunionism."

The same Stringfellow (so appropriately named), in a
letter to the "Montgomery Advertiser," wrote: "We have
now laws more efficient to protect slave-property than any
State in the Union. These laws have just taken effect
(Sept. 1, 1855), and have already silenced Abolitionists; for
in spite of their heretofore boasting, these know they will be

enforced to the very letter and with the utmost rigor." Let us see, then, what these laws were, which John Brown was even then journeying towards Kansas, through Illinois and Missouri, to confront and overthrow. Mr. Gladstone says of this Missouri-born Legislature : —

" Being in haste to give a code of laws to Kansas, they transferred into a volume of more than a thousand pages the greater part of the laws of their own State, substituting the words 'Territory of Kansas' for 'State of Missouri.' In protection of slavery they enacted far more rigorous laws than obtain in Missouri, or than were ever before conceived of, — making it a felony to utter a word against the institution, or even to have in possession a book or paper which denies the right to hold slaves in Kansas. It will be seen that for every copy of a Free-State paper which a person might innocently purchase, the law would justify that person's condemnation to penal servitude for two or five years, dragging a heavy ball and chain at his ankle, and hired out for labor on the public roads or for the service of individuals at the fixed price of fifty cents *per diem.* So comprehensive did these legislators make their slave-code, that by the authority they thus gave themselves they could in a very short time have made every Free-State man a chained convict, standing side by side, if they so pleased, with their slaves, and giving years of forced labor for the behoof of their proslavery fellow-citizens. The Legislature proceeded also to elect officers for the Territory. Even the executive and judiciary were made to hold office from itself; and a board of commissioners chosen by the Legislature, instead of the inhabitants themselves, was empowered to appoint the sheriffs, justices of the peace, constables, and all other officers in the various counties into which the Territory was divided. Every member of succeeding legislatures, every judge of election, every voter, must swear to his faithfulness on the test questions of slavery. Every officer in the Territory, judicial, executive, or legislative, every attorney admitted to practice in the courts, every juryman weighing evidence on the rights of slaveholders, must attest his soundness in the interest of slavery, and his readiness to indorse its most repugnant measures. For further security the members of the assembly submitted their enactments to the chief-justice [1] for confirmation. This judicial

---

[1] " Had he not the Chief-Justice," said Burke, in his impeachment of Warren Hastings, — "the tamed and domesticated Chief-Justice, who waited on him like a familiar spirit ?" The Kansas dignitary of this name and function was he of whom John Brown once said, "he had *a perfect right* to be hung."

confirmation was gratefully given. All they had done was declared
legal; and the sheriffs and other local officers appointed by the Legislature were equally ready with their aid in the execution of these
unjust laws."

To show that our English visitor, in his blunt indignation
at the iniquity he found flagrant in Kansas, has exaggerated
nothing, let me cite the very words of this slave-code: —

CHAPTER CLI.   *Slaves.   An Act to punish Offences against Slave
Property.*

.   .   .   .

SEC. 3. If any free person shall, by speaking, writing, or printing, advise, persuade, or induce any slaves to rebel, conspire against,
or murder any citizen of this Territory, or shall bring into, print, write,
publish, or circulate, or cause to be brought into, printed, written,
published, or circulated, or *shall knowingly aid or assist in the bringing into, printing, writing, publishing, or circulating, in this Territory any book, pamphlet, paper, magazine, or circular, for the purpose
of exciting insurrection, rebellion, revolt, or conspiracy on the part of
the slaves, free negroes, or mulattoes,* against the citizens of the Territory or any part of them, such person shall be guilty of felony, *and
suffer death.*

SEC. 4. If any person shall entice, decoy, or carry away out of this
Territory any slave belonging to another, with intent to deprive the
owner thereof of the services of such slave, or with intent to effect or
procure the freedom of such slave, he shall be adjudged guilty of
grand larceny, and on conviction thereof, *shall suffer death,* or be
imprisoned at hard labor for not less than ten years.

SEC. 5. If any person shall aid or assist in enticing, decoying,
persuading, or carrying away, or sending out of this Territory any
slave belonging to another, with intent to effect or procure the freedom of such slave, or with intent to deprive the owner thereof of the
services of such slave, he shall be adjudged guilty of grand larceny,
and on conviction thereof *he shall suffer death,* or be imprisoned at
hard labor for not less than ten years.

SEC. 6. If any person shall entice, decoy, or carry away out of
any State or other Territory of the United States any slave belonging
to another, with intent to procure or effect the freedom of such slave,
or to deprive the owners thereof of the services of such slave, and shall
bring such slave into this Territory, he shall be adjudged guilty of
grand larceny, in the same manner as if such slave had been enticed,
decoyed, or carried away out of this Territory; and in such case the

larceny may be charged to have been committed in any county of this Territory into or through which such slave shall have been brought by such person; and on conviction thereof, the person offending *shall suffer death*, or be imprisoned at hard labor for not less than ten years.

. . . .

SEC. 9. If any person shall resist any officer while attempting to arrest any slave that may have escaped from the service of his master or owner, or shall rescue such slave when in the custody of any officer or other person, or shall entice, persuade, aid, or assist such slave from the custody of any officer or other person who may have such slave in custody, whether such slave have escaped from the service of his master or owner in this Territory or in any other State or Territory, the person so offending shall be guilty of felony, and punished by imprisonment at hard labor for a term not less than two years.

. . . .

SEC. 11. If any person print, write, introduce into, publish, or circulate, or cause to be brought into, printed, written, published, or circulated, or shall knowingly aid or assist in bringing into, printing, publishing, or circulating within this Territory any book, paper, pamphlet, magazine, handbill, or circular containing *any statements, arguments, opinions, sentiment, doctrine, advice, or innuendo calculated to produce a disorderly, dangerous, or rebellious disaffection among the slaves of this Territory, or to induce such slaves to escape from the service of their masters, or resist their authority, he shall be guilty of felony, and be punished by imprisonment at hard labor for a term not less than five years.*

SEC. 12. If any free person, by speaking or by writing, assert or maintain that persons have not the right to hold slaves in this Territory, or shall introduce into this Territory, print, publish, write, circulate, or cause to be printed, published, written, circulated, or introduced into this Territory, any book, paper, magazine, pamphlet, or circular containing any denial of the right of persons to hold slaves in this Territory, such person shall be deemed guilty of felony, and punished by imprisonment at hard labor for a term not less than two years.

SEC. 13. No person who is conscientiously opposed to holding slaves, or who does not admit the right to hold slaves in this Territory, shall sit as a juror on the trial of any prosecution for any violation of any of the sections of this act.

It is plain at a glance, that Thomas Jefferson, through whom the existence of Kansas as a part of the United States

was made possible, and who wrote the first charter of our
national existence, the Declaration of Independence, had he
been living in Kansas under these detestable laws, could not
have held office nor sat on a jury ; nay, he would have been
liable to punishment as a felon, certainly under section eleven,
and probably to the punishment of death under section three.
If he dreaded in 1785 some mild "misapplication of law"
which would have prevented the circulation of his "Notes
on Virginia," what would he have said in 1855 of that worse
than British or French tyranny which punished all generous
sentiments in favor of the poor slave with imprisonment
and with death ?   Yet the men who enacted these laws, and
the baser men at Washington who had them enforced by the
national courts and the national army, were the professed
followers of Jefferson, and one of them, the Secretary of
War, bore his name.[1]

Such a crisis could not escape the eye nor fail to command
the presence of John Brown. The disciple of Franklin and
Jefferson, he could not be other than the sworn foeman of
Franklin Pierce and Jefferson Davis, whom God, for our
sins, had allowed to be set in authority over us and over
Kansas. He went far beyond Jefferson and Franklin, those
founders of American democracy, in his sternness of hostility to oppression. Jefferson had said, quoting an imaginary
epitaph on Bradshaw the regicide, " Rebellion to tyrants is
obedience to God ; " and the spirit of that maxim had sought
expression in the escutcheon of Virginia, with its proud
legend, " Sic semper tyrannis."   But Brown found in the
tenets of Calvinism, in the practice of his Puritan ancestors,
and in the oracles of the Bible, a more imperative and practical duty enjoined, which he hastened to perform at Pottawatomie and elsewhere.   There rang in his ears those deep
notes of "the ballad-singer of Calvinism " (as Emerson called
Isaac Watts) chanting in Puritan verse the avenging justice
of the Hebrew Jehovah : —

---

[1] *Jefferson* Davis was Secretary of War under *Franklin* Pierce ; but
Franklin and Jefferson, for whom they were named, could both have been
shot or hanged in Kansas under their administration, if then living and
maintaining the doctrines which gave them renown.

"Judges who rule the world by laws,
Will ye despise the righteous cause,
When th' injured poor before you stands?
Dare ye condemn the righteous poor,
And let rich sinners 'scape secure,
While gold and greatness bribe your hands?

"Have ye forgot, or never knew,
That God will judge the judges too?
High in the heavens his justice reigns;
Yet you invade the rights of God,
And send your bold decrees abroad
To bind the conscience in your chains.

"Break out their teeth, eternal God! —
Those teeth of lions dyed in blood, —
And crush the serpents in the dust!
As empty chaff, when whirlwinds rise,
Before the sweeping tempest flies,
So let their hopes and names be lost.

"Thus shall the justice of the Lord
Freedom and peace to men afford;
And all that hear shall join and say,
'Sure there 's a God that rules on high,
A God that hears his children cry,
And all their sufferings will repay.' "

Until Brown arrived on the scene in Kansas, few blows
had been struck in the Lord's cause.   Mr. Gladstone, who
reached Kansas City May 22, 1856, at the very moment
when Brown heard of the burning of Lawrence, says : —

"Among all the scenes of violence I witnessed it is remarkable
that the offending parties were invariably on the proslavery side.
The Free-State men appeared to me to be intimidated and overawed
in consequence, not merely of the determination and defiant boldness
of their opponents, but still more through the sanction given to these
acts by the Government."

He was deeply impressed with the wild and fierce aspect
of the Border Ruffians, as he first saw them.   He says : —

"It was on the night of May 22, 1856, that I first came in contact
with the Missourian patriots.   I had just arrived in Kansas City, and
shall never forget the appearance of the lawless mob that poured into
the place, inflamed with drink, glutted with the indulgence of the

vilest passions, displaying with loud boasts the 'plunder' they had
taken from the inhabitants, and thirsting for the opportunity of repeating the sack of Lawrence on some other offending place. Men,
for the most part of large frame, with red flannel shirts and immense
boots worn outside their trousers, their faces unwashed and unshaven,
still reeking with the dust and smoke of Lawrence, wearing their
most savage looks, and giving utterance to the most horrible imprecations and blasphemies; armed, moreover, to the teeth with rifles
and revolvers, cutlasses, and bowie-knives, — such were the men I
saw around me. Some displayed a grotesque intermixture in their
dress, having crossed their native red rough shirt with the satin vest
or narrow dress-coat, pillaged from some Lawrence Yankee, or having
girded themselves with the cords and tassels which the day before had
adorned the curtains of the Free-State Hotel. Looking around at these
groups of drunken, bellowing, blood-thirsty demons, who crowded
around the bar of the hotel, shouting for drink, or vented their furious
noise on the levee outside, I felt that all my former experiences of
Border men and Missourians bore faint comparison with the spectacle
presented by this wretched crew, who appeared only the more terrifying from the darkness of the surrounding night. The hotel in Kansas City, where we were, was the next, they said, that should fall, —
the attack was being planned that night: and such, they declared,
should be the end of every place which was built by Free-State men,
or harbored 'those rascally Abolitionists.' Happily, this threat was
not fulfilled."

Nor was the astonished Englishman left in any doubt
what all this meant. He had visited New York, Washington, and most of the Southern States before going to Kansas,
and went there from Mississippi. He says: "When in South
Carolina and other Southern States, I witnessed extraordinary meetings, presided over by men of influence, at which
addresses of almost incredible violence were delivered on
the necessity of 'forcing slavery into Kansas,' of 'spreading
the beneficent influence of Southern institutions over the
new Territories,' of driving back at the point of the bayonet
the nigger-stealing scum poured down by Northern fanaticism." He knew what was the temper of Pierce, Cushing,
Davis, Mason, and Toombs at Washington ; and he had not
learned, as many of his countrymen did a few years later,
to identify the oligarchy of slavery with the aristocracy of
Europe, and to exult in the anticipated downfall of democratic freedom in America.

Long before Mr. Gladstone's arrival in Kansas, the real inhabitants of that Territory had declared their purpose to resist the "bogus" laws of the usurping Legislature. At a convention held in "Big Springs," Sept. 5, 1855, General Lane and ex-Governor Reeder had each brought forward resolutions, somewhat inconsistent with each other, but which the convention adopted. Those written by Reeder, which the Kansas people afterward fully confirmed by their action, contained these declarations : "We owe no allegiance or obedience to the tyrannical enactments of this spurious Legislature ; their laws have no binding force upon the people of Kansas, and every freeman among us is at full liberty (consistent with all his obligations as a citizen and a man) to resist them if he chooses so to do. We will endure and submit to these laws no longer than the best interests of the Territory require as the least of two evils, and will resist them to a bloody issue so soon as we ascertain that peaceable remedies shall fail, and forcible resistance shall furnish any reasonable prospect of success. In the mean time we recommend to our friends throughout the Territory the organization and discipline of volunteer companies, and the procurement and preparation of arms." Upon this platform John Brown (who was not in Kansas when it was adopted, although four of his sons were) consistently acted from 1855 to 1859, when he finally left the Territory with a party of rescued slaves whom he carried to Canada early in 1859, in utter defiance of the Kansas laws and the Fugitive Slave Law of Senator Mason. What his course had been in the mean time will be seen in the following chapters. The contest in Kansas went forward, with many changes and reverses, in those four years ; and towards the close of 1859, just before Brown's death, the other great martyr of emancipation, Abraham Lincoln, came for a few days to look upon the scene of conflict. Mr. Wilder, the Kansas historian, speaking at Wathena, in Doniphan County, July 4, 1884, said : —

"The greatest man who ever set foot in this township arrived here on the first day of December, 1859, — a warm and beautiful day. The late Judge Delahay and I met him at the depot in St. Joseph, Mo.,

that day, and rode up town with him; took him to a barber's shop on
Francis Street, just east of the Planter's House, where there is now a
planing-mill; and I went up to Woolworth's news-stand, in the next
block, and bought him the latest papers. Then the three went down
to the ferry landing, near the old Robidoux building, and sat down in
the dirt, on the bank, waiting for Captain Blackiston's boat. Mr. Lincoln's talk, sitting on that bank, was of Douglas and Colonel Thomas
L. Harris, the famous Illinois Congressman. Mr. Lincoln always
spoke kindly, almost tenderly, of his political opponents. On some
occasion I asked him about John Calhoun, the first surveyor-general
of Kansas and Nebraska, the president of the Lecompton Constitutional Convention, and probably the ablest Democratic manager we
have ever had in Kansas. Mr. Lincoln spoke of Calhoun in terms
of the highest esteem, and with affection. Mr. Calhoun had given
him a surveying job when he was poor, needy, unknown; and the
great and good man had never forgotten it. Calhoun did his best —
and that was much — to plant slavery in Kansas, but he was not the
monster that our papers and speeches pictured him. By the way,
Mr. Lincoln made Mark Delahay Surveyor-General, and when Delahay resigned, gave the place to me without my asking for it. Mr.
Lincoln made a speech that evening at the Great Western Hotel, in the
dining-room, — a very great speech, — to an audience called together
by a man who went through the town sounding a gong. The next
day, December 2d, the day on which John Brown was hanged, he
spoke at Troy; and I think Colonel Ege replied to him, and fully
vanquished the future President. He also spoke in Asahel Low's
hotel in Doniphan; and that completes the great man's connection
with this county."

The audiences in Kansas, even on the threshold of civil
war, could not recognize the full greatness of the plain, awkward Illinois lawyer who was to lead his people like a true
shepherd through dark and bloody ways. The qualities of
John Brown were more obvious, and they attracted more
attention in Kansas; yet it was only here and there that his
real rank was seen and appreciated, and by a singular ingratitude it is in Kansas that his most malicious enemies
are now found. Their malice cannot harm his renown; he
is as much above their reach now as he was above their
comprehension while he fought in their cause, and traversed
their prairies to make them glorious. "In a great age,"
says Cousin, speaking of Pascal, "everything is great."

John Brown, like Abraham Lincoln, came to prominence in
an age by no means grand or noble ; but such was his own
heroic character that he conferred importance on events in
themselves trivial.   His petty conflicts in Kansas and the
details of his two days' campaign in Virginia will be remembered when a hundred battles of our Civil War are forgotten.   He was one of ten thousand, and, as Thoreau said,
could not be tried by a jury of his peers, because his peers
did not exist ; yet so much was he in accord with what is
best in the American character, that he will stand in history
for one type of our people, as Franklin and Lincoln do, —
only with a difference.   He embodied the distinctive qualities of the Puritan, but with a strong tincture of the more
humane sentiments of later times.   No man could be more
sincere in his faith toward God, more earnest in love for man ;
his belief in foreordination was absolute, his courage not
less.   The emotion of fear seemed quite unknown to him,
except in the form of diffidence, — if that were not rather a
sort of pride.   He was diffident of his power in speech or
writing ; yet who, of all his countrymen, has uttered more
effective, imperishable words ?   Part of the service he rendered to his country was by this heroic impersonation of
traits that all mankind recognize as noble.   The cause of
the poor slave had need of all the charm that romantic
courage could give it ; his defenders were treated with the
contempt which attached to himself.   They were looked
upon with aversion by patriots ; they were odious to trade,
distasteful to fashion and learning, impious in the sight of
the Church.   At the stroke of Brown's sword all this was
changed : the cause that had been despised suddenly became
hated, feared, and respected ; and out of this new fear and
hatred our national safety was born.

It was on the soil of Kansas that this transformation began, though it was not completed until Brown's desperate
onset and valiant death in Virginia.   In Kansas he had with
him the hopes and the support of millions, to whom he was
then the defender of white men's rights ; in Virginia he
stood almost alone, — the omen and harbinger of that national calamity which was to avenge the black man's wrongs.
But in his devout mind the two causes united, as they were

soon seen to unite in the event of the Civil War, to
which the course and the result of the Kansas skirmish
were as beacons lighting the way, and warning against useless concession.   *O navis! fortiter occupa portum*, was the
lesson of Kansas.

NOTE. — On page 162, the statement that the Kansas-Nebraska Act left
the people free "at each election to determine the existence of slavery for
themselves" is too strong, and interprets this juggling bill of Douglas too
favorably.   All that it did was to declare that the Territory, "*at the time
of its admission into the Union as a State*, shall be received with or without
slavery, as its Constitution may provide."   But it also declared the right
of the people "to form and regulate their domestic institutions in their
own way, *subject only to the Constitution of the United States*."   The mischief in this clause lay in the fact that by the Dred Scott decision the Federal Constitution was interpreted to hold slavery forever in a Territory, —
as Abraham Lincoln forcibly showed in his speech at Springfield, Ill., June
17, 1858, saying, "The second point of the Dred Scott decision is that,
'subject to the Constitution of the United States,' *neither Congress nor a
Territorial Legislature can exclude slavery from any United States Territory*."   I am indebted to Mr. T. Dwight Thacher, of Topeka, for calling
my attention to this.

JOHN BROWN.

[1855.]

CHAPTER VIII.

THE BROWN FAMILY IN KANSAS.

THE long contest against Southern slavery ended at last in a revolution, of which Kansas saw the first outbreak. Then followed a bloody civil war, after which the South was reorganized, — or, as it was called, "reconstructed," — with the corner-stone of its old social structure, negro slavery, left out, and emancipation, "the stone which the builders rejected," at last adopted in its place. In this contest, continuing for almost a century, but active and violent for about fifty years, there were four distinct parties or groups of men, varying in number as the struggle proceeded, but now nearly all merged in one great antislavery party, just as the persecution of the Christians ended in the conversion of the whole Roman world to Christianity. These parties were — (1) the Abolitionists, beginning with Franklin, Jefferson, and George Mason, and ending with Garrison, Lincoln, and Phillips; (2) the proslavery men; (3) the great body of neutrals; and (4) the Brown family, by which I mean John Brown of Osawatomie, his father Owen Brown, and his children. This one household constituted itself an outpost of emancipation when the early Abolitionists had been defeated and Jefferson had grown silent; it was an active force long before Garrison began his agitation (about 1830), and it continued in the service until the freedom of the slaves was assured. There was no discharge in that war for the Brown family. As one generation passed away, another took its place; and when the struggle became one of arms, the sons replaced each other in the fight, as the children of the old clansman in Scott's romance came forward to die one by one for their chieftain. "Another for Freedom!" was as potent a call with them as "Another for

Hector ! " with the sons of the defeated clan. The Browns
too were defeated, but only for a time, and in such a way
that their renown was increased thereby. From a local
leader John Brown became a world-famous martyr.

" Are you Captain Brown of Kansas ? " asked the Virginian at Harper's Ferry of the old hero, as he recovered
from the stabs and blows of Lee's soldiers.

" I am sometimes called so."

" Are you Osawatomie Brown ? "

" *I tried to do my duty there.*"

So long as these manly answers and the manly acts that
preceded them remain on the record; so long as the public
murder of John Brown for the crime of emancipation is a
part of the history of that republic which within five years
completed emancipation at the cost of half a million lives, —
so long will the deeds and sufferings of the Brown family
in Kansas be as important a chapter in the history of that
State as any that can be written.

Let us then resume the homely series of family letters in
which the father and his children told each other the story
of their pilgrimage to Kansas in 1854–55, and what befell
them there; beginning with the account given in November,
1883, by the present head of the family, John Brown, Jr.,
of the circumstances attending and preceding this removal
from Ohio and the Adirondac forest to Osawatomie in Kansas. The town of this name is ten miles from the various settlements of the Brown family on the branches of the
Pottawatomie Creek (properly a river); but the brother-in-
law of Brown, the Rev. S. L. Adair, established himself at
Osawatomie in 1854, and his log-cabin served as a rendezvous for the family so long as they remained in Kansas.
John Brown, Jr., says: —

" During the years 1853 and 1854 most of the leading Northern
newspapers were not only full of glowing accounts of the extraordinary fertility, healthfulness, and beauty of the Territory of Kansas,
then newly opened for settlement, but of urgent appeals to all lovers
of freedom who desired homes in a new region to go there as settlers,
and by their votes save Kansas from the curse of slavery. Influenced
by these considerations, in the month of October, 1854, five of the
sons of John Brown, — John, Jr., Jason, Owen, Frederick, and Sal-

mon, — then residents of the State of Ohio, made their arrangements to emigrate to Kansas. Their combined property consisted chiefly of eleven head of cattle, mostly young, and three horses. Ten of this number were valuable on account of the breed. Thinking these especially desirable in a new country, Owen, Frederick, and Salmon took them by way of the lakes to Chicago, thence to Meridosia, Ill., where they were wintered; and in the following spring drove them into Kansas to a place selected by these brothers for settlement, about eight miles west of the town of Osawatomie. My brother Jason and his family, and I with my family followed at the opening of navigation in the spring of 1855, going by way of the Ohio and Mississippi rivers to St. Louis. There we purchased two small tents, a plough, and some smaller farming-tools, and a hand-mill for grinding corn. At this period there were no railroads west of St. Louis; our journey must be continued by boat on the Missouri at a time of extremely low water, or by stage at great expense. We chose the river route, taking passage on the steamer 'New Lucy,' which too late we found crowded with passengers, mostly men from the South bound for Kansas. That they were from the South was plainly indicated by their language and dress; while their drinking, profanity, and display of revolvers and bowie-knives — openly worn as an essential part of their make-up — clearly showed the class to which they belonged, and that their mission was to aid in establishing slavery in Kansas.

"A box of fruit-trees and grape-vines which my brother Jason had brought from Ohio, our plough, and the few agricultural implements we had on the deck of that steamer looked lonesome; for these were all we could see which were adapted to the occupations of peace. Then for the first time arose in our minds the query: Must the fertile prairies of Kansas, through a struggle at arms, be first secured to freedom before free men can sow and reap? If so, how poorly we were prepared for such work will be seen when I say that, for arms, five of us brothers had only two small squirrel rifles and one revolver. But before we reached our destination other matters claimed our attention. Cholera, which then prevailed to some extent at St. Louis, broke out among our passengers, a number of whom died. Among these brother Jason's son Austin, aged four years, the elder of his two children, fell a victim to this scourge; and while our boat lay by for repair of a broken rudder at Waverley, Mo., we buried him at night near that panic-stricken town, our lonely way illumined only by the lightning of a furious thunderstorm. True to his spirit of hatred of Northern people, our captain, without warning to us on shore, cast off his lines and left us to make our way by stage to Kansas City, to which place we had already paid our fare by boat. Before we reached there, however, we became very hungry, and endeavored to buy food at various farm-houses on the way; but the occupants, judging from our speech that we were not from the South, always denied us, saying, ' We have nothing for you.' The only exception to this answer was at the stage-house at Independence, Mo.

" Arrived in Kansas, her lovely prairies and wooded streams seemed to us indeed like a haven of rest. Here in prospect we saw our cattle increased to hundreds and possibly to thousands, fields of corn, orchards, and vineyards. At once we set about the work through which only our visions of prosperity could be realized. Our tents would suffice for shelter until we could plough our land, plant corn and other crops, fruit-trees, and vines, cut and secure as hay enough of the waving grass to supply our stock the coming winter. These cheering prospects beguiled our labors through late spring until midsummer, by which time nearly all of our number were prostrated by fever and ague that would not stay cured; the grass cut for hay mouldered in the wet for want of the care we could not bestow, and our crop of corn wasted by cattle we could not restrain. If these minor ills and misfortunes were all, they could be easily borne; but now began to gather the dark clouds of war. An election for a first Territorial Legislature had been held on the 30th of March of this year. On that day the residents of Missouri along the borders came into Kansas by thousands, and took forcible possession of the polls. In the words of Horace Greeley, ' There was no disguise, no pretence of legality, no regard for decency. On the evening before and the morning of the day of election, nearly a thousand Missourians arrived at Lawrence in wagons and on horseback, well armed with rifles, pistols, and bowie-knives, and two pieces of cannon loaded with musket balls. Although but 831 legal electors in the Territory voted, there were no less than 6,320 votes polled. They elected all the members of the Legislature, with a single exception in either house, — the two Free-Soilers being chosen from a remote district which the Missourians overlooked or did not care to reach.'

" Early in the spring and summer of this year the actual settlers at their convention repudiated this fraudulently chosen Legislature, and refused to obey its enactments. Upon this, the border papers of Missouri in flaming appeals urged the ruffian horde that had previously invaded Kansas to arm, and otherwise prepare to march again into the Territory when called upon, as they soon would be, to ' aid in enforcing the laws.' War of some magnitude, at least, now appeared to us brothers to be inevitable; and I wrote to our father, whose home was in North Elba, N. Y., asking him to procure and send to us, if he could, arms and ammunition, so that we could be better prepared to defend ourselves and our neighbors. He soon obtained them; but instead of sending, he came on with them him-

self, accompanied by my brother-in-law Henry Thompson, and my
brother Oliver.   In Iowa he bought a horse and covered wagon ;
concealing the arms in this and conspicuously displaying his surveying implements, he crossed into Missouri near Waverley, and at that
place disinterred the body of his grandson, and brought all safely
through to our settlement, arriving there about the 6th of October."

In August, 1854, when John Brown, Jr., had first mentioned to his father his purpose of emigrating to Kansas, it
was not the intention of the father to accompany them,
although he was willing and rather desirous his children
should go. In a letter written from Akron (Aug. 21, 1854),
he said to John : " If you or any of my family are disposed to
go to Kansas or Nebraska, with a view to help defeat *Satan*
and his legions in that direction, I have not a word to say ;
but I feel committed to operate in another part of the field. If
I were not so committed, I would be on my way this fall.
Mr. Adair [who married Brown's half-sister Florilla] is
fixing to go, and wants to find 'good men and true' to go
along. I would be glad if Jason would give away his Rock
and go. Owen is fixing for some move ; I can hardly say
what." In fact, the four brothers, — John, Jason, Owen, and
Frederick Brown, — as above mentioned, set out for Kansas
in 1854, arriving there in the early spring of 1855, and settling near their uncle Mr. Adair. John Brown himself soon
changed his mind and prepared to follow them, first visiting North Elba and New England ; and at this point his letters to his family at North Elba may be taken up, relating,
in their simple way, the domestic history in these removals,
and the frugal plans he formed for the maintenance and
comfort of those dependent on him or under his guidance.
Here will be found little speech of the great objects he had
in view, but much concerning cattle and household affairs :
as in the correspondence, were it preserved, of some Oriental
patriarch migrating from land to land in Scripture times.

John Brown to his Children.

AKRON, OHIO, Jan. 3, 1855.

DEAR CHILDREN, — Last night your letters to Jason were received (dated December 26), and I had the reading of them. I

conclude from the long time mine to you from Albany was on the way, that you did not reply to it. On my return here from North Elba I was disappointed of about three hundred dollars for cattle sold to brother Frederick, and am still in the same condition, — he having gone to Illinois just before I left to go East, and not having returned nor written me a word since. This puts it out of my power to move my family at present, and will until I get my money, unless I sell off my Devon cattle, — which I cannot, without great sacrifice, before spring opens. Your remarks about hay make me doubt the propriety of taking on any cattle till spring, as I have here an abundance of feed. I am now entirely unable to say whether we can get off before spring or not. All are well here, so far as we know. Owen and Frederick were with their uncle Edward in Meridosia, Ill. (where they expect to winter), on the 23d December; they were well, and much pleased with the country, and with him. You can write them at that place, care of Edward Lusk, Esq. I may send on one of the boys before the family go, but am not now determined. Can write no more now for want of time. Write me, on receipt of this, any and every thing of use or interest.

Your affectionate father,   JOHN BROWN.

AKRON, OHIO, Feb. 13, 1855.

DEAR CHILDREN, — I have deferred answering your very acceptable letter of January 30 for one week, in the hope of having some news to write you about Owen and Frederick; but they are so negligent about writing that I have not a word to send now. I got quite an encouraging word about Kansas from Mr. Adair the other day. He had before given quite a gloomy picture of things. He and family were all well. The friends here were all well a few days since. John and Wealthy have gone back to Vernon, John taking with him my old surveyor's instruments, in consideration of having learned to survey. I have but little to write that will interest you, so I need not be lengthy. I think we may be able to get off in March, and I mean to sell some of our Devon cattle in order to effect it, if I can do no better. I should send on Watson within a few days, if I thought I could manage to get along with the family and cattle without his help. I may conclude to do so still before we get away. The last of January and February, up to yesterday, have been very remarkable for uninterrupted cold weather for this section. We were glad to learn that you had succeeded in getting the house so comfortable. I want Johnny should be so good a boy that " 95 will not turn him off." Can you tell whether the Stout lot was ever redeemed in December or not by the owners ?

ROCKFORD, WINNEBAGO COUNTY, ILL., May 7, 1855.

DEAR CHILDREN, — I am here with my stock of cattle to sell, in order to raise funds so that I can move to North Elba, and think I may get them off in about two weeks. Oliver is here with me. We shall get on so late that we can put in no crops (which I regret), so that you had perhaps better plant or sow what you can conveniently on "95."[1] I heard from John and Jason and their families (all well) at St. Louis on the 21st April, expecting to leave there on the evening of that day to go up the Missouri for Kansas. My family at Akron were well on the 4th inst. As I may be detained here some days after you get this, I wish you to write me at once what wheat and corn are worth at Westport now, as near as you can learn. People are here so busy sowing their extensive fields of grain, that I cannot get them even to see my cattle now. Direct to this place, care of Shepard Leach, Esq.

ROCKFORD, WINNEBAGO COUNTY, ILL., June 4, 1855.

DEAR CHILDREN, — I write just to say that I have sold my cattle without making much sacrifice, and expect to be on my way home to-morrow. Oliver expects to remain behind and go to Kansas. After I get home I expect to start with my family for North Elba as soon as we can get ready. We may possibly get off this week, but I hardly think we can. I have heard nothing further as yet from the boys in Kansas. All were well at home a few days since.

HUDSON, OHIO, June 18, 1855.

DEAR CHILDREN, — I write to say that we are (after so long a time) on our way to North Elba, with our freight also delivered at the Akron depot; we look for it here to-night. If this reaches you before we get on, I would like to have some one with a good team go out to Westport on next Tuesday afternoon or Wednesday forenoon, to take us out or a load of our stuff. We have some little thought now of going with our freight by the Welland Canal and by Ogdensburgh to Westport, in which case we may not get around until after you get this. All are well here, so far as we know.

Your affectionate father,   JOHN BROWN.

To his Wife.

SYRACUSE, June 28, 1855.

DEAR WIFE AND CHILDREN, — I reached here on the first day of the convention, and I have reason to bless God that I came ; for

---

[1] Brown's farm at North Elba.

13

I have met with a most warm reception from all, so far as I know, and — except by a few sincere, honest peace friends — a most hearty approval of my intention of arming my sons and other friends in Kansas. I received to-day donations amounting to a little over sixty dollars, — twenty from Gerrit Smith, five from an old British officer;[1] others giving smaller sums with such earnest and affectionate expressions of their good wishes as did me more good than money even. John's two letters were introduced, and read with such effect by Gerrit Smith as to draw tears from numerous eyes in the great collection of people present. The convention has been one of the most interesting meetings I ever attended in my life; and I made a great addition to the number of warm-hearted and honest friends.

Letters from John Brown's Sons in Kansas to their Father.

BROWNSVILLE, BROWN Co.,[2] K. T.,
Friday Morning, June 22, 1855.

DEAR FATHER, — Day before yesterday we received a letter from you dated Rockford, Ill., 24th May, which for some unaccountable cause has been very long delayed on the road. We are exceedingly glad to hear from you, and that you still intend coming on. Our health is now excellent, and our crops, cattle, and horses look finely. We have now about twelve acres of sod corn in the ground, more than a quarter acre of white beans, two and a half bushels seed potatoes planted and once hoed, besides a good garden containing corn, potatoes, beets, cabbages, turnips, a few onions, some peas, cucumbers, melons, squashes, etc. Jason's fruit-trees, grape-vines, etc., that survived the long period of transportation, look very well : probably more than half he started with are living, with the exception of peaches ; of these he has only one or two trees. As we arrived so late in the season, we have but little expectation of harvesting much

---

[1] This was Charles Stewart, a retired captain of the British army, who had served under Wellington in India or Spain, afterwards emigrated to America, and who became one of the zealous associates of Gerrit Smith in the antislavery crusade of 1835-50. He was visiting at Mr. Smith's house in 1855 ; and I found him there again in February, 1858, when I met Brown in Mrs. Smith's parlor, to hear the disclosure of his Virginia plans. The money given to Brown at Syracuse, in June, 1855, was in part expended by him at Springfield, in July, for arms. He then saw his old friend Thomas Thomas, the Maryland freedman, and urged him to join in the Kansas expedition ; but Thomas, who had made his arrangements to live in California, declined, and never met Brown again.

[2] This is now Cutler, in Franklin County.

corn, and but few potatoes. The rainy season usually commences here early in April or before, and continues from six to eight weeks, during which a great amount of rain falls. This year we had no rain of any consequence before the 12th or 15th of May; since then have had two heavy rains accompanied with some wind and most tremendous thunder and lightning; have also had a number of gentle rains, continuing from one to twenty-four hours; but probably not more than half the usual fall of rain has yet come. As the season last year was irregular in this respect, probably this will be to some extent. We intend to keep our garden, beans, and some potatoes watered if we can, so as to have something if our corn should be a failure. As it is, the prospect is middling fair, and the ground is ploughed ready for early planting next year. Old settlers here say that people should calculate on having the spring's sowing and planting all done by the middle of April; in that case their crops are more abundant. The prairies are covered with grass, which begins to wave in the wind most beautifully; shall be able to cut any quantity of this, and it is of far better quality than I had any idea.

In answer to your questions: Good oxen are from $50 to $80 per yoke, — have been higher; common cows, from $15 to $25, — probably will not be higher; heifers in proportion. Limited demand as yet for fine stock. Very best horses from $100 to $150 each; average fair to good, $75 to $80. No great demand now for cattle or horses. A good strong buggy would sell well, — probably a *Lumberee* best. Mr. Adair has had several chances to sell his. Very few *Lumberee* buggies among the settlers. White beans, $5 per bushel; corn meal, $1.75 per bushel of fifty pounds, tending downward; flour, $7 per hundred pounds; dried apples, 12½ cents per pound; bacon, 12 to 14 cents here; fresh beef, 5 to 6 cents per pound. Enclosed is a slip cut from a late number of the "Kansas Tribune" giving the markets there, which differ somewhat from prices in this section. It is the paper published at Lawrence by the Speers.

I have no doubt it would be much cheaper and healthier for you to come in the way you propose, with a "covered lumber buggy and one horse or mule," especially from St. Louis here. The navigation of the Missouri River, except by the light-draught boats recently built for the Kansas River, is a horrid business in a low stage of water, which is a considerable portion of the year. You will be able to see much more of the country on your way, and if you carry some provisions along it is altogether the cheaper mode of travelling; besides, such a conveyance is just what you want here to carry on the business of surveying. You can have a good road here whithersoever you may wish to go. Flour, white beans, and dried fruit will doubtless continue for some time to come to be high. It is believed that a much larger emigration will arrive here this fall than before. Should you buy anything to send by water, you can send it either to Lawrence, thirty-five miles north of us, or to Kansas City, Mo., care of Walker & Chick, sixty miles northeast of us.

A surveyor would soon find that great numbers are holding more land, and especially timber, than can be covered by 160 acres, or even 320, and that great numbers are holding claims for their friends; so that I have no doubt people will find a sufficient amount of timber yet for a long time. Owing to the rapid settlement of the country by squatters, it does not open a good field for speculators.

The land on which we are located was ceded by the Pottawatomie Indians to the Government. The Ottawa lands are soon to be sold, each person of the tribe reserving and choosing two hundred acres; the remainder open to pre-emption after their choice is made. The Peoria lands have been bargained for by the Government, and are to be sold to the highest bidder without reservation. But Missourians have illegally gone on to these Peoria lands, intending to combine and prevent their going higher than $1.25 per acre, and then claim. if they go higher, a large amount of improvements, — thus cheating the Indians. The Ottawas intend to divide into families, and cultivate the soil and the habits of civilized life, as many of them are now doing. They are a fine people. The Peorias are well advanced, and might do the same but for a bad bargain with our Government.

[Here is drawn a plan of the Brown settlement or claim.]

There is a town site recently laid out on the space marked " village plat ; " as there are two or three in sight, it is uncertain which will be taken. The semicircle is even ground, sloping every way, and affording a view in every way of from twenty to thirty miles in every direction, except one small point in the direction of Osawatomie; the view from this ground is beautiful beyond measure. The timbered lands on Middle Creek are covered with claims; the claimants, many of them from Ohio, Illinois, and the East, are mostly Free-State folks. There are probably twenty families within five or six miles of us.

Day before yesterday Owen and I ran the Peoria line east to see if there might not be found a patch of timber on some of the numerous small streams which put into the Osage, and which would be south of the Peoria line. We found on a clear little stream sufficient timber for a log-house, and wood enough to last say twenty families for two or three years, perhaps more, and until one could buy and raise more. Here a good claim could be made by some one. The prairie land which would be included is of the very best I have ever seen ; plenty of excellent stone on and adjoining it. Claims will soon be made here that will have no more than two or three acres of timber ;

and after these are exhausted prairie claims will be taken, the claimants depending on buying their timber. Already this is the case, and
many are selling off twenty, thirty, and forty acres from their timber
claims to those who have none.

The above, though without signature, is in the handwriting of John Brown, Jr.; and the plan of "Brown's Station" is drawn in his neat surveyor's manner. In the same
envelope evidently went the two following letters from Jason
Brown (familiarly called "Jay" by his family) and Salmon,
the eldest son of the second marriage.

OSAWATOMIE, K. T., June 23, 1855.

DEAR FATHER, MOTHER, BROTHERS, AND SISTERS, — We received a few days since a letter from mother, since then one from
father, which we were all very glad to get. I should have written you
before, but since we laid little Austin in the grave I have not felt as
if I could write. I shall not attempt to say much now. We fully
believe that Austin is happy with his Maker in another existence;
and if there is to be a separation of friends after death, we pray God
to keep us in the way of truth, and that we may so run our short
course as to be able to enjoy his company again. Ellen feels so
lonely and discontented here without Austin, that we shall go back
to Akron next fall if she does not enjoy herself better. I am well
pleased with the country, and can be as well content here as anywhere else if it proves to be healthy. It is a very rich and beautiful
country. I should think it would be altogether best for father to
come by land from St. Louis. Salmon has a very good claim (as
well as the rest of us), and seems to be very much pleased with it.
We are all living together in tents and in the wagon, and have no
houses yet. I used all the money I had for freight and passage before I got here, and had to borrow of John. We have no stoves; I
wish now that we had brought ours along. We would all like to
hear from you often. All well.

Your affectionate son and brother,

J. L. BROWN.

P. S. If you should come by Akron on your way here, and could
buy and box up a middle-sized stove and furniture, with about four
lengths of pipe, and send or bring it to me at Kansas City, I will
contrive some way to pay you for it. I think they can be got there
and shipped here cheaper than they can be bought here. I would
like to have you inquire, if you will.

OSAWATOMIE, K. T., June 22, 1855.

DEAR FATHER, — We received your letter from Rockford, Ill., this week, and are very glad that you are going to get through there soon, and that you are going to be here before fall. In answer to your questions about what you will need for your company, I would say that I have one acre of corn that looks very well, and some beans and squashes and turnips. You will want to get some pork and meal, and beans enough to last till the crop comes in, and then I think we will have enough grain to last through the winter. I will have a house up by the time that you will get here. My boots are very near worn out, and I shall need some summer pants and a hat. I bought an axe, and that you will not have to get. There are slaves owned within three miles of us.

Your affectionate son,

SALMON BROWN.

From Oliver Brown to his Mother at North Elba.

ROCKFORD, WINNEBAGO COUNTY, ILL., Aug. 8 [1855].

DEAR MOTHER, — I just received yours of the 31st, and also of the 1st, and was very much pleased to hear that you were all well. I also received letters from father and Ruth at the same time, which I was very glad to get; but I much more expected to see father than to hear from him. My health is very good at present, but has been very poor for a week or ten days back. I am working now for a man named Goodrich, getting $1.50 per day, which I have to earn, every cent of it. I never worked so hard before. I am quite sorry to hear that you are likely to have rather tough times of it for a year to come. Was I certain that father would not be distressed for money when he gets here, I would send you enough to buy another cow; but I think we must try and see what we can do for you when we get to Kansas. Have written to Salmon twice, but have received no answer as yet. My shirts hold out very well so far, but I think the ones you were going to send by father will come in play in course of the season. I very much hope to see Alexis Hinkley with him. Should much like to have Watson with us, but do not see that it is possible. I hope to see you all in Kansas in the course of a year or two. It has been very dry here, but crops look very well. I received that receipt for cholera medicine, and went at once and got the whole dose mixed up. I do not think of more at present, so please all write me soon; and Wat. you must spur up about writing, and Anna too.

From your affectionate son,

OLIVER BROWN.

From John Brown to his Family at North Elba.

CHICAGO, ILL., Aug. 23, 1855.

DEAR WIFE AND CHILDREN, EVERY ONE, — I see that Henry has given you so full a history of our matters that I have but little to say now, but to add that we start from here this morning, all well. We have a nice young horse, for which we paid here $120, but have so much load that we shall have to walk a good deal — enough probably to supply ourselves with game. We have provided ourselves with the most of what we need on our outward march. If you get this on Tuesday and answer it on Wednesday, some of you directing on the outside to Oliver, at Rock Island, Ill., we should probably get your answer there. Oliver's name is not so common as either Henry's or mine. We shall write you often, and hope you will do so by us. You may direct one to Oliver at Kansas City, Mo., as we may go there, and shall be very glad to hear from you. Write us soon at Osawatomie, Kansas, and may God Almighty bless you all!

Your affectionate husband and father,

JOHN BROWN.

SCOTT COUNTY, IOWA, Sept. 4 [1855], in Morning.

DEAR WIFE AND CHILDREN, ALL, — I am writing in our tent about twenty miles west of the Mississippi, to let you know that we are all in good health and how we get along. We had some delay at Chicago on account of our freight not getting on as we expected; while there we bought a stout young horse that proves to be a very good one, but he has been unable to travel fast for several days from having taken the distemper. We think he appears quite as well as he has, this morning; and we hope he will not fail us. Our load is heavy, so that we have to walk most of the time; indeed, all the time the last day. The roads are mostly very good, and we can make some progress if our horse does not fail us. We fare very well on crackers, herring, boiled eggs, prairie chicken, tea, and sometimes a little milk. Have three chickens now cooking for our breakfast. We shoot enough of them on the wing as we go along to supply us with fresh meat. Oliver succeeds in bringing them down quite as well as any of us. Our expenses before we got away from Chicago had been very heavy; since then very light, so that we hope our money will not entirely fail us; but we shall not have any of account left when we get through.

We expect to go direct through Missouri, and if we are not obliged to stop on account of our horse, shall soon be there. We mean to write you often when we can. We got to Rock Island too soon for any letter from you, but shall not be too early at Kansas City, where we hope to hear from you. The country through which we have travelled from Chicago has been mostly very good; the worst fault is want of living streams of water. With all the comforts we have along our journey, I think, could I hope in any other way to answer the end of my being, I would be quite content to be at North Elba.

I have directed the sale of the cattle in Connecticut, and to have the rest sent in a New York draft payable to Watson's order, which I hope will make you all quite comfortable. Watson should get something more at Elizabethtown than the mere face of the draft. He will need to write his name across the back of the draft when he sells it: about two inches from the top end would be the proper place. I want you to make the most of the money you get, as I expect to be very poor about money from any other source. Commend you all to the mercy and infinite grace of God. I bid you all good-by for this time.

Your affectionate husband and father,

JOHN BROWN.[1]

OSAWATOMIE, K. T., Oct. 13, 1855.
Saturday Eve.

DEAR WIFE AND CHILDREN, EVERY ONE, — We reached the place where the boys are located one week ago, late at night; at least Henry and Oliver did. I, being tired, stayed behind in our tent, a mile or two back. As the mail goes from here early Monday morning, we could get nothing here in time for that mail. We found all more or less sick or feeble but Wealthy and Johnny.[2] All at Brownsville appear now to be mending, but all sick or feeble here at

---

[1] The following receipts belong in this portion of the family papers : the first one is for arms purchased with money contributed by Gerrit Smith and others for use in Kansas ; the second is for the wagon in which Brown made the journey to Kansas : —

SPRINGFIELD, MASS., July 24, 1855.

Received of John Brown one box firearms and flasks, to be forwarded by railroad to Albany, and consigned to him at Cleveland, Ohio, care of H. B. Spellman of that place.

THOMAS O'CONNELL,
For W. R. R. Company.

$100.   Received of John Brown one hundred dollars in full for a heavy horse wagon, this day sold him, and which we agree to ship immediately to J. B., Iowa City, Iowa, care of Dr. Jesse Bowen.

BILLINGS & BRYANT.

[2] Son of John Brown, Jr.

Mr. Adair's. Fever and ague and chill-fever seem to be very general. Oliver has had a turn of the ague since he got here, but has got it broken. Henry has had no return since first breaking it. We met with no difficulty in passing through Missouri, but from the sickness of our horse and our heavy load. The horse has entirely recovered. We had, between us all, sixty cents in cash when we arrived. We found our folks in a most uncomfortable situation, with no houses to shelter one of them, no hay or corn fodder of any account secured, shivering over their little fires, all exposed to the dreadful cutting winds, morning and evening and stormy days. We have been trying to help them all in our power, and hope to get them more comfortable soon. I think much of their ill health is owing to most unreasonable exposure. Mr. Adair's folks would be quite comfortable if they were well. One letter from wife and Anne to Salmon, of August 10, and one from Ruth to John, of 19th September, is all I have seen from any of you since getting here. Henry found one from Ruth, which he has not shown me. Need I write that I shall be glad to hear from you? I did not write while in Missouri, because I had no confidence in your getting my letters. We took up little Austin and brought him on here, which appears to be a great comfort to Jason and Ellen. We were all out a good part of the last night, helping to keep the prairie fire from destroying everything; so that I am almost blind to-day, or I would write you more.

Sabbath Eve, October 14.

I notice in your letter to Salmon your trouble about the means of having the house made more comfortable for winter, and I fondly hope you have been relieved on that score before now, by funds from Mr. Hurlbut, of Winchester, Conn., from the sale of the cattle there. Write me all about your situation; for, if disappointed from that source, I shall make every effort to relieve you in some other way. Last Tuesday was an election day with Free-State men in Kansas, and hearing that there was a prospect of difficulty we all turned out most thoroughly armed (except Jason, who was too feeble); but no enemy appeared, nor have I heard of any disturbance in any part of the Territory. Indeed, I believe Missouri is fast becoming discouraged about making Kansas a slave State, and I think the prospect of its becoming free is brightening every day. Try to be cheerful, and always " hope in God," who will not leave nor forsake them that trust in him. Try to comfort and encourage each other all you can. You are all very dear to me, and I humbly trust we may be kept and spared to meet again on earth; but if not, let us all endeavor earnestly to secure admission to that eternal home,

where will be no more bitter separations, " where the wicked shall
cease from troubling and the weary be at rest." We shall probably
spend a few days more in helping the boys to provide some kind of
shelter for winter, and mean to write you often. May God in infinite
mercy bless, comfort, and save you all, for Christ's sake !

Your affectionate husband and father,

JOHN BROWN.

In addition to the account given by John Brown, Jr., of
the pilgrimage to Kansas, the following notice of it, written
by the father, and found among his papers at North Elba,
may here be cited. He wrote thus : —

" In 1854 the four eldest sons of John Brown, named John, Jr.,
Jason, Owen, and Frederick (all children by a first wife), then living
in Ohio, determined to remove to Kansas. John, Jr., sold his place,
a very desirable little property, near Vernon, in Trumbull County.
Jason Brown had a very valuable collection of grape-vines, and also of
choice fruit-trees, which he took up and shipped in boxes at a heavy
cost. The other two sons held no landed property, but both were
possessed of some valuable stock (as were also the two first-named)
derived from that of their father, which had been often noticed by
liberal premiums, both in the State of New York and also of Ohio.
The two first-named, John and Jason, both had families. Owen had
none. Frederick was engaged to be married, and was to return for
his wife.

" In consequence of an extreme dearth in 1854 the crops in Northern Ohio were almost an entire failure ; and it was decided by the
four brothers that the two youngest should take the teams and entire
stock, cattle and horses, and move them to Southwestern Illinois to
winter, and to have them on early in the spring of 1855. This was
done at a very considerable expense, and with some loss of stock to
John, Jr., some of his best stock having been stolen on the way.
The wintering of the animals was attended with great expense, and
with no little suffering to the two youngest brothers, — one of them,
Owen, being to some extent a cripple from childhood by an injury
of the right arm ; and Frederick, though a very stout man, was subject to periodical sickness for many years, attended with insanity.
It has been stated that he was idiotic ; nothing could be more false.
He had subjected himself to a most dreadful surgical operation but
a short time before starting for Kansas, which had well-nigh cost
him his life, and was but just through with his confinement when
he started on his journey, pale and weak. They were obliged to

husk corn all winter, out of doors, in order to obtain fodder for their animals. Salmon Brown, a very strong minor son of the family, eighteen years old, was sent forward early in 1855, to assist the two last-named, and all three arrived in Kansas early in the spring."

In such patriarchal fashion did the Browns enter the land which they were foreordained to defend. These young men were of the true stuff, worthy sons of such a sire; active, enterprising persons, fond of labor, inured to hardship, and expecting, as their father had taught them, to earn their living with the toil of their own hands. The narrow circumstances of the family made it necessary that these young men should support themselves somewhere. Love of freedom, love of adventure, and a desire for independence in fortune combined to tempt them; but the father, besides his wish to aid them, had constantly in view his main object, as the last letter shows.

More Family Letters.

BROWNSVILLE, K. T., Nov. 2, 1855.

DEAR WIFE AND CHILDREN, EVERY ONE, — We last week received Watson's letter of October 3, too late to answer till now. I felt grateful to learn that you were all then well, and I think I fully sympathize with you in all the hardships and discouragements you have to meet; but you may be assured you are not alone in having trials. I believe I wrote you that we found every one here more or less unwell but Wealthy and Johnny, without any sort of a place where a stout man even could protect himself from the cutting cold winds and storms, which prevail here (the winds, I mean, in particular) much more than in any place where we have ever lived; and that no crops of hay or anything raised had been taken care of; with corn wasting by cattle and horses, without fences; and, I may add, without any meat; and Jason's folks without sugar, or any kind of breadstuffs but corn ground with great labor in a hand-mill about two miles off. Since I wrote before, Wealthy, Johnny, Ellen, and myself have escaped being sick. Some have had the ague, but lightly; but Jason and Oliver have had a hard time of it, and are yet feeble. They appear some better just now. Under existing circumstances we have made but little progress; but we have made a little. We have got a shanty three logs high, chinked, and mudded, and roofed with our tent, and

a chimney so far advanced that we can keep a fire in it for Jason.[1]
John has his shanty a little better fixed than it was, but miserable
enough now; and we have got their little crop of beans secured,
which, together with johnnycake, mush and milk, pumpkins, and
squashes, constitute our fare. Potatoes they have none of any account; milk, beans, pumpkins, and squashes a very moderate supply,
just for the present use. We have also got a few house-logs cut for
Jason. I do not send you this account to render you more unhappy,
but merely to let you know that those here are not altogether in
paradise, while you have to stay in that miserable frosty region.
We had here, October 25, the hardest freezing I ever witnessed south
of North Elba at that season of the year.

After all, God's tender mercies are not taken from us, and blessed
be his name forever! I believe things will a little brighten here
before long, and as the winter approaches, and that we may be able
to send you a more favorable account. There is no proper officer
before whom a deed can be acknowledged short of Lawrence, and
Jason and Owen have not been able to go there at all since we got
here. I want to learn very much whether you have received any
return from the cattle of Mr. Hurlbut, in Connecticut, so that I may
at once write him if you have not. I trust you will not neglect this,
as it takes so long to get letters through, and it will greatly lessen my
anxiety about your being made in some measure comfortable for the
winter. We hear that the fall has been very sickly in Ohio and other
States. I can discover no reason why this country should continue
sickly, but it has proven exceedingly so this fall. I feel more and
more confident that slavery will soon die out here, — and to God be
the praise! Commending you all to his infinite grace, I remain

Your affectionate husband and father,

JOHN BROWN.

To his Family.

OSAWATOMIE, K. T., Nov. 23, 1855.

DEAR WIFE AND CHILDREN, ALL, — Ruth's letter to Henry,
saying she was about moving, and dated 23d October (I think),
was received by last week's mail. We were all glad to learn again
of your welfare; and as to your all staying in one house, I can see
no possible objection, if you can only be well agreed, and try to

---

[1] His home was a freezing cabin,
  Too bare for the hungry rat;
Its roof was thatched with ragged grass,
  And bald enough of that.
          HOLMES, *The Pilgrim's Vision.*

make each other as comfortable as may be. Nothing new of account
has occurred amongst us since I wrote. Henry, Jason, and Oliver
are unable to do much yet, but appear to have but little ague now.
The others are all getting middling well. We have got both families
so sheltered that they need not suffer hereafter ; have got part of the
hay (which had lain in cocks) secured ; made some progress in preparation to build a house for John and Owen ; and Salmon has caught
a prairie wolf in the steel trap. We continue to have a good deal of
stormy weather, — rains with severe winds, and forming into ice as
they fall, together with cold nights that freeze the ground considerably. " Still God has not forsaken us," and we get " day by day
our daily bread," and I wish we all had a great deal more gratitude
to mingle with our undeserved blessings. Much suffering would be
avoided by people settling in Kansas, were they aware that they
would need plenty of warm clothing and light warm houses as much
as in New Hampshire or Vermont; for such is the fact.

Since Watson wrote, I have felt a great deal troubled about your
prospects of a cold house to winter in, and since I wrote last I have
thought of a cheap ready way to help it much, at any rate. Take
any common straight-edged boards, and run them from the ground
up to the eaves, barn fashion, not driving the nails in so far but that
they may easily be drawn, covering all but doors and windows as
close as may be in that way, and breaking joints if need be. This
can be done by any one, and in any weather not very severe, and the
boards may afterwards be mostly saved for other uses. I think much,
too, of your widowed state, and I sometimes allow myself to dream a
little of again some time enjoying the comforts of home ; but I do
not dare to dream much. May God abundantly reward all your
sacrifices for the cause of humanity, and a thousandfold more than
compensate your lack of worldly connections ! We have received two
newspapers you sent us, which were indeed a great treat, shut away
as we are from the means of getting the news of the day. Should
you continue to direct them to some of the boys, after reading, we
should prize them much.

Your affectionate husband and father,

JOHN BROWN.

These letters disclose the hardships of the first year of
pioneer life in Kansas, suffered from the elements and natural causes alone. Yet the troubles of this family were but
just begun when the inclemency of the season had been in
some measure guarded against. The Browns had " located,"
as already mentioned, ten or twelve miles from Osawatomie ;

their kinsman Mr. Adair living between them and the
village. James Hanway, another pioneer, living on the
Pottawatomie, near Dutch Henry's Crossing, in Franklin
County, a few miles southeast of Brownsville (which is
now in the township of Cutler), thus speaks of the location : " On North Middle Creek, on the farm of Mr. Day,
eight miles southeast of Ottawa, John Brown caused to be
erected a cabin for the purpose of pre-empting a claim for
his brother-in-law Mr. Day, the father of the present occupant of the farm ; but I never learned that Brown lived on
it, for after the month of May, 1856, he was never station-
ary, but all the time on the war-path, until he left Kansas
for a season. After the Pottawatomie tragedy occurred,
the John Brown, Jr., cabin, with a valuable library, was
burned down by the ruffians. This cabin was located a
short distance south of the Day cabin. The other sons of
John Brown had claims about one and a half miles south,
now known as 'Brown's Run.' " The family were therefore
within a circuit of two miles of each other, and at some distance from any other settlers. Their post-office was Osawatomie; for there was then no town at Ottawa, which is now
a thriving village, with a third part of the whole county
population. The township of Pottawatomie, in which the
Shermans and Doyles lived, was about as far south from
the Browns as Osawatomie was on the east.

Scarcely had the Brown family got over the first hardships of the sickly season and the frosty autumn, when they
were called upon to arm and muster for the defence of their
threatened neighbors at Lawrence. The murdering of Free-
State men had begun (Oct. 25, 1855) with the shooting of
Samuel Collins at Doniphan by Pat Laughlin, a noisy proslavery Irishman, who was aided in his attack by three or
four armed associates. No attempt was made to punish
Laughlin. Four weeks later, November 21, Charles Dow
was murdered by Franklin Coleman, a proslavery bully,
near Hickory Point. The next night, Jacob Branson, a witness against Coleman, was arrested by the proslavery sheriff
Jones, for taking part in a Free-State meeting, contrary to
the " bogus laws ; " but before Jones and his *posse* could
carry their prisoner to the proslavery capital, Lecompton,

they were waylaid by an equal force of Free-State men, who
rescued Branson, near Blanton's Bridge, on the very night
of his arrest. J. R. Kennedy, now of Colorado, has given a
graphic account of the rescue scene, which I will quote in
his own words, for the sake of showing what men and what
events might be heard of at any time in Kansas.[1] The date
is Nov. 22, 1855; the men acting on the Free-State side
were Major James B. Abbott, Captain Philip Hutchinson,
Philip Hupp, and his son Miner Hupp, Colonel Samuel N.
Wood (an Ohio man, six months resident in Kansas), Elmore
Allen, Edmund Curless, Lafayette Curless, William Hughes,
Paul Jones, J. R. Kennedy, Collins Holloway, Isaac Shap-
pet, John Smith, and —— Smith. The party were waiting
at Abbott's house at eleven o'clock at night, when the
chronicle begins. Kennedy says: —

" While I was standing by the door, still on the watch, I heard
Philip Hupp (and no braver man ever lived) say, ' Well, boys, I
tell you what's the matter; they have taken Branson and crossed the
Wakarusa at Cornelius's Crossing, and have him at old Crane's hotel.
All we have to do, and what we ought to do, is to march right down
there, and if Branson is in the house, tell him to come out, — that he
is a free man, and will be protected.' Just at this time I walked out
a little from the door, and looking south saw fifteen or twenty mounted
men riding slowly along the road toward the house. Stepping quickly
back to the door, I caught Major Abbott's eye, and beckoned him to
come out, which he did. I showed him the men, and exclaiming,
' That's the party ! ' he rushed into the house, telling the boys they

---

[1] Mr. Wilder, the Kansas historian, with the national turn for humor,
says : " We had a Kansas war here once, — civil, internecine, fratricidal.
Some fellow in long hair and buckskin breeches, armed and mounted like
Jesse James, would ride up to you and kill you because you could read and
write, and were a Yankee. He controlled the elections in that way for
several years. Those who fought you at the polls also counted the votes
after the election. There was a proslavery bully here — name happily forgotten — who made it a business to fight on election day, to knock down
and drag out, and to keep timid men from the polls. But at one election
the bully woke up the wrong passenger, — namely, John Lawler, of Elwood.
When John came home that night, after taking a square Free-State drink,
he said he had found the way to carry a Free-State election : ' Break a
Democratic leg early in the morning.' And that was just what John had
done."

were coming, and to go out quick. Mrs. Abbott handed the boys
their guns, and they did go out with a rush, Abbott going first, followed by Philip Hupp ; then came Captain Hutchinson, Paul Jones,
and others. We turned to the left around the corner of the house
into the road a few rods in front of the horsemen. Phil Hupp was
the first man who crossed the road. He said afterwards he was
watching the man on the gray horse, Sheriff Jones ; and he did
watch him, sure enough. Next to Hupp was Paul Jones, and both
were armed with squirrel rifles. Next came Captain Hutchinson,
armed with two large stones ; next were Holloway and myself, — I
thinking Captain Hutchinson was a good man to stay with, as he
had been three years in the Mexican War. The rest of the boys
ranged along the side of the road near the house. This was about the
order we occupied when the party approached close to those in the
road, and very close to those by the side of the road. Mr. Hupp
being in front, and seeing the boys scattered along from where he was
to the side of the house, called out, ' Boys, what the hell are you
doing there ? Here is the place for you.' They then all crowded
rapidly up in front of the other party, when one of these said,
' What 's up ? ' Major Abbott replied, ' That is what we want to
know,' — which remark was followed by a shot on our side. (The
Major had a self-cocking revolver, and he had, in his excitement,
pulled it a little too hard, causing it to go off.) Then the question
was asked him again by the other side, ' What 's up ? ' Thinking of
what Mr. Hupp had said in the house, I said to Major Abbott, ' Ask
them if Branson is there.' He did so, and the answer was, ' Yes, I
am here, and a prisoner.' Three or four of our men spoke at once,
— Major Abbott, Colonel Wood, and others whom I do not remember, — saying, ' Come out of that,' or ' Come over to your friends,'
or perhaps both were said. Branson replied, ' They say they will
shoot me if I do.' Colonel Sam Wood answered quickly, ' Let
them shoot and be damned ; we can shoot too.' Branson then said,
' I will come if they do shoot,' starting his mule. (The man who
was leading it let the halter slip through his hands very quietly.)
The rest of the proslavery party raised their shot-guns and cocked
them. Our little crowd raised their guns, and were ready in as
good time as the others. Sam Wood and two or three of our
men helped Branson. Wood asked Branson, ' Is this your mule ? '
' No,' was the reply, whereupon Wood kicked the mule and said,
' Go back to your masters, damn you.' In the mean time Branson
had disappeared, and was seen no more by these brave ' shot-gun '
men.

" About this time some one of them said, ' Why, Sam Wood, you
are very brave to-night ; you must want to fight.' Colonel Wood

replied that he ' was always ready for a fight.' Just at this moment
Sheriff Jones interposed, saying, ' There is no use to shed blood in
this affair ; but it will be settled soon in a way that will not be very
pleasant to Abolitionists,' and started to ride through those standing
in the road. He did not then know old Philip Hupp, but soon made
his acquaintance ; and I do not think he will be stopped by death any
quicker than Phil Hupp stopped him that night.   Just as soon as
he started, old Philip set the trigger and cocked his old squirrel rifle
quicker than he or any other man ever did it before, and said to Sheriff
Jones, ' Halt ! or I will blow your damned brains out in a moment.'
He stopped, and stayed right there, saying gently to Mr. Hupp,
' Don't shoot.' There was then a general talk among all hands, and
we were told about the ' Kansas militia, three thousand strong, that in
three days' time would wipe that damned Abolition town Lawrence
out, and corral all the Abolitionists and make pets of them.' However, Colonel Sam Wood and others out-talked them so bad that they
were glad to get away on any terms.   Miner Hupp, who wanted to
square accounts with his two men,[1] was prevented from doing so. It
was not his fault, for he had a ' bead ' on them several times ; but his
father was watching him all the time after he got Sheriff Jones in
shape."

As the affair, thus described, was the first instance of
combined and forcible resistance to the usurping authorities
created by the fraudulent elections of March 30, 1855, it
was naturally looked upon as very serious by both parties.
Sheriff Jones (the notorious ruffian who afterward led the
successful attack on Lawrence in May, 1856) was full of
wrath and cursing.   He rode on with his *posse* that night to
a little village near Lawrence, then called Franklin, where
they decided to appeal both to Wilson Shannon (the drunken
governor of Kansas, who had superseded Governor Reeder),
and to Colonel Boone, of Westport, Mo. (Jones's father-in-
law and a descendant of Daniel Boone), for aid in punishing
the rebellious Yankees.   Jones wrote a despatch to Westport, which he sent by a mounted messenger, saying, as the

---

[1] This alludes to a previous saying of young Hupp, that he "wanted to
square accounts with two of the *posse* that had threatened and abused him
a day or two before, and was afraid the ball would be over before he got
there." The above account is part of a letter written by Kennedy from
Colorado Springs, where he was living in 1879, and may not be minutely
accurate ; but it is the best I have seen.

14

man rode off, "That man is taking my despatch to Missouri, and, by God! I will have revenge before I see Missouri
again." Being reminded that he had not notified his official superior Governor Shannon, he next sent a message to
him at the Shawnee Mission by one Hargous, who was an
accessory to the murder of Dow two days before. Meantime the Free-State men were not idle. They held a public
meeting, November 27, at Lawrence, at which Branson the
rescued prisoner spoke, telling the story of his friend's
murder and his own arrest. Dow, he said, was a mild and
peaceable young man, esteemed by those who knew him, — an
immigrant from Ohio. who was boarding at Branson's house.
Coleman had repeatedly threatened to kill him, and on the
morning of the 21st, when Dow went on some errand to the
blacksmith's shop, Branson advised him to take his gun,
but Dow did not. On his return to Branson's, and when a
few steps from the shop, hearing the click of a gun, he turned
round. and received in his breast the charge of a double-
barrelled shot-gun loaded with slugs. This happened about
one o'clock ; and the body was left lying by the side of the
road where he fell until sundown, when some of the acces-
sories sent word to Branson "that a dead body was lying by
the roadside." He had begun to fear some ill had befallen
his friend, and at once recognizing the body, conveyed it to
his house. Coleman then took refuge with Governor Shannon at the Shawnee Mission, and was nominally arrested by
Jones, who was serving as sheriff of Douglas County in Kansas, while living at Westport, and acting postmaster there.
Branson had taken no part in the affair; but the next morning a proslavery justice at Lawrence, named Cameron, issued
a " peace-warrant " against Branson on the complaint of a
proslavery neighbor at Hickory Point, where the murder
occurred. That evening, after Branson had gone to bed with
his family, Sheriff Jones, with a party of mounted men, rode
up to his lone cabin upon the prairies, a half-mile from
neighbors, knocked at the door, and to the question " Who
is there ? " replied, " A friend." " Come in then ; " and
the little cabin was at once full of rough, savage, armed
men. Jones went to the bedside, and, presenting his
pistol to Branson's breast, said, " You are my prisoner."

Branson asked, "By what authority?" Oaths, and the threat "I will blow you through," were the only answer; the ruffians, with guns cocked, gathered round, and took him prisoner, — an innocent, defenceless man, kidnapped from his home and family by a gang of twenty-five half-drunken men, showing no papers of arrest, and answering with oaths and threats of death any question of their authority.

Such was the story told by Branson and the other speakers at the Lawrence meeting.   Branson, a plain elderly farmer, "of quiet and modest deportment," says Mrs. Robinson,[1] then went on to say, "with tears at times stealing down his weather-beaten cheeks," that he had been requested by some friends to leave Lawrence, to seek some other place of safety, so that no excuse could be given to the enemy for an attack upon Lawrence.   He said he would go, — Lawrence should not be involved in difficulty on his account; if it was the decision of the majority, he would go to his home, and die there, and be buried by the side of his friend.   This statement was met by cries of "No! no!"   The principal speakers after Branson were Grosvenor P. Lowry, a young lawyer from Pennsylvania, who proposed a committee of ten for the common defence ; Colonel Wood, who had taken part in the rescue ; and Martin F. Conway (born in Maryland in 1828), who had emigrated to Kansas in October, 1854, and had resigned his seat in the fraudulent Territorial Council of 1855.[2]

What Mr. Conway said had much weight, as coming from the best lawyer in Kansas.   He advised them to move cautiously, but boldly, having a care to take every step properly. They had ignored and repudiated the Legislature at the Shawnee Mission : they would never give their allegiance

---

[1] Kansas : Its Exterior and Interior Life, pp. 105–110.

[2] Mr. Conway was among the ablest of the men who made Kansas a free State, and was a steady friend of John Brown.   He had been bred a Democrat, and was a protégé of Henry May, a Democratic Congressman from Baltimore, but was hostile to slavery, and a radical in his construction of the Constitution and laws.   He was chosen Chief-Justice of Kansas under the Topeka Constitution, and was the first Congressman from the State. He died at Washington in 1883.

to such a monstrous iniquity. To the United States authorities, to the organic act, to the courts created under it, and
to the judges and marshals appointed by the President, they
would yield obedience. These might oppress them, but they
would submit, and seek redress for grievances at the United
States Supreme Court, which would give them a fair hearing.[1] He did not dissuade them from defending their rights
and insisting on all the safeguards of the law. Fortunately,
however, the friends of Kansas in New England and New
York had not suffered their emigrants to rely wholly upon
what proved to be a broken reed, — the protection of the
courts. Notwithstanding the protest of Mr. Amos Lawrence and others before the Congressional Investigating
Committee of May and June, 1856, that "the Emigrant Aid
Company had never invested a dollar in cannon or rifles, in
powder or lead, or in any of the implements of war," the
truth is, that the officers and agents of this company (and
Mr. Lawrence among the foremost) raised money and purchased arms, which were sent to Kansas in May, 1855, in
August, 1855, and at other times. The chief agent of this
company in Kansas was Charles Robinson, who despatched
G. W. Deitzler to Massachusetts in April, 1855, to obtain
weapons, and again sent Major Abbott (already mentioned
as the leader in the rescue of Branson) in July for the same
purpose. Robinson gave Abbott a letter to Eli Thayer,
the originator of the Emigrant Aid Company, in which he
told Mr. Thayer that "the rifles in Lawrence [the so-called
'Beecher Bibles'] have had a very good effect, and I
think the same kind of instruments in other places would
do more to save Kansas than almost anything else." This
was John Brown's opinion also, as was shown by his starting for Kansas at that time with a supply of weapons. Mr.
Branscomb, a Boston agent of the Emigrant Aid Company, indorsed Robinson's suggestion, and "cheerfully recommended Mr. J. B. Abbott to the public," under date of

---

[1] Judge Conway then supposed — what the events of the next year sadly
disproved by Taney's atrocious Dred Scott decision — that the court of Marshall and Story would decree justice, and not hasten to make itself the mere
tool of the slave-power, as Pierce and Buchanan were. In fact, the United
States Court in Kansas anticipated Taney in this submission.

August 10, 1855. Mr. Lawrence, vice-president of the company, on the next day (August 11) wrote to Major Abbott at Hartford, Conn. (where Sharpe's rifles were then made), as follows: —

" Request Mr. Palmer to have one hundred Sharpe's rifles packed in casks, like hardware, and to retain them subject to my order; also to send the bill to me by mail. I will pay it either with my note, according to the terms agreed on between him and Dr. Webb,[1] or in cash, less interest at seven per cent per annum."

August 20.

This instalment of carbines is far from being enough, and I hope the measures you are taking will be followed up until every organized company of trusty men in the Territory shall be supplied. Dr. Cabot[2] will give me the names of any gentlemen here who subscribe money, and the amount, of which I shall keep a memorandum, and promise them that it shall be repaid, either in cash or rifles, whenever it is settled that Kansas shall not be a province of Missouri. Therefore keep them in capital order, and, above all, take good care that they do not fall into the hands of the Missourians after you once get them into use. You must dispose of these *where they will do the most good;* and for this purpose you should advise with Dr. Robinson and Mr. Pomeroy.[3]

August 24.

The rifles ought to be on the way. Have you forwarded them? How much money have you received? The Topeka people will require half of these.

---

[1] Secretary of the Emigrant Aid Company, and a devoted friend of free Kansas.

[2] Samuel Cabot, Jr., M.D., a noted surgeon in Boston, and one of the most active in raising money for rifles and other material aid to the Kansas farmers in 1855-57. He has preserved a list of the subscribers to the arms fund, which the historian of Kansas should print in his volume.

[3] In view of these manly letters of Mr. Lawrence, his statements to the Massachusetts Historical Society (May 8, 1884) in praise of the peaceful character of Charles Robinson are very grotesque. Mr. Lawrence then said : " Charles Robinson *never bore arms,* nor omitted to do whatever he considered to be his duty. *He sternly held the people to their loyalty to the Government,* against the arguments and the example of the ' higher law ' men, *who were always armed."* One of these "higher law" men was Major Abbott, who rescued Branson contrary to law, and who was armed by Mr. Lawrence himself, at the urgent request of Robinson ! Sad is the effect of time on the human memory.

In presenting these letters of Robinson and Lawrence to
the Kansas Historical Society in 1882, Major Abbott said,
among other things : " I went to the Emigrant Aid folks in
Boston, and to Amos A. Lawrence, who immediately gave
the money for the purchase of one hundred Sharpe's rifles.
His action and these letters show what a friend of Kansas
he was at that early period, and how quick he was to comprehend the character of the struggle into which we had
been precipitated. When I reached home, the latter part
of September, I found the rifles, which I had sent ahead of
me, at Lawrence, and ready for use. The howitzer came
later, but was in time to be brought to the defence of Lawrence at the invasion in December, 1855, the pretence for
which was the rescue of Branson, — which rescue, as it
happened, I had a hand in." To meet this invasion Robinson was made a major-general, and in that capacity commissioned John Brown as captain.[1]

The story of the arms earlier sent out by the "Emigrant
Aid folks" may here be given as told by General Deitzler
and the Rev. Edward E. Hale in 1879. General Deitzler
said : —

" Some six weeks after my arrival in the Territory, and only a few
days after the Territorial election of March 30, 1855, at which time

---

[1] The position of Robinson towards Major Abbott and the rescuers of
Branson may be inferred from the fact that they reported at Robinson's
house, ten miles from Blanton's Bridge, before sunrise, November 23, the
day after the affair. Mrs. Robinson thus tells the story in her book : "The
slight form of the leader stood a little nearer the door ; and when his peculiarly dry manner of speech fell upon the ear in his brief inquiry, 'Is Dr.
R. in ?' his identity was also known. The Doctor opened the door and
invited them in. The fact of the rescue was stated, and Mr. Branson, being in the ranks, was ordered to 'step forward and tell his story,' which
he did with much feeling, and with the appearance of a person who is
heart-broken. I shall never forget the appearance of the men in simple
citizen's dress, some armed and some unarmed, standing in unbroken line,
just visible in the breaking light of a November morning. This little band
of less than twenty men had, through the cold and upon the frozen ground,
walked ten miles since nine o'clock of the previous evening. Mr. Branson —
a large man, of fine proportions — stood a little forward of the line, with his
head slightly bent, which an old straw hat hardly protected from the cold,
looking as though, in his hurry of departure from home in charge of the
ruffianly men, he took whatever came first."

Kansas was invaded by an armed force from the Southern States and the actual Free-State settlers were driven from the polls, Governor Charles Robinson requested me to visit Boston with a view to securing arms for our people, to which I assented. . Preparations were quickly and quietly made, and no one knew of the object of my mission except Governor Robinson and Joel Grover. At Worcester I presented my letter from Governor Robinson to Mr. Eli Thayer, just as he was leaving his Oread Home for the morning Boston train. Within an hour after our arrival in Boston, the Executive Committee of the Emigrant Aid Society held a meeting, and delivered to me an order for one hundred Sharpe's rifles, and I started for home on Monday morning. The boxes were marked 'Books.' I took the precaution to have the (cap) cones removed from the guns, and carried them in my carpet-sack, which would have been missing in the event of the capture of the guns by the enemy. On the Missouri River I met John and Joseph L. Speer for the first time. They did not know me, but may remember the exciting incidents at Booneville and other points along the river. I arrived at Lawrence with the 'Beecher Bibles' several days before the special election in April, called by Governor Reeder. But no guns were needed upon that occasion, as the ruffians ignored said election; and when the persons elected upon that day presented their credentials at Pawnee, they were kicked out without ceremony. . . . It was perhaps the first shipment of arms for our side; and it incited a healthy feeling among the unarmed Free-State settlers, which permeated and energized them until even the Quakers were ready to fight." [1]

Mr. Hale gave his recollections as follows : —

" In the spring of 1855 my friend Mr. Deitzler came on in haste to New England, to say that fighting was certain, and that you must have more weapons. The breech-loading rifle was then a new and costly arm. It was then that we gave to the Sharpe's Rifle Company the first of a series of orders which became historical. In the next year Henry Ward Beecher won the nickname which he has never lost, 'Sharpe's Rifle Beecher;' and I fancy there is no nickname of which he is more proud. With your permission I will read the answer of the company to that order, and then I will ask our friend Mr. Adams to accept that letter as an historical document for his Society." [2]

[1] Kansas Memorial, 1879, pp. 184, 185.
[2] Ibid., p. 147.

SHARPE'S RIFLE MANUFACTURING CO.,
HARTFORD, May 7, 1855.

DEAR SIR, — Annexed find invoice of one hundred carbines, ammunition, etc., delivered Mr. Deitzler this morning. For balance of account, I have ordered on Messrs. Lee, Higginson, & Co., at thirty days from this date, for $2,155.65, as directed by you. We shall be pleased to receive further orders from you, and will put up arms at our lowest cash prices to the trade, with interest added for time. The sample carbine for your use shall go forward immediately. Our negotiations with you I trust will be entirely confidential, as the trade in Boston and elsewhere might take offence if they understood that we had made you better terms than we grant to others.

Your obedient servant,

J. C. PALMER, Pres.

THOS. H. WEBB, ESQ.

Dr. Webb was then, and continued to be, the secretary of the Emigrant Aid Company; and when Mr. Hale said "we," he meant the managers of that company, whose best title to the gratitude of Kansas and the nation is this very gift of arms to the emigrants, without which the invasion of Lawrence in December, 1855, could not have been met. This invasion was made under a proclamation issued by Governor Shannon, November 29, calling out the "Kansas militia." He meant thereby the Missouri men, as appears by an early message sent from Woodson, the governor's secretary, to a proslavery commander at Leavenworth, named Eastin, who had been appointed by the usurping Legislature to be general of the Territorial militia.

(*Private.*)

DEAR GENERAL, — The Governor has called out the militia, and you will hereby organize your division, and proceed forthwith to Lecompton. As the Governor has no power, you may call out the Platte Rifle Company. They are always ready to help us. Whatever you do, do not implicate the Governor.

DANIEL WOODSON.

On the same day (November 27) a despatch was sent from Westport to the capital of Missouri in these words : —

Hon. E. C. McClarem, *Jefferson City*, — Governor Shannon has ordered out the militia against Lawrence. They are now in open rebellion against the laws. Jones is in danger.

From another border town in Missouri, this despatch was sent : —

Weston, Mo., November 30.

The greatest excitement continues to exist in Kansas. The officers have been resisted by the mobocrats, and the interposition of the militia has been called for. A secret letter from Secretary Woodson to General Eastin has been written, in which the writer requests General Eastin to call for the Rifle Company at Platte City, Mo., *so as not to compromise Governor Shannon*. Four hundred men from Jackson County are now *en route* for Douglas County, K. T. St. Joseph and Weston are requested to furnish each the same number. The people of Kansas are to be subjugated at all hazards.

The invasion took place, and resulted in threats on the Missouri side, fortifications and drilling on the Lawrence side; and finally this little " Wakarusa war " was ended by a treaty with Shannon, who conceded all that the Free-State men had asked. Brown and his family rallied to the defence of their neighbors and their cause, and were said to be the best-armed men that came forward for service. They were mustered in as Kansas militia; John Brown was made captain, and his son John lieutenant, in the Osawatomie company. His own report of this affair is as follows : —

BROWN'S FIRST CAMPAIGN: THE WAKARUSA WAR.

Osawatomie, K. T., Dec. 16, 1855.
Sabbath Evening.

Dear Wife and Children, every one, — I improve the first mail since my return from the camp of volunteers, who lately turned out for the defence of the town of Lawrence in this Territory; and notwithstanding I suppose you have learned the result before this (possibly), will give a brief account of the invasion in my own way.

About three or four weeks ago news came that a Free-State man by the name of Dow had been murdered by a proslavery man by the name of Coleman, who had gone and given himself up for trial to the proslavery Governor Shannon. This was soon followed by further news that a Free-State man who was the only reliable witness against the murderer had been seized by a Missourian (appointed sheriff by the bogus Legislature of Kansas) upon false pretexts, examined, and held to bail under such heavy bonds, to answer to those false charges, as he could not give; that while on his way to trial, in charge of the bogus sheriff, he was rescued by some men belonging to a company near Lawrence; and that in consequence of the rescue Governor Shannon had ordered out all the proslavery force he could muster in the Territory, and called on Missouri for further help; that about two thousand had collected, demanding a surrender of the rescued witness and of the rescuers, the destruction of several buildings and printing-presses, and a giving up of the Sharpe's rifles by the Free-State men, — threatening to destroy the town with cannon, with which they were provided, etc.; that about an equal number of Free-State men had turned out to resist them, and that a battle was hourly expected or supposed to have been already fought.

These reports appeared to be well authenticated, but we could get no further account of matters; and I left this for the place where the boys are settled, at evening, intending to go to Lawrence to learn the facts the next day. John was, however, started on horseback; but before he had gone many rods, word came that our help was immediately wanted. On getting this last news, it was at once agreed to break up at John's camp, and take Wealthy and Johnny to Jason's camp (some two miles off), and that all the men but Henry, Jason, and Oliver should at once set off for Lawrence under arms; those three being wholly unfit for duty. We then set about providing a little corn-bread and meat, blankets, and cooking utensils, running bullets and loading all our guns, pistols, etc. The five set off in the afternoon, and after a short rest in the night (which was quite dark), continued our march until after daylight next morning, when we got our breakfast, started again, and reached Lawrence in the forenoon, all of us more or less lamed by our tramp. On reaching the place we found that negotiations had commenced between Governor Shannon (having a force of some fifteen or sixteen hundred men) and the principal leaders of the Free-State men, they having a force of some five hundred men at that time. These were busy, night and day, fortifying the town with embankments and circular earthworks, up to the time of the treaty with the Governor, as an attack was constantly looked for, notwithstanding the negotiations then pending. This state of things continued from Friday until Sunday evening.[1] On the evening we left Osawatomie a company of the invaders, of from fifteen to twenty-five, attacked some three or four Free-State men, mostly unarmed, killing a Mr. Barber from Ohio, wholly unarmed. His body was afterward brought in and lay for some days in the room after-

[1] December 7–9.

ward occupied by a part of the company to which we belong (it being organized after we reached Lawrence). The building was a large unfinished stone hotel, in which a great part of the volunteers were quartered, who witnessed the scene of bringing in the wife and other friends of the murdered man. I will only say of this scene that it was heart-rending, and calculated to exasperate the men exceedingly, and one of the sure results of civil war.

After frequently calling on the leaders of the Free-State men to come and have an interview with him, by Governor Shannon, and after as often getting for an answer that if he had any business to transact with any one in Lawrence, to come and attend to it, he signified his wish to come into the town,[1] and an escort was sent to the invaders' camp to conduct him in. When there, the leading Free-State men, finding out his weakness, frailty, and consciousness of the awkward circumstances into which he had really got himself, took advantage of his cowardice and folly, and by means of that and the free use of whiskey and some trickery succeeded in getting a written arrangement with him much to their own liking. He stipulated with them to order the proslavery men of Kansas home, and to proclaim to the Missouri invaders that they must quit the Territory without delay, and also to give up General Pomeroy (a prisoner in their camp), — which was all done; he also recognizing the volunteers as the militia of Kansas, and empowering their officers to call them out whenever in their discretion the safety of Lawrence or other portions of the Territory might require it to be done. He (Governor Shannon) gave up all pretension of further attempt to enforce the enactments of the bogus Legislature, and retired, subject to the derision and scoffs of the Free-State men (into whose hands he had committed the welfare and protection of Kansas), and to the pity of some and the curses of others of the invading force.

So ended this last Kansas invasion, — the Missourians returning with *flying colors*, after incurring heavy expenses, suffering great exposure, hardships, and privations, not having fought any battles, burned or destroyed any infant towns or Abolition presses; leaving the Free-State men organized and armed, and in full possession of the Territory; not having fulfilled any of all their dreadful threatenings, except to murder one *unarmed* man, and to commit some robberies and waste of property upon defenceless families, unfortunately within their power. We learn by their papers that they boast of a great victory over the Abolitionists; and well they may.[2] Free-State

---

[1] December 7, 8.

[2] Brown seems to have been divided in mind concerning this treaty with Shannon, at first denouncing it strongly, as well as the manner of making

men have only hereafter to retain the footing they have gained, and *Kansas is free.* Yesterday the people passed upon the Free-State constitution. The result, though not yet known, no one doubts.

One little circumstance, connected with our own number, showing a little of the true character of those invaders : On our way, about three miles from Lawrence, we had to pass a bridge (with our arms and ammunition) of which the invaders held possession ; but as the five of us had each a gun, with two large revolvers in a belt exposed to view, with a third in his pocket, and as we moved directly on to the bridge without making any halt, they for some reason suffered us to pass without interruption, notwithstanding there were some fifteen to twenty-five (as variously reported) stationed in a log-house at one end of the bridge. We could not count them. A boy on our approach ran and gave them notice. Five others of our company, well armed, who followed us some miles behind, met with equally civil treatment the same day. After we left to go to Lawrence, until we returned when disbanded, I did not see the least sign of cowardice or want of self-possession exhibited by any volunteer of the eleven companies who constituted the Free-State force; and I never expect again to see an equal number of such well-behaved,

it, and afterward seeing the respite it gave the Kansas farmers to make good their position. Mr. E. A. Coleman writes me : " When Lawrence was besieged, we sent runners to all parts of the Territory, calling on every settler. We met at Lawrence. Robinson was commander-in-chief ; I was on his staff, appointed of course by order of the commander. We had gathered to the number of about two hundred and fifty, all told. The ruffians were gathered at Franklin, four miles east, with four or five hundred men. We were not well armed, all of us, — at the same time being somewhat afraid of getting into trouble with the General Government. Robinson sent to Shannon, at Lecompton, to come down and see if something could not be done to prevent bloodshed. He came ; we all knew his weakness. We had plenty of brandy, parleyed with him until he was drunk, and then he agreed to get the ruffians to go home, — which he did by telling them *we* had agreed to obey all the laws, which was a *lie.* As soon as Brown heard what had been done, he came with his sons into our council-room, the maddest man I ever saw. He told Robinson that what he had done was all a farce ; that in less than six months the Missourians would find out the deception, and things would be worse than they were that day (and so it was) ; that he came up to help them fight, but if that was the way Robinson meant to do, not to send for him again." Mr. Foster, of Osawatomie, meeting Brown on his return from Lawrence, asked him about Robinson and Lane. " They are both men without principle," said Brown ; " but when worst comes to worst, Lane will fight, — and there *is no fight in Robinson.*"

cool, determined men, — fully, as I believe, sustaining the high character of the Revolutionary fathers. But enough of this, as we intend
to send you a paper giving a more full account of the affair. We
have cause for gratitude in that we all returned safe and well, with
the exception of hard colds, and found those left behind rather
improving.

We have received fifty dollars from father, and learn from him
that he has sent you the same amount, — for which we ought to be
grateful, as we are much relieved, both as respects ourselves and you.
The mails have been kept back during the invasion, but we hope to
hear from you again soon. Mr. Adair's folks are well, or nearly so.
Weather mostly pleasant, but sometimes quite severe. No snow of
account as yet. Can think of but little more to-night.

Monday Morning, December 17.

The ground for the first time is barely whitened with snow, and it is
quite cold; but we have before had a good deal of cold weather, with
heavy rains. Henry and Oliver and, I may [say], Jason were disappointed in not being able to go to war. The disposition at both our
camps to turn out was uniform. I believe I have before acknowledged the receipt of a letter from you and Watson. Have just taken
one from the office for Henry that I think to be from Ruth. Do
write often, and let me know all about how you get along through
the winter. May God abundantly bless you all, and make you
faithful.

Your affectionate husband and father,

John Brown.[1]

---

[1] Soon after this "Wakarusa war," and perhaps in consequence of his
service therein, Brown became the owner of one small share in the Emigrant
Aid Company, as appears by this certificate : —

No. 638.   Boston, Jan. 15, 1856.

This is to certify that John Brown, Lawrence. K. T., is proprietor of one share, of
the par value of twenty dollars each, in the capital stock of the New England Emigrant
Aid Company, transferable on the books of said Company, on the surrender of this
certificate.

John M. S. Williams, Vice-President.

Thomas H. Webb, Secretary.

This paper is indorsed, in John Brown's handwriting, "Emigrant Aid
Co., Certificate," and was found among his papers after his death. He
derived no profit from it, as indeed was the case with the other sharehold-
ers ; but it perhaps gave him some standing among his Kansas neighbors to have even this connection with a corporation supposed to be very
rich.

During this arctic winter Brown wrote as follows to the family at North Elba, where it was still more arctic: —

John Brown to his Family.

OSAWATOMIE, K. T., Feb. 1, 1856.

DEAR WIFE AND CHILDREN, EVERY ONE, — Yours and Watson's letters to the boys and myself, of December 30 and January 1, were received by last mail. We are all very glad to hear again of your welfare, and I am particularly grateful when I am noticed by a letter from *you*. I have just taken out two letters for Henry [Thompson], one of which, I suppose, is from Ruth. Salmon and myself are so far on our way home from Missouri, and only reached Mr. Adair's last night. They are all well, and we know of nothing but all are well at the boys' shanties. The weather continues very severe, and it is now nearly six weeks that the snow has been almost constantly driven, like dry sand, by the fierce winds of Kansas. Mr. Adair has been collecting ice of late from the Osage River, which is nine and a half inches thick, of perfect clear solid ice, formed under the snow. By means of the sale of our horse and wagon, our present wants are tolerably well met, so that, if health is continued to us, we shall not probably suffer much. The idea of again visiting those of my dear family at North Elba is so calculated to unman me, that I seldom allow my thoughts to dwell upon it, and I do not think best to write much about it; suffice it to say, that God is *abundantly* able to keep both us and you, and in him let us all trust. We have just learned of some new and shocking outrages at Leavenworth, and that the Free-State people there have fled to Lawrence, which place is again threatened with an attack. Should that take place, we may soon again be called upon to "buckle on our armor," which by the help of God we will do, — when I suppose Henry and Oliver will have a chance. My judgment is, that we shall have no general disturbance until warmer weather. I have more to say, but not time now to say it; so farewell for this time. Write!

Your affectionate husband and father,

JOHN BROWN.

OSAWATOMIE, K. T., Feb. 6, 1856.

DEAR WIFE AND CHILDREN, EVERY ONE, — . . . Thermometer on Sunday and Monday at twenty-eight to twenty-nine below zero. Ice in the river, in the timber, and under the snow, eighteen inches thick this week. On our return to where the boys live we found Jason again down with the ague, but he was some better yesterday.

Oliver was also laid up by freezing his toes, — one great toe so badly frozen that the nail has come off. He will be crippled for some days yet. Owen has one foot some frozen. We have middling tough times (as some would call them), but have enough to eat, and abundant reasons for the most unfeigned gratitude. It is likely that when the snow goes off, such high water will prevail as will render it difficult for Missouri to invade the Territory; so that God by his elements may protect Kansas for some time yet. . . . Write me as to all your wants for the coming spring and summer. I hope you will all be led to seek God " with your whole heart:" and I pray him, in his mercy, to be found of you. All mail communications are entirely cut off by the snowdrifts, so that we get no news whatever this week. . . .

OSAWATOMIE, K. T., Feb. 20, 1856.

DEAR WIFE AND CHILDREN, EVERY ONE, — Your letter to Salmon, and Ruth's to Henry and Ellen, of 6th and 16th January, were received by last week's mail. This week we get neither letter nor paper from any of you. I need not continually repeat that we are always glad to hear from you, and to learn of your welfare. I wish that to be fully understood. Salmon and myself are here again, on our way back from Missouri, where we have been for corn, — as what the boys had raised was used up, stock and families having to live on it mainly while it lasted. We had to pay thirty cents per bushel for corn. Salmon has had the ague again, while we have been gone, and had a hard shake yesterday. To-day is his well day. We found Henry and Frederick here helping Mr. Adair; and I have been helping also yesterday and to-day. Those behind were as well as usual a day or two since. I have but little to write this time, except to tell you about the weather, and to complain of the almost lack of news from the United States. We are very anxious to know what Congress is doing. We hear that Frank Pierce means to crush the men of Kansas. I do not know how well he may succeed; but I think he may find his hands full before it is all over. For a few days the snow has melted a little, and it begins to seem like early March in Ohio. I have agreed either to buy the line-backed cow of Henry, or to pay five dollars for the use of her and keep her a year, whichever may hereafter appear best; so that, if she lives, you can calculate on the use of her. I have also written Mr. Hurlbut, of Connecticut, further in regard to the cattle, and think you will soon hear something from him. No more now. May God Almighty bless you and all good friends at North Elba!

Your affectionate husband and father,

JOHN BROWN.

Brown seems to have written about this time to his former representative in Congress, Mr. Giddings of Ohio, to inquire the purpose of the Government, and was thus answered : —

HALL OF REPRESENTATIVES, U. S.,
March 17, 1856.

MY DEAR SIR, — We shall do all we can, but we are in a minority, and are dependent on the " Know Nothings "[1] for aid to effect anything, and they are in a very doubtful position ; we know not how they will act. All I can say is, we shall try to relieve you. In the mean time you need have no fear of the troops. The President never will *dare* employ the troops of the United States to shoot the citizens of Kansas. The death of the first man by the troops will involve every free State in your own fate. *It will light up the fires of civil war throughout the North, and we shall stand or fall with you.* Such an act will also bring the President so deep in infamy that the hand of political resurrection will never reach him. Your safety depends on the supply of men and arms and money which will move forward to your relief as soon as the spring opens. I am confident there will be as many people in Kansas next winter as can be supplied with provisions. I may be mistaken, but I feel confident there will be no war in Kansas.

Very respectfully,
J. R. GIDDINGS.

JOHN BROWN, ESQ.

In this last prediction Mr. Giddings was wide of the mark; for within two months from the time this letter reached Kansas, the Territory was again invaded, Lawrence was captured and pillaged, and the Pottawatomie executions had taken place. These events had been preceded by many others, which can here be noticed only briefly, though they were of great importance. An election had been held, Jan. 15, 1856, for State officers and a Legislature. under the Free-State constitution adopted at Topeka in 1855. At some points in Kansas, particularly at Leavenworth, the usurping proslavery men forbade this election ; and an adjourned election was held for that county at Easton (a few miles northwest of Leavenworth and near Kickapoo, where that infamous Border-Ruffian military company, the "Kickapoo Rangers," had their headquarters) on the 17th of

---

[1] A political party (the "Native Americans") so designated.

January. That night, very late, while a Free-State man named Sparks was returning home with his sons, he was surrounded by the ruffians, and rescued by R. P. Brown (no relative of John Brown), who was a leader of the Free-State men in Leavenworth County, and a member elect of the Topeka Legislature, as Sparks also was. The next morning, as Brown, with seven other Free-State men, — among whom was Henry J. Adams, afterward Mayor of Leavenworth, — was returning to his home, about half-way between Easton and Leavenworth, and near Kickapoo, he was surrounded by a force of fifty men or more, all armed, and some of them drunk, who took them prisoners. The drunken ruffians tried to kill the Free-State men, but were prevented by their leaders, among whom were several persons holding Territorial or United States office. The prisoners were carried by this howling mob back to Easton; but Brown was separated from them. A rope was purchased and shown to the prisoners, who were threatened with hanging. Unwilling that all these men should be murdered, Martin, the Kickapoo captain, allowed Adams and the other prisoners to escape. Adams hastened to Fort Leavenworth in hopes of getting United States troops to rescue Brown, but was refused. Meantime Brown had surrendered his arms, and was helpless. His enemies, who dared not face him the night before, though they had a superior force, crowded around him; and one of the "Rangers," a drunken wretch named Gibson, inflicted the fatal blow, — a large hatchet gash in the side of the head, penetrating the skull and brain. The gallant man fell, while his enemies jumped on him and kicked him. Desperately wounded, he said, "Don't abuse me! it is useless; I am dying." One of the mob (afterward United States deputy marshal) stooped over the prostrate man, and spat tobacco juice in his eyes. Finally a few of the ruffians, whom a little spark of conscience or fear of punishment animated, raised the dying man, still groaning, and placing him in a wagon, in a cold winter day, drove him to the grocery, where they dressed his wounds; but seeing the hopelessness of his case they took him home to his wife, to whom he said, "I have been murdered by a gang of cowards in cold blood."

15

To one of the neighbors who came to Brown's house at
three o'clock on the morning of January 19, and found him
lying on the floor soaked in blood, the murdered man said,
" I am dying, but in a good cause." " I sat down," says
this neighbor, " took his head upon my lap, and examined
the wound in his head; opened his vest, but found no other
wound. He raised apparently from one side, as if he
wanted to turn over, exclaimed, 'I am dying,' and immediately died, with his head on my lap. Charles Dunn [a
Border-Ruffian 'captain,' who brought Brown home] told
me that after receiving the wound Brown had made his
escape, fled to the woods, had been caught and brought
back, and that he [Dunn] had been instrumental in keeping
them from shooting or hanging him. Dunn was at that
time very much intoxicated."

The offence that this murdered man had committed was,
first, voting; second, defending the ballot-box from drunken
ruffians who tried to break up the election; and, finally, with
fifteen men, rescuing his neighbor Sparks from twenty or
thirty of these ruffians. A proslavery man of the better
class, Pierce Rively, who kept a store near Brown's farm
in " Salt Creek Valley," testified before the Congressional
Committee, four months later: " I do not know that the
grand jury has made any inquiry into this matter, or has
ever attempted it. I have been a member of the grand
jury since, and nothing was said about it; " yet Rively was
present when Brown received his death-blow, and helped
the drunken Dunn to put him into the wagon. The wife
and child of Brown went to live with a neighbor until
spring, and then went back to Michigan. The wife of
Stephen Sparks, the Free-State man whom Brown rescued,
testified that on the day Brown was murdered a party of
proslavery horsemen, commanded by Dunn, rode up to her
cabin on Stranger Creek, four miles south of Easton. They
first gave chase to two Free-State men near by, shooting at
them and shouting, " Kill the damned Abolitionists," and
then returned to the Sparks cabin, where Dunn cried,
" Now we will take the house : shoot Captain Sparks at
sight ! " Whereupon, Mrs. Sparks says : —

" I then told them I had an afflicted son, and that anything that excited him threw him into spasms right at once, and that his father and all but him were away from home. When I stepped back to the door and looked in, I saw Captain Dunn with a six-shooter presented at my son's breast. I did not hear the question asked, but I heard my son's answer, ' I am on the Lord's side ; and if you want to kill me, kill me! I am not afraid to die.' Dunn then left him, and turned to my little son, twelve years old, put the pistol to his breast, and asked him where his father's Sharpe's rifle was. My son told him he had none. Dunn then asked where those guns were, — pointing to the racks, — and told him if he did not tell the truth he would kill him. My son told him ' the men-folks generally took care of the guns.' When they came out, I asked Captain Dunn, ' What does all this mean ?' He answered that ' they had taken the law into their own hands, and they intended to use it.' Late in February eight men came to the house ; two men came up first, and the others followed. They asked for Mr. Sparks, and left a paper with me, ending thus : ' Believing that your further residence among us is incompatible with the peace and welfare of this community, we advise you to leave as soon as you can conveniently do so.' This was signed by forty men, only one of whom is an actual resident in the neighborhood ; most of them are Kickapoo Rangers and Missourians. One of the two who first came to the door said his name was Kennedy, from Alabama ; the other, I think, emigrated from Missouri. I asked him what he had against Mr. Sparks. He said he had nothing against him ; but he ' was too influential in his party, and they intended to break it down ;' that I must tell Mr. Sparks to leave by March 10 or abide the consequences. A night or two before the 10th of March four men came into the house, about ten o'clock, and searched for Mr. Sparks, but did not find him. They asked for the ' notice to leave,' and if I had given it to Mr. Sparks, — and made many threats, and charged us to leave at that time, saying that if he was there they would cut him to pieces." [1]

[1] This testimony was given by Mrs. " Esseneth " Sparks (who signed with a mark because she could not write), May 24, 1856, — the very day that Brown with his party was executing the Doyles and other ruffians on the Pottawatomie. Stephen Sparks was a Missourian, who had lived in Platte County from 1845 to 1854, then moved into Kansas, and was in 1856 elected to the Free-State Legislature. He was a man of cool courage, who behaved well throughout the violent scenes of January 17-19, and told the Congressional Committee, " I belong to the Free-State party, but am no Abolitionist, either." On the night of the 17th, as he said, " My son was wounded (and knocked down within six or eight feet of me) in

The Topeka Legislature (of which Sparks and the murdered Brown were members, as well as John Brown, Jr., and Major Abbott, the rescuer of Branson) met on the 4th of March, and remained in session four days, adjourning to July 4. During this session they elected James H. Lane (who had commanded an Indiana regiment in the Mexican War and distinguished himself at Buena Vista) one of the United States senators from Kansas, not yet admitted as a State. On the 19th of March the House of Representatives at Washington voted a special committee (W. A. Howard of Michigan, John Sherman of Ohio, and M. N. Oliver of Missouri) to investigate the troubles of Kansas; and on the 24th of March General Cass presented in the United States Senate the Topeka Free-State Constitution. Early in April, Jefferson Buford, of Eufaula, Ala., who had left his home in March, reached Kansas with a large force of Southern men, armed champions of slavery, and encamped not far from Osawatomie; while on the 16th of April the Free-State men round there — John Brown and his son John, O. V. Dayton, Richard Mendenhall, Charles A. Foster of Massachusetts, and others — met in public assembly, and agreed not to pay taxes to the usurping Legislature, for which they were afterward indicted as conspirators. These occurrences should be borne in mind when reading John Brown's next letter.

John Brown to his Family at North Elba.

BROWN'S STATION, K. T., April 7, 1856.

DEAR WIFE AND CHILDREN, EVERY ONE, — I wrote you last week, enclosing New York draft for thirty dollars, made payable to Watson; twenty dollars of which were to be given to Ruth, in part payment for the spotted cow, the balance to be used as circumstances might require. I would have sent you more, but I had no way to do it, and money is very scarce with me indeed. Since I wrote last, three letters have been received by the boys from Ruth, dated March 5 and 9, and one of same date from Watson. The general tone of those letters I like exceedingly. We do not want you to borrow

the arm and head slightly ; but he raised again and fired." See Report of the Special Committee on the Troubles in Kansas, 1856, pp. 981–1020.

trouble about us, but trust us to the care of " Him who feeds the young ravens when they cry." I have, as usual, but little to write. We are doing off a house for Orson Day, which we hope to get through with soon; after which we shall probably soon leave this neighborhood, but will advise you further when we do leave. It may be that Watson can manage to get a little money for shearing sheep if you do not get any from Connecticut. I still hope you will get help from that source. We have no wars as yet, but we still have abundance of "rumors." We still have frosty nights, but the grass starts a little. There are none of us complaining much just now, all being able to do something. John has just returned from Topeka,[1] not having met with any difficulty; but we hear that preparations are making in the United States Court for numerous arrests of Free-State men.[2] For one, I have no desire (all things considered) to have the slave-power cease from its acts of aggression. " Their foot shall slide in due time." No more now. May God bless and keep you all!

Your affectionate husband and father.

It was in the early part of May that John Brown executed a manœuvre which has often been related, not always in the same manner, and which he may have repeated when necessary, — his visit to the camp of the proslavery men in the guise of a land-surveyor. Mr. Foster, now living in Quincy, Mass., but then a young lawyer at Osawatomie, newly married and beginning to practise in Miami County,

---

[1] The meeting of the Free-State Legislature.

[2] James Hanway, of Pottawatomie, speaking of his old log-cabin, not far from Dutch Henry's Crossing, said, some years since : " It was in this cabin that the Pottawatomie Rifle Company, under Captain John Brown, Jr., stacked their arms when they paid a friendly visit to Judge Cato's court, in April, 1856. The Free-State settlers were anxious to learn what position Judge Cato would take, in his charge to the grand jury, concerning the celebrated ' bogus laws ' of the Shawnee Mission. This visit of our citizens was .construed by the court as a demonstration unfavorable to the execution of the bogus laws. Before daylight the next morning Cato and his proslavery officials had left (they were on their way to Lecompton), and the grand jury was dismissed from further labor. This was the first and the last time that this section of the country was visited by proslavery officials." But we shall see, when we come to consider the Pottawatomie executions, that this court did take action ; and perhaps their action led to the killing of the five proslavery men near Dutch Henry's.

is authority for one version of it.   Mention has just been
made of the arrival of Jefferson Buford from Alabama,
with an armed company, which divided into colonies.   Two
of these directed their course towards the town of Osawatomie, — one settling in a block-house on the Miami
Reserve, about a mile and a half from the town; the other,
and larger, colony made their first halt in the Osage bottom,
near the town of Stanton, about eight miles from where the
Shermans, Wilkinson, and the Doyles lived.   At this time
John Brown was not generally known, although he had been
in the country six months.   It was a matter of importance
to the Free-State men to know what was the purpose of these
bodies of armed men, so that they might shape their action
accordingly.   Brown, without consulting any one, determined to visit their camp and ascertain their plans.   He
therefore took his tripod, chain, and other surveying implements, and with one of his younger sons started for the
camp.   Just before reaching the place he struck his tripod,
sighted a line through the centre of the camp, and then
with his son began "chaining" the distance.   The Southern
men supposed him to be a Government surveyor (in those
times, of course, proslavery), and were very free in telling
him their plans.   They were going over to Pottawatomie
Creek to drive off all the Free-State men; and there was a
settlement of Browns on North Middle Creek, who had some
of the finest stock, — these also they would "clean out," as
well as the Dutch settlement between the two rivers.[1]   They
were asked who had given them information about the
Browns, etc., and who was directing them about the county;
and without any hesitation the Shermans, Doyles, Wilkinson, George Wilson, and others were named.   In the midst
of the talk these men walked into the camp, as Mr. Foster
says, and were received with manifestations of pleasure.   A
few days after, the camp was moved over to Pottawatomie
Creek, and the men began stealing horses, arms, etc.   This

[1] This was the neighborhood where Benjamin, Bondi, and Wiener had
settled, and where the valuable warehouse of Wiener was afterward burned.
The Doyles and Wilkinson were not far off, and the Shermans at Dutch
Henry's Crossing were between the "Dutch settlement" and Buford's
camp.

had been going on for some weeks when the attack upon Lawrence was made in May.[1]

The immediate occasion of the invasion of Lawrence a second (or rather a third) time was the resistance of the Lawrence Free-State men to an attempt made by Sheriff Jones, as deputy marshal of the United States, to arrest S. N. Wood, one of the rescuers of Branson the previous November. Jones made the first attempt April 19, tried again on the 20th, and on the 23d came with a file of United States troops to support him. He arrested several citizens, but not Wood, and at night was himself shot at and wounded slightly. Advantage was taken of this act to inflame the minds of the Missourians; and the United States District Court, which was organized by this time, with Judge Lecompte at its head, took up the matter as an affair of rebellion and treason. Early in May Lecompte gave a charge to the grand jury at the town named for him (Lecompton), in which he said : —

" This Territory was organized by an act of Congress, and so far its authority is from the United States. It has a Legislature elected in pursuance of that organic act. This Legislature, being an instrument of Congress by which it governs the Territory, has passed laws. These laws, therefore, are of United States authority and making ; and *all that resist these laws resist the power and authority of the United States, and are therefore guilty of high-treason.* Now, gentlemen, if you find that any persons have resisted these laws, then you must, under your oaths, find bills against them for high-treason. If you find that *no such resistance has been* made, but that combinations have been formed for the purpose of resisting them, and individuals of influence and notoriety have been aiding and abetting in such combinations, *then must you still find bills for constructive treason.*"

It was under this monstrous instruction, by which usurpation was made legal and put on a level with the existence of the United States, that indictments were soon found against the Browns, Robinson, and others for treason, conspiracy, etc. Robinson, who was seeking to leave Kansas, was arrested May 10, and held a prisoner four months, when

[1] See Mr. Coleman's version of this surveying adventure in the next chapter.

he was released on bail. The grand jury then proceeded to indict other persons, and even the new hotel at Lawrence, — thus giving an air of burlesque to the tragedy they had begun. One of this jury, a Free-State man named Legate, who has since been conspicuous in Kansas now in one way and now in another, has told this amusing story of the secret proceedings at the Lecompton court-house : [1] —

" I was honored, as I have been oftentimes, by holding distinguished positions in the State of Kansas, — being a member of the grand jury ; and what a sweet-scented jury it was ! Uncle Jimmy McGee and myself were members from Lawrence. We had a caucus semi-occasionally. There were seventeen members, all told. Uncle Jimmy and I were temperate, but there were at least fifteen bottles of whiskey in the room all the time. The first and most important case to be tried was the indictment of Sam Wood and John Speer. I have forgotten whether it was John Speer for assuming to hold an office that he was not legally elected to, and Sam Wood for resisting an officer, or *vice versa*. Attorney-General Isaacs was sent for. Like a great many Yankees I was inquisitive, and there was a very important point to be decided, in my mind ; so I said to him, ' You have John Speer charged with treason. Under what law or circumstance do you make his offence treason ?' ' Well, sir,' said he, taking hold of the flask of whiskey, ' the facts are these : a man who pretends to hold an office, having once held that office, and is defunct, and assumes to still hold it against the constituted authorities, commits treason.' Said I, ' What about Sam Wood ?' He replied, ' If a man undertakes to carry out the decrees of such an officer, he commits treason also.' I thought that was good enough. There were thirteen votes, — Stuart not voting. Uncle Jimmy McGee and I voted no.[2]

[1] See " The Kansas Memorial," 1879, pp. 62, 63. This volume contains much material for history, undigested and ill-arranged, along with some worthless stuff.

[2] " Uncle Jimmy McGee " was a Kansas settler of Scotch-Irish descent, a Methodist of some property, who when the defenders of Lawrence were throwing up rifle-works said to them, " Work away, boys ! there 's two thousand bushels of corn in Jimmy McGee's crib, and while it lasts ye sha'n't starve." James F. Legate himself is a Massachusetts man (born in Leominster in 1829), who saw a great deal of the machinery that in 1855–56 was used to produce political effect in Kansas and in the East. He said in this speech of 1879 : " I remember, twenty-five years ago, when the Free-State men of Kansas (that meant Lawrence, Topeka, and a few fellows over

"The next thing was this 'cussed' Emigrant Aid Society. They had built a hotel here in Lawrence with about a foot and a half of wall above the roof, and fitted it up with port-holes, and they called that the Fort. It was designed to protect the town against the officers of the law from executing the decrees of court, they said. About that time I remembered that I had a pressing engagement out at old Judge Wakefield's. So I went out afoot (that is the way we used to ride a good deal in those days), and got a pony and saddle there, rode up to Tecumseh, where I had a talk with John Sherman, Governor Robinson, and Mr. Howard; and I gave them a pretty clear idea of what was going on, — that is, I intimated it to them. I then went back to Judge Wakefield's, slept about an hour, walked over to Lecompton, and was arrested for contempt of court. I went into the court-room, and the court wanted to know what excuse I had. I gave a truthful answer, as I always do. I said I went over to Judge Wakefield's, went to sleep, and had overslept myself. I was excused; and I went back to Judge Wakefield's, got the pony, and came over to Lawrence. I do not think Governor Robinson was there at the time. I believe he had pressing duties which called him East, and he went as far as Lexington, where he found a stopping-place. He came back by way of Leavenworth to Lecompton. They made some arrests in Lawrence, and then they went about abating the nuisance of the Fort hotel. They had a cannon on the opposite side of the street; and old Atchison got down on his knees, took deliberate aim at the hotel, and shot clear over it, and struck the hill near where a crowd of women were, who had left the town for safety. Their gunners were so good (?) that they could not hit the whole side of a hotel across the street. However, they finally demolished it."

In this humorous chronicle Mr. Legate has comprised all the time from the 8th to the 20th of May, closing with the attack on Lawrence by the United States marshal and his *posse*, — Sheriff Jones, too, with his *posse*, — including the

in Leavenworth) would hold a convention as often as the Yankees eat in hay-time, — and that is, three regular meals a day and a luncheon between. And a solemn convention it would be, with 'Dr. Charles Robinson, president,' 'George W. Brown, secretary' (now and then Joel K. Goodin or John Speer for secretary), and about a dozen awfully ragged, deplorably forlorn-looking cusses (who wanted to get back East again, and had n't the money to take them there) to make up the audience. And W. A. Phillips, Jim Redpath, and Hinton would report it, and it would make two and a half and sometimes three columns in the 'New York Tribune.'" It was after coming out of some such convention that John Brown said, "Great cry and little wool, — all talk and no cider."

Border Ruffians, and Atchison, lately Vice-President of the United States, at their head. The marshal, Donaldson, acted under Judge Lecompte, and collected his men by this proclamation, dated May 11 : —

" Whereas certain judicial writs have been directed to me, by the First District Court of the United States, etc., to be executed within the county of Douglas; and whereas an attempt to execute them by the United States deputy marshal was violently resisted by a large number of the citizens of Lawrence; and as there is every reason to believe that an attempt to execute these writs will be resisted by a large body of armed men, — now, therefore, the law-abiding citizens of the Territory are commanded to be and appear at Lecompton, as soon as practicable, and in numbers sufficient for the proper execution of the law."

Atchison, on the morning of May 20, made a foul speech near Lawrence to five hundred Border Ruffians,[1] among whom were the Kickapoo Rangers, who had murdered Brown at Easton. He said : —

" Boys, this day I am a Kickapoo Ranger, by God! This day we have entered Lawrence with ' Southern Rights ' inscribed upon our banner, and not one damned Abolitionist dared to fire a gun. Now, boys, this is the happiest day of my life. We have entered that damned town, and taught the damned Abolitionists a Southern lesson that they will remember until the day they die. And now, boys, we will go in again, with our highly honorable Jones, and test the strength of that damned Free-State Hotel, and teach the Emigrant Aid Company that Kansas shall be ours. Boys, ladies should, and I hope will, be respected by every gentleman.

---

[1] I quote this speech, with all its profanity and drunken gravity, because in no other way than by reading their utterances can the men of to-day understand how vile and coarse were the men who were carrying out in Kansas the behests of the Southern slaveholders and their willing tools at Washington. The term " Border Ruffians " is also used for the same purpose, since none could be so descriptive of these men who followed Atchison and his comrades. Among their leaders were men of cultivation, wealth, and humanity; and such persons did much to mitigate the horrors of the brutal mob-despotism which then prevailed, by intervals, where the flag of the nation should have secured peace and justice to all who lived under it. But from the rabble who filled the ranks came in due time such outlaws as Quantrell, who in 1863 sacked Lawrence and murdered one hundred and fifty of its people ; and the James brothers, who were in his band.

But when a woman takes upon herself the garb of a soldier by carrying a Sharpe's rifle, then she is no longer worthy of respect. Trample her under your feet as you would a snake! Come on, boys! Now do your duty to yourselves and your Southern friends. Your duty I know you will do. If one man or woman dare stand before you, blow them to hell with a chunk of cold lead."

As soon as Atchison concluded, the men moved towards the town until near the hotel, when the advance company halted. Jones said the hotel must be destroyed; he was acting under orders; he had writs issued by the First District Court of the United States to destroy the Free-State Hotel, and the offices of the "Herald of Freedom" and "Free State." The grand jury at Lecompton had indicted them as nuisances, and the court had ordered them to be destroyed. Here is the indictment : —

"The Grand Jury sitting for the adjourned term of the First District Court, in and for the County of Douglas, in the Territory of Kansas, beg leave to report to the Honorable Court, from evidence laid before them showing it, that the newspaper known as 'The Herald of Freedom,' published at the town of Lawrence, has from time to time issued publications of the most inflammatory and seditious character, denying the legality of the *Territorial authorities ;* addressing and commanding forcible resistance to the same; demoralizing the popular mind, and rendering life and property unsafe, even to the extent of advising assassination as a last resort.

"Also, that the paper known as 'The Kansas Free State' has been similarly engaged, and has recently reported the resolutions of a public meeting in Johnson County, in this Territory, in which resistance to the *Territorial laws* even unto blood has been agreed upon. And that we respectfully recommend their abatement as a nuisance. Also, that we are satisfied that the building known as the 'Free-State Hotel' in Lawrence has been constructed with the view to military occupation and defence, regularly parapeted and portholed for the use of cannon and small arms, and could only have been designed as a stronghold of resistance to law, thereby endangering the public safety and encouraging rebellion and sedition in this country, and respectfully recommend that steps be taken whereby this nuisance may be removed.

"OWEN C. STEWART, *Foreman.*"

Incredible as it may now appear, this indictment was
carried out: the hotel was destroyed, the offending newspaper had its type and press thrown into the Kansas River;
and all this was done under the cover of United States
authority. The President (Pierce), his Cabinet, in which
Jefferson Davis was a controlling member, the Senate of
the United States, and the national courts appeared as the
accomplices of murder, arson, and pillage, and as the champions of pettier tyrants who would hesitate at no crime.
It was under these circumstances that John Brown now
took the field; and he shall be his own reporter.

BROWN'S SECOND CAMPAIGN IN KANSAS.

NEAR BROWN'S STATION, K. T., June, 1856.

DEAR WIFE AND CHILDREN, EVERY ONE, — It is now about five
weeks since I have seen a line from North Elba, or had any chance
of writing you. During that period we here have passed through
an almost constant series of very trying events. We were called to
go to the relief of Lawrence, May 22, and every man (eight in all),
except Orson, turned out; he staying with the women and children,
and to take care of the cattle.[1] John was captain of a company to
which Jason belonged; the other six were a little company by ourselves. On our way to Lawrence we learned that it had been already
destroyed, and we encamped with John's company overnight. Next
day our little company left, and during the day we stopped and
searched three men.

Lawrence was destroyed in this way : Their leading men had (as
I think) decided, in a very *cowardly* manner, not to resist any process having any Government official to serve it, notwithstanding the
process might be wholly a bogus affair. The consequence was that
a man called a United States marshal came on with a horde of
ruffians which he called his posse, and after arresting a few persons
turned the ruffians loose on the defenceless people. They robbed the
inhabitants of their money and other property, and even women of
their ornaments, and burned considerable of the town.

On the second day and evening after we left John's men we
encountered quite a number of proslavery men, and took quite a

---

[1] "Orson" was Mr. Orson Day, a brother of Mrs. John Brown. The
"other six" were probably John Brown, Owen, Frederick, Salmon, Oliver,
and Henry Thompson.

number prisoners. Our prisoners we let go; but we kept some four or five horses.[1] We were immediately after this accused of murdering five men at Pottawatomie, and great efforts have since been made by the Missourians and their ruffian allies to capture us. John's company soon afterward disbanded, and also the Osawatomie men.[2]

Jason started to go and place himself under the protection of the Government troops; but on his way he was taken prisoner by the Bogus men, and is yet a prisoner, I suppose. John tried to hide for several days; but from feelings of the ungrateful conduct of those who ought to have stood by him, excessive fatigue, anxiety, and constant loss of sleep, he became quite insane, and in that situation gave up, or, as we are told, was betrayed at Osawatomie into the hands of the Bogus men. We do not know all the truth about this affair. He has since, we are told, been kept in irons, and brought to a trial before a bogus court, the result of which we have not yet learned. We have great anxiety both for him and Jason, and numerous other prisoners with the enemy (who have all the while had the Government troops to sustain them). We can only commend them to God.[3]

---

[1] This is all that Brown says in this letter about the events of that night in May when the Doyles were executed. Doubtless his text for the next morning was from the Book of Judges: "Then Gideon took ten men of his servants, and did as the Lord had said unto him; and so it was that he did it by night. And when the men of the city arose early in the morning, behold the altar of Baal was cast down. And they said, one to another, Who hath done this thing? And when they inquired and asked, they said, Gideon, the son of Joash, hath done this thing."

[2] In the original something has been erased after this, to which this note seems to have been appended: "There are but very few who wish real facts about these matters to go out." Then is inserted the date "June 26," as below.

[3] John Brown, Jr.'s, own account of this campaign, as given by him to a reporter of the "Cleveland Leader," April, 1879, is as follows: "During the winter of 1856 I raised a company of riflemen from the Free-State settlers who had their homes in the vicinity of Osawatomie and Pottawatomie Creek, and marched with this company to the defence of Lawrence, May, 1856, but did not reach the latter place in time to save it from being burned by the Missourians at that time. On this march I was joined by three other companies, and was chosen to the command of the combined forces. Returning to our homes, we found them burned to the ground by Buford's men from Alabama, who had marched in from Missouri on our rear. Our cattle and horses were driven off and dispersed, there only being three or four which we ultimately recovered. In that destruction of our houses I lost my library, consisting of about four hundred volumes, which I had been accumulating since I was sixteen. Reaching

The cowardly mean conduct of Osawatomie and vicinity did not save them ; for the ruffians came on them, made numerous prisoners, fired their buildings, and robbed them.   After this a picked party of the Bogus men went to Brown's Station,[1] burned John's and Jason's houses, and their contents to ashes ; in which burning we have all suffered more or less.   Orson and boy have been prisoners, but were soon set at liberty.   They are well, and have not been seriously injured.   Owen and I have just come here for the first time to look at the ruins.   All looks desolate and forsaken, — the grass and weeds fast covering up the signs that these places were lately the abodes of quiet families.   After burning the houses, this self-same party of picked men, some forty in number, set out as they supposed, and as was the fact, on the track of my little company, boasting, with awful profanity, that they would have our scalps.   They however passed the place where we were hid, and robbed a little town some four or five miles beyond our camp in the timber.[2]   I had omitted to say that some murders had been committed at the time Lawrence was sacked.

On learning that this party were in pursuit of us, my little company, now increased to ten in all, started after them in company of a Captain Shore, with eighteen men, he included (June 1).   We were all mounted as we travelled.   We did not meet them on that day, but took five prisoners, four of whom were of their scouts, and well armed.   We were out all night, but could find nothing of them until

Osawatomie, my brother Jason and I were arrested on the charge of treason against the United States, by United States troops, acting as *posse* for the marshal of the Territory, and taken to Paola, where Judge Cato was to hold a preliminary examination ; but he did not hold his court.   It was from the latter place that I was tied by Captain Wood of the United States cavalry, and driven on foot at the head of the column a distance of nine miles at full trot to Osawatomie.   My arms were tied behind me, and so tightly as to check the circulation of the blood, especially in the right arm, causing the rope, which remained on me twenty-seven hours, to sink into the flesh, leaving a mark upon that arm which I have to this day.   The captain of that company was, I think, a Georgian, and finally, I believe, entered the Confederate service during the late war.   From there we were marched, chained two by two, carrying the chain between us, to a camp near Lecompton, where we met the other treason prisoners and were turned over to the custody of Colonel Sacket, who had command of a regiment of United States cavalry.   We were held here until September of 1856, when we were released on bail ; and a few days after I took part in the defence of Lawrence against the third attack.   At that time Franklin was burned, a few miles from Lawrence."

[1] Ten miles west of Osawatomie.

[2] This town was Palmyra.

about six o'clock next morning, when we prepared to attack them at once, on foot, leaving Frederick and one of Captain Shore's men to guard the horses. As I was much older than Captain Shore, the principal direction of the fight devolved on me. We got to within about a mile of their camp before being discovered by their scouts, and then moved at a brisk pace, Captain Shore and men forming our left, and my company the right. When within about sixty rods of the enemy, Captain Shore's men halted by mistake in a very exposed situation, and continued the fire, both his men and the enemy being armed with Sharpe's rifles. My company had no long-shooters. We (my company) did not fire a gun until we gained the rear of a bank, about fifteen or twenty rods to the right of the enemy, where we commenced, and soon compelled them to hide in a ravine. Captain Shore, after getting one man wounded, and exhausting his ammunition, came with part of his men to the right of my position, much discouraged. The balance of his men, including the one wounded, had left the ground. Five of Captain Shore's men came boldly down and joined my company, and all but one man, wounded, helped to maintain the fight until it was over. I was obliged to give my consent that he[1] should go after more help, when all his men left but eight, four of whom I persuaded to remain in a secure position, and there busied one of them in shooting the horses and mules of the enemy, which served for a show of fight. After the firing had continued for some two to three hours, Captain Pate with twenty-three men, two badly wounded, laid down their arms to nine men, myself included, — four of Captain Shore's men and four of my own. One of my men (Henry Thompson)[2] was badly wounded, and after continuing his fire for an hour longer was obliged to quit the ground. Three others of my company (but not of my family) had gone off. Salmon was dreadfully wounded by accident, soon after the fight; but both he and Henry are fast recovering.

A day or two after the fight, Colonel Sumner of the United States army came suddenly upon us, while fortifying our camp and guarding our prisoners (which, by the way, it had been agreed mutually should be exchanged for as many Free-State men, John and Jason included), and compelled us to let go our prisoners without being exchanged, and to give up their horses and arms. They did not go more than two or three miles before they began to rob and injure Free-State people. We consider this as in good keeping with the

[1] By "he" is apparently meant Captain Shore.

[2] Brown's son-in-law, the husband of Ruth Brown. The agreement with Pate, referred to above, is still in existence to confirm this letter; both copies of it having found their way to the Historical Library at

cruel and unjust course of the Administration and its tools throughout this whole Kansas difficulty. Colonel Sumner also compelled us to disband; and we, being only a handful, were obliged to submit.

Since then we have, like David of old, had our dwelling with the serpents of the rocks and wild beasts of the wilderness; being obliged to hide away from our enemies. We are not disheartened, though nearly destitute of food, clothing, and money. God, who has not given us over to the will of our enemies, but has moreover delivered them into our hand, will, we humbly trust, still keep and deliver us. We feel assured that He who sees not as men see, does not lay the guilt of innocent blood to our charge.

I ought to have said that Captain Shore and his men stood their ground nobly in their unfortunate but mistaken position during the early part of the fight. I ought to say further that a Captain Abbott, being some miles distant with a company, came onward promptly to sustain us, but could not reach us till the fight was over. After the fight, numerous Free-State men who could not be got out before were on hand; and some of them, I am ashamed to add, were very busy not only with the plunder of our enemies, but with our private effects, leaving us, while guarding our prisoners and providing in regard to them, much poorer than before the battle.

If, under God, this letter reaches you so that it can be read, I wish it at once carefully copied, and a copy of it sent to Gerrit Smith. I know of no other way to get these facts and our situation before the world, nor when I can write again.

Topeka, where Mr. F. G. Adams, the secretary, showed them to me in 1882. Here is a copy : —

This is an article of agreement between Captains John Brown, Sr., and Samuel T. Shore of the first part, and Captain H. C. Pate and Lieutenant W. B. Brockett of the second part ; and witnesses that, in consideration of the fact that the parties of the first part have a number of Captain Pate's company prisoners, that they agree to give up and fully liberate one of their prisoners for one of those lately arrested near Stanton, Osawatomie, and Pottawatomie, and so on, one of the former for one of the latter alternately, until all are liberated. It is understood and agreed by the parties that the sons of Captain John Brown, Sr. — Captain John Brown, Jr., and Jason Brown — are to be among the liberated parties (if not already liberated), and are to be exchanged for Captain Pate and Lieutenant Brockett, respectively. The prisoners are to be brought on neutral ground and exchanged. It is agreed that the neutral ground shall be at or near the house of John T. (or Ottawa) Jones of this Territory, and that those who have been arrested and have been liberated will be considered in the same light as those not liberated ; but they must appear in person, or answer in writing that they are at liberty. The arms, particularly the side arms of each one exchanged, are to be returned with the prisoners ; also the horses, so far as practicable.

(Signed)   JOHN BROWN.
S. T. SHORE.
H. C. PATE.
W. B. BROCKETT.

PRAIRIE CITY, K. T., June 2, 1856.

Owen has the ague to-day. Our camp is some miles off. Have heard that letters are in for some of us, but have not seen them. Do continue writing. We heard last mail brought only three letters, and all these for proslavery men. It is said that both the Lawrence and Osawatomie men, when the ruffians came on them, either hid or gave up their arms, and that their leading men counselled them to take such a course.

May God bless and keep you all!

Your affectionate husband and father,

JOHN BROWN.

P. S. Ellen and Wealthy are staying at Osawatomie.

The above is a true account of the first regular battle fought between Free-State and proslavery men in Kansas. May God still gird our loins and hold our right hands, and to him may we give the glory! I ought in justice to say, that, after the sacking and burning of several towns, the Government troops appeared for their protection and drove off some of the enemy.   J. B.

June 26. Jason is set at liberty, and we have hopes for John. Owen, Salmon, and Oliver are down with fever (since inserted); Henry doing well.

With this chapter of Brown's commentaries on the Kansas war may properly go the following papers, although they were not written until some months later, — the first in August, 1856, and the second after Brown left Kansas in October, 1856. The first is addressed to his friend Edmund B. Whitman, who then lived at Lawrence.

For Mr. Whitman.

Names of sufferers and persons who have made sacrifices in endeavoring to maintain and advance the Free-State cause in Kansas, within my personal knowledge.

1. Two German refugees (thoroughly Free-State), robbed at Pottawatomie, named Benjamin and Bondy (or Bundy). One has served under me as a volunteer; namely, Bondy. Benjamin was prisoner for some time. Suffered by men under Coffee and Pate.

2. Henry Thompson. Devoted several months to the Free-State cause, travelling nearly two thousand miles at his own expense for the purpose, leaving family and business for about one year. Served under me as a volunteer; was dangerously wounded at Palmyra, or Black Jack; has a bullet lodged beside his backbone; has had a

16

severe turn of fever, and is still very feeble. Suffered a little in burning of the houses of John Brown, Jr., and Jason Brown.

3. John, Jr., and Jason Brown. Both burned out ; both prisoners for some time, one a prisoner still : both losing the use of valuable, partially improved claims. Both served repeatedly as volunteers for defence of Lawrence and other places, suffering great hardships and some cruelty.

4. Owen and Frederick Brown. Both served at different periods as volunteers under me; were both in the battle of Palmyra ; both suffered by the burning of their brothers' houses ; both have had sickness (Owen a severe one), and are yet feeble. Both lost the use of partially improved claims and their spring and summer work.

5. Salmon Brown (minor). Twice served under me as a volunteer; was dangerously wounded (if not permanently crippled) by accident near Palmyra ; had a severe sickness, and still feeble.

6. Oliver Brown (minor). Served under me as a volunteer for some months; was in the battle of Palmyra, and had some sickness.

7. [B. L.] Cochran (at Pottawatomie). Twice served under me as a volunteer ; was in the battle of Palmyra.[1]

8. Dr. Lucius Mills devoted some months to the Free-State cause, collecting and giving information, prescribing for and nursing the sick and wounded at his own cost. Is a worthy Free-State man.

9. John Brown has devoted the service of himself and two minor sons to the Free-State cause for more than a year ; suffered by the fire before named and by robbery ; has gone at his own cost for that period, except that he and his company together have received forty dollars in cash, two sacks of flour, thirty-five pounds bacon, thirty-five do. sugar, and twenty pounds rice.

I propose to serve hereafter in the Free-State cause (provided my needful expenses can be met), should that be desired ; and to raise a small regular force to serve on the same condition. My own means are so far exhausted that I can no longer continue in the service at present without the means of defraying my expenses are furnished me.

I can give the names of some five or six more volunteers of special merit I would be glad to have particularly noticed in some way.

J. BROWN.

The second paper is part of the notes which Brown drew up for his speeches at Hartford, Boston, Concord, and other New England towns, in the spring of 1857. In this speech he laid stress not only on the sins of the Border Ruffians

---

[1] Better known as Black Jack.

and the unpatriotic conduct of the National Government, but on the pecuniary loss which he and the other settlers had undergone in being kept from their work, at the busiest season of the year, by the raids from Missouri. This gives a strange air to the paper, which is otherwise noticeable for the facts set forth.

AN IDEA OF THINGS IN KANSAS.

I propose, in order to make this meeting as useful and interesting as I can, to try and give a correct idea of the condition of things in Kansas, as they were while I was there, and as I suppose they still are, so far as the great question at issue is concerned. And here let me remark that in Kansas the question is never raised of a man, Is he a Democrat? Is he a Republican? The questions there raised are, Is he a Free-State man? or, Is he a proslavery man?

I saw, while in Missouri in the fall of 1855, large numbers on their way to Kansas to vote, and also returning after they had so done, as they said. I, together with four of my sons, was called out to help defend Lawrence in the fall of 1855, and travelled most of the way on foot, and during a dark night, a distance of thirty-five miles, where we were detained with some five hundred others, or thereabout, from five to fifteen days, — say an average of ten days, — at a cost to each per day of $1.50 as wages, to say nothing of the actual loss and suffering it occasioned; many of them leaving their families at home sick, their crops not secured, their houses unprepared for winter, and many of them without houses at all. This was the case with myself and all my sons, who were unable to get any house built after our return. The loss in that case, as wages alone, would amount to $7,500. Loss and suffering in consequence cannot be estimated. I saw at that time the body of the murdered Barber, and was present when his wife and other friends were brought in to see him as he lay in the clothes he had on when killed, — no very pleasant sight!

I went, in the spring of last year, with some of my sons among the Buford men, in the character of a surveyor, to see and hear from them their business into the Territory; this took us from our work. I and numerous others, in the spring of last year, travelled some ten miles or over on foot, to meet and advise as to what should be done to meet the gathering storm; this occasioned much loss of time. I also, with many others, about the same time travelled on foot a similar distance to attend a meeting of Judge Cato's court, to find out what kind of laws he intended to enforce; this occasioned further loss of time. I with six sons and a son-in-law was again called out to defend Lawrence, May 20 and 21, and travelled most of the way on foot and during the night, being thirty-five miles. From that date none of us could do any work about our homes, but lost our whole time until we left, in October last, excepting one of my sons, who had a few weeks to devote to the care of his own and his brother's family, who had been burned out of their houses while the two men were prisoners.

From about the 20th of May of last year hundreds of men like ourselves lost their whole time, and entirely failed of securing any kind of crop whatever. I believe it safe to say that five hundred Free-State men lost each one hundred and twenty days, at $1.50 per day, which would be, to say nothing of attendant losses, $90,000. I saw the ruins of many Free-State men's houses at different places in the Territory, together with stacks of grain wasted and burning, to the amount of, say $50,000; making, in lost time and destruction of property, more than $150,000. On or about the 30th of May last two of my sons, with several others, were imprisoned without other crime than opposition to bogus enactments, and most barbarously treated for a time, — one being held about one month, the other about four months. Both had their families in Kansas, and destitute of homes, being burned out after they were imprisoned. In this burning all the eight were sufferers, as we all had our effects at the two houses. One of my sons had his oxen taken from him at this time, and never recovered them. Here is the chain with which one of them was confined, after the cruelty, sufferings, and anxiety he underwent had rendered him a maniac, — yes, a maniac.

On the 2d of June last my son-in-law was terribly wounded (supposed to be mortally), and two other Free-State men, at Black Jack. On the 6th or 7th of June last one of my sons was wounded by accident in camp (supposed to be mortally), and may prove a cripple for life. In August last I was present and saw the mangled and shockingly disfigured body of the murdered Hoyt, of Deerfield, Mass., brought into our camp. I knew him well. I saw several other Free-State men who were either killed or wounded, whose names I cannot now remember. I saw Dr. Graham, who was a prisoner with the ruffians on the 2d of June last, and was present when they wounded him, in an attempt to kill him, as he was trying to save himself from being murdered by them during the fight of Black Jack. I know that for much of the time during the last summer the travel over a portion of the Territory was entirely cut off, and that none but bodies of armed men dared to move at all. I know that for a considerable time the mails on different routes were entirely stopped, and that notwithstanding there were abundant United States troops at hand to escort the mails, such escorts were not furnished as they might or ought to have been. I saw while it was standing, and afterward saw the ruins of, a most valuable house, full of good articles and stores, which had been burned by the ruffians for a highly civilized, intelligent, and most exemplary Christian Indian, for being suspected of favoring Free-State men. He is known as Ottawa Jones, or John T. Jones. In September last I visited a beautiful little Free-State town called Stanton, on the north side of the Osage or Marais des Cygnes River, as it is called, from which every inhabitant had fled (being in fear of their lives), after having built them, at a heavy expense, a strong block-house or wooden fort for their protection. Many of them had left their effects liable to be destroyed or carried off, not being able to remove them. This was a most gloomy scene, and like a visit to a vast sepulchre.

During last summer and fall deserted houses and cornfields were to be met with in almost every direction south of the Kansas River. I saw the burning of Osawatomie by a body of some four hundred ruffians, and of Franklin afterward by some twenty-seven hundred men, — the first-named on August 30, the last-named September 14 or 15. Governor Geary had been for some time in the Territory, and might have saved Franklin with perfect ease. It would not have cost the United States one dollar to have saved Franklin.

I, with five sick and wounded sons and son-in-law, was obliged for some time to lie on the ground, without shelter, our boots and clothes worn out, destitute of money, and at times almost in a state of starvation, and dependent on the charities of the Christian Indian and his wife whom I before named.[1] I saw, in September last, a Mr. Parker,

---

[1] Notwithstanding the losses and charities of this good Indian in 1856, he was the next year in condition to make further gifts to Brown, as appears by this letter : —

OTTAWA CREEK, K. T., Oct. 13, 1857.

MR. JOHN BROWN.

DEAR SIR, — Respecting the account you have against us as a band, I would respectfully inform you that I have presented the matter before them two or three different times, and I cannot persuade them but what was paid by them was all that could be reasonably demanded of them, from the bargain they entered into with Jones the agent. For my part I think the charge is just, and it ought to be paid. The Ottawa payment comes off some time this week, and I will present your case before them again, and do what I can to induce them to attend to the account, though I entertain no hopes of its being allowed ; but nothing like trying. In contributing my mite in aiding you in your benevolent enterprise, I enclose you ten dollars on the State Bank of Indiana (I presume it is good, though hundreds of other banks are worthless), and throw in the young man's bill and horse-hire, which amounts to four dollars. Accept it, sir, as a free-will offering from your friend.

Times are coming round favorably in Kansas. Mr. Parrott for Congress will have 8,000 to 10,000 majority over Ransom, and both branches of the Legislature the same in proportion. I am quite encouraged that all things will work together for good for those who are trying to work out righteousness in the land. May God bless you in your work

whom I well know, with his head all bruised over and his throat partly cut, having before been dragged, while sick, out of the house of Ottawa Jones, the Indian, when it was burned, and thrown for dead over the bank of the Ottawa Creek.

I saw three mangled bodies of three young men, two of which were dead and had lain on the open ground for about eighteen hours for the flies to work at, the other living with twenty buckshot and bullet-holes in him. One of those two dead was my own son.

Here, then, we may pause to review the position of the Brown family in Kansas, twelve months after John Brown had set forth from Illinois to support his children in making free and peaceful homes on those beautiful prairies. One of his sons was dead; another a prisoner charged with treason; a third was desperately wounded; a fourth stricken down with illness; all had lost their cabins, their crops, their books and papers; their wives and children were scattered or far away. Only one son of the six remained in fighting condition; all were in extreme poverty; the cause of freedom, for which they had ventured so much, seemed almost lost. Everything was subdued except the inexorable will of John Brown.[1] That remained; his faith in God and his obedience to the voice of God were as quick as ever; and he had begun the warfare against slavery by a dire blow, which was destined in its consequences to make Kansas free, even as his master-stroke in Virginia, three years later, was to set in motion the avalanche that destroyed slavery in the whole land. This blow was the execution at Pottawatomie on the 24th of May.

of benevolence and philanthropy : and may God reward you more than double for your toil and losses in the work to bring about liberty for all men ! Write me if you can, and let me know how you are getting along, etc.

I remain your sincere friend,   JOHN T. JONES.

By "us as a band" is meant the Ottawa tribe of Indians, and their "payment" was the allowance periodically given to them by the Federal Government. I saw one of the last nomadic Indians of this tribe sitting bareheaded on his pony in the busy streets of Ottawa, in August, 1882, staring with his stolid eye at the white man's way of life.

[1] Audire magnos jam videor duces
Non indecoro pulvere sordidos,
Et cuncta terrarum subacta
Præter atrocem animum Catonis.

HORACE, *Odes*, lib. ii. car. i.

CHAPTER IX.

THE POTTAWATOMIE EXECUTIONS.

THE story of John Brown will mean little to those who do not believe that God governs the world, and that He makes His will known in advance to certain chosen men and women who perform it, consciously or unconsciously. Of such prophetic, Heaven-appointed men John Brown was the most conspicuous in our time, and his life must be construed in the light of that fact, — as the career of Cromwell must be, and has been, since Carlyle set it forth to the world in its true colors. Cotton Mather, in 1720, intimated to the young friend for whom he wrote his quaint "Directions for a Candidate of the Ministry," that he must not look at Cromwell through Clarendon's glasses. "I do particularly advertise you," said Mather, "that this *mighty man* has never yet had his *history* fully and fairly given; and when you read it given with the greatest *impartiality* wherein you have hitherto seen it, you may bear this in your mind, that the *principal stroke* in his character, and the *principal spring* of his conduct, is forever *defectively* related." Brown has not suffered so much as Cromwell in this way, for his worldly success was not so great, and therefore he offered a lesser mark for envy and malice; he was also a more simple and ingenuous Calvinist than Cromwell, and could not lay himself so open to the charge of hypocrisy and self-seeking. But the source of his greatness and the motive of his public conduct were essentially the same, — an impression that God had called him to a high and painful work, and that he must accomplish this even with bloodshed and at the loss of friends, life, and reputation. Milton, in so many points like Cromwell, though in more like Brown (I speak not of his genius, but of his character),

understood this, — and also that there is a divine antinomi-
anism as well as a loose and diabolic one. Therefore he
said in one of those matchless choral passages of the
" Samson," —

> " Just are the ways of God,
> And justifiable to men ;
> Unless there be who think not God at all.
> If any be, they walk obscure ;
> For of such doctrine never was there school,
> But the heart of the fool, —
> And no man therein doctor but himself.
>
> Yet more there be who doubt His ways not just,
> As to His own edicts found contradicting ;
> .   .   .   .
> As if they would confine th' Interminable,
> And tie Him to His own prescript,
> Who made our laws to bind us, not Himself,
> And hath full right to exempt
> Whom it so pleases Him by choice
> From national obstriction, without taint
> Of sin or legal debt ;
> For with His own laws He can best dispense."

This is a high doctrine, applying only to heroes; but it
holds good of John Brown, and particularly in regard to
the Pottawatomie executions of May, 1856. Such a deed
must not be judged by the every-day rules of conduct, which
distinctly forbid violence and the infliction of death for
private causes; branding the act, and justly, by the odious
names of "murder" and "assassination." The cause here
was a public one ; the crisis was momentous, and yet invisible
to all but the eyes divinely appointed to see it and to foresee
its consequences. Upon the swift and secret vengeance of
John Brown in that midnight raid hinged the future of Kansas, as we can now see ; and on that future again hinged the
destinies of the whole country. Had Kansas in the death-
struggle of 1856 fallen a prey to the slaveholders, slaveholding would to-day be the law of our imperial democracy ;
the sanctions of the Union and the Constitution would now
be on the side of human slavery, as they were from 1840 to
1860. And the turning point in the Kansas conflict was

that week of May, 1856, when the whole power of the
United States was shamefully put forth to conquer the little
town of Lawrence, to abase the free spirit of the Northern
farmers on the Kansas prairies, and to give supremacy
to the vilest and most inhuman elements in the American
nationality. The attack on Lawrence (May 20) was coin-
cident in time with the close of Charles Sumner's great
speech in the Senate on the "Crime against Kansas;" and
the temporary downfall of the Free-State cause west of
the Missouri was echoed at Washington in the contrived
and almost completed murder of Sumner by the weapons of
South Carolina, as he sat in the Senate chamber two days
after (May 22, 1856). One shout of exultation went up
from the slaveholding States over the two events; and one
thrill of anguish ran through the free North when the
tidings came in the same day from Kansas and from Washington. A venerable citizen of Boston, — Josiah Quincy,
then in his eighty-fifth year, — who had seen the Independence of America declared by Jefferson and maintained by
Washington, Franklin, and Lafayette, raised his aged voice
in protest against the degeneracy of their descendants.
Writing to Judge Hoar, of Concord (May 27, 1856), Mr.
Quincy said : —

"My mind is in no state to receive pleasure from social
scenes and friendly intercourse. I can think and speak of
nothing but the outrages of slaveholders at Kansas, and the
outrages of slaveholders at Washington, — outrages which,
if not met in the spirit of our fathers of the Revolution
(and I see no sign that they will be), *our liberties are but a
name, and our Union proves a curse.* But, alas! sir, I see
no principle of vitality in what is called freedom in these
times. The palsy of death rests on the spirit of freedom in
the so-called free States."

Thus Quincy spoke; and in the same sense, to a result
such as Quincy could not foresee, John Brown had already
acted. He also felt that "our liberties are but a name and
our Union proves a curse," if the deeds done at Lawrence,
preceded by murders and followed by the flight of freemen
from Kansas, were not to be met with retaliation. The
blow at Pottawatomie followed, as a signal to every Kansas

ruffian that blood must recompense blood. For every cold-blooded murder heretofore perpetrated, — for Dow, Barber, Brown, Stewart, and Jones, — the sabres of Pottawatomie requited life with life. Five representative defenders of slavery were struck down in a single night, in reprisal for the five sons of liberty slain in the previous six months. The lesson was terrible, but salutary; the oppressors of Kansas never forgave it, but they could not forget it, — and it wrought their defeat in the end. It shocked the Free-State men, no doubt; but it soon gave them confidence that God's justice did not sleep, and that their cause was not lost. I have already cited what Charles Robinson said of it in 1878, — that he had always believed John Brown to be the author of the Pottawatomie executions, because he was the only man then in Kansas who comprehended the situation, and had the nerve to strike the blow. John Brown, Jr., in this respect agrees with Robinson, and says : " It has never been asserted by me, nor by any one else who comprehended the situation at that time, that the killing of those men at Pottawatomie was wholly on account of the emergency in that neighborhood. That blow was struck for Kansas and the slave ; and he who attempts to limit its object to a mere settlement of accounts with a few proslavery desperadoes on that creek, shows himself incapable of rendering a just judgment in the case." When Jason Brown met his father for the first time after the executions, near the empty cabins from which the Brown families had fled for safety to Osawatomie, the tender-hearted son said : " Father, did you have anything to do with that bloody affair on the Pottawatomie ? " Brown's reply was, " I approved of it." Jason then said : " Whoever did it, the act was uncalled for and wicked." Brown answered, " God is my judge, — the people of Kansas will yet justify my course." This prediction was true. An old friend of his, James Hanway, who lived near the scene of the executions, and at first strongly abhorred them, has given this testimony on the point : —

" In the month of January, 1859, the last time I met John Brown before he left the Territory for the last time, he asked me, in the presence of my family, ' What do the old settlers now think about the affair?' alluding to the killing of the Doyles, etc. My reply was, 'A great change in public opinion has taken place; it is not now looked upon with that feeling of horror which prevailed soon after the event took place.' Brown replied, 'I knew all good men who loved freedom, when they became better acquainted with the circumstances connected with the case, would approve of it. The public mind was not ready then to accept such hard blows.' Captain Brown firmly believed that he was an instrument in the hands of Providence to smite the slave-power, and roll back its blasphemous threats. The question with him was the proper time to strike the blow. He thought the hour had come, and the Pottawatomie tragedy was the result."

The scene of this act of wild justice was one of the most romantic in Kansas. The broad prairies of that State are fertile and sunny, but they have the tameness and sameness of landscape that soon wearies the eye of the traveller. Around Osawatomie, however, this monotony is broken by winding streams, swelling hills, and steep ravines; while along the streams is a noble border of woodland. That instinctive love of the picturesque which led John Brown and his sons to the forests of Ohio, the mountains of the Adirondac wilderness, and the snow-capped heights of California, guided their steps in Kansas also, and pitched their tents in this wildest tract of a tame region. Two copious rivers, though condescending to bear the commonplace name of "creek," — the Marais des Cygnes, and the Pottawatomie, — unite near Osawatomie, in what was then the home of Indian tribes, to form the Osage River, the largest tributary of the Missouri below the mountain-torrents. Each of these Kansas rivers is formed by tributary streams, and all wind gracefully among fringes of woodland, below which in many places the banks shelve steeply down to the lazy waters.[1]

[1] I visited Osawatomie, August 21, 1882, and made this entry in my journal : "Crossed the Marais des Cygnes by a bridge on the road from Paola between the insane asylum and the village of Osawatomie, — a large stream with high banks, heavily timbered, perhaps one hundred feet wide at this season, and in some places twenty or thirty feet deep ; so that men fording it have often been drowned. It was on the northern bank of this river, one mile or more from the village, that John Brown was encamped (August 29, 30) before the battle of Osawatomie. I saw one of Brown's friends, — the

Beyond this forest selvage stretches broad and grand the
grassy, flower-enamelled prairie, now dotted at many points
with orchards, groves, farm-houses and villages, — but in
1856 a virgin soil, which the plow had only scarred a little
now and then, and over which ranged and flitted countless
beasts and birds, with here and there a herd of cattle, or
a group of half-wild horses. The Indian hunter pursued
his game there, and the buffalo had not wholly forsaken his
old grazing-ground. The villages of Osawatomie, which
gave John Brown a distinctive name, and of Lane, which
has grown up near the old ford of the Pottawatomie in
the township of that ilk, once known as Dutch Henry's
Crossing, are neither of them large or specially flourishing,
but a historic interest attaches to both from their association with Brown's career. Lane is southwest of Osawatomie, and therefore, as the river runs, above it; and
above the old Crossing, where there is now a modern
bridge, are the neighborhoods which Brown visited on
that tragic night. Professor Spring, the latest historian
of Kansas, thus describes the country as he saw it three
years ago : —

" The Dutch Henry's Crossing of 1882 is a paradise of rural peace
and happiness. The fiercest sounds I heard during a visit to that
region were the clatter of agricultural machinery and the fervent
hallelujahs of a ' holiness ' camp-meeting. Here quiet and security
seem to have reached their utmost limit. The Pottawatomie — half
limpid, with slighter mixtures of discoloring mud than any Kansas
stream that I have seen — winds languidly between beautifully
shaded banks toward the Marais des Cygnes. The vast fields of

Sniders of the Trading Post massacre, — a blacksmith of Osawatomie now,
standing tall and swarthy in his shop at the village ; and then drove the
next morning two miles farther west to the log-house of Rev. S. L. Adair,
on the high prairie along which the Missourians came the morning of the
fight. The road from the village to Mr. Adair's is steep and rocky, — more
so than any I have yet seen in Kansas. His house is the one he built in
the spring of 1855, though it has since been enlarged ; it is the common
cabin of squared logs, chinked in with clay, and the main room has two
beds in it. In this room John Brown was sick with typhoid fever for six
weeks, in 1858, — Kagi and the Adairs taking care of him. The house has
orchards about it, and in front two or three pine-trees which Mr. Adair
brought from the East about 1860, one of which is now twenty feet high."

corn and wheat, with their picturesque borders of orange hedge, lie mapped upon the rolling prairie in every direction, —

> ' As quietly as spots of sky
> Among the evening clouds.'

" The Dutch Henry's Crossing of 1856 stands in antithesis to all this Arcadian repose. Then there was no law but force, no rule but violence, in the Territory of Kansas. A veritable reign of terror was inaugurated. Marauders were prowling about in whose eyes nothing was sacred that stood in the way of their passions. The opposing factions into whose hands the question of slavery or no slavery for Kansas had fallen, hunted each other like wolves. Pistol-shots and sword-slits were the prevailing style of argument. For purposes of ambush and concealment this location was admirably chosen. The surface is cut up by gulches affording natural defences which ten resolute men could hold against a hundred. I spent half a day in exploring this region with one of Brown's men, who had not been on the ground for twenty-six years, in an effort to recover the exact site of Brown's bivouac of May 23. But so marked is the change which time has wrought in the landscape, so great the number and similarity of the ravines, that all our efforts failed. Indeed, nothing here remains as it was in the Border period. The earliest cabins have been pulled down, frontier characteristics are gone, and the customs of older civilizations appear. The ford retains its quaint and primitive name of Dutch Henry's Crossing, but has ceased to be used. The once broad and travelled road leading down to it has now shrunk to a narrow, weed-choked path, right across which lies a half-decayed tree. I found one direct, and to me pathetic, memorial of the Pottawatomie raid (even that is being rapidly obliterated), — the grave of three of its victims. They were buried coffinless in one shallow trench. No stone or tablet marks their resting-place, — only a slight heaving of the turf, in an open field near the ford."

The two Shermans, — Dutch Henry and Dutch William, — who lived here and gave their name to the ford, were brothers, from Oldenburg in Germany, who had been long in America, and were among the earliest white settlers of this region. They were men of harsh and brutal character, who profited by the neighborhood of peaceful Indians to advance their own interests at the expense of the red men, and who looked upon Indians and negroes with equal contempt. Their house was a sort of tavern, as many of the prairie cabins were in those days, and their most acceptable

visitors were the proslavery men from Missouri and farther
south.   At this very time, in the words of John Brown the
younger, "the Doyles, Wilkinsons, and Shermans were furnishing places of rendezvous and active aid to the armed
men who had sworn to kill us and others."   With the Browns
it was simply a question as to which, to use a Western phrase,
should "first get the drop" on the others.   Upon this point,
which of late years has been the subject of controversy, the
testimony is clear and ample.   The men who suffered death
were not only leagued with the Missouri invaders, but had
themselves committed gross outrages, such as they had
threatened a year before their death.   An early citizen of
Kansas (now or recently a police magistrate at Salina), August Bondi by name, went to settle, in May, 1855, on the
Musquito branch of the Pottawatomie, four miles from Dutch
Henry's.   Being a German, and having two compatriots
(Theodore Wiener and Jacob Benjamin) owning near him,
Bondi went to call on Henry Sherman, whom he had heard
of as a German also, and therefore sought his acquaintance.
After a short conversation with him, Henry Sherman said
" he had heard that Bondi and Benjamin were Freesoilers,
and therefore would advise them to clear out, or they might
meet the fate of Baker," — a Vermont man whom the Border Ruffians had taken from his cabin on the Marais des
Cygnes, whipped, and hanged upon a tree, but had cut him
down before death, and released him upon his promise to
leave Kansas.   Allen Wilkinson, who was a member of the
usurping Legislature, talked to Bondi in much the same way.
The two Germans (Bondi and Benjamin, for Wiener had
not yet arrived) took counsel what should be done.   Benjamin, who had worked several days at the settlement on the
Marais des Cygnes, reported that no help could be expected
thence, where the settlers were all from Missouri or Arkansas.   He had heard, however, of a small settlement of Ohio
men about five miles to the northeast, and both agreed that
these ought to be seen.   Next morning Benjamin went there,
and about noon returned with Frederick Brown, who brought
word from his three brothers that they would always be
found ready to assist Bondi and his friend.   No attack was
made that summer, during which there was a large immi-

gration into the Pottawatomie region, both from the North
and the South, — the Northern men in the majority, but the
proslavery men having the advantage of being generally
well armed and under better organization. On their side,
too, were the gangs of robbers and murderers on the borders
of Missouri and the Indian Territory.

But in the spring of 1856 the Shermans and their comrades began to carry out their threats. George Grant, who
then lived on the Pottawatomie, testified in 1879 : —

"My father, John T. Grant, came from Oneida County, N. Y.,
and settled on Pottawatomie Creek, in 1854. We were near neighbors of the Shermans, of the Doyles, and of Wilkinson, who were
afterward killed. There was a company of Georgia Border Ruffians
encamped on the Marais des Cygnes, about four miles away from us,
who had been committing outrages upon the Free-State people; and
these proslavery men were in constant communication with them.
They had a courier who went backward and forward carrying messages. When we heard on the Pottawatomie that the Border Ruffians were threatening Lawrence, and that the Free-State men wanted
help, we immediately began to prepare to go to their assistance.
Frederick Brown, son of John Brown, went to a store at Dutch
Henry's Crossing, kept by a Mr. Morse, from Michigan, known as
old Squire Morse, a quiet, inoffensive old Free-State man, living
there with his two boys, and bought some bars of lead, — say twenty
or thirty pounds. He brought the lead to my father's house on Sunday morning, and my brother Henry C. Grant and my sister Mary
spent the whole day in running Sharpe's and other rifle bullets for
the company. As Frederick Brown was bringing this lead to our
house, he passed by Henry Sherman's house, and several proslavery
men, among them Doyle and his sons, William Sherman, and others,
were sitting on the fence, and inquired what he was going to do with
it. He told them he was going to run it into bullets for Free-State
guns. They were apparently much incensed at his reply, as they
knew that the Free-State company was then preparing to go to
Lawrence. The next morning, after the company had started to go
to Lawrence, a number of these proslavery men — Wilkinson, Doyle,
his two sons, and William Sherman, known as 'Dutch Bill' — took
a rope and went to old Squire Morse's house, and said they were
going to hang him for selling the lead to the Free-State men. They
frightened the old man terribly; but finally told him he must leave
the country before eleven o'clock, or they would hang him. They
then left and went to the Shermans' and went to drinking. About

eleven o'clock a portion of them, half drunk, went back to Mr.
Morse's, and were going to kill him with an axe. His little boys —
one was only nine years old — set up a violent crying, and begged
for their father's life. They finally gave him until sundown to leave.
He left everything and came at once to our house. He was nearly
frightened to death. He came to our house carrying a blanket and
leading his little boy by the hand. When night came he was so
afraid that he would not stay in the house, but went out doors and
slept on the prairie in the grass. For a few days he lay about in the
brush, most of the time getting his meals at our house. He was
then taken violently ill and died in a very short time. Dr. Gilpatrick
attended him during his brief illness, and said that his death was
directly caused by the fright and excitement of that terrible day when
he was driven from his store. The only thing they had against Mr.
Morse was his selling the lead, and this he had previously bought of
Henry Sherman, who had brought it from Kansas City. While the
Free-State company was gone to Lawrence, Henry Sherman [1] came
to my father's house and said: 'We have ordered old Morse out of
the country, and he has got to go, and a good many others of the
Free-State families have got to go.' The general feeling among the
Free-State people was one of terror while the company was gone,
as we did not know at what moment the Georgia ruffians might come
in and drive us all out."

[1] Mr. Foster, already quoted, who knew the Shermans and their reputation, tells this story of the brutality of "Dutch Bill," who was one of the
five men executed by Brown : "In the spring of 1856 William Sherman
had taken a fancy to the daughter of one of his Free-State neighbors, and
had been refused by her. The next time he met her he used the most vile
and insulting language toward her, in the midst of which Frederick Brown
appeared and was besought for protection, which was readily granted.
Sherman then drew his knife, and, speaking to the young woman, said :
'The day is soon coming when all the damned Abolitionists will be driven
out or hanged ; we are not going to make any half-way work about it ; and
as for you, Miss, you shall either marry me or I'll drive this knife to the
hilt until I find your life.' Frederick Brown quietly warned Sherman
that if he attempted any violence he would be taken care of ; when, with
an oath and threat, Sherman left them." His viler brother, Henry Sherman, who escaped Brown's avenging hand, was shot not long afterward, I
have heard, by one of Brown's soldiers, — not a member of the party which
slew William Sherman. The chief wonder was, that a wretch so outrageous as Dutch Henry, in a country so full of tumult as Southern Kansas,
had not been killed sooner. His house has long been destroyed, and only
a few apple-trees remain to mark the spot where he lived and persecuted
his Free-State neighbors.

Notwithstanding the controversy which has so long been kept up concerning these executions, the facts are plain and simple, and are now almost universally accepted. The character of the men slain was notoriously bad, as has been shown; and they had long been plotting with the Missourians, and more recently with Buford's armed colonists from the South, to exterminate the Free-State settlers along the Pottawatomie and its tributaries. While the Free-State men were on their way to the defence of Lawrence, and their families were left unprotected, word was sent to the camp of John Brown, Jr., who commanded the Pottawatomie Rifles, that the Free-State families along the Creek were to be attacked and driven out. This news followed hard upon the tidings that Lawrence had been captured and burned by the Missouri ruffians. After that dismal message, John Brown, who was a member of his son's company, proposed marching at once on Lawrence. But word soon came from that town requesting the company not to come, since the ruffians had gone back to Missouri, and the Free-State men were short of provisions. A vote was therefore taken in the company not to visit Lawrence, but to go into camp near the house of Captain Shore on the Middle Ottawa Creek; and this was done on the night of May 22. The place is about five miles from the town of Palmyra, and not more than ten miles from where Brown afterward won the fight of Black Jack. James Hanway, already quoted, was a member of the Pottawatomie Rifles, and a witness of entire credibility. He says : —

"When we were in camp on Middle Ottawa Creek, in Franklin County, a young man, son of Mr. Grant,[1] brought the intelligence that certain proslavery citizens of the Pottawatomie had visited some of the Free-State families, and threatened them with death, and their property with destruction, if they did not leave the neighborhood by the following Saturday or Sunday night. Old John Brown, who had a firm belief that Providence directed his steps in all undertakings, immediately raised a small party of men, and visited those who had been the instigators of this threatened movement. I think it was May 23, about two P. M., that John Brown and his party left our

---

[1] Others say another was the messenger.

17

camp. When Brown was packing up his camp kettles, etc., at Middle Ottawa Creek, I was invited to become one of the party, by one of the eight who formed the company. I was informed at the time of the purpose of the expedition, and the necessity there was to carry out the programme.

"The following day we camped at Palmyra. We had heard of the arrest of Governor Robinson, and our object was to rescue him if they brought him by the Santa Fé road to Lecompton. On Sunday morning, May 25, we broke camp, and took up quarters near Prairie City, on Liberty Hill. It was then and there that four persons came riding across the prairie, and reported what had taken place on the Pottawatomie. That night we camped in the yard of Ottawa Jones, and during the night John Brown's party, who had left our company *several days before,* made their appearance. I was with Jason Brown in what was called the Brown tent. John Brown asked if his son John was there. I replied no; he was in Ottawa Jones's house. This was about the middle of the night."

Between the departure of John Brown from his son's camp early in the afternoon of May 23, and his return thereto in the night of May 25–26, the deed of death was done. Those who accomplished it were under Brown's orders, and were directed in all their movements by him. Of this there is now no doubt, although at the time, and for many years afterward, John Brown's presence at the executions was denied; and this denial was supposed to be supported by his words. But upon inquiry of all those who talked with him on the subject, it does not appear that he ever denied his presence at the scene, while he constantly justified the act. One of the earliest witnesses has already been cited, — Jason Brown. John Brown, Jr., was not informed of the deed by his father. An old Kansas settler, E. A. Coleman, now living near Lawrence, where he was in 1855–56, bears witness thus: —

"John Brown frequently visited me at my house, and stayed with me. In fact, my latch-string was always out for such men. John Brown knew where his friends lived, and could go to them night or day. One evening, not long before the fight at Osawatomie, we ate supper out of doors in the shade of my cabin at five o'clock. As soon as supper was over, Captain Brown commenced pacing back and forth in the shade of the house. My wife stood by the dishes, and I sat in my chair. I finally said, 'Captain Brown, I want to ask you one question, and you can answer it or not as you please, and I shall not be offended.' He stopped his pacing, looked me square in the face, and said, 'What is it?' Said I, 'Captain Brown, did you kill those five men on the Pottawatomie, or did you not?' He replied, 'I did not; but I do not pretend to say they were not killed by my order; and in doing so I believe I was doing God's service.' My wife spoke and said, 'Then, Captain, you think that God uses you as an instrument in his hands to kill men?' Brown replied, 'I think he has used me as an instrument to kill men; and if I live, I think he will use me as an instrument to kill a good many more.' He went on and said: 'Mr. Coleman, I will tell you all about it, and you can judge whether I did right or wrong. I had heard that these men were coming to the cabin that my son and I were staying in [I think he said the next Wednesday night] to set fire to it and shoot us as we ran out. Now, that was not proof enough for me; but I thought I would satisfy myself, and if they had committed murder in their hearts, I would be justified in killing them. I was an old surveyor, so I disguised myself, took two men to carry the chain, and a flagman. The lines not being run, I knew that as soon as they saw me they would come out to find out where their lines would come.' And taking a book from his pocket, he said, 'Here is what every man said that was killed. I ran my lines close to each man's house. The first that came out said, "Is that my line, sir?" I replied, "I cannot tell; I am running test lines." I then said to him, "You have a fine country here; great pity there are so many Abolitionists in it." "Yes, but by God we will soon clean them all out," he said. I kept looking through my instrument, making motions to the flagman to move either way, and at the same time I wrote every word they said. Then I said, "I hear there are some bad men about here by the name of Brown." "Yes, there are; but next Wednesday night we will kill them." So I ran the lines by each one of their houses, and I took down every word; and here it is, word for word, by each one. [Shows wife and me the book]. I was satisfied that each one of them had committed murder in his heart, and according to the Scriptures they were guilty of murder, and I felt justified in having them killed; but, as I told you, I did not do it myself.' He then said, 'Now, Mr. Coleman, what do you think?' I told him I thought he did right, and so did my wife. This statement we are both willing to be sworn to."[1]

[1] See "The Kansas Memorial," 1879, pp. 196, 197. I have a letter from Mr. Coleman, written in 1885, in which he repeats this striking conversation, with some variations, but in substance as recited above. He says :

John Brown, Jr., has thus expressed himself concerning the mystery which long concealed the true facts in this affair; and no person who knows him will doubt his word:

"The only statement that I ever heard my father make in regard to this was, 'I did not myself kill any of those men at Pottawatomie, but I am as fully responsible as if I did.' This statement of his is strictly in accordance with the facts, as I have now abundant evidence. The statements of others, giving a different version, I believe

"The Browns were hunted as we hunt wolves to-day; and because they undertook to protect themselves, they are called cold-blooded murderers, — merely because they 'had the dare,' and were contented to live and die as God intended them to. Brown was a Bible-man, — he believed it all; and though I am not, I give him credit for being honest, and the most consistent so-called Christian I have ever met. Brown and his sons had claims, and worked them, as I did mine, when these devils were not prowling about, killing a man now and then, stealing our stock and running them off to Missouri."

John Brown, Jr.'s, version of the surveying adventure, and doubtless the more correct one, is as follows: "Early in the spring of 1856, Colonel Buford, of Alabama, arrived with a regiment of armed men, mostly from South Carolina and Georgia. They came with the openly declared purpose to make Kansas a slave State at all hazards. A company of these men was reported to us as being encamped near the Marais des Cygnes, a little south of the town now called Rantoul, I think, and distant from our place about two miles. Father took his surveyor's compass, and with him four of my brothers, — Owen, Frederick, Salmon, and Oliver, — as chain-carriers, axman, and marker, and found a section line which, on following, led through the camp of these men. The Georgians indulged in the utmost freedom of expression. One of them, who appeared to be the leader of the company, said: 'We've come here to stay. We won't make no war on them as minds their own business; but all the Abolitionists, such as them damned Browns over there, we're going to whip, drive out, or kill, — any way to get shut of them, by God.' The elder Doyle was already there among them, having come from the Pottawatomie, a distance of nine miles, to show them the best fords of the river and creek."

Upon reading Mr. Coleman's letter, John Brown has written me thus: "While we had in the spring of 1856 abundant and entirely satisfactory evidence that our family were marked for destruction, I am not aware of any information having been received by any of our number that a particular day had been decided upon for the undertaking. It is probable that father related to Mr. Coleman the story of his running that line through a camp of Buford's men and of the information he obtained; but further than this I think he did not go. The running of that line occurred a few days before our second call to assist Lawrence, May 20, 1856."

have been made in good faith upon reports which they supposed were true, or upon their interpretation of father's words as given above. I have yet to learn of any authentic statement made by him touching this matter which in substance differs from his words as I have given them. In the fall of 1856 I was told by one who as I supposed was in possession of the facts, that when my father and his men, on their return from our camp near Ottawa Creek, had reached Middle Creek, his party divided; that he and some of the men crossed the Marais des Cygnes to reconnoitre the position of a party of Buford's men, and that consequently he was several miles away when those men were killed on the Pottawatomie. I accepted this statement as true, and whenever I had occasion to refer to the matter I stated it in accordance with what I supposed was fact. It was not until July, 1860, that I was more correctly informed by one who had himself participated in that affair. At that time a large reward was offered by the State of Virginia for my capture. Soon after, stimulated by that reward, kidnappers attempted the work of my abduction; and from that time until the close of the Civil War other matters more urgent claimed my attention than the correction of my own statements in regard to Pottawatomie, or of Mr. Redpath's mistake, which I have no doubt was as innocently made as my own." [1]

The most direct statement made by any of the party who accompanied John Brown on his expedition of May 23, that was made public before the Civil War, is, I think, a letter from one of his sons, who undertook, a few weeks after his father's death, to answer a question on the subject which was asked of his mother. She had no knowledge concerning the matter, as she told me in 1882; but knowing that her son Salmon had been Brown's constant companion in Kansas, she requested him to reply. He was then living with her at North Elba, and he wrote as follows: —

NORTH ELBA, Dec. 27, 1859.

DEAR SIR, — Your letter to my mother was received to-night. You wish me to give you the facts in regard to the Pottawatomie execution, or murder, and to know whether my father was a participator in the act. I was one of his company at the time of the homicide, and was never away from him one hour at a time after we took up arms in Kansas; therefore I say positively that he was not a

[1] In confirmation of this, I may say that my last letters from Mr. Redpath continued to declare that John Brown was not at the executions.

participator in the deed, — although I should think none the less of him if he had been there; for it was the grandest thing that was ever done in Kansas. It was all that saved the Territory from being overrun with drunken land-pirates from the Southern States. That was the first act in the history of Kansas which proved to the demon of Slavery that there was as much room to give blows as to take them. It was done to save life, and to strike terror through their wicked ranks.

Yours respectfully,

SALMON BROWN.

The member of Brown's company of eight who first disclosed the details of the expedition of May 23–25, was James Townsley, a Maryland man, who had emigrated to Kansas in October, 1855, and settled on the Pottawatomie, a mile west of the present town of Greeley. This is several miles southwest of Dutch Henry's Crossing, and therefore higher up on the creek. Townsley had been a cavalry soldier in the United States army from 1839 to 1844, and had fought against Indians in Florida; by trade he was a painter, and he was an acquaintance of Martin and Jefferson Conway, who like himself migrated from Maryland to Kansas, but were opposed to slavery. He set out from Baltimore with his wife and four children and eleven hundred dollars in money, and, leaving his family in Kansas City, went into the Pottawatomie region and bought a "claim," for which he paid eighty dollars, put up a rude cabin, and moved his family into it. They suffered much from cold during the winter, and were just beginning to plant their land in the spring, when Townsley, who had joined the "Pottawatomie Rifles" in April, was called upon to march for the protection of Lawrence. This was on the afternoon of May 21. What followed has thus been told by himself: —

"About two miles south of Middle Creek we were joined by the Osawatomie company, under Captain Dayton, and proceeded to Mount Vernon, where we waited about two hours until the moon rose. We then marched all night, camping the next morning (the 22d) for breakfast, near Ottawa Jones's. Before we arrived at this point news had been received that Lawrence had been destroyed, and a question was raised whether we should return or go on. During the forenoon, however, we proceeded up Ottawa Creek to within

1856.] THE POTTAWATOMIE EXECUTIONS.

about five miles of Palmyra, and went into camp near the residence of Captain Shore. Here we remained undecided over night. About noon the next day, the 23d, old John Brown came to me and said he had just received information that trouble was expected on the Pottawatomie, and wanted to know if I would take my team and take him and his boys back, so that they could keep watch of what was going on. I told him I would do so. The party — consisting of John Brown, Frederick Brown, Owen Brown, Watson Brown, Oliver Brown, Henry Thompson (John Brown's son-in-law), and Mr. Wiener — were soon ready for the trip, and we started, as near as I can remember, about two o'clock P. M. All of the party except Mr. Wiener, who rode a pony, rode with me in my wagon. When within two or three miles of the Pottawatomie Creek we turned off the main road to the right, drove down into the edge of the timber between two deep ravines, and camped about one mile above Dutch Henry's Crossing. After my team was fed and the party had taken supper, John Brown told me for the first time what he proposed to do. He said he wanted me to pilot the company up to the forks of the creek, some five or six miles above, into the neighborhood in which I lived, and show them where all the proslavery men resided; that he proposed to sweep the creek as he came down of all the proslavery men living on it. I positively refused to do it. He insisted upon it; but when he found that I would not go he decided to postpone the expedition until the following night. I then wanted to take my team and go home, but he refused to let me do so, and said I should remain with them. We remained in camp that night and all day the next day. Sometime after dark we were ordered to march."

Townsley has related, not always in the same manner, and with more or less variation from the fact (as in the above statement, which is somewhat incorrect, though mainly true), how the five men were called out and despatched, — alleging that he had no hand in the actual slaughter, but that John Brown had.[1] I have talked with those present, and find reason to doubt this. Whatever Townsley's part may have been, I am convinced that John Brown did not raise his own hand or discharge his weapon against his victims. He was no less responsible for their death than if he had done so, and this he never denied. But for some reason he chose not to strike a blow himself; and this is what Salmon Brown meant when he declared that his father " was

[1] Owen Brown and Henry Thompson deny this.

not a participator in the deed." It was a very narrow interpretation of the word "participator" which would permit
such a denial; but it was no doubt honestly made, although
for the purpose of disguising what John Brown's real agency
in the matter was. He was, in fact, the originator and per-
former of these executions, although the hands that dealt
the wounds were those of others. The actual executioners
were but three or four. The weapons used were short cutlasses, or artillery sabres, which had been originally worn by
a military company in Ohio, and were brought from Akron
in 1855 by John Brown.[1] They were straight and broad,
like an old Roman sword, and were freshly ground for this
expedition at the camp of John Brown, Jr.[2] When the
bodies of the dead were found, there went up a cry that they
had been mutilated; but this was because of the weapons
used. Their death was speedy and with little noise, the use
of fire-arms being forbidden. A single shot was fired during
the five executions; but when, and for what purpose, the
witnesses are in dispute. The Doyles were first slain, then

---

[1] The swords used were not sabres exactly, but weapons made like the
Roman short-sword, of which six or eight had been given to Brown in
Akron, Ohio, just before he went to Kansas, by General Bierce of that
city, who took them from an old armory there. They had been the swords
of an artillery company, then disbanded, which General Bierce had something to do with, and there were also some guns and old bayonets among
these arms. The bayonets would not fit any guns the Kansas people
had ; and so in December, 1855, when the Browns went up to defend
Lawrence for the first time, they fastened some of them on sticks, and
intended to use them in defending breastworks. They were thrown
loosely "into the bed of the wagon," — not set up about it for parade, as
some have said. There were also some curved swords among these Akron
arms.

[2] When Brown called for volunteers to go on a secret expedition, his son
at first questioned the wisdom of reducing his main force in this way ; but
as only eight men were wanted no serious opposition was made, and John
Brown, Jr., says : "We aided him in his outfit, and I assisted in the
sharpening of his cutlasses. James Townsley, who resided near Pottawatomie Creek, volunteered to return with his team, and offered to point out
the abodes of such as he thought should be disposed of. No man of our
entire number could fail to understand that a retaliatory blow would fall ;
yet when father and his little band departed, they were saluted by all our
men with a rousing cheer." All the survivors of the " little band," except
Townsley, deny that Brown " proposed to sweep the creek."

Wilkinson; and finally the Shermans were visited, their guests captured and questioned, but only William Sherman executed. The testimony of James Harris, one of the comrades of William Sherman, who was allowed to go unpunished, was given in these words before the Congressional Committee of 1856:[1]—

"On Sunday morning, May 25, 1856, about two A. M., while my wife and child and myself were in bed in the house where we lived, near Henry Sherman's, we were aroused by a company of men who said they belonged to the Northern army, and who were each armed with a sabre and two revolvers, two of whom I recognized; namely, a Mr. Brown, whose given name I do not remember (commonly known by the appellation of ' old man Brown'), and his son Owen Brown. They came into the house and approached the bedside where we were lying, and ordered us, together with three other men who were in the same house with me, to surrender; that the Northern army was upon us, and it would be no use for us to resist. The names of these other men who were then in the house with me were William Sherman and John S. Whiteman ; the other man I did not know. They were stopping with me that night. They had bought a cow from Henry Sherman, and intended to go home the next morning. When they came up to the bed, some had drawn sabres in their hands, and some revolvers. They then took into their possession two rifles and a bowie-knife, which I had there in the room (there was but one room in my house), and afterwards ransacked the whole establishment in search of ammunition. They then took one of these three men, who were staying in my house, out. (This was the man whose name I did not know.) He came back. They then took me out, and asked me if there were any more men about the place. I told them there were not. They searched the place, but found no others but us four. They asked me where Henry Sherman was. (Henry was a brother to William Sherman.) I told them he was out on the plains in search of some cattle which he had lost. They asked me if I had ever taken any hand in aiding proslavery men in coming to the Territory of Kansas, or had ever taken any hand in the last troubles at Lawrence ; they asked me whether I had ever done the Free-State party any harm, or ever intended to do that party any harm ; they asked me what made

---

[1] James Hanway, who talked with Harris more than once after the affair, says that this testimony differed from the accounts Harris privately gave.

me live at such a place. I then answered that I could get higher
wages there than anywhere else. They asked me if there were any
bridles or saddles about the premises. I told them there was one
saddle, which they took; and they also took possession of Henry
Sherman's horse, which I had at my place, and made me saddle him.
They then said if I would answer no to all the questions which they
had asked me, they would let me loose. Old Mr. Brown and his son
then went into the house with me. The other three men — Mr. William Sherman, Mr. Whiteman, and the stranger — were in the house
all this time. After old man Brown and his son went into the
house with me, old man Brown asked Mr. Sherman to go out with
him; and Mr. Sherman then went out with old Mr. Brown, and another man came into the house in Brown's place. I heard nothing
more for about fifteen minutes. Two of the Northern army, as they
styled themselves, stayed in with us until we heard a cap burst, and
then these two men left. That morning, about ten o'clock, I found
William Sherman dead in the creek near my house. I was looking
for him; as he had not come back, I thought he had been murdered.
I took Mr. William Sherman out of the creek and examined him.
Mr. Whiteman was with me. Sherman's skull was split open in
two places, and some of his brains was washed out by the water. A
large hole was cut in his breast, and his left hand was cut off except
a little piece of skin on one side. We buried him."

Mr. Hanway used to declare that this James Harris told
him that when the avenging party first entered the house
his wife supposed they were Missouri men, arrived there for
the purpose of driving out the Free-State settlers. Mrs.
Wilkinson, an unfortunate woman who had tried in vain to
keep her husband from engaging in the outrages against
their Free-State neighbors, was visited early in the morning after the executions by Dr. Gilpatrick and Mr. Grant,
two Free-State men, who went to her house (which was the
post-office) to get their mail. They found the poor woman
weeping, and saying that a party of men had been to the
house during the night and taken her husband out; she had
heard that morning that Mr. Doyle had been killed within
the night, and she was afraid that her husband had been
killed also. Among other reasons that she gave for fearing
this, he had said to her the night before that there was going
to be an attack made upon the Free-State men, and that
by the next Saturday night there would not be a Free-State

settler left on the creek.   These, she said, were his last
words to her the night before as they were going to sleep.
Her testimony before the Congressional Committee was as
follows : —

. . . "On the 25th of May last, somewhere between the hours of
midnight and daybreak, I cannot say exactly at what hour, after we
all had retired to bed, we were disturbed by the barking of the dog.
I was sick with the measles, and woke up Mr. Wilkinson, and asked
him if he heard the noise, and what it meant.   He said it was only
some one passing about, and soon after was again asleep.   It was
not long before the dog raged and barked furiously, awakening me
once more ; pretty soon I heard footsteps as of men approaching ;
saw one pass by the window, and some one knocked at the door.   I
asked, ' Who is that ? '   No one answered.   I awoke my husband,
who asked, ' Who is that ? '   Some one replied, ' I want you to
tell me the way to Dutch Henry's.'   He commenced to tell them,
and they said, ' Come out and show us.'   He wanted to go, but I
would not let him ; he then told them it was difficult to find his
clothes, and could tell them as well without going out of doors.   The
men out of doors after that stepped back, and I thought I could hear
them whispering ; but they immediately returned, and as they approached, one of them asked my husband, ' Are you a Northern
armist ? '   He answered, ' I am.'   I understood the answer to
mean that my husband was opposed to the Northern or Free-Soil
party.   I cannot say that I understood the question.   My husband
was a proslavery man, and was a member of the Territorial Legislature held at Shawnee Mission.   When my husband said, ' I am,'
one of them said, ' You are my prisoner ; do you surrender ? '   He
said, ' Gentlemen, I do.'   They said, ' Open the door.'   Mr. Wilkinson told them to wait till he made a light, and they replied, ' If
you don't open it, we will open it for you.'   He opened the door
against my wishes ; four men came in to ; my husband was told to put
on his clothes, and they asked him if there were not more men about.
They searched for arms, and took a gun and powder-flask, — all the
weapon that was about the house.   I begged them to let Mr. Wilkinson stay with me, saying that I was sick and helpless, and could
not stay by myself.   The old man, who seemed to be in command,
looked at me, and then around at the children, and replied, ' You
have neighbors.'   I said, ' So I have ; but they are not here, and I
cannot go for them.'   The old man replied, ' It matters not.'   They
then took my husband away.   One of them came back and took two
saddles ; I asked what they were going to do with him, and he said,
' Take him a prisoner to the camp.'   I wanted one of them to stay

with me. He said 'he would, but they would not let him.' After
they were gone, I thought I heard my husband's voice in complaint,
but do not know; went to the door, and all was still.   Next morning Mr. Wilkinson was found about one hundred and fifty yards from
the house, in some dead brush. I believe that one of Captain Brown's
sons was in the party who murdered my husband; I heard a voice
like his. I do not know Captain Brown himself. The old man who
seemed to be commander wore soiled clothes and a straw hat, pulled
down over his face. He spoke quick; is a tall, narrow-faced,
elderly man. I would recognize him if I could see him.   My husband was a quiet man, and was not engaged in arresting or disturbing
anybody." [1]

There is little reason to doubt that this account is substantially correct. The particulars of the action, like the
deed itself, were bloody, and it is not pleasant to read them
or relate them; but they were the opening scenes of war, and
in requital for bloodier and quite inexcusable deeds which
had preceded them. Brown long foresaw the deadly conflict
with the slave-power, which culminated in the Civil War, and
was eager to begin it, that it might be the sooner over. He
knew — what few could then believe — that slavery must
perish in blood; [2] and, though a peaceful man, he had no
scruples about shedding blood in so good a cause. The
American people a few years after engaged in organized
bloodshed for the attack and defence of slavery, and hundreds
of thousands of men died in the cause that Brown had killed
and been killed to maintain. Yet we who praise Grant for
those military movements which caused the bloody death
of thousands, are so inconsistent as to denounce Brown for
the death of these five men in Kansas. If Brown was a
murderer, then Grant and Sherman, and Hancock and the
other Union generals, are tenfold murderers, — for they
simply did on a grand scale what he did on a small one.
War is murder, — in one of its aspects it is deliberate and
repeated murder; and yet the patriot warrior who goes

[1] On the contrary, Mr. Grant and his other neighbors speak of him as
a vicious, malignant man, who ill-treated his wife as well as the Free-State
men.

[2] "Without the shedding of blood there is no remission of sins," was a
favorite text with Brown.

to battle in behalf of his country is not arraigned for murder, but honored as a hero. This is so even when by stratagem, or midnight assault, he slays hundreds of defenceless people; for the cause in which he fights is supposed to excuse all atrocious deeds. A like excuse must serve for this violent but salutary act of John Brown; [1] and it was in this way that he defended it to those who served under him, and by whose hands the deed was done. I have talked with more than one of these men, and from one of them I had this statement: —

" John Brown did no shooting in my presence, and I think he had nothing to do with the killing of any of the five men. At a consultation on Middle Creek the question came up who would join; I opposed the scheme for a time, and ——— opposed it all the time, and had nothing to do with it, except that he went along with us. John Brown thought it a matter of duty that there should be a little bloodletting on both sides; he not only approved these executions, but planned and carried them through very successfully.[2] I reflected that these men were influential persons, leading men, and among the worst holding office [referring particularly to Wilkinson and George Wilson], and I agreed with Brown it was a matter of duty; yet I

[1] Charles Robinson, who had as many minds about the Pottawatomie affair as his Democratic friends used to have about slavery itself, characterized it thus in a letter of Dec. 21, 1879, published in the Topeka "Commonwealth" of Jan. 8, 1880 (he has since called John Brown all sorts of names, *jussit quod splendida bilis*): "It had the effect to strike terror into the hearts of all proslavery men, and had its influence in the general melee. The proslavery party could take no exceptions to it, as it had inaugurated the war, and all the Free-State men can say in its defence is, it was an incident of the civil war set on foot by the slave-power. . . . But was John Brown at heart a murderer in this butchery? I think not. He worshipped the God of Joshua and David, who ordered all the enemies of his people slaughtered, including non-combatants, women, and children, flocks and herds, and ' everything that breathed.' John Brown seemed to believe he was the special messenger and servant of this God ; and he may have been as sincere as was Abraham when he stretched forth his hand to take the knife to slay his own son, or as Joshua when he slaughtered all that breathed of his enemies."

[2] The following anecdote is said to rest on the testimony of James Christian, a Kansas Democrat. How good authority this may be I cannot say, but give it as I find it: "Jerome Glanville was the man who was stopping at Dutch Henry's on the night of the massacre, and was taken out to be killed, as the others were. On examination he was found

was opposed to doing it myself. I saw the inconsistency of this, and afterwards *acted consistently.* I had seen Doyle and his boys two or three times, and knew them; they harbored the worst ruffians, and I thought them as guilty as if they had done the deeds themselves. There was a signal understood, and no firing done in the first operation (at Doyle's). The signal was when John Brown was to raise a sword; then we were to begin, and there were to be no shots fired. I heard but one shot when I was keeping guard over the family of Henry Sherman; it was fired down the creek, half a mile away, and I did not know what it meant. The antislavery people in the Territory disapproved of the killing, — Mr. Adair among them. He said to one of us, 'You are a marked man. You see what a terrible calamity you have brought upon your friends, and the sooner you go away the better.' The reply was, 'I intend to be a marked man.' The Border Ruffians had for their watchword 'War to the knife, and the knife to the hilt,' in the spring before the Pottawatomie executions; after that, they thought the knife might come from the other side. Liberty can only live or survive by the shedding of blood."

Townsley declares that when he and others of the party were unwilling to slay men taken by surprise and unarmed, John Brown argued that it was a just and necessary stroke of war; and said, "It is better that ten guilty proslavery men should die, than that one Free-State settler should be driven out." Townsley adds that he was unwilling to have the proslavery men who lived in his neighborhood (Anderson County, near Greeley) attacked by Brown, because some of them were good men, and others had wives who had been kind to his wife. He thought as ill as Brown did of the proslavery probate judge Wilson, then supposed to be at Dutch Henry's, and was willing to have the attack made there. He was also ready to go to the Doyles, who, "when they had drunk a little whiskey, were ready to do what-

to be only a traveller, but was kept a prisoner until morning and then discharged. He informed me personally who were the principal actors in that damning midnight tragedy, and said that the next morning, while the old man raised his hands to Heaven to ask a blessing, they were stained with the dried blood of his victims. For being too free in his expressions about the matter he was soon after shot in his wagon, between Black Jack and the head of Bull Creek, while on his way to Kansas City."

ever Dutch Henry told them." According to Townsley, Wilkinson was born in the North, but had married a Tennessee wife, and adopted her view of slavery; he was the postmaster at Shermansville (now called Lane), and was an active proslavery leader, like Henry Sherman and George Wilson.[1] Townsley and all the witnesses agree that the horses of the Shermans were taken and carried with the party to the camp of John Brown, Jr., near Ottawa Jones's, where they arrived late on the night of the 24th. The next morning Oliver Brown showed his brother John a horse with his mane and tail sheared, saying, "Did you ever see that horse before? That is Dutch Henry's gray pony." This horse was soon after taken to northern Kansas by some Free-State men, who gave in exchange for that and other horses captured on the Pottawatomie some fast Kentucky horses, on one of which Owen Brown afterward escaped from his pursuers. August Bondi says of the executions: —

"Late in the evening of May 25 I arrived at my claim, in company with an old neighbor, Austin, who was afterward named Old Kill Devil, from a rifle he had of that name. The family of Benjamin (whom we had left when we departed for camp) had disappeared, and no cattle were to be seen. This latter was a serious matter, for there was nothing left in the shape of provisions. When I told Austin that I was willing to stay with him until the last of the Border Ruffians had left the country, he encouraged me, and assured me that he would find Benjamin's family and protect them at all events. This the old man faithfully did. The next evening (May 26) I arrived, tired and hungry, at the camping-ground of John Brown, a log-cabin on the banks of Middle Creek upon the claim of his brother-in-law Orson Day. This is one of the houses which, under the name of 'John Brown's cabin,' has since become famous. The Browns built it as a first shelter in the winter of 1855–56, and Day dwelt

---

[1] Mrs. Rising, a New Hampshire woman, who then lived next neighbor to the Wilkinsons, told a friend of mine that she knew Mrs. Wilkinson very well before and after the killing of her husband; that Mrs. Wilkinson said she had persuaded him to take the proslavery side, but was sorry for it, since he was a worse man after it than before, and had treated her badly. Mrs. Rising added that he was harsh and cruel to his wife, who was a delicate, sickly woman; and that he was a bad man in other respects.

in it after March, 1856. It stands west from Osawatomie on the
bottom land of North Middle Creek. Here also I found my friend
Wiener,[1] from whom I first heard an account of the killing of Doyle
and his sons, Wilkinson, and Dutch Henry's brother William. In
this account Wiener never expressed himself positively as to who
killed those persons, and I could only guess about it. I was astonished, but not at all displeased. The men killed had been our
neighbors, and I was sufficiently acquainted with their characters
to know that they were of the stock from which afterwards came the
James brothers, the Youngers, and the rest, who never shrank from
perpetrating crime if it was done in the interest of the proslavery
cause. As to their antecedents, — the Doyles had been 'slave-
hunters' before they came to Kansas, and had brought along two of
their blood-hounds. Dutch Bill (Sherman), — a German from
Oldenburg, and a resident of Kansas since 1845, — had amassed considerable property by robbing cattle droves and emigrant trains. He
was a giant, six feet four inches high, and for the last weeks before
his death had made it his pastime (in company with the Doyles) to
break in the doors of Free-State settlers, frightening and insulting
the families, or once in a while attacking and ill-treating a man
whom they encountered alone. Wilkinson was one of the few
Southerners who were able to read and write, and who prided himself accordingly. He was a member of the Border Ruffian Legislature, and a principal leader in all attempts to annoy and extirpate
the Free-State men. Although he never directly participated in the
murders and robberies, still it was well understood that he was always
informed a short time before an invasion of Missourians was to occur ;
and on the very day of his death he had tauntingly said to some Free-
State men that in a few days the last of them would be either dead
or out of the Territory. In this he referred to the coming invasion
of Cook, at the head of two hundred and fifty armed men from Bates
County, Mo., who made his appearance about the 27th of May and
plundered the whole region."

A startling tale has been told, but without good authority,
concerning the effect produced in the camp on the Ottawa

[1] Wiener, who took part in the Pottawatomie executions, was residing
in St. Louis, September, 1855, but then agreed with Benjamin to go to
Kansas and open a store on Bondi's claim. He invested some $7,000 in
goods, and took them to Kansas just after Bondi had gone back to St.
Louis, in November. In May, 1856, Wiener went there to buy more
goods, and Bondi returned to Kansas with him. Wiener furnished as a
gift all the provisions needed by the two rifle companies of sixty-five men,
when they set out for Lawrence.

by the return of John Brown, — how his son resigned the command and became insane, and how general was the execration against Brown for his bloody deed. No doubt it was regretted by most of the company, and it is true that John Brown, Jr., resigned his captaincy. But this was for other reasons, and the insanity which soon appeared had other causes. Jason Brown, who was in his brother's company, says: "On the afternoon of Monday, May 26, a man came to us at Liberty Hill (eight miles north of Ottawa Jones's house), his horse reeking with sweat, and said, 'Five men have been killed on the Pottawatomie, horribly cut and mangled; and they say old John Brown did it.' Hearing this, I was afraid it was true, and it was the most terrible shock that ever happened to my feelings in my life; but brother John took a different view. The next day, as we were on the east side of Middle Creek, I asked father, 'Did you have any hand in the killing?' He said, 'I did not, but I stood by and saw it.' I did not ask further, for fear I should hear something I did not wish to hear. Frederick said, 'I could not feel as if it was right;' but another of the party said it was justifiable as a means of self-defence and the defence of others. What I said against it seemed to hurt father very much; but all he said was, 'God is my judge, — we were justified under the circumstances.'" The occasion upon which John Brown, Jr., resigned his command had occurred the day before, — the setting free by him of some slaves, who were afterward returned to their master. On the Sunday following the Pottawatomie executions, but before the tidings reached him, he had gone with Captain Abbott, the rescuer of Branson, to see the ruins of Lawrence, and on his way back with a file of men, John Brown, Jr., liberated two slaves from their Missouri master, near Palmyra, and took them up to his camp, while the master fled to Missouri.

The arrival of these slaves in camp caused a commotion. The act of freeing them, though attended by no violence or bloodshed, was freely denounced, and in accordance with a vote given by a large majority of the men they were ordered to go back to their master. The driver of the team which carried them back, overtaking him on his way to

18

Westport, received a side-saddle as his reward from the grateful slaveholder. Young Brown, feeling insulted by this act of his men, refused to command them any longer. But in the mean time (so fast did events move that day), while the company from Osawatomie was still at Liberty Hill, two or three miles south of Palmyra, a company of United States dragoons came up, and their leader, a lieutenant, asked to see the commander of the Free-State force. John Brown, Jr., who had not yet resigned, sent word that if the lieutenant would come forward without his men he (Brown) would meet him. Thereupon, says John Brown, Jr., " A solitary horseman from their number came toward us, and I rode out and met him. He introduced himself as Lieutenant Ives, if I am not mistaken, and told me that he had been sent by Colonel Sumner, then in command of the Federal troops in Kansas, with an order for all armed bodies of men on either side to disperse and return to their homes, — adding that Colonel Sumner had undertaken to prevent hostile meetings of armed men. The lieutenant hoped we would not delay in complying with the order, and further said that he was then on his way to disperse the force of Georgians, who, he had been informed, were in camp a few miles east. He and his men then rode away in that direction, while I returned and related what the lieutenant had said. It gave much satisfaction; for we were all anxious to be at home and attend to the planting of our spring crops, which had seemed likely to be prevented, in accordance with the openly avowed plan of our enemies. We did not return to our first place of encampment, but at once began our homeward march, and reached Ottawa Jones's place, where we met my father, about ten o'clock that evening." The attack of insanity, which came on after this, does not seem to have been caused by the news from Pottawatomie, but by the hardships, exposure, and anxiety to which John Brown, Jr., had been subjected, and which were soon to be redoubled by the harsh treatment of his captors

The tidings of the executions inflamed the Border Ruffians greatly, as was natural, and gave an excuse for the activity of the Federal troops on the side of the slaveholders. Warrants had already been issued for the arrest of the Browns as conspirators against the Territorial government; and these were now served by civil officers who had a strong military force behind them. We saw in the last chapter John Brown's explanation of his sons' capture.[1] I will now give in the words of those sons the events accompanying it. John Brown, Jr., says : —

" We got back to Osawatomie from our five days' campaign, toward evening on the 26th of May. The same night I went to the house of Mr. Adair, where I found my wife and son, Jason and his wife and their little boy. Jason and I remained there all night; but next morning, learning that a man named Hughes, of Osawatomie, a pretended Free-State man, was heading a party to capture us, Mr. Adair did not consider it prudent for us to stay longer, and advised us to secrete ourselves in a ravine on his place well filled with small undergrowth. He told us he had received word that the United States Marshal had warrants for us and all of our family, — also for Mr. Williams, William Partridge, and several others, — and that Hughes wanted to distinguish himself by taking us, though pretending to be friendly. Jason started at once on foot for Lawrence, saying that if there was a warrant out for him he would go there and give himself up to a United States officer rather than be taken by a *posse* made up of Missourians and Buford's men. While on his way to Lawrence he was captured near Stanton (now called Rantoul) by just such a gang as he hoped to avoid, and was taken at once to Paola, then called Baptisteville. I took my rifle and horse and went into the ravine on Mr. Adair's land, remaining there through that day (May 27) and the following night. About four o'clock P. M. I was joined by my brother Owen, who had been informed at Mr. Adair's of my whereabouts. He brought with him into the brush a valuable running horse, mate of the one I had with me. These horses had been taken by Free-State men near the Nebraska line and exchanged for horses obtained in the way of reprisals further south ; and while on foot a few miles south of Ottawa Jones's place, May 26, I had been offered one of these to ride the remaining distance to Osawatomie. Owen's horse was wet with sweat; and he told me of the narrow escape he had just had from a number of armed proslavery men who had their headquarters at Tooley's, — a house at the foot of the hill, about a mile and a half west of Mr. Adair's. Their guards, seeing him in the road coming down the hill, gave a signal,

---

[1] See Brown's Second Campaign in Kansas, p. 237.

and at once the whole gang were in hot chase. The superior fleet-
ness of the horse Owen rode alone saved him. He exchanged horses
with me, and that night forded the Marais des Cygnes, and going by
Stanton (or Standiford, as it was sometimes called), recrossed the
river to father's camp about a mile north of the house of Mr. Day.
Until Owen told me that night, I did not know where father could be
found. The next morning early I went to Mr. Adair's house; and
was there but a few moments when there suddenly rode up a number
of United States cavalry, whom I was quite willing to see; but while
in conversation with them a large number of mounted Missourians
came up also, and with them the United States Marshal, whom I
knew, but did not wish to see. He read to me a warrant for my
arrest, which charged me with treason against the United States.
Resistance was of course out of the question. It was then I discovered that the soldiers were there simply as a *posse* to aid the
marshal; and I went along in a wagon accompanied by all of
these as far as where Captain Wood of the cavalry had his camp,
near Osawatomie, when the soldiers returned to their camp, and
the others went on with me to Paola. There I found Jason and
several others of our men, including Mr. Williams, Mr. Partridge,
and, I think, Mr. Benjamin."

Such were the adventures of one brother, before he joined
the other in captivity at Baptisteville,[1] now called Paola.
Jason's adventures were even more romantic. He had
parted from his father, May 26, early in the morning, after
the conversation already quoted, and had returned with a
heavy heart to Osawatomie, where his family were. His
brother John was suffering from his sleepless anxieties, although he afterward became much worse;[2] and the conduct

[1] This is a town of some importance between Osawatomie and the
Missouri border, and about ten miles northeast of Mr. Adair's house.
Its name in 1856 (pronounced colloquially "Batteesville") was given
in honor of an Indian, — Baptiste Peoria, — from whose last name, by
corruption, the present title of the town seems to be derived. It was a
proslavery settlement at that time, while Osawatomie was celebrated for
its antislavery character.

[2] Mr. Adair told me, when I visited him in 1882, among his orchards
and vines at Osawatomie, that John Brown, Jr., was "beside himself"
when he came to the Adair place Monday night, May 26, with Jason; that
he had been without sleep several nights, and was perhaps disturbed also
by the killing of the Doyles, etc. Thinking him in such a condition as
made it unsafe to have him, fully armed, in the house, some of his friends,

of his father at Pottawatomie weighed on Jason's compassionate mind. His uncle Adair could give them no protection, and was endangered himself by their presence. Jason therefore set forth alone and on foot across the prairie north of the Marais des Cygnes, to go back to the friendly house of Ottawa Jones, the Christian Indian, and thence to Lawrence, where he meant to give himself up to " Uncle Sam's " troops, and not to the Border Ruffians. He had not gone far when he saw in the distance towards Paola a dozen horsemen, whom he took to be Missourians, moving southwest toward the Browns' settlement on Middle Creek, while he was travelling northwest from Osawatomie. Their lines of travel soon intersected, and Jason, going up to one of the horsemen, inquired the way to Ottawa Jones's. The leader of the party with an oath exclaimed : " You are one of the men we're hunting for;" and levelled his rifle at him. Jason stood still, and the men began to question him rapidly. "What is your name?" "Jason Brown." — "The son of old John Brown?" "Yes." — " Are you armed? " "Yes, with a revolver." — "Give it up. Have you any money?" He produced two or three dollars, which he happened to have, and gave that up. "Now step in front of the horses." Upon this, he knew they meant to shoot him; so he stepped backward, facing them, opened his bosom, and said: "I am an Abolitionist; I believe that slavery is wrong, and that Kansas ought to be a free State. I never knowingly harmed any man in the world. If you want to take my blood for believing in the doctrines of the Declaration of Independence, do it now." When he said this with emphasis,[1] three or four of the Missourians laid their rifles across their saddles, but the rest kept aiming at him. The leader, who proved to be Martin White, a proslavery preacher (the same who afterward shot Frederick Brown), said, "Well, we won't shoot you now, but make a

---

or those who professed to be such, tried to have him give up his arms, and be himself given up to the United States troops and put under their protection. Owen Brown, who spent some hours with John the night before his arrest, denies this alleged insanity at that time.

[1] " I could talk then," said the modest man, telling me the story ; " I can't talk now."

prisoner of you;" and they took him back toward Paola. On the way they halted, and he, overcome with fatigue, sat down on the ground and fell asleep. He was waked by men who seemed to be threatening his life again; but he began to talk to them, denouncing slavery and declaring himself an Abolitionist, with the reasons why. One or two of the company, who seemed more intelligent than the rest, listened to him; and when they reached Paola, these men — Judge Cato and Judge Jacobs, as they were called — caused their prisoner to be put in a good bed, and returned his money and revolver to him. He met his brother John the next day; and there soon happened to them another adventure, which is related by the elder brother, and is a good example of the fear inspired by John Brown: —

"The day after we were taken to Paola, a proslavery man from near Stanton brought in and gave to the Missourians and Buford's men who held our little company as prisoners a scrap of paper containing only these words: 'I am aware that you hold my two sons, John and Jason, prisoners. — *John Brown.*' The bearer of the paper said he brought it under the assurance that his own life depended on its delivery. Brother Jason and I occupied a room which contained a bed and a small lamp-stand or table. Two others also occupied the room as guards. The early part of the night of this day had been spent by our guards at card-playing at the little table. Jason, without removing his clothes, had lain down on the front side of the bed, and was in deep sleep. Occupying in like manner the side of the bed next the wall, at about midnight, as near as I can judge, I was awakened by the sudden opening of the outside door and the rushing in of a number of men with drawn bowie-knives. Seizing the candle, and saying, 'Which are they?' they crowded around our bed with uplifted knives. Believing that our time had come, and wishing to save Jason, still asleep, from prolonged suffering, I opened the bosom of his shirt, and pointing to the region of his heart, said, 'Strike here!' At this moment the sudden and loud barking of dogs outside and a hurrying of steps on the porch caused a most lively stampede of our assailants within, and this attack was ended without a blow. From the hour at Pottawatomie, father had become to slaveholders and their allies in Kansas an omnipresent dread, filling them with forebodings of evil by day and the spectre of their imaginings at night. Owing to that fear, our lives were saved.'

The next day they were placed in custody of Captain
Walker, of the United States cavalry, a Southerner, who
himself tied John's arms back in such a manner as to produce the most intense suffering, with one end of a long rope,
of which he gave the other end to a sergeant; the captive
was then placed a little in advance of the column headed by
Captain Walker, and to avoid being trampled by the horses
which had been ordered to trot, he was driven at this pace
in the hot sun to Osawatomie, a distance of nine miles.
The rope had been tied so tight as to stop circulation.   Instead of loosening it at camp, a mile south of Osawatomie,
no change was made in it through that day, all the following night, nor until about noon the next day.   By that time
the poor man's arms and hands had swollen to nearly double
their size, and turned black as if mortified.   On removing
the rope, a ring of the skin came off; and the scar of this,
which he calls "slavery's bracelet," is still visible on Mr.
Brown's arms.   Such treatment, of course, increased his
insanity, throwing him into a kind of fever, and for some
time his recovery was doubtful.   During this period he was
sometimes chained with a common trace-chain, — which his
father afterward obtained, and occasionally exhibited in
his journeys through the North, to show his hearers what
slavery could do for white men in Kansas.

John Brown, meanwhile, was pursuing the course described by him in the long letter of June, 1856, printed in
the last chapter.   His fame was wonderfully increased by
the bloody deed of Pottawatomie, which rumor instantly
ascribed to him, and which was not doubted to be his act at
the time, in Kansas or Missouri.   He had counted, most
likely, on this very result, and profited in his campaign by
the terror and rage it inspired.   The two or three weeks
that intervened between the attack on Lawrence and the
successful skirmishes of Brown in June, were the critical
period of the contest for the Free-State men.   Had he not
held up the standard then, and checked the insolence of the
slaveholders, Kansas would have been given up to them,
and the immigration of Northern men prevented.   This
opinion has been expressed to me by many of the Kansas

people; while others, who do not go so far, admit that Brown's course was very useful to the cause. Colonel Walker, of Lawrence, in quoting to me Brown's saying in August, 1882, — "the Pottawatomie execution was a just act, and did good," — added, "I must say he told the truth. It did a great deal of good by terrifying the Missourians. I heard Governor Robinson say this himself in his speech at Osawatomie in 1877; he said he rejoiced in it then, though it put his own life in danger, — for he [Robinson] was a prisoner at Lecompton, when Brown killed the men at Pottawatomie."

This also was the deliberate and often-expressed opinion of Judge Hanway, who lived near the scene of the executions, and who knew all the circumstances. This worthy man published the following statement in December, 1879, in addition to what I have already quoted : —

"I was informed by one of the party of eight who left our camp on Ottawa Creek, May 22, 1856, to visit the Pottawatomie, what their object and purposes were. I protested, and begged them to desist. Of course my plea availed nothing. After the dreadful affair had taken place, and after a full investigation of the whole matter, I, like many others, modified my opinion. Good men and kind-hearted women in 1856 differed in regard to this affair in which John Brown and his party were the leading actors. John Brown justified it, and thought it a necessity; others differed from him then, as they do now. I have had an excellent opportunity to investigate the matter, and like others of the early settlers was finally forced to the conclusion that the Pottawatomie 'massacre,' as it is called, prevented the ruffian hordes from carrying out their programme of expelling the Free-State men from this portion of the Territory of Kansas. It was this view of the case which reconciled the minds of the settlers on the Pottawatomie. They would whisper one to the other : 'It was fortunate for us ; for God only knows what our fate and condition would have been, if old John Brown had not driven terror and consternation into the ranks of the proslavery party.'"

Upon this result, as well as upon the ground first named in this chapter, — that Brown believed himself to be, and in fact was, divinely inspired to make a slavish peace in Kansas impossible, — must rest his justification for the bloody act I have described. Men will continue to doubt

whether his justification is ample; but such he held it to
be, and was willing to rest his cause with God, and with posterity. A few men who now denounce him for this deed long
upheld it, and have profited by its good consequences, —
among them Charles Robinson, whose emphatic approval
in 1878 has already been cited.[1] With the excuses of such
men for their change of tone, history has nothing to do.
During the period when they must have best known the
circumstances attending Brown's act, — its provocations,
its timeliness, and its results, — they publicly excused it,
and honored him. Their voice in accusation and malicious interpretation of Brown will now be judged at its
true value. Those of us who long refused to believe that
Brown participated in these executions would not perhaps

---

[1] At a public meeting held in Lawrence, Dec. 19, 1859 (according to
the newspaper reports at the time), the citizens passed resolutions concerning the Pottawatomie executions, declaring "that according to the ordinary
rules of war said transaction was not unjustifiable, but that it was performed from the sad necessity which existed at that time to defend the
lives and liberties of the settlers in that region." This resolution was
supported by Charles Robinson, who said that he had always believed
that John Brown was connected with that movement. Indeed, he believed
Brown had told him so, or to that effect; and when he first heard of the
massacre, he thought it was about right. A war of extermination was in
prospect, and it was as well for Free-State men to kill proslavery men, as
for proslavery men to kill Free-State men. All he wanted to know was
that these men were put out of the world decently, not hacked and cut to
pieces, as was R. P. Brown. G. W. Brown believed the murder of those
men on Pottawatomie Creek was not justifiable; but he (Robinson) thought
it was. Mr. Adair, a nephew of John Brown, remarking that he had
heard his uncle say he was present and approved of the deed, but that he
did not raise a finger himself to injure the men, — that his skirts were clear
of blood, — Robinson said it made no difference whether he raised his hand
or otherwise. John Brown was present, aiding and advising; he did not
attempt to stop the bloodshed, and is of course responsible, though justifiable according to Robinson's understanding of the matter. He added
that while the war in Kansas continued, he was pleased with the co-operation of John Brown; but after peace was restored, and the offices passed
into Free-State hands, he thought the sheriffs of the several counties should
have been called upon to preserve the peace. With them the responsibility
should have rested, not with the unauthorized individuals, — old John
Brown or anybody else; and any interference of Brown subsequent to
the troubles in 1856 he repudiated.

have honored or trusted him less had we known the whole truth. I for one should not; though I should have deeply regretted the necessity for such deeds of dark and providential justice.

> " Not yet the wise of heart would cease
> To hold his hope through shame and guilt,
> And, with his hand against the hilt,
> Would pace the troubled land like Peace ;
> Would love the gleams of good that broke
> From either side, nor veil his eyes ;
> *And if some dreadful need should rise,*
> *Would strike, and firmly, and one stroke.*"

CHAPTER X.

THE KANSAS STRUGGLE CONTINUED.

THE events already chronicled are but a small part of those which took place in Kansas while John Brown maintained his connection with the friends of freedom there. It was more than three years from his first arrival at Osawatomie before he finally withdrew (late in January, 1859) from the Territory, whose admission as a free State was then secure, although the date was delayed. But he spent less than half those three years in Kansas. His first summer there, in 1856, was the most eventful portion of that period; and this has been in part described. But much remains to be told, although the incidents of that summer, which then seemed so momentous, have shrunk almost into insignificance in comparison with the campaigns of the Civil War that so soon followed. What we used to call "battles" in Kansas, if the whole sum of them were thrown together, would hardly equal in their numbers or tangible results a single heavy skirmish along the front of Grant's army. The total loss of life on both sides during 1856, by the casualties of war, did not exceed a hundred men, and the property destroyed was hardly so much as a hundred thousand dollars. Yet though this computation makes the struggle appear trivial, it was not so in fact; while in the qualities of mind which it developed it became all-important. In Kansas, first of all, the patient and too submissive citizen of the North learned to stand firm against Southern arrogance and assumption; for that scantily settled prairie exhibited more courage to the square mile than the most populous Northern States had before displayed. John Brown alone was worth all the trouble that Kansas gave the nation, and his significance atones for the littleness of the affair, even as we now view it.

Yet, in truth, the creation of a free State, colonized by the best yeomanry of the North, on the western frontier of the slaveholding South, was in itself a great event; and the possibility of success in the enterprise aroused an interest throughout the country that nothing else had excited. The attempt was made, too, on the eve of one of our periodic political contests, — the election of President; and this issue became inevitably connected with the canvass. It was the fear of losing the presidential vote of Pennsylvania for James Buchanan in 1856 that inspired the recall of the worst Territorial governors of Kansas, — Shannon and Woodson, — and the appointment, just before the decisive October election, of that upright Pennsylvania Democrat Governor Geary. His private instructions were said to be, "Quiet the Territory at any cost; for if the warfare continues in Kansas, Pennsylvania will vote for Fremont." This, as the other States then stood, would have defeated Buchanan. Just before Geary's appointment, Jefferson Davis (of all men in the world), who was then Secretary of War, had directed General Persifor Smith, who commanded the United States forces at Leavenworth, to put down the "open rebellion" of the freemen of Kansas.[1] But more patriotic and peaceful counsels prevailed; Governor Geary quieted the Territory, and Buchanan was elected President.

The occasion for this manifesto from Jefferson Davis was the lively campaign, offensive as well as defensive, which had been carried on by John Brown, General Lane, Major Abbott, Captain Walker, and others, during the three months between the Pottawatomie executions and the burning of Osawatomie at the end of August. Having already published

[1] Davis wrote to General Smith : "The President has directed me to say to you that you are authorized from time to time to make requisitions upon the Governor [of Kansas] for such militia force as you may require to enable you to suppress the insurrection against the government of the Territory of Kansas. Should you not be able to derive from the military of Kansas an adequate force for the purpose, you will derive such additional number of militia as may be necessary from the States of Illinois and Kentucky. . . . The position of the insurgents is that *of open rebellion against the laws and constitutional authorities*, with such manifestation of purpose to spread devastation over the land as no longer justifies further hesitation or indulgence."

John Brown's report to his family of the fight at Black Jack, near Palmyra, early in June, I will next quote from other authorities, and finally from Brown himself, some historical notes of this disturbed summer. One of his soldiers, Luke F. Parsons, has within a few years made this statement respecting his own conduct in the Kansas feud : —

RECOLLECTIONS OF L. F. PARSONS.

" At daylight on the morning of the 3d of June, 1856, Major Hoyt and I galloped to Black Jack, where I tendered my services to Captain Brown, and was immediately put on guard; and I was the only post sentinel who challenged Colonel Sumner when he came to release our prisoners. Again, sometime in the latter part of August I met John Brown in Lawrence ; he told me he came to get help to defend Osawatomie. I told him to try the 'Stubs' (which was a Lawrence Sharpe's rifle company to which I belonged). He replied that he had, but they would not leave Lawrence. I told him I would get my rifle and go with him. He said he would surely show me how to fight, if the rascals would give him a chance. When I went for my gun Lieutenant Cutler asked what I was going to do. I told him, and he said, ' The guns belong to the company, and shall not be taken away.' Brown borrowed a Sharpe's rifle of Captain Harvey for me, and I went with him to his camp near Osawatomie.

" Aug. 30, 1856, we were camped a half-mile east of that town, at Mr. Crane's place. While we were cooking breakfast, before sunrise, a man dashed into camp, saying the Border Ruffians were coming from the west, and had just killed Fred Brown and David Garrison near Mr. Adair's. Brown started right off, and said, ' Men, *come on !*' He did not say *go*. I started with him, and it was some minutes before any overtook us. While we were hurrying on by ourselves, Brown said, ' Parsons, were you ever under fire ? ' I replied, ' No ; but I will obey orders. Tell me what you want me to do.' He said, ' Take more care to end life well than to live long.'

" When we reached the blockhouse in the village he motioned to several to go in, myself with the rest. He then said to me, ' Hold your position as long as possible, and hurt them all you can ; while we will go into the timber and annoy them from that side.' I fastened the door with a large bar, and thought all secure. Soon firing commenced up the Marais des Cygnes, where Brown had gone. There was a second floor in the blockhouse, and part of the boys had gone up there. While we all selected our port-hole, Brown had drawn their attention, so that we were not molested. After some twenty minutes or so, some one on the second floor called out : ' They have cannon, and will blow us all to pieces in here. I am going to get out of this.' I said : ' No, you must stay.' Old man Austin said, ' Stay here, and let them blow us to hell and back again !' I went upstairs to get a better view of the enemy, and before I knew it the door was opened and most of the men gone. I don't know even where they went. Austin and I, and I think two others, — four in all, — then went up the Marais des Cygnes River, in the timber, and joined Brown at the fight, on his left. Cline had gone before this. We had not been there long when we all fell back across the river. Partridge was shot while in the river.

" At this place the water was deep, and I said to Austin, ' I cannot swim with my gun,' which I soon threw into the river. So we both ran down the river. The bank was high, so we were most of the time out of sight. I ran too fast for the old man [Austin], and he called to me not to leave him. As we approached the old saw-mill the bank became lower, and we were seen by the ruffians, three of whom were after us. I told Austin that as I could see the bottom, I would cross. He replied, ' I won't run another inch ; ' and dropped down behind a large log. I waded through ; but the opposite bank was steep and high ; and as I was clinging to brush and scrambling up, I heard the words ' Halt ! halt ! halt !' in rapid succession, and immediately several guns were fired, and the dirt torn up by my side. I was on the bank in a twinkle, and returned their salute as well as I could. Two were putting spurs to their horses the best they could. One horse bore an empty saddle, and one man was kicking his last kick ; and Austin jumped up and came over to me. As we went up the river he told me that they did not see him, but passed rather in front of him, and all shot at me ; while he shot one in the back just at the very moment they shot at me. In an hour or so after this we got together at a log-house on the north side of the river. Dr. Updegraff was then in the house, shot in the thigh. Brown was with him. But before we got together the smoke of the burning town was seen. They burned twenty-nine houses.

" The next day we moved to the south side, to a Mr. Häuser's. We commenced to fell timber round a place selected by Brown as possessing natural advantages for defence. We felled the tree-tops out, and trimmed them with sharp points. Most of the men became sick with the ague, and work was suspended. Soon after this, I too was taken with fever, and Brown hauled me to Lawrence. I was very sick. Brown asked me if he should take me to the hospital. I told him that I would rather go to Mrs. Killum's (a boarding-house where I had previously lodged), if she would take care of me. He went and found her, and returned saying, ' Mrs. Killum says,

" Bring him here : I would do as much for Luke Parsons as for my own son." ' Under her care I recovered so that I was again under Brown's command. I shouldered my gun and marched out to meet the twenty-eight hundred men who came up from Missouri in September. If I remember aright, in about a year after this I went with John E. Cook to Tabor, Iowa, where I next saw Brown, and from Tabor went on to Springdale.

" I also take pride in saying that I was under arms in Topeka, on July 4, 1856, when Colonel Sumner dispersed the Legislature. I was with Captain Walker in the capture of Colonel Titus, near Lecompton. I claim to be the man who shot Colonel Titus.

" I was near our Captain Shombre when he was struck by the fatal ball. I received a very sore but slight wound there. It was on my shin, made by a very small ball or a buck-shot.

" Kansas was admitted into the Union in 1861, with every inch free soil, and still the object for which Brown fought was not entirely accomplished. I enlisted in the Union army, and fought for nearly four years, until that object *was fully attained,* and there was nowhere to be found a ' slave to clank his chains by the graves of Monticello or the shades of Mt. Vernon.' "

The name of this soldier of Brown's company appears in the " Articles of Enlistment and By-Laws of the Kansas Regulars, made and established by the commander, A. D. 1856, in whose handwriting it is," — as Brown described the book to me when he gave me a copy in April, 1857. Here are its contents, given, as to spelling and punctuation, in exact accordance with the original : —

KANSAS TERRITORY, A. D. 1856.

1. *The Covenant.*

We whose names are found on these and the next following pages do hereby enlist ourselves to serve in the Free-State cause under John Brown as Commander : during the full period of time affixed to our names respectively and we severally pledge our word and our sacred honor to said Commander ; and to each other, that during the time for which we have enlisted we will faithfully and punctually perform our duty (in such capacity or place as may be assigned to us by a majority of all the votes of those associated with us : or of the companies to which we may belong as the case may be) as a regular volunteer force for the maintainance of the rights & liberties of the Free-State Citizens of Kansas : and we further agree ; that as

individuals we will conform to the *by Laws of this Organization* &
that *we will insist* on their regular & punctual *enforcement* as a first
& last duty: & in short that we will observe & maintain a strict &
thorough Military discipline at all times untill our term of service
expires.

*Names, date of enlistment, and term of service on next Pages.
Term of service omitted for want of room (principally for the
War).*

2. *Names and date of enlistment.*

Aug. 22.[1] Wm. Patridge (imprisoned), John Salathiel, S. Z.
Brown, John Goodell, L. F. Parsons, N. B. Phelps, Wm. B.
Harris.

Aug. 23. Jason Brown (son of commander; imprisoned).

Aug. 24. J. Benjamin (imprisoned).

Aug. 25. Cyrus Taton, R. Reynolds (imprisoned), Noah Frazee
(1st Lieut.), Wm. Miller, John P. Glenn, Wm. Quick, M. D. Lane,
Amos Alderman, August Bondie, Charles Kaiser (murdered Aug.
30), Freeman Austin (aged 57 years), Samuel Hereson, John W.
Troy, Jas. H. Holmes (Capt.).

Aug. 26. Geo. Patridge (killed Aug. 30), Wm. A. Sears.

Aug. 27. S. H. Wright.

Aug. 29. B. Darrach (Surgeon), Saml. Farrar.

Sept. 8. Timothy Kelly, Jas. Andrews.

Sept. 9. W. H. Leman, Charles Oliver, D. H. Hurd.

Sept. 15. Wm. F. Haniel.

Sept. 16. Saml. Geer (Commissary).

3. *Bylaws of the Free-State regular Volunteers of Kansas enlisted under John Brown.*

Art. I. Those who agree to be governed by the following articles
& whose names are appended will be known as the Kansas
Regulars.

Art. II. Every officer connected with organization (except the
Commander already named) shall be elected by a majority of the
members *if above a Captain;* & if a Captain; or under a Captain,
by a majority of the company to which they belong.

Art. III. All vacancies shall be filled by vote of the majority of
members or companies as the case may be, & all members shall be
alike eligible to the highest office.

Art. IV. All trials for misconduct of Officers; or privates; shall
be by a jury of Twelve; chosen by a majority of Company, or

[1] 1856.

companies as the case may be. Each Company shall try its own members.

Art. V. All valuable property taken by honorable warfare from the enemy, shall be held as the property of the whole company, or companies, as the case may be : equally, without distinction ; to be used for the common benefit or be placed in the hands of responsible agents for sale : the proceeds to be divided as nearly equally amongst the company : or *companies* capturing it as may be : except that no person shall be entitled to any dividend from property taken before he entered the service ; and any person guilty of desertion, or convicted of gross violation of his obligations to those with whom he should act, *whether officer or private :* shall forfeit his interest in all dividends made after such misconduct has occurred.

Art. VI. All property captured shall be delivered to the receiver of the force, or company as the case may be ; whose duty it shall be to make a full inventory of the same (assisted by such person, *or persons* as may be chosen for that purpose), a coppy of which shall be made into the Books of this organization ; & held subject to examination by any member, on all suitable occasions.

Art. VII. The receiver shall give his receipts in a Book for that purpose for all moneys & other property of the regulars placed in his hands ; keep an inventory of the same & make copy as provided in Article VI.

Art. VIII. Captured articles when used for the benefit of the members : shall be receipted for by the Commissary, the same as moneyes placed in his hands. The receiver to hold said receipts.

Art. IX. A disorderly retreat shall not be suffered at any time & every Officer & private is by this article fully empowered to prevent the same by force if need be, & any attempt at leaving the ground during a fight is hereby declared disorderly unless the consent or direction of the officer then in command have authorized the same.

Art. X. A disorderly attack or charge ; shall not be suffered at any time.

Art. XI. When in camp a thorough watch both regular and Piquet shall be maintained both by day, & by Night : and visitors shall not be suffered to pass or repass without leave from the Captain of the guard and under common or ordinary circumstances it is expected that the Officers will cheerfully share this service with the privates for examples sake.

Art. XII. Keeping up Fires or lights after dark ; or firing of Guns, Pistols or Caps shall not be allowed, except Fires and lights when unavoidable.

Art. XIII. When in Camp neither Officers shall be allowed to leave without consent of the Officer then in command.

19

Art. XIV. All uncivil ungentlemanly profane, vulgar talk or conversation shall be discountenanced.

Art. XV. All acts of petty theft needless waste of the property of the members or of Citizens is hereby declared disorderly : together with all uncivil, or unkind treatment of Citizens or of prisoners.

Art. XVI. In all cases of capturing property, a sufficient number of men shall be detailed to take charge of the same ; all others shall keep in their position.

Art. XVII. It shall at all times be the duty of the quarter Master to select ground for encampment subject however to the approbation of the commanding officer.

Art. XVIII. The Commissary shall give his receipts in a Book for that purpose for all moneys provisions, and stores put into his hands.

Art. XIX. The Officers of companies shall see that the arms of the same *are in constant good order* and a neglect of this duty shall be deemed disorderly.

Art. XX. *No person* after having first surrendered himself a prisoner shall be *put to death :* or *subjected to corporeal punishment,* without *first* having had the benefit of an impartial trial.

Art. XXI. A Waggon Master and an Assistant shall be chosen for each company whose duty it shall be to take a general care and oversight of the teams, waggons, harness and all other articles or property pertaining thereto : and who shall both be exempt from serving on guard.

Art. XXII. The ordinary use or introduction into the camp of any intoxicating liquor, *as a beverage :* is hereby declared disorderly.

Art. XXIII. A Majority of Two Thirds of *all the Members* may at any time alter or amend the foregoing articles.

4. *List of Volunteers either engaged or guarding Horses during the fight of Black Jack or Palmyra, June 2, 1856.*

1. Saml. T. Shore (Captain). 2. Silas More. 3. David Hendricks (Horse Guard). 4. Hiram McAllister. 5. Mr. Parmely (wounded). 6. Silvester Harris. 7. O. A. Carpenter (wounded). 8. Augustus Shore. 9. Mr. Townsley (of Pottawatomie). 10. Wm. B. Hayden. 11. John Mewhinney. 12. Montgomery Shore. 13. Elkana Timmons. 14. T. Weiner. 15. August Bondy. 16. Hugh Mewhinney. 17. Charles Kaiser. 18. Elizur Hill. 19. William David. 20. B. L. Cochran. 21. Henry Thompson (wounded). 22. Elias Basinger. 23. Owen Brown. 24. Fredk. Brown (horse guard ; murdered Aug. 30). 25. Salmon Brown. 26. Oliver Brown. 27. This blank may be filled by Capt. Shore as he may have the name.   JOHN BROWN.

5. *List of names of the wounded in the Battle of Black Jack (or Palmyra) and also of the Eight who held out to receive the surrender of Capt. Pate and Twenty-Two men on that occasion. June 2, 1856.*

1. Mr. Parmely wounded in Nose, & Arm obliged to leave. 2. Henry Thompson dangerously wounded but fought for nearly one Hour afterward. 3. O. A. Carpenter Badly wounded and obliged to leave. 4. Charles Kaiser, murdered Aug. 30. 5. Elizur Hill. 6. Wm. David. 7. Hugh Mewhinney (17 yrs. old). 8. B. L. Cochran. 9. Owen Brown, 10. Salmon Brown. Seriously wounded (*soon after by accident*). 11. Oliver Brown — 17 years old.

In the battle of Osawatomie Capt. (or Dr.) Updegraph ; and Two others whose names I have lost were severely (*one of them shockingly*) wounded before the fight began Aug. 30, 1856.

JOHN BROWN.

In these lists appear a few of the men who afterward fought under Captain Brown at Harper's Ferry; but only a few, for most of them seem to have been settlers in Kansas who would fight to protect themselves, but not to attack slavery at a distance. The dates given in the list, when this man or that was " murdered," denote the day on which Brown's most famous engagement — that of Osawatomie, Aug. 30, 1856 — was fought. The fight at Black Jack, or Palmyra, on the 2d of June, 1856, was more remarkable, though the whole force engaged on both sides was less than eighty. I have quoted Brown's report of it, but will here describe it more fully.

Brown had taken to the prairie for guerilla warfare against the Missourians and other Southern invaders of Kansas, after the Pottawatomie executions. Among their leaders was Captain Pate, a Virginian. Brown, hearing of the capture of his sons, pursued Pate, and came up with him on Monday, the 2d of June, at his camp on the Black Jack Creek (so called from the black oak growing on its banks), within the present limits of Palmyra.

In the interval between the Pottawatomie executions and the fight at Black Jack, during which the sons of John Brown were captured as has been related, many important events occurred ; but I will confine my narrative chiefly to

those in which the Brown family were directly concerned.
Several witnesses are still alive who took part in them; but
my chief reliance will be (besides the letters of John Brown)
the detailed statements made by Owen Brown and by
August Bondi (the German citizen of Kansas already mentioned), both of whom were in camp, or rather in hiding,
with John Brown while the Border Ruffians and the United
States dragoons were scouring the country between Lawrence and Osawatomie to find the perpetrators of the bloody
deed of May 24. Bondi has published a minute report, in
which he says that he rode, with nine others, on the morning of May 26, to the claim of John Brown, Jr., on "Vine
Branch, a mile and a half from Middle Creek Bottom,"
where they halted, and were joined in the afternoon by
O. A. Carpenter, a Free-State man then living on Ottawa
Creek, not far from Prairie City, who came to request John
Brown in the name of the settlers there that he would come
and protect them against the Missourians. This little village of Prairie City (described by Redpath as "a munici-
pality consisting of two log-cabins and a well") is a part
of the township of Palmyra, and now figures as a railroad
station on the route from Lawrence to the Indian Territory
and Texas. It has been eclipsed by Baldwin City in the
same township, which is the nearest station (on the Southern Kansas Railway) to the field of Black Jack. Baldwin
City had three hundred and twenty-five inhabitants in 1880;
while Prairie City has disappeared from separate enumera-
tion, and contributes its few citizens to the aggregate population of Palmyra township, — about twenty-five hundred.
These places are in the southeastern corner of Douglas
County, of which Lawrence is the chief town, and so near
the Shawnee Mission and the Missouri border that they
were peculiarly exposed to raids by the Ruffians. Moreover
they lay near the road from Lawrence to Osawatomie (some
forty miles apart), and the protection of the Free-State men
there was important in keeping up communications between
central and southern Kansas, as those terms were then used.
South of Palmyra, in Miami County, was the armed colony
of Buford's men, and eastward were the Missouri counties
of Cass and Jackson. Carpenter's mission was, then, to

secure Brown's small band as a protection for the southern part of Douglas County, checking the thieving raids which were then so frequent, and, if necessary, making reprisals. Brown accepted the duty, and at dusk on the 26th of May, with his force now increased to nine men besides himself, set out under Carpenter's guidance towards Prairie City, twenty miles northeastward. Bondi says : —

"There were ten of us, — Captain Brown, Owen, Frederick, Salmon, and Oliver Brown; Henry Thompson, Theodore Wiener, James Townsley, Carpenter, and myself. Our armament was this: Captain Brown carried a sabre and a heavy seven-shooting revolver ; all his sons and his son-in-law were armed with revolvers, long knives, and the common 'squirrel rifle ;' Townsley with an old musket, Wiener with a double-barrelled gun, I with an old-fashioned flint-lock musket, and Carpenter with a revolver. The three youngest men — Salmon Brown, Oliver, and I — rode without saddles. By order of Captain Brown, Fred Brown rode first, Owen and Carpenter next; ten paces behind them, old Brown ; and the rest of us behind him, two and two. Our way from Middle Creek to Ottawa Creek was along the old military road between Fort Scott and Fort Leavenworth. When we had nearly reached the crossing of the old California road at the ford of the Marais des Cygnes, we saw by the fading watch-fires of a camp, hardly a hundred and fifty steps before us, an armed sentinel pacing. While Fred Brown rode slowly forward, Carpenter turned back and told Captain Brown that here was probably a division of United States dragoons who were acting as *posse* for the marshal. Brown thereupon gave Carpenter his instructions in a few words. We were to ride forward slowly with no indication of the least anxiety, and otherwise to imitate his example. The sentry let Fred Brown and Carpenter approach within twenty-five paces, and then cried, 'Who goes there ?' Fred answered just as loud, 'Free-State.' The sentry called the officer of the guard, and while he was coming the rest of us rode, by Brown's order, within five paces of where Fred and Carpenter were halted, forming ourselves in an irregular group. When the officer appeared, Carpenter spoke up and said we were farmers, living not far from Prairie City, who had gone to Osawatomie upon invitation of the settlers to protect them against an expected invasion from Missouri ; had been there two days, seen and heard nothing of the Missourians, and so had resolved to return home. Upon this Lieutenant McIntosh, the commanding officer, appeared, and Carpenter repeated what he had said. None of the rest of us said a word ; but the deputy marshal came forward and requested the lieutenant to detain us till daylight, so that he might make further inquiries. McIntosh replied sternly : ' I have no orders to stop peaceable travellers, such as these people are ; they are going home to their farms ;' adding to Carpenter and the rest of us : ' Pass on ! pass on !' We defiled slowly through the camp, forded the stream, and when the soldiers were a mile behind us pushed on rapidly. About four o'clock in the morning of May 27 we reached the secluded spot on Ottawa Creek which Carpenter had indicated to us as a safe place for camping. In the midst of a primeval wood, perhaps half a mile deep before you come to the creek, we pitched our camp beside a huge fallen oak, and tethered our horses in the underwood. Old Brown inspected the region, and set guards ; Carpenter brought corn for the horses and coarse flour for ourselves, and then Brown began to get breakfast."

In this secure retreat they remained until June 1, when they set forth to find the enemy, whom they defeated at Black Jack ; and it was here that James Redpath on May 30, and Colonel Sumner on June 5, visited Brown. Redpath was at that time a Kansas correspondent of the "New York Tribune" and other Eastern newspapers, and was spending a few days near Prairie City to watch the movements of the Missourians and the dragoons, and, if possible, to give some aid to the Free-State men. His horse had been stolen in Palmyra by one of the Border Ruffians, and he was arrested himself the next day on suspicion of stealing dragoon horses, but soon discharged. While looking about on Friday for an old preacher who lived near Ottawa Creek, and who was to carry his New York letter for mailing to Kansas City, some twenty miles off, the lively newspaper correspondent stumbled upon the hiding-place of John Brown, whom he then saw for the first time. Redpath's description of the adventure, somewhat abridged, is this : —

" The creeks of Kansas are all fringed with wood. I lost my way, or got off the path that crosses Ottawa Creek, when suddenly, thirty paces before me, I saw a wild-looking man, of fine proportions, with pistols of various sizes stuck in his belt, and a large Arkansas bowie-knife prominent among them. His head was uncovered ; his hair was uncombed ; his face had not been shaven for many months. We were similarly dressed, — with red-topped boots worn over the pan-

taloons, a coarse blue shirt, and a pistol-belt. This was the usual
fashion of the times.

"'Hello!' he cried, 'you're in our camp!'

"He had nothing in his right hand, — he carried a water-pail in his
left; but before he could speak again I had drawn and cocked my
eight-inch Colt. I only answered in emphatic tones: 'Halt! or I'll
fire!' He stopped, and said that he knew me; that he had seen me
in Lawrence, and that I was true; that he was Frederick Brown,
the son of old John Brown; and that I was now within the limits of
their camp. After a parley of a few minutes I was satisfied that I
was among my friends, shook hands with Frederick, and put up my
pistol. He talked wildly as he walked before me, turning round
every minute as he spoke of the then recent affair of Pottawatomie.
His family, he said, had been accused of it; he denied it indignantly,
with the wild air of a maniac. His excitement was so great that he
repeatedly recrossed the creek, until, getting anxious to reach the
camp, I refused to listen to him until he took me to his father. He
then quietly filled his pail with water, and after many strange turnings
led me into camp. As we approached it we were twice challenged
by sentries, who suddenly appeared before trees, and as suddenly
disappeared behind them.

"I shall not soon forget the scene that here opened to my view.
Near the edge of the creek a dozen horses were tied, all ready saddled for a ride for life, or a hunt after Southern invaders. A dozen
rifles and sabres were stacked against the trees. In an open space,
amid the shady and lofty woods, there was a great blazing fire with
a pot on it; three or four armed men were lying on red and blue
blankets on the grass; and two fine-looking youths were standing,
leaning on their arms, near by. One of them was the youngest son
of old Brown, and the other was 'Charley,' the brave Hungarian,
who was subsequently murdered at Osawatomie. Old Brown himself
stood near the fire, with his shirt-sleeves rolled up, and a large fork
in his hand. He was cooking a pig. He was poorly clad, and his
toes protruded from his boots. The old man received me with great
cordiality, and the little band gathered about me. But it was only
for a moment, for the Captain ordered them to renew their work.
He respectfully but firmly forbade conversation on the Pottawatomie
affair; and said that if I desired any information from the company
in relation to their conduct or intentions, he as their captain would
answer for them whatever it was proper to communicate. In this
camp no manner of profane language was permitted; no man of immoral character was allowed to stay, except as a prisoner of war.

". . . It was at this time that the old man said to me: 'I would
rather have the small-pox, yellow fever, and cholera all together in

my camp, than a man without principles. It's a mistake, sir,' he continued, ' that our people make, when they think that bullies are the best fighters, or that they are the men fit to oppose these Southerners. Give me men of good principles; God-fearing men; men who respect themselves, — and with a dozen of them, I will oppose any hundred such men as these Buford ruffians.' I remained in the camp about an hour. Never before had I met such a band of men. They were not earnest, but earnestness incarnate. Six of them were John Brown's sons." [1]

Bondi remembers this adventure of Redpath, and relates some other conversation that then took place. Their chance visitor told them it looked well for their neighbors that in spite of the great rewards already offered for their arrest, no traitor had been found to pilot the enemy to that camp, although many in the neighborhood had by that time come to know where it was. He told them further that on their perseverance might depend the success of the good cause in Kansas; that when he should go back to Lawrence he would try to have the Lawrence "Stubs," a small military company, join them; and meantime hoped they would not forsake Douglas County, as Brown had threatened to do, unless the settlers took up arms to aid him in his warfare. The cheerful counsel of the young correspondent encouraged them, and, as Bondi says, "they felt as if they were the extreme outpost of the free North in Kansas." Doubtless they were; and with prophetic insight Brown said that day, " We shall stay here, young man; we will not disappoint the hopes of our friends." [2]

" Charley, the brave Hungarian," of whom Redpath speaks, was Charles Kaiser, a Bavarian, who had settled

[1] In fact, there were but four of Brown's sons here, and his son-in-law Thompson. In some other points the account is exaggerated; but in the main it gives a true picture of the scene, as remembered by Bondi, Owen Brown, and others. At this time John and Jason Brown were prisoners, on their way to Lecompton. Jason was soon discharged; but John Brown, Jr., remained at Lecompton until September 10, when he was released on bail and went to Lawrence.

[2] According to Bondi, Brown had suggested, a day or two before, that if they had to leave Kansas on account of the cowardice or indifference of their friends, they might go to Louisiana and head an uprising of the slaves there, to make a diversion in favor of Kansas.

in Hungary when young, and in 1849 had served in the Hungarian revolutionary army as a hussar.   His face, says Bondi, was marked with lance and sabre-cuts ; and he had a taste for war.   He was living on a claim three or four miles from this camp, and had made the acquaintance of Brown in the " Wakarusa war " the winter before.   Recognizing in Bondi and Wiener fellow-countrymen of the same political opinions, he became intimate with them as soon as he joined Brown's company on the 28th of May. The same day they had been joined by Ben Cochrane, a member of the Pottawatomie Rifles, and a neighbor of Bondi and Wiener, who told them how their houses had been burned, their cattle driven off, and their goods plundered a day or two before ; while the United States dragoon officer refused to interfere on behalf of the settlers on the Pottawatomie, saying, " I have no orders."   Bondi goes on to say : —

" The next day (May 29), Captain Shore, of the Prairie City Rifles, and Dr. Westfall, a neighbor of Carpenter, came to our camp and told us that many horses and other property had been stolen near Willow Springs, ten or fifteen miles distant.   They asked Brown ' what he calculated to do ? '   Brown replied, ' Captain Shore, how many men can you furnish me ? '   Shore answered that his men were just now very unwilling to leave home ; to which Brown said, ' Why did you send Carpenter after us ?   I am not willing to sacrifice my men, without having some hope of accomplishing something.'   That evening (May 29) Shore visited us again, and brought some flour, of which we had great need, as a present.   Brown then said to him that if his neighbors did not soon take the offensive, he should certainly be compelled to leave that region, for the Missourians would sooner or later find out our hiding-place.   Captain Shore asked him to delay his departure a few days, saying that he knew the Missourians suspected we were in ambush somewhere near Prairie City, and that nothing save the fear of us had protected this neighborhood so long against attack and pillage : but should Shannon's militia find out that we were away, it would be all over with the Free-State men.   Brown gave him till next Sunday to gather the settlers, so that with combined forces we might hunt for the militia and offer them battle wherever we might find them ; Shore promised to do his best. and so the matter stood when Redpath visited us.   The day after his visit (May 31) Shore came to tell us that a large band of Shannon's militia were encamped on the Santa Fé road, by Black Jack Spring, and at ten o'clock P. M. returned with Carpenter and Mewhinney bringing serious news. They said that three men from the Black Jack camp had attacked a block house in Palmyra, three miles from Prairie City, where several neighbors' families were visiting; that the seven Free-State men there, though well armed, had, upon a simple demand, given up to the three Missourians three rifles, three revolvers, and five double-barrelled guns. Such a disgrace, our visitors thought, could not be endured patiently; and Shore said he had sent word to all the settlers to muster at Prairie City by ten the next morning (Sunday), where he would expect us with our arms and horses. Captain Brown grasped his hand and said, 'We will be with you!' and our friends departed about midnight. The next morning Brown had breakfast earlier than common, and when Carpenter came back about nine o'clock, to escort us to Prairie City, we were ready to start. Carpenter, Kaiser, and Townsley assisted Wiener to empty his bottle. Captain Brown called out, 'Ready, Forward, March!' and we were on the road towards the enemy. Our appearance was indescribable. Except Kaiser, none of us had proper attire; for our clothes readily showed the effects of bush-whacking, continued for the last eight days; we had come down to wearing ideas, suspicions, and memories of what had once been boots and hats. Still in the best of spirits, and with our appetite still better, just whetted by our scant breakfast, we followed Captain Brown, — he alone remaining serious, and riding silent at our front." [1]

Prairie City is half-way between Lawrence and Osawatomie, and near by is Hickory Point, where Dow was murdered by Coleman. Pate had been encamped a day or two among the "black-jack oaks," which gave an uncouth name to the stream, and though Brown's force was much the smaller, — only twenty-eight men including Brown himself, — he did not hesitate to attack at once. The day was Sunday, and Brown had attended a prayer-meeting at Prairie City; while there, three men who had been at the sack of Lawrence came up and brought exact word of Pate's whereabouts. Brown set out that night, and at four o'clock the next morning reached a patch of black oaks on a slope to-

[1] I have abridged this account from the letters of Bondi, printed both in German and English in the Kansas newspapers of 1883-84. Occasionally the English version varies from the German, and I follow the latter in preference. Prairie City is about five miles southwest of Black Jack.

wards the north near Pate's camp, but away from the water.
Leaving the horses there in the charge of his son Fred, he
marched his other twenty-six men in double file until he
came within reach of the enemy's fire, and still pushed forward under fire until he gained a place of shelter in sight
of Pate's tents, but screened by the slope of land, where he
took position in a ravine ten feet deep. The firing began a
little after six A. M., and lasted until one or two o'clock in
the afternoon. During this time many of the men on both
sides deserted; but Captain Brown crept round on his hands
and knees behind the ridge, and persuaded some of the de-
serters to fire on the horses of the enemy. At this point
Fred Brown (who "was a little flighty," as his brother
Owen says) came riding up on Ned Scarlet, Owen's colt,
waving his sword, and shouting, "Hurrah! come on, boys!
we 've got 'em surrounded; we 've cut off all communication." He could be heard a long way off; and his great size
and odd gestures alarmed the enemy. He was shot at, but
not hit, and the firing upon Pate's horses was kept up by the
stragglers. Alarmed at all this, Captain Pate tied a white
handkerchief on a ramrod as a flag of truce, and sent a lieutenant forward to meet Captain Brown, who was returning
from his successful ruse.[1] Brown said to the lieutenant,
" Are you the captain of that company ? " " No." " Then
stay with me and send your companion back to call the captain out ; I will talk with him, and not with you." Thus
summoned, Captain Pate himself appeared, saying that he
was an officer acting under orders of the United States Marshal of Kansas, and that he supposed they did not intend to
fight against the United States. He was going on in this

---

[1] Owen Brown adds (April, 1885) : " When my brother Frederick rode
' Ned Scarlet ' entirely around where the fight was going on, he was not so
flighty but he knew well what he was doing ; he made a dashing appearance, brandished his sword, and shouted so loud that all could distinctly
hear, ' Come on, boys, we 've got them surrounded, and have cut off their
communications.' At this very time Pate's horses and mules were tumbling down pretty lively, and within five or eight minutes Pate came out
with his white handkerchief tied to a ramrod, and with him a Free-State
prisoner. I think Fred's riding around there as he did, happened just at
the right time, and had a most excellent effect." Like all the witnesses,
Owen praises the courage of Captain Shore.

way when Brown stopped him by saying, "I understand
exactly what you are, and do not wish to hear any more
about it. Have you any proposition to make me?" There
being no definite answer to this query, Brown continued,
"Very well; I have one to make to you: you must surrender unconditionally." Then, taking his pistol in hand,
Brown returned with Captain Pate to the enemy's line,
leading with him eight of his own men, and among them
Owen Brown, to receive the surrender of the one-and-twenty
men who were left under Pate's orders. As they drew near
the line, where Pate's lieutenant Brockett was in command,
Brown called upon him also to surrender. He hesitated; and
Captain Pate, to whom Brown turned requesting that he
should order his lieutenant to yield, also hesitated, seeing
the great apparent superiority of his force over Brown's.
Quick as thought, Brown placed his pistol at Pate's head,
and cried in a terrible voice, "Give the order!" The Virginian yielded, and bade his men lay down their arms, which
they sullenly did. Brown's force of eight unwounded men
then took the guns and other arms of the discomfited party,
threw them into wagons, and marched off the twenty odd
prisoners to their own position. Here a treaty or agreement was drawn up and signed by John Brown and Captain
Shore on one side, and Captain Pate and Lieutenant Brockett
on the other.

This agreement (or rather Pate's copy of it) seems to have
been folded as a letter, and indorsed or addressed on the back
as follows: "United States Marshal Hays, Colonel Coffey,
General Heiskell, or Judge Cato, or friends at Baptiste Paola, K. T." These were the persons into whose hands Pate
and Brockett hoped the paper would fall; and it did apparently reach William A. Heiskell, of Paola, one of the persons
named, whose widow a few years since sent it to the Kansas
Historical Society.[1] The agreement was not carried out, for

[1] Two copies of this agreement were made, one of which Brown kept,
and it was sent by his widow, long after his death, to the Kansas Historical
Society at Topeka, where it has been for six or eight years. Sometime
after this, the duplicate, which had been retained by Pate, was also sent
to the librarian of the Historical Society, Mr. F. G. Adams; and now
the two papers, torn and faded, but still legible, are exhibited side by

a knowledge of the capture of Pate (communicated to his friends perhaps by this very paper, sent to Paola) brought from Missouri a large force under General Whitfield to rescue him. Brown also was presently largely reinforced; and a sanguinary battle seemed imminent. But on the 5th of June Colonel Sumner appeared with a force of United States troops and summoned Captain Brown to an interview, which resulted in his prisoners being set at liberty. It is said that Pate was at the sacking of Osawatomie two days afterward, while John Brown, Jr., was not liberated till the 10th of September following.

Brown's report of his men after the fight, made to a committee at Lawrence, was much the same as the list already given : —

(On the face of the sheet.)

List of names of men wounded in the battle of Palmyra or Black Jack; also of eight volunteers who maintained their position during that fight, and to whom the surrender was made June 2d, 1856.

O. A. Carpenter, } wounded badly, Thompson dangerously.
Henry Thompson, }
Mr. Parmely, wounded slightly in nose, also in arm so that he had to leave the ground.
Charles Keiser.
Elizur Hill.
Wm. David.
Hugh Mewhinney.
Mr. Cochran, of Pottawatomie (B. L.).
Owen Brown.
Salmon Brown, accidentally wounded after the fight, and liable to remain a cripple.
Oliver Brown.

(Names of all who either fought or guarded the horses during the fight at Palmyra, June 2d, 1856, will be found on other side.)

Respectfully submitted by   JOHN BROWN.
Messrs. WHITMAN, ELDRIGE, and others.

side in Mr. Adams's invaluable collection. The copy printed on page 240 was obtained by Mr. Robinson, of Paola, from Mrs. Heiskell of the same town, which in the address is termed " Baptiste Paola." The form of the agreement and the order of signatures proves that Captain Brown and not Captain Shore was the real leader at Black Jack, — a fact which some have questioned.

(On the back of the sheet.)

*List of volunteers, either engaged or guarding horses during the fight
at Palmyra or Black Jack, June 2d, 1856.*

Saml. T. Shore, Captain.	O. A. Carpenter, badly wounded.
Silas More.	Augustus Shore.
David Hendricks, Horse Guard.	Mr. Townsley, of Pottawatomie.
Hiram McAllister.	Wm. B. Hayden.
Mr. Parmely, wounded.	John Mewhinney.
Silvester Harris.	Montgomery Shore.
Elkanah Timmons.	Henry Thompson, dangerously
T. Weiner.	wounded.
A. Bondy.	Elias Basinger.
Hugh Mewhinney.	Owen Brown.
Charles Keiser.	Fred'k Brown, Horse Guard.
Elizur Hill.	Salmon Brown, wounded &
Wm. David.	crippled.
Mr. Cochran, of Pottawatomie.	Oliver Brown.
—— —— (this blank to be filled).	
	(Signed) JOHN BROWN.

(Indorsed in Brown's handwriting, " List of Volunteers, etc., at
Black Jack.")

It will be noticed that Brown omits his own name in
these lists, except as signed to the report ; and also that he
puts Captain Shore first, as being next himself in rank.
Apparently the fight would not have ended with the capture
of Pate and his men had it not been for the daring of Brown
and his sons, who were the true heroes of the day ; although
others did well. These sons were all worthy of their father ;
they knew as little how to give way or to fear odds as he
did. Owen Brown once said to me of his brothers, " I never
could discover the least sign of cowardice about those boys ;"
and to another person he said, "None of us ever made much
pretension to being scared."

Mrs. Robinson, wife of the nominal Free-State governor
of Kansas, whose husband had been under arrest for some
weeks when the fight at Black Jack occurred, returned to
Kansas from Massachusetts two days after this fight, and
about ten days after the Pottawatomie executions. She
came up the Missouri River from St. Louis by steamboat,

and reached Kansas City, on the Missouri side of the
Kansas border, at midnight of June 3, 1856. She says
in her book: —

"The last day or two of the trip on the Missouri River rumors of
war became more frequent. Inflammatory extras were thrown upon
the boats at different landings. People at Lexington and other
points along the river were much excited and preparing for a new
invasion. The extras stated the murder of eight proslavery men by
the Abolitionists and the cruel mutilation of their bodies, the death
of the United States Marshal, of H. C. Pate, and J. McGee. Deeds
of blood and violence, of which they were hourly guilty, were charged
upon the Free-State men. The following is a sample of the incendiary extras which flew through the border counties: 'Murder is
the watchword and midnight deed of a scattered and scouting band of
Abolitionists, who had courage only to fly from the face of a wronged
and insulted people when met at their own solicitation. Men, peaceable and quiet, cannot travel on the public roads of Kansas without
being caught, searched, imprisoned, and their lives perhaps taken.
No Southerner dare venture alone and unarmed on her roads!'"

Concerning the fight at Black Jack, Mrs. Robinson says:

"After a two hours' fire Pate sent forward one of his men with a
prisoner and a white flag, and surrendered unconditionally. A few of
his company fled into Missouri; among them was Coleman the murderer. Twenty-six men were taken prisoners by Captain Brown, and
a quantity of goods stolen from Lawrence was found in their wagons.
The delegate to Congress, Whitfield (a proslavery man), left his seat
before the Congressional Investigating Committee, June 2, at the
head of a large body of armed men, his stated object being to relieve
Pate. While Governor Shannon in every instance has stationed
troops in a town after it has been sacked, he now saw the Free-State
men rallying to protect themselves, and feared the slave-power would
lose the ground gained through his servility. He heard, too, of aid
coming from out of Kansas, and issued a proclamation on the 4th,
'commanding all persons belonging to military companies unauthorized by law, to disperse, otherwise they would be dispersed by
the United States troops.' The President's proclamation of February 11 was appended, and Governor Shannon stated that it would
be strictly enforced. A requisition was also made upon Colonel
Sumner for a force sufficient to compel obedience to the proclamation. On the 5th of June Colonel Sumner broke in upon the Free-
State camp and released Captain Pate and his fellow-prisoners.

Colonel Sumner ordered the Free-State men to return quietly to their homes; and then, turning to Pate, said: 'What business have you here?'

" 'I am here by orders of Governor Shannon.'

" 'I saw Governor Shannon yesterday, and your case was specially considered; and he asserted you were not here by his orders.' He then added: 'You are Missourians, all of you, and when you crossed your State line you trampled on State sovereignty. Now, go, sir, in the direction whence you came;' and as he closed his remarks Colonel Sumner waved his hand for Pate and his party to leave. So the brave Pate returned to Westport[1] and Kansas City. He acknowledged the bravery of Brown, for he said Captain Brown rode about them sword in hand and commanded a surrender, and they were obliged to make it. He spoke well of them in their treatment of him while a prisoner."

The victory of Brown at Black Jack roused the proslavery men in Missouri and in Kansas to new fury, while it stimulated the freemen of Kansas to new efforts. Both parties mustered in large force near Palmyra; and on the 5th of June a battle seemed unavoidable, until Colonel Sumner, as Mrs. Robinson mentions, came down with a force of United States cavalry and put a stop to hostilities. He also sent for Captain Brown, as soon as he heard where he was, desir-

---

[1] The title of this unfortunate Captain Pate, who was an editor in Westport, was derived from his commanding the Westport Sharpshooters, — a Border Ruffian company, which seems to have emulated the reputation of the Kickapoo Rangers. With his command he had obeyed the war proclamation of Governor Shannon, been mustered in as a part of the Kansas militia, though living in Missouri, and in that capacity had escorted Gaius Jenkins and George W. Brown, two of the Lawrence men arrested for treason, from Westport to a point near Lecompton, where they arrived on the evening of the 19th of May. He was present, taking part with his command, at the sacking of Lawrence; after which he visited Lecompton, where he learned on the evening of the 25th of the executions on the Pottawatomie. As a United States deputy marshal he resolved to arrest John Brown and his party wherever found. " Without following his steps in detail to Palmyra and Prairie City, and noting the outrages which Pate perpetrated at these places and in their vicinity, — enough to cover his name with infamy," says an enemy of Brown, — "the two men came in contact at a place on the Santa Fé road known as Black Jack." What resulted from that contact we know; the would-be captor was himself captured, held a prisoner for three days by Brown, and then released by the United States, only to engage again in the same career.

ing an interview. Brown left his intrenched camp on the Ottawa and went into the camp of Colonel Sumner, who at once visited Brown's camp and came to terms with him, bidding him release his prisoners, but making no attempt to arrest or punish him,[1] except to ask the civil officer who accompanied him if he had not some warrants to serve. The officer declared that he saw no one whom he wished to arrest; and Brown with his men, though charged with murder at the Pottawatomie, as well as with treason and conspiracy against the Territorial laws, was allowed to go forth unpunished and without being disarmed. Captain Pate and his men were chided by Colonel Sumner, as Mrs. Robinson says; but their horses, arms, etc., were restored to them, even though their guns might have been stolen from the national arsenal in Missouri, as was done a few months before. Brown felt and complained of this injustice, but to no avail. He and his little band dispersed at Colonel Sumner's command; but they soon came together again, and kept up their organization during the whole summer.

John Brown himself was near Topeka, July 4, when the proslavery usurpers in Kansas had determined to disperse

---

[1] All this is concisely described by John Brown in his letter of June, printed in a former chapter. The account by Mrs. Robinson varies in some points from that of Brown; but in such variations Brown is almost always correct. The dispersal of the Free-State legislature at Topeka by Colonel Sumner, July 4, is described by William A. Phillips in the "Atlantic Monthly" for 1879, who brings in Brown as present and advising resistance, even to Federal authority. It is doubtless true that Brown did more than once, while in Kansas, declare that the Federal troops might properly be resisted when they upheld the usurping rulers of the Territory; but there is no evidence that he ever sought to attack them. He did finally attack an arsenal of the United States in Virginia; but that was when he had fully proved the complicity of the national Government in every evil design of the slave-power. The Government which he would have resisted in Kansas had Jefferson Davis for one of its ministers; and the cabinet officer controlling the arsenal at Harper's Ferry was Floyd, who afterward put government arms into the hands of rebels, and led a division himself. In fact, the Federal authority from 1856 to 1861 was but a mask for the slave oligarchy. Colonel Phillips commanded a regiment of Indians during the Civil War, then served in Congress, and now lives at Washington. I have condensed a little his "Atlantic" paper.

the Free-State legislature, which had adjourned to meet there on that day. Mr. W. A. Phillips has given some interesting details of this period. He met Brown at Lawrence, July 2, and rode with his party from Mount Oread, where the Kansas University now stands, along the California road, by Coon Point, and within four miles of Lecompton, the proslavery capital (where Brown's son was a prisoner), until they reached Big Springs. Mr. Phillips says : —

"There we left the road, going in a southwesterly direction for a mile, when we halted on a hill, and the horses were stripped of their saddles, and picketed out to graze. The grass was wet with dew. The men ate of what provision they had with them, and I received a portion from the captain, — dry beef (which was not so bad), and bread made from corn bruised between stones, then rolled in balls and cooked in the ashes of the camp fire. Captain Brown observed that I nibbled it very gingerly, and said, ' I am afraid you will be hardly able to eat a soldier's harsh fare.'

" We next placed our two saddles together, so that our heads lay only a few feet apart. Brown spread his blanket on the wet grass, and, when we lay together upon it, mine was spread over us. It was past eleven o'clock, and we lay there until two in the morning, but we slept none. He seemed to be as little disposed to sleep as I was, and we talked ; or rather he did, for I said little. I found that he was a thorough astronomer ; he pointed out the different constellations and their movements. ' Now,' he said, ' it is midnight,' as he pointed to the finger-marks of his great clock in the sky. The whispering of the wind on the prairie was full of voices to him, and the stars as they shone in the firmament of God seemed to inspire him. ' How admirable is the symmetry of the heavens ; how grand and beautiful ! Everything moves in sublime harmony in the government of God. Not so with us poor creatures. If one star is more brilliant than others, it is continually shooting in some erratic way into space.'

" He criticised both parties in Kansas. Of the proslavery men he said that slavery besotted everything, and made men more brutal and coarse ; nor did the Free-State men escape his sharp censure. He said that we had many noble and true men, but too many broken-down politicians from the older States, who would rather pass resolutions than act, and who criticised all who did real work. A professional politician, he went on, you never could trust ; for even if he had convictions, he was always ready to sacrifice his principles for his advantage.[1]   One of the most interesting things in his conversation that night, and one that marked him as a theorist, was his treatment of our forms of social and political life.   He thought society ought to be organized on a less selfish basis; for while material interests gained something by the deification of pure selfishness, men and women lost much by it.   He said that all great reforms, like the Christian religion, were based on broad, generous, self-sacrificing principles.   He condemned the sale of land as a chattel, and thought that there was an infinite number of wrongs to right before society would be what it should be, but that in our country slavery was the 'sum of all villanies,' and its abolition the first essential work.   If the American people did not take courage and end it speedily, human freedom and republican liberty would soon be empty names in these United States.

"He ran on during these midnight hours in a conversation I can never forget.   The stars grew sharper and clearer, and seemed to be looking down like watchers on that sleeping camp.   My companion paused for a short time, and I thought he was going to sleep, when he said: 'It is nearly two o'clock, and it must be nine or ten miles to Topeka; it is time we were marching,' — and he again drew my attention to his index marks in the sky.   He rose and called his men, who responded with alacrity.   In less than ten minutes the company had saddled, packed, and mounted, and was again on the march.   He declined following the road any farther, but insisted on taking a straight course over the country, guided by the stars.   It was in vain that I expostulated with him, and told him that three or four creeks were in the way, and the country rough and broken, so that it would be difficult to find our way in the dark.   We had a rough time of it that night, and day broke while we were floundering in the thickets of a creek-bottom some miles from Topeka.   As soon as daylight came and we could see our way, we rode more rapidly; but the sun had risen above the horizon before we rode down the slopes.   Across the creek and nearly two miles to the right we saw the tents, and in the morning stillness could hear the bugles blow in Colonel Sumner's camp.   Brown would not go into Topeka, but halted in the timber of the creek, sending one of his men with me as a messenger to bring him word when his company was needed.   He had his horse picketed, and walked down by the side of my horse to the place where I crossed the creek.   He sent messages to one or two gentlemen in town, and, as he wrung my hand at parting, urged that we should have

---

[1] In a later conversation with Phillips, speaking of a Kansas politician, he took out his pocket compass, uncovered it, and said: "You see that needle: it wobbles about, and is mighty unsteady; but it wants to point to the North.   Is your friend like that needle?"

the Legislature meet, resist all who should interfere with it, and fight, if necessary, even the United States troops. He had told me the night before of his visit to many of the fortifications in Europe, and criticised them sharply, holding that modern warfare did away with them, and that a well-armed brave soldier was the best fortification. He criticised all the arms then in use, and showed me a fine repeating-rifle which he said would carry eight hundred yards; but, he added, ' the way to fight is to press to close quarters.' "

In August Brown joined the forces of General James H. Lane in northern Kansas, having first carried his wounded son-in-law, Henry Thompson, into Iowa to be taken care of. Returning about the 10th of August with General Lane, he proceeded with him to Lawrence and to Franklin, where there was some skirmishing; and from the middle of August to the 20th of September he was in the field with his company, fighting the Missourian invaders. The following despatch invited him to join Lane (under the name of Cook) in an expedition : —

Mr. Brown, — General Joe Cook wants you to come to Lawrence this night, for we expect to have a fight on Washington Creek. Come to Topeka as soon as possible, and I will pilot you to the place.   Yours in haste,

                                                    H. Stratton.
Topeka, 7 o'clock, p. m., Aug. 12, 1856.

Concerning this affair Mr. Stratton (who now lives in Colorado) writes me in these words : —

" John Brown was with us when ' Fort Saunders,' on Wakarusa Creek (I think), was destroyed, and commanded the cavalry. A few days before this event Major Hoyt had been murdered at Fort Saunders, where he had gone trusting to the fact that he was a Free Mason ; but he was murdered, and partially buried out on the prairie. General Lane sent out an expedition under Captain Shombre,[1] who was afterwards shot in the groin at Lecompton, and died from the wound. I was second in command of the expedition. We discovered Major Hoyt's remains, and removed them to our camp, which I believe was on the Wakarusa, west of Lawrence. The next day we marched on Fort Saunders. General Lane drew up his forces in front of the fort, Captain Brown occupying the right wing

[1] Or Chambrée.

with his cavalry. A charge was ordered, and the fort taken ; but the murderers had fled into the timber and escaped.

"Large stores of bacon, sugar, flour, etc., were captured and loaded into our train-wagons. The dinner was left untasted on the tables by the ruffians, so precipitate had been their flight. Captain Brown, with his men, was among the first to reach the fort, which was surrounded by a high rail fence, inside of which heavy earth-works had been thrown up. I was acting as Aid to General Lane, and that night piloted him to Topeka. This is the only time I can call to mind when I was with Captain Brown on any expedition, though I used to meet him often at different points. I am not certain about Captain Brown being with our party when we came in from Nebraska, but think he was. While with General Lane I was charged with his personal safety, as a price had been offered for his head. If I could sit down with some one who was an active participant during the border war, I presume in talking over old times I could recall many incidents that have now escaped me."

By this time Brown's name had become such a terror, that wherever the enemy were attacked they believed he was in command. In an appeal to the citizens of Lafayette County, Missouri, urging them to take horses and guns and march into Kansas, General Atchison wrote thus, under date of Aug. 17, 1856 : —

"On the 6th of August *the notorious Brown*, with a party of three hundred abolitionists, made an attack upon a colony of Georgians,[1] murdering about two hundred and twenty-five souls, one hundred and seventy-five of whom were women, children, and slaves. Their houses were burned to the ground, all their property stolen, — horses, cattle, clothing, money, provisions, all taken away from them, and their plows burned to ashes. August 12, at night, three hundred abolitionists, *under this same Brown*, attacked the town of Franklin, robbed, plundered, and burned, took all the arms in town, broke open and destroyed the post-office, captured the old cannon ' Sacramento,' which our gallant Missourians captured in Mexico, and are now turning its mouth against our friends. August 15 *Brown, with four hundred abolitionists*, mostly Lane's men, mounted and armed, attacked Treadwell's Settlement, in Douglas County, numbering about thirty men. They planted the old cannon ' Sacramento' towards the colony, and surrounded them."

[1] At Baptisteville, ten miles northeast of Osawatomie, on an Indian reservation. " Preacher Stewart " really commanded the Free-State men.

It is not necessary (nor was it in 1856) to believe all the stories of battles and sieges which were related on one side or the other during this Kansas imbroglio. Even when there was a desire to tell the truth, circumstances often proved too strong for the narrator. But the great reputation of Brown as a partisan leader is as fully proved by these fictions as by the authentic reports.

The following letters from John Brown, Jr., in prison at Lecompton, seem to be in reply to a suggestion from his father that he might be visited and rescued : —

From John Brown, Jr., to his Father.

LECOMPTON, Aug. 14, 1856.

You can, at any time you think it best, come to camp and see me, especially at evening, without observation. Come to the house of Mrs. Wesley, about fifty rods east from the camp, and she will send up her boy to let me know that a man wants to see me. You could no doubt find a temporary stopping-place either at Captain Thome's or at Mr. Lewis's, about a mile south of our camp, near the California road. In coming here you will notice two camps ; *ours* is the more *easterly*. If you wish to see me, come at evening, early, to the captain's tent, and say that you wish to see the prisoners, and you will be admitted, without a doubt. The captain is very accommodating ; you can come and go *incog.* The captain of Company I says he has been after you more than two months. Don't let them get you. I very much want to see you, but don't run any great risk on this account. At any time you wish to write me, direct to X. Y. Z., and enclose in an *envelope* to C. W. Babcock, Lawrence.

Aug. 16, 1856.

The prospect now appears so favorable for us that it does seem as though I had better not try to meet you just now. The prospect is that there will be either a writ of *habeas corpus* issued, or a change of *venue*, which will in either case take us into the States for trial. Have sent you several letters lately by persons going to Topeka, and I enclose one which I wrote on the 13th.[1] The bearer of it, not seeing you there, has returned it. I was in hearing of the attack on Colonel Titus this morning. A messenger has just come in, stating that he (Titus) and several others were taken prisoners ; Titus wounded. He also reports that a Free-State man was either killed

[1] Not extant.

yesterday or last night, as he was found at Titus's stiff and cold. I saw the fire of Titus's house. Well, it seems that Heaven is smiling on our arms. The case may be that within a few days I shall think it *altogether* best to try to meet you. A very few days will determine. All well. May God bless you! Good-by.

I should be very glad to see you, if you think it prudent to visit me. There is nothing here, that I know of, in the way. If you come just at edge of evening, no one need know it is you ; but don't risk yourself if you are aware of danger. There are *spies* around. In view of present prospects, the prisoners think best that no attempt should be made at present to release them. We are all well treated here. Captain Sackett is a noble man. Should be very glad to know where I could communicate with you from time to time.   J. B., JR., *in prison.*

Indorsed by John Brown.

The allusion to the attack on " Titus," in the above letter, will be made more clear by a longer letter to Jason Brown, written in part on the same day, but apparently begun earlier in the day. The same letter contains some notice of what had been happening in Kansas since the middle of July. These chronicles are not wholly exact; but it was not possible then to obtain precise information in Kansas, and the news sent to the prisoners was likely to come from both sides. They were not held in strict confinement, and, after a while at first, did not suffer much hardship. Indeed, they might easily have escaped, as will soon appear.

From John Brown, Jr.

CAMP OF U. S. CAVALRY, NEAR LECOMPTON, KANSAS,
Aug. 16, 1856.

DEAR BROTHER JASON AND OTHERS, — Agreeably with my promise to write often, I have sent you lately not less than four letters, — one or two by private hands, the others by mail. Events of the most stirring character are now passing within hearing distance. I should think more than two hundred shots have been fired within the past half hour, and within a mile of our camp. Have just learned that some eighty of our Free-State men have " pitched into " a proslavery camp this side of Lecompton, which was commanded by a notorious proslavery scoundrel named Titus, one of the Buford party from Alabama. A dense volume of smoke is now rising in the vicinity of his house. The firing has ceased, and we are most impatient to learn the result.

During the past month the Ruffians have been actively at work, and have made not less than five intrenched camps, where they have in different parts of the Territory established themselves in armed bands, well provided with provisions, arms, and ammunition. From these camps they sally out, steal horses, and rob Free-State settlers (in several cases murdering them), and then slip back into their camp with their plunder. Last week a body of our men made a descent upon Franklin,[1] and after a skirmishing fight of about three hours took their barracks, and recovered some sixty guns and a cannon, of which our men had been robbed some months since, on the road from Westport. Our loss was one man killed and two severely wounded, but it is thought they will recover. The enemy were in a log building, from which they kept up a sharp fire, while they themselves were quite unexposed. Our men then had recourse to a system of tactics not laid down in Scott. They procured a wagon loaded with hay, and running it down against the building set it on fire, when the rascals immediately surrendered. Yesterday our men had invested another of their fortified camps on Washington Creek, a south branch of the Wakarusa ; and it was expected that an attack would be made upon it last night.

Hurrah for our side! A messenger has just come in, stating that on the approach of our men, some two hundred and fifty or three hundred in number, at Washington Creek yesterday, towards evening, the enemy broke and fled, leaving behind, to fall into the hands of our men, a lot of provisions and a hundred stand of arms. But this is not all. The notorious Colonel Titus, who only a day or two since was heard to declare that "Free-State men had only two weeks longer to remain in Kansas," went out last night on a marauding expedition, in which he took six prisoners and a lot of horses. This morning our men followed him closely and fell upon his camp, killed two of his men, liberated the prisoners he had taken, took him and ten other prisoners, set fire to his house, and with a lot of arms, tents, provisions, etc., returned, having in the fight had only one of our men seriously wounded.

August 19.

The affair last mentioned was conducted with such expedition that the United States troops, located about a mile off, had not time to reach the scene before it was all over and our men on their return, marching in good order. Our men numbered four hundred, and had

---

[1] Four miles south of Lawrence. The fights that followed are those mentioned by Atchison on page 309.

the cannon which they had taken at Franklin. With this they fired six balls, out of seven shots, through Colonel Titus's house before his gang surrendered. This series of victories has caused the greatest fear among the proslavery men. While the firing was going on, the citizens at Lecompton fled across the river in the greatest consternation. Great numbers are leaving for Missouri. Colonel Titus was seriously wounded by a Sharpe's-rifle ball passing through his hand, and lodging in his shoulder too deep to be reached. It is thought the wound will prove fatal.

Day before yesterday Governor Shannon and Major Sedgwick of the army went to Lawrence to obtain the prisoners our men had taken; but our men would consent to give them up only on condition that they on the other side should give up the prisoners that had been taken on warrants at Franklin, the next day after the battle there, for participating in it; and, as a further condition, that they should give up the cannon which had been taken from Lawrence at the time it was sacked; and still further agree to do all in their power to break up the camps of armed desperadoes, as well as to prevent their coming in from Missouri. These terms were complied with; and yesterday the prisoners were exchanged and the cannon at Lecompton given up to our men, and it is now once more in Lawrence. Thus you see they have themselves set their own laws at nought by that exchange of prisoners whom they had taken on warrants for those we had taken by the *might of the people*. Lane's men were on hand and did good service. The Chicago company that had been turned back on the Missouri River were on hand and in the thickest of the fight. Some say Colonel Lane was in it himself. Father returned with the overland emigrants, leaving in Nebraska Henry Thompson, Owen, Salmon, Frederick, and Oliver, much improved in health. He was in the fight at Franklin, and also aided in routing the gang on Washington Creek, as well as in the capture of Titus and his crew. By this time he is in Iowa, or some other distant region. He is an omnipresent dread to the ruffians. I see by the Missouri papers that they regard him as the most terrible foe they have to encounter. He stands very high with the Free-State men who will fight; and the great majority of these have made up their minds that nothing short of war to the death can save us from extermination. Say to the men of Osawatomie to become thoroughly prepared, for at any time their lives may depend upon their efficiency and vigilance; that military organization is needed for something else than *amusement*. Don't fail to urge the enrolment of every able-bodied Free-State man, and place yourselves in a position to act both offensively and defensively in the most efficient manner. Stringfellow and Atchison are said to be again raising a force to come in from

Missouri and carry out their long-cherished plan to drive out or exterminate our people. If our men are wide awake we shall gain the day. The prospect for Kansas becoming a free State never looked brighter. Now is the time to prepare, and continue prepared.

Have not yet learned of any definite action of Congress in regard to us prisoners, but we doubtless shall in a few days. Wealthy continues to have the chills and fever every few days. Write often.

Ever your affectionate brother,

JOHN.

The last fight at Osawatomie, which for some reason or other was more celebrated than any of the encounters in which Brown engaged during 1856, was the third skirmish that had taken place at or near that historic village. The first was on June 2, and is mentioned by Brown in his letter of June 24; the second was early in August, and is probably the same as the attack on Buford's men about Middle Creek, soon to be spoken of, which occurred August 5;[1] the third was on the 30th of August, and was provoked by the defeat of Buford's men. In both these August encounters John Brown had some share.

A Boston clergyman (Rev. J. W. Winkley), who was in Kansas as a young man in 1856, has described to me with some detail John Brown on the war-path, as he saw him during the fights of August. Mr. Winkley was then living on the South Pottawatomie, twenty miles above Osawatomie, and had enlisted to join Brown there, with twenty others, upon the news of an invasion of Missourians. They travelled all night, reached Osawatomie in the morning, breakfasted there, and then went with Captains Cline and Shore (seventy men in all) to attack the enemy, whom they surprised and defeated to the number of two hundred or more. Soon after, Brown came up from Osawatomie and congratulated the men on their victory, at which he had not been present. A Missourian, mortally wounded, wished greatly to see Brown before he died. The old hero rode up to the wagon where the wounded man was, and said with some sternness : "You wish to see me ; here I am. Take a good look at me, and tell your friends when you get back to Missouri what sort of man you saw." Then in a gentler

---

[1] This is one of the battles reported by Atchison.

tone he added: "We wish no harm to you or your companions. Stay at home, let us alone, and we shall be friends. I wish you well." Meantime the wounded man had with an effort raised himself up, viewed Brown from head to foot, as if feasting his eyes on the greatest curiosity, and then sank back exhausted, saying: "I don't see as you are so bad; you don't look or talk like it." Then, reaching out his hand, the dying Missourian said: "I thank you." Brown clasped his hand, said "God bless you!" and rode away with tears in his eyes. Mr. Winkley also describes an onset made by Brown upon some of his own men, supposing them to be the enemy, the next morning. He had taken volunteers the day before, after the fight, and ridden away on some excursion, bidding the rest go home to their farms. They went back and camped where they had met the enemy that morning. While at breakfast Brown came upon them suddenly, supposed them to be foes, and in a moment went charging down upon them at the head of his little band of thirty men. Before he attacked he discovered who they were; but had they been Missourians he would have put them to rout by his ready courage.

The condition of matters in Kansas and Missouri was such at this time that it was almost impossible to obtain correct information of what was going on, even from eye-witnesses. Owen Brown, who had been badly injured after the campaign of June, and afterward very ill in Iowa, whither he had gone to regain his health, wrote just before the fight at Osawatomie the following letter to his mother in the Adirondacs, which illustrates the exaggerations then everywhere current; while it gives some true touches concerning men and things:

Owen Brown to his Mother at North Elba.

TABOR, FREMONT COUNTY, IOWA, Aug. 27, 1856.

DEAR MOTHER, — The last news we had from Kansas, father was at Lawrence, and had charge of a company, — the bravest men the Territory could afford. Those who come through here from the Territory say that father is the most daring, courageous man in Kansas. You have no doubt heard that the Free-State men have taken two forts, or blockhouses, with a fine lot of arms, several prisoners, and two cannon. Shannon was obliged to flee for his life;

afterwards came to Lane to negotiate for peace. He proposed that the Free-State men should give up the prisoners and arms they had taken; at the same time they (the enemy) should still hold our men as prisoners, and keep all the arms they had taken from the Free-State men. But Lane would not consent to that; he required Shannon to deliver up the howitzer they had taken at Lawrence, release some prisoners, disarm the proslavery men in the Territory, and do all in his power to remove the enemy from the Territory. With fear and trembling, Shannon consented to all of Lane's demands.

There is now at this place a company of volunteers from Maine, Massachusetts, and Michigan, — about eighty in all. We hear lately that about three thousand Missourians have crossed at St. Joe and other places, and have gone armed into the Territory; that Governor Woodson has sent four hundred mounted men on to the frontier to intercept our volunteers and prevent them from carrying in provisions and ammunition, which are much needed now in Kansas. The last information comes from reliable sources, and is probably true, — a portion of it. We also learn that the Free-State men have melted up all the old lead-pipe they can get hold of for ammunition; and now the news comes from reliable sources that Lane is about to enter Leavenworth with two thousand men; that he has sent word to the citizens of Leavenworth, requiring them to deliver up a few prisoners they had taken, with some wagons and other property, or he will destroy the town forthwith. Colonel Smith, of Leavenworth, commander of Government troops, refuses to protect the proslavery men of the Territory, replying that Lane is able to dress them all out, troops and all. Shannon made a speech to them, urging them to cease hostilities, — that he could not defend them (that is, our enemies). At present our enemies and the Missourians are trembling in their boots, if reports are true.

I have gained strength quite fast, and am now determined to go back into the Territory, and try the elephant another pull. We hope that men will volunteer by the thousands from the States, well armed, with plenty of money to buy provisions with, which are scarce in Kansas Territory. There are probably several thousand acres less of corn in Kansas than there would have been had it not been for the war. We look hard for help: now comes the tug of war. We have sent on men to learn the state of affairs on the frontier, and will move on into the Territory shortly. We are now waiting for one other company, which is within a few days' drive of here. For the want of time I leave out many particulars in connection with the taking of those forts, which would be quite interesting, and show Yankee skill and strategy, at least. If any

of our folks write to us, or to me (I assume another name, George
Lyman), direct to George Lyman, Tabor, Fremont County, Iowa,
care Jonas Jones, Esq. Mr. Jones will take them out of the office
here and send them on by private conveyance. We cannot hear
from you in any other way. Perhaps you know of a different way,
but I do not.

Your affectionate son,

OWEN BROWN.

P. S. Have not heard from Fred since Oliver and William
Thompson took him into the camp ; nor have I heard from Henry,
Salmon, William, and Oliver since they left this place to go home.

" Fred " was John Brown's son Frederick, who three days
after this letter was written was shot down by Missourians
near his uncle Adair's house in Osawatomie, the morning
of the fight there. William Thompson was the brother of
Henry, and had just come from North Elba.

John Brown made two written reports of the Osawatomie engagement of August 30. The more concise is that
sent to his family ten days after. A longer report of the
same date, which he published in the newspapers, follows
it immediately : —

John Brown to his Family.

LAWRENCE, KANSAS TERRITORY, Sept. 7, 1856.

DEAR WIFE AND CHILDREN, EVERY ONE, — I have one moment
to write to you, to say that I am yet alive, that Jason and family
were well yesterday; John and family, I hear, are well (he being
yet a prisoner). On the morning of the 30th of August an attack
was made by the Ruffians on Osawatomie, numbering some four
hundred, by whose scouts our dear Frederick was shot dead without
warning, — he supposing them to be Free-State men, as near as we
can learn. One other man, a cousin of Mr. Adair, was murdered by
them about the same time that Frederick was killed, and one badly
wounded at the same time. At this time I was about three miles
off, where I had some fourteen or fifteen men over night that I had
just enlisted to serve under me as regulars. These I collected as
well as I could, with some twelve or fifteen more; and in about
three quarters of an hour I attacked them from a wood with thick
undergrowth. With this force we threw them into confusion for
about fifteen or twenty minutes, during which time we killed or
wounded from seventy to eighty of the enemy, — as they say, — and

then we escaped as well as we could, with one killed while escaping, two or three wounded, and as many more missing. Four or five Free-State men were butchered during the day in all. Jason fought bravely by my side during the fight, and escaped with me, he being unhurt. I was struck by a partly-spent grape, canister, or rifle shot, which bruised me some, but did not injure me seriously. "Hitherto the Lord has helped me," notwithstanding my afflictions. Things seem rather quiet just now, but what another hour will bring I cannot say. I have seen three or four letters from Ruth, and one from Watson, of July or August, which are all I have seen since in June. I was very glad to hear once more from you, and hope that you will continue to write to some of the friends, so that I may hear from you. I am utterly unable to write you for most of the time. May the God of our fathers bless and save you all !

Your affectionate husband and father,

JOHN BROWN.

Monday morning, Sept. 8, 1856.

Jason has just come in ; left all well as usual. John's trial is to come off or commence to-day.   Yours ever,

JOHN BROWN.

THE FIGHT OF OSAWATOMIE.

Early in the morning of the 30th of August the enemy's scouts approached to within one mile and a half of the western boundary of the town of Osawatomie. At this place my son Frederick (who was not attached to my force) had lodged, with some four other young men from Lawrence, and a young man named Garrison, from Middle Creek. The scouts, led by a proslavery preacher named White, shot my son dead in the road, while he — as I have since ascertained — supposed them to be friendly. At the same time they butchered Mr. Garrison, and badly mangled one of the young men from Lawrence, who came with my son, leaving him for dead. This was not far from sunrise. I had stopped during the night about two and one half miles from them, and nearly one mile from Osawatomie. I had no organized force, but only some twelve or fifteen new recruits, who were ordered to leave their preparations for breakfast and follow me into the town, as soon as this news was brought to me.

As I had no means of learning correctly the force of the enemy, I placed twelve of the recruits in a log-house, hoping we might be able to defend the town. I then gathered some fifteen more men together, whom we armed with guns ; and we started in the direction of the enemy. After going a few rods we could see them approaching the town in line of battle, about half a mile off, upon a hill west of the village. I then gave up all idea of doing more than to annoy, from the timber near the town, into which we were all retreated, and which was filled with a thick growth of underbrush; but I had no time to recall the twelve men in the log-house, and so lost their assistance in the fight. At the point above named I met with Captain Cline, a very active young man, who had with him some twelve or fifteen mounted men, and persuaded him to go with us into the timber, on the southern shore of the Osage, or Marais des Cygnes, a little to the northwest from the village. Here the men, numbering not more than thirty in all, were directed to scatter and secrete themselves as well as they could, and await the approach of the enemy. This was done in full view of them (who must have seen the whole movement), and had to be done in the utmost haste. I believe Captain Cline and some of his men were not even dismounted in the fight, but cannot assert positively. When the left wing of the enemy had approached to within common rifle-shot, we commenced firing, and very soon threw the northern branch of the enemy's line into disorder. This continued some fifteen or twenty minutes, which gave us an uncommon opportunity to annoy them. Captain Cline and his men soon got out of ammunition, and retired across the river.

After the enemy rallied we kept up our fire, until, by the leaving of one and another, we had but six or seven left. We then retired across the river. We had one man killed — a Mr. Powers, from Captain Cline's company — in the fight. One of my men, a Mr. Partridge, was shot in crossing the river. Two or three of the party who took part in the fight are yet missing, and may be lost or taken prisoners. Two were wounded; namely, Dr. Updegraff and a Mr. Collis. I cannot speak in too high terms of them, and of many others I have not now time to mention.

One of my best men, together with myself, was struck by a partially spent ball from the enemy, in the commencement of the fight, but we were only bruised. The loss I refer to is one of my missing men. The loss of the enemy, as we learn by the different statements of our own as well as their people, was some thirty-one or two killed, and from forty to fifty wounded. After burning the town to ashes and killing a Mr. Williams they had taken, whom neither party claimed, they took a hasty leave, carrying their dead and wounded with them. They did not attempt to cross the river, nor to search for us, and have not since returned to look over their work.

I give this in great haste, in the midst of constant interruptions. My second son was with me in the fight, and escaped unharmed.

This I mention for the benefit of his friends. Old Preacher White,
I hear, boasts of having killed my son. Of course he is a lion.

JOHN BROWN.

LAWRENCE, KANSAS, Sept. 7, 1856.

Jason Brown ("my second son"), who was his father's
body-guard in this fight, relates this incident of the
campaign : —

"Captain Shore is a good and brave man, but I cannot learn that
he claims to be the hero of Black Jack. I care nothing for the
honors of war. It matters but little whether the battles of Black
Jack and Osawatomie are looked upon as victories or defeats. I
was at the latter engagement, but I do not know whether I had the
honor of *killing* (as it is looked upon by some persons) anybody at
Osawatomie or not. If I did, I would gladly transfer the honor of
the whole slaughtering part of it to the Rev. David N. Utter, and to
his brother in divinity, Rev. Martin White. The only real comforting recollection of my part in it is, that I did all in my power to
alleviate the sufferings of a young and very intelligent Mississippian
named Kline, if I remember correctly, who was terribly wounded,
but able to talk. He had been wounded a day or two before, in an
attack by Free-State men on a camp of Georgians, seven or eight
miles southeast of Osawatomie. The weather was hot, and the
wound below the knee of the right leg, which was terribly shattered
by a Sharpe's-rifle ball, was filled with maggots. How it was that
he did not have the right care I do not know. All about the house
where he was lying was excitement and hurry, to be ready to meet
the enemy we expected soon to attack us. I got help, cleansed his
wound of the vermin, dressed it, bathed him, and changed his
clothes. While this was being done he asked my name. I told
him. He said, 'I thought the Abolitionists were savages before I
was brought here.' As he lay there, pale and exhausted from loss of
blood and suffering, he spoke of his home and friends in Mississippi,
and how he wished he had never come to Kansas. He said he would
soon be at rest. He asked me if I would not take care of him for
the few hours he had to live. I told him I would. As I was sitting
by his bed and saw the tears flowing from a heart full of sorrow and
trouble, alone among strangers, and far from home, I thought this :
If these are some of the things which make war glorious and honorable, deliver me from the honors of war. In a moment more I was
suddenly called away to defend my own life, and probably to do more
of such work. I would rather have the real good it did me then to
care as best I could for a few hours for a misguided dying enemy,

than to have all the glory ever gained by the proudest and most
successful warrior that ever shook the earth with the thunder of his
guns and the tread of his mighty armies of beasts and men, since the
world began. I heard afterwards that this young man was rescued
from 'the abolition fiends' by Reid's army, and thrown into a
wagon with other wounded men, and died somewhere on the way to
Missouri. I don't know that this is true."

A contemporary proslavery account of this fight is as
follows, copied from a Missouri newspaper : —

" The attack on Osawatomie was by part of an army of eleven
hundred and fifty men, of whom Atchison was major-general. General Reid, with two hundred and fifty men and one piece of artillery,
moved on to attack Osawatomie ; he arrived near that place, and was
attacked by two hundred Abolitionists under the command of the notorious John Brown, who commenced firing upon Reid from a thick
chaparral four hundred yards off. General Reid made a successful
charge, killing thirty-one, and took seven prisoners. Among the
killed was Frederick Brown. The notorious John Brown was also
killed, by a proslavery man named White, in attempting to cross the
Marais des Cygnes. The proslavery party have five wounded. On
the same day Captain Hays, with forty men, attacked the house of
the notorious Ottawa Jones, burned it, and killed two Abolitionists.
Jones fled to the cornfield, was shot at by Hays, and is believed to
be dead."

The Indian missions in Kansas were little centres of civilization, and that which was first established near the crossing
of the Ottawa River, near what is now Ottawa, was long an
oasis in the desert. There the Presbyterians and Baptists
started missions ; thither the Rev. Joseph Meeker, in 1834,
brought the first printing-press, and there the first Kansas
book was printed ; there lived the famous Indian and his
excellent white missionary wife, John Tecumseh Jones
(usually called " Tawey Jones," Ottawa being properly pronounced Ot-*taw*-wa). There John Brown and his friends
were always welcome, and the great house of this Christian
Indian was " long the hospitable headquarters of Free-State
men," as Wilder says, with whom Horace Greeley made this
part of his tour in Kansas in 1859, — spending a night at
Jones's house. Brown said of it and its owner in 1857 : " I

saw while it was standing, and afterwards saw the ruins of,
a most valuable house, the property of a highly civilized, intelligent, and exemplary Christian Indian, which was burned
to the ground by the Ruffians, because its owner was suspected of favoring Free-State men." [1] The house was afterwards rebuilt. Its destruction by the Missouri invaders, —
a detachment from the force that burned Osawatomie, August 30, — has been described to me by Jason Brown : —

" On the 29th of August word came to my father, who was posted
a mile from Osawatomie, on the road to Paola and Westport, on
the Missouri side of the Marais des Cygnes, near where the State
Insane Asylum now stands, that the Missourians were on their way
from Westport. At the same time that they attacked Osawatomie,
they sent a force of fifty men to burn the house of our friend Jones,
and kill him if possible. He was a tall and stout Christian Indian,
who had married a Miss Emery from Vermont ; he owned much
land, had two or three hundred head of cattle, improved breeds of
all domestic animals, and had committed no offence, except being
friendly to the Free-State men. A little after midnight he heard a
great noise among his dogs, and sprang out of bed ; as he did so, he
heard the scabbards of the Missourians strike on the flag-stones in
front of his house as they dismounted from their horses. They had
let down his cornfield fences, and ridden on all sides, hoping to
find a force of Free-State men there in his double log-house, —
at that time the best in Kansas ; but there was nobody in it except
Jones and his wife, an Indian boy, and a ' neutral ' named Parker

---

[1] Mr. Adair wrote from Osawatomie, July 16, 1856, to " Bro. John
Brown," by Jason, informing him that of $49.50 received in June from
" Bro. J. R. B.," he had assigned $25 to John Brown, Sr., and his unmar-
ried sons ; $10 to J. B., Jr. ; $7.25 to Jason, and $7.28 to S. L. Adair.
He says he had sent him $10 immediately, — but it had come back to him,
and he had now sent it by George Partridge to " you or some of your sons "
at Ottawa Jones's : $8 was paid to Frederick and $7 to Henry Thompson,
July 2, at Jones's. This shows that the house of this Indian farmer was a
rendezvous for Brown and his party, while they were under arms in that
anxious summer, and while they were hunted like wolves over the prairie.
Sarah Brown says : " On the day that my brother Frederick was killed,
near Osawatomie, my father lost his hat in fighting. When he found the
body of his son he was forced to take his hat to cover his own head. Afterward, the Indian (Ottawa Jones), of whom he often spoke, gave him a cap.
When on one of his visits home, at North Elba, he brought the cap with
him, and said he wanted it kept in memory of Ottawa Jones."

from Missouri. The Ruffians shouted, 'We've got you now, —
come out, come out!' Nobody replying, and fearing an ambush,
they cried, 'Fire the house!' and began to do so, setting it on fire in
several places. Jones had seized his gun and stood in his front hall,
thinking what he could do. 'I knew we must shoot,' he told me;
'we must fight, or make our escape the best way we could.' He
opened the door and cocked his gun; the enemy hearing it called
out, 'Don't shoot!' whereupon he sprang out in his night-clothes,
and ran as far as he could into a thirty-acre cornfield close by, the
enemy shooting at him, but missing him. It was a wet and cold
night (August 29). He ran through his corn, and far beyond, about
two miles in all; looking back, he saw his house burning. The
guide in this attack was Henry Sherman, of Pottawatomie, who had
worked for Jones and knew the house well. Mrs. Jones, in the
mean time, had put about four hundred dollars in gold and silver
into a bag, and tried to conceal it and herself in the house. The
captain of the Ruffians, looking through the door, saw her and said:
'Come out! we won't hurt *you*, — you have been kind to us.' As
she went out, she dropped the money in the grass, and it was picked
up by Sherman or some of the band.   They found Parker, the Missourian, ill in bed; as they approached him with their weapons, he
said, 'Don't kill me, — I'm sick.' 'We always find a good many
sick men when we come round,' was the reply, — and with that they
dragged him out into the road, knocked him on the head and cut his
throat, but did not sever the jugular vein; then dragged him to the
bank of the Ottawa and threw him in among some brush.   I found
him afterward in a hospital at Lawrence, able to tell his story; to
which he added, 'I'm not a neutral any more; I'm a Free-State
man now; they'll never take me alive again.' The Ruffians sacked
the house, which was burned to the ground, as described by my father
in one of his speeches."

A marble monument now stands at Osawatomie, erected
in 1877 to commemorate the battle there, and bearing on
one side this legend: —

THIS INSCRIPTION IS ALSO IN COMMEMORATION OF THE
HEROISM OF CAPTAIN JOHN BROWN, WHO COM-
MANDED AT THE BATTLE OF OSAWATOMIE,
AUG. 30, 1856, WHO DIED AND CON-
QUERED AMERICAN SLAVERY
AT CHARLESTON, VA.,
DEC. 2, 1859.

In dedicating this monument on the twenty-first anniversary of the fight (Aug. 30, 1877), Charles Robinson, of Lawrence, who presided, said among other things : —

"This is an occasion of no ordinary merit, being for no less an object than to honor and keep fresh the memory of those who freely offered their lives for their fellow-men. We are told that 'scarcely for a righteous man will one die, yet peradventure for a good man some would dare to die;' but the men whose death we commemorate this day, cheerfully offered themselves a sacrifice for strangers and a despised race. They were men of convictions, though death stared them in the face. They were cordial haters of oppression, and would fight injustice wherever found ; if framed into law, then they would fight the law ; if upheld and enforced by government, then government must be resisted. They were of Revolutionary stock, and held that when a long train of abuses had put the people under absolute despotism, it was right and duty to throw off such government and provide guards for future security. The soul of John Brown was the inspiration of the Union armies in the emancipation war, and it will be the inspiration of all men in the present and distant future who may revolt against tyranny and oppression ; because he dared to be a traitor to the government that he might be loyal to humanity. To the superficial observer John Brown was a failure. So was Jesus of Nazareth.[1] Both suffered ignominious death as traitors to the

---

[1] The comparison here drawn by this speaker is too close and literal to be accepted by all Christians, but it was designed to express the deepest reverence for John Brown, and to indicate that his memory is immortal. In fact, this Ohio Puritan is the best-known name in Kansas ; not that the million people, — white, black, and red, — who now dwell in this State, all know accurately who he was and what he did ; but they have all heard of him, and keep his memory alive by tales and disputes. And in the districts where he moved about, armed at all points, the air is full of legends concerning him, — some true, some false, and most of them neither true nor false, but a mixture of both. This is specially the case in the region around Osawatomie, that village of a single street and a few detached houses, in the angle where those two romantic rivers, — the Marais des Cygnes (or as Brown spelled it, "Merodezene") and the Pottawatomie, — come together and form the Osage. The town takes its name from the first three letters of "Osage" prefixed to the last three syllables of "Pottawatomie." This centaur-like epithet was the work of another Brown, who early settled in this spot, but who is now quite forgotten in the greater fame of his namesake. The Marais des Cygnes has a more picturesque name, as if the old French *voyageurs* who gave the title had found the swan swimming there. They never did, but it was some other great bird to which they gave the

government, yet one is now hailed as the savior of a world from sin, and the other of a race from bondage."

On the 8th of September, after hearing the particulars of the Osawatomie fight, John Brown, Jr., wrote to his father at Lawrence thus : —

MONDAY MORNING, Sept. 8, 1856.

DEAR FATHER AND BROTHER, — Colonel Blood has just handed me your letter, for which I am most grateful. Having before heard of Frederick's death and that you were missing, my anxiety on your account has been most intense. Though my dear brother I shall never again see here, yet I thank God you and Jason still live. Poor Frederick has perished in a good cause, the success of which cause I trust will yet bring joy to millions.

My "circumstances and prospects" are much the same as when I last wrote you. The trial of Mr. Williams and me is before Cato, in October, — I believe the 4th. Don't know whether or not the others will get any trial here. Judge Lecompte is reported sick, and as no notice of the names of the jurors and witnesses has been served on them, it looks as if the intention is to hold them over to another term.

Wealthy has the chills and fever almost every day. She succeeds in checking it only a short time. It would afford us a great satisfaction to see you and Jason; he, and I have no doubt you, could come up with some one without any risk. If Governor Geary should not release us, I still think of going with you, whenever you think it best, to some place out of reach of a re-arrest. I can, I have no doubt, succeed in making my escape to you from here, where W. and Johnny

---

old poetic name ; and here, too, on this " Marsh of the Swans," the vulture of slavery croaked its foulest note before committing suicide. A long, slow, winding, and sombre stream, fringed everywhere with dark woods, it creeps through the counties south of Lawrence, where the worst ruffians had their roosts, and where the darkest deeds were done. The annals of theft and murder and arson on the Scotch border, around which Walter Scott and the older ballad-makers cast an atmosphere of romance, were repeated in ruder ways in these Missouri Marches, of which John Brown and James Montgomery came to be the self-appointed wardens. Montgomery was himself a Scotchman by descent, whose great-grandfather had fought for the young Chevalier at Culloden ; but Brown was of the unmixed Puritan breed, and inherited from deacons and captains of Connecticut " the sword of the Lord and of Gideon." Montgomery's widow and sons still live in Kansas, but none of the Browns remain there alive.

might join us. There is some talk of our being removed to Leavenworth soon. If we are, I suppose the difficulty of escape would be very much increased. I am anxious to see you both, in order to perfect some plan of escape in case it should appear best. Come up if you *consistently* can.

The battle of Osawatomie is considered here as *the great fight* so far, and, considering the enemy's loss, it is certainly a great victory for us. Certainly a very dear burning of the town for them. This has proven most unmistakably that "Yankees" *will* "fight." Every one I hear speaking of you is loud in your praise. The Missourians in this region show signs of great fear. Colonel Cook [1] was heard to say that if our party were prudent in view of their success, there was nothing to prevent our having everything our own way.

Hoping to see you both soon, I am as ever

Your affectionate son and brother.

(Not signed.)

On the reverse, "Captain J. B———, Lawrence."

Near the above, in John Brown's handwriting, is "J. Brown, Jr., in prison."

In connection with this fight, I may quote from a letter concerning John Brown which I received after his death from Richard Mendenhall, a Quaker, then living near Osawatomie. He said: "I was at a public meeting held in the spring of 1856 at Osawatomie, for the purpose of considering what course should be pursued relative to submitting to the 'bogus laws' (of Governor Shannon's Territorial Legislature), more especially the payment of taxes under them. I was very unexpectedly chosen chairman of the meeting. John Brown was present, and made a very earnest, decisive, and characteristic speech. For the action of that meeting in taking a bold stand against the 'bogus laws' we were all indicted, but the warrants were never served. I next met John Brown again on the evening before the battle of Osawatomie. He with a number of others was driving a herd of cattle which they had taken from proslavery men. He rode out of the company to speak to me, when I playfully asked him where he got those cattle. He replied, with a characteristic shake of the head, that 'they were good

---

[1] Of the United States Army.

Free-State cattle now.' In the tenth month, 1858, John
Brown and two others — one of them Stevens — came to my
house and stayed several days, being detained by high water.
I found him capable of talking interestingly on almost every
subject. He had travelled a good deal in Europe on account
of his business, and he imparted to me some valuable hints
on different branches of business. I once heard a stranger
ask the Rev. S. L. Adair if he knew what John Brown's
principles were; and he replied that his relation to John
Brown gave him a right to know that Brown had an idea
impressed upon his mind from childhood that he was an
instrument raised up by Providence to break the jaws of
the wicked; and his feelings becoming enlisted in the affairs
of Kansas, he thought this was the field for his operations.
Last winter, when Brown took those negroes from Missouri,
he sent them directly to me; but I had a school then at my
house, and the children were just assembling when they
came. I could not take them in, and was glad of an excuse,
as I could not sanction his mode of procedure." Nevertheless, Richard Mendenhall added, much in the spirit of John
A. Andrew's phrase ("Brown himself was right"), "Men
are not always to be judged so much by their actions as by
their motives. I believe that John Brown was a good man,
and that he will be remembered for good in time long hence
to come."

The state of affairs immediately preceding the fight was
made known by many letters such as the following, written
by a Kansas farmer, Cyrus Adams, who emigrated from
Massachusetts, to his brother at home: —

LAWRENCE, KANSAS, Aug. 24, 1856.

DEAR BROTHER, — You probably learn of the state of affairs here
in Kansas as well as I can describe them. We live under a republican form of government, so called, — a form of government which
allows its people to be murdered every day, and lifts no hand for
their protection; and so we are all of us liable to be murdered any
day. Every little while we are set upon by bands of ruffians acting
under the officers of the General Government; towns are sacked and
burned, men murdered, and property destroyed. Until lately the
Free-State folks have not offered much resistance to these outrages.

It was known that bands of these ruffians encamped in the vicinity, where they carried on their trade of horse-stealing and robbery; and murdered a man with whom I was well acquainted: he was riding by near one of these camps, and was shot dead by some of the guard. His name was Major Hoyt, of Deerfield, Mass. Another man was shot near the same place. A few days ago a brother-in-law of Mr. Nute, whom you saw in Concord, came into the Territory. He intended to stop in Leavenworth. He brought his wife, and left her with Mr. Nute until he could go back and put up a house. When returning, and within two miles of Leavenworth, he was shot, and, horrible to relate, was scalped in the Indian fashion. A man — or a beast — took his scalp and carried it about the streets of Leavenworth on a long pole, saying that he "went out to get a damned Abolition scalp, and got one." Another man went to Kansas City for a load of lumber; he was shot and scalped in the same way. So you may judge of the folks we have to deal with. If they catch a man alone they show no mercy.

Two weeks after the date of this letter, Governor Geary reached Kansas to supersede Shannon and his proslavery secretary Woodson, who was acting governor. At that time Lawrence was a military camp. All the roads leading thither were blockaded by armed bodies of Southern marauders, and every day violence was offered to Free-State citizens. Guerilla parties of Free-State men were also abroad, making reprisals on proslavery men. Between these bodies there was little safety for any one. Geary at once distributed large numbers of his proclamations, ordering all bodies of armed men to lay down their arms and retire to their homes and ordinary occupations. He declared his intention to protect the Territory from further violence, and this promise was tolerably well kept. When questioned by the people at Lawrence (which he visited for the first time September 12) whether it would be safe for them to go to their homes in other parts of the Territory, he replied: "You had better stay in town a few days longer, for mutual protection; but be careful that you do nothing in violation of the spirit of my proclamation. To defend yourselves against an attack will not incur my displeasure." At this time there were some eight hundred Free-State men assembled in Lawrence, but a few days after the number was much reduced. Soon after Geary's removal by Buchanan, he wrote a "Farewell Address to the People of Kansas," dated March 12, 1857, in which he fully describes the condition of things on his first arrival, — the time of which I am writing. He says : " I reached Kansas, and entered upon the discharge of my official duties in the most gloomy hour of her history. Desolation and ruin reigned on every hand ; homes and firesides were deserted ; the smoke of burning dwellings darkened the atmosphere ; women and children, driven from their habitations, wandered over the prairies and among the woodlands, or sought refuge and protection even among the Indian tribes. The highways were infested with numerous predatory bands, and the towns were fortified and garrisoned by armies of conflicting partisans, each excited almost to frenzy, and determined upon mutual extermination. Such was, without exaggeration, the condition of the Territory at this period."

It was in the midst of such scenes that the Border Ruffians, provoked by the recent successes of the Kansas farmers, raised an army of twenty-seven hundred men for their last great invasion of the Territory, and what they meant should be a final attack on Lawrence, where John Brown then was. While this force was mustering, Charles Robinson, who had just been discharged from prison, wrote a few letters to John Brown, of which the first is as follows : —

Lawrence, Sept. 13, 1856.

Captain John Brown.

Dear Sir, — Governor Geary has been here and *talks very well.* He promises to protect us, etc. There will be no attempt to arrest any one for a few days, and I think no attempt to arrest you is contemplated by him. He talks of letting the past be forgotten, so far as may be, and of commencing anew. If convenient, can you not come to town and see us?[1] I will then tell you all that the governor said, and talk of some other matters.

Very respectfully,

C. Robinson.

[1] The interview solicited by Robinson did take place at a house in Lawrence, and in course of it, according to John Brown, Jr., who was present, Robinson not only did not censure Brown for his Pottawatomie

On the same sheet of letter-paper is a longer letter to
Brown from his son John, written the same day : —

John Brown, Jr., to his Father.

All seem to be pleased with Geary. They think that while he
must *talk* of enforcing the Territorial laws, he has intended to let
them lie a dead letter; says no Territorial officer or court shall arrest
or try. Although he says in his proclamation that all armed men
must disband, yet he says our men better hold together a few days
until he can clear the Territory of the *militia ;* requests our men to
enroll themselves, choose *their own officers,* and consider him as chief
and themselves as his guard. I am inclined to the belief that unless
something unusual shall turn up within a few days, you had better
return home, as I have no doubt an attempt will be made to arrest
you, as well as Lane, whom Geary says he is under obligations to arrest. His plan, no doubt, will be to get the assistance of Free-State
men to aid in making arrests. Don't allow yourself to be trapped
in that way. Captain Walker thinks of going East *via* Nebraska
soon. I do hope you will go with him, for I am sure that you will
be no more likely to be let alone than Lane. *Don't go into that
secret military refugee plan as talked of by Robinson, I beg of you.*
I shall go into Mr. Whitman's house, about two and a half miles west
of Lawrence, where I shall make arrangements for Jason and commence cutting hay.

Robinson to John Brown.

LAWRENCE, Sept. 14, 1856.

CAPTAIN JOHN BROWN.

MY DEAR SIR, — I take this opportunity to express to you
my sincere gratification that the late report that you were among
the killed at the battle of Osawatomie is incorrect. Your course,
so far as I have been informed, has been such as to merit the
highest praise from every patriot, and I cheerfully accord to you
my heartfelt thanks for your prompt, efficient, and timely action
against the invaders of our rights and the murderers of our citizens. History will give your name a proud place on her pages,
and posterity will pay homage to your heroism in the cause of God

executions, but urged him to undertake similar work elsewhere ; to which
Brown replied, "If you know of any job of that sort that needs to be done,
I advise you to do it yourself," or words to that effect. Robinson now
denies that he made such a proposition.

and humanity.   Trusting that you will conclude to remain in Kansas, and serve " during the war " the cause you have done so much to sustain, and with earnest prayers for your health, and protection from the shafts of death that so thickly beset your path, I subscribe myself,   Very respectfully, your obedient servant,

C. ROBINSON.

LAWRENCE, Sept. 14, 1856.

To THE SETTLERS OF KANSAS, — If possible, please render Captain John Brown all the assistance he may require in defending Kansas from invaders and outlaws, and you will confer a favor upon your co-laborer and fellow-citizen,

C. ROBINSON.

At this time, as these letters prove, there was no question among the Free-State men of Kansas concerning the services which Brown had rendered.   The feeling against him in consequence of the Pottawatomie affair had subsided ; nor was it till years afterward that this feeling was maliciously revived.   The general effect of Brown's deadly blow has been described ; but it may be asked what were its immediate consequences in the region where it was directly felt.   There are no better witnesses to this than the two neighbors of the men that suffered, — George Grant and James Hanway, — already quoted.   Grant said in 1880 : " Both parties were greatly alarmed at first.   The proslavery settlers almost entirely left at once, and the Free-State people were constantly fearful of vengeance.   As a matter of fact, there was no more killing on either side in that neighborhood.   Dutch Henry, — Henry Sherman, — was killed in the spring of 1857, but politics had nothing to do with it."   Judge Hanway, who died in 1881, said : —

" It was thought that the effect of the Pottawatomie affair would be disastrous to the settlers who had taken up their quarters in this locality.[1]   For a few weeks it looked ominous.   I spent most of my

[1] As to the wisdom of John Brown's general policy of brave resistance and stern retaliation, the sagacious Judge Hanway says : " In the early Kansas troubles, I considered the extreme measures which he adopted as not the best under the circumstances.   We were weak and cut off, as it were, from our friends.   Our most bitter enemies received their support from an adjoining State.   We were not in a condition to resist by force the power of

time in the brush. The settlement was overrun by the 'law and
order' men, who took every man prisoner whom they came across,
'jay-hawked' horses and saddles, and even, in several cases, work
cattle ; but after these raids ceased, the proslavery element became
willing to bury the hatchet and live in peace. The most ultra of
those who had been leaders left the Territory, only to return at
periods to burn the house of some obnoxious Free-State man. The
Pottawatomie affair sent a terror into the proslavery ranks, and those
who remained on the creek were as desirous of peace as any class of
the community."

Brown's only autograph account, so far as I know, of the
attack on Lawrence, in September, 1856, is the following,
written in January, 1857, as part of his address before New
England audiences : —

THE LAWRENCE FORAY.

" I well know, that, on or about the 14th of September last, a large
force of Missourians and other ruffians, numbering twenty-seven hundred (as stated by Governor Geary), invaded the Territory, burned
Franklin, and while the smoke of that place was going up behind
them, they, on the same day, made their appearance in full view of,
and within about a mile of, Lawrence. And I know of no possible
reason why they did not attack and burn that place except that about
one hundred Free-State men volunteered to go out on the open plain
before the town and there give them the offer of a fight, which they declined, after getting some few scattering shots from our men, and then
retreated back towards Franklin. I saw that whole thing. The
government troops at this time were with Governor Geary at Lecompton, a distance of twelve miles *only* from Lawrence, and, notwithstanding several runners had been to advise him in good time of the
approach or of the setting out of the enemy, who had to march some

the Border Ruffians, backed and supported as they were by the administration at Washington. Events afterward proved that the most desperate
remedies, as in the Pottawatomie affair, were best. In place of being
the forerunner of additional strife and turmoil, the result proved it was a
peace measure." Charles Robinson, in an article written for the "Kansas
Magazine" many years ago, said of the executions by Brown: "They had
the effect of a clap of thunder from a clear sky. The slave men stood
aghast. The officials were frightened at this new move on the part of
the supposed subdued free men. This was a warfare they were not prepared to wage, as of the *bona fide* settlers there were four free men to one
slave man."

forty miles to reach Lawrence, *he did not on that memorable occasion* get a single soldier on the ground until after the enemy had retreated back to Franklin, and had been gone for more than five hours.   He did get the troops there about midnight afterwards; and that is the way he *saved* Lawrence, as he boasts of doing in his message to the bogus Legislature !

" This was just the kind of protection the administration and its tools have afforded the Free-State settlers of Kansas from the first. It has cost the United States more than half a million, for a year past, to harass poor Free-State settlers in Kansas, and to violate *all law, and all right, moral and constitutional,* for the *sole and only purpose of forcing slavery* upon that Territory. I challenge this whole nation to prove before God or mankind the contrary. Who paid this money to enslave the settlers of Kansas and worry them out ?   I say nothing in this estimate of the money wasted by Congress in the management of this horrible, tyrannical, and damnable affair."

In what Brown here says of Governor Geary, he does some injustice to that officer, who proved to be the best governor that Kansas had during the reign of terror in 1855–56.   His motives were political, no doubt; but he had the heart of a man and the courage of a soldier, and soon placed himself, in effect, on the Free-State side.   He might have dispersed the invaders about Lawrence more speedily, but he was not then wholly master of the situation, or did not feel himself to be.   As the course of events at Lawrence, September 14–15, has been variously represented, I will here cite the evidence of eye-witnesses and contemporary reporters. H. L. Dunlop, then of Lawrence, but now of Topeka, says : —

" I was at that time a member of John Wright's company.   What name I went by on the rolls I will not say.   Many of us went under fictitious names.   My next younger brother, who was with me in that command, went by the name of Henry Preston.   You will find his name on the list of Lecompton prisoners.   He was captured at Hickory Point with Colonel Harvey.   On the day preceding the attack on Lawrence (September 13), I went east of Lawrence, through the town of Franklin, with a detachment of Captain Wright's men, on a scout, the balance of Captain Wright's company having gone with Colonel Harvey.   We found a large body of men crossing at the lower ford of the Wakarusa; they camped that night on the bottom.

We counted their tents to ascertain about how many there were, as near as possible. The next morning they commenced to advance. We fell back slowly through Franklin, ducking their advance-guard occasionally. They fired the mill at Franklin and came on, and when we arrived near Lawrence their advance was pressing us closely. The Stub Rifles, Captain Walker's men, came up and deployed on our right, and we went into position in the rifle pits near the head of Massachusetts Street. John Brown was there. I think he had on a reddish plush cap, which had side pieces to turn down. I heard him talk to some of the boys who were playing cards, ' that it was no time or place for that,' saying that the pro-slavery men would soon be there. He cautioned them to fire low, and talked quite awhile. At this time Walker's men had opened fire on the proslavery advance, and they were falling back.

" Just before sunset John Brown pointed out to me a stone building that stood south and west of where we were, and asked me to take some men and hold the position ready for the morrow. I called for volunteers, and selected ten or twelve men. They were mostly Wright's men. We marched to the spot. The building was not completed; no floor laid. I had boards laid so that we could fire from the window openings, and placed some videttes out. The balance went to sleep in the building. During the night I heard a rattling of sabres and a command to halt. I went to one of the sentinels, who was on the Santa Fé trail leading west towards Lecompton. I found there a detachment of United States troops, and conversed with the officer in command, gave him a detailed account of the day's doings and the positions of the different forces. He said he would take a position between us, and marched his men past. In the morning the regulars were between us and the proslavery men. You, no doubt, recollect that on the disbandment of the proslavery men it was proposed that a portion of them should cross the river at Lawrence, whereupon several of us notified Governor Geary that we should fire on them from the buildings, and the order was changed, and they crossed at De Soto."

John Brown, who was in Lawrence September 8, soon after went to Topeka, and was on his way from that town to Osa-watomie, when the Missourians began to show themselves about Lawrence, September 12 or 13. The latter was the date of an expedition sent out from Lawrence to capture a fort of the Border Ruffians at Hickory Point. On the 14th, while many of the armed men of Lawrence were absent on this expedition, the people of the town were alarmed by the

news "that twenty-eight hundred Missourians were marching down upon Lawrence, with drums beating and with
eagles upon their banners." The actual number reported
by Governor Geary, who visited their camp at Franklin on
Monday the 15th, was twenty-seven hundred, and their
leaders were General John W. Reid, David R. Atchison, B.
F. Stringfellow, etc., — the same who had led an invasion
three weeks before. The whole number of fighting-men in
Lawrence that Sunday did not exceed two hundred, and
many of them were unarmed; but Brown was there, and
soon made himself known. He was asked to take command
of the defences of the town, and though he declined this, he
did his whole duty. Between four and five o'clock in the
afternoon he assembled the people in the main street, and,
mounted on a dry-goods box in the midst of them, made
this speech, which is reported by one who heard him : —

" GENTLEMEN, — It is said there are twenty-five hundred Missourians down at Franklin, and that they will be here in two hours.
You can see for yourselves the smoke they are making by setting fire
to the houses in that town. Now is probably the last opportunity
you will have of seeing a fight, so that you had better do your best.
If they should come up and attack us, don't yell and make a great
noise, but remain perfectly silent and still. Wait till they get within
twenty-five yards of you; get a good object; be sure you see the
hind sight of your gun, — then fire. A great deal of powder and lead
and very precious time is wasted by shooting too high. You had
better aim at their legs than at their heads. In either case, be sure
of the hind sights of your guns. It is from the neglect of this that I
myself have so many times escaped; for if all the bullets that have
ever been aimed at me had hit, I should have been as full of holes as
a riddle."

After this exhortation, which reminds one of John Stark
at Bunker Hill and Bennington, Brown sent a small force
to the few defences about the town, and others ordered all
the men who had the far-shooting Sharpe's rifle — then a new
weapon — to go out upon the prairie, half a mile south, where
by this time the invading horsemen could be seen, two miles
off. After a halt for reconnoitring purposes, the enemy made
an advance upon Brown's left, and came within half a mile
of his advance guard, just as the sun was setting. Under

cover of the dusk some approached nearer; but the discharge of a few Sharpe's rifles and the coming of a brass cannon, which had been ordered up to support the rifles, caused the enemy (who may have been only a reconnoitring party) to turn and retreat; and no further attack was made. The stone building which Dunlop mentions was a stone church, still standing, on the southwest side of Lawrence; and John Brown, Jr., was one of thirty or forty men sent out to hold that position. He is my authority for the statement that Brown placed men armed with pitchforks (for want of better weapons) in places of defence where they could be useful with such arms. He heard his father make the speech above cited, and says it was longer than reported, but the substance of it was caught and printed. Colonel Walker, of Lawrence, told me in 1882 that on the 14th of September, 1856, Brown was not in command, " but went about with his rifle on his shoulder." In Lane's absence on an expedition the chief command fell to Captain Abbott, the rescuer of Branson, who was " officer of the day." There was little fighting, but much firing on both sides at long range. Walker himself went out toward Franklin with ten or fifteen mounted men, to reconnoitre; saw the enemy, — two or three thousand in number, as he judged, — and fell back toward Lawrence, followed by two hundred or more of them. When these men came near Lawrence they were fired at by the few men who were there, but there was no engagement. If the main body had come up then, they might have captured Lawrence, in Colonel Walker's opinion.

During his excursion northward, early in August, we get a glimpse of John Brown as he appeared to the armed emigrants from Massachusetts and New York. A brother of Brown's wounded son-in-law, on learning of the casualties at Black Jack, at once left North Elba, and joined the second Massachusetts company of emigrants at Buffalo. Brown rode into their camp in Nebraska, inquiring if William Thompson was there, found him, and they left the camp together. " The Captain was riding a splendid horse, and was dressed in plain white summer clothing. He wore a large straw hat, and was closely shaven: everything about him was scrupulously clean." He made a great impression on several of the company, who, without knowing him, at once declared that he must be a distinguished man in disguise. Brown and his party then proceeded to Tabor, in Iowa, left the wounded man and his brother there, and went back to Kansas in company with General Lane and Colonel Walker.

Let me make a digression here, in order to introduce some anecdotes which I heard from Colonel Walker concerning Captain Brown and General Lane, the two Kansas men who were always ready for fighting. Colonel Walker was a Pennsylvania Democrat when he settled in Kansas, a little earlier than John Brown went there. He has always lived there, except when in the military service; and no man's character for truth and courage stands higher. He told me that he first saw Brown when he came with his sons in a wagon from Osawatomie to Lawrence, to help defend it from the Missourians in the "Wakarusa War" of 1855. They were then the best-armed men he had seen in Kansas. There was no fighting then, but earthworks were thrown up near Governor Robinson's old house on Mount Oread, where now the State University stands; and these old lines are still visible. Walker was sent by Robinson in August, 1856, to meet General Lane, then coming on with a party of emigrants who had crossed Iowa and Nebraska, and to prevent him from being intercepted by General Richardson and the Missourians or the United States troops, on his way into Kansas with his company of armed emigrants. Walker rode up to the Nemaha River, and found what he supposed was a camp of Missourians, but which turned out to be John Brown, with his sick son Owen and a few men, working their way along northward to where he was to leave Owen at Tabor, in Iowa. Brown and Walker then went northward together until they came near where Lane was. When Walker told Lane that he must not come into Kansas with his emigrants, for if he did he would certainly be arrested by the United States troops. Lane said: "Then I will shoot myself to-night; for I have told the Kansas people that I am coming back, and I have told these emi-

22

grants that I am going in with them ; if I give it up now it
will be said that I deserted them, and there will be no way
of disproving it. I *must* go back into Kansas."

Walker then told Lane that he must disguise himself.
" So we tried nitrate of silver on his face, but it would not
change him ; and then we tried putting old clothes on him ;
but the worse clothes we put on, the more like Jim Lane
he looked." Then Walker said he would take him back
under escort, with Brown's help ; and they started so, with
twenty or thirty men, and Brown among them. When
they camped for the night, Brown, according to his custom,
went away to sleep by himself ; and Walker describes him
as sitting bolt upright on his saddle, with his back against
a tree, his horse " lariated " to the saddle-peak, and Brown
asleep with his rifle across his knees. At early dawn
Walker went up to waken Brown, and as he touched him
on the shoulder Brown sprang up "quick as a cat," levelled, cocked, and discharged his piece, which Walker
threw up with his hand in time to escape death ; but the
bullet grazed his shoulder. " That shows how quick he
was ; but he was frightened afterward, when he saw it was
I he had fired at." Then, said Walker, " As we rode along
together, Brown was in a sort of study ; and I said to him,
' Captain Brown, I would n't have your thoughts for anything in the world.' Brown said, ' I suppose you are thinking about the Pottawatomie affair.' Said I, ' Yes.' Then
he stopped and looked at me, and said, ' Captain Walker, I
saw that whole thing, but I did not strike a blow. I take
the responsibility of it ; but there were men who advised
doing it, and afterward failed to justify it,' " — meaning,
as Walker supposed, Lane and Robinson. Walker now
believes Brown, and cannot think that Townsley's statement about Brown's shooting Doyle through the head is
correct ; " for Brown would never tell me what was not
true, and would not deny to me anything he had really
done."

In respect to Governor Geary's friendly feeling toward
Brown, Walker said that one morning, after a deed of Brown
which had made much noise, Geary sent a note to Walker,
as he was drilling his men out on the field, telling him to get

word to Brown that a warrant was out against him, which *must* be served, and that Brown must get away. Walker saw a man looking on whom he had before seen in Brown's camp; he took him one side, showed him Geary's note, and told him to find and warn Brown. Not long after came an orderly from Governor Geary with a warrant against Brown, which Walker must serve with his *posse.* "Take him dead or alive; and for this I shall hold you, Captain Walker, personally responsible," was the order. Walker took the warrant and made search for Brown; but of course he had gone. At that time Brown's camp was on the Wakarusa, eight or ten miles from Lawrence. The man who warned Brown, Walker afterwards found, was James Montgomery, who succeeded to the reputation of Brown as a good fighter in southern Kansas.

Soon after Governor Geary came to Kansas, he persuaded Walker to become a deputy marshal of the United States, and to summon jurymen, serve processes, and make arrests. At first Walker refused, saying there were thirty-seven indictments against himself found by the proslavery grand-jury; and he feared he should be arrested if he undertook to serve warrants on other men. It was finally agreed that the District Attorney should refuse to prosecute (*nol. pros.*) these indictments, and then Walker should be sworn in as a deputy marshal of the United States, and should use his armed band of Free-State men as his *posse* in making arrests. Before the matter was thus settled, Governor Geary came to Lawrence from Lecompton one day, and sent word that he would dine at Walker's house; but, as it happened, that very day the other United States Marshal with a *posse* of mounted proslavery men came into Lawrence to arrest Walker, went to his house, and was fired upon there by the people inside, — Walker being on the street with Governor Geary at the time. His little boy came running up to him in the street, and said before the Governor, "Mother says the Marshal and his men are surrounding the house and firing; and you must not come home." Geary turned white with anger, and said, "You're mistaken, boy; they are firing at birds." But he found it was the Marshal, and went back at once to Lecompton and put a stop to such proceedings. Soon after, Walker was sworn in; and his first act was to summon a jury of Free-State men. He had his pocket full of warrants against Free-State men, some of which he served and some he would not serve. Several were against John Ritchie, with whom Walker often spent the night; when Ritchie, who was a brave Free-State soldier, would say to him: "Walker, I like you as well as any man in Kansas; but if you try to serve your warrants on me, by God, I'll kill you!" "I never did try," said Walker; "but by and by another deputy — a Free-State man — had the warrants given him to serve, and thought he must try it; he did so, and Ritchie shot him."

It was probably upon the hint which Walker gave through Montgomery, that John Brown left Kansas in 1856, pursued by the United States troops. He started for northern Kansas before the 20th of September, journeying with his four sons and with a fugitive slave, whom he picked up on the way. The old hero was sick, as he often was, and travelled slowly: appearing to be a land-surveyor on a journey. He had a light wagon in which he rode, with his surveyor's instruments ostentatiously in sight; and inside, covered up in a blanket, was the fugitive slave. Sometimes he pitched his camp at night near the dragoons who were ordered to arrest him, but who little suspected that the formidable fighter was so near them in the guise of a feeble old man. A spy had notified the dragoons that Brown was on the road, and they were on the watch for him, — five hundred mounted men, as one of his sons told me, with four cannon. Early in the morning two of the sons, John and Jason, rose early and made a long circuit round the camp, while their father, ill and weak, followed on later in the day. It was proposed to carry him along this dangerous part of his journey concealed in the wagon, as his fugitive slave was. "No," said Brown, who scorned to hide himself; "I may as well die by the enemy as be jolted to death in the wagon." At Plymouth, not far from the Nebraska border, Redpath, in one of his journeys through the Territory, found him lying ill in a log hut, while his four sons were camped near by. A few hours after, the dragoons, hearing he was so near them, came up to arrest him; but he had crossed the border into

Nebraska, and was out of their reach.   He went forward till he came to Tabor in Iowa, not far northeast of Nebraska City, and there remained among friends for two weeks in early October.   In the latter part of that month he reached Chicago, and made himself known to the National Kansas Committee, which then had headquarters in that city.[1]   Afterward he travelled eastward, to Ohio, to Peterboro', N. Y., where he visited his friend Gerrit Smith ; to Albany and Springfield, and finally to Boston, where I first saw him in the early part of January, 1857.

That Brown was in Chicago as early as October 25 will be seen by the two following letters, — the first by General J. D. Webster, then a member of the National Kansas Committee, and the other by Mr. Horace White, its assistant secretary : —

NATIONAL KANSAS COMMITTEE ROOMS,
CHICAGO, Oct. 25, 1856.

DEAR SIR, — We have requested Captain Brown to join you and give you the benefit of his counsel in reference to the safe transportation of your freight.[2]   Colonel Dickey will also be able to assist you. We hope every precaution will be taken.   Captain Brown says the immediate introduction of the supplies is not of much consequence compared to the danger of *losing* them.   We trust your foresight and

---

[1] On his way from Kansas to Chicago he passed one of his sons, who was going to join his father in Kansas, as appears by this letter : —

ST. CHARLES, IOWA, Oct. 30, 1856.

DEAR MOTHER, BROTHERS, AND SISTERS, — I sent you a draft for thirty dollars a few days ago in a sheet of paper with a very few words on it, — they being all I had time to write then.   We are well and in fine spirits, besides being in good company.   We are in the company of a train of Kansas teams loaded with Sharpe's rifles and cannon.   I heard a report that father had gone East.   We travel very slow ; you can write to us at Tabor. On our way we saw Gerrit Smith, F. Douglass, and other old friends.   We have each a Sharpe's rifle.   Oliver, your watch was all that saved us.   I want you to write and let us know how you get along.   No more now.

Yours truly,   WATSON BROWN.

From this it would seem that Oliver Brown, the youngest son, had gone back to North Elba in advance of his father.   Watson also turned back and joined his father at Chicago, and then returned home to the Adirondacs, where I saw him in the summer of 1857.

[2] This " freight " included the two hundred rifles sent forward in September by the Massachusetts Kansas Committee, and afterward carried by Brown to Virginia when he attacked Harper's Ferry.

discretion will prevent any loss, and be of essential aid to the good cause.

Yours truly,   J. D. WEBSTER.

Dr. J. P. Root.

OFFICE NATIONAL KANSAS COMMITTEE,
CHICAGO, Oct. 26, 1856.

CAPTAIN BROWN, — We expect Mr. Arny, our general agent, just from Kansas, to be in to-morrow morning. He has been in the Territory particularly to ascertain the condition of certain affairs for our information. I know he will very much regret not having seen you. If it is not absolutely essential for you to go on to-night, I would recommend you to wait and see him. I shall confer with Colonel Dickey on this point. Rev. Theodore Parker, of Boston, is at the Briggs House, and wishes very much to see you.

Yours truly,

HORACE WHITE, *Assist. Sec., etc.*

P. S. If you wish one or two of those rifles,[1] please call at our office between three and five this afternoon, or between seven and eight this evening.

In his testimony before Senator Mason's investigating committee in January, 1860, Mr. White thus explained the allusion to rifles in the letter just cited: "Our committee sent John Brown twenty-five navy revolvers of Colt's manufacture, in August, 1856, by Mr. Arny, our agent; but they never reached him. They were sent to Lawrence and stored there for a time, subject to Brown's order; but he did not come forward to claim them, and they were loaned to a military company in Lawrence called the 'Stubs;' but Brown never afterward appeared to claim them. He told me that the reason was, he had had so much trouble and fuss and difficulty with the people of Lawrence, that he never would go there again to claim anything. I gave no other arms to Brown himself, but gave rifles to two of his sons. After all the arms of the committee had been distributed in Kansas, or all but two or three, Mr. Brown made his appearance at the committee-rooms with two of his sons in October, 1856. One of them was Watson, and the other, I think, was Owen Brown. We had three or four rifles left, and I gave one to

---

[1] These were perhaps from the Massachusetts stock of rifles, but most likely belonged to another lot which was then on its way to Kansas.

each of those sons; and, as they were very poorly clad, I went down to a fur store in Chicago and purchased each of them a pair of fur gloves and fur overshoes and caps." Mr. White also fitted out Captain Brown with a new suit of clothes, in which he made his visits that winter to his New England friends, who had begun to take a strong interest in his course, as the following note from the Emigrant Aid Office in Boston sufficiently indicates: —

BOSTON, Sept. 22, 1856.
No. 3 Winter Street.

JOHN BROWN, ESQ.

DEAR SIR, — The Messrs. Chapin, who keep the Massasoit House in Springfield, in this State, wish to give you fifty or one hundred dollars, as a testimonial of their admiration of your brave conduct during the war. Will you write to them, stating how they can send you the money? Call upon Mr. S. N. Simpson, of Lawrence. He will tell you who I am.

Yours truly,
CHARLES H. BRANSCOMB.

Indeed, at this time Brown had the confidence of all lovers of liberty.

NOTE. — While these events were occurring in Kansas, Congress was in session at Washington, adjourning Aug. 30, 1856. The Senate was controlled by Senator Mason and his slaveholding associates, who were obediently followed by Cass, Douglass, and the other Northern "dough-faces," as John Randolph called such persons. The House, under the lead of the Speaker, — General Banks, of Massachusetts, — was on the side of freedom, and voted that the Territorial laws of Kansas were oppressive; it also refused for some weeks to pass the Army Bill, except with a clause forbidding the "dough-face" President Pierce to use the army against the freemen of Kansas. Finally, a few Northern men yielded, and the bill passed the House as Mason and Douglass forced it through the Senate (Aug. 30, 1856). The American news from Kansas and Washington, "through some certain strainers well refined," reached London in a damaged state; for Lord Malmesbury wrote in his diary, Sept. 6, 1856: "Civil war has broken out in the United States between the Abolitionists and the proslavery party, and a great deal of blood has been already shed. The Government refused to take part with either side, upon which the slave-party in Congress would not vote the supplies for the army, which accordingly must be disbanded." As this peer had been Foreign Secretary, he might have been supposed to know something about America; but he writes in 1865, after the fighting around Richmond, that Grant and Sheridan "drove Lee into Pittsburg." Such is English material for American history!

CHAPTER XI.

JOHN BROWN AND THE KANSAS COMMITTEES.

THE committees appointed from 1854 to 1859 to attend to Kansas and its affairs were legion, and as various in kind as possible. The Boston Emigrant Aid Company was the first of these committees; next the Free-State men of Lawrence formed a singular secret committee in 1855, to protect themselves from the Border Ruffians; and of this the chief members were General Lane and Charles Robinson. A penitent or treacherous member, who had been admitted to this secret committee, disclosed what he said were its oaths and signs; but there was much exaggeration in what Dr. Francis swore to before the next Kansas committee, — that of Congress, sent out in the spring of 1856. Some parts of his testimony may here be cited to show what he wished to have us believe : —

THE KANSAS REGULATORS.[1]

.   .   .   .

"Offers were made to me by various persons to introduce me to a secret political organization. The only name I ever received as a member of the lodge was Kansas Regulators. . . . I went with

---

[1] John Brown, Jr., says : I belonged to this secret organization, though I cannot say it had this name : it seems to me the name was "Kansas Defenders." I was initiated by Lane himself, in a room of Garvey's Hotel at Topeka, in the spring of 1856, at the time of the first assembling of the legislature under the Topeka Constitution. The oath, as stated by Dr. Francis, is the same substantially as administered by Lane to me. I do not think we were required by our *oath* to resist United States authorities in attempts to enforce the bogus laws, though it was understood by us that we might be driven to do so, when we *would* so resist, rather than tamely submit. Our badge was a narrow black ribbon, from six to eight inches long, tied in the button-hole of the shirt collar.

Colonel Lane to the law-office of John Hutchinson, as I afterward
found out.   Governor Reeder did not go into the room where I was
initiated. Dr. Robinson was standing just before the door with a
lady, I should think. Colonel Lane asked him to leave the lady and
go into the office with us.   Robinson rather objected at first, but
finally came in with us, and said he would explain the nature of the
organization he was about to initiate me into.   The substance of
the explanation was, that Kansas was a beautiful country and well
adapted to freedom, and the best Territory in the world for the
friends of freedom to operate on, — more especially for those who were
engaged in the free white State cause. After proceeding in that
strain for a while, he asked me if I was willing to pledge my word
and honor that I would keep secret what I saw there, and whom I
saw there, provided he would pledge his word and honor that there
was nothing which would interfere with my duties as a citizen, or that
was disloyal in any respect."

The oath was this : —

" I furthermore promise and swear that I will at all times and
under all circumstances bear upon my person a weapon of death;
that I will at all times and under all circumstances keep in my house
at least one gun, with a full supply of ammunition ; that I will at
all times and under all circumstances, when I see the sign of distress
given, rush to the assistance of the person giving it, where there is
a greater probability of saving his life than of losing my own. I
furthermore promise and swear that I will, to the utmost of my
power, oppose the laws of the so-called Kansas Legislature; and
that when I hear the words of danger given I will repair to the place
where the danger is. . . .

" . . . The regalia was this: The private members wore a black
ribbon tied upon their shirt-bosoms; the colonel wore a red sash ;
the lieutenant-colonel a green sash, the major a blue sash, the adju-
tant a black sash, the captains white sashes, the lieutenants yellow
sashes, the orderly sergeant a very broad black ribbon upon his
shirt-bosom. . . . Colonel Lane wore the red sash, and some one
else, but I am not certain who it was. I do not recollect seeing any
body with a green sash. Dr. Robinson had a beautiful sash on,
looking like a blue and red one joined together, trimmed with gold
lace. I was told it denoted some higher office than colonel; but I
did not learn what it was. . . .

" In regard to the laws which were to be resisted, I understood
from Dr. Robinson and Colonel Lane that they were the laws of
the late Territorial Legislature. Colonel Lane said : ' We will not

submit to any laws passed by that Legislature ; and we are making preparations to place in the hands of every Free-State man a
Sharpe's rifle and a brace of Colt's revolvers ; and, if need be, we
will resist even the United States troops if they attempt to enforce
those laws.' He also stated at the same time that an attack had
been anticipated on the town of Lawrence the day before, and that
he saw five hundred men there, at their business in the streets,
armed. . . . Dr. Robinson and Col. Lane told me they expected
to form lodges or councils in every county in the Territory. They
proclaimed me a Kansas Regulator ; and that was all the name
I learned for a member of the organization ; and they gave me
authority to institute lodges, and conferred upon me a sort of brevet
rank of captain. This was at the time I was initiated. During the
first Lawrence war they sent me a commission as captain, which I
never used."

A Free-State man, Mr. G. P. Lowrey, testified thus : —

" . . . I have no distinct recollection of all the oath, but I know
Dr. Francis testifies to matters as being in the oath which were not
contained in it. The oath required us to keep fire-arms and ammunition ; to use all lawful and honorable means to make Kansas a free
State ; to wear at all times upon our persons a weapon of death ;
and I think to go to the assistance of a brother when the probability
of saving his life was greater than of losing our own. I do not
recollect anything in the oath which required us to deal with Free-
State men in preference to proslavery men, or to wear upon the person at all times the insignia of the order, or to obey at all times the
orders of superior officers even unto death."

That Brown had something to do with both these committees is probable, — almost certain. He was at times in
close relations with the officers of the Emigrant Aid Company, and, as we have seen, was a small stockholder therein. There is no record that he was ever initiated in the
secret order of Robinson and Lane ; but it has been asserted
that he executed the five men on the 24th of May in accordance with a decree of these " Regulators." I have seen no
good evidence of this, but have no doubt that some of the
" Regulators " counselled such acts and justified them when
done. The committees under which Brown chiefly acted
however, when he would connect himself with any such
organizations at all, were the National Kansas Committee,

which was formed in Buffalo in the summer of 1856, and
the State Kansas Committee of Massachusetts, formed about
the same time, but continuing much longer in its work.
The creation of such unofficial bodies for public service was
natural enough, and in accord with a national custom. The
people of the North had resolved that Kansas should be controlled by freemen, and that slavery should never be toler-
ated there. In pursuance of this resolution, they formed
these societies and committees to colonize Kansas with
Northern men, who would never vote to establish slavery;
and by one of these organizations, — the New England
Emigrant Aid Company, — a portion of Kansas was in fact
colonized during the years 1854 and 1855. At that time I
was in college, and so occupied with my private affairs that,
except to vote and read the newspapers, I took little interest in those of the public. But upon leaving college and
going to reside in Concord in 1855, I became more actively
concerned in regard to the political situation, and early took
up the opinion that the battle between the North and the
South was first to be fought in Kansas. In the spring of 1856
one of my brothers became a Kansas colonist. Soon after,
the outrages of the Missouri invaders of Kansas grew so frequent and alarming that the indignation of Massachusetts
and of the whole North was roused, and further action began to be taken in this form. "Kansas committees" were
organized in towns, counties, and States, and very soon a
national committee, among the members of which were
Abraham Lincoln, Gerrit Smith, and Dr. S. G. Howe. Mr.
Lincoln never acted, so far as I know; but the committee
did much work for a year, and raised thousands of dollars
to colonize towns and support armed colonists in Kansas.
Between May, 1856, and January, 1857, I passed through
all the grades of these Kansas committees, — beginning in
June, 1856, as secretary of the Concord town committee;
then in July helping to organize a county committee for
Middlesex, of which I was secretary; then serving as secretary to the Massachusetts State Kansas Committee, from
December, 1856, until the committee dissolved in 1858–59;
and finally serving upon the National Committee at its last
meeting, in January, 1857, as proxy for Dr. Howe.

What a few years later the Sanitary Commission did for the Union armies as a whole, these committees of 1856–57 did for the pioneers of Kansas. Something more was done, too ; for they supplied rifles, cartridges, and cannon to the defenders of freedom in Kansas, — a work which the Sanitary Commission could leave to the National Government. The first large sum of money raised to buy arms for Kansas was that contributed in Boston during the spring of 1855, — some thousands of dollars, which were expended in the purchase of Sharpe's rifles. The Faneuil Hall Committee, of Boston, organized in May, 1856, pledged itself to raise money for use "in a strictly lawful manner" in Kansas; but most of the other committees were not so scrupulous, and gave their money freely to arm the colonists who went out to defend the Free-State cause. The National Kansas Committee, which had its headquarters at Chicago, had received and forwarded many of these arms ; but some members of this committee soon became distrustful of Captain Brown, who was too radical for them. A general meeting of this National Committee, which was made up of one or more members from each free State, assembled in New York on the 23d of January, 1857. At this meeting, which took place at the Astor House, and remained in session two days, Captain Brown was present, urging his plan to organize a company of mounted rangers for service in Kansas and Missouri. I was there as a delegate from Massachusetts, and caused a resolution to be introduced, transferring the custody of two hundred Massachusetts rifles to our own State committee. This was passed without much opposition ; but another resolution, introduced I think by Mr. Newton, the delegate from Vermont, and appropriating five thousand or ten thousand dollars to Captain Brown for his special purposes, was vehemently opposed by Mr. Henry B. Hurd, of Chicago, and a few others, — among them Mr. Arny, of Illinois, who had taken Abraham Lincoln's place on the committee. The reasons given by these gentlemen were that Captain Brown was so ultra and violent that he would use the money, if voted, in ways which the committee would not sanction; and I remember that Mr. Hurd, when Captain Brown had withdrawn, urged this argument very earnestly. The views of the more radical Eastern members prevailed however, and the money was voted, although only one hundred and fifty dollars of it was ever paid over to Captain Brown.

The friends of Kansas in Massachusetts, and particularly the State Kansas Committee (which grew out of the Faneuil Hall Committee and some others appointed in the Massachusetts counties), had no hesitation in buying rifles and ammunition, and did, in fact, buy the rifles which John Brown carried to Harper's Ferry. This State committee, and its auxiliaries in the towns and counties, raised throughout Massachusetts, during 1856, nearly one hundred thousand dollars in money and supplies, which were sent to the Kansas people. Some towns, Concord for example, raised in proportion to their population much more than this ; for it was estimated that if all Massachusetts had contributed as freely as Concord, the amount raised in the State would have been nearly a million dollars. Personally, I undertook to canvass Middlesex County that summer and autumn, and visited more than half the towns to appoint committees, hold meetings, or solicit subscriptions. Enough was subscribed, in Massachusetts and the other Northern States, to carry our colonists in Kansas through their worst year ; and but for these supplies of money, arms, and clothing, it is quite possible they would have been driven out or conquered by the Missourians, the United States troops, and their other enemies.[1]

---

[1] The records of the Massachusetts Kansas Committee, including its large correspondence, were in my possession for a few years as secretary. Before the attack on Harper's Ferry, or soon after, I transferred them to the custody of the chairman of the committee, George L. Stearns, and some of them have since been destroyed. They contained much historical information and some curious revelations concerning political movements in those years. They will also confirm the statements made in the " Atlantic Monthly " in 1872, concerning the ownership of the arms carried by Brown to Virginia. The Massachusetts Committee voted them to John Brown as its agent in 1857, and though they were nominally reclaimed in 1858, they were never out of his custody till captured in Maryland. They had ceased to be the property of the committee, except in name, before the correspondence of May, 1858 (printed in Senator Mason's Report of 1860, pp. 176, 177), in which Mr. Stearns, the real owner of the arms, warned

Mr. Stearns, before Senator Mason's committee in 1860, gave this account of the State committee : —

" In the spring of 1856 I went to the Boston Committee for the relief of sufferers in Kansas, and offered my services. I worked for them until June of that year; and then being willing to devote all my time to the cause, I was made chairman of the Kansas State Committee of Massachusetts, which took the place of the first-named committee, and continued the work throughout the State. In five months, including August and December of that year (1856), I raised, through my agents, about $48,000 in money : and in the same time my wife commenced the formation of societies for contributions of clothing, which resulted in sending from $20,000 to $30,000 more, in supplies of various kinds. In January, 1857, our work was stopped, by advices from Kansas that no more contributions were needed except for defence. If we had not been thus stopped, our arrangements then made would have enabled us to have collected $100,000 in the next six months. Soon after our State committee had commenced work, — I think in August, 1856, — a messenger from Kansas, who came through Iowa (for the Missouri River was then closed by the Missourians to all Free-State travellers), came to us asking earnestly for arms and ammunition for defence of the Free-State party. Our committee met the next day, and immediately voted to send two hundred Sharpe's rifles, and the necessary quantity of ammunition, — which was procured and sent to the National Kansas Com-

Brown not to use them for any other purpose than the defence of Kansas, " and to hold them subject to my order as chairman of the committee." On the 20th of May, 1858, Mr. Stearns wrote thus to Colonel Higginson, then cognizant of Brown's designs, but not a member of the Kansas Committee : " I have felt obliged, for reasons that cannot be written, to recall the arms committed to B——'s custody. We are all agreed on that point; and if you come to Boston, I think we can convince you that it is for the best." That this recall was only nominal appears from a memorandum made by Higginson when he did " come to Boston " early in June. " I found," he says, " that the Kansas Committee had put some five hundred dollars in gold into Brown's hands, *and all the arms*, with only the understanding that he should go to Kansas, and then be left to his own discretion." In fact, no member of the committee who was consulted ever suggested the *actual* recall of the arms from Brown, well knowing that he would not give them up unless he pleased. Nor, according to my recollection, did any member who gave advice (probably only Mr. Stearns, Dr. Howe, and myself, who had long been the three acting members of a committee practically defunct, were consulted) desire to have Brown surrender them.

mittee at Chicago, to be by them forwarded through Iowa to Kansas. From some cause, which I have never heard explained, these arms were delayed in Iowa; and in November or December of that year we directed an agent to proceed to Iowa at our charge, and take possession of them as our property.   Early in January, 1857, John Brown, of whom I had heard, but had not seen, came to Boston and was introduced to me by one of our Kansas agents; and after repeated conferences with him, being strongly impressed with his sagacity, courage, and stern integrity, I, through a vote of our committee, made him our agent to receive and hold these arms and the ammunition, for the defence of Kansas, appropriating $500 to pay his expenses.   Subsequently, in April of that year, we authorized him to sell one hundred rifles, if expedient, and voted $500 more to enable him to proceed to Kansas with his armament.   About this time, on his representing that the force to be organized in Kansas ought to be provided with revolvers, I authorized him to purchase two hundred from the Massachusetts Arms Company, and when they were delivered to him in Iowa, paid for them from my own funds; the amount was $1,300.   At the same time I gave him, by a letter of credit, authority to draw on me at sight for $7,000 in sums as it might be wanted, for the subsistence of one hundred men, provided that it should be necessary at any time to call that number into the field for active service in the defence of Kansas, in 1857.   As the exigency contemplated did not occur, no money was drawn under it, and the letter was subsequently returned to me. Besides these transactions, which were for specific purposes, I have given him money from time to time, — how much I do not know, as I never keep any account of my personal expenses, or of money I give to others; it is all charged to my private account as paid me.   I should think it might amount to, say, from $1,500 to $2,000.   In addition to what I have before stated, I raised money and sent an agent to Kansas to aid the Free-State party in the Lecompton election, and again for the election of 1858.

"*Question.* Was it at Brown's request that you put him in possession of those arms in January, 1857?

"*Answer.* No, sir; but because we needed an agent to secure them.   They were left in Iowa, and under circumstances that made it doubtful whether they would not be lost entirely; and we put them into his hands because it was necessary to have some agent to proceed there and reclaim them from the hands they were in, and take proper care of them."

The operations of the National Kansas Committee (to which Gerrit Smith contributed one thousand dollars a month during the summer and autumn of 1856) were active and efficient for a time.[1]

This committee, through its assistant-secretary Horace White, reported, Jan. 25, 1857, at New York, as follows:

" There have been forwarded by this committee about two thousand emigrants. These have gone exclusively by the land route of Iowa and Nebraska. The committee have expended between $20,000 and $30,000 in provisions and groceries for the needy settlers. These supplies have been purchased mostly in Western Missouri, where food is cheap and abundant. There were also forwarded prior to the 1st of December about four hundred boxes of clothing, valued at $60,000. The receipts in money have been as follows, classified by States:

Massachusetts	$26,107.17
New York	33,707.39
Illinois	8,882.00
Ohio	2,709.41
Connecticut	3,182.13
Wisconsin	3,054.35
Michigan	2,519.15
Pennsylvania	1,360.19
Indiana	1,349.20
Vermont	956.25
Rhode Island	643.37
New Hampshire	138.00
Iowa	313.85
Minnesota	10.00
New Jersey	254.00
The Slave States	10.00
Unknown	10.00

[1] The following were the names of its members : —

Dr. Samuel Cobb, Jr., } Boston,
Dr. S. G. Howe,   } Mass.
B. B. Newton, St. Albans, Vt.
Governor W. W. Hoppin, Providence, R. I.
W. H. Russell, New Haven, Conn.
Thaddeus Hyatt, New York City.
Alexander Gordon, Pittsburgh, Pa.
W. H. Stanley, Cleveland, Ohio.
John W. Wright, Logansport, Ind.
W. F. M. Arny, Bloomington, Ill.

S. S. Barnard, Detroit, Mich.
J. H. Tweedy, Milwaukee, Wis.
W. Penn Clark, Iowa City, Iowa.
F. A. Hunt, St. Louis, Mo.
A. H. Reeder, Kansas.
S. W. Eldridge, Kansas.
J. D. Webster,   }
H. B. Hurd,   } Chicago.
G. W. Dole,   }
J. Y. Scammon,   }

OFFICERS.

Thaddeus Hyatt, *President*, N. Y. City.
J. D. Webster, *Vice-President*, Chicago.
H. B. Hurd, *Secretary*, Chicago.
Horace White, *Assistant Secretary*, Chicago.
G. W. Dole, *Treasurer*, Chicago.

Eli Thayer, *Agent for Organization of States,* Worcester, Mass.
Edward Daniels, *Agent of Emigration*, Chicago.
E. B. Whitman, *General Agent*, Lawrence, Kansas.

" The New York ' Tribune ' Fund and Gerrit Smith's donations are included in the amount from New York. Gerrit Smith has paid in $10,000. These accounts do not indicate the entire amount contributed for the Free-State cause by the various Northern States. Wisconsin, Illinois, Michigan, and Ohio have given liberally through State organizations. Massachusetts has been the recipient of donations from other States, and has herself contributed largely without the intervention of the National Committee.

" Of clothing, our committee have received seven hundred and sixty-three packages, valued at $110,000, and have incurred an expense on the same, up to the present date, of $4,108.79.

" I have prepared a schedule exhibiting the receipts of clothing from each of the States by towns. The following are the totals received from each of the States in the order of their precedence : —

	Packages.
Massachusetts	310
New York	134
Illinois	96
Ohio	51
Michigan	26
Wisconsin	25
New Hampshire	8
Connecticut	6
Pennsylvania	6
Rhode Island	5
Vermont	4
Indiana	2
Unknown	89
Total	762

" It is proper to state that contributions from some of the New England States were forwarded to the Boston and Massachusetts State Relief committees, and by them forwarded to us at Chicago, and also, without our intervention, to the Territory direct. Thus, for example, — Maine, which has very liberally contributed, her population and resources considered, does not appear on my list, her donations being included in the list of packages forwarded by Dr. Cabot. The State of Iowa should also receive credit for large contributions in clothing, grain, provisions, and money presented to the conductors of our different overland companies of emigrants."

Mr. Redpath, who reported this meeting of the committee at New York, said at the time : " At least $250,000, in cash and clothing, have been contributed by the Republicans of

the North in various ways for the relief and protection
of their brethren in Kansas." Of this sum, not less than
$100,000 came from the single State of Massachusetts ; [1] and
the whole amount of money alone raised there was more
than $60,000, of which at least $20,000 was paid for the
purchase and forwarding of arms to the Free-State men.
Yet of all these supplies only a few rifles and a few hundred dollars in money went into the hands of John Brown
and his men in 1856. He sought to obtain a greater share
in 1857, when, during the winter and spring, he was busily
engaged in efforts to raise money enough to arm and equip
a hundred mounted men for service in Kansas and Missouri,
but without much success. Although the National Committee at its Astor House meeting voted him an appropriation of five thousand dollars, he received nothing under this
vote except one hundred and fifty dollars, and that not until
the summer of 1857. The money voted him by the Massachusetts Committee about the same time was soon exhausted,
and so were the small collections he had made in New England from January to April, 1857. The efforts made for
legislative appropriations in Massachusetts, New York, and
other Northern States in aid of the Kansas colonists all
failed. Brown had labored in person for such an appropriation in Massachusetts, going before the joint committee of
the legislature in the State House at Boston, on the 18th

---

[1] Mr. White (who has since been editor of the " Chicago Tribune," and
connected with the "Evening Post" and other journals in New York) said
at the close of his report, Jan. 26, 1857 : "I desire to bring before your
notice the remarkable services rendered by Dr. Samuel Cabot, Jr., of Boston, from whom we received directly and indirectly over two hundred and
fifty boxes of clothing within the short space of two months. Let us not
forget, however, that it is to women almost solely that the people of Kansas are indebted for this invaluable aid. Everywhere they have been the
most devoted and untiring friends of freedom. It is impossible to notice
all who deserve especial mention : but I might specify the young ladies of
the Oread Institute, at Worcester, Mass., who contributed forty-two water-
proof overcoats for the 'Stubs' of Lawrence ; the ladies of Norwalk, Ohio,
who furnished one hundred new bed-comforters ; Mrs. Captain Cutter, of
Warren, Mass., Mrs. Dr. Cabot, of Boston, Mass., Mrs. H. L. Hibbard, of
Chicago, and Mrs. H. M. T. Cutler, of Dwight, Ill., who have been particularly active in organizing the efforts of the ladies of the North."

of February, and giving his testimony as an eye-witness of what had happened in Kansas the year before.

With this preliminary explanation, I may now give some correspondence of these committees with Brown and others, beginning with a letter sent by the Massachusetts Kansas Committee, before they saw Brown, to the late Senator Grimes, of Iowa, — then Governor of that State.

STATE KANSAS AID COMMITTEE ROOMS,
BOSTON, Dec. 20, 1856.

DEAR SIR, — Your letter of the 16th has been received, and we are glad to find that the importance of State action in regard to Kansas is appreciated in Iowa as well as here. The first question seems to be, Is such action really needed? And I will state what I believe to be substantially the views of this committee, who are now laboring to obtain an appropriation from our legislature.

There can be no doubt that the measures of which you speak (the purchase of land, erection of mills, etc.) could not well be engaged in by a State; and certainly no grant for that purpose could be obtained here. But although present destitution may be relieved in Kansas, it is by no means certain that there will not be great suffering there in the spring, before any crops can be raised, — especially if for any cause business should not be active. Then who can be sure that the scenes of last summer will not be acted again? True, things look better; but the experience of the past ought to teach us to prepare for the future. But even if things go on prosperously there, money may still be needed. Men have been subjected to unjust punishments, or at least threatened with them, under the unconstitutional laws of the Territory. It is desirable that these cases should be brought before a higher tribunal; while the accused person may be a poor man unable to bear the expense of such a suit. The State appropriations could then be drawn upon for this purpose, and used to retain counsel, furnish evidence, and in other ways to forward the suit of the injured man.

Would it not therefore be well for each State to make an appropriation, which should remain in the hands of the Governor, as in Vermont, or of a committee, until it should be needed in Kansas? It would thus be a contingent fund, to be drawn on only in cases of necessity, and it would be ready against any emergency. It might never be called for, or only a portion of it might be used; but should occasion arise, it would save our citizens in Kansas from many of the horrors which have afflicted them the past year. A bill embodying these ideas will be introduced into our legislature; and from the tone of our people we have good hope that it will pass. If a similar bill could pass your legislature I have no doubt the example would be followed by New York, Maine, Michigan, Connecticut, and perhaps by Ohio, New Hampshire, and Rhode Island. A general movement of this kind would give us all we want; and we might make Kansas free, I think, without expending a dollar of the money voted. The moral effect of such action on emigration from the North, and on the employment of capital, would be very important. Security would be given that the rights of emigrants would be supported; and the first result would be the emigration of thousands as soon as spring opens; so that by July we should have a force of Northern settlers there, enough to sustain any form of law which might be set up. Without this, I fear that next year, in spite of the flattering promises of the present, will only see the last year's history repeated. There will be no confidence in the tranquillity of the Territory: capital will shun it; emigration be almost stopped; and a year hence we may be no better off than now, — and perhaps worse. With these opinions, we look on State appropriations as the salvation of Kansas, and hope that the whole North may be led to the same view.

With much respect,

F. B. SANBORN,
Corresponding Secretary of State Committee.

Although my name is signed to this letter, it was the joint composition of the chairman (Mr. Stearns) and myself; and had been preceded by the following letters: —

BOSTON, Dec. 18, 1856.
H. H. VAN DYCK, Esq.

DEAR SIR, — Since my return I have received a letter from Governor Robinson, a copy of which is enclosed.

In Connecticut they are ready to form a strong State committee to co-operate with New York and Massachusetts, but, like you, are waiting for light. In Philadelphia they have a very large committee, and are taking measures for the ultimate formation of a State committee. We are taking measures to have a petition to our legislature signed in every town in our State, and find it meets the general approval of our citizens. We have also taken measures to get full information from Chicago and Kansas as to the past, which, when sent us, we will forward to you. Please let me know how you progress in the work, and believe me

Your sincere friend,

GEORGE L. STEARNS,
Chairman M. S. K. Committee.

BOSTON, Dec. 18, 1856.
E. B. WHITMAN, ESQ.

DEAR SIR, — We have to-day written to H. B. Hurd, Esq., asking for permission for an examination of his committee's doings and accounts by you. We have endeavored from time to time to get from them definite information of their operations; and now, when grave charges are brought in our newspapers by Kansas men against them and their agents (the Central Committee in Kansas), we are entirely without the means of contradicting these assertions, and can only oppose our general knowledge of their good character and belief in their wise conduct to the positive statements now daily current. We therefore wish you to inform yourself as fully as possible of all their operations from the commencement to the present time, taking such minutes of your researches as will enable you to give a full and close account to us, and also before our legislature, should you be called upon for that purpose. We want to know the disposition made of the money we have sent to them (about $21,600, and two hundred rifles), an account of which you have enclosed. We hope soon to see you in good health, and are

Truly your friends,
GEORGE L. STEARNS,
Chairman M. S. K. Committee.

In connection with the letter to Mr. Whitman given above, a letter was sent to Mr. Hurd, the Secretary of the National Committee, portions of which are as follows : —

STATE KANSAS COMMITTEE ROOMS, 17 NILES BLOCK,
BOSTON, Dec. 18, 1856.
H. B HURD, ESQ., CHICAGO, ILL.

DEAR SIR, — Yours of the 10th was received to-day, and the arrangement which you have made with regard to the money will no doubt be satisfactory. I am sorry to say, however, that our committee are not satisfied with the infrequent and irregular communication which exists between us and you. It is now more than four months since our committee has been expecting and hoping for an account of the money we have sent you, . . . and yet we can get no definite information as to the way in which your agents have expended our money ; nor have we had from time to time much knowledge of the general course of your operations. You say that you have no time for such communications; but certainly a committee like ours, representing so many people and so much money, ought to take precedence in a correspondence with individuals. Such information as we seek is absolutely necessary to our acting in concert with you; and for want of it we are now compelled to act by ourselves. In order to satisfy the committee and our contributors as to what has been done, it is necessary that we should have copies of your accounts, — so far, at least, as they relate to our money; and therefore we ask for the copy mentioned in the indorsed vote. And I am further directed to request that you will give our agent, Mr. E. B. Whitman, such information on this point as he may desire. . . . All that our committee wish is a full and business-like statement of what you have done and are doing; for want of this they are compelled to cease acting as collectors of money for which they can obtain no sufficient vouchers.

Truly yours,

F. B. SANBORN,
Corresponding Secretary Mass. State Committee.

These letters, together with the movement to obtain legislative appropriations (one being actually voted by the State of Vermont), were the occasion of calling together the National Committee at the Astor House late in January. But previously it was found needful to notify that committee as follows : —

STATE KANSAS COMMITTEE ROOMS,
BOSTON, Jan. 3, 1857.

H. B. HURD, ESQ., *Secy. National Kansas Committee.*

DEAR SIR, — The Massachusetts Kansas Committee have thought it best to rescind the vote by which certain rifles owned by S. Cabot, Jr., are made subject to the order of the Kansas Central Committee, and to resume possession of the same. They were taken on to Tabor, it is understood, by Dr. J. P. Root; but they seem to be still at Tabor, and not to be at present needed in Kansas. Any information which you can give our agent Mr. Clark, or any directions to your agents which will facilitate his business, we hope you will give him. The necessary expense of transporting the rifles will be reimbursed by this committee when they have obtained actual possession of them; and they will be held in trust for the people of Kansas for the present.

Truly yours,

F. B. SANBORN,
Cor. Sec. Mass. S. K. Com.

These were the very rifles which were carried to Maryland by Brown, for use in Virginia, two years and a half later; but at this time there was no thought of any such campaign. Brown's purpose, as he disclosed it in Boston in January, 1857, was to equip and arm a hundred mounted men for defence and reprisal in Kansas; and it was upon this plan that the National Committee, when it assembled, held a warm discussion, in which Brown himself took part. His request was for arms and money which he might be at liberty to use in his own way, his past conduct being his guaranty that he would use them wisely. A compromise was the result. The arms chiefly in question were voted back to the Massachusetts Committee, who, it was understood, would place them in Brown's hands; and an appropriation of five thousand dollars was made from the almost empty treasury of the National Committee for his benefit; while he was also to have the reversion of any arms in their possession not otherwise disposed of. This appears by the following votes: —

At a meeting of the National Kansas Committee, held at the Astor House, in the city of New York, on the twenty-fourth day of January, A. D. 1857, the following resolutions were adopted: —

1. *Resolved*, That the treasurer be directed to reserve in the treasury, out of any unappropriated moneys in his custody, or which may be hereafter sent to the National committee, the sum of five thousand dollars, to be used by the committee in aid of Captain John Brown in any defensive measures that may become necessary; and that Captain Brown be, and he is hereby, authorized to draw upon the treasurer for the sum of five hundred dollars, as a portion of said sum, at such time as he may deem it expedient, for the said purposes.

2. *Resolved*, That such arms and supplies as the committee may have, and which may be needed by Captain Brown, are appropriated to his use, *provided*, that the arms and supplies be not more than enough for one hundred men; and that a letter of approbation be given him by this committee.

H. B. HURD,
Sec. National Kansas Com.

Any person having property covered by the above Resolution is requested to deliver the same to Mr. John Brown or his agent.

H. B. HURD.

In furtherance of these votes, Brown at once made out the following schedule, which he called a "Memorandum of small outfit:" —

Memorandum of articles wanted as an outfit for fifty volunteers to serve under my direction during the Kansas war, or for such specified time as they may each enlist for ; together with estimated cost of the same, delivered in Lawrence or Topeka.

2 substantial (but not heavy) baggage wagons with good covers	$200.00
4 good serviceable wagon-horses	400.00
2 sets strong plain harness	50.00
100 good heavy blankets, say at $2 or $2.50	200.00
8 substantial large-sized tents	100.00
8 large camp-kettles	12.00
50 tin basins	5.00
50 tin spoons	2.00
4 plain strong saddles and bridles	80.00
4 picket ropes and pins	3.00
8 wooden pails	2.00
8 axes and helves	12.00
8 frying-pans (large size)	8.00
8 large size coffee-pots	10.00
8 " " spiders or bake-ovens	10.00
8 " " tin pans	6.00
12 spades and shovels	18.00
6 mattocks	6.00
2 weeks provisions for men and horses	150.00
fund for horse-hire and feed ; loss and damage of same	500.00
	$1774.00

Upon this list Mr. White remarked as follows : —

ASTOR HOUSE, NEW YORK, Jan. 27, 1857.

CAPTAIN JOHN BROWN.

DEAR SIR, — I am unable yet to give you the schedule of articles which the committee propose placing in your hands. Please address me at Chicago, stating whether a letter may be still sent to you at the Massasoit House. It will be necessary for me to examine shipping-books, etc., in our office at Chicago. I brought your matters before the notice of the committee yesterday. Resolutions were passed directing the secretary to instruct Mr. Jones, of Tabor, to retain the supplies, etc., in his hands until you had made your selections. Resolutions were also adopted empowering me to ship clothing, boots, etc., to you at Tabor, which will be done on the opening of navigation.   Very truly,

HORACE WHITE.

OFFICE NATIONAL KANSAS COMMITTEE,
11 MARINE BANK BUILDING, CHICAGO, Feb. 18, 1857.

JOHN BROWN, ESQ.

MY DEAR SIR, — The articles specified in the schedule and order which you gave me in New York will be forwarded next week. I think we shall be able to make out the whole number required, filling the blanks with 100. They will be shipped as directed, and freight paid through. Mr. Jones has been notified to expect them. We hope to hear from you soon.

Very truly,

HORACE WHITE,
Ass't Sec. N. K. Com.

If any evidence were needed of Mr. White's entire confidence in Brown at this time, it would be furnished by this letter : —

CHICAGO, March 21, 1857.

CAPTAIN JOHN BROWN.

MY DEAR FRIEND, — I find it quite impossible to prepare a schedule of the property which belongs to you under the New York resolution. It can only be ascertained in the Territory. I am going there myself about the first of next month, and I need not say that you may command my services at all times. Mr. Arny is there, and with the help of him and Mr. Whitman we shall probably be able to secure everything. At any rate we will work for it. Please let me hear how you are prospering. Write me a line directed to Chicago. If I am not here it will be forwarded to me. State when you expect to be in Kansas. If you should think it undesirable to have one of your letters sent through Missouri, you need not sign your name to it. I shall know the handwriting. I anticipate perilous times ; and when the Philistines are upon us, I may possibly be found carrying a bayonet on the right side.

Very truly,

HORACE WHITE.

P. S. I suppose the Boston people will fix you out with a return ticket. Perhaps it may not be amiss to send you the enclosed note. If you have other means of procuring just as well a free ticket, I would prefer you would not use this, because the railroads have done very liberally by us, and I do not wish to seem to be bleeding them.

I would rather no one but yourself should have the benefit of the enclosed, because our credit with the companies for the future depends somewhat upon the fairness which they experience this summer.[1]

Again very truly,

H. W.

Mr. Arny, General Agent of this committee, also wrote to Brown as follows : —

LOUISVILLE, KY., March 11, 1857.

CAPTAIN BROWN.

DEAR SIR, — I last week packed fourteen boxes clothing for you, marked "J. B., care Jonas Jones, Tabor, Iowa." In one of the boxes I put three mills to grind wheat or corn for bread, which I think will be useful to the men of your settlement. I could not get in every instance the full amount of clothing required ; but have done the best I could. Anything I can do further for you, please let me know ; and please acknowledge the receipt of this, directed to me, care of Simmons & Leadbeater, St. Louis, Mo.

As ever your friend and well-wisher,

W. F. M. ARNY.

On the opposite page you will find a statement of the contents of the boxes.[2]

---

[1] The note enclosed runs thus : —

OFFICE NATIONAL KANSAS COMMITTEE, 11 MARINE BANK BUILDING,
CHICAGO, March 21, 1857.

DEAR SIR, — Allow me to introduce Captain John Brown, of Osawatomie, Kansas Territory. If you could consistently give him a trip pass over your road it would be regarded a special favor by the committee, and a personal one to most of us. We shall not be in the habit of making such requests, but in the present instance it is peculiarly wanted, and will be rightly appreciated.

Very respectfully,

HORACE WHITE,
Assistant Secretary N. K. Committee.

To C. B. GREENOUGH, ESQ., General Ticket Agent, New York & Erie Railroad, New York.

WILLIAM R. BARR, ESQ., General Agent Lake Shore Railroad, Buffalo, N. Y.

DUDLEY P. PHELPS, ESQ., General Ticket Agent, Michigan Southern Railroad, Toledo, Ohio.

Upon which is the following indorsement in the handwriting of John Brown : " Horace White, March 21, 1857."

[2] These were given thus : —

" CONTENTS : Box No. 1, — 5 coats, 6 pairs pants, 1 vest, 6 quilts, 8 pairs boots, 10 caps, 20 pairs socks, 10 pairs drawers, 22 shirts, and 5 pairs mits. Box No. 2, — 24 coats, 22 pants, 12 vests, 12 quilts, 12 pairs drawers, 12 shirts. Box No. 3, — 4 coats, 12 pants, 2 vests, 12 quilts, 2 pairs boots, 2 caps, 13 socks, 5 shirts, 9 pairs mits. Box No. 4, — 12 pairs boots. Box No. 5, — 12 pairs boots. Box No. 6, — 18 pairs pants, 6 vests, 11 quilts, 13 pairs boots, 18 caps, 42 socks, 1 pair drawers, 18 shirts, .

These votes and letters, with the letters which had preceded them, and served as Brown's introduction where he was not personally known, fully refute the statements made many years later that Brown was looked upon with indifference or aversion by the friends of Kansas in 1856–57.

The letter of Charles Robinson, dated Sept. 14, 1856, at Lawrence (printed on page 330), was filled with praise of John Brown, and when it reached me in Boston, Jan. 2, 1857, it bore these two indorsements : —

Governor Chase's Indorsement.

COLUMBUS, Dec. 20, 1856.

Captain John Brown, of Kansas Territory, is commended to me by a highly reputable citizen of this State as a gentleman every way worthy of entire confidence. I have also seen a letter from Governor Charles Robinson, whose handwriting I recognize, speaking of Captain Brown and his services to the cause of the Free-State men in Kansas in terms of the warmest commendation. Upon these testimonials I cordially recommend him to the confidence and regard of all who desire to see Kansas a free State.

S. P. CHASE.[1]

13 pairs mits. Box No. 7, — 15 quilts. Box No. 8, — 19 quilts. Box No. 9, — 2 coats, 4 pants, 3 vests, 12 socks, 12 drawers, 16 shirts. Box No. 10, — 12 pairs boots. Box No. 11, — 48 coats, 4 quilts, 12 pairs boots. Box No. 12, — 41 pairs pants, 15 vests, 9 quilts, 9 boots, 46 caps, 16 pairs socks. Box No. 13, — 1 coat, 2 pants, 7 quilts, 9 pairs socks, 56 pairs drawers, 31 shirts. Box No. 14, — 17 quilts. Whole amount as follows : 84 coats, 105 pairs pants, 39 vests, 100 quilts and blankets, 68 pairs boots, 76 caps, 112 pairs socks, 91 pairs drawers, 104 shirts, 27 pairs mits. 3 hand-mills for grinding grain."

Upon all which is the following indorsement in the handwriting of John Brown : " W. F. M. Arny. Answered March 21."

[1] This eminent man, afterward Senator from Ohio and Chief-Justice of the United States, sent another letter to Brown six months later, but while he was still Governor of Ohio. It is interesting as showing that Governor Chase either did not know or did not choose to recognize the *alias* of " Nelson Hawkins," by which Brown was then addressed to avoid the opening of his letters by proslavery postmasters.

COLUMBUS, OHIO, June 6, 1857.

NELSON HAWKINS.

MY DEAR SIR. — Captain John Brown lately wrote me, requesting that I put a subscription paper in aid of the cause of freedom in Kansas in the hands of some reliable and efficient person here. I am sorry to say that on consideration I do not find there is

Gerrit Smith's Letter.

PETERBORO', Dec. 30, 1856.

CAPTAIN JOHN BROWN, — You did not need to show me letters from Governor Chase and Governor Robinson to let me know who and what you are. I have known you many years, and have highly esteemed you as long as I have known you. I know your unshrinking bravery, your self-sacrificing benevolence, your devotion to the cause of freedom, and have long known them. May Heaven preserve your life and health, and prosper your noble purposes!

GERRIT SMITH.

I may also cite here a letter from one of Brown's neighbors in Osawatomie, and still a resident of that town, written a year later than Robinson's, but breathing the same admiration and respect for the old captain : —

Letter from Henry H. Williams.

OSAWATOMIE, Oct. 12, 1857.

CAPTAIN BROWN.

DEAR SIR, — Learning that there is a messenger in town from you, I will take the opportunity to drop you a line. We are just through with the October election, and as far as this county is concerned it went off bright. This was owing in a great measure to our thorough military organization here, and the well-known reputation that *our* boys have for fighting. There were about four hundred and twenty-five votes cast in this county : about three hundred and fifty Free-State. I have a company organized here of about eighty men, and we drilled twice a week for several weeks previous to election, which no doubt had a wholesome effect upon the *borderers*. Our company is a permanent institution. We have sent on to St. Louis for three drums and two fifes. We are very

any probability of obtaining any contributions here beyond the twenty-five dollars which I obtained for the Captain when here early last winter. The capital of a State, where calls are so constant and must have attention, is a hard place to raise money ; and there are very few indeed who can be brought to see that the cause of freedom in Kansas at this time requires further contributions. I write this note to you at the request of Captain Brown, who speaks of you as his special friend.

Very respectfully and truly,

S. P. CHASE.

Upon which is the following indorsement in the handwriting of John Brown : " S. P. Chase. Requires no reply." Probably the twenty-five dollars was Mr. Chase's own gift.

poorly supplied with arms. However, I understand that you have
some arms with you which you intend to bring into the Territory.
I hope that you will not forget the *boys* here, a considerable number
of whom have smelt gunpowder, and have had their courage tried on
several occasions. I do not like to boast, but I think we have some
of the best fighting stock here that there is in the Territory. Speaking of arms reminds me that there was a box containing five dozen
revolvers sent to you at Lawrence last fall to be distributed by you to
your *boys*. K. and W. — two renegade Free-State men from here —
went up to Lawrence about that time, told a pitiful tale, and said
that they were *your boys ;* and the committee that had the revolvers
in charge gave them each one, and a Sharpe's rifle. A few days after,
I was in Lawrence, and applied to the committee to know if they
intended to distribute the revolvers ; if they did, that I would like to
have one. They refused, however, to let me have one, because for-
sooth I could not tell as big a yarn about what I had done for the
Free-State cause as K. and W. could. I have since learned that
the committee have distributed the revolvers to the "Stubs" and
others about Lawrence, with the understanding that they are to
return them at your order. But I think it is doubtful if you get
them. There has been plenty of Sharpe's rifles and other arms distributed at Manhattan and other points remote from the Border,
where they never have any disturbances, and a Border Ruffian is a
curiosity ; while along the Border here, where we are liable to
have an outbreak at any time, we have had no arms distributed
at all.

Two or three weeks before election I visited the Border counties
south of this, and organized a company of one hundred men on the
Little Osage, and a company on Sugar Creek ; also at Stanton and
on the Pottawatomie above this point. According to the election
returns, we have done much better in this and the Border counties
south than they have in the Border counties north of this point.
The *boys* would like to see you and shake you by the hand once
more. Nearly all would unite in welcoming you back here ; those
that would not, you have nothing to fear from in this locality. The
sentiment of the people and the strength and energy of the Free-
State party here exercise a wholesome restraint upon those having
Border Ruffian proclivities.

Yours as of old for the right,   .

HENRY H. WILLIAMS.[1]

---

[1] This letter was addressed "To Captain John Brown, Tabor, Fremont
County, Iowa," and among Brown's papers was accompanied with the
following memorandum of the distribution made at Lawrence of the arms

These letters, covering the whole period in 1856–57 during which Brown was absent from Kansas, are conclusive proof of the estimation in which he was held by the Free-State settlers during "the time that tried men's souls." The votes and letters of the National Committee show that they, too, as they came to know Brown better, trusted him more. But their affairs had not been very well managed, and their treasury became empty; so that the money voted at New York did not appear, and when Brown wrote for it from New England, he received the following reply : —

which Mr. Williams mentions, and which are the same spoken of by Mr. White in his testimony on page 342.

Memorandum of William Hutchinson, Lawrence.

Bloomington.	A. Curtis,	Navy Revolver.	No. 50,400
Osawatomie.	N. King,	" "	" 49,860
"	J. B. Way,	" "	" 50,906
Keokuk.	J. M. Arthur, eight revolvers with accoutrements. Numbers not taken.		
Pottawatomie.	Wm. Partridge,	Navy Revolver.	No. 50,410
Lawrence.	E. C. Harrington,	" "	" 51,171
"	A. Cutler,	" "	" 50,995
Minniola.	O. A. Bassett,	" "	" 51,140

The following are the numbers of others given to the "Stubs" : —

49,986,   51,208,   50,992,   50,410,   51,203,   50,963,   49,947,   51,101,
50,998,   50,969,   50,944,   51,043,   51,021,   51,033,   51,195,   50,994,
50,980,   49,741,   50,446,   50,040,   51,019,   51,218,   51,200,   51,204.
51,059,   50,948,   51,149,   50,958,   51,255,

Mr. Whitman has one, and I think the others were distributed by Eldridge without taking receipts.

Feeling too unwell to walk the distance, I gave up going to my sister's, and have looked up the above numbers.   Sorry to hear of your ill-health. Still it is nothing unusual to hear of sickness all over the Territory.   I have waited for Eldridge to act; but he has left, I think, without doing anything for you, and as soon as I can take the time I will make one more earnest effort for you in this place, and am sure that *some* can be obtained. Say to Mr. Kagi I gave the order for Parsons's gun into the hands of Mr. Lyon's family, and they promised to bring it to town, but it has not come yet.

If you get any news of importance, please inform me.

Yours again,

WM. HUTCHINSON.

Upon which is the following indorsement in the handwriting of John Brown : "Wm. Hutchinson's letter."   The date is not given, but it must be in 1857–58.

OFFICE NATIONAL KANSAS COMMITTEE,
11 MARINE BANK BUILDING,
CHICAGO, April 1, 1857.

CAPTAIN JOHN BROWN, Springfield, Mass.

At a meeting of the National Kansas Committee, held this day, it was

Resolved, That as according to the present state of the public feeling, evinced by the almost total cessation of contributions to the funds of the committee, it appears that the means of carrying on our operations will not be forthcoming from the usual sources; therefore, it is expedient to take immediate measures to settle the liabilities, and close the accounts of the committee, and to reduce the current expenses to the lowest possible point; and that the secretary be instructed to take measures accordingly.

Resolved, further, That the secretary be instructed to write to the members of the committee residing in other cities, — to Messrs. Greeley & McElrath, Hon. Gerrit Smith, and other prominent donors and friends, — setting forth the fact of the cessation of contributions as above stated, and the necessity we are under of closing our operations, unless immediately sustained by liberal contributions.

We are sorry to be obliged to come to the above conclusion, but are compelled to do so. There are several important undertakings now in hand, which we shall have to abandon, unless further means are forthcoming. The committee are at present out of money, and are compelled to decline sending you the five hundred dollars you speak of. They are sorry this has become the case, but it was unavoidable. I need not state to you all the reasons why. The country has stopped sending us contributions, and we have no means of replenishing our treasury. We shall need to have aid from some quarter to enable us to meet our present engagements.

I send you a copy of the list of articles selected for you by Mr. Arny. Our opinion is that some things have been selected that you do not need; such, for instance, as quilts, unless it is intended to supply the families of the company, and mits, which I suppose means ladies' mits. If he means mittens they would be useful.[1]

Yours, etc.,

H. B. HURD.
Secretary National Kansas Committee.

Thus ended the hopes of further material aid from the National Committee. The Massachusetts Committee kept

---

[1] Upon this is the following indorsement in the handwriting of John Brown: "H. B. Hurd. Needs no comment."

its word better. Before the Astor House meeting it had
made Brown the custodian of the two hundred rifles at Tabor,
and had suggested to him the following receipt, which, with
its erasures, is among the Brown Papers at Topeka: —

STATE KANSAS AID COMMITTEE ROOM,
BOSTON, Jan. 7, 1857.

Received of George L. Stearns, Chairman of the Massachusetts
Kansas Aid Committee, an order on Edward Clark, Esq., of Lawrence, K. T., for two hundred Sharpe's rifles, carbines, with four
thousand ball cartridges, thirty-one thousand military caps, and six
iron ladles, — the same to be delivered to said committee, or to their
order, on demand. It being further understood and agreed that I
(*am at liberty to distribute one hundred of the carbines, and to use
the ammunition for maintaining the cause of freedom in Kansas and
in the United States, and that such distribution and use shall be considered a delivery to said committee*). [Have authority to use one
hundred of the carbines, and all the ammunition, as I may think the
interests of Kansas require. Keeping an account of my doings] ;
and that such delivery and use shall be considered as such delivery.[1]

A week later I wrote to Edward Clark, another agent of
our committee (Jan. 15, 1857) : —

" We have made the rifles subject to Captain Brown's order, as we
wrote you. From Mr. Winchell's account, we conclude that you will
find them in the Territory, and in the hands of the Central Committee.[2] In the quarrel between the National and the Central Committees, we hope you will keep yourself strictly neutral, and inform us
how the case really stands. We hear charges of misconduct from both

---

[1] The words in parentheses are marked across in the original, evidently
for the purpose of erasure ; the words in brackets are in a different handwriting from the rest of the paper. There is no indorsement except the
word " Boston " written twice in Brown's handwriting.

[2] Originally they had been forwarded to this committee, as appears by
the following note : —

STATE KANSAS AID COMMITTEE ROOMS,
BOSTON, Sept. 30, 1856.

DEAR SIR, — At a meeting of this committee it was *voted*, That the arms purchased
by Dr. Cabot, in accordance with a vote of the committee, passed September 10, be
forwarded to the Kansas Central Committee at Lawrence, with instructions that they
be loaned to actual settlers for defence against unlawful aggressions upon their rights
and liberties.

GEORGE L. STEARNS, *Chairman.*

H. B. HURD, ESQ., Chicago.

sides. The order of Captain Brown will not probably be issued till spring, if it is at all, since his use of the rifles depends on a contingency which may not occur."

On Jan. 30, 1857, still later instructions followed to Mr. Clark : —

"The National Committee, at their meeting in New York, voted to resign all claim to the rifles at Tabor to our committee ; and Mr. Hurd is to notify you of the fact officially. If, therefore, you have commenced any proceedings to get possession of them from the National Committee, you may suspend all action until you receive Mr. Hurd's letter, which will give you full power in the premises. We learn that the rifles are at Tabor, in charge of a certain Jonas Jones, and that they are properly stored and cared for. If this should not be so, or if the Central Committee at Lawrence have interfered with them at all, you may take measures to get immediate possession, as directed by us. All matters at issue between our committee and the National Committee have been satisfactorily settled, and we trust there will be no further misunderstandings. Mr. Hurd has been in Boston and arranged all things. We have been expecting a letter from you for some days. By the time this reaches you, you will have been at Tabor, we presume. There write us a full account of your proceedings, and also of the present condition of things in Kansas, the position of the Central Committee, etc. Much business was done at the New York meeting ; but no final settlement of accounts could be made, by reason of the absence of important persons and papers. Conway and Whitman are here, preparing to appear before the legislative committee about a State appropriation."

The closing sentence of this letter indicates that the Massachusetts Committee, in furtherance of the policy explained to Governor Grimes, was preparing to obtain a State appropriation from the legislature which was then in session at Boston. John Brown was summoned as a witness before this legislature, and gave his testimony in the hall of the House of Representatives, February 18, 1857, the committee on Federal Relations holding a hearing in that place for the purpose. There are but few letters from Brown at this time. Here is one of them : —

24

John Brown to the Rev. S. L. Adair.

BOSTON, MASS., Feb. 16, 1857.

DEAR BROTHER AND SISTER ADAIR, — It is a long time since I have heard a word from you, but I suppose it is because I have been continually shifting about since my return to the States. I am getting quite anxious to hear from you, and to get your views on your own prospects and present condition, together with your ideas of Governor Geary and of Kansas matters generally. I have not heard a word from Hudson or Akron since December; but that is owing to the fact that I have had no place fixed upon, till of late, where to receive letters. This has been from a kind of necessity; but I can now say, do write me at Springfield, Mass., care of the Massasoit House, leaving the title of Captain off. I now expect to go to Kansas (quietly) before long; but I do not wish it noised about at all. Can you tell me what has become of Captain Holmes of your place? I expect to appear before a committee of the Massachusetts legislature in a day or two. My family were well about a week ago.   Your affectionate brother,

JOHN BROWN.

It fell to my lot to introduce Brown to the legislative committee, February 18; and I did so in these words : —

"As one of the petitioners for State aid to the settlers of Kansas, I appear before you to state briefly the purpose of the petition. No labored argument seems necessary; for if the events of the last two years in Kansas, and the prospect there for the future, are not of themselves enough to excite Massachusetts to action, certainly no words could do so. We have not provided ourselves with advocates, therefore, but with witnesses; and we expect that the statements of Captain Brown and Mr. Whitman will show conclusively that the rights and interests of Massachusetts have suffered gross outrage in Kansas, — an outrage which is likely to be repeated unless measures are taken by you to prevent so shameful an abuse. Your petitioners desire that a contingent appropriation be made by the legislature, to be placed in the hands of a commission of responsible and conservative men, and used only in case of necessity to relieve the distress of the settlers of Kansas, — especially such as have gone from our own State. It is possible that no such necessity will occur; but nothing, in the opinion of your petitioners, would do so much to obviate it as the proposed appropriation. Such an act would both encourage our friends in Kansas and dishearten their oppressors; and the moral effect of it would be greater than any which would follow from the expenditure of a much larger sum.

" Let it not be understood, however, that the petitioners ask for this as a simple act of charity, or are willing to rest their case on the common arguments for a charitable donation. The question involved is not merely whether the hungry shall be fed, the naked clothed, and the houseless sheltered ; it reaches far beyond this : it is the issue between freedom and slavery, in Kansas and in the nation. Why should we refuse to see this manifest fact ?

" Viewed in this light, we feel justified in regarding our petition as the most important matter which the General Court has now to consider. The interests of banks and railroads, points of etiquette between different branches of the government, — even the solemn discussions which involve the lives of condemned men, — all seem trivial beside this most public and pressing business. I think, Mr. Chairman, that the people of Massachusetts will soon ask, if they have not already begun, ' What preparation are our Senators and Representatives making for the crisis which they were elected specially to meet ? How are they raising themselves to the height of this great argument ? ' Is it not true, sir, that yourself and nine tenths of your colleagues in this body were elected as declared supporters of two all-important measures, — the re-election of Charles Sumner and the establishment of freedom in Kansas ? And do you believe that the one which you have so triumphantly accomplished is one whit more dear to the people than the other ? Let the liberal contributions of the whole State, in money and clothing, and the numerously signed petitions which are presented here daily, answer that. Can you hesitate, then, to give expression to the will of the people, — not merely in words, which cost nothing and are worth nothing, but in substantial deeds ?

" It has been suggested that some persons doubt the constitutionality of the proposed measure. That is rather a question to be decided by the legislature than a point to be argued by the petitioners ; but should it be necessary, which I can hardly think possible, I have no doubt they can fully show its constitutionality, of which they make no question. The name of Judge Parker, attached to the Cambridge petition, and the decided opinion of several eminent jurists, confirm their belief. We have invited Captain Brown and Mr. Whitman to appear in our behalf, because these gentlemen are eminently qualified either to represent Massachusetts in Kansas or Kansas in Massachusetts. The best blood of the ' Mayflower ' runs in the veins of both, and each had an ancestor in the army of the Revolution. Mr. Whitman, seventh in descent from Miles Standish, laid the foundation of the first church and the first schoolhouse in

Kansas; John Brown, the sixth descendant of Peter Browne, of the 'Mayflower,' has been to Kansas what Standish was to the Plymouth Colony. These witnesses have seen the things of which they testify, and have felt the oppression we ask you to check. Ask this gray-haired man, gentlemen, — if you have the heart to do it, — where lies the body of his murdered son; where are the homes of his four other sons, who a year ago were quiet farmers in Kansas. I am ashamed, in presence of this modest veteran, to express the admiration which his heroism excites in me. Yet he, so venerable for his years, his integrity, and his courage, — a man whom all Massachusetts rises up to honor, — is to-day an outlaw in Kansas. To these witnesses, whose unsworn testimony deserves and will receive from you all the authority which an oath confers, I will now yield place."

Brown then addressed the committee and a large audience who had assembled to hear him. He made in substance the same speech which he gave that winter at Hartford, at Concord, and elsewhere; reading from his manuscript (which I have already cited) an account of the destruction of property and of life by the Missouri invaders in 1855–56, and speaking of the inactivity of the Federal Government, except in the protection of these invaders. He described modestly the last attack on Lawrence, and denied that it had been saved from destruction by Governor Geary. In answer to questions by the chairman of the committee (Senator Albee, of Marlborough) he gave the account — since so well known — of his visiting Buford's men near Osawatomie in the guise of a surveyor; and quoted them as telling him that the Yankees could not be coaxed, driven, or whipped into a fight, and that one Southerner could whip a dozen Abolitionists; they intended to drive out the whole Free-State population of Kansas, if that should be necessary to establish slavery in the new State; if Kansas was free, Missouri could not maintain slavery, they told him. When asked what sort of emigrants were needed to make Kansas free, Brown replied, " We want good men, industrious and honest, who respect themselves, and act only from principle, from the dictates of conscience; men who fear God too much to fear anything human." Questioned by Senator Albee concerning the probable need and effect of such an appropriation as was sought for, Brown replied: " Whenever we heard last year that the people of the North were doing anything for us, we were encouraged and strengthened to keep up the contest. At present there is not much danger of an invasion from Missouri. God protects us in winter; but when the grass gets high enough to feed the horses of the Border Ruffians we may have trouble, and should be prepared for the worst. Things do not look one iota more encouraging now — except that the winter is milder — than they did last year at this time. You may remember that from the Shannon treaty, which ended the Wakarusa war, till early in May, 1856, there was general quiet in Kansas. No violence was offered to our citizens when they went to Missouri. I frequently went there myself to buy corn and other supplies. I was known there; yet they treated me well. I do not know that there will be another invasion, but should expect one. Yet the actual settlers who go to Kansas from the slave States have many of them turned to be the most determined Free-State men, — fighting in all our battles. The comparative strength of the parties as regards numbers, intelligence, industry, and good habits generally, is all on our side; but the machinery of a genuine territorial government is not yet in operation, while the Federal Government is wholly on the side of slavery."

The movement for a State appropriation was unsuccessful, but the Massachusetts Committee continued their contributions to John Brown.

Among the contributors to his fund was Mr. Amos Lawrence, of Boston, who wrote to Brown as follows the day after the speech in the State House : —

BOSTON, Feb. 19, 1857.

MY DEAR SIR, — Enclosed you will find seventy dollars. Please write to John Conant, of East Jaffrey, N. H., and acknowledge receipt; or write to me saying you have received the Jaffrey money, and I will send your letter to them. It is for your own personal use, and not for the cause in any other way than that. I am sorry not to have seen you before you left. It may not be amiss to say that you may find yourself disappointed if you rely on the National Kansas Committee for any considerable amount of money. Please to consider this as confidential; and it is only my own opinion, without *definite* knowledge of their operations. I hope they will get a great deal of money, but think they will not. The old managers have not inspired confidence, and therefore money will be hard for them to get now and hereafter. This check, you will see, needs your indorsement.

May God bless you, my dear sir, is the wish of your friend,

AMOS A. LAWRENCE.

While Brown was ordering his pikes in Connecticut, Mr. Lawrence wrote him again in these words : —

(*Private*.)

BOSTON, March 20, 1857.

MY DEAR SIR, — Your letter from New Haven is received. I have just sent to Kansas near fourteen thousand dollars to establish a fund to be used, first, to secure the best system of common schools for Kansas that exists in this country; second, to establish Sunday-schools.

The property is held by two trustees in Kansas, and cannot return to me. On this account, and because I am always short of money, I have not the cash to use for the purpose you name. But in case anything should occur, while you are engaged in a great and good cause, to shorten your life, you may be assured that your wife and children shall be cared for more liberally than you now propose. The family of "Captain John Brown of Osawatomie" will not be turned out to starve in this country, until Liberty herself is driven out.

Yours with regard,

AMOS A. LAWRENCE.

I hope you will not run the risk of arrest.

I never saw the offer to which you refer, in the "Telegraph," and have now forgotten what it was. Come and see me when you have time.

A. A. LAWRENCE.

Soon after the Boston hearing, Brown visited his family at North Elba; and early in March returned to New England, where he revisited the graves of his ancestors in Connecticut. These letters relate to this period : —

John Brown to his Wife.

HARTFORD, CONN., March 6, 1857.

DEAR WIFE, — I enclose with this a letter from Owen, written me from Albany. He appeared to be very much depressed before he left me; but there was no possible misunderstanding between us that I knew of. I did not pay Samuel Thompson all that I ought to have given him for carrying us out, and wish you would make it up to him, if you can well, out of what I have sent you. If you get hay of him, I will send or fetch the money soon to pay for it. I shall send you some newspapers soon to let you see what different stories are told of me. None of them tell things as I tell them. Write me, care of the Massasoit House, Springfield, Mass.

Your affectionate husband,

JOHN BROWN.

SPRINGFIELD, MASS., March 12, 1857.

DEAR WIFE AND CHILDREN ALL, — I have just got a letter from John. All middling well, March 2, but Johnny, who has the ague by turns. I now enclose another from Owen. I sent you some papers last week. Have just been speaking for three nights at Canton, Conn., and at Collinsville, a village of that town. At the two places they gave me eighty dollars. Canton is where both father and mother were raised. They have agreed to send to my family at North Elba grandfather John Brown's old granite monument, about eighty years old, to be faced and inscribed in memory of our poor Frederick, who sleeps in Kansas.[1] I prize it very highly, and the family all will, I think. I want to see you all very much, but cannot tell when I can go back yet. Hope to get something from you here soon. Direct as before. May God bless you all!

Your affectionate husband and father.

Mr. Rust, to whom the next letters were written, says that he had a "store" at Collinsville in 1857, and John Brown was there in April, showing to various persons the bowie-knife that he captured with Pate in Kansas. As he did so, Brown said: "Such a blade as this, mounted upon a strong shaft, or handle, would make a cheap and effective weapon. Our friends in Kansas are without arms or money

---

[1] This note from a friend in Connecticut shows how soon the gravestone was removed to North Elba: —

COLLINSVILLE, April 17, 1857.

CAPTAIN J. BROWN.

DEAR SIR, — Your favor of the 16th is just at hand. The pistols I shall send to-morrow morning. I received the package for S. Brown, and delivered it. The expense on the parcel was one dollar fifty, but I am very willing to pay that myself. Your friends have sent the old stone to your place. Hoping to see you soon, I remain

Yours respectfully,

H. N. RUST.

to get them; and if I could put such weapons into their
hands, they could make them very useful. A resolute woman, with such a pike, could defend her cabin door against
man or beast. What can such a weapon be made for ? " Mr.
Rust guessed for a dollar each, in quantity. "Very well,"
said Brown; "I would be glad to pay that price for a
thousand;" and it was agreed that Mr. Rust should try to
get them made in Collinsville for that price, by Charles
Blair. Mr. Rust further says: —

"During one of his visits I carried him to Canton to see his
relatives. Not far from their house he noticed a tombstone leaning
against the stone wall by the roadside. He got out and examined it,
and found it to be his grandfather's; whereupon he said, ' I will go
back and see if my cousins will let me have it.' They consented,
and afterwards brought it to me at Collinsville; and I sent it to his
address at North Elba. ' That stone,' said he, ' formerly marked
the grave of my grandfather, who died fighting for the liberties of
his country; my son has just been murdered in the same cause in
Kansas, and the Government applauded the murderer. This stone
shall bear his name also; and I will have it set up at North
Elba.' "

John Brown to H. N. Rust.

SPRINGFIELD, MASS., April 16, 1857.

H. N. RUST, ESQ.

MY DEAR SIR, — Your favor of the 9th is received. Please forward to me by express the pistols you have received, and also send
me *with them the amount you had to pay on the whole package.* Be
kind enough to say to my friend Blair that I expect *funds within a
day or two to meet my engagement,* and that I mean to call on him.
Please direct the package to John (not Captain) Brown, care Massasoit House, Springfield, Mass. Did you receive the package for
Selden H. Brown?

Very respectfully your friend,

JOHN BROWN.

SPRINGFIELD, MASS., April 25, 1857.

H. N. RUST, ESQ.

MY DEAR SIR, — I did not see you the other morning before I
left, as I expected. Please hand line and draft to Mr. Blair at once.
The sabre you got is the identical one taken from Lieutenant
Brocket at Black Jack surrender. I would on no account have you

buy it of me, as you really have done, but that I am literally driven
to beg, — which is very humiliating.

Very respectfully your friend,

JOHN BROWN.

(Note by Mr. Rust.)

The draft was spoken of in the letter of April 16, and was
handed to Mr. Blair; the sabre was a present to me from Captain
Brown, received with the pistols; the pay spoken of was the bill
for the pistols, which I did not send him as requested. The pistols
had been used in Kansas and sent East for repairs; the funds spoken
of were to be the first payment for the pikes which had been ordered
not long before.

CHARLES BLAIR'S CONTRACT.

COLLINSVILLE, CONN., March 30, 1857.

The undersigned agree to the following: First, Charles Blair, of
this place, is to make and deliver at the railroad depot in Collinsville one thousand spears with handles fitted, of equal quality to one
dozen already made and sent to Springfield, Mass. The handles are
to be six feet in length, and the ferules to be made of strong malleable
iron. The handles to be well tied in bundles; and the blades with
screws for fastening to be securely packed in strong boxes suitable
for the transportation of edge tools. In consideration whereof, John
Brown, late of Kansas, agrees to deposit five hundred dollars with
Samuel W. Collins within ten days from this date, in part payment;
and four hundred and fifty dollars as payment in full for the above-
named one thousand spears and handles within thirty days thereafter.
The whole money to be deposited with said Collins at Collinsville,
and the spears and handles to be held subject to the order of said
Brown, on or before the first of July next.

CHARLES BLAIR.
JOHN BROWN.

COLLINSVILLE, March 30, 1857.

Received of John Brown, Esq., fifty dollars on account of spear
contract.

CHARLES BLAIR.

Received on the within contract one hundred dollars.

COLLINSVILLE, April 22, 1857.

Received the same date two hundred dollars.

Letters to John Brown by C. Blair.

HARTFORD, April 15, 1857.

MR. BROWN.

DEAR SIR, — I received yours in relation to the funds which you expected from the Kansas Committee, and I would say that I have not taken any further measures with the spears than to ascertain where I can get the handles and ferules, etc. If you do not find it convenient to raise the funds for a thousand, I will make you five hundred at the same rate. I should think the committee were not treating you very fairly by not honoring your drafts after the promise they had made you. I shall wait further orders from you before I proceed further.

Truly yours,

CHARLES BLAIR.

COLLINSVILLE, CONN., Aug. 27, 1857.

MR. BROWN.

DEAR SIR, — Yours of the 14th instant came to hand last Saturday. In regard to those articles, I have to say that I commenced the whole number; have all the handles well seasoned, the ferules and guards, screws, etc., and have some over five hundred of them ground, but not hearing anything further from you, I have let them rest until such times as you can make your arrangements. I thought I would not make any further outlay upon them, at least until I heard from you. I did not know but things would take such a turn in Kansas that they would not be needed. Of this you can judge better than I can. I did not feel able to bear the loss of having them left on my hands after I had finished them up, as you are aware that we did not expect *much* profit on the manufacture of the articles; but I am not disposed to cast the least blame upon you. I very well know that when a man is depending upon the public for *money* he is very liable to be disappointed, and I judge from the tenor of your letter that you will not blame me for *stopping* them, as I had used up the funds. I therefore wait your further orders whether to finish them up or to let them rest where they are. Don't give yourself any uneasiness about the affair, for if I go no further with them, I shall lose nothing, or but little; and I have no doubt you and I can make the matter satisfactory in some way. Your son (Oliver) is in the village, but is not now at work for me. My work in the shop was too hard for him in the hot weather, and he has been out at haying. I think he may get some job in the shop soon. Let me hear from you when convenient.

Very respectfully yours,

CHARLES BLAIR.

In speaking at Hartford and Canton, Brown used the
same manuscript as at Boston; but at the end of his address made this appeal to the citizens of Connecticut, where
he felt more at home than in Massachusetts : —

"I am trying to raise from twenty to twenty-five thousand dollars in the free States, to enable me to continue my efforts in the
cause of freedom. Will the people of Connecticut, *my native State,*
afford me some aid in this undertaking? Will the gentlemen and
ladies of Hartford, where I make my first appeal in this State, set
the example of an earnest effort? Will some gentleman or lady
take hold and try what can be done by small contributions from
counties, cities, towns, societies, or churches, or in some other way?
I think the little beggar-children in the streets are sufficiently interested to warrant their contributing, if there was any need of it, to
secure the object. I was told that the newspapers in a certain city
were dressed in mourning on hearing that I was killed and scalped
in Kansas, but I did not know of it until I reached the place. Much
good it did me. In the same place I met a more cool reception than
in any other place where I have stopped. If my friends will hold up
my hands while I live, I will freely absolve them from any expense
over me when I am dead. I do not ask for pay, but shall be most
grateful for all the assistance I can get."

At the same time, or a little earlier, Brown published
this letter in the "New York Tribune" of March 4,
1857 : —

To the Friends of Freedom.

The undersigned, whose individual means were exceedingly limited when he first engaged in the struggle for liberty in Kansas,
being now still more destitute, and no less anxious than in time past
to continue his efforts to sustain that cause, is induced to make this
earnest appeal to the friends of freedom throughout the United
States, in the firm belief that his call will not go unheeded. I ask
all honest lovers of liberty and human rights, both male and female,
to hold up my hands by contributions of pecuniary aid, either as
counties, cities, towns, villages, societies, churches, or individuals.
I will endeavor to make a judicious and faithful application of all
such means as I may be supplied with. Contributions may be sent
in drafts to W. H. D. Callender, cashier State Bank, Hartford,
Conn. It is my intention to visit as many places as I can during
my stay in the States, provided I am first informed of the disposition

of the inhabitants to aid me in my efforts, as well as to receive my visit. Information may be communicated to me (care of Massasoit House) at Springfield, Mass. Will editors of newspapers friendly to the cause kindly second the measure, and also give this some half-dozen insertions ? Will either gentlemen or ladies, or both, who love the cause, volunteer to take up the business ? It is with *no little sacrifice of personal feeling* that I appear in this manner before the public.

JOHN BROWN.

About a month after his address in the State House at Boston, Brown visited me in Concord, and held a successful public meeting there. He afterwards spoke in Worcester, and the following correspondence relates to matters there : —

Letters of Eli Thayer.

WORCESTER, March 18, 1857.

FRIEND BROWN, — I have just returned from Albany, and find your favor of the 16th. I am glad you had a good meeting at Concord, — as I knew you would have, for the blood of heroes is not extinct in that locality. I will see some of our friends here to-morrow, and we will decide at once about your speaking here. If you are to speak, you will do well to be here a day or two in advance, and converse with some of our citizens. I will write you again to-morrow.

Truly yours,

ELI THAYER.

WORCESTER, March 19, 1857.

FRIEND BROWN, — I have seen some of our friends to-day, and they say you had better come here next Monday. There is to be an antislavery meeting in the evening, and I think it will be a very good time for you to present your cause, — which is the Free-State cause of Kansas. which is the cause of mankind. I shall expect you to do me the favor of stopping at my house.

Truly yours,

ELI THAYER.

Upon both these letters is this indorsement in the hand-writing of John Brown : " Eli Thayer. Answered March 23d in person." This means that he went to Worcester,

Monday, the 23d, and spoke that night at the antislavery meeting,[1] of which he had been notified.

WORCESTER, March 30, 1857.

CAPTAIN BROWN, — I have received your letter from Easton, Penn. Some of the men engaged in the Virginia scheme care nothing for slavery or antislavery but to make money. Of course such will do nothing for Kansas; but most of us have been doing, and shall continue to do, till the thing is settled. We have not the remotest idea of relinquishing Kansas, — not at all. I have just seen Mr. Higginson, and he informs me that our county committee will let you have fifty dollars. Perhaps, also, something will be raised by subscription, — I gave the papers to Mr. Higginson. He will write to you. Please let me know when you are coming this way. Do not pay postage on your letter to me, — let Uncle Sam do his part.   Truly yours,

ELI THAYER.[2]

While Brown was at Worcester on this second visit, he was introduced by Mr. Thayer to the manufacturers of arms

---

[1] Dr. Wayland, of Philadelphia, who was then a young clergyman in Worcester, thus writes respecting the occasion : —

"In the spring of 1857, just after the Dred Scott decision of the Supreme Court, I, being then a resident of Worcester, was getting up a lecture for Frederick Douglass, at which the then Mayor of the city for the first time in an American city presided at an address of Mr. Douglass. I called at the house of Eli Thayer, afterwards member of Congress from that District, to ask him to sit on the platform. Here I found a stranger, a man of tall, gaunt form, with a face smooth-shaven, destitute of the full beard that later became a part of history. The children were climbing over his knees ; he said, 'The children always come to me.' I was then introduced to John Brown of Osawatomie. How little one imagined then that within less than three years the name of this plain home-spun man would fill America and Europe ! Mr. Brown consented to occupy a place on the platform, and at the urgent request of the audience spoke briefly. It is one of the curious facts, that many men who *do* it are utterly unable to *tell* about it. John Brown, a flame of fire in action, was dull in speech.''

[2] This letter is indorsed by John Brown, " Hon. Eli Thayer. Answered 1st April," — which was soon after Brown's return from a visit he had made with Martin Conway and myself to Governor Reeder at his home at Easton, in the hope of persuading him to go back and take the lead of the Free-State men in Kansas in place of Robinson, who had lost the confidence of the people.

in that city, of which this note and the subsequent correspondence is evidence : —

APRIL 4, 1857.

MESSRS. ALLEN & WHEELOCK, — Captain Brown wishes to get a cannon and rifle which I have given him so sighted as to secure accuracy. I hope you will attend to his wishes.

Truly yours,

ELI THAYER.

What the further errand of the Kansas hero was with this firm will be seen below : —

Letters to and from Eli Thayer, etc.

SPRINGFIELD, MASS., April 16, 1857.

Hon. ELI THAYER.

MY DEAR SIR, — I am advised that one of " Uncle Sam's hounds is on my track ; " and I have kept myself hid for a few days to let my track get cold. I have no idea of being taken, and intend (if God will) to go back with irons in rather than upon my hands. Now, my dear sir, let me ask you to have Mr. Allen & Co. send me by express one or two navy-sized revolvers as soon as may be, together with his best cash terms (he warranting them) by the hundred with good moulds, flasks, etc. I wish the sample pistols sent to John (not Captain) Brown, care of Massasoit House, Springfield, Mass. I now enclose twenty dollars towards repairs done for me and revolvers ; the balance I will send as soon as I get the bill. I have written to have Dr. Howe send you by express a rifle and two pistols, which with the guns you gave me and fixings, together with the rifle given me by Mr. Allen & Co., I wish them to pack in a suitable strong box, perfectly safe, directing to J. B., care of Orson M. Oviatt, Esq., Cleveland, Ohio, as freight, to keep dry. For box, trouble, and packing I will pay when I get the bill. I wish the box very plainly marked, and forwarded to Cleveland, as soon as you receive the articles from Dr. Howe. I got a fine list in Boston the other day, and hope Worcester will not be entirely behind. I do not mean you or Mr. Allen & Co.

Very respectfully your friend,

JOHN BROWN.

P. S. Direct all letters and bills to care of Massasoit House. Please acknowledge.

April 17, 1857.

FRIEND BROWN, — I have received your letter containing twenty dollars, and have given it over with contents to Allen & Wheelock, who will attend to your requests. I shall leave to-night for New York City, and may not be back again to look after the things. Please send any directions you wish to Allen & Wheelock. The Boston people have done nobly, especially Mr. Stearns. Dr. Howe has not forwarded the articles named in your letter. As soon as received, I will place them in the hands of Allen & Wheelock. I thought it best to give them your letters, so that they might attend to your requests understandingly. They will be secret.

Will you allow me to suggest a name for your company? I should call them "the Neighbors," from Luke, tenth chapter: "Which thinkest thou was *neighbor* to him who fell among thieves?"

Our Virginia scheme is gaining strength wonderfully.[1] Every mail brings me offers of land and men. The press universally favors it, — that is, so far as we care for favor. It is bound to go ahead. You must have a home in Western Virginia.

Very truly your friend,

ELI THAYER.

WORCESTER, April 20, 1857.

JOHN BROWN, ESQ.

DEAR SIR, — Your letter to Mr. Thayer was handed us by him with the twenty dollars, and in reply would say that we are very sorry we cannot send you the sample revolvers, owing to great delay in some of our work, etc. We shall not be able to supply you with any at present, and recommend that you obtain Colt's pistols for your immediate use. We will send you one or more as soon as we can get them ready, if we can know where to send them, and would then be glad to supply you with what you may want. We have got the large gun ready; and at the request of Mr. Thayer we have been and got the cannon and brought it here; and are waiting for the rifle and pistols that you wrote were to be sent from Dr. Howe, on the receipt of which we shall forward them, together with the cannon, rifles, etc., as you directed; which we hope will be safely received in due time. Yours truly,

ALLEN & WHEELOCK.

---

[1] Lest it should be thought that this refers to Brown's plan for compulsory emancipation (which was not then disclosed), I hasten to say that this "Virginia scheme" was a combination of political campaigning and land speculation, which Mr. Thayer had originated and put in motion at a place named by him Ceredo, in West Virginia.

Eli Thayer, whose support of Brown in his most aggressive measures was at this time cordial and active, was one of the chief managers of the Emigrant Aid Company. Other managers took a like interest in Brown's character or his plans, or in both. Mr. Charles Higginson, a Boston cousin of Wentworth Higginson (who was then preaching at Worcester), had written somewhat earlier as follows:

EMIGRANT AID ROOMS, BOSTON, Jan. 10, 1857.
CAPTAIN JOHN BROWN OF OSAWATOMIE.

DEAR SIR, — I have a small fund in my hands to be used for the benefit of Kansas men. I enclose thirty dollars, with the request that you will use it as you see fit, — remembering that you are to regard yourself and your sons as entitled to your consideration as well as any others.   Respectfully yours,

C. J. HIGGINSON.[1]

Meantime the Massachusetts Kansas Committee had completed the transaction concerning the rifles at Tabor, and given Brown the following orders and votes to show his authority. The first is dated at Boston, Jan. 8, 1857:

DEAR SIR, — Enclosed we hand you our order on Edward Clark, Esq., of Lawrence, K. T., for two hundred Sharpe's rifled carbines, with four thousand ball cartridges, thirty-one thousand military caps, and six iron ladles, — all, as we suppose, now stored at Tabor in the State of Iowa. We wish you to take possession of this property, either at Tabor or wherever it may be found, as our agent, and to hold it subject to our order. For this purpose you are authorized to draw on our treasurer, Patrick T. Jackson, Esq., in Boston, for such sums as may be necessary to pay the expenses as they accrue, to an amount not exceeding five hundred dollars.

Truly yours,

GEORGE L. STEARNS,
Chairman Massachusetts State Kansas Committee.

MR. JOHN BROWN,
Of Kansas Territory.

---

[1] Upon this is the following indorsement in Brown's handwriting: "C. J. Higginson, or H. L. Higginson." The latter was a kinsman of Charles Higginson; and has since been known as the wealthy Boston banker, who supplies his native city with cheap concerts of the best music. I suppose he may have handed the above note or the money to Captain Brown.

Boston, April 15, 1857.

Dear Sir, — By the enclosed vote of the 11th instant we place in your hands one hundred Sharpe's rifles to be sold in conformity therewith, and wish you to use the proceeds for the benefit of the Free-State men in Kansas; keeping an account of your doings as far as practicable. Also a vote placing a further sum of five hundred dollars at your disposal, for which you can, in need, pass your draft on our treasurer, P. T. Jackson, Esq.

Truly yours,

GEORGE L. STEARNS,
Chairman Massachusetts State Kansas Committee.

Mr. John Brown,
Massasoit House, Springfield, Mass.

Boston, April 15, 1857.

At a meeting of the executive committee of the State Kansas Aid Committee of Massachusetts, held in Boston, April 11, 1857, it was

Voted, That Captain John Brown be authorized to dispose of one hundred rifles, belonging to this committee, to such Free-State inhabitants of Kansas as he thinks to be reliable, at a price not less than fifteen dollars; and that he account for the same agreeably to his instructions, for the relief of Kansas.

At the same meeting it was

Voted, That Captain John Brown be authorized to draw on P. T. Jackson, treasurer, for five hundred dollars, if on his arrival in Kansas he is satisfied that such sum is necessary for the relief of persons in Kansas.

GEORGE L. STEARNS,
Chairman Massachusetts State Kansas Committee.

Having assumed so much responsibility for the property of the committee, Captain Brown, before leaving Boston, made the following will for the protection of his friends:

I, John Brown, of North Elba, N. Y., intending to visit Kansas, and knowing the uncertainty of life, make my last will as follows: I give and bequeath all trust funds and personal property for the aid of the Free-State cause in Kansas, now in my hands or in the hands of W. H. D. Callender, of Hartford, Conn., to George L. Stearns, of Medford, Mass., Samuel Cabot, Jr, of Boston, Mass., and William H. Russell, of New Haven, Conn., to them and the survivor or survivors and their assigns forever, in trust that they will administer said funds and other property, including all now collected or hereafter to be collected by me or in my behalf for the aid of the Free-State cause in Kansas, leaving the manner of so doing entirely at their discretion.

Signed at Boston, Mass., this 13th day of April, A. D. 1857, in presence of us, who, in presence of said Brown and of each other, have at his request affixed our names as witnesses of his will. The words "and personal property" and "and other property" interlined before signature by said Brown, and "said Callender," erased.

(Signed)   JOHN BROWN.

DANIEL FOSTER, }
MARY ELLEN RUSSELL, } *Witnesses.*
THOMAS RUSSELL, }

The purposes of the Massachusetts Committee will be seen by the letter of Mr. Stearns to a New York committee, dated May 18, 1857. He said : —

" Since the close of the last year we have confined our operations to aiding those persons in Kansas who were, or intended to become, citizens of that Territory, — believing that sufficient inducements to immigrate existed in the prosperous state of affairs there; and we now believe that should quiet and prosperity continue there for another year, the large influx of Northern and Eastern men will secure the State for freedom. To insure the present prosperity we propose —

" 1. To have our legislature make a grant of one hundred thousand dollars, to be placed in the hands of discreet persons, who shall use it for the relief of those in Kansas who are, or may become, destitute through Border-Ruffian outrage. We think it will be done.

" 2. To organize a secret force, well armed, and under control of the famous John Brown, to repel Border-Ruffian outrage and defend the Free-State men from all alleged impositions. This organization is strictly to be a defensive one.

" 3. To aid by timely donations of money those parties of settlers in the Territory who from misfortune are unable to provide for their present wants.

" I am personally acquainted with Captain Brown, and have great confidence in his courage, prudence, and good judgment. He has control of the whole affair, including contributions of arms, clothing, etc., to the amount of thirteen thousand dollars. His presence in the Territory will, we think, give the Free-State men confidence in their cause, and also check the disposition of the Border Ruffians to impose on them. This I believe to be the most important work to be done in Kansas at the present time. Many of the Free-State leaders being engaged in speculations are willing to accept peace on any terms.

Brown and his friends will hold to the original principle of making Kansas free, without regard to private interests. If you agree with me, I should like to have your money appropriated for the use of Captain John Brown. If not that, the other proposition, to aid parties of settlers now in the Territory, will be the next best."

As has already been mentioned, Captain Brown, in company with Martin F. Conway and myself, representing the Massachusetts Committee, met by appointment at the Metropolitan Hotel in New York late in March, 1857, and proceeded in company to Easton, Penn., where Mr. Reeder, a former governor of Kansas, was living, for the purpose of inducing him, if possible, to return to Kansas and become the leader of the Free-State party there. The journey was undertaken at the request of the Massachusetts Committee, of which both Brown and Conway were agents. It resulted in nothing; for Mr. Reeder was unwilling to leave his family and his occupations at Easton to engage again in the political contests of Kansas. Captain Brown had quite a different conception of his own duty to his family, as compared with his duty to the cause. Although he had been absent from home nearly two years, he refrained from a visit to North Elba, where his family then were, until he had arranged his military affairs in Boston and New York; and he finally reached his rough mountain home late in February. He found his daughter Ellen, whom he had left an infant in the cradle, old enough to hear him sing his favorite hymn, "Blow ye the trumpet, blow!" to the old tune of Lenox. "He sung all his own children to sleep with it," writes his daughter Anne, "and some of his grandchildren, too. He seemed to be very partial to the first verse; I think that he applied it to himself. When he was at home (I think it was the first time he came from Kansas), he told Ellen that he had sung it to all the rest, and must to her, too. She was afraid to go to him alone [the poor child had forgotten her father in his two years' absence], so father said that I must sit with her. He took Ellen on one knee and me on the other and sung it to us." His sons were now inclined to give up war and remain at North Elba, and so his wife wrote him, March 21. He replied : —

To his Wife.

SPRINGFIELD, MASS., March 31, 1857.

DEAR WIFE, — Your letter of the 21st is just received.   I have only to say as regards the resolution of the boys to "learn and practice war no more," that it was not at my solicitation that they engaged in it at first; and that while I may perhaps feel no more love of the business than they do, still I think there may be possibly in their day what is more to be dreaded, if such things do not now exist. . . . I have just got a long letter from Mr. Adair.   All middling well, March 11, but had fears of further trouble after a while.

Your affectionate husband,

JOHN BROWN.

He found means to overcome the reluctance of his children to sacrifice themselves for the cause of the slave, and this in spite of many discouragements of his own.   In reply to Mr. Adair, he wrote this short note : —

SPRINGFIELD, MASS., March 31, 1857.

DEAR BROTHER AND SISTER ADAIR, — I received Mr. Adair's most welcome letter to-day, and am greatly obliged for it indeed.   I also yesterday saw your letter to Mr. Burt, at Canton, Conn.   Mr. Burt died in January.   In him truth, right, and humanity lost a faithful friend.   I have but a moment to write, and but little to say that would afford you any interest, except that friends are well, so far as I know, and that I think of going West somewhere, soon.   The excitement is getting up this way in view of Supreme Court proceedings,[1] Walker's appointment as governor of Kansas, etc.   May God still preserve and keep you all!

Your affectionate brother,

JOHN BROWN.

It was about this time that Brown made the unlucky acquaintance of Hugh Forbes, was pleased with him, and engaged him to drill his soldiers at a salary of one hundred dollars a month, even going so far as to pay him six hundred dollars in advance, early in April.   Mr. Callender, of the State Bank in Hartford, thus testified before Senator Mason's committee : —

---

[1] The Dred Scott decision.

" I had instructions from Mr. Brown to pay Forbes six hundred dollars ; that was about the 1st of April, 1857 ; the two drafts I have with me.

[The witness produced two drafts, which are in the following words and figures : —

No. —. $400.   NEW YORK, April 27, 1857.

At sight, pay to the order of Ketchum, Howe, & Co. four hundred dollars, value received, and charge the same to account of
(Signed)   HUGH FORBES.
Indorsed : Cr. our account,
KETCHUM, HOWE, & Co.

No. —. $200.   NEW YORK, April 29, 1857.

Pay to the order of Ketchum, Howe, & Co. two hundred dollars, value received, and charge the same to account of
(Signed)   HUGH FORBES.
W. H. D. CALLENDER, ESQ., Hartford, Conn.]

" Mr. Brown told me that Mr. Forbes might draw upon me for six hundred dollars ; that was about the 1st of April, 1857 ; these drafts soon afterwards came on, and I paid them.   Brown furnished me, I think, with four hundred dollars, which came from Springfield."

The fish had swallowed the golden hook, but it was not easy to " land " him.   He should have followed Brown to the West in May, but he loitered in New York, and Brown was forced to warn him as follows.   Mr. Callender says : —

" Here is an order drawn by John Brown, dated the 22d of June, 1857, upon Colonel H. Forbes, at New York City, in these words :

' SIR, — If you have drawn on W. H. D. Callender, Esq., cashier at Hartford, Conn., for six hundred dollars, or any part of that amount, and are not prepared to come on and join me at once, you will please pay over to Joseph Bryant, Esq., who is my agent, six hundred dollars, or whatever amount you have so drawn.'

" The indorsement on it is,

' I did not present this to the colonel, as I presumed it would be of no use ; and then he is, I am persuaded, acting on good faith.
(Signed)   JOSEPH BRYANT.' "

Forbes was printing his precious Manual in New York, and also enjoying the advantages of the city, instead of hurrying away to the prairies.   Mr. Bryant at various dates thus reports him : —

June 1. I this day saw your friend Colonel Forbes; he is trying to raise funds to get his family brought to this country, but I fear he will not succeed very well. I will have, when collected, some six dollars only in my hands; this I intend passing into his hands. I may get a few dollars more, but the prospects are not very good here at present to raise money. The colonel says he is getting along well in getting his printing done (and is losing no time).

June 16. I called on the colonel last night; found him well, except very anxious about getting his family to this country. He is not ready to join you; thinks nothing will be needed out West before winter, — not till Congress have met and acted in favor of the constitution about being framed; so he thinks. He is getting along, he tells me, as fast as possible with his book; will have it ready in about ten days; has as yet raised no funds to pay the passage of his family. Thinks they will have to come in the third class passage, which grieves him very much, as his wife is not in good health. I had promised what money was in my hands to defray the expenses of publishing his book; this I promised him on account of your introduction to me of him.

June 25. Yours of the 22d was duly received by me on yesterday, and I, according to your request, called on the colonel. I learned that he intends to leave here to join you in about ten days (*certainly, barring accidents*). I learned, too, that he had drawn the money, and I think it is pretty well used up by this time. I did not say anything about his refunding, as he assured me, in the most positive way he could, that he would set out as soon as he got his book finished, which would be done in about a week. He says he is as anxious as you are to do everything that can be done; but he still thinks that there will be no need of action before winter. Yet he admitted it was best to be ready; and he thinks his book of extracts is all-important, — a part of the necessary tools to work with. He has given up the idea of getting his family over to this country, and is about sending his daughter back to her mother. She will leave in a few days. He sent his family (I understood from himself) about one hundred and twenty dollars some time ago of the money he drew, and I suppose it will take some hundred dollars for his daughter to go home on; yet I think the colonel *is acting in good faith*, and is an *honorable* man.

The character of Hugh Forbes and his final connection with Brown will be considered hereafter. It is enough to say, now, that he was unfitted for the work given him to do, and that the money paid to him was worse than thrown away; yet the lack of this sum — six or seven hundred dollars — embarrassed Brown at every step of his course in the summer of 1857, and prevented his reaching Kansas until late in the year. Meantime his friends there were expecting him, and he was corresponding with them at intervals. Through one of these friends, Augustus Wattles, then living at Lawrence, he sent messages to others; and one of these letters expresses so pungently his opinion of Kansas affairs in the early spring of 1857, that I will quote it here : —

BOSTON, MASS., April 8, 1857.

MY DEAR SIR, — Your favor of the 15th March, and that of friend Holmes of the 16th, I have just received. I cannot express my gratitude for them both. They give me just that kind of news I was most of all things anxious to hear. I bless God that he has not left the Free-State men of Kansas to pollute themselves by the foul and loathsome embrace of the old rotten whore. I have been trembling all along lest they might " back down " from the high and holy ground they had taken. I say, in view of the wisdom, firmness, and patience of my friends and fellow-sufferers in the cause of humanity, let God's name be eternally praised! I would most gladly give my hand to all whose " garments are not defiled ; " and I humbly trust that I shall soon again have opportunity to rejoice (or suffer further if need be) with you in the strife between heaven and hell. I wish to send my most cordial and earnest salutation to every one of the chosen. My efforts this way have not been altogether fruitless. I wish you and friend Holmes both to accept this for the moment ; may write soon again, and hope to hear from you both at Tabor, Fremont County, Iowa, — care of Jonas Jones, Esq.

Your sincere friend,

NELSON HAWKINS.

AUGUSTUS WATTLES, ESQ., Lawrence, K. T.

" Friend Holmes " was Brown's youngest lieutenant, who thus wrote to him after he had left New England for North Elba : —

Letters of J. H. Holmes to John Brown.

LAWRENCE, KANSAS, April 30, 1857.

MY DEAR FRIEND BROWN, — I have been anxiously expecting to hear from you direct, but have only heard through Mr. Wattles. I want to see you as soon as possible after you arrive in the Territory.

I have settled at Emporia, six miles above the junction of the Neosho and the Cottonwood. My address is either Emporia or Lawrence, as you may choose. My letters all come and go safe. War, ere six months shall have passed away, is inevitable. Secretary Stanton has made a public speech in Lawrence, and says that those laws (the bogus) shall be enforced, and that the taxes shall be paid. The people shout, " Never ! " " Then," he says, " there is war between you and me, — war to the knife, and the knife to the hilt." There will be no voting ; no paying of taxes ; and I think the Free-State men will remove the Territorial Government and set up their own. Then we want you. Please write. All your friends, as far as I know, are well.   Very truly yours,

JAMES H. HOLMES.[1]

This letter was immediately followed by another, in which Holmes opens a little of the mystery of Kansas politics in this third year of the struggle there : —

LAWRENCE, KAN., 3 o'clock, P. M., April 30, 1857.

DEAR FRIEND BROWN, — This morning I received your letter which came by the way of Tabor, and also your letter which came through the mail. I had previously written you a short letter. I now write to let you know that I have received them, and to answer them hastily ; though I presume you will leave Springfield for Kansas ere this reaches you. I do not think there is any disposition to " back down " by the Free-State men, other than by the speculators ; and they are, as a class, never to be relied on, of course. I have full faith in the virtue of the Free-State men of Kansas. You have something to learn in the political world here.

You will hear of me either at Lawrence, through J. E. Cook, of the firm of Bacon, Cook, & Co., or I may be at Emporia, where I have taken a claim and make it my home. At any rate, Cook can tell you where I may be. A case has recently occurred of kidnapping a Free-State man, which is this : Archibald Kandell, a young fellow who came in with Redpath under Eldridge, last fall, and has been all winter on a claim near Osawatomie, was some two weeks since enticed out under pretence of trading horses, by four men, and abducted into Missouri. Archy was in my company, and is a good

[1] Holmes was at this time nineteen years old, the son of a New York broker, and had gone to Kansas to aid the cause of freedom. He has since been a journalist, and under President Lincoln was secretary of New Mexico. Brown used to call him " my little hornet."

brave fellow. How long he is to remain incarcerated and in chains I will not in this place and time attempt to predict.

Judge Conway is here, radical and right. Dr. Robinson recently made a proposition with some leading proslavery men to compromise. The Free-State men won't do it. We are talking of running Phillips for governor next fall.

Very truly your constant friend,

JAMES.

This letter was months in reaching Brown, who did not answer it until September 9. Mr. Wattles wrote in the summer, touching upon matters political, and in reply to a second letter from Brown, who was meditating his proposed attack on slavery in Missouri, and for this time called himself " James Smith," instead of " Hawkins."

John Brown to A. Wattles.

HUDSON, OHIO, June 3, 1857.

MY DEAR SIR, — I write to say that I started for Kansas some three weeks or more since, but have been obliged to stop for the fever and ague. I am now righting up, and expect to be on my way again soon. Free-State men need have no fear of my *desertion.* There are some half-dozen men I want a visit from at Tabor, Iowa, to come off in the most QUIET WAY ; namely, *Daniel Foster,* late of Boston, Massachusetts ; *Holmes, Frazee,* a Mr. *Hill,* and *William David,* on Little Ottawa Creek ; a Mr. Cochran, on Pottawatomie Creek ; or I would like *equally* well to see *Dr. Updegraff* and *S. H. Wright,* of Osawatomie ; or *William Phillips,* or CONWAY, or *your honor.* I have some very important matters to confer with some of you about. Let there be *no words* about it. Should any of you come out to see me, wait at Tabor if you get there first. Mr. Adair, at Osawatomie, may supply fifty dollars (if need be) for expenses, on my account, on presentation of this. Write me at Tabor, Iowa, Fremont County. Very respectfully yours,

JAMES SMITH.[1]

[1] The persons mentioned in this letter were supposed by Brown to be specially friendly and true to him. Foster was a clergyman, formerly settled at Concord, Mass., but then in Kansas. Holmes was Brown's lieutenant in 1856, and afterward in 1858-59. Frazee was Brown's teamster and soldier in 1856, and fought at Black Jack, as did B. L. Cochran. Dr. Updegraff fought at Osawatomie. Concerning David, Hill, and Wright I have little information. Phillips was afterwards Congressman.

The Reply.

LAWRENCE, K. T., June 18, 1857.

JAMES SMITH, ESQ.

DEAR SIR, — Your favor of the 3d instant was duly received. I am much pleased to hear from you. We talked over matters here, and concluded to say, come as quietly as possible, or not come at present, as you may choose. Holmes is at Emporia, plowing; Conway is here, talking politics; Phillips is here, trying to urge the Free-State men to galvanize the Topeka constitution into life. Dr. Robinson's absence at the assembling of the Free-State Legislature last winter dispirited the Free-State party. It is difficult to make them rally again under him. Foster I do not know. Frazee has not returned. The others are as you left them. We are prospering finely. You will hear much against G. W. Brown and the "Herald of Freedom," but be careful about believing it. Brown is as good as ever.

Most truly your friend,

AUGUSTUS WATTLES.[1]

In reply to a letter of Brown, sent in August from Tabor, Mr. Wattles wrote again on Kansas politics, and more definitely.

Letters from Kansas Friends.

LAWRENCE, K. T., Aug. 21, 1857.

DEAR SIR — Your favor of August 8 came duly to hand, as did yours to Dr. Prentice. The business you speak of was put into the hands of Mr. Realf. Mr. Whitman and Mr. Edmonds[2] are both gone East. In regard to other inquiries, I can hardly tell you satisfactorily. I think Dr. Robinson's failure to meet the legislature last winter disheartened the people so that they lost confidence in him and in the movement. Although in the Convention we invited him to withdraw his resignation (which he did), yet the masses could never be vitalized again into that enthusiasm and confidence which they had before. Another mistake which he made, equally fatal, was his attack upon George W. Brown and the "Herald of Freedom;" thus leading off his friends into a party by themselves, and leaving all who doubted and hated him in another party. This war between the leaders settled the question of resistance to outside

---

[1] Indorsed by John Brown: "A. Wattles, No. 2. Requires no reply."
[2] Two names for the same man.

authority at once. Those who had entertained the idea of resistance
have entirely abandoned it. Dr. Robinson was not alone in his blun-
ders. Colonel Lane, Mr. Phillips, and "The Republican" made
equally fatal ones. Colonel Lane boasted in his public speeches
that the Constitutional Convention would be driven into the Kaw
River, etc., by violence. Mr. Phillips boasted this, and much more,
in the "New York Tribune." "The Republican" boasted that old
Captain Brown would be down on Governor Walker and Co. like an
avenging god, etc. This excited Walker and others to that degree
they at once took refuge under the United States troops. Whatever
might have been intended, much more was threatened and boasted
of than could possibly have been performed, unless there was an
extensive conspiracy. This, I believe, Governor Walker says was
the case.

I saw Conway to-day. He says he thinks all will go off quietly
at the election. Phillips, you will see by the "Tribune," has come
out in favor of voting in October. They intend to cheat us; but we
expect to beat them. Walker is as fair as he can be, under the
circumstances.　　　　　　Yours truly,

A. WATTLES.[1]

A few days earlier than this letter was written, Holmes,
who differed a little from Wattles, sent a word of warning
to his captain, along with other information, thus : —

LAWRENCE, K. T., Aug. 16, 1857.

MY DEAR FRIEND, — I received your letter of the 8th inst. yesterday. I am glad to hear that you are so near. Messrs. Realf,
Phillips, and Wattles also received letters from you yesterday. I
have a word of caution to say in regard to Mr. Wattles. He is a
friend whom I most highly esteem ; yet he is so connected in politics
that I think it unsafe for you to communicate to him any plans you
would not like to communicate *directly* to Governor Walker. For
this reason : Mr. Wattles is under George W. Brown ; and both believe in submitting in good faith, under Governor Walker, to the Territorial authorities. Governor Walker comes to town frequently, and
stops at the "Herald of Freedom" office, in secret conclave with
G. W. Brown. When you come here (if you should), you can judge
for yourself.

[1] Indorsed by John Brown : "A. Wattles, No. 6." The rest of these
letters are not in my hands. The election mentioned was to occur in
October, and was carried by the Free-State men. "Walker" was the
new Governor, — R. J. Walker, of Pennsylvania.

Messrs. Phillips, Wattles, and Realf I have seen; they will write to you themselves, and I will merely give you my own mind on the subject. I do not know what you would have me infer by "business." I presume, though, by the word being emphasized, that you refer to the business for which I learn you have a stock of material with you. If you mean this, I think quite strongly of a good(?) opening for this business about the first Monday in October [1] next. If you wish other employments, I presume you will find just as *profitable* ones. I am sorry that you have not been here in the Territory before. I think that the sooner you come the better, so that the people and the Territorial authorities may become familiarized with your presence. This is also the opinion of all other friends with whom I have conversed on this subject. You could thus exert more influence. Several times we have needed you very much. I have much to communicate to you, which I cannot do through this medium; therefore you must try to let me know of your approach or arrival as soon as possible, through Mr. Phillips, or through the Lawrence postoffice. I presume Mr. Phillips wrote to you in regard to *teams* and means, which, as Mr. Whitman is now East, will be, I fear, scarce.

Most sincerely your friend,

JAMES H. HOLMES.

This letter was directed to "Captain Brown," and so was, perhaps, sent by a safe messenger; for the Free-State men had much distrust of the mails. This was one reason for the change of names which John Brown adopted; another was, that he was still proscribed in Kansas, as he had been in 1856, and might be arrested at any time by the Territorial authorities. Mr. Whitman wrote to him soon after, and wishing to free him from this anxiety, chose as his messenger the Englishman Realf, of whom we shall soon hear more: —

LAWRENCE, June 30, 1857.

DEAR SIR, — I send you by the bearer, Richard Realf, one hundred and fifty dollars, minus the reasonable expenses of the messenger on his way up. You will please make arrangements for him to return with you. Your friends are desirous of seeing you. The dangers that threatened the Territory and *individuals* have been removed, in the shape of quashed indictments. Your *furniture* can

---

[1] Election day.

be brought and safely stored while you are seeking a location; and your *family* can find board among the settlers. Hoping to see you soon in good health, I remain, as ever,

Yours truly,   E. B. W.

To CAPTAIN BROWN.

Mr. Phillips, afterward in Congress from Kansas, and a general during the Civil War, wrote thus : —

LAWRENCE, K. T., June 24, 1857.

MY DEAR FRIEND, — I received your letter, dated from Ohio the 9th instant, a few days ago. I fear I shall not be able to meet you at Tabor. I have just received (on the 13th) the task of superintending and taking the census for the State election. As means are limited, those who can must do this. I have therefore assumed the task, which will require my presence and most active efforts until the 15th of July. I have tried to arrange it so as to get off for a week ; but it is impossible without a sacrifice of duty. Should it be so, or if no one else can go, I will still try. Holmes I have seen ; he is busy, and will not be able to come up. Several of those you mentioned are gone, and others cannot go to Tabor. I sent a message to Osawatomie, and enclosed your letter to Mr. Adair; told him that Holmes and the others could not go, and urged that some go from Osawatomie, if possible. I have not yet heard from him. I start to Osawatomie when I finish this ; I will make it on my round, appointing deputies and taking the census. Two young men from this place have promised me that they will go if possible ; but they have no horses, and horses cannot be hired for such a journey. I still hope to have a few friends at Tabor to meet you in a week.

As to your future action, for fear I should be prevented from going to meet you, let me say I think you should come into Kansas, provided you desire to do so. I think it will be our duty to see you protected. There is no necessity for active military preparations at this time ; but so far as you have the elements of defence at your command, I think *they are safer with you than with any one else.* Your old claim has, I believe, been jumped. If you do not desire to contest it, let me suggest that you make a new settlement at some good point, of which you will be the head. Lay off a town and take claims around it. You would thus rally round you a class of useful men, who could be prepared for an emergency at the same time that they furthered their own interests, which they have a right to do. Any information I could render as to the best sites or otherwise you may cheerfully call upon. Should I not be able to come to meet you, I hope at least to see you shortly after you enter. I have not time to detail the present condition of the Free-State party. Until I see you, adieu.   Respectfully,

WILLIAM A. PHILLIPS.

JAMES SMITH.[1]

Mr. Whitman's messenger reached Tabor nearly a month before Brown got there, and went back to Kansas again, leaving this note : —

TABOR, IOWA, July 6, 1857.

JOHN BROWN, ESQ.

DEAR SIR, — I arrived here to-day from Lawrence, bringing $150, minus my expenses up and down. These will amount to about $40, leaving you $110. Mr. Whitman could not, as you will see from his note signed "Edmunds," spare you more; and the mule team you asked for could not be procured. I am sorry you have not arrived: I should like to have gone back with you. The Governor has instructed the Attorney-General of Kansas to enter a *nolle prosequi* in the case of the Free-State prisoners; so that you need be under no apprehension of insecurity as to yourself or the munitions you may bring with you. By writing a line to me or Mr. Whitman or Phillips at Lawrence immediately on your arrival here, we will come and meet you by way of Topeka. God speed you!

Truly,   RICHARD REALF.

Brown reported to me at the end of September his progress then made, as follows : —

TABOR, FREMONT COUNTY, IOWA, Oct. 1, 1857.

F. B. SANBORN, Concord, Mass.

MY DEAR SIR, — Two days since I received your very kind letter of the 14th September; also one from James Hunnewell, Esq., saying he had sent me $72.68 through P. T. Jackson, Esq., of Boston; for both which I am very glad.[2] I cannot express my gratitude for

---

[1] Indorsed by John Brown : "William A. Phillips. Requires no reply. No. 1." The tone of this letter shows how Brown was regarded in Kansas as the custodian of arms, — which, of course, was the "furniture" mentioned by Mr. Whitman.

[2] This note explains the source and object of this seasonable contribution : —

BOSTON, Sept. 14, 1857.

NELSON HAWKINS, ESQ., care of Jonas Jones, Tabor, Iowa.

DEAR SIR, — By order of the (Mass.) Middlesex County Kansas Aid Committee, I have sent to you through P. T. Jackson, Esq., treasurer of the State Committee, $72.68, "to be appropriated to the use of Captain John Brown, now at Tabor, Iowa, in support of the cause of freedom in Kansas."

Very respectfully yours,

JAMES HUNNEWELL,

Treasurer of Middlesex County Kansas Aid Committee.

your earnest and early attention to my wants and those of my family. I regret that Mr. Hunnewell did not at once send me either a check or a draft on New York or Boston, as it will probably be one month or more before I can realize it; and I have not the means of paying my board bill here, not having as yet received anything from Mr. Whitman toward a balance of five hundred dollars, nor heard from him. If I get the money from Mr. Hunnewell and Mr. Whitman, it will answer my present wants, except the secret service I wrote you about. I have all the arms I am likely to need, but am destitute of saddle-bags or knapsacks, holsters and belts; have only a few blankets, no shovels or spades, no mattocks, but three or four adzes (ought to have been one hundred), and am nearly destitute of cooking utensils. The greater part of what I have just named I must do without till another spring, at any rate. I found here one brass field-piece complete, and one damaged gun-carriage, with some ammunition suitable for it; some seventy to seventy-five old damaged United States rifles and muskets, one dozen old sabres, some powder and lead (enough for present use; weight not known), — I suppose sent by National Committee. Also one dozen boxes and barrels of clothing, boots, etc., with three hand gristmills, sent to Nebraska City, from same source. I also got from Dr. Jesse Bowen, of Iowa City, one old wagon, which broke down with a light load on the way; also nine full-rigged tents, three sets tent-poles (additional), eleven pairs blankets, and three axes, sent there by National Committee. Also from Mr. Hurd I got an order for fifty dollars' worth of tents, wagon-covering, ropes, etc., at Chicago, which was paid me. I find one hundred and ninety-four carbines, about thirty-three hundred ball cartridges, all the primers, but no iron ladles. This, I believe, with the teams and wagon I purchased, will give you a pretty good idea of the stuff I have. I had a gun and pair of pistols given me by Dr. Howe, and some three or four guns made for experiment by Mr. Thayer (a little cannon and carriage is one of them), and one nice rifle by the manufacturing company at Worcester.[1] I had also a few revolvers, common guns, and sabres left on hand, that I took on with me in 1855. While waiting here I and my son have been trying to learn a little of the arts of *peace* from Colonel F., who is still with us. That is the school I alluded to.

Before I reached here, I had written particularly to friends in Kansas, saying that I wanted help to meet me here, and to wait for me should I be detained on the way. I also arranged with Mr. Whitman in regard to it in Chicago. He sent one man with one hundred and fifty dollars; forty of it he kept, and went immediately

---

[1] These are the arms mentioned in Eli Thayer's letters.

back. From that time I send you copies of some of the correspondence between Kansas and me, as rather essential to give you a correct idea of things in connection with my statements yet to be made. When I got on here I immediately wrote Mr. Whitman and several others what was my situation and wants. He (Mr. Whitman) has not written me at all since what I send. Others have written, as you will see. I wrote the man Mr. Whitman sent me, among the rest, but get no word from him since what I now send.

As to the policy of voting on Monday next, I think Lane hit his mark at the convention of Grasshopper's, if never before; I mean "An escape into the filthy sluice of a prison." I had not been able to learn by papers or otherwise distinctly what course had been taken in Kansas till within a few days; and probably the less I have to say, the better.

I omitted above to say that I paid out five hundred and fifty dollars on a contract for one thousand superior pikes, as a cheap but effectual weapon to place in the hands of entirely unskilful and unpractised men, which will not easily get out of order, and require no ammunition. They will cost, handles and all complete, a little short of one dollar each. That contract I have not been able to fulfil; and *wise* military men may ridicule the idea; but "I take the whole responsibility of that job," — so that I can only get them.

On hearing that Lane had come into Nebraska, I at once sent a young man with a line, saying I had been hurt, and was exceedingly anxious to see him early in September. To this he sent me no reply, unless Redpath's letter be one. I am now so far recovered from my hurt as to be able to do a little ; and foggy as it is, " we do not give up the ship." I will not say that Kansas, watered by the tears and blood of my children, shall yet be free or I fall. I intend at once to put the supplies I have in a secure place, and then to put myself and such as may go with me where we may get more speedy communications, and can wait until we know better how to act than we now do. I send this whole package to you, thinking Concord a less offensive name just now than Boston at this end of the route. I wish the whole conveyed to my friend Stearns and other friends, as old Brown's last report.

Until further advised, I wish all communications addressed to Jonas Jones, Esq., Tabor, Fremont County, Iowa, *outwardly ;* and I hope you will all write often.

I had forgotten to say, that day before yesterday one single man, with no team at all, came from Lane to have me start at once for Kansas, as you will see by copies. He said he had left ten fine fellows about thirty miles back. The names he gave me were all strange to me, as well as himself. Tabor folks (some of them) speak slightingly of him, notwithstanding that he too is a general.

October 3, 1857.

Yours, covering check, is this moment to hand, and will afford most seasonable relief. Express goes to K. at once to see how the land lies. You will hear again soon.

Yours most truly,

J. BROWN.

The following correspondence will find its key in the letter just given. General Lane was at the head of the organization mentioned, and Mr. Whitman was his quarter-master-general.

(*Private.*)

LAWRENCE, Sept. 7, 1857.

SIR, — We are earnestly engaged in perfecting an organization for the protection of the ballot-box at the October election (first Monday). Whitman and Abbot have been East after money and arms for a month past; they write encouragingly, and will be back in a few days. We want you, with all the materials you have. I see no objection to your coming into Kansas publicly. I can furnish you just such a force as you may deem necessary for your protection here and after your arrival. I went up to see you, but failed. Now what is wanted is this: write me concisely what transportation you require, how much money, and the number of men needed to escort you into the Territory safely; and if you desire it I will come up with them.

Yours respectfully,

J. H. LANE.

To CAPTAIN JOHN BROWN, Tabor.

Brown's answer was as follows : —

TABOR, FREMONT COUNTY, IOWA, Sept. 16, 1857.

GENERAL JAMES H. LANE.

MY DEAR SIR, — Your favor of the 7th inst. is received. I had previously written you expressive of my strong desire to see you. I suppose you have my letter before this. As to the job of work you inquire about, I suppose that three good teams, with *well covered* wagons, and ten *really ingenious, industrious* (*not gassy*) men, with about one hundred and fifty dollars in cash, could bring it about in the course of eight or ten days.

Very respectfully your friend,

JOHN BROWN.

This letter was returned to Brown by Mr. Jamison, September 30, and the following note from General Lane came with it. Falls City is in southern Nebraska, comparatively near Tabor. In addressing Brown as "Dear General," Lane had in mind the fact that he had made Brown a brigadier of the new army which Lane had organized : —

FALLS CITY, Sept. 29, 1857.

DEAR GENERAL, — I send you Mr. Jamison (quartermaster-general second division), to assist you in getting your articles into Kansas in time. Mr. Whitman wrote us a week ago he would be at Wyandotte yesterday, and that he was supplied with the things; but he had not arrived when I left. It is *all-important* to Kansas that your things should be in at the *earliest possible moment*, and that you should be much nearer at hand than you are. I send you all the money I have (fifty dollars), and General Jamison has some more. We want every gun and all the ammunition. I do not know that we will have to use them, but I do know we should be prepared. I send you ten true men. You can rely upon the General; and what he tells you comes from me.   Yours ever,

J. H. LANE.

To GENERAL JOHN BROWN, Tabor.

To this Brown replied : —

TABOR, FREMONT COUNTY, IOWA, Sept. 30, 1857.

GENERAL JAMES H. LANE.

MY DEAR SIR, — Your favor from Falls City by Mr. Jamison is just received; also fifty dollars sent by him, which I also return by same hand, as I find it will be *next to impossible in my poor state of health* to go through on such very short notice, four days only remaining to get ready, load up, and go through. I think, considering all the uncertainties of the case, want of teams, etc., that I should do wrong to set out. I am disappointed in the extreme.[1]

Very respectfully your friend,   JOHN BROWN.

John Brown to E. B. Whitman.

TABOR, FREMONT COUNTY, IOWA, Oct. 5, 1857.

E. B. WHITMAN, ESQ.

DEAR SIR, — Please send me by Mr. Charles P. Tidd what money you have for me, — not papers. He is the second man I have sent in

---

[1] Brown explained this refusal to comply with Lane's request in his letter to me of October 1, already given, as well as in the letter which follows.

order to get the means of taking me through.   General Lane sent a
man who got here *without any team*, with but fifty dollars of Lane's
money (as he said), which I returned to him, and wanted me to start
right off, with only four days' time to load up and drive through before
this bogus election day, — which my state of health and the very wet
weather rendered it impossible to do in time; and I did not think it
right to start from here under such circumstances.   Do try to make
me up the money, all in good shape, before Mr. Tidd returns, and
also write me everything you know about the aspect of things in
Kansas.   Please furnish Mr. Tidd with a horse to take him to Osawatomie, and greatly oblige me.   The fifty dollars Lane sent was
only about enough to pay up my board bill here, with all I had on
hand.   *I need not say my disappointments have been extreme.*
Your friend,
JOHN BROWN.

P. S.   Before any *teams are now sent*, I want to hear further from
Kansas.

What was the object of Lane's organization will appear
by Mr. Whitman's report below : —

(Order No. 2.)

QUARTERMASTER'S DEPARTMENT, HEADQUARTERS KANSAS
VOLUNTEERS FOR THE PROTECTION OF THE BALLOT-BOX,
LAWRENCE, Oct. 19, 1857.

Whereas, On the 3d day of August an order was issued from this
department requesting the appointment of company, brigade, and
division quartermasters, and an immediate return to be made of the
number and description of all arms available for the use of the respec-
tive companies; and *whereas*, said returns have been generally made:
Now, therefore, in reply, and in explanation of the failure to furnish
an entire supply for the deficiency, it is deemed proper to declare, that
while no efforts were spared by this department, and by the entire
staff, promptly to supply the necessary quota of arms, yet the unexpected obstacles which the great financial pressure threw in their
way have prevented the anticipated success for the time being.   It
is, however, a cause for congratulation, that while the reports show
a considerable deficiency, yet the entire armament is by no means
insignificant.

The immense immigration of the past year, composed largely of
those who deceived by official promises of protection had anticipated
no occasion for personal defence, readily accounts for this deficiency.
In our disappointment we may rejoice that the effect of the organiza-

tion, with all its imperfections, has been in the highest degree satisfactory. The knowledge that an outraged people had at length banded themselves together, almost to a man, for the protection of the most sacred rights of freemen, and were ready to die in their defence, has most manifestly deterred an organized invasion. Voting-lists ready manufactured and false returns have been made to supply its place; against this the organization could afford no protection.

It remains to be seen whether the people of Kansas will have any further use for this organization. It is always true that the surest way to prevent an evil is to be prepared to meet it, and three years' experience in the past should teach us not to indulge in any premature feelings of security and safety. In view of possible contingencies, this department hereby announces that it will still continue its exertions to furnish the means of protection and defence to all who may be destitute of them, and in all cases first to supply those localities most exposed to invasion and attack.

E. B. WHITMAN,

Quartermaster-General Kansas Volunteers.

Approved: J. H. LANE, *Organizer*.

Mr. Whitman replied as follows to Brown's letter of October 5: —

LAWRENCE, Oct. 24, 1857.

MY DEAR FRIEND, — Your first two messengers are sick at Tecumseh. I helped them start back with the information that you should soon hear from me, but they were taken sick on their way. Mr. Tidd has been waiting some time for me to receive remittances from the East; but as the crisis approaches I feel in a hurry to get him off. You are wanted here a week from Tuesday. I will wait no longer, but by great personal exertion have raised on my personal responsibility one hundred and fifty dollars. General Lane will send teams from Falls City, so that you may get your goods all in. Leave none behind if you can help it. Come direct to this place and see me before you make any disposition of your plunder, except to keep it safe. Make the Tabor people wait for what you owe them. *They must.* Make the money I send answer to get here, and I hope by that time to have more for you. Mr. Tidd will explain all.

Very truly yours,

E. B. WHITMAN.[1]

Finally, this correspondence closes with a letter from Lane.

[1] Indorsed by Brown: "Received at Tabor, Nov. 1."

FALLS CITY, Oct. 30, 1857.

DEAR SIR, — By great sacrifice we have raised, and send by Mr. Tidd, one hundred and fifty dollars. I trust this money will be used to get the guns to Kansas, or as near as possible. If you can get them to this point, we will try to get them on in some way. The probability is Kansas will never need the guns. One thing is certain: if they are to do her any good, it will be in the next few days. Let nothing interfere in bringing them on.

Yours,   J. H. LANE.

Brown accepted this invitation, and entered Kansas; but without the rifles, and with only a part of his other supplies.

These tedious delays in the armed expedition under Brown's direction, from which the Massachusetts Committee and the majority of the National Committee hoped so much, were very annoying to Brown himself, — more so, as it happened, than to those who had placed the arms and money in his hands. "God protects us in winter," he had told his Massachusetts friends; and the same protection was extended throughout the whole year 1857 to the poor farmers of Kansas, who had suffered in 1856 to the verge of ruin. The resignation of Governor Geary in March and the appointment of Governor Walker had not led, as was feared, to a repetition of the scenes of Shannon's administration. Peace was preserved, emigrants flocked into Kansas, and the political campaign which ended in the October election had a result unexpectedly favorable to the Free-State men. Consequently the rifles and cannon of Brown were not needed, and but few of them ever were carried into Kansas. Had he gone in with them in June, as he expected, the result would not have been materially different, although his presence would have given more confidence to the radical wing in the Free-State party, which ultimately triumphed. In truth, Brown had done his work during the summer of 1856 — that season of hardship and terror — so thoroughly that there was no need to continue it in 1857. When resumed in 1858–59, it was chiefly to protect the settlers in the border counties, and to aid the escape of slaves in Missouri. What Brown thought and felt during this year of inaction may be inferred from these letters, which begin with his final departure from New England in April: —

John Brown to his Family and Friends.

NEW HAVEN, CONN., April 23, 1857.

DEAR CHILDREN, — I received your letter of the 6th and 8th inst. Will endeavor to get the article Ruth wrote for. I now expect to buy the place of Franklin and Samuel. I would be very glad to have some of the friends take a horse-team and meet me at Westport as soon as this is received. Inquire for me at Mr. Judd's, Elizabethtown. I want to get a passage, and to have some things taken out. Have but a moment to write. If I am not found at Westport, wait a little for me.

Your affectionate father,

JOHN BROWN.

VERGENNES, VT., May 13, 1857.

GEORGE L. STEARNS, ESQ., Boston, Mass.

MY DEAR SIR, — . . . In regard to the security you mention, for being responsible for Colonel Carter, I will say, it is most reasonable; but as I deem it most uncertain what will become of things I carry into the war, and as I need arms "more than I do bread," I propose not to draw on you for the amount named, — thirteen hundred dollars, — and will not.

This, I trust, will be entirely satisfactory to you, and a vastly better security. I am exceeding glad of the arrangement with Colonel Carter, whom I have written. I leave here for the West to-day, with health some improved, and shall be much gratified with getting a line from you, addressed to Orson M. Oviatt, Esq., Cleveland, Ohio. Please remember me to Mrs. S., family, and other friends; and believe me

Your sincere friend,

JOHN BROWN.

The allusion above is to the generous offer of Mr. Stearns to guarantee the payment for two hundred revolvers, made by him in these letters of May, 1857: —

May 4. I have written to Colonel Carter that I will be responsible for the payment of thirteen hundred dollars for two hundred revolvers, as you propose, and have requested him to write to you if .

he accepts my proposal.[1] If he does not, I will write to you again. If I pay for these revolvers, I shall expect that all the arms and ammunition, rifles as well as revolvers, *not used* for the defence of Kansas, shall be held as pledged to me for the payment of this amount. To this our committee have assented by a vote passed on Saturday, and I have no doubt you will assent to it. If you do not, let me know your reasons.

May 6. I think you ought to go to Kansas as soon as possible, and give Robinson and the rest some backbone.

May 11. I am glad to know that you are on your way to Kansas: the Free-State leaders need somebody to talk to them. I hope you will see Conway very soon after your arrival. I did not expect you to return, or hold pledged to me, any arms you used in Kansas, but only such as were not used.

Truly yours,
GEORGE L. STEARNS.

Although Mr. Stearns had given authority to draw on him for seven thousand dollars during 1857, what John Brown actually did was to abstain from drawing for a dollar, to take nothing from this abundance either for his own comforts or the wants of his family, but to push forward with the work he had undertaken, burdened in heart, but faithful to the trust his friends reposed in him. They, alas! were not always so thoughtful for him as he for them; they did not consider that the promises of rich men to poor men should be kept not only sacredly but promptly. *Bis dat qui cito dat* would have been Greek to John Brown; but the meaning of that maxim was burned into his soul by the delay in that petty subscription which Mr. Lawrence had undertaken for the relief of Brown's family. Here are some of the letters which Mr. Stearns and I received from him in the spring and summer of 1857: —

---

[1] Mr. Stearns's letter to Colonel Carter, agent of the Massachusetts Arms Company, was as follows: —

BOSTON, May 4, 1857.

DEAR SIR, — Being desirous of aiding Captain Brown in his Kansas enterprise, I am willing to purchase of you the two hundred revolvers, to be delivered to him as proposed, and to pay you by my note at four months from date of delivery. This will give me time to get the money, should I wish to raise the amount by subscription. Should you accept my proposition, you will please notify Captain Brown that you are ready to deliver; and your draft, accompanied by his receipt for the property, will be accepted.

To Mr. Stearns.

VERGENNES, VT., May 13, 1857.

Some days since, while on my way home [to North Elba, N. Y.], sick with fever and ague, I got your favor of the 29th April, saying, "Mr. Lawrence has agreed with me that the one thousand dollars shall be made up, and will write to Gerrit Smith to-day or to-morrow, to say that he can depend on the money from him." After getting home I agreed with two young men (by the name of Thompson) who had bargained with Mr. Smith for the farm several years ago, and paid him in part for it, and who had made the improvements on it, that I would take the farm, pay the balance due Mr. Smith (some two hundred dollars), and the remainder, about eight hundred dollars, to them; which would enable them to pay for another farm which they had before bought of a Mr. Lawton, and were unable to pay for. Three days ago one of these men set out for Peterboro' (the home of Gerrit Smith) to meet me there, on my way West, and have the thing completed. I will now say ("frankly," as you suggest) that I must ask to have the one thousand dollars made up *at once* and forwarded to Gerrit Smith. I did not start the measure of getting up any subscription for me (although I was sufficiently needy, as God knows), nor had I a thought of further burdening either of my dear friends Stearns or Lawrence.

To F. B. Sanborn.

PETERBORO', N. Y., May 15, 1857.

Your most kind letter of the 26th of April I did not get till within the last two or three days, and then I was on my way West, full of cares, and in feeble health. I have just written my friend Stearns a letter of explanation, in which I frankly ask that the one thousand dollars' donation I was so generously encouraged to expect for the permanent assistance of my wife and children be, under the circumstances as so explained, promptly raised. This, I think, much the cheapest and most proper way to provide for them, and far less humiliating to my wife, who, though not above getting her bread over the washtub, will never tell her trials or her wants to the world. This I know by the experience of the past two years, while I was absent; but I would never utter a syllable in regard to it, were I not conscious that I am performing that service which is equally the duty of millions, who need not forego a single hearty dinner by the efforts they are called on to make. I did not mean to burden my friends Stearns and Lawrence further with the thing. I do not love to "ride free horses till they fall down dead."

In reply to Brown's letter of May 13, Mr. Stearns wrote on the 19th a letter containing this passage, — the reference to Gerrit Smith on my authority being understood by me to concern Brown's main work, and not this purchase of land : —

BOSTON, May 19, 1857.

Your favor of the 13th was received yesterday. Mr. Lawrence agreed with me that the one thousand dollars should be made up for you, and requested me to write you so. The next day he sent me a note stating that he had written to Mr. Smith to receive from him six hundred dollars, and let you mortgage for four hundred dollars. I learn to-day from Mr. Sanborn that Gerrit Smith intends to aid you in this, and also obtain something for your enterprise in his neighborhood. My agreement with Mr. Lawrence was that he having five hundred and fifty dollars towards the one thousand dollars, I would be responsible for one-half of the deficiency, if he would provide the other half, and when he returns I shall tell him he must fulfil the agreement with me. He will be home the 1st of June.

To this Brown replied at once : —

AKRON, OHIO, May 23, 1857.

GEORGE L. STEARNS, ESQ., Boston, Mass.

MY DEAR SIR, — On my arrival at Cleveland yesterday, I found with O. M. Oviatt, Esq., your favors of the 16th and 19th inst. I had made no previous arrangement with Mr. Smith about the land, other than to say that I wanted the contract with the Thompsons made over to me on payment, or to that effect. He had given me no encouragement of any help about it from him ; and when I met one of the Thompsons there,[1] all I could do was to get both parties to agree to the arrangement, and to wait until the money could get on from Boston. Mr. Smith had before written me that his last year's efforts for Kansas had embarrassed him, but that when the struggle was renewed he would do all he could. He gave me fifty dollars, Mrs. S. ten dollars and some little useful articles ; Peterboro' friends gave me thirty-one dollars, and I came on with the understanding that probably the thousand dollars would soon be sent on to Mr. Smith. I lost about one week on my way to my family with ague and fever, and left home feeble, and am still so. I could promise Colonel Carter no more than pay for primings, which I had not bargained for. I shall redeem my promise to you as soon as I am able

---

[1] At Peterboro'.

to do so. Please write me next to Dr. Jesse Brown, Iowa City,
Iowa, on envelope. I send my earnest good wishes to Mrs. S. and
the children. Am disappointed in not having Mr. Foster and child
for company.

Very respectfully your friend,

JOHN BROWN.

Upon this statement of the case, Mr. Stearns proposed
to Mr. Lawrence that the money should be sent on at
once. To this proposition he finally assented, but in the
mean time wrote to Mr. Stearns as follows : —

JUNE 3 [1857].

MY DEAR SIR, — I did not intend to do any more than to write a
" heading " for a subscription for Captain Brown, and subscribe for
myself. But he was desirous to have me do more, and I have, as
the paper shows. I wish I could do the whole. But I am behind-
hand in everything. My business extends through a large part of
the twenty-four hours, and prevents my devoting as much time as
would be desirable to push on this and similar good projects for
individual advantage. If Captain Brown should be killed or dis-
abled, then I should be held for the one thousand dollars.[1]

Yours truly,

A. A. LAWRENCE.

HUDSON, OHIO, May 27, 1857.

DEAR WIFE AND CHILDREN, EVERY ONE, — . . . I have got
Salmon's letter of the 19th instant, and am much obliged for it.
There is some prospect that Owen will go on with me. If I should
never return, it is my particular request that no other monument
be used to keep me in remembrance than the same plain one that
records the death of my grandfather and son ; and that a short story,
like those already on it, be told of John Brown the fifth, under that
of grandfather. I think I have several good reasons for this. I
would be glad that my posterity should not only remember their
parentage, but also the cause they labored in. I do not expect to
leave these parts under four or five days, and will try to write again

---

[1] I take it this last sentence implies that Brown was going to "bear
arms," that he was on a dangerous errand, and that Mr. Lawrence approved
of what he was going to do with the arms and money in his hands. At this
time there was no talk of the Virginia plan, nor did any property of the
Kansas Committee go for that plan, — but the property of individual members who gave it freely, knowing what might be done with it.

before I go off. I am much confused in mind, and cannot remember what I wish to write. May God abundantly bless you all! . . .

Your affectionate husband and father,

JOHN BROWN.

These letters are all brief and to the point.

WASSONVILLE, IOWA, July 17, 1857.

DEAR WIFE AND CHILDREN, EVERY ONE, — Since I last wrote I have made but little progress, having teams and wagons to rig up and load, and getting a horse hurt pretty badly. Still we shall get on just as well and as fast as Providence intends, and I hope we may all be satisfied with that. We hear of but little that is interesting from Kansas. It will be a great privilege to hear from home again; and I would give anything to know that I should be permitted to see you all again in this life. But God's will be done. To his infinite grace I commend you all.

Your affectionate husband and father,

JOHN BROWN.

TABOR, IOWA, Aug. 8, 1857.

GEORGE L. STEARNS, ESQ., Boston, Mass.

MY DEAR SIR, — In consequence of ill-health and other hindrances too numerous and unpleasant to write about, the least of which has *not been* the lack of sufficient means for freight bills and other expenses, I have never as yet returned to Kansas. This has been unavoidable, unless I returned without securing the principal object for which I came back from the Territory; and I am now waiting for teams and means to come from there to enable me to go on.[1] I obtained two teams and wagons, as I talked of, at a cost of seven hundred and eighty-six dollars, but was obliged to hire a teamster and to drive one team myself. This unexpected increase of labor, together with being much of the time quite unwell and depressed with disappointments and delays, has prevented my writing sooner. Indeed, I had pretty much determined not to write till I should do it from KANSAS. I will tell you some of my disappointments. I was flattered with the expectation of getting one thousand dollars from Hartford City and also one thousand dollars from New Haven. From Hartford I did get about two hundred and sixty dollars, and a little over in some repair of arms. From New Haven I got twenty-five dollars; at any rate, that is all I can get any advice of. Gerrit Smith supplied me with three hundred and fifty dollars,

---

[1] Have here and at Nebraska City five full loads.

or I could not have reached this place. He also loaned me one hundred and ten dollars to pay to the Thompsons who were disappointed of getting their money for the farm I had agreed for and got possession of for use. I have been continually hearing from them that I *have not fulfilled*, and that I told them I should not leave the country till the thing was completed. This has exceedingly mortified me. I could tell you much more had I room and time. *Have not given up.* Will write more when I get to Kansas.

Your friend,

JOHN BROWN.

To F. B. Sanborn.

TABOR, FREMONT COUNTY, IOWA, Aug. 13, 1857.

Much as I love to communicate with you, it is still a great burden for me to write when I have nothing of interest to say, and when there is something to be active about. Since I left New England I have had a good deal of ill-health ; and having in good measure exhausted my available means toward purchasing such supplies as I should certainly need if again called into active service, and without which I could accomplish next to nothing, I had to begin my journey back with not more than half money at any time to bear my expenses through and pay my freights. This being the case, I was obliged to stop at different points on the way, and to go to others off the route to solicit help. At most places I raised a little ; but it consumed my time, and my unavoidable expenses so nearly kept pace with my incomes that I found it exceedingly discouraging. With the help of Gerrit Smith, who supplied me with sixty dollars at Peterboro', and two hundred and fifty dollars at Chicago, and other smaller amounts from others, I was able to pay freights and other expenses to this place; hiring a man to drive one team, and driving another myself ; and had about twenty-five dollars on hand, with about one hundred dollars' worth of provisions, when I reached here. Among all the good friends who had promised to go with me, *not one* could I get to stick by me and assist me on my way through. I have picked up, at different times on the way, considerable value in articles (indispensable in active service) which were scattered on the way, and had been provided either by or for the National Committee. On reaching here I found one hundred and ten dollars, sent me by Mr. Whitman, from sale of articles in Kansas, sent there by the National Committee. This is all the money I have got from them on their appropriation at New York. On the road one of my horses hurt himself so badly that I lost about ten days in consequence, not being in condition to go on without him, or to buy or to hire another.   I find the arms and ammunition voted me by the Massachusetts State Committee nearly all here, and in middling good order, — some a little rusted.   Have overhauled and cleaned up the worst of them, and am now waiting to know what is best to do next, or for a little escort from Kansas, should I and the supplies be needed.   I am now at last within a kind of hailing distance of our Free-State friends in Kansas.

On the way from Iowa City I and my third son (the hired man I mentioned), in order to make the little funds we had reach as far as possible, and to avoid notice, lived exclusively on herring, soda crackers, and sweetened water for more than three weeks (sleeping every night in our wagons), except that twice we got a little milk, and a few times some boiled eggs.   Early in the season, in consequence of the poor encouragement I met with, and of their own losses and sufferings, my sons declined to return; and my wife wrote me as follows : " The boys have all determined both to practise and learn war no more."   This I said nothing about, lest it should prevent my getting any further supplies.   After leaving New England I could not get the scratch of a pen to tell whether anything had been deposited at Hartford, from New Haven and other places, for me or not; until, since I came here, a line comes from Mr. Callender, dated 24th July, saying nothing has been deposited, in answer to one I had written June 22, in which he further says he has answered all my letters.   The parting with my wife and young uneducated children, without income, supplies of clothing, provisions, or even a comfortable house to live in, or money to provide such things, with at least a fair chance that it was to be a *last* and *final separation*, had lain heavily on me, and was about as much a matter of self-sacrifice and self-devotion on the part of my wife as on my own, and about as much her act as my own.   When Mr. Lawrence, of his own accord, proposed relieving me on that score, it greatly eased a burdened spirit; but I did not rely upon it absolutely, nor make any certain bargain on the strength of it, until after being positively assured by Mr. Stearns, in writing, that it should, and by yourself that it would, certainly be done.

It was the poor condition of my noble-hearted wife and of her young children that made me follow up that encouragement with a tenacity that disgusted him and completely exhausted his patience. But after such repeated assurances from friends I so much respected that I could not suspect they would trifle with my feelings, I made a positive bargain for the farm ; and when I found nothing for me at Peterboro', I borrowed one hundred and ten dollars of Mr. Smith for the men who occupied the farm, telling him it would certainly be refunded, and the others that they would get all their money very soon, and even before I left the country. This has brought me only extreme mortification and depression of feeling; for all my letters from home, up to the last, say not a dime has been paid in to Mr. Smith. Friends who never know the lack of a sumptuous dinner little comprehend the value of such trifling matters to persons circumstanced as I am. But, my noble-hearted friend, I am " though faint, yet pursuing." My health has been much better of late. I believe my anxiety and discouragements had something to do with repeated returns of fever and ague I have had, as it tended to deprive me of sleep and to debilitate me. I intend this letter as a kind of report of my progress and success, as much for your committee or my friend Stearns as yourself. I have been joined by a friend since I got here, and get no discouraging news from Kansas.   Your friend,

J. BROWN.

TABOR, IOWA, Aug. 17, 1857.

DEAR WIFE AND CHILDREN, EVERY ONE, — I have just received the letter of Henry and Ruth, of 26th and 27th July, enclosing one from Mr. Day. We are very glad to learn that all were well so lately; and I am pleased to discover that Mr. Day is willing I should pay Henry, if I have any funds of his in my hands. This I shall certainly *try to do*, should that prove to be the case. I do not know how that is, as I have not yet had time to overhaul some papers left by me last fall in my old chest with Owen. Shall try to do that soon. I wrote home from here week before last, on Saturday. Since then we have been waiting either for news or for a small escort of men and teams to go with us. We get no special news from the West as yet. We are beginning to take lessons, and have (we think) a very capable teacher. Should no disturbance occur, we may possibly think best to work back eastward ; [1] cannot determine yet. I hope you will continue to write me *here* till I say to you where else ; and I want you to give me all the particulars concerning your welfare. God bless you all !

N. HAWKINS.

TABOR, FREMONT COUNTY, IOWA, Sept. 12, 1857.

DEAR WIFE AND CHILDREN, EVERY ONE, — It is now nearly two weeks since I have seen anything from home, and about as long since I wrote. . . . We get nothing very definite from Kansas yet,

---

[1] Here is the first intimation in these letters of a purpose to use his armed force against slavery in the eastern States, as he did two years after.

but think we shall in the course of another week. . . . Got a most
kind letter from Mr. F. B. Sanborn yesterday; also one from Mr.
Blair, where Oliver was living. You probably have but little idea
of my anxiety to get letters from you constantly ; and it would afford
me great satisfaction to learn that you all regularly attend to reading
your Bibles, and that you are all punctual to attend meetings on
Sabbath days. I do not remember ever to have heard any one complain of the time he had lost in that way.

> Your affectionate husband and father,
>
> JOHN BROWN.

Of all the Brown family who had settled in Kansas two
years before, there now remained only the household of
the Rev. Mr. Adair, Brown's brother-in-law, who wrote him
at Tabor thus : —

OSAWATOMIE, K. T., Oct. 2, 1857.

MR. J. B.

DEAR FRIEND, — Yours of September 5 was received yesterday,
having been mailed at Lawrence the day before. Your whereabouts
had for some time been to us unknown. The letter you sent to "Mr.
Addis" was forwarded to me in the latter part of June.[1] I secured the
sum of money requested, but the men failed to go. I was in Lawrence about a month since; Mr. Whitman was East. "Mr. Addis"
said that the last he had heard of you, you had gone to Chicago,
but expected you would return to Tabor again before long; thought
some persons would go and meet you, — talked some of going himself. You desire much a personal interview with me, and also definite information about matters as they "really are" now in the
Territory. As to a personal interview, I should be happy to have
one ; but the state of my own health and of my family forbids my
going to Tabor at present. For nearly five weeks past I have spent
most of my time in taking care of the sick, when able to do anything.
I had a man hired to work for me, who about the 1st of September
was taken very sick (fever and internal inflammation); has been
better, and again worse, and is still dangerous. I was absent nearly
one week at Lecompton, as a witness in the case of the Osawatomie
town site ; some outsiders having tried to preempt a part of it.
Had to hire a man during my absence, to take care of the sick man.
Since my return I have been much troubled with illness, sometimes
severe when I exercise much. Florella and the babe have very sore
throats ; the babe is teething, has chills sometimes, and requires

---

[1] I suppose "Mr. Addis" was W. A. Phillips.

much care. Charles and Emma are well at present. Mrs. Garrison [1] and babe have been with us since the first of June until last week. She came back, went to Lecompton to preempt her claim in June, just before the land-office closed ; but did not succeed, because I could not swear that she had as a widow built, or caused to be built, a house on the claim. The house her husband built they would not recognize as being built by her *" as a widow."* She had to return and have another built, which has been done. She went last week and preempted, and has returned to Ohio. For a number of weeks before she left she and her babe had both been sick. Though we have not had much sickness among the members of our own family proper, yet we are in a measure worn out taking care of the sick. We greatly feel the need of rest and quiet. There is a good deal of sickness around, — chiefly among the more recent emigrants. It has been drier here this year than last. My corn and potatoes are almost an entire failure. Mine were planted early ; later crops have done better.

As to political matters, I have my own views of things. Walker has disgraced himself, — has not fulfilled a pledge made in his Topeka speech ; indeed, I never had confidence to believe he would. But the Free-State men have determined to go into the October election, and many are sanguine that they will carry it. I may be disappointed, but cannot see things in so favorable a light as they do. An invasion such as we had in '54 and '55 I do not expect ; but doubtless many voters from slave States will be smuggled in, and fraudulent returns will be made ; nor do I suppose it will be possible for the Free-State men to show up the frauds so as to gain their ends. The showing up of frauds does not amount to much where those who are to decide upon the frauds are abettors or perpetrators of them, and the highest rewards are given from headquarters for the most bold and outrageous perpetrators. Hence I rather expect that the proslavery men will carry the day October 5. If disappointed, I shall rejoice. What course things will take if the Free-State men fail, I do not know. Some prophesy trouble right along. This would not surprise me were it to occur. But I would deplore a renewal of war. If it is to be commenced again, the boil had better be probed in the centre, at Washington, where the corruption is the worst. The proslavery men in the Territory are but petty tools.

No recent word from Hudson, Akron, or Grafton. We have now a tri-weekly mail to Westport, and also to Lawrence ; mails generally regular. I know of no means of sending you by private

[1] Widow of a neighbor killed August 30, 1856.

conveyance. Send by mail, addressing on the envelope as you requested.

S. L. ADAIR.

P. S. A letter from you to me by mail would probably reach me without much risk.

Such letters depict the every-day situation of matters in Kansas at this time. But Brown was meditating a stroke which should accomplish more than the most garrulous chronicler could narrate.

NOTE. — It will be plain from the letters given in this chapter that Brown was regarded in Kansas, at the close of 1857, by all the leading Free-State men, and by their friends in New England and New York, as neither a dangerous nor a deceitful man. They actually felt that reliance upon him which these letters express ; any subsequent opinion of theirs to the contrary was an afterthought. The active hostility of Robinson and G. W. Brown to John Brown began in 1858.

27

CHAPTER XII.

THE PLANS DISCLOSED.

JOHN BROWN'S long-meditated plan of action in Virginia was wholly his own, as he more than once declared; and it was not until he had long formed and matured it that he made it known to the few friends outside of his own household who shared his confidence in that matter. I cannot say how numerous these were; but beyond his family and the armed followers who accompanied him, I have never supposed that his Virginia plan was known to fifty persons. Even to those few it was not fully communicated, though they knew that he meant to fortify himself somewhere in the mountains of Virginia or Tennessee, and from that fastness, with his band of soldiers, sally out and emancipate slaves, seize hostages and levy contributions on the slaveholders. Moreover, from the time he first matured it, there were several changes amounting at last to an entire modification of the scheme. As he disclosed it to me in 1858, in the house of Gerrit Smith at Peterboro', it was very different from the plan he had unfolded to Thomas and to that other Maryland freedman Frederick Douglass, at Brown's own house in Springfield in 1847.[1] I have already quoted Douglass's description of this house and its master, whose guest he was. In respect to his disclosure of the great plan, Douglass says in his "Life and Times" (edition of 1881, pp. 279–282) : —

" Captain Brown cautiously approached the subject which he wished to bring to my attention, for he seemed to apprehend opposition to his views. He denounced slavery in look and language

[1] This house, on Franklin Street, north of the railroad station, near which was Brown's wool-warehouse, is still standing. It was rented by Brown, who never owned a house in New England, nor lived so long in any there as in that where he was born at Torrington.

fierce and bitter ; thought that slaveholders had forfeited their right
to live, and that the slaves had the right to gain their liberty in any
way they could ; did not believe that 'moral suasion' would ever
liberate the slave, nor that political action would abolish the system.
He had long had a plan which could accomplish this end, and had
invited me to his house to lay that plan before me ; he had been
some time looking for colored men to whom he could safely reveal
his secret, and at times he had almost despaired of finding such men ;
but now he was encouraged, for he saw heads of such rising up in all
directions. He had observed my course, at home and abroad, and he
wanted my co-operation. His plan, as it then lay in his mind, had
much to commend it. It did not, as some suppose, contemplate a
general rising among the slaves, and a general slaughter of the
slavemasters : an insurrection, he thought, would only defeat the
object ; but his plan did contemplate the creating of an armed force
which should act in the very heart of the South. He was not averse
to the shedding of blood, and thought the practice of carrying arms
would be a good one for the colored people to adopt, as it would give
them a sense of their manhood. No people, he said, could have self-
respect, or be respected, who would not fight for their freedom. He
called my attention to a map of the United States, and pointed out
to me the ranges which stretch away from the borders of New York
into the Southern States. ' These mountains,' he said, ' are the basis
of my plan. God has given the strength of the hills to freedom ; they
were placed here for the emancipation of the negro race ; they are
full of natural forts, where one man for defence will be equal to a
hundred for attack ; they are full also of good hiding-places, where
large numbers of brave men could be concealed, and baffle and elude
pursuit for a long time. I know these mountains well, and could
take a body of men into them and keep them there, despite of all the
efforts of Virginia to dislodge them. The true object to be sought is,
first of all, to destroy the money-value of slave property ; and that
can only be done by rendering such property insecure. My plan,
then, is to take at first about twenty-five picked men, and begin on
a small scale ; supply them arms and ammunition, and post them in
squads of five on a line of twenty-five miles. The most persuasive
and judicious of them shall then go down to the fields from time to
time, as opportunity offers, and induce the slaves to join them, seeking and selecting the most restless and daring.' He saw that in this
part of the work the utmost care must be used to avoid treachery and
disclosure. Only the most conscientious and skilled should be sent
on this perilous duty ; with care and enterprise he thought he could
soon gather a force of a hundred hardy men, who would be content
to lead the free and adventurous life to which he proposed to train

them. When these were properly drilled, and each man had found the place for which he was best suited, they would begin work in earnest; they would run off the slaves in large numbers, retain the brave and strong ones in the mountains, and send the weak and timid to the North by the 'underground railroad;' his operations would be enlarged with increasing numbers, and would not be confined to one locality.

"When I asked him how he would support these men, he said emphatically he would subsist them upon the enemy. Slavery was a state of war, and the slave had a right to anything necessary to his freedom. 'But,' said I, 'suppose you succeed in running off a few slaves, and thus impress the Virginia slaveholders with a sense of insecurity in their slaves, — the effect will only be to make them sell their slaves farther South.' 'That,' said he, 'will be first what I want to do; then I would follow them up. If we could drive slavery out of one county, it would be a great gain; it would weaken the system throughout the State.' 'But they would employ bloodhounds to hunt you out of the mountains.' 'That they might attempt,' said he, 'but the chances are we should whip them: and when we should have whipped one squad, they would be careful how they pursued.' 'But you might be surrounded and cut off from your means of subsistence.' He thought that could not be done so they could not cut their way out; but even if the worst came, he could but be killed, and he had no better use for his life than to lay it down in the cause of the slave. When I suggested that we might convert the slaveholders, he became much excited, and said that could never be; 'he knew their proud hearts, and that they would never be induced to give up their slaves until they felt a big stick about their heads.' He thought I might have noticed the simple manner in which he lived, adding that he had adopted this in order to save money to carry out his purposes. This was said in no boastful tone, for he felt that he had delayed already too long, and had no room to boast either his zeal or his self-denial. Had some men made such display of rigid virtue, I should have rejected it as affected, false, or hypocritical, but in John Brown I felt it to be as real as iron or granite. From this night spent with John Brown in 1847, while I continued to write and speak against slavery, I became all the less hopeful of its peaceful abolition. My utterances became more and more tinged by the color of this man's strong impressions." [1]

---

[1] Mr. Douglass adds the true version of a famous anecdote: "Speaking at an antislavery convention in Ohio, I expressed my apprehension that slavery could only be destroyed by bloodshed, when I was suddenly and sharply interrupted by my good old friend Sojourner Truth, with the ques-

There can be no question that what Brown saw and did in Kansas gave a new tone to his scheme. I do not much rely upon the memory of Mr. Arny, who as a witness before Senator Mason's committee showed himself apt at forgetting and misplacing events; but a part of his testimony bearing upon this matter must have some foundation in fact. He mentions a conversation held with Brown in Kansas late in 1858, in which Brown said the only way to abolish slavery was to post a company of men somewhere in the mountains of the slave States to assist slaves in escaping, and thus make the system of slavery insecure. "I told him that I thought he was doing an injury to the whole country in pursuing that course; that it was contrary to his former views on the subject; that I did not suppose he could get any person to assist him in it; that I felt satisfied his good friend Gerrit Smith would not assist him, because Mr. Smith had placed in our hands ten thousand dollars, and made it an especial condition that every dollar of it should go for food or medicine, and not for matters of war; he professed to be a peace man. I told him I knew he was acquainted with Dr. Howe, and I did not suppose Dr. Howe would do anything of that sort: no Republican would. His answer was, that he disliked the do-nothing policy of the Abolitionists; they would never effect anything by their milk-and-water principles. As to the Republicans, they were of no account, for they were opposed to carrying the war into Africa; they were opposed to meddling with slavery in the States where it existed. He said his doctrine was to free the slaves by the sword. I then again asked him how

tion, 'Frederick, is God dead?' 'No,' I answered, 'and because God is not dead, slavery can only end in blood.' My quaint old sister was of the Garrison school of non-resistants, and was shocked at my sanguinary doctrine ; but she, too, became an advocate of the sword when the war for the maintenance of the Union was declared." I have slightly abbreviated Douglass's statement here and there. Possibly in writing from memory, after Brown's death, he may have unconsciously mingled with the scheme of 1847 features that did not take shape in Brown's mind until after his Kansas experiences. Thomas Thomas assures me that Brown's plan before 1851 was to occupy land at the South as a slaveholder, using trusty colored men as his nominal slaves, and through them indoctrinating the real slaves with the hopes of freedom.

he reconciled such opinions with his peace principles that he held when I first knew him in Virginia, more than twenty years ago. He said that the aggressions of slavery, the murders and robberies perpetrated upon himself and members of his family, the violation of the laws by Atchison and others in Kansas in 1855, and from that time down to the murders on the Marais des Cygnes, convinced him that peace was but an empty word."

It was a year before this that Brown, in September, 1857, began to prepare the minds of his Eastern friends for the full scope of his purposes. He was then at Tabor, in Western Iowa, where he had opened a small school for military drill, at the head of which was the Garibaldian Briton, Hugh Forbes, the adventurer already described. Brown wrote to Theodore Parker, September 11, —

MY DEAR SIR, — Please find on other side first number of a series of tracts lately gotten up here. I need not say I did not prepare it; but I would be glad to know what you think of it, and much obliged for any suggestions you see proper to make. My particular object in writing is to say that I am in immediate want of some five hundred or one thousand dollars for secret service, and no questions asked. I want the friends of freedom to "prove me now herewith." Will you bring this matter before your congregation, or exert your influence in some way to have it, or some part of it, raised and placed in the hands of George L. Stearns, Esq., of Boston, subject to my order? I should highly prize a letter from you, directed on the envelope to Jonas Jones, Esq., Tabor, Fremont County, Iowa. Have no news to send *by letter.*

Very respectfully your friend,

JOHN BROWN.

The tract enclosed was a dull and heavy paper entitled "The Duty of the Soldier," and bearing on its face the inscription, "Presented with respectful and kind feelings to the officers and soldiers of the United States army in Kansas." Parker probably caused Brown to know what was his opinion of this tract, as I did when I received a similar letter. It was not easy for any of us in that autumn, when business was greatly depressed, to raise money for an object so indefinite. I sent him some money (seventy-two dollars), which he received Oct. 3, 1857, and others no doubt contributed something; but no movement was made before winter, nor did he further disclose his purposes to us at that time. But when he reached Kansas at last, in November, he hastened to communicate them in general terms to Kagi, Cook, Stephens, and others who afterward joined him in his Virginia campaign. Cook's confession, while in prison, is explicit on this point, and is confirmed by Parsons, Moffat, and others, who received some part of the plan from Brown in Kansas. Cook said: —

" I became acquainted with Captain Brown in his camp on Middle Creek, K. T., just after the battle of Black Jack, and was with him in camp until it was broken up and his company disbanded by Colonel Sumner, of the First Cavalry. I next saw him at the convention at Topeka, July 4, and some days afterward in Lawrence. I did not see him again until the fall of 1857, when I met him at the house of E. B. Whitman, four miles from Lawrence, about the first of November. I was then told that he intended to organize a company for the purpose of putting a stop to the aggressions of the proslavery men. I agreed to join him, and was asked if I knew of any other young men, who were perfectly reliable, who I thought would join. I recommended Richard Realf, Luke F. Parsons, and R. J. Hinton. I received a note from Brown the next Sunday morning while at breakfast, in Lawrence, requesting me to come up that day, and to bring Realf, Parsons, and Hinton with me. Realf and Hinton were not in town. Parsons and myself went, and had a long talk with Captain Brown. A few days afterward I received another note which read as follows: —

CAPTAIN COOK.

DEAR SIR, — You will please get everything ready to join me at Topeka by Monday night next. Come to Mrs. Sheridan's, two miles south of Topeka, and bring your arms, ammunition, clothing, and other articles you may require. Bring Parsons with you if he can get ready in time. Please keep very quiet about the matter.

Yours, etc.,

JOHN BROWN.

" I made all my arrangements for starting at the time appointed. Parsons, Realf, and Hinton could not be ready. I left them at Lawrence and started for Topeka; stopped at the hotel over night, and left early the next morning for Mrs. Sheridan's to meet Captain Brown. At Topeka we were joined by Stephens, Moffat, and Kagi. Left Topeka for Nebraska City, and camped at night on the prairie northeast of Topeka. Here for the first time I learned that we were to leave Kansas to attend a military school during the winter in Ashtabula County, Ohio. Next morning I was sent back to Lawrence to get a draft of eighty dollars cashed, and get Parsons, Realf, and Hinton to come back with me. Captain Brown had given me orders to take boat to St. Joseph, Mo., and stage from there to Tabor, Iowa. Hinton could not leave at that time. I started with Realf and Parsons on a stage for Leavenworth, and then left for Weston, where we took stage for St. Joseph, and thence to Tabor. I found C. P. Tidd and Leeman at Tabor, where we stayed some days, making preparations to start. Here we found that Captain Brown's ultimate destination was the State of Virginia. Some warm words passed between him and myself in regard to the plan, which I had supposed was to be confined entirely to Kansas and Missouri. Realf and Parsons were of the same opinion with me. After a good deal of wrangling we consented to go on, as the rest of the party were so anxious that we should go with them. At Tabor we procured teams for the transportation of about two hundred Sharpe's rifles, which had been brought on as far as Tabor a year before, awaiting the order of Captain Brown. There were also other stores, consisting of blankets, clothing, boots, ammunition, and about two hundred revolvers of the Massachusetts Arms patent, all of which we transported across Iowa to Springdale, and from there to Liberty, at which place they were shipped for Ashtabula County, Ohio, where they remained till brought to Chambersburg, Pa., and from there transported to the Kennedy Farm, which Brown had rented for six months, and which was about five miles from Harper's Ferry. It was the intention of Captain Brown to sell his teams in Springdale, and with the proceeds to go on with the rest of the company to some place in Ashtabula County, Ohio, where we were to have a good military instructor during the winter; but he was disappointed in the sale, and it was decided we should remain in the neighborhood of Springdale, and that our instructor, Colonel Forbes, should be sent to us from the East. We stopped over winter at Mr. Maxon's, where we pursued a course of military studies."

It thus appears that Brown had started for Virginia with a few men, and with the Kansas rifles and revolvers, at least three months before he communicated to Mr. Stearns, the owner of the arms, that he had any purpose of using them outside of Kansas and Missouri. It is also plain that he imparted his purposes little by little to his armed followers. Edwin Coppoc, an Iowa youth, who joined Brown at Spring-

dale, said to the Virginians who captured and hung him:
" I am a Republican philanthropist, and came here to aid in
liberating negroes. I made the acquaintance of Captain
Brown in Iowa as he returned from Kansas, and agreed to
join his company. Brown wrote to me in July to come on
to Chambersburg, where he first revealed the whole plot.
The whole company was opposed to making the first demonstration at Harper's Ferry, but Captain Brown would have
it his own way, and we had to obey orders." [1]

C. W. Moffat, of Montour, Iowa, who was one of Brown's
company in the winter of 1857–58, says : —

" We spent the winter in the vicinity of Iowa City. Our efforts
there were directed towards starting a Sharpe's rifle military school,
of which a man named Stephens, — known better in Kansas as
Whipple, — was to be the instructor ; but our plans were interfered
with by pecuniary embarrassments. Then Brown went to Ohio (for
which we had started in the first place) to form another school.
There was also to be one in Canada, — three in all. When Brown
left he gave Whipple charge of the school, and I had sent Forbes
round by water to Ohio. Forbes had been engaged as drill-master
at a hundred dollars a month, and when we stopped in Iowa Brown
said he would have to give Forbes the choice of the schools : if Forbes
would come back to Iowa, Whipple would take the school in Ohio
or in Canada. But when he got to Ohio, Brown found that Forbes
had gone away, and so gave up the Ohio school."

This is as good a place as any to speak once for all of
this Hugh Forbes, who proved to be the false member of
the little band, and betrayed the confidence of his employer
through vanity and emptiness of head, rather than through
malice of heart. I have already spoken of his employment
by Brown eight months before ; but his earlier history and
his general character were thus portrayed by Horace Greeley,
in his usual lively manner, in October, 1859, after Forbes
had promulgated some futile disclosures of Brown's plans :

"This Forbes appeared in New York sometime after the explosion
of the European revolution of 1848, and claimed to have borne an
important part in that movement. Of course he was needy, and the

---

[1] See Owen Brown's statement in chap. xv.

Herald says he was 'at one time a reporter or translator on the Tribune.' This is quite probable, though I do not recollect it. Some time late in 1856 (I think it was) [1] I was apprised that he was going out to Kansas to help the Free-State men, then threatened with annihilation by the Border Ruffians of Missouri, backed by Federal functionaries and troops. Lawrence had then been twice beleaguered and once sacked; Osawatomie had been twice ravaged and burned; Leavenworth had been swept clean of Free-State men by a Missouri raid, — William Phillips being butchered while defending his own house, his brother badly wounded and captured, while those who made no resistance were sent down the river at an hour's notice. As Forbes professed to be a capable and experienced military officer, especially qualified for guerilla or border warfare, and as he had always claimed to be an earnest Red Republican and foe of every form of human slavery, I thought his resolution natural and commendable. Knowing him to be poor, I gave him twenty dollars as he was starting; others gave him larger sums, — how much in all I do not know; but I think his total receipts from friends of Free Kansas cannot have fallen below seven hundred dollars. He went — was absent some months — came back: that is all *I* know of his services to the Free-State cause in any shape. Whether he was not needed, or was not trusted, or was found incompetent, I do not know; I only know that he did nothing, and was practically worth nothing. [2] I believe he spent part of the money given him in printing a pamphlet embodying his notions of guerilla or partisan warfare: of course, no dollar ever came back. I think I heard of him before his return, clamoring for more money. In due time, he reappeared in New York, and came to me (as to others) with complaints that he had been deceived, misled, swindled, beggared, his family (in

---

[1] Really in April, 1857.

[2] Forbes could not rest quiet under Greeley's censure, and published in the " Herald " this card : —

NEW YORK, Oct. 25, 1859.

There having appeared in yesterday's "Tribune " a false and malicious attack upon me, I shall, after the trial of John Brown, publish the correspondence between himself, his friends, and myself, which correspondence commenced about two years ago, and was continued during the spring of 1859. Some Abolitionists of good judgment insisted strongly that I should make Brown desist from his projects, which they considered would prove fatal to the antislavery cause ; and as there were sundry persons in the free States interested, copies of most of the letters were furnished to each of them and to Brown. I could not myself take all the copies, therefore some friends occasionally copied for me. I feel sure that none of these letters were suffered to be seen by the Secretary of War : first, because I have faith in the reliability of those who had them in their hands ; and, secondly, because it is absolutely impossible that, had such authentic evidence been placed before him, he could have been taken so by surprise as he was at Harper's Ferry.

H. FORBES.

Paris) turned into the streets to starve, etc. I tried to ascertain *who*
had deceived him, what promises made to him had been broken, etc.,
but with little success.   All I could make out was that some one —
he now says it was Brown — had promised him something in the
way of pecuniary recompense for his services, which had not been
made good, and that his family were consequently reduced to the
brink of starvation.   *I do not believe that John Brown ever wilfully
deceived him or any one else.*   I am very sure that no one was ever
authorized to engage the services of 'Colonel Forbes' in behalf of
the Free-State men of Kansas on condition that said Forbes should
be authorized to charge his own price for those services and draw at
pleasure on some responsible party for payment.   I have never heard
of any one's version of the matter but Forbes's; and I confidently
infer from this, that, if there was mutual misunderstanding and disappointment in the premises, the employing party had decidedly the
worst of it."

In December, 1857, there began to arrive a series of letters written by this Forbes to Dr. Howe, Charles Sumner,
and myself, which greatly puzzled us all.   Brown's Massachusetts friends, either from his inadvertence, or because he
was not yet ready to disclose his ultimate purpose, had not
been informed by him who Forbes was; they had never
seen him, and only heard of him casually and incidentally.
They had never been consulted by Brown in regard to paying Forbes, nor of course had Brown given Forbes any
assurances that they would pay him the salary stipulated
for his services; of which, in fact, they knew nothing whatever.   It was therefore with much surprise and mystifica-
tion that about Christmas-time, 1857, we received passionate
and denunciatory letters, written by Forbes, complaining of
ill-treatment at our hands, and assuming to hold us responsible for the termination of his engagement with Brown;
by which, he said, he had been reduced to poverty, and his
family in Paris, deprived of pecuniary aid from him, had
suffered great hardship.   Two of these letters were addressed to Senator Sumner, and were forwarded by him to
Dr. Howe and to me, who, in great ignorance as to what
such abusive epistles meant, answered them with curtness
and severity.   This correspondence temporarily closed in
January, 1858, and the substance of it was communicated

to Brown, then in Iowa, with the request that he would explain the meaning of Forbes's course, and state what their relations with each other were. I also communicated the matter to Theodore Parker, with whom I was then in frequent correspondence; and, as it happens, my letter of January, 1858, to Parker has been preserved. I wrote: —

F. B. Sanborn to T. Parker.

CONCORD, Jan. 15, 1858.

DEAR FRIEND, — I send you a letter this day received from Forbes. During the week I have received a note from Mr. Sumner, who sent me two letters of Forbes to him, in which he says these same things. Now, if it were not for the wife and children, who are undoubtedly in suffering, the man might be hanged for all me, — for his whole style towards me is a combination of insult and lunacy. But I fear there was such an agreement between him and Brown, though Brown has told me nothing of it; and if so, he has a claim upon somebody, though not particularly upon us. Is there anything that can be done for him? I have written to Brown inquiring about the matter, but cannot get an answer before the middle of February. Have you heard anything from Brown or Whitman? When you do, please let me hear of it. Forbes's threats are of no account, and they, with the vulgar abuse which he uses, show what sort of man he is. I shall answer his letter, and send him ten dollars.

January 17.

Mr. Sumner suggests that in my note to Forbes I might have been "less sharp;" but the character of F.'s epistles convinces me that, if I erred at all, it was on the side of gentleness. I have since received a letter from Forbes himself, in which he goes over the same charges and insinuations with "damnable iteration." This I have also answered, explaining more fully my position in the matter. Forbes threatens terrible things, — meaning, as I conjecture, to give notice at the South of Brown's position and designs. Should he do this, he would deserve all the suffering which his own carelessness has brought on his family; but their suffering troubles me, and I am trying to do something to relieve it, and also to find out from Brown the true condition of affairs.

Yours affectionately,

F. B. SANBORN.

I wrote thus to Forbes himself, and cite the letter here only because it preserves some facts and dates which might otherwise be lost : —

F. B. Sanborn to Hugh Forbes.

CONCORD, Jan. 15, 1858.

SIR, — Yours of the 9th and 14th is received. I regret that you should have continued the abusive strain of your letter to Mr. Sumner, towards a person of whom you are wholly ignorant, and whose character you so greatly mistake. Let me give you some facts, which you may believe or not, as you choose. I became acquainted with Captain Brown a little more than a year ago, and have since been his warm friend and admirer. Being a member of the Massachusetts Kansas Committee, I interested myself with my colleagues in his behalf, and we furnished him with some five thousand dollars in arms and money. As a temporary member of the National Committee, I procured the passage of a resolution appropriating five thousand dollars from that committee also, of which, however, only five hundred dollars has been paid. I also introduced him to a public meeting of my townsmen, who raised something for him. In the summer I visited Mr. Gerrit Smith, and made arrangements with him for the settlement of property worth one thousand dollars on the wife and daughter of Captain Brown. The money was raised in Boston by the men whom you calumniate. I visited the families in the wilderness where they live, and arranged the transfer of property. Mr. Smith first mentioned your name to me, — unless it were a member of his family, Mr. Morton. Captain Brown had never done so, nor did any one hint to me that there was any agreement between you and him of the kind you mention. I think I wrote to Brown from Peterboro', informing him that you were at Davenport, having seen your letter to Mr. Smith announcing that fact. On September 14 I received Mr. Smith's letter, asking that some money be raised for your family, but merely on general grounds. I was pledged to aid and support Brown, and could not give money to persons of whom I knew little or nothing. Had Brown or yourself informed me of your agreement, the case would have been different. I kept Mr. Smith's draft just a week, returning it to him September 21; it was out of his hands just eleven days. Since then, I have had a few letters from Brown, and have seen some from you, but have heard nothing of any compact. To answer Brown's call for " secret service " money, I procured about six hundred dollars to be sent him, which, as he has not yet come into active operations, has probably been sufficient. My property is small, — my income this year hardly up to my expenses; but to carry out the plan which Captain Brown has matured, if the time seemed favorable, I would sacrifice both income and property, as he very well knows. But it is probable that Captain Brown placed too much confidence in the expectations of others, and that he may have mistaken *hopes* for *promises*. Does he join in your vituperation of his Boston friends ? I know he does not.

I can excuse much to one who has so much reason for anxiety as you have in the distress of your family. Yet be assured that if you had written to me (or if Captain Brown had done so) the true nature of your compact with him, I would have supported your wife and children rather than have allowed what has happened to take place. You knew my address, — why, then, did you not write to me rather than send a slanderous letter to Mr. Sumner ?

As for your threats, you are at liberty to speak, write, and publish what you please about me, — only be careful to keep within the limits of your knowledge ; do not tax your imagination for facts. I have written to Captain Brown for his statement of the relation between you, and have also sent to Mr. Gerrit Smith for any information in his possession. In the mean time I send you ten dollars, promising that if I find you have any further claim on me, either in law, justice, or humanity, I will discharge it to the uttermost.

The gentlemen with whom I am associated, and for whose action I am in any way responsible, are honorable men, and as far from deserving the vulgar slanders you heap upon them as your language is lacking in common courtesy and justice. They always keep and always will keep their engagements ; but they have made none with you. You cite the people of New Haven. I have nothing to do with them, nor with the other towns which have failed in their promises.

I never saw Hugh Forbes, and have no personal reason to esteem him, since his entire correspondence with me and with my Boston friends was absurdly violent and unreasonable. Horace Greeley, and those who were bored by him in person, at New York and Washington, have spoken of him with much impatience, declaring that he was at once fanatical and mercenary, and wholly wanting in common-sense. In New York he was a fencing-master and a hanger-on at the "Tribune" office, while his wife and daughter lived in Paris upon remittances sent by him from New York. Gerrit Smith, at whose house he once spent a day or two, spoke of him to me as a handsome, soldierly-looking man, skilful in the sword-exercise, and with some military experience, picked up under Garibaldi in 1848–49. He had been a silk-merchant of some sort at Sienna, it was said, before he joined Garibaldi. Judged by his letters, his little book ("Manual of the Patriotic Volunteer"), and the various accounts given by persons who knew him, he was a brave, vainglorious, undisciplined person, with little discretion, and quite wanting in the qualities which would fit him to be a leader of American soldiers. Yet he was ambitious, eager to head a crusade against slavery, and apparently desirous of taking Brown's place as commander of what he regarded as a great antislavery movement, supported by thousands in the Northern States. Accustomed to see European insurrections managed by committees outwardly similar to the various antislavery committees which he found or heard of in America, he hastily inferred that these American committees were all working for the same revolutionary end, and were ready to promote a design which Brown had as yet communicated to none of them, and which none of them would have aided, had they known it. He was really connected with Brown's enterprise but a few months; having joined his rendezvous at Tabor, in Iowa, on the 9th of August, 1857, and parted from him in early November of the same year. His complaining letters were the first intimation received by the Boston friends of Brown that there was any peculiar relation between him and the Kansas hero; and these letters, by a singular chance, occasioned the first disclosure of Brown's plans to his Boston friends.

Frederick Douglass says of Forbes, whom he saw in November, 1857, and afterwards kept track of for a while : —

"After remaining with Brown a short time, he came to me in Rochester with a letter from him, asking me to receive and assist him. I was not favorably impressed with Forbes at first; but I 'conquered my prejudices,' took him to a hotel, and paid his board while he remained. Just before leaving, he spoke of his family in Europe as in destitute circumstances, and of his desire to send them some money. I gave him a little, — I forget how much, — and through

Miss Ottilia Assing, a German lady deeply interested in the John Brown scheme, he was introduced to several of my German friends in New York. But he soon wore them out by his endless begging; and when he could make no more money by professing to advance the John Brown project, he threatened to expose it and all connected with it. I think I was the first to be informed of his tactics, and I promptly communicated them to Captain Brown. Through my friend Miss Assing I found that Forbes had told Brown's designs to Horace Greeley, and to the government officials at Washington, of which I informed Captain Brown; and this led to the postponement of the enterprise another year. It was hoped that by this delay the story of Forbes would be discredited; and this calculation was correct, — for nobody believed the scoundrel, though he told the truth."

Brown's own method of dealing with the loquacious betrayer of his counsels (with which so slight a person should never have been intrusted) was peculiar. While at the house of Douglass, in Rochester, he received, early in February, a letter from Forbes, forwarded by John Brown, Jr., from West Andover, Ohio, where the latter was then living. Upon this he wrote to his son as follows: —

To John Brown, Jr.

DEAR SON JOHN, — Forbes's letter to me of the 27th of January I enclose back to you, and will be glad to have you return it to him with something like the following (unless you can think of some serious objection), as I am anxious to draw him out more fully, and would also like to keep him a little encouraged and avoid an open rupture for a few weeks, at any rate. Suppose you write Forbes thus: —

"Your letter to my father, of 27th January, after mature reflection, I have decided to return *to you*, as I am unwilling he should, with all his other cares, difficulties, and trials, be vexed with what I am apprehensive he will accept as *highly offensive and insulting,* while I know that he is disposed to do all he consistently can for you, and will do so, unless you are yourself the cause of his disgust. I was trying to send you a little assistance myself, — say about forty dollars; but I must hold up till I feel different from what I now do. I understood from my father that he had *advanced* you already six hundred dollars, or six months' pay (disappointed as he has been), to enable you to provide for your family; and that he was to give you one hundred dollars per month for just so much time as you continued in his service. Now, you in your letter undertake to *instruct* him to say that he had positively engaged you for one year. I fear he will not accept it well to be asked or told to state what he considers an *untruth*. Again, I suspect you have greatly mistaken the man, if you suppose he'will take it kindly in you, or any living man, to assume to instruct him how he should conduct his own business and correspondence. And I suspect that the seemingly spiteful letters you say you have written to some of his particular friends have not only done you great injury, but also weakened his hands with them. While I have, in my poverty, deeply sympathized with you and your family, *who*, I ask, is likely to be moved by any exhibition of a wicked and spiteful temper on your part, or is likely to be dictated to by you as to their duties ?

"I ask you to look over your letter again. You begin with saying, 'With a little energy, all will yet be right.' Is that respectful? and does it come with a good grace *from you* to the man you thus address? Look it all over; and if, after having done so, you wish him to have it, — go on! you can do so. But as a friend I would advise a very different course."

As I conclude Forbes does not hold you as deeply committed to him, he may listen to you; and I hope he will. I want to see how a sharp but well-merited rebuke will affect him; and should it have the desired effect, I would like to get a draft for forty dollars, payable to his order, and remit him at once. I do not mean to dictate to you, as he does to me; but I am anxious to understand him fully before we go any further, and shall be glad of the earliest information of the result. . . .

Your affectionate father,

JOHN BROWN.

Having established his little company at Springdale, in Iowa, under the military instruction of Stephens, who had served in the United States Army, Brown came eastward in January, 1858, — first to West Andover, in Ohio, where his son John was then living, and soon after to Rochester, N. Y., where he showed himself, early in February, to his good friend Frederick Douglass, and took shelter from observation in his house. Douglass says : "Brown desired to stop with me several weeks, but added, 'I will not stay unless you will allow me to pay board.' Knowing that he was no trifler, but meant all he said, and desirous of retaining him under my roof, I charged three dollars a week. While here he spent most of his time in correspondence. He wrote often to George L. Stearns, of Boston, Gerrit Smith, of Peterboro', and many others, and received many letters in return. When he was not writing letters, he was writing and revising a constitution, which he meant to put in operation by the men who should go with him in the Virginia mountains. He said that to avoid anarchy and confusion, there should be a regularly constituted government, which each man who came with him should be sworn to honor and support. I have a copy of this constitution, in Captain Brown's own handwriting, as prepared by himself at my house." Douglass adds: —

" His whole time and thought were given to this subject. It was the first thing in the morning, and the last thing at night; till, I confess, it began to be something of a bore to me. Once in a while he would say he could, with a few resolute men, capture Harper's Ferry and supply himself with arms belonging to the Government at that place; but he never announced his intention to do so. It was, however, very evidently passing in his mind as a thing that he might do. I paid but little attention to such remarks, although I never doubted that he thought just what he said. Soon after his coming to me he asked me to get for him two smoothly planed boards, upon which he could illustrate, with a pair of dividers, by a drawing, the plan of fortification which he meant to adopt in the mountains. These forts were to be so arranged as to connect one with the other by secret passages, so that if one was carried another could be easily fallen back upon, and be the means of dealing death to the enemy at the very moment when he might think himself victorious. I was less interested in these drawings than my children were; but they showed that the old man had an eye to the means as well as to the end, and was giving his best thought to the work he was about to take in hand."

From Douglass's house Brown wrote again to Theodore Parker in these words: —

ROCHESTER, N. Y., Feb. 2, 1858.

MY DEAR SIR, — I am again out of Kansas, and am at this time concealing my whereabouts; but for very different reasons, however, from those I had for doing so at Boston last spring. I have nearly perfected arrangements for carrying out an important measure in which the world has a deep interest, as well as Kansas; and only. lack from five to eight hundred dollars to enable me to do so, — the same object for which I asked for secret-service money last fall. It is my only errand here; and I have written to some of our mutual friends in regard to it, but they none of them understand my views so well as you do, and I cannot explain without their first committing themselves more than I know of their doing. I have heard that Parker Pillsbury and some others in your quarter hold out ideas similar to those on which I act; but I have no personal acquaintance with them, and know nothing of their influence or means. Cannot you either by direct or indirect action do something to further me? Do you not know of some parties whom you could induce to give their abolition theories a thoroughly practical shape? I hope this will prove to be the last time I shall be driven to harass a friend in such a way. Do you think any of my Garrisonian friends, either at Boston, Worcester, or any other place, can be induced to supply a little " straw," if I will absolutely make " bricks"? I have written George L. Stearns, Esq., of Medford, and Mr. F. B. Sanborn, of Concord; but I am not informed as to how deeply-dyed Abolitionists those friends are, and must beg you to consider this communication strictly confidential, — unless you know of parties who will feel and act, and hold their peace. I want to bring the thing about during the next sixty days. Please write N. Hawkins, care William J. Watkins, Esq., Rochester, N. Y.

Very respectfully your friend,

JOHN BROWN.[1]

Brown's letters of the same date and for a few weeks after, to Colonel Higginson and to me, were of a similar tenor, though rather more explicit; but they conveyed no distinct intimation of his plans. He wrote to Higginson, February 2, from Rochester: "I am here, concealing my whereabouts for good reasons (as I think), — not, however, from any anxiety about my personal safety. I have been told that you are both a true man and a true Abolitionist, and I partly believe the whole story. Last fall I undertook to raise from five hundred to one thousand dollars for secret service, and succeeded in getting five hundred dollars. I now want to get, for the perfecting of by far the most important undertaking of my whole life, five hundred to eight hundred dollars within the next sixty days. I have written Rev. Theodore Parker, George L. Stearns, and F. B. Sanborn, Esqs., on the subject, but I do not know as either Mr.

---

[1] Weiss's Life of Theodore Parker, vol. ii. pp. 163, 164.

Stearns or Mr. Sanborn are Abolitionists. I suppose they are." On the 12th of February he wrote again, in response to a remark in Higginson's reply about the Underground Railroad in Kansas: "Railroad business on a somewhat extended scale is the identical object for which I am trying to get means. I have been connected with that business, as commonly conducted, from my boyhood, and never let an opportunity slip. I have been operating to some purpose the past season; but I now have a measure on foot that I feel sure would awaken in you something more than a common interest if you could understand it. I have just written my friends G. L. Stearns and F. B. Sanborn, asking them to meet me for consultation at Peterboro', N. Y. I am very anxious to have you come along, certain as I feel that you will never regret having been one of the council." It was inconvenient for any of the persons addressed to take the long journey proposed; and on the 13th I wrote for myself and Mr. Stearns, inviting Brown to visit Boston, and offering to pay his travelling expenses. To this request Brown replied, February 17: "It would be almost impossible for me to pass through Albany, Springfield, or any of those parts. on my way to Boston, and not have it known; and my reasons for keeping quiet are such that when I left Kansas I kept it from every friend there; and I suppose it is still understood that I am hiding somewhere in the Territory; and such will be the idea until it comes to be generally known that I am in these parts. I want to continue that impression as long as I can, or for the present. I want very much to see Mr. Stearns, and also Mr. Parker, and it may be that I can before long; but I must decline accepting your kind offer at present, and, sorry as I am to do so, ask you both to meet me by the middle of next week at the furthest. I wrote Mr. Higginson, of Worcester, to meet me also. It may be he would come on with you. My reasons for keeping still are sufficient to keep me from seeing my wife and children, much as I long to do so. I will endeavor to explain when I see you." [1]

[1] This letter was written from Douglass's house, at Rochester, but fixed the place of meeting at Gerrit Smith's house in Peterboro'. At this time one of my Kansas correspondents sent word that Brown had disappeared

On the 7th of February my friend Edwin Morton wrote me from Gerrit Smith's house, giving the substance of a similar letter which Smith had just received from Brown. " He wants from five to eight hundred dollars for secret service, and thinks he can do more with it than all that has yet been done. That is his errand. He wishes to avoid publicity, and so does not come here, and will not see his family. Meantime he is staying with Fred Douglass under the *nom de guerre* of N. Hawkins, — to which name he desires letters addressed, care of Douglass. This is news, — he 'expects to overthrow slavery' in a large part of the country." On the 19th of February Morton wrote me again : " John Brown is here, and asks me to say he is waiting here to see you. If you cannot come within the time he named, — say the middle of next week, — let him know by letter here (Peterboro'), enclosed to me, when you can come. He says 't is not possible for him to go East under the circumstances. He would very much like to see you. He is pleased to find Mr. Smith more in harmony with his general plan than he thought he might be." On the next day (February 20) Brown himself wrote as follows to his son : —

PETERBORO', N. Y., Feb. 20, 1858.

DEAR SON JOHN, — I am here with our good friends Gerrit Smith and wife, who, I am most happy to tell you, are ready to go in for a share in the whole trade. I will say (in the language of another), in regard to this most encouraging fact, " My soul doth magnify the Lord." I seem to be almost marvellously helped ; and to His name be praise ! I had to-day no particular thing to write, other than to let you share in my encouragement. I have been looking for a letter from you to be forwarded from Rochester ; and may get one to-day. When I get one, will write you further. I do not expect to remain here long, but shall be glad to have you write me here, enclosing to Caleb Calkins,[1] Esq., Peterboro', Madison County, N. Y. Jason and family well on the 8th.

Your affectionate father,   JOHN BROWN.

from among them, and that some of the Kansas people thought him insane. All this, combined with the complaints and intimations of Forbes, led me to imagine that Brown had some plan for an uprising of slaves ; but, if so, I supposed it would be on the Kansas border, or in some part of Missouri.

[1] This was the faithful clerk of Gerrit Smith, to whose hands most of

I have still need of all the help I can possibly get, but am greatly encouraged in asking for it. Mr. Smith thinks you might operate to more advantage in New England, about Boston, than by going to Washington, — say in the large country towns. I think he may be right. Do as you think best.

Yours ever,   J. B.

Theodore Parker and George Stearns being at the time unable to accept this second and pressing request from Brown for a meeting at Peterboro', I determined to go, and invited Colonel Higginson to join me at Worcester, February 20. But in fact I made the journey alone, and reached Canastota, ten miles from Peterboro', on the afternoon of Monday, February 22. There I either took the stage-coach, or was met by Mr. Smith's sleigh, and drove up over the hills to his house, where I arrived early in the evening of Washington's birthday. Brown had been there since the preceding Thursday, and had unfolded much of his plan to the Smiths. After dinner, and after a few minutes spent with other guests in the parlor, I went with Mr. Smith, John Brown, and my classmate Morton, to the room of Mr. Morton in the third story. Here, in the long winter evening which followed, the whole outline of Brown's campaign in Virginia was laid before our little council, to the astonishment and almost the dismay of those present. The constitution which he had drawn up for the government of his men, and of such territory as they might occupy, was exhibited by Brown, its provisions recited and explained, the proposed movements of his men indicated, and the middle of May was named as the time of the attack. To begin this hazardous adventure he asked for but eight hundred dollars, and would think himself rich with a thousand. Being questioned and opposed by his friends, he laid before them in detail his methods of organization and fortification ; of settlement in the South, if that were possible, and of retreat through the

his large pecuniary affairs were intrusted, and whose business it was in such matters as this to " hear and see, and say nothing." Morton, at that time the tutor of Mr. Smith's son, was born in Plymouth, Mass., of the Pilgrim stock.

North, if necessary ; and his theory of the way in which
such an invasion would be received in the country at large.
He desired from his friends a patient hearing of his statements, a candid opinion concerning his plan, and, if that
were favorable, then such aid in money and support as we
could give him. We listened until after midnight, proposing
objections and raising difficulties ; but nothing could shake
the purpose of the old Puritan. Every difficulty had been
foreseen and provided against in some manner ; the grand
difficulty of all, — the manifest hopelessness of undertaking
anything so vast with such slender means, — was met with
the text of Scripture : " If God be for us, who can be against
us ?" He had made nearly all his arrangements : he had so
many men enlisted, so many hundred weapons ; all he now
wanted was the small sum of money. With that he would
open his campaign in the spring, and he had no doubt that
the enterprise " would *pay*," as he said.

On the 23d of February the discussion was renewed, and,
as usually happened when he had time enough, Captain
Brown began to prevail over the objections of his friends.[1]
At any rate, they saw that they must either stand by him,
or leave him to dash himself alone against the fortress he
was determined to assault. To withhold aid would only
delay, not prevent him ; nothing short of betraying him to
the enemy would do that. As the sun was setting over the
snowy hills of the region where we met, I walked for an
hour with Gerrit Smith among those woods and fields (then
included in his broad manor) which his father had purchased
of the Indians and bequeathed to him. Brown was left at
home by the fire, discussing points of theology with Charles
Stewart, an old captain under Wellington, who also happened to be visiting at the house. Mr. Smith restated in
his eloquent way the daring propositions of Brown, whose
import he understood fully ; and then said in substance :
" You see how it is ; our dear old friend has made up his
mind to this course, and cannot be turned from it. We
cannot give him up to die alone ; we must support him. I

---

[1] " Ah, gentlemen," said Edwin Coppoc at Harper's Ferry, " you don't
know Captain Brown : when *he* wants a man to do a thing he does it."

will raise so many hundred dollars for him; you must lay
the case before your friends in Massachusetts and perhaps
they will do the same. I see no other way." For myself,
I had reached the same conclusion, and engaged to bring
the scheme at once to the attention of the three Massachusetts men to whom Brown had written, and also of Dr.
S. G. Howe, who had sometimes favored action almost as
extreme as this proposed by Brown. I returned to Boston
on the 25th of February, and on the same day communicated the enterprise to Theodore Parker and Wentworth
Higginson. At the suggestion of Parker, Brown, who had
gone to Brooklyn, N. Y., was invited to visit Boston secretly,
and did so the 4th of March, taking a room at the American
House, in Hanover Street, and remaining for the most part
in his room [1] during the four days of his stay. Mr. Parker
was deeply interested in the project, but not very sanguine of its success. He wished to see it tried, believing
that it must do good even if it failed. Brown remained at
the American House until Monday, March 8, when he departed for Philadelphia. On the 6th of March he wrote to
his son John from Boston : " My call here has met with a
most hearty response, so that I feel assured of at least tolerable success. I ought to be thankful for this. All has been
effected by quiet meeting of a few choice friends, it being
scarcely known that I have been in the city."

Before visiting Gerrit Smith, and while doubly occupied
in managing his delicate negotiation with Forbes, and arranging for a full disclosure of his purposes to his wealthy
friends, John Brown, from his hiding-place in Rochester,
addressed this pathetic letter to his household in the wintry
forest of North Elba : —

To his Family.

ROCHESTER, N. Y., Jan. 30, 1858.

MY DEAR WIFE AND CHILDREN, EVERY ONE, — I am (praised
be God !) once more in York State. Whether I shall be permitted
to visit you or not this winter or spring, I cannot now say ; but it is
some relief of mind to feel that I am again so near you. Possibly, if
I cannot go to see you, I may be able to devise some way for some

---

[1] This was No. 126, I remember.

one or more of you to meet me somewhere. The anxiety I feel to see my wife and children once more I am unable to describe. I want exceedingly to see my big baby and Ruth's baby, and to see how that little company of sheep look about this time. The cries of my poor sorrow-stricken despairing children, whose " tears on their cheeks " are ever in my eyes, and whose sighs are ever in my ears, may however prevent my enjoying the happiness I so much desire. But, courage, courage, courage ! — the great work of my life (the unseen Hand that " guided me, and who has indeed holden my right hand, may hold it still," though I have not known him at all as I ought) I may yet see accomplished (God helping), and be permitted to return, and " rest at evening."

O my daughter Ruth ! could any plan be devised whereby you could let Henry go " to school " (as you expressed it in your letter to him while in Kansas), I would rather now have him " for another term " than to have a hundred average scholars. I have a particular and very important, but not dangerous, place for him to fill in the " school," and I know of no man living so well adapted to fill it. I am quite confident some way can be devised so that you and your children could be with him, and be quite happy even, and safe; but God forbid me to flatter you into trouble ! I did not do it before. My dear child, could you face such music if, on a full explanation, Henry could be satisfied that his family might be safe ? I would make a similar inquiry of my own dear wife ; but I have kept her tumbling here and there over a stormy and tempestuous sea for so many years that I cannot ask her such a question. The natural ingenuity of Salmon in connection with some experience he and Oliver have both had, would point him out as the next best man I could now select ; but I am dumb in his case, as also in the case of Watson and all my other sons. Jason's qualifications are, some of them, like Henry's also.

Do not noise it about that I am in these parts, and direct to N. Hawkins, care of Frederick Douglass, Rochester, N. Y. I want to hear how you are all supplied with winter clothing, boots, etc.

God bless you all !

Your affectionate husband and father, JOHN BROWN.

Ruth's reply to this letter should not fail to be quoted here : —

Ruth Thompson to John Brown.

NORTH ELBA, Feb. 20, 1858.

MY DEAR FATHER, — Your letter of January 30 we received this week, it having lain in the postoffice a week. Oliver went to the office and got our news; there were two letters for me, but the postmaster did not give him yours. We did not get it this week in time to answer it, or we should have done so immediately. I am sorry for such a delay. We were rejoiced to hear that you were so near us, and we hope that you can visit us yet before leaving York State. It really seems hard that we cannot see you, when you have been so long from home; yet we are glad that you still feel encouraged. Dear father, you have asked me rather of a hard question. I want to answer you wisely, but hardly know how. I cannot bear the thought of Henry leaving me again; yet I know I am selfish. When I think of my poor despised sisters, that are deprived of both husband and children, I feel deeply for them; and were it not for my little children, I would go almost anywhere with Henry, if by going I could do them any good. What is the place you wish him to fill? How long would you want him? Would my going be of any service to him or you? I should be very glad to be with him, if it would not be more expense than what good we could do. I say *we;* could I not do something for the cause? Henry's feelings are the same that they have been. He says: "Tell father that I think he places too high an estimate on my qualifications as a scholar; and tell him I should like much to see him." I wish we could see you, and then we should know better what to do; but will you not write to us and give us a full explanation of what you want him to do? . . . Please write often.

Your affectionate daughter,

RUTH THOMPSON.

In a letter of February 24 from Gerrit Smith's house, Brown wrote to his wife: "I have been here for a short time, and am making middling good progress, I think. Mr. Smith and family go all lengths with me." A week later he was more explicit: —

To his Wife.

NEW YORK, March 2, 1858.

MY DEAR WIFE, — I received yours of the 17th of February yesterday; was very glad of it, and to know that you had got the ten dollars safe. I am having a constant series of both great encouragements and discouragements, but am yet able to say, in view of all, "hitherto the Lord hath helped me." I shall send Salmon something as soon as I can, and will try to get you the articles you mention. I find a much more earnest feeling among the colored people

than ever before ; but that is by no means unusual. On the whole,
the language of Providence to me would certainly seem to say,
" Try on." I flatter myself that I may be able to go and see you
again before a great while ; but I may not be able. I long to see
you all. All were well with John and Jason a few days since. I
had a good visit with Mr. Sanborn at Gerrit Smith's a few days ago.
It would be no very strange thing if he should join me. May God
abundantly bless you all ! No one writes me but you.

Your affectionate husband,

JOHN BROWN.

As this letter shows, Brown had left Peterboro' in order to visit and confer with the colored people of New
York, Brooklyn, and Philadelphia concerning his main
plan. He was to have visited Philadelphia with Douglass
before going to Boston ; but while in Brooklyn he received
this letter from Douglass : —

SYRACUSE, Feb. 27, 1858.

MY DEAR FRIEND, — When we parted, we were to meet in Phila-
delphia on Friday, March 5. I write now to postpone going to
Philadelphia until Wednesday, March 10. Please write me at
Rochester if this will do, and if you wish me to come at that time.
You can, I hope, find work enough in and about New York up to
that date. Please make my warmest regards to Mrs. and Mr.
Gloucester, and accept that and more for yourself.

FRED DOUGLASS.

JOHN BROWN, ESQ.

Brown answered this note March 2, and had previously
written me from Brooklyn as follows : —

BROOKLYN, Feb. 26, 1858.

F. B. SANBORN, ESQ., Concord, Mass.

MY DEAR FRIEND, — I want to put into the hands of my young
men copies of Plutarch's " Lives," Irving's " Life of Washington,"
the best-written Life of Napoleon, and other similar books, together
with maps and statistics of States. Could you not find persons who
might be induced to contribute old copies (or other ones) of that
character, or find some person who would be willing to undertake to
collect some for me ? I also want to get a quantity of best white
cotton drilling, — some hundred pieces, if I can get it. The use of
this article I will hereafter explain. Mr. Morton will forward your

letter here to me. Anything you may be disposed to say to me within two or three days please enclose to James N. Gloucester, No. 265 Bridge Street, Brooklyn, N. Y.

Very respectfully your friend,

JOHN BROWN.

P. S. Persons who would devote their time to the good work, as agents in different parts, might do incalculable good. Can you find any such ?

Yours,   J. B.

From Gerrit Smith's house, the day I departed for Boston, Brown wrote to me one of those touching and prophetic letters which so seldom flowed from his pen, and which I have cherished as the most complete evidence of his confidence in my friendship and unison with him : —

John Brown to F. B. Sanborn.

PETERBORO', N. Y., Feb. 24, 1858.

MY DEAR FRIEND, — Mr. Morton has taken the liberty of saying to me that you felt half inclined to make a common cause with me. I greatly rejoice at this ; for I believe when you come to look at the ample field I labor in, and the rich harvest which not only this entire country but the whole world during the present and future generations may reap from its successful cultivation, you will feel that you are out of your element until you find you are in it, an entire unit. What an inconceivable amount of good you might so effect by your counsel, your example, your encouragement, your natural and acquired ability for active service ! And then, how very little we can possibly lose ! Certainly the cause is enough to *live* for, if not to —— for. I have only had this one opportunity, in a life of nearly sixty years ; and could I be continued ten times as long again, I might not again have another equal opportunity. God has honored but comparatively a very small part of mankind with any possible chance for such mighty and soul-satisfying rewards. But, my dear friend, if you should make up your mind to do so, I trust it will be wholly from the promptings of your own spirit, after having thoroughly counted the cost. I would flatter no man into such a measure, if I could do it ever so easily.

I expect nothing but to " endure hardness ;" but I expect to effect a mighty conquest, even though it be like the last victory of Samson. I felt for a number of years, in earlier life, a steady, strong

Peterboro, N.Y. 24th Feb, 1858.

F B Sanborn Esqr

My Dear Friend

Mr Morton
has taken the liberty of saying to me that you felt ½
inclined to make a common cause with me. I
greatly rejoice at this; for I believe when you come to
look at the ample field I labour in; & the rich
harvest which (not only this entire country, but) the whole
world during the present & future generations may reap
from its successful cultivation: you will feel that
you are out of your element until you find you are
in it; an entire Unit. What an inconceivable amount
of good you might so effect; by your counsel, your example, your encouragement, your natural, & acquired ability; for active service. And then how
very little we can possibly loose? Certainly the cause
is enough to live for: if not to   for. I have only had
this one opportunity in a life of nearly Sixty years, &
could I be continued Ten times as long again, I might
not again have another equal opportunity. God has honored but comparatively a very small part of mankind with any

possible chance for such mighty & soul satisfying re—
wards. But my dear friend if you should make up
your mind to do so I trust it will be wholly from the promptings of your own spirit; after having thoroughly counted
the cost. I would flatter no man into such a measure if
I could do it ever so easily. I expect nothing but to "endure
hardness": but I expect to effect a mighty conquest even though it be
like the last victory of Samson. I felt for a number of
years in earlier life: a steady, strong, desire: to die: but since
I saw any prospect of becoming a "reaper" in the great harvest I
have not only felt quite willing to live: but have enjoyed
life much; & am now rather anxious to live for a few
years more.   Your Sincere Friend
                        John Brown

desire to die; but since I saw any prospect of becoming a " reaper "
in the great harvest, I have not only felt quite willing to live, but
have enjoyed life much; and am now rather anxious to live for a
few years more.

Your sincere friend,

JOHN BROWN.[1]

Till I follow my noble friend to that other world on
which his hopes were fixed, I can never read this letter
without emotion. Yet it did not persuade me to comply
with his wish. Long accustomed to guide my life by lead-
ings and omens from that shrine whose oracles may destroy
but can never deceive, I listened in vain, through months
of doubt and anxiety, for a clear and certain call. But it
was revealed to me that no confidence could be too great,
no trust nor affection too extreme, towards this aged poor
man whom the Lord had chosen as his champion. In any
event of his designs, — had he failed as conspicuously as
he has succeeded, — I could still have had nothing to regret
in the little aid I afforded him, except that I could not aid
him more. The work upon which he entered was dangerous, and even desperate; none saw this better than those
who stood with him: but his commission was from a Court
that could bear him out, whatever the result. It is a
maxim even of worldly prudence that desperate diseases
require desperate remedies, — *in rebus arduis ac tenui spe
fortissima quæque consilia sunt optima.* But it is also the

---

[1] This letter, which is now in possession of Mrs. Stearns, was received
by me soon after my return to Concord. On my way through Boston I
had communicated to Theodore Parker (at his house in Exeter Place, to
which I had taken Brown in January, 1857, and where he met Mr. Garrison and other Abolitionists) the substance of Brown's plan; and upon
receiving the letter I transmitted it to Parker. He retained it, so that it
was out of my possession in October, 1859, when I destroyed most of the
letters of Brown and others which could compromise our friends. Some
time afterward, probably in 1862, when Parker had been dead two years,
my letters to him came back to me, and among them this epistle. It has
to me an extreme value, from its association with the memory of my best
and noblest friends; but in itself it is also a remarkable utterance. That
it did not draw me into the field as one of Brown's band was due to the
circumstance that the interests of other persons were then too much in my
hands and in my thoughts to permit a change of my whole course of life.

privilege of heroism, as of beauty and of sanctity, to impose its own conditions upon the beholder: they claim and they receive their due homage. A casual glance, a frivolous mind, might be deceived in John Brown. His homely garb and plain manners did not betoken greatness, but neither could they disguise it. That antique and magnanimous character which amid wounds and fetters and ferocious insults suddenly fastened the gaze of the whole world; those words of startling simplicity uttered among the corpses of his men, or before his judges, or in his prison cell, and listened to by all mankind, — all things that were peculiar to John Brown and distinguished him among the multitude, lost nothing of their force when he was seen at nearer view and heard within the walls of a chamber. That impressive personality, whose echoes so long filled the air of our camps, lacked nothing of its effect upon the few who came within his influence before the world recognized him. We saw this lonely and obscure old man choosing poverty before wealth, renouncing the ties of affection, throwing away his ease, his reputation, and his life for the sake of a despised race and for " zeal to his country's ancient liberties." Moved by this example, shamed by this generosity, was it to be imagined that young men and devoted Abolitionists would examine cautiously the grounds of prudence, or timidly follow a scrupulous conservatism? Without accepting Brown's plans as reasonable, we were prepared to second them merely because they were his, — under the impulse of that sentiment to which Andrew afterward gave utterance when he said: " Whatever might be thought of John Brown's acts, John Brown himself was *right*." Three courses were open to us, — to aid him so far as we could; to discountenance and oppose his plans; or to remain neutral. Of course there was no thought of betraying his confidence, nor of treating him as a madman incapable of counsel. And it was soon evident that where Brown was concerned there could be no neutrality and no indifference.

In the winter and spring of 1858 the Kansas rifles, pistols, etc., were in the care of John Brown, Jr., to whom his father wrote from Mr. Smith's house, Feb. 23, 1858 : —

" I have become satisfied that it will be entirely best to have all
my freight removed from Conneaut, and stored away safe with very
quiet friends, and all marks removed from the boxes.[1] I have lately
learned of some circumstances which satisfy me that this will certainly
be a prudent measure; and I wish you to effect it as soon as you can
without extra effort and sacrifice. Have not heard from you for some
days. Write N. Hawkins, care of F. Douglass."

The arrival of Brown in Boston was thus indicated,
Parker being the first to learn it : —

Brown to Theodore Parker.

American House, Boston, March 4, 1858.

My dear Sir, — I shall be most happy to see you at my room
(126) in this house, at any and at all hours that may suit your own
convenience, or that of friends. Mr. Sanborn asked me to be here
by Friday evening, and as I was anxious to have all the time I could
get, I came on at once. Please call by yourself and with friends as
you can. Please inquire for Mr. (not Captain) Brown, of New
York.   Your friend,   John Brown.

Parker was one of the first persons who called on Brown
during his short visit to Boston, which it was then supposed would be his last until he should have struck his
great blow in Virginia. I had come from Gerrit Smith's
house directly to Parker's house in Boston, and had communicated Brown's plans to Parker at Brown's request and
Smith's. On the same day at Worcester,[2] and the next day
at Boston, I told Higginson and Dr. S. G. Howe, as Brown
desired me to do. I asked him what I should say to Mr.

---

[1] See note at the end of Chapter XIII., for the disposal of these arms
and their removal to Harper's Ferry.

[2] Before Brown had quite converted us to his support at Peterboro', on
the 23d of February, I began a letter to Higginson which was never finished, but on the back of which Brown that day drew rude outlines of his
Virginia forts. I have this sheet still ; the fragment runs thus : "Dear
Friend, — You ought to be here to see our friend Hawkins, who is about
entering largely into the wool business, in which he has been more or less
engaged all his life. He now has a plan — the result of many years' careful study — " Here the note ends ; and on the other side of the sheet are
Brown's pencillings, above which I then wrote, "Woollen machinery, invented by N. Hawkins."

Stearns. Brown replied that he would make the communication himself in Boston, as he did about March 5. He desired that Wendell Phillips should not be informed, nor did he ever reveal his plans fully to Phillips. On the succeeding Friday, Saturday, and Sunday he saw Parker, Dr. Howe, Mr. Stearns, Mr. Higginson, and two or three other persons. He did not think it prudent to show himself at Parker's Sunday-evening reception, on the 7th of March, as he had done when in Boston the year before; and therefore he wrote Mr. Parker a letter, which I carried to him that afternoon.

Brown to Theodore Parker.

BOSTON, MASS., March 7, 1858.

MY DEAR SIR, — Since you know I have an almost countless brood of poor hungry chickens to " scratch for," you will not reproach me for scratching even on the Sabbath. At any rate, I trust God will not. I want you to undertake to provide a substitute for an address you saw last season, directed to the officers and soldiers of the United States Army. The ideas contained in that address I of course like, for I furnished the skeleton. I never had the ability to clothe those ideas in language at all to satisfy myself; and I was by no means satisfied with the style of that address, and do not know as I can give any correct idea of what I want. I will, however, try.

In the first place it must be short, or it will not be generally read. It must be in the simplest or plainest language, without the least affectation of the scholar about it, and yet be worded with great clearness and power. The anonymous writer must (in the language of the Paddy) be " afther others," and not " afther himself at all, at all." If the spirit that communicated Franklin's Poor Richard (or some other good spirit) would dictate, I think it would be quite as well employed as the " dear sister spirits " have been for some years past. The address should be appropriate, and particularly adapted to the peculiar circumstances we anticipate, and should look to the actual change of service from that of Satan to the service of God. It should be, in short, a most earnest and powerful appeal to men's sense of right and to their feelings of humanity. Soldiers are men, and no man can certainly calculate the value and importance of getting a single " nail into old Captain Kidd's chest." It should be provided beforehand, and be ready in advance to distribute by all persons, male and female, who may be disposed to favor the right.

I also want a similar short address, appropriate to the peculiar circumstances, intended for all persons, old and young, male and female, slaveholding and non-slaveholding, to be sent out broadcast over the entire nation. So by every male and female prisoner on being set at liberty, and to be read by them during confinement. I know that men will listen, and reflect too, under such circumstances. Persons will hear your antislavery lectures and abolition lectures when they have become virtually slaves themselves. The impressions made on prisoners by kindness and plain dealing, instead of barbarous and cruel treatment, such as they might give, and instead of being slaughtered like wild reptiles, as they might very naturally expect, are not only powerful but lasting. Females are susceptible of being carried away entirely by the kindness of an intrepid and magnanimous soldier, even when his bare name was but a terror the day previous.[1] Now, dear sir, I have told you about as well as I know how, what I am anxious at once to secure. Will you write the tracts, or get them written, so that I may commence colporteur?

Very respectfully your friend,

JOHN BROWN.

P. S. If I should never see you again, please drop me a line (enclosed to Stephen Smith, Esq., Lombard Street, Philadelphia), at once, saying what you will encourage me to expect. You are at liberty to make any prudent use of this to stir up any friend.

Yours for the right,

J. B.

Perhaps Brown was not aware how hard was the task imposed by these masterly directions in the art of writing. Parker, who was then overweighted with work, never undertook to write the tracts desired, nor were they written by any one else; but Parker sent Brown from his library on this Sunday the report of General McClellan on the European armies, which was then a new book, and was thought likely to be of service to Brown. At the same time Brown praised Plutarch as a book he had read with great profit for

---

[1] A Kansas newspaper said in 1859: "At the sacking of Osawatomie one of the most bitter proslavery men in Lykins County was killed. His name was Ed. Timmons. Sometime afterward Brown stopped at the loghouse where Timmons had lived. His widow and children were there, and in great destitution. He inquired into their wants, relieved their distresses, and supported them until their friends in Missouri, informed through Brown of the condition of Mrs. Timmons, had time to come to her and carry her to her former home. Mrs. Timmons fully appreciated the great kindness thus shown her, but never learned that John Brown was her benefactor."

29

its military and moral lessons, and particularly mentioned the life of Sertorius, the Roman commander who so long carried on a partisan warfare in Spain. He wished, as he had before written me, to get a few copies of Plutarch for his men to read in camp, and inquired particularly about the best edition.

Although Brown communicated freely to the four persons just named his plans of attack and defence in Virginia, it is not known that he spoke to any but me of his purpose to surprise the arsenal and town of Harper's Ferry. Both Dr. Howe and Mr. Stearns testified before Mason's committee, in 1860, that they were ignorant of Brown's plan of attack; which was true so far as the place and manner of beginning the campaign were concerned. It is probable that in 1858 Brown had not definitely resolved to seize Harper's Ferry; yet he spoke of it to me beside his coal-fire in the American House, putting it as a question, rather, without expressing his own purpose. I questioned him a little about it; but it then passed from my mind, and I did not think of it again until the attack had been made, a year and a half afterward. That it was then seriously a part of his plan may be inferred, however, from letters to his son John written from Douglass's house, Feb. 4–5, 1858, in which he said: "I have been thinking that I would like to have you make a trip to Bedford, Chambersburg, Gettysburg, and Uniontown, in Pennsylvania, travelling slowly along, and inquiring out every man on the way, or every family of the right stripe, and getting acquainted with them as much as you could. When you look at the location of those places, you will readily perceive the advantage of getting up some acquaintance in those parts." After advising his son to go to Washington and call on such members of Congress as Mr. Giddings and John Sherman of Ohio, Dr. Chaffee and Mr. Burlingame of Massachusetts, and Mr. Olin, of Troy, N. Y., in hopes to raise five hundred or one thousand dollars by their aid for secret service ("Mr. Burlingame gave me fifty dollars at Boston"), Brown writes: "You can say to our friends that I am out from Kansas for that express purpose. I think Mr. Sherman and Giddings will give you a good lift. Eli Thayer is a particular friend. I have no doubt he would

hook on his team. . . . Do not lisp my plans or theories of
any kind, other than by mere hints to such persons as will
first commit themselves. You may say we are as strong
Abolitionists as Gerrit Smith." March 4, Brown wrote
from Boston: "As it may require some time to hunt out
friends at Bedford, Chambersburg, Gettysburg, Hagerstown,
Md., *or even Harper's Ferry, Va.*, I would like to have you
arrange your business so as to set out very soon, unless you
hear to the contrary from me right away. Have pretty
much concluded not to have you go to Washington. I have
but little 'trust in princes' myself; still I have no doubt
but something might be done there. I expect to go from
here to Philadelphia with our Rochester friend in three or
four days." March 6, he wrote again from Boston: "My
call here has met with a most hearty response, so that I feel
assured of at least tolerable success. I ought to be thankful
for this; all has been effected by quiet meetings of a few
choice friends, it being scarcely known that I have been
in the city. I go from here to Philadelphia, to be there
by the 10th instant. I want you to meet me there, if
possible, on or before the 15th, as I will wait until then
to see or learn from you. (Day before yesterday, when I
wrote, I did not fully understand what my success would
be here.) I expect to meet our Rochester and other choice
friends there, and to be accompanied by one, at least, from
here."

John Brown, Jr., accordingly met his father, with Douglass, Henry Highland Garnet, Stephen Smith, and other colored men at Philadelphia, conferred with them there, and
then went on with his father to New York and New Haven, where they called (March 18) at the house of Mr. W. H.
Russell. From New Haven they went, March 19, to New
York, and thence to North Elba, where they arrived March
23, having travelled on foot from Elizabethtown to save
time and money. They remained at North Elba a few days,
and reached the house of Gerrit Smith, at Peterboro', as Mr.
Smith's diary shows, April 2, 1858.[1] They remained there

---

[1] About a month before the Forbes disclosures, which caused the postponement of the attack until 1859.

from ten o'clock that day till the next morning at six, and reported to Mr. Smith ("who seemed then fully acquainted with the Virginia plan, and in hearty sympathy with it," says John Brown, Jr.) what had been said and done at Boston and Philadelphia. I had already written to Mr. Smith, according to our agreement of February 23, what Brown's Boston friends could and would do. Both father and son discussed the plan with Mr. Smith in his study, and Mrs. Smith took part in the conversation, as she had done when I was at Peterboro' six weeks before. During the afternoon Brown and Smith walked out to Mr. Smith's former home, a mile or two away, and talked over the scheme alone. When they returned, Mr. Smith (says John Brown, Jr.,) "was buoyant and hopeful about it, and showed great animation and interest."

From Peterboro' the father and son went to the house of Douglass, in Rochester, where they separated about April 4, 1858, John Brown proceeding at once to St. Catherine's in Canada, whence he wrote to his son on the 8th of April as follows : —

"I came on here direct with J. W. Loguen the day after you left Rochester. I am succeeding, to all appearance, beyond my expectations. Harriet Tubman hooked on his whole team at once.[1] He (Harriet) is the most of a man, naturally, that I ever met with. There is the most abundant material, and of the right quality, in this quarter, beyond all doubt. Do not forget to write Mr. Case (near Rochester) at once about hunting up every person and family of the reliable kind about, at, or near Bedford, Chambersburg, Gettysburg, and Carlisle, in Pennsylvania, and also Hagerstown and vicinity, Maryland, and *Harper's Ferry, Va.* The names and residences of all, I want to have sent me at Lindenville."

This shows that Brown was constantly thinking of the place where he finally made the attack ; yet John Brown, Jr., declares that he did not suppose that to be the place fixed upon, but some less accessible spot in the mountains near by. He testified on this point in 1867 : "According to the plans of John Brown, as explained to me by him, and talked over at an interview between John Brown, Gerrit

[1] This was a woman. See p. 453.

Smith, and myself in the summer of 1859,[1] Harper's Ferry was not designated as the place of attack, nor was any particular place named; but it was expressly stated that the first blow would be struck at some place in Virginia or Maryland; and the news of the attack on Harper's Ferry surprised me, both on account of the place upon which it had been made and the time when it occurred, as I did not expect it at so early a period."

On the 14th of April Brown was still at St. Catherine's among the Canadian fugitives from slavery. The woman of whom he spoke in his letter of April 8 was temporarily living there among those she had helped away from bondage; but her more permanent home was in Auburn, N. Y., on some property she had bought of Senator Seward. She was fully conversant with Brown's plans, and did what she could in her wild sibylline way to further them. From Canada he went to Chicago, where he was on the 25th of April. But on his way westward he sent this cautionary letter to North Elba: —

To his Family.

INGERSOL, CANADA WEST, April 16, 1858.

DEAR WIFE AND CHILDREN, EVERY ONE, — Since I wrote you I have thought it possible, though not probable, that some persons might be disposed to hunt for any property I may be supposed to possess, on account of liabilities I incurred while concerned with Mr. Perkins. Such claims I ought not to pay if I had ever so much given me for my service in Kansas, as most of you well know I gave up all I then had to Mr. Perkins while with him. I think if Henry and Ruth have not yet made out a deed, as was talked of, they had better not do it at present, but merely sign a receipt I now

---

[1] Allusion is here made to a second visit of John Brown and his son together at Peterboro' a few months before the attack. When in consultation with Mr. Smith, says John Brown, Jr., "My father informed him that he had so far got his plans perfected that within a few months at least he should strike the blow. The place in Pennsylvania at which arms, etc., should be first sent had been fixed upon previous to this time. It was Chambersburg; and the whole plan, as far as then matured, was fully made known to Mr. Smith. The exact place had not been determined on, but it had been determined to commence operations in the vicinity of Harper's Ferry."

send, which can be held by Watson; and I also think that when the contract of Gerrit Smith with Franklin and Samuel Thompson is found, he had better lay it by carefully with the receipt, and that all the family had better decline saying anything about their land matters. Should any disturbance ever be made, it will most likely come directly or indirectly through a scoundrel by the name of Warren, who defrauded Mr. Perkins and me out of several thousand dollars. He may set persons we suppose to be friends (who may, in fact, be so) to inquiring out matters. It can do no harm to decline saying much about such things; you can very properly say the land belongs to the family.[1] If a deed has been made by Henry and Ruth, it need not be recorded at present. I expect to leave for Iowa in a few days; write me at Chicago, directing to Jason Brown, care of John Jones, Esq., Box 764. May God bless you all!

Your affectionate husband and father,

JOHN BROWN.

P. S. Show this to John when he gets on. Henry and Ruth should both sign the receipt.

SPRINGDALE, IOWA, April 27, 1858.

DEAR WIFE AND CHILDREN, EVERY ONE, — We start from here to-day, and shall write you again when we stop, which will be in two or three days. I have just bought eight barrels of flour for you, which will be shipped to Watson, care of James A. Allen, Westport. You can divide it among the different branches of the family so as to make all as comfortable as may be. If I should not be able to send you money to pay the freight, you can perhaps sell some of it to some of your neighbors for cash, and pay the freight in that way. I shall try to send you some pork and leather soon. I am trying to arrange so as to have Henry come out to see me at Pennsylvania with Oliver (and any others), if it can be consistently done. I shall write Oliver and any others when and where to find us, and also provide about travelling expenses. They will not probably be called on before the middle of May, and possibly not so soon. May God bless you all! Write Jason Brown at Chatham, Canada West.

Yours ever,

JOHN BROWN.

P. S. The flour, taken either by John, Henry, Watson, or Salmon, may be credited to their mother. Do not fail to write, all of you, — Ellen as well as the others.   Yours,

J. B.

---

[1] This relates to the farms bought with the subscription of one thousand dollars from Boston in 1857.

CHICAGO, ILL., April 28, 1858.

DEAR WIFE AND CHILDREN, EVERY ONE, — The letters of Henry, Ruth, and Oliver are all received, and most glad were we to get them. I am entirely satisfied with the arrangement about who shall go out surveying. Would it be entirely satisfactory all round to have Henry manage the farms for both families, and let Watson go with Oliver and friend Hinkley? Say frankly, wife and all concerned. Ten of the company got here this morning; three more will probably be on to-morrow. We that are now here leave for Canada West this evening. Owen is here, and is well. Write as directed before. I now enclose two drafts (amount, twenty-five dollars) to help pay travelling expenses, and shall send more. Acknowledge these. Will write again soon. God bless you all!

Your affectionate husband and father,

JOHN BROWN.

CHATHAM, CANADA WEST, May 12, 1858.

MY DEAR WIFE AND CHILDREN, EVERY ONE, — I have just received Oliver's letter of the 14th of April; also one from wife and Oliver, of the 5th inst. I am most glad of them; and I am thankful to be able to say that all here were well yesterday, when Owen and some others left for the eastward. I with others remain behind to wait for funds to arrive. I have also a letter from John, dated April 22, enclosing lines from Forbes, with printed slips attached. It seems now, by what we can learn, that his management may occasion some hindrance; that being the case, you at home will have the more time to prepare, and will wait for further advice in the matter. It would seem as though F. has a correspondent somewhere. Can it be at Lindenville or New York? I wish John would think over the matter, and see if he can get any light on the subject, and write me, enclosing what F. has lately written him, and also the substance of what he has lately written F. I suspect some one in Dr. McCune Smith's confidence is furnishing F. with information. It must be traced out, and the utmost care observed in doing it, as well as prudence exercised in all that is said, written, or done. I shall write you as often as I can, and shall assist you all I can. I cannot say what either flour or pork will be worth when you get them; you can easily find that out when you have them. Shall send you more money as soon as I can. It may be best to sell off much of the flour. I expect to leave here shortly, but I want to hear from you right away. Enclose in a sealed envelope, the outer one directed to James M. Bell, Chatham, as above. Was very glad to hear from Ellen. May God bless and finally save you all! Had a good Abolition convention here, from different parts, on the 8th and 10th inst. Constitution slightly amended and adopted, and society organized. Great unanimity prevailed. I hope you may be able to get the old granite monument home this summer.

Your affectionate husband and father,

JOHN BROWN.

CHATHAM, CANADA WEST, May 25, 1858.

DEAR WIFE AND CHILDREN, EVERY ONE, — Oliver's letter of the 19th is just received. I have to commend him for his promptitude in replying to mine, as well as the comprehensiveness, brevity, and spirit of that reply. We are completely nailed down at present, for want of funds; and we may be obliged to remain inactive for months yet, for the same reason. You must all learn to be patient, — or, at least, I hope you will. If you have not been obliged to use the two drafts (amount, twenty-five dollars) before you get this, do try and hold them till I write you further. I have heard nothing from John since in March, and feel quite anxious on his account. You need not reply till further advised.

Your affectionate husband and father,

JOHN BROWN.

Meanwhile the Boston friends of Brown were receiving plain information that Forbes was at Washington, betraying the Virginia plan to Republican Senators, and perhaps to members of the proslavery Administration. Startled by this, some of us wrote to Brown at Chatham, May 10, to which he soon replied thus : —

John Brown to F. B. Sanborn.

CHATHAM, CANADA WEST, May 14, 1858.

MY DEAR SIR, — Your much-prized letter of the 10th inst. is received. I have only time to say at this moment that as it is an invariable rule with me to be governed by circumstances, or, in other words, not to do anything while I do not know what to do, none of our friends need have any fears in relation to hasty or rash steps being taken by us. As knowledge is said to be power, we propose to become possessed of more knowledge. We have many reasons for begging our Eastern friends to keep clear of F. personally, unless he throws himself upon them. We have those who are thoroughly posted up to put on his track, and we beg to be allowed to do so. We also beg our friends to supply us with three or four hundred dollars without delay, pledging ourselves not to act other than to secure perfect knowledge of facts in regard to what F. has really done, or will do, so that we may ourselves know how we ought to act. None of us here or with you should be hasty, or decide the course to be taken, while under excitement. " In all thy ways acknowledge Him, and He shall direct thy paths." A good cause is sure to be safe in the hands of an all-good, all-wise, and all-powerful Director and Father. Dear Sir, please send this to the friends at Boston and Worcester at once ; and in the mean time send me on a plain copy of all that F. may hereafter write and say. The copy, together with fifteen dollars, is received. Direct all communications on outside envelope to James M. Bell, Chatham, Canada West; the inside, sealed, to Jason Brown.

Yours ever.

(No signature.)

P. S. You can say with perfect truth to F. that you do not know what has become of me ; and you might ask him when he last heard from me, and where I was at the time.

The narration must now go back a few weeks in order to take up events as they occurred at the East while Brown was making his arrangements for a foray in Virginia, by visiting Canada and the West.

Brown's first request in 1858 was for a fund of a thousand dollars only ; with this in hand he promised to take the field either in April or May. Mr. Stearns acted as treasurer of this fund, and before the 1st of May nearly the whole amount had been paid in or subscribed, — Stearns contributing three hundred dollars, and the rest of our committee smaller sums. It soon appeared, however, that the amount named would be too small, and Brown's movements were embarrassed from lack of money before the disclosures of Forbes came to his knowledge. I do not find among my papers the precise language of Forbes's threats, but the effect of them is visible enough in the letters extant. On the 20th of April, 1858, I had written thus to Higginson of the secret committee : —

" I have lately had two letters from Mr. Hawkins, who has just left Canada for the West, on business connected with his enterprise. He has found in Canada several good men for shepherds, and, if not embarrassed by want of means, expects to turn his flock loose about the 15th of May. He has received four hundred and ten dollars of the five hundred guaranteed him in Massachusetts, but wants more; and we must try to make up to him the other five hundred dollars. Part of it is pledged, and the rest ought to be got, though with some difficulty. . . . Hawkins's address is 'Jason Brown,' under cover to John Jones, Chicago. He has gone West to move his furniture and bring on his hands. He has received two hundred and sixty dollars from other sources than our friends, and is raising more elsewhere, but got little in New York or Philadelphia."

On the 28th of April Brown was still at Chicago, ignorant of Forbes's treachery, and was on his way a day or two later, with a dozen or twenty "shepherds," for the "market" at Chatham in Canada, where he wrote his Massachusetts friends to meet him. But just then came a letter to me from Forbes, followed by one to Dr. Howe, threatening to make the matter public. On the 2d of May, Dr. Howe, Mr. Stearns, and myself met for consultation on the new aspect of affairs presented by these letters from Washington, where Forbes then was. Parker was also consulted on the same day, and I wrote the result (May 5) to Higginson as follows : —

" It looks as if the project must, for the present, be deferred, for I find by reading Forbes's epistles to the doctor that he knows the details of the plan, and even knows (what very few do) that the doctor, Mr. Stearns, and myself are informed of it. How he got this knowledge is a mystery. He demands that Hawkins be dismissed as agent, and *himself* or some other be put in his place, threatening otherwise to make the business public. Theodore Parker and G. L. Stearns think the plan must be deferred till another year ; the doctor does not think so, and I am in doubt, inclining to the opinion of the two former."

On the 7th of May Gerrit Smith wrote me : [1] " It seems to me that in these circumstances Brown must go no further, and so I write him. I never was convinced of the wisdom of his scheme. But as things now stand, it seems to me it would be madness to attempt to execute it. Colonel Forbes would make such an attempt a certain and most disastrous failure. I write Brown *this evening*." On the 9th

---

[1] This letter is now in Colonel Higginson's possession.

of May Higginson wrote to Parker a brief note from Brattleboro, protesting against delay. "I regard any postponement," he said, "as simply abandoning the project; for if we give it up now, at the command or threat of H. F., it will be the same next year. The only way is to circumvent the man somehow (if he cannot be restrained in his malice). When the thing is well started, who cares what he says?" He soon after wrote more fully to Parker, giving many arguments against delay. Parker replied: "If you knew all we do about 'Colonel' Forbes, you would think differently. Can't you see the wretch in New York?" At the same time Dr. Howe wrote to Higginson: "T. P. will tell you about matters. They have held a different view from the one I have taken, which agrees mainly with yours. I think that the would-be traitor is now on the wrong track. I told him some truth, which he will think to be false [1] (for he

[1] Dr. Howe wrote to Forbes as follows : " I said to Senator Sumner that I *had confidence* in the *integrity* and ability of Captain Brown ; but it is utterly absurd to infer from that any responsibility for his acts. I have confidence in the integrity and ability of scores and hundreds of men for whose words and acts I am in no wise responsible. I never made myself responsible, as a member of the Kansas Committee, or as an individual, neither legally nor morally, for any contract between Captain Brown and you. I was an active member of the committee from its formation until it ceased active operations (which was long, long ago), and never heard of any contract with you ; and I know that the committee never delegated power to any one to bind it by any legal or even moral obligation with you. So the brains are out of that allegation, and I will not heed any ghosts of it which you may parade before me or the public. Your mistaken notion about my being in any way responsible for Captain Brown's actions is the key, I suppose, to certain enigmatical allusions in your last letter to some projected expedition of his ; as though I was to be responsible through all time for him ! I infer from your language that you have obtained (in confidence) some information respecting an expedition which you think to be commendable, provided *you* could manage it, but which you will *betray* and *denounce* if he does not give it up ! You are, sir, the guardian of your own honor ; but I trust that for your children's sake, at least, you will never let your passion lead you to a course that might make them blush. In order, however, to disabuse you of any lingering notion that I, or any of the members of the late Kansas Committee (whom I know intimately) have any responsibility for Captain Brown's actions, I wish to say that the very last communication I sent to him was in order to signify the earnest wish of certain gentlemen, whom you name as his supporters (in your letter and in the

thinks evil), and he will probably be bungling about in the
dark and hesitating until the period for his doing harm has
passed.   Forbes has disclosed what he knows to Senator
Seward, or *says* he has." A few days after this, Dr. Howe
also admitted that the enterprise must be postponed.   I
was in almost daily consultation with him, and on the 18th
of May I wrote to Higginson : " Wilson as well as Hale and
Seward, and God knows how many more, have heard about
the plot from Forbes.   To go on in the face of this is mere
madness, and I place myself fully on the side of Parker,
Stearns, and Dr. Howe.   Mr. Stearns and the doctor will
see Hawkins in New York this week, and settle matters
finally."

Following up Parker's hint, but without being able to
meet Forbes in New York, Higginson wrote to him a letter
which after a time found him out, and to which Forbes replied from Philadelphia, June 6, — some days after Brown
had definitely agreed to the postponement, and had left New
England for Kansas.   The letter was long and rambling,
and reads more like the epistle of a lunatic than the proposition of a military leader, such as Forbes professed to be.
He said : —

" The patent business which called me to Washington detained
me longer than I anticipated ; besides, certain financial difficulties
threw obstacles in my way. . . . I am little disposed to trust certain
letters by the United States mail addressed to obnoxious individuals.
You can get from F. B. Sanborn and Dr. S. G. Howe a sight of my
letters to them, unless Dr. H. may have thrown them behind the
fire, as he said he would do if he did not like their tone, — as if he

anonymous one), that he should go at once to Kansas and give his aid in
the coming elections.   Whether he will do so or not, we do not know.   I
may, perhaps, save you trouble by declaring that though I am willing to
do my uttermost to aid your family, or any distressed family, and though
I am willing to listen to any supposed claim of yours upon me, or any of
my friends, I will not read letters couched in such vituperative and abusive
language as you have hitherto used to Mr. Sanborn and me.   I will read
only far enough to see the spirit of the communication ; and if it is similar
to that of your former letters, I shall put it in the fire, with a real feeling
of regret at seeing a man of ability and acquirements wilfully injuring
himself and his family by his own passions."   With this plain statement, -
all correspondence with Forbes from Boston closed.

thought himself the Pope, or the autocrat of Austria, Japan, or China. I have been grossly defrauded in the name of humanity and antislavery. . . . I have for years labored in the antislavery cause, without wanting or thinking of a recompense. Though I have made the least possible parade of my work, it has nevertheless not been entirely without fruit; the very protest presented to the United States Senate and House against the Clayton clause of the organic act, which deprived foreigners of the right of voting in Kansas, was mainly my doing. . . . I consider, therefore, that if my family were from any circumstance to be in distress, that distress ought cheerfully and effectually to be alleviated by the antislavery men of every school. . . . Patience and mild measures having failed, I reluctantly have recourse to harshness. Let them not flatter themselves that I shall eventually become weary and shall drop the subject; it is as yet quite at its beginning. The Massachusetts senators, — Sumner and Wilson, — wrote to Boston about it; but Howe, Lawrence, Sanborn, and associates prefer to accumulate injury on injury rather than acknowledge their fallibility by redressing a wrong they have committed. I am on my way to New York, but I shall stop in this city (Philadelphia) for three days, because I wish to see some antislavery people here. I had letters to Mr. Miller McKim, but by him I was told that I could expect nothing from the Pennsylvania wing of the antislaveryites, because my remedy lay in New England, and because funds were low and prospects gloomy," etc.

On the 14th of May (the day when Brown's letter last cited was written), Mr. Stearns had sent to Brown in Canada an important letter, to which he added a second on the 15th. Here they are : —

BOSTON, May 14, 1858.

MR. JOHN BROWN, Chatham, Canada West.

DEAR SIR, — Enclosed please find a copy of a letter to Dr. Howe from Hon. Henry Wilson. You will recollect that you have the custody of the arms alluded to, to be used for the defence of Kansas, as agent of the Massachusetts State Kansas Committee. In consequence of the information thus communicated to me, it becomes my duty to warn you not to use them for any other purpose, and to hold them subject to my order as chairman of said committee. A member of our committee will be at Chatham early in the coming week, to confer with you as to the best mode of disposing of them.

Truly your friend,

GEORGE L. STEARNS,

Chairman Mass. State Kansas Committee.

MAY 15, 1858.

MR. JOHN BROWN, Chatham, Canada West.

DEAR SIR, — I wrote to you yesterday informing you that a member of the Massachusetts State Kansas Committee would visit Chatham, to confer about the delivery of the arms you hold. As I can find no one who can spare the time, I have to request that you will meet me in New York City sometime next week. A letter to me, directed to care of John Hopper, 110 Broadway, New York, will be in season. Come as early as you can. Our committee will pay your expenses.   Truly yours,

GEORGE L. STEARNS,
Chairman Mass. State Kansas Committee.

Dr. Howe will go on as soon as he knows you are in New York.

On or before the 20th of May Mr. Stearns met Brown in New York by appointment, and wrote to Higginson from there that "we are all agreed" about the recall of these arms from Virginia, "for reasons that cannot be written." Previously, on the 12th and 15th of May, Dr. Howe had replied to Senator Wilson's letter of May 9 as follows : —

BOSTON, May 12, 1858.

DEAR SIR, — I have just received your letter of the 9th. I understand perfectly your meaning. No countenance has been given to Brown for any operations outside of Kansas *by the Kansas Committee.* I had occasion, a few days ago, to send him an earnest message from some of his friends here, urging him to go at once to Kansas and take part in the coming election, and throw the weight of his influence on the side of the right. There is in Washington a disappointed and malicious man, working with all the activity which hate and revenge can inspire, to harm Brown, and to cast odium upon the friends of Kansas in Massachusetts. You probably know him. He has been to Mr. Seward. Mr. Hale, also, can tell you something about him. God speed the right!

MAY 15, 1858.

When I last wrote to you, I was not aware fully of the true state of the case with regard to certain arms belonging to the late Kansas Committee. Prompt measures have been taken, and will be resolutely followed up, to prevent any such monstrous perversion of a trust as would be the application of means raised for the defence of Kansas to a purpose which the subscribers of the fund would disapprove and vehemently condemn.   Faithfully yours,

S. G. HOWE.

Dr. Howe, with his usual ardor to act, had at first agreed with Brown and with Higginson; but, as these letters show, he was moved by the awkward complication which Brown's possession of these Kansas rifles created to acquiesce in a different view, and favor postponement of the attack, — as Parker, Stearns, and Sanborn did. For since these rifles, which had been purchased by the Massachusetts Kansas Committee and intrusted to Brown, were still, so far as Senator Wilson and the public knew, the property of that committee (though really, as has been explained, the personal property of Mr. Stearns), it would expose the Kansas Committee, who were ignorant of Brown's later plans, to suspicions of bad faith if those arms were used by him in any expedition to Virginia. Brown saw that nothing further could then be done, and yielded, though with regret, to the postponement.

When, about May 20, Mr. Stearns met Brown in New York, it was arranged that hereafter the custody of the Kansas rifles should be in Brown's hands as the agent, not of this committee, but of Mr. Stearns alone. It so happened that Gerrit Smith, who seldom visited Boston, was coming there late in May, to deliver an address before the Peace Society at its anniversary. He arrived and took rooms at the Revere House, where, on the 24th of May, 1858, the secret committee (organized in March, and consisting of Smith, Parker, Howe, Higginson, Stearns, and Sanborn) held a meeting to consider the situation. It had already been decided to postpone the attack, and the arms had been placed under a temporary interdict, so that they could only be used, for the present, in Kansas. The questions remaining were whether Brown should be required to go to Kansas at once, and what amount of money should be raised for him in future. Of the six members of the committee only one (Higginson) was absent, and as this was the only occasion when Smith acted personally with his associates, who met in his chamber at the Revere House, he was made chairman of the meeting. It was unanimously resolved that Brown ought to go to Kansas at once.

As soon as possible after this, Brown visited Boston (May 31), and while there held a conversation with Higginson, who made a record of it at the time, — saying that

Brown was full of regret at the decision of the Revere
House council to postpone the attack till the winter or
spring of 1859, when the secret committee would raise for
Brown two or three thousand dollars; "he meantime to
blind Forbes by going to Kansas, and to transfer the property so as to relieve the Kansas Committee of responsibility, and they in future not to know his plans. On probing
Brown," Higginson goes on, "I found that he . . . considered delay very discouraging to his thirteen men, and to
those in Canada. Impossible to begin in the autumn; and
he would not lose a day [he finally said] if he had three
hundred dollars; it would not cost twenty-five dollars apiece
to get his men from Ohio, and that was all he needed. The
knowledge that Forbes could give of his plan would be
injurious, for he wished his opponents to underrate him;
but still . . . the increased terror produced would perhaps
counterbalance this, and it would not make much difference.
If he had the means he would not lose a day." He complained that some of his Eastern friends were not men of
action; that they were intimidated by Wilson's letter, and
magnified the obstacles. Still, it was essential that they
should not think him reckless, he said; "and as they held
the purse, he was powerless without them, having spent
nearly everything received this campaign, on account of
delay, — a month at Chatham, etc." Higginson notes down
a few days later that Dr. Howe told him Brown left Boston,
June 3, with five hundred dollars in gold, and liberty to
retain all the arms, and that "he went off in good spirits."
He visited North Elba, Ohio, and Iowa, on his way to Kansas, and finally reached Lawrence, June 25, 1858.[1]

---

[1] The relation of the Kansas Committee of Massachusetts to the rifles they
had bought was one thing; that of Mr. Stearns, chairman of that committee, to these arms was quite another thing in 1858. He had then virtually
bought back the two hundred rifles from the committee, which at this time,
though never formally dissolved, and still continuing at intervals to pass
votes and write letters in its executive committee, had long been practically defunct, for the very good reason that its funds were exhausted and
there was little expectation of raising more. It had supplied the starving
people of Kansas with wheat and clothing in 1857; and in order to do this
had advanced money far beyond the amount raised in that year. I remember this with some distinctness, because I had myself advanced two or three

It is still a little difficult to explain this transaction concerning the arms without leaving a suspicion that there was
somewhere a breach of trust; but it will be seen that Mr.
Stearns, and those of his colleagues who acted with him,
although they could not in honor disclose what Brown had
imparted to them, took pains to free their uninformed asso-

hundred dollars at that time; but the principal advances were made by
our chairman, Mr. Stearns, whose liberality where his heart was interested
knew no bounds. At the time, therefore, when his Massachusetts friends
first heard of the Virginia plans of Brown, and gave them their reluctant
approval, as has been mentioned, the rifles in Brown's possession, though
nominally belonging to the Massachusetts Kansas Committee, were pledged
to Mr. Stearns, along with the other property, for the reimbursement of
his advances. I have forgotten how many thousand dollars he paid in this
way, but it was so many that the value of the arms was not enough to reimburse him; and it was agreed that he should not only have these, but
should also be at liberty to reimburse himself out of the avails of promis-
sory notes given by the Kansas farmers in payment for the wheat and other
supplies furnished to them in 1857. At the time these notes were given it
was hoped that most of them would be paid, and some of them were; but
I fancy very little of the money ever came into the hands of Mr. Stearns.
Some of it was paid to John Brown, as the agent of the committee, in the
summer and autumn of 1858, by the agents of Mr. Whitman, in whose
hands most of the notes were first placed. I have before me, in Brown's
handwriting, an "account of money, etc., collected of E. B. Whitman's
agents on National Kansas Committee account," in which something less
than two hundred dollars, mostly in small sums, is set down as received
from S. L. Adair, William Partridge, William Hutchinson, and other
Kansas residents, between Aug. 21, 1858, and Jan. 20, 1859. Mr. Whitman acted as agent both for the National Committee and for the Massachusetts Committee; and the business had become so complicated in
one way and another that when Brown levied upon the agents for
moneys claimed by him under votes of the committees, it excited a lively
dispute in Kansas. The Massachusetts Committee, however, stood firmly
by Brown, even after its three active members (Stearns, Howe, and Sanborn) were apprised of his Virginia plans, — as they were before he began
to collect money on their notes in 1858. In reality everything that *the
committee* had done was completely regular, and appropriate to the exigency of 1856–57. They had collected much money, had expended it
judiciously, and had allowed a generous individual, their chairman, to
place in their hands more money, for which he was willing to wait without
payment until the property of the committee could be turned into cash;
then, to give him all the security in its power, the committee had made
over this property to him, with no restriction as to what he should do with
it; and Mr. Stearns had chosen to give it to Brown.

ciates of the old Kansas Committee from all reproach of having aided Brown in his Virginia campaign. They were themselves indifferent to this reproach; but they could not bear to be charged with diverting other people's money into his hands. The public had not been notified in 1857 that the Kansas Committee had overdrawn its account on Dr. Howe, Mr. Stearns etc.; and that the arms had been pledged to the chairman, to meet this overdraft, long before any of us knew aught of Brown's Virginia scheme. When we did know this, it was too late to inform the public, except in the manner undertaken by Dr. Howe in his letters to Senator Wilson. As soon as possible after Brown had consented to the alternative of going to Kansas in the summer of 1858, the business of the Kansas Committee was put in such shape that its responsibility for the arms in Brown's possession should no longer fetter his friends in aiding his main design.

Moreover, it was agreed that Brown should not inform them of his plans in detail, nor burden them with knowledge that would be to them both needless and inconvenient. They were willing to trust him with their money, and did not want him to report progress except by action. This was the general sentiment of the six persons who formed the secret committee of 1858–59, — Gerrit Smith, Theodore Parker, Dr. Howe, Mr. Stearns, Wentworth Higginson, and myself, — and it was thus pithily expressed by Mr. Smith, when I wrote to him six weeks after Brown had left Boston: —

PETERBORO', July 26, 1858.

Mr. F. B. SANBORN.

MY DEAR SIR, — I have your letter of the 23d instant. I have great faith in the wisdom, integrity, and bravery of Captain Brown. For several years I have frequently given him money toward sustaining him in his contests with the slave-power. Whenever he shall embark in another of these contests I shall again stand ready to help him; and I will begin by giving him a hundred dollars. I do not wish to know Captain Brown's plans; I hope he will keep them to himself. Can you not visit us this summer? We shall be very glad to see you.

With best regards, your friend,

GERRIT SMITH.

Peterboro July 26 1858

W. F. Brinkerhoff

My dear Sir

I have your letter of
23 inst.

I have great spirit in the [uncommon]
integrity & bravery of Capt. Brown. For
several years I have frequently given
him money toward sustaining him in
his contests with the slave-power.
Whenever he shall embark in
another of these contests, I shall
again stand ready to help him & I
will begin with giving him what I
enclose. I enclose ($100)

I do not wish to know Capt. Brown's
plans. I hope he will keep them to
himself —

Can you not visit me this summer
now? We shall be very glad to
see you —

With friendly regard
your friend
Gerrit Smith

Thus matters stood fifteen months before the foray at Harper's Ferry, so far as Brown's last committee were concerned. His own movements in Canada and Kansas will soon be related; but I may here continue the record of Mr. Smith's hospitality toward the old hero. Early in the spring of 1859, Brown again directed his steps to Peterboro', where he arrived with a single follower (Jerry Anderson), April 11, 1859. My classmate Morton was still residing in Mr. Smith's family, and wrote me as follows at the dates named : —

Wednesday Evening, April 13, 1859.

You must hear of Brown's meeting this afternoon, — few in numbers, but the most interesting I perhaps ever saw. Mr. Smith spoke well; G. W. Putnam read a spirited poem; and Brown was exceedingly interesting, and once or twice so eloquent that Mr. Smith and some others wept. Some one asked him if he had not better apply himself in another direction, and reminded him of his imminent peril, and that his life could not be spared. His replies were swift and most impressively tremendous. A paper was handed about, with the name of Mr. Smith for four hundred dollars, to which others added. Mr. Smith, in the most eloquent speech I ever heard from him, said : " If I were asked to point out — I will say it in his presence — to point out the man in all this world I think most truly a Christian, I would point to John Brown." I was once doubtful in my own mind as to Captain Brown's course. I now approve it heartily, having given my mind to it more of late.[1]

April 18.

Brown left on Thursday the 14th, and was to be at North Elba to-morrow the 19th. Thence he goes " in a few days " to you. [He actually reached my house in Concord, Saturday, May 7, and spent half his last birthday with me.] He says he must not be trifled with, and shall hold Boston and New Haven to their word. New Haven advises him to forfeit five hundred dollars he has paid on a certain

---

[1] When I first met Brown at Peterboro', in 1858, Morton played some fine music to us in the parlor, — among other things Schubert's "Serenade," then a favorite piece, — and the old Puritan, who loved music and sang a good part himself, sat weeping at the air.

> "Northward he turneth through a little door,
> And scarce three steps ere music's golden tongue
> Flattered to tears this aged man and poor.
> But, no; already had his death-bell rung;
> The joys of all his life were said and sung."

contract, and drop it. He will not. From here he went in good spirits, and appeared better than ever to us, barring an affection of the right side of his head. I hope he will meet hearty encouragement elsewhere. Mr. Smith gave him four hundred dollars, I twenty-five, and we took some ten dollars at the little meeting. . . . . " L'expérience démontre, avec toute l'évidence possible, que c'est la société que prépare le crime, et que le coupable n'est que l'instrument que l'exécute." Do you believe Quetelet ?

June 1.

Mr. Smith has lately written to John Brown at New York to find what he needed, meaning to supply it. He now sends to him according to your enclosed address. I suppose you know the place where this matter is to be adjudicated. Harriet Tubman suggested the 4th of July as a good time to " raise the mill."

June 30.

News from Andover, Ohio, a week or more since, from our friend. He had received two hundred dollars more from here,[1] was full of cheer, and arranging his wool business; but I do not look for a result so soon as many do.

This message from Brown, about June 20, 1859, shows that he was already mustering his men and moving his arms toward Virginia; and it was about the 4th of July, as Harriet Tubman the African Sibyl had suggested, that Brown first showed himself in the counties of Washington and Jefferson, on opposite sides of the lordly Potomac. Before relating his adventures there, I must pause to recite his last Kansas episode.

[1] That is, from Gerrit Smith.

CHAPTER XIII.

FROM CANADA, THROUGH KANSAS, TO CANADA.

IT is now a humiliating thought that in 1858–59 Canada was the only safe refuge of the American fugitive slave. That simple hero, whose guide was the North Star, and to whom the roar of Niagara meant freedom, used to call his resort to British protection "shaking the paw of the Lion." "Slaves could not breathe in England" a hundred years ago; but the atmosphere of Canada was as wholesome to the freedmen in Judge Taney's time as that of England was in Lord Mansfield's. When John Brown wished to organize quietly his foray against Virginian slavery, he withdrew to Chatham, in Canada, where, in May, 1858, he held his little convention among the fugitives, and promulgated his "Provisional Constitution." Here is the beginning of the instrument, as it came from the mind and the pen of John Brown: —

PROVISIONAL CONSTITUTION [1] AND ORDINANCES FOR THE PEOPLE OF THE UNITED STATES.

Preamble.

Whereas, Slavery, throughout its entire existence in the United States, is none other than a most barbarous, unprovoked, and unjustifiable war of one portion of its citizens upon another portion —

---

[1] On the 10th of May, 1858, when the Chatham convention adjourned, it was voted "that John Brown (commander-in-chief), J. H. Kagi (secretary of war), Richard Realf (secretary of state), Charles P. Tidd, E. Whipple (A. D. Stephens), C. W. Moffat, John E. Cook, Owen Brown, Stewart Taylor, *Osborne P. Anderson, A. M. Ellsworth, Richard Richardson,* W. H. Leeman, and *John Lawrence* be, and hereby are, appointed a committee to whom is delegated the power of the convention to fill by election all the offices specially named in the Provisional Constitution which may be vacant after the adjournment of this convention." Those in italics were colored men.

the only conditions of which are perpetual imprisonment and hopeless servitude or absolute extermination — in utter disregard and violation of those eternal and self-evident truths set forth in our Declaration of Independence :

Therefore, We, citizens of the United States, and the oppressed people who by a recent decision of the Supreme Court are declared to have no rights which the white man is bound to respect, together with all other people degraded by the laws thereof, do, for the time being, ordain and establish for ourselves the following Provisional Constitution and Ordinances, the better to protect our persons, property, lives, and liberties, and to govern our actions :

Qualifications for Membership.

ART. I. All persons of mature age, whether proscribed, oppressed, and enslaved citizens, or of the proscribed and oppressed races of the United States, who shall agree to sustain and enforce the Provisional Constitution and Ordinances of this organization, together with all minor children of such persons, shall be held to be fully entitled to protection under the same.

This whole constitution, much ridiculed in 1859, will bear a careful examination, and will be found well suited to its purpose, — the government of a territory in revolt, of which the chief occupants should be escaped slaves. Mr. Bagehot once said that "the men of Massachusetts could work any constitution;" and so perhaps Brown and his men might have done.

Upon the intelligence received from Boston, in May, 1858, the little party of liberators in Canada separated, some going one way, some another. Richard Realf wrote to Brown, May 31, from Cleveland, Ohio : —

"I learn from George Gill that a certain Mr. Warner, living at Milan, has been told that a quantity of material was located in a certain county[1] (name correctly given), and that this Warner has

---

[1] At this time the arms of Brown were stored at Lindenville, Ohio, in charge of Mr. E. A. Fobes, to whom Brown had written from Chatham, May 11, saying : "The conduct of Colonel Forbes has been so strange of late as to render it important that he get no clew to where the arms are stored, or other articles, and that he should know nothing of my whereabouts. You will greatly oblige me and many other friends of freedom by

mentioned it to another man. All these are, Gill says, true men; but I do not like the idea any more for that. Nor am I better pleased to learn from the same source that a certain Mr. Reynolds (colored), who attended our convention, has disclosed its objects to the members of a secret society (colored) called 'The American Mysteries,' or some other confounded humbug. I suppose it is likely that these people are good men enough; but to make a sort of wholesale divulgement of matters at hazard is too steep even for me, who am not by any means over-cautious. Cook also, I learn, conducted himself here in a manner well calculated to arouse suspicion. According to Parsons, he stated in his boarding-house that he was here on a secret expedition, and that the rest of the company were under his orders. He made a most ostentatious display of his equipments; was careful to let it be known that he had been in Kansas; stated, among other recitals of impossible achievements, that he had killed five men; and, in short, drew largely on his imagination in order to render himself conspicuous. He found out and called upon a lady friend whom he knew in Connecticut, talked a great deal too much to her; and wound up his performances by proposing to Parsons, Gill, and Taylor a trip to the *same* locality on the *same* errand in the event of postponement.[1] He has taken his tools with him. It pains me to be obliged to say these things of one whom I have known so long; but I should be lacking in common honesty if I withheld them from you, — and especially now, when we have to tread with double care. I am not at all sure but that, in the event of deferment, our chief danger will accrue from him and his dreadful affliction of the *cacoëthes loquendi*, which, rendered into English, means 'rage for talking,' or 'tongue malady.'"

At the time Realf wrote, Brown was in Boston; June 9 he was at North Elba; a few days later, at West Andover, Ohio; June 22, at Chicago; and on Sunday, June 25, he reached Lawrence, in Kansas; where James Redpath met him in company with Richard Hinton. Redpath says: —

"We were at supper that day at a hotel in Lawrence, when a stately old man, with a flowing white beard, entered the room and took a seat at the public table. I immediately recognized in the stranger John Brown. Yet many persons who had previously known him did not penetrate his patriarchal disguise."

getting all who may know anything about either to observe the utmost secrecy about the whole matter."

[1] This trip to Harper's Ferry is perhaps that mentioned in Brown's last interview with Cook, Dec. 2, 1859.

The narrative is continued by Hinton, who says: —

" On this Sunday I held a conversation with Captain Brown, which lasted nearly the whole afternoon. The purport of it was, on his part, inquiries as to various public men in the Territory, and the condition of political affairs. He was very particular as to the movements and character of Captain Montgomery. The massacre of the Marais des Cygnes was then fresh in the minds of the people. I remember an expression which he used. Warmly giving utterance to my detestation of slavery and its minions, and impatiently wishing for some effectual means of injuring it, Captain Brown said to me most impressively, ' Young men must learn to wait. Patience is the hardest lesson to learn. I have waited for twenty years to accomplish my purpose.' He reminded me of a message that I had sent him in 1857, and said he hoped I meant what I said, for he should ask the fulfilment of that promise, and perhaps very soon; further adding that he wanted to caution me against rash promises. Young men were too apt to make them, and should be very careful. The promise given was of great importance; and I must be prepared to stand by it, or disavow it now. Kagi, who was present at the same time, gave me to understand that their visit to Kansas was caused by the betrayal of their plans by Colonel Forbes to the Administration; and that they wished to give a different impression by coming to the West. Both said they intended to stay some time; and that night Captain Brown announced that they should go to southern Kansas in the morning, to see Captain Montgomery and visit the Adairs near Osawatomie.

" I did not see Brown again until September, when I met him at Mr. Adair's. Both he and Kagi were sick with the fever and ague, and had been for some time. In the interim Brown had been in Linn and Bourbon Counties, and other parts of southern Kansas. One of his first acts was to negotiate with Snyder the blacksmith, upon whose claim the massacre of the Marais des Cygnes occurred, for its purchase. This claim is about half a mile from the State line, — the buildings in an admirable position for defence. Brown saw both the moral and material advantages of the position, and was desirous of obtaining possession. Snyder agreed to sell; but soon after, having a better offer, he broke the contract. The Captain had in the interval, with the assistance of Kagi, Tidd, Stephens, Leeman, and another member of his company, prepared a very strong fortification, where they could have successfully resisted a large force. In my journey through the border counties I found that a general feeling of confidence prevailed among our friends because John Brown was near. Over the border the Missourians were remarkably·

quiet from June until October, in the belief that the old hero was in their vicinity. When the farm was abandoned, Brown and Kagi came to Mr. Adair's, where I met them. . . . Brown was then more nervous and impatient in his manner than I had before observed. Captain Montgomery's name was introduced, and Brown was enthusiastic in praise of him, avowing perfect confidence in his integrity and purposes. 'Captain Montgomery,' he said, 'is the only soldier I have met among the prominent Kansas men. He understands my system of warfare exactly. He is a natural chieftain, and knows how to lead.' He spoke of General Lane and his recent killing of Gaius Jenkins ; said he would not say one word against Lane in his misfortunes, but he told the General himself that he was his own worst enemy. Of his own early treatment at the hands of ambitious leaders, he said : 'They acted up to their instincts. As politicians they thought every man wanted to lead, and therefore supposed I might be in the way of their schemes. While they had this feeling, of course they opposed me. Committees and councils could not control my movements, therefore they did not like me. Many men did not like the manner in which I conducted warfare, and they too opposed me. But politicians and leaders soon found that I had different purposes, and forgot their jealousy. They have all been kind to me since.' "

Brown preferred Montgomery to the other Kansas leaders; and on the 9th of July he wrote to his son John from Sugar Mound, in southern Kansas: "I am now writing in the log-cabin of the notorious Captain James Montgomery, whom I deem a very brave and talented officer, and, what is infinitely more, a very intelligent, kind, gentlemanly, and most excellent man and lover of freedom." [1]

Not long after this letter Brown wrote to me from the region made famous by the Marais des Cygnes murders, where he was then residing under the name of Captain Shubel Morgan, with a small company whom he had enlisted according to this compact, which he signed by his assumed name : —

ARTICLES OF AGREEMENT FOR SHUBEL MORGAN'S COMPANY.

We, the undersigned, members of Shubel Morgan's company, hereby agree to be governed by the following rules : —

---

[1] James Montgomery, one of the bravest partisans on the Kansas border, and during the Civil War colonel of a black regiment in South Carolina.

I. A gentlemanly and respectful deportment shall at all times and places be maintained towards all persons; and all profane or indecent language shall be avoided in all cases.

II. No intoxicating drinks shall be used as a beverage by any member, or be suffered in camp for such purpose.

III. No member shall leave camp without leave of the commander.

IV. All property captured in any manner shall be subjected to an equal distribution among the members.

V. All acts of petty or other thefts shall be promptly and properly punished, and restitution made as far as possible.

VI. All members shall, so far as able, contribute equally to all necessary labor in or out of camp.

VII. All prisoners who shall properly demean themselves shall be treated with kindness and respect, and shall be punished for crime only after trial and conviction, being allowed a hearing in defence.

VIII. Implicit obedience shall be yielded to all proper orders of the commander or other superior officers.

IX. All arms, ammunition, etc., not strictly private property, shall ever be held subject to, and delivered up on, the order of the commander.[1]

NAMES.	DATE, 1858.	NAMES.	DATE, 1858.
Shubel Morgan,	July 12.	E. W. Snyder,	July 15.
C. P. Tidd,	" "	Elias J. Snyder,	" "
J. H. Kagi,	" "	John H. Snyder,	" "
A. Wattles,	" "	Adam Bishop,	" "
Saml. Stevenson,	" "	Wm. Hairgrove,	" "
J. Montgomery,	" "	John Mikel,	" "
T. Homyer [Wiener ?],	" "	Wm. Partridge,	" "
Simon Snyder,	" 14.		

John Brown on Guard at Fort Snyder.

MISSOURI LINE (ON KANSAS SIDE), July 20, 1858.

F. B. SANBORN, ESQ., AND FRIENDS AT BOSTON AND WORCESTER, — I am here with about ten of my men, located on the same quarter-section where the terrible murders of the 19th of May were committed, called the Hamilton or trading-post murders. Deserted farms and dwellings lie in all directions for some miles along the

---

[1] This paper is in Kagi's handwriting, and contains the signature of Montgomery as a private.

line, and the remaining inhabitants watch every appearance of persons moving about, with anxious jealousy and vigilance. Four of the persons wounded or attacked on that occasion are staying with me. The blacksmith Snyder, who fought the murderers, with his brother and son, are of the number. Old Mr. Hairgrove, who was terribly wounded at the same time, is another. The blacksmith returned here with me, and intends to bring back his family on to his claim within two or three days. A constant fear of new troubles seems to prevail on both sides of the line, and on both sides are companies of armed men. Any little affair may open the quarrel afresh. Two murders and cases of robbery are reported of late. I have also a man with me who fled from his family and farm in Missouri but a day or two since, his life being threatened on account of being accused of informing Kansas men of the whereabouts of one of the murderers, who was lately taken and brought to this side. I have concealed the fact of my presence pretty much, lest it should tend to create excitement; but it is getting leaked out, and will soon be known to all. As I am not here to seek or secure revenge, I do not mean to be the first to reopen the quarrel. How soon it may be raised against me I cannot say; nor am I over anxious. A portion of my men are in other neighborhoods. We shall soon be in great want of a small amount in a draft or drafts on New York, to feed us. We cannot work for wages, and provisions are not easily obtained on the frontier.

I cannot refrain from quoting, or rather referring to, a notice of the terrible affair before alluded to, in an account found in the "New York Tribune" of May 31, dated at Westport, May 21. The writer says: "From one of the prisoners it was ascertained that a number of persons were stationed at Snyder's, a short distance from the Post, a house built in the gorge of two mounds, and flanked by rock-walls, — a fit place for robbers and murderers." At a spring in a rocky ravine stands a very small open blacksmith's-shop, made of thin slabs from a saw-mill. This is the only building that has ever been known to stand there, and in that article is called a "fortification." It is to-day, just as it was on the 19th of May, — a little pent-up shop, containing Snyder's tools (what have not been carried off) all covered with rust, — and had never been thought of as a "fortification" before the poor man attempted in it his own and his brother's and son's defence. I give this as an illustration of the truthfulness of that whole account. It should be left to stand while it may last, and should be known hereafter as *Fort Snyder*.

I may continue here for some time. Mr. Russell and other friends at New Haven assured me before I left, that if the Lecompton abomination should pass through Congress something could be done there to relieve me from a difficulty I am in, and which they understand. Will not some of my Boston friends " stir up their minds " in the matter? I do believe they would be listened to.[1]

You may use this as you think best. Please let friends in New York and at North Elba[2] hear from me. I am not very stout; have much to think of and to do, and have but little time or chance for writing. The weather, of late, has been very hot. I will write you all when I can.

I believe all honest, sensible Free-State men in Kansas consider George Washington Brown's " Herald of Freedom " one of the most mischievous, traitorous publications in the whole country.

July 23. Since the previous date another Free-State Missourian has been over to see us, who reports great excitement on the other side of the line, and that the house of Mr. Bishop (the man who fled to us) was beset during the night after he left, but on finding he was not there they left. Yesterday a proslavery man from West Point, Missouri, came over, professing that he wanted to buy Bishop's farm. I think he was a spy. He reported all quiet on the other side. At present, along this part of the line, the Free-State men may be said, in some sense, to " possess the field; " but we deem it wise to " be on the alert." Whether Missouri people are more excited through fear than otherwise, I am not yet prepared to judge. The blacksmith (Snyder) has got his family back; also some others have returned, and a few new settlers are coming in. Those who fled or were driven off will pretty much lose the season. Since we came here about twenty-five or thirty of Governor Denver's men have moved a little nearer to the line, I believe.

August 6. Have been down with the ague since last date, and had no safe way of getting off my letter. I had lain every night without shelter, suffering from cold rains and heavy dews, together with the oppressive heat of the days. A few days since, Governor Denver's officer then in command bravely moved his men on to the line, and on the next adjoining claim with us. Several of them immediately sought opportunity to tender their service to me secretly. I however advised them to remain where they were. Soon after I

---

[1] The allusion here is to Brown's contract with Charles Blair, who was to make the thousand pikes. Brown had not been able, for lack of money, to complete the payment, and was afraid his contract would be forfeited, and the money paid would be lost. He therefore communicated the facts to Mr. Russell, who was then the head of a military school at New Haven, and had some assurance from him of money to be raised in Connecticut to meet this contract.

[2] Gerrit Smith, and his own family.

came on the line my right name was reported; but the majority did not credit the report.

I am getting better. You will know the true result of the election of the 2d inst. much sooner than I shall, probably. I am in no place for correct general information. May God bless you all!

Your friend,

JOHN BROWN.

When recovering from fever he wrote this shorter letter:

OSAWATOMIE, KANSAS, Sept. 10, 1858.

DEAR FRIEND, AND OTHER FRIENDS, — Your kind and very welcome letter of the 11th July was received a long time since, but I was sick at the time, and have been ever since until now; so that I did not even answer the letters of my own family, or any one else, before yesterday, when I began to try. I am very weak yet, but gaining well. All seems quiet now. I have been down about six weeks. As things now look I would say that if you had not already sent forward those little articles,[1] do not do it. Before I was taken sick there seemed to be every prospect of some business very soon; and there is some now that requires doing; but, under all the circumstances, I think not best to send them.

I have heard nothing direct from Forbes for months, but expect to when I get to Lawrence. I have but fourteen regularly employed hands, the most of whom are now at common work, and some are sick. Much sickness prevails. How we travel may not be best to write. I have often met the "notorious" Montgomery, and think very favorably of him.

It now looks as though but little business can be accomplished until we get our mill into operation. I am most anxious about that, and want you to name the earliest date possible, as near as you can learn, when you can have your matters gathered up. Do let me hear from you on this point (as soon as consistent), so that I may have some idea how to arrange my business. Dear friends, do be in earnest; the harvest we shall reap, if we are only up and doing.

Sept. 13, 1858.

Yours of the 25th August, containing draft of Mr. S. for fifty dollars is received. I am most grateful for it, and to you for your kind

---

[1] The whistles, etc., mentioned in this note, sent to me from Brooklyn in March, 1858. "Please get for me (if you can) a quantity of whistles such as are used by the boatswain on ships of war. They will be of great service. Every ten men ought to have one at least. Also some little articles as marks of distinction, which I mentioned to you."

letter. This would have been sooner mailed but for want of stamps and envelopes. I am gaining slowly, but hope to be on my legs soon. Have no further news.

Mailed, September 15. Still weak.

Your friend.

To his Family.

OSAWATOMIE, KANSAS, Sept. 9, 1858.

DEAR WIFE AND CHILDREN, ALL, — I received Henry's letter of the 21st July a long time ago, but was too sick to answer it at the time, and have been ever since till now. I am still very weak, but gaining pretty well. I was never any more sick. I left the Missouri line about six weeks since; soon after, I was taken down. Things are now very quiet, so far as I know. What course I shall next take, I cannot tell, till I have more strength. I have learned with pain that the flour did not go on, and shall try to send you some money instead of it, so that Mr. Allen may be well paid for the barrel he lent. I can write you no more now, but I want to know how you all get along. Enclose everything to Augustus Wattles, Moneka, Linn County, Kansas, in sealed envelope, with my name only on it. God bless you all!

Your affectionate husband and father.

OSAWATOMIE, KANSAS, Sept. 13, 1858.

DEAR WIFE, — Your letter of the 25th August I was most glad to get, notwithstanding it told me of your trials; and I would be thankful that the same hand that brought me your letter brought me another, supplying me with the means of sending you some relief. I hope you will all learn to put your trust in God, and not become discouraged when you meet with poor success and with losses. I wrote you two or three days ago, telling you how I had been sick, but was getting better. I am still very weak, and write with great labor. I enclose draft for fifty dollars, payable to Watson. I want Mr. Allen paid out of it, to his full satisfaction, for the barrel of flour lent, as a first thing, and the balance used to supply substantial comforts for the family, or to pay any little debts. I shall have the means, after a while, of paying for another yoke of oxen, and I hope to have it soon; but of that I cannot be certain. It would be well to make considerable inquiry for a good, youngish yoke, without faults, and also to find where you can get them most reasonably for the money. Do not, any of you, go in debt for a team. You may, perhaps, hire a few days' work of some good team to log with, or of some good man to help to pile logs without a team, and I will endeavor to send the pay

on for that soon. Do the best you can, and neither be hasty nor discouraged. You must acknowledge the receipt of this at once, and
tell me all how you get along. May God abundantly bless you all!
                                  Your affectionate husband.

                        OSAWATOMIE, KANSAS, Oct. 11, 1858.

DEAR WIFE AND CHILDREN, ALL, — I wrote you sometime
since, enclosing G. Smith's check for fifty dollars, payable to order
of Watson. Since then I have no word from any of you, but am in
hopes of getting something to-morrow. I have been very feeble ever
since, but have improved a good deal now for about one week. I can
now see no good reason why I should not be located nearer home, as
soon as I can collect the means for defraying expenses. I still intend
sending you some further help as soon as I can. Will write you how
to direct to me hereafter. No more now.
                           Your affectionate husband and father.

                           MONEKA, KANSAS, Nov. 1, 1858.

DEAR WIFE AND CHILDREN, ALL, — I have just written to John
H. Painter, of Springdale, Cedar County, Iowa, to send you a New
York draft, payable to Oliver. I have strong hopes of your getting
one to the amount of his note. At any rate, it is all the means I now
have of giving you a little further help. Should you get it, you need
not send him the note, as my letter is good against the note. I would
be glad to have you pay the taxes, if you can so manage as to do it and
be comfortable. I shall do all I can to help you, and as fast as I can.
How soon I shall be able to see you again, I cannot tell, but I still
live in hopes. I cannot now tell you how to direct to me, but will
advise you further as soon as I can. Things at this moment look
quite threatening along the line. I am much better in health than I
was when I wrote last, but not very strong yet. May God bless you
all!
                           Your affectionate husband and father.

                           MONEKA, KANSAS, Nov. 1, 1858.

DEAR FRIENDS, — Your letter of the 10th October from Hudson
was received in good time, but I was not then in a condition to reply
at once. Things at this moment look rather threatening in this immediate neighborhood; but what will come up I cannot say. I am
obliged to you for your efforts to prevent Watson from going to California, and will try to express my gratitude by hinting to you that a
business and copartnership, such as you allude to, would be very likely
to require a good deal of the capital (real or fictitious) of others, where-

by you would be likely to run into debt, and into some other entanglements. Could you not do moderately well by taking a dairy again? That business has for the last half century been subject to as few fluctuations in Ohio as any other (I think). Beside that, I suppose you already understand it, tolerably well at least. I may take wholly a wrong view of the subject. My health is some improved, but I am still weak. Shall write to you where to direct when I know where to do so.

May God bless you all!   Your friend.

These letters are not signed, because Brown was still a proscribed person in Kansas, and was liable at any time to engage in new contests which might lead to his arrest by the Democratic governor or the Federal troops. At the date of the last letter, Governor Denver, who had succeeded Walker and Stanton, had resigned, and there was a short interregnum. Captain Montgomery, with an armed force much larger than any that Brown had commanded, for some months patrolled southern Kansas, and retaliated on the Border Ruffians as he saw occasion. Montgomery was Brown's friend, and had carried Brown's opinions very far. Just before April 1, 1858, while pursued by United States troops, he turned and put them to flight, firing upon them and killing two dragoons, — the first and last time that the national soldiers were fired upon by the Free-State men in Kansas. These troubles in southern Kansas were mainly over when Brown wrote the following letter to his family, just a year before his execution : —

John Brown to his Children in Ohio.

OSAWATOMIE, KANSAS, Dec. 2, 1858.

DEAR CHILDREN, — I have a moment to write you, and I hasten to improve it. My health is some improved since I wrote you last, but still I get a shake now and then. Other friends are middling well, I believe. In some of the border counties south, there is the worst feeling at this time, which affords but little prospect of quiet. Other portions of the Territory are comparatively undisturbed. The winter may be supposed to have fairly set in, which may compel parties to defer hostilities at least. I want you to write my family to inquire particularly whether they are so circumstanced as to be able to get through the winter without suffering, so that I may hear from them when I know where to have you direct to me. I have but this moment returned from the south, and expect to go back at once.

P. S.   Am still preparing for my other journey.   Yours.

P. S.   I want you, some of you, for the present, to write John, saying all about the condition of your different families, and whether you are suffering for anything, or are likely to be, and for what, that I may get the information by-and-by, through him, when there is any chance. You may depend on my doing all in my power to make you comfortable. To God and his infinite grace I commend you all.

By his "other journey," Brown meant his Virginia expedition; but he was then preparing also for his raid into Missouri, to rescue slaves from one or two plantations there. He has told the story of this raid in his own inimitable manner, summing up in a short letter the history of the whole year 1858 in southern Kansas. It was addressed to the "New York Tribune," and published both there and in the Lawrence "Republican": —

JOHN BROWN'S PARALLELS.

TRADING POST, KANSAS, January, 1859.

GENTLEMEN, — You will greatly oblige a humble friend by allowing the use of your columns while I briefly state two parallels, in my poor way.

Not one year ago eleven quiet citizens of this neighborhood, — William Robertson, William Colpetzer, Amos Hall, Austin Hall, John Campbell, Asa Snyder, Thomas Stilwell, William Hairgrove, Asa Hairgrove, Patrick Ross, and B. L. Reed, — were gathered up from their work and their homes by an armed force under one Hamilton, and without trial or opportunity to speak in their own defence were formed into line, and all but one shot, — five killed and five wounded. One fell unharmed, pretending to be dead. All were left for dead. The only crime charged against them was that of being Free-State men. Now, I inquire what action has ever, since the occurrence in May last, been taken by either the President of the United States, the Governor of Missouri, the Governor of Kansas, or any of their tools, or by any proslavery or Administration man, to ferret out and punish the perpetrators of this crime?

Now for the other parallel.[1] On Sunday, December 19, a negro man called Jim came over to the Osage settlement, from Missouri, and stated that he, together with his wife, two children, and another negro man, was to be sold within a day or two, and begged for help to get away. On Monday (the following) night, two small companies were made up to go to Missouri and forcibly liberate the five slaves, together with other slaves. One of these companies I assumed to direct. We proceeded to the place, surrounded the buildings, liberated the slaves, and also took certain property supposed to belong to the estate. We however learned before leaving that a portion of the articles we had taken belonged to a man living on the plantation as a tenant, and who was supposed to have no interest in the estate. We promptly returned to him all we had taken. We then went to another plantation, where we found five more slaves, took some property and two white men. We moved all slowly away into the Territory for some distance, and then sent the white men back, telling them to follow us as soon as they chose to do so. The other company freed one female slave, took some property, and, as I am informed, killed one white man (the master), who fought against the liberation.

Now for a comparison. Eleven persons are forcibly restored to their natural and inalienable rights, with but one man killed, and all "hell is stirred from beneath." It is currently reported that the

---

[1] On the back of the original draft of "Old Brown's Parallels," in Brown's handwriting, is the following indorsement by him in pencil of stations on the "Underground Railroad" through Kansas : —

Raynard, Holton.	Nemaha City.
Dr. Fuller, six miles.	On River Road, Martin Stowell, Mount Vernon.
Smith, Walnut Creek, fifteen.	non.
Mills and Graham (attorneys), Albany, twenty-five.	Dr. Whitenger and Sibley, Nebraska City. Mr. Vincent, Ira Reed, Mr. Gardner.

Besides these entries appear the following : —

Teamsters, Dr. To cash each, $1.00 . . . . $2.00
Linsley, Dr. at Smith's 1.00

On the other end of the same page, —

Cash received by J. Brown on his private account, of J. H. Painter on note $100.00
Cash received by J. Brown on his private account, of J. H. Painter for saddle 10.00
Cash received by J. Brown on his private account, of J. H. Painter for wagon 88.10

"J. Brown paid for company : For G. Gill, $5.70 ; to Pearce, $39.00 ; to Painter, $8.00 ; to Townsend for shoes, $1.65 ; to Pearce, $3.00 ; to Carpenter, $10.00 ; to Kagi, $8.00 ; to Carpenter for making shirts, $2.00." These are part of the cost of the journey, no doubt.

Governor of Missouri has made a requisition upon the Governor of
Kansas for the delivery of all such as were concerned in the last-
named "dreadful outrage." The Marshal of Kansas is said to be
collecting a *posse* of Missouri (not Kansas) men at West Point, in
Missouri, a little town about ten miles distant, to "enforce the laws."
All proslavery, conservative, Free-State, and dough-face men and
Administration tools are filled with holy horror.

Consider the two cases, and the action of the Administration party.

Respectfully yours,

JOHN BROWN.

When Brown was about to set forth from Osawatomie
with his freedmen, Gerrit Smith, who had heard of his foray
in Missouri, and rejoiced at it, sent me this letter: —

PETERBORO', Jan. 22, 1859.

MY DEAR SIR, — I have yours of the 19th. I am happy to learn
that the Underground Railroad is so prosperous in Kansas. I cannot
help it now, in the midst of the numberless calls upon me. But I
send you twenty-five dollars, which I wish you to send to our noble
friend John Brown. Perhaps you can get some other contributions
to send along with it. He is doubtless in great need of all he can
get. The topography of Missouri is unfavorable. *Would that a
spur of the Alleghany extended from the east to the west borders of
the State!* Mr. Morton has not yet returned. We hope he may
come to-night.   In haste, your friend,

GERRIT· SMITH.

P. S. Dear Theodore Parker! May Heaven preserve him to us!

It was not far from January 20 when Brown started
northward with his freedmen from the neighborhood of the
Pottawatomie, where he had sheltered them. The following letter was received by Brown while tarrying a day at
Major J. B. Abbott's house on the Wakarusa, near Lawrence,
with the eleven fugitives, — the same brave Abbott who
rescued Branson three years before. It was written in reply
to one sent from Brown by messenger to Judge Conway;
upon the back of it is a pencil memorandum in the handwriting of Brown, apparently giving the names of safe
stopping-places on the route northward, as follows: "Sheridan's, Hill, Holton, Fuller's, Smith's, Plymouth, Indians,
Little Nemeha, Dr. Blanchard's, Tabor."

Judge Conway to John Brown.

LAWRENCE, K. T., Jan. 23, 1859.

DEAR SIR, — I have been able to see Whitman but once since I got your previous letter, and then he promised to come and see me about it; but he has not done so. I am of opinion that you will not be able to get any funds from him. He expressed himself to me since his return from the East as dissatisfied at your proceedings in Lawrence when you were here before. He has always complaints to make about his pecuniary sufferings in connection with the National Kansas Committee. Still, it may be as well for you to look after him at this time. Anything I can do for you I will do ; but I am extremely pinched for money, and am unable to do anything in that way. If, however, you can suggest anything within my power by which I may aid you, I am at your service. You know Mr. Whitman is living out of town. He does not come in very often. I shall keep " entirely dark," of course.

Very truly your friend,   M. F. CONWAY.

The retreat from southern Kansas with his freedmen, and particularly the first stage of his journey from Osawatomie to Lawrence, was one of the boldest adventures of Brown. With a price on his head, with but one white companion, himself an outlaw, with twelve fugitives who had been advertised the world over, and with their property loaded into an odd-looking wagon and drawn by the cattle taken from the slave-owner in Missouri, Brown pushed forward, in the dead of winter, regardless of warnings and threats, but relying on the mercy of God and on his own stout heart. His next and most dangerous stage was from Holton in Jackson County, thirty miles north of Topeka, to the Nebraska border. At Holton he occupied the cabin of Albert Fuller, and went forth from there with his Topeka reinforcements, to win "the battle of the spurs." It was at this encounter that he made that capture of his pursuers concerning which Brown's biographers have romanced a little, saying, among other things, that he forced his prisoners to pray or be shot. The truth of that matter is better narrated thus : —

" One of the party captured was Dr. Hereford, a young physician from Atchison, — a wild, rattling, devil-may-care kind of fellow,

always ready for an adventure, but who really had nothing very bad
in his composition. Brown took him under his especial care. One
evening he called upon the doctor to offer prayer.

"'By God!' said the doctor, 'I can't pray.'

"'Did your mother never teach you to pray?'

"'Oh, yes; but that was a long time ago.'

"'But you still remember the prayer she taught you,' said
Brown.

"'Yes.'

"'Well, for lack of a better one, say that.' And the doctor repeated before black and white comrades of the camp that night the
rhyme, 'Now I lay me down to sleep,' etc., to the amusement of his
fellow-prisoners and others.

"On his return home he related this, and said with an oath that
John Brown was the best man he had ever met, and knew more
about religion than any man. When asked whether Brown had
ever treated them badly, or used harsh language while they were
with him, he said, 'No,' — that they were all treated like gentlemen;
had the same fare as the others; but it did go a little against the
grain to eat with and be guarded by 'damned niggers.'" [1]

Brown appears to have made no written report of his
retreat with the freedmen through Kansas, Nebraska, Iowa,
Illinois, and Michigan to Canada; but I find copious accounts
of it by others. He reached Lawrence January 24, 1859,
and travelled northward slowly. About thirty miles from
Topeka he found shelter in a vacant log-cabin, belonging to
Dr. Fuller.

"Our party," says a comrade, "consisted only of the captain,
myself, and a man known by the name of Whipple in Kansas, but
afterward as Stephens at Harper's Ferry. Kagi and Tidd had stayed
at Topeka to procure provisions, and our teamster had been sent back
to bring them along. While waiting for them, we found ourselves
surrounded by a band of human bloodhounds, headed by the notorious
deputy-marshal of the United States, Wood. I afterward learned

[1] The prisoners all cursed terribly at their ill luck in being captured.
Brown said to them : "Gentlemen, you do very wrong to thus take the
name of God in vain. Besides, it is very foolish ; for if there is a God
you can gain nothing by such profanity ; and if there is no God, how foolish it is to ask God's curses on anything !" The men saw their folly,
ceased swearing, and joined willingly in the morning and evening prayers
of the party during the five days they were held prisoners.

that he was put on our track by a traitor from New Hampshire, named Hussey. Whipple lived alone in a small empty cabin near the one we occupied. There had been heavy rains, which produced a freshet; and one day as he walked a short distance from the cabin to see whether the waters had subsided, eight of the marshal's men came upon him suddenly, and asked him if he had seen any negroes thereabout. He told them if they would come with him he would show them some, and conducted them to his cabin where he had left his rifle. He came back immediately and pointed his rifle at the leader, commanding him to surrender, which he did at once. The other men put spurs to their horses, and rode off as fast as possible. From that time I was the sole bodyguard of Captain Brown, the eleven fugitives, and the prisoner who had surrendered, — Whipple keeping a sharp lookout as our sentry. We were detained at this place about three days. At last our provisions arrived, and we were joined by a band of Topeka boys who had walked down in the night to aid us. We then started on our journey. A short distance from our road was Muddy Creek, where the marshal, supposing our party must pass that way, stationed himself on the opposite side of the creek, with eighty armed men, for he had made careful preparations, well knowing that it was no joke to attack old Brown. Captain Brown had with him only twenty-three white men, all told. He placed them in double file, in front of the emigrant wagons, and said, 'Now go straight at 'em, boys! They'll be sure to run.' In obedience to this order, we marched towards the creek, but scarcely had the foremost entered the water when the valiant marshal mounted his horse, and rode off in haste. His men followed as fast as possible, but they were not all so lucky as he was in untying their horses from the stumps and bushes. The scene was ridiculous beyond description; some horses were hastily mounted by two men. One man grabbed tight hold of the tail of a horse, trying to leap on from behind, while the rider was putting the spurs into his sides; so he went flying through the air, his feet touching the ground now and then. Those of our men who had horses followed them about six miles, and brought back with them four prisoners and five horses. Meanwhile Captain Brown and the rest of his company succeeded in drawing the emigrant wagons through the creek by means of long ropes. This battle of Muddy Creek was known ever after in Kansas as 'The Battle of the Spurs.' When we resumed our journey, the captain did not think it prudent to allow the five prisoners to mount their horses lest they should escape and bring a fresh party to attack us. So he told them they must walk; but as he meant them no unkindness, he would walk with them. They went on together, he talking with them all the way concerning the wickedness of slavery, and the meanness of

slavehunting. He kept them with us all night; in the morning he
told them that they might make the best of their way back on foot.
Their horses were retained from prudential motives, as it was obviously not for the safety of our colored emigrants to have these men
return very speedily. The horses captured from Marshal Wood's
posse were given to the brave Topeka boys who had walked so far
to help us."

Another comrade, Jacob Willetts, of Topeka, says : —

" I lived on a farm a short distance from Topeka at the time
Brown was last in Kansas. When he came up north he stopped
with my near neighbor, Mr. Sheridan, and sent for me. When I got
there he wanted me to go to town on business for him. I came down
that night with him to cross the river, and on the way he told me he
had some colored people with him, who were in need, and asked me if
I could do anything to help them. They had no shoes, and but little
to eat. I went out among the houses and into several stores and got
a number of pairs of shoes and some little money for the good cause.
As we were going down to the river, I noticed Brown shivering, and
that his legs trembled a good deal. I suspected something, and as I
sat beside him on my horse I reached down and felt of his pantaloons, and found they were of cotton, thin and suited to summer, not
to the cold weather we had then. I asked him : ' Mr. Brown, have
you no drawers?' He said he had not. ' Well,' I said, ' there is no
time to go to the store now ; but I have on a pair that were new to-
day, and if you will take them you can have them and welcome.'
After a few words he agreed to it. We got down beside the wagons
on the boat ; I took the drawers off, and he put them on. I don't remember what day this was ; but one Sunday morning, not a great
while after, we got word that Brown was surrounded near Holton. I
could not go just then, but got started during the day, and when we
got to Holton we found that the way had been cleared and Brown
had gone on."

Another writer continues the narrative thus : —

" The trip after leaving Holton was accompanied with great hardships. By pressing through rapidly, despite extremely cold weather
and drifted roads, the crossing of the Missouri was made at Nebraska
City before a force could be gathered to intercept them. At Tabor
Brown had formerly been received with great hospitality and treated
in the friendliest manner; but the very people who had formerly contributed to his wants so liberally now felt called upon to assemble and
resolve that Brown's conduct in crossing into a slave State and forcing

negroes away was inconsistent with the teachings of the Bible and with Christianity. This was very disagreeable to Brown, who supposed the good men of Tabor were the friends of fugitives. But the Tabor people, though good Republican voters, were alarmed, and declared such fugitives contraband. A public meeting was called for Monday morning, and announced in the churches of that whole region on the Sunday preceding. The people flocked in, and a Missouri slaveholder was there as well as John Brown and his lieutenant John Henry Kagi, who was killed at Harper's Ferry. The meeting was addressed by a deacon, who had hitherto been reckoned an Abolitionist, but now called on his fellow-Christians to declare that the forcible rescue of slaves was robbery and might lead to murder, and that the citizens of Tabor had no sympathy with John Brown in his late acts.[1] When the deacon had offered his resolution and made his speech, another resolution was offered as a substitute by James Vincent, but drawn up by Kagi, to this effect : —

' *Whereas,* John Brown and his associates have been guilty of robbery and murder in the State of Missouri,

' *Resolved,* That we, the citizens of Tabor, repudiate his conduct and theirs, and will hereupon take them into custody, and hold them to await the action of the Missouri authorities.'

" 'The meeting evaded this caustic test of its sincerity, but went on denouncing Brown and his acts. In the midst of these natural but disgraceful proceedings, John Brown arose, and left the meeting, in aggrieved silence."

He never returned to Tabor, but from Springdale, a week or two later, he wrote to a friend in Tabor as follows : —

RECEPTION OF BROWN AND PARTY AT GRINNELL, IOWA, COMPARED WITH PROCEEDINGS AT TABOR.

SPRINGDALE, IOWA, Feb. 25, 1859.

1. Whole party and teams kept for two days free of cost.

2. Sundry articles of clothing given to the captives.

3. Bread, meat, cakes, pies, etc., prepared for our journey.

4. Full houses for two nights in succession, at which meetings Brown and Kagi spoke, and were loudly cheered and fully indorsed.

---

[1] Here is the resolution adopted by the citizens of Tabor, Feb. 7, 1859 :

. *Resolved,* That while we sympathize with the oppressed, and will do all that we conscientiously can to help them in their efforts for freedom, nevertheless we have no sympathy with those who go to slave States to entice away slaves and take property or life when necessary to attain that end.

J. S. SMITH, *Secretary.*

Three Congregational clergymen attended the meeting on Sabbath evening (notice of which was given out from the pulpit). All of them took part in justifying our course and in urging contributions in our behalf. There was no dissenting speaker present at either meeting. Mr. Grinnell spoke at length; and has since labored to procure us a free and safe conveyance to Chicago, and effected it.

5. Contributions in cash amounting to $26.50.

6. Last, but not least, public thanksgiving to Almighty God offered up by Mr. Grinnell in the behalf of the whole company for His great mercy and protecting care, with prayers for a continuance of those blessings.

As the action of Tabor friends has been published in the newspapers by some of her people (as I suppose), would not friend Gaston or some other friend give publicity to all the above ?

Respectfully your friend,   JOHN BROWN.

P. S. Our reception among the Quaker friends here has been most cordial.   Yours truly,   J. B.

To quiet the scruples of some persons in the North, Brown made these notes for a speech : —

"VINDICATION OF THE INVASION, ETC.

" The Denver truce was broken; and (1) It was in accordance with my settled policy ; (2) It was intended as a discriminating blow at slavery ; (3) It was calculated to lessen the value of slaves ; (4) It was (over and above all other motives) right.

" Duty of all persons in regard to this matter.

"Criminality of neglect in this matter.

" Suppose a case.

" Ask for further support."

The family letters at this period are few, but I find some. The first was written while in southern Kansas with his fugitives, waiting for a favorable time to take them to Canada; but he did not trust the tidings of what he had done or exactly where he was to a letter, which might be taken from the mails in Missouri.

To his Family.

OSAWATOMIE, KANSAS, Jan. 11, 1859.

DEAR CHILDREN, ALL, — I have but a moment in which to tell you that I am in middling health ; but have not been able to tell you as yet where to write me. This I hope will be different soon. I suppose you get Kansas news generally through the papers.[1] May God ever bless you all!

Your affectionate father,

JOHN BROWN.

TABOR, IOWA, Feb. 10, 1859.

DEAR WIFE AND CHILDREN, ALL, — I am once more in Iowa, through the great mercy of God. Those with me, and other friends, are well. I hope soon to be at a point where I can learn of your welfare, and perhaps send you something besides my good wishes. I suppose you get the common news. May the God of my fathers be your God!

SPRINGDALE, CEDAR COUNTY, IOWA, March 2, 1859.

DEAR WIFE AND CHILDREN, ALL, — I write to let you know that all is yet well with me, except that I am not very strong. I have something of the ague yet hanging about me. I confidently expect to be able to send you some help about team, etc., in a very few days. However, if I should be delayed about it longer than I could wish, do not be discouraged. I was much relieved to find on coming here that you had got the draft sent by Mr. Painter. He has been helping me a little in advance of its being due, since I got on. Do not be in haste to buy a team until you can have time to get further word from me. I shall do as fast as I can; and may God bless and keep you all!

Your affectionate husband and father.

Iowa City is not far from Springdale, and it may have been the proslavery postmaster there concerning whom this anecdote is told: In the midst of a crowd on the street-corner a quiet old countryman was seen listening to a champion of slavery, who was denouncing Brown as a reckless, bloody outlaw, — a man who never dared to fight fair, but skulked, and robbed, and murdered in the dark; adding,

---

[1] They would thus learn that he had made his foray, and that both Governor Medary of Kansas and President Buchanan had set a price on his head. Charles Robinson's account of this foray (published twenty years later in the "Topeka Commonwealth") is characteristic: "Brown and his heroes went over the line into Missouri, killed an old peaceable citizen, and robbed him of all the personal effects they could drive or carry away. Such proceedings caused the Free-State men to organize to drive him from the Territory; and he went to Harper's Ferry, where he displayed his wonderful generalship in committing suicide."

"If I could get sight of him I would shoot him on the spot; I would never give him a chance to steal any more slaves." "My friend," said the countryman in his modest way, "you talk very brave; and as you will never have a better opportunity to shoot Old Brown than right here and now, you can have a chance." Then, drawing two revolvers from his pockets he offered one to the braggart, requesting him to take it and shoot as quick as he pleased. The mob orator slunk away, and Brown returned his pistols to his pocket.

When this affair happened, Brown's expedition from Kansas back to Canada was nearly over. On the 12th of March, 1859, he saw his twelve freedmen (among them a new-born infant) safely ferried across from Detroit to Windsor, where "the paw of the Lion" protected them.[1] After Brown's capture in Virginia, public attention was directed to them; and their condition was described by several friends who visited them. When they heard Brown's speech in court read to them they burst into tears and sobs, declaring that they wished they could die instead of their liberator; and one woman said, "If the Bible is true, he will have his reward in heaven, for he followed the Bible in this world." His action, however, like that of earlier Christians, brought much reproach upon himself at first. Even his stanch friend Dr. Howe, who as a young man had taken part in the Greek revolution, the French revolution of July, and the Polish revolution of 1831, was distressed, on his return from Cuba in the spring of 1859, to find that Brown had actually been taking the property of slaveholders to give their escaping slaves an outfit, — and for a time withdrew his support. Nor did he ever sustain Brown's Virginia scheme again so heartily as he had done before this visit to Cuba and Carolina.[2] Meanwhile, the

[1] When he parted from them Brown said: "Lord, permit Thy servant to die in peace; for mine eyes have seen Thy salvation! I could not brook the thought that any ill should befall you, — least of all, that you should be taken back to slavery. The arm of Jehovah protected us."

[2] Dr. Howe, returning from Cuba (whither he accompanied Theodore Parker in February, 1859), journeyed through the Carolinas, and there accepted the hospitality of Wade Hampton and other rich planters; and it shocked him to think that he might be instrumental in giving up to fire

secret committee were not idle. The fifty dollars sent
to Brown in Kansas, Aug. 25, 1858, and acknowledged by
him September 13, came from Gerrit Smith, who first and
last gave him more than a thousand dollars.[1] The long
letters from Kansas were sent by me to Higginson, Oct. 13,
1858, with this comment: —

" I received the enclosed letter from our friend a week or two
since. You see he is anxious about future operations. Can you do
anything for him before next March ; and if so, what ? The partners
in Boston have talked the matter over, but have not yet come to any
definite proposal. I send you also an older letter, which should have
been sent to you, but by some fault of others was not."

Higginson expressed the hope that the enterprise would
not be deferred longer than the spring of 1859, and made
some contribution to the fund ; as did also Parker and
the other members of the secret committee. No active
movement to raise money was undertaken, however, until
the next spring. On the 19th of January, 1859, three
weeks after Brown's incursion into Missouri, I wrote to
Higginson : —

" I have had no private advices from J. B. since I wrote you.
He has begun the work in earnest, I fancy, and will find enough to do
where he is, for the present. I earnestly hope he may not fall into
the hands of the United States or Missouri. If he does not, I think
we may look for great results from this spark of fire. If Forbes is a
traitor, he will now show his hand, and we can pin him in some
way."

and pillage their noble mansions. But the Civil War did that five or six
years later, with Howe's full consent.

[1] Most of the smaller sums which Brown received during the years
1858 and 1859, I suppose, passed through my hands ; while the larger
sums were paid to him directly by Mr. Stearns or other contributors.
Most of the correspondence on this Virginia business also went through
my hands ; it being Brown's custom to write one letter, to be read by the
half-dozen persons with whom he desired to communicate ; and this letter
generally (by no means always) coming to me in the first instance. My
custom was to show it to Mr. Parker and Dr. Howe, when they were at
home, then to send it to Mr. Stearns, who sometimes forwarded it to
Higginson or some more distant correspondent, and sometimes returned it
to me.

I also wrote later, as follows : —

March 4.

" Brown was at Tabor on the 10th of February, with his stock in fine condition, as he says in a letter to G. Smith. He also says he is ready with some new men to set his mill in operation, and seems to be coming East for that purpose. Mr. Smith proposes to raise one thousand dollars for him, and to contribute one hundred dollars himself. I think a larger sum ought to be raised; but can we raise so much as this? Brown says he thinks any one of us who talked with him might raise the sum if we should set about it; perhaps this is so, but I doubt. As a reward for what he has done, perhaps money might be raised for him. At any rate, he means to do the work, and I expect to hear of him in New York within a few weeks. Dr. Howe thinks John Forbes and some others not of our party would help the project if they knew of it." [1]

Following up this last suggestion, I sounded several anti-slavery men of wealth and influence in the spring of 1859, and did obtain subscriptions from persons who were willing to give to a brave man forcibly interfering with slavery, without inquiring very closely what he would do next. But Parker (who never returned to Boston, but died in Florence soon after Brown's execution) contributed nothing after 1858; nor did Higginson give so much, or interest himself so warmly in the enterprise after its first postponement. All this would have made it more difficult to raise the money which Brown needed, had it not been for the munificence of Mr. Stearns, who at each emergency came forward with his indispensable gifts. After placing about twelve hundred dollars in Brown's hands in the spring and summer of 1859, he still continued to aid him, in one way and

---

[1] Dr. Howe gave me the following letter at New York, Feb. 5, 1859 : —

JOHN M. FORBES, ESQ.

DEAR SIR, — If you would like to hear an honest, keen, and veteran backwoodsman disclose some plans for delivering our land from the curse of slavery, the bearer will do so. I think I know him well. He is of the Puritan militant order. He is an enthusiast, yet cool, keen, and cautious. He has a martyr's spirit. He will ask nothing of you but the pledge that you keep to yourself what he may say.

Faithfully yours,

S. G. Howe.

I never used this letter, but personally introduced Brown to Mr. Forbes in May, 1859, at his house in Milton, near Boston.

another, until almost the day of the attack at Harper's Ferry. Gerrit Smith, also, was better than his word, and gave Brown more than seven hundred dollars between his return to Canada in March and his interview with Frederick Douglass in September, 1859.

From Canada Brown went to Ohio, where he publicly sold the horses he had captured in Kansas, warning the purchasers of a possible defect in the title.[1] He then reported for counsel and encouragement at North Elba, at Peterboro', and finally, in May, 1859, at Concord and Boston.

[1] A Vermont judge refused to recognize a slave as property, until his owner could bring before the court "a bill of sale from the Almighty." Brown fancied he held these horses by such a title.

Note. — John Brown, Jr., says : " In the winter of 1857-58 I brought the arms from the railroad at Conneaut to Cherry Valley, stored them in the furniture warerooms of the King Brothers, and covered the boxes with a lot of ready-made coffins. In the following spring I was made slightly anxious one day by a visit from the township assessor, who in the line of his duty went up into the room where they were stored and took the number of the coffins in a somewhat hurried way, but fortunately without examining what was beneath them. On receipt of the letter from father, of May 11, 1858, I moved the arms (two wagon-loads) by night to the western part of the next township of Wayne, and stored them in the barn of a farmer named William Coleman, who helped me by night to build a little store-room under his hay-mow. There they remained perfectly secreted (his wife, even, did not know it) until I took them, again by night, to the canal at Hartstown, Penn., early in the summer of 1859, and shipped them as hardware to Chambersburg." This refers to the rifles, etc., afterward captured at the Kennedy farm.

CHAPTER XIV.

JOHN BROWN AND HIS FRIENDS.

IN the broad and permanent sense of that comforting word "friendship," John Brown had innumerable friends. When Wordsworth, in the flush of the noble pantheism which breathes through his earlier verse, addressed the fallen Toussaint L'Ouverture in his French dungeon, he described the state of John Brown, and every generous champion of God's cause : —

> "Live, and take comfort ! Thou hast left behind
> Powers that will work for thee, — air, earth, and skies.
> There's not a breathing of the common wind
> That will forget thee ; thou hast great allies :
> Thy friends are exultations, agonies,
> And Love, and man's unconquerable Mind."

In the same sense, but more definitely, Emerson said at Salem five weeks after Brown's execution,[1] —

"I am not a little surprised at the easy effrontery with which political gentlemen, in and out of Congress, take it upon them to say that there are not a thousand men in the North who sympathize with John Brown. It would be far safer and nearer the truth to say that all people, in proportion to their sensibility and self-respect, sympathize with him. For it is impossible to see courage and disinterestedness and the love that casts out fear, without sympathy. All women are drawn to him by their predominance of sentiment. All gentlemen, of course, are on his side. I do not mean by 'gentlemen' people of scented hair and perfumed handkerchiefs, but men of gentle blood and generosity, 'fulfilled with all nobleness,' who, like the Cid, give the outcast leper a share of their bed ; like the dying Sidney, pass the cup of cold water to the wounded soldier who

---

[1] Emerson's "Miscellanies" (Boston, 1884), pp. 262, 263.

needs it more. For what is the oath of gentle blood and knighthood? What but to protect the weak and lowly against the strong oppressor? Nothing is more absurd than to complain of this sympathy, or to complain of a party of men united in opposition to slavery. As well complain of gravity or the ebb of the tide. Who makes the Abolitionist? The slaveholder. The sentiment of mercy is the natural recoil which the laws of the universe provide to protect mankind from destruction by savage passions. And our blind statesmen go up and down, with committees of vigilance and safety, hunting for the origin of this new heresy. They will need a very vigilant committee, indeed, to find its birthplace, and a very strong force to root it up. For the arch-Abolitionist, older than Brown, and older than the Shenandoah Mountains, is Love, whose other name is Justice, — which was before Alfred, before Lycurgus, before slavery, and will be after it."

But in the narrower meaning of men and women who knew the purposes of John Brown, and gave him aid and comfort while he most needed them, he had but few friends, and some of those fell away from him when the hour of trial came. In his own family he was always understood, and had no cause to feel the full bitterness of that Scripture, " A man's foes shall be they of his own household." But beyond that family the number of persons who at any time both understood and sympathized with him in his main purpose was very small, — so that he valued and cherished disproportionately, perhaps, those who accepted his mission and helped it forward even by words and friendly listening.[1] There may have been a thousand men who knew that he meant to harass the slaveholders in some part of the South, with an armed force; but of those who knew with any fulness the details of his Virginia enterprise, I suppose the number never at any one time exceeded a hundred, — and these were scattered over the whole country from Boston to Kansas, from Maryland to Canada.

The earliest, most devoted, most patient, and noblest friend of Brown in this enterprise was his second wife, of whom too little has hitherto been known. Now that death has

---

[1] " It is some relief to a poor body," says Izaak Walton, speaking of George Herbert, " to be but heard with patience ; " and it was not every one who did Brown that justice.

released her from her long bereavement, and her modest reserve can no more be wounded by the public mention of her virtues, it is due to her silent and tender constancy that the tale of her life should be told. Mary Anne Brown (the daughter of Charles Day, a blacksmith of New England ancestry, but settled in New York until about 1825) was born in Granville, N. Y., April 15, 1816. Her only school education was acquired before the age of ten, when she removed with her father and his younger children to a farm near Meadville, Penn., not far from the Delamaters (with whom she was connected) and from John Brown's tannery in Randolph.[1] Early in life she became a member of the Congregational Church, and continued in its communion until her death. When but sixteen years of age she became the wife of John Brown, and assumed the care of his five children, the eldest of whom was near her own age. She brought to the task good health, a strong, well-balanced mind, and an earnest desire to discharge every duty conscientiously. She became the mother of thirteen children, seven of whom died in childhood, — three of them in one week. She once remarked, " That was the time in my life when all my religion, all my philosophy, and all my faith in God's goodness were put to the test. My husband was away from home, prostrated by sickness; I was helpless from illness; in one week three of my little ones died of dysentery, — this but three months before the birth of another child. Three years after this sad time another little one, eighteen months old, was burned to death. Yet even in these trials God upheld me."

She was of a large and firm mould, like a Roman mother, but with all the susceptible and yearning affection which the milder types of constancy display. She labored with her hands, and taught all her children to do the same; she was trained to endure long absences from her husband and her sons, and that in periods of great anxiety, and when they were ill-spoken of among her neighbors. She soon became separated from her own kindred, and, like Ruth in the Scrip-

---

[1] The Delamaters are of Huguenot descent, and had intermarried with the Days, as well as with wealthier families of New York.

tures, she silently said to her much-wandering husband:
" Whither thou goest, I will go ; and where thou lodgest, I
will lodge ; thy people shall be my people, and thy God my
God ; the Lord do so to me, and more also, if aught but
death part thee and me." But in his perilous campaigns,
and with his scanty means, she could not accompany him
save in prayers and wishes; she was even denied that facility
in writing letters which so often beguiles the weariness of
absence.[1] This modern Penelope had her loom and spindle,
like the fabled one, but her labors were real, and supported
her household.

During all the time her husband was in Kansas she remained at North Elba with her three young daughters, and
sometimes with no son to till her rocky farm.   When the
struggle at Harper's Ferry was terminated, and she knew
that her husband's life-work was ended, she visited him and
received his last messages ; her warrior was brought home
to her and buried by her door.   After all was over, she remained in her lonely home until 1863 ; and in the following
year, in company with her son Salmon and her daughters,
made the long journey across the plains to California.
For six years their home was at Red Bluff, and then in the
town of Rohnerville for ten years.   About 1880, with two
daughters, she removed to Saratoga, Santa Clara County,
which was her home until death.   She had long felt a desire
to return to the East, to visit scenes with which she had
been familiar, and to greet friends from whom she had long
been separated ; but the narrowness of her fortunes had prevented this.   She was not even able to revisit the grave of
her husband, to which thousands of strangers resorted.   In
1882, as she told me when I met her at North Elba, the
way was providentially opened for the accomplishment of
this desire, and she accepted the opportunity.   Her journey
was pleasant and mournful.   In course of it she was permitted to recover the remains of her son Watson, and to see
him buried, with the praise of friends and neighbors, beside
his father on the Adirondac hillside.   Public receptions were

---

[1] Heaven first taught letters for some wretch's aid,
     Some banished lover, or some captive maid. — POPE.

tendered to her at Chicago, Boston, Springfield, and at the capital of Kansas; she visited the battle-grounds of her family there, and saw for the first time the dark waters of the Marais des Cygnes and the Ottawa.[1]

Returning to California, the fatigues of her journey and the strain upon her deep sensibilities, little perceived at the time (such was her silent fortitude), began to tell upon her robust constitution. During a visit to her son Salmon among the sheep-walks of northern California she was attacked with a lingering disease, from which she never recovered. The last two months of her life were spent in San Francisco for medical treatment, carefully watched over by her daughter Sarah, to whom she had been sister as well as mother, so strong was the bond of sympathy between them.

The wife of John Brown was of a type more common in our age than is the austere Puritanic order to which he belonged, but by no means frequent, — resembling those mothers in Israel, diligent and God-fearing, of whom her Bible told her. She was far from the culture of modern life, but keenly alive to great ideas, and of a broad catholicity in spirit, which embraced slaveholders and murderers in its love, and never sought vengeance as justice. She read the Bible daily, and with humble attention. A true Christian of the antique pattern, she gladly recognized as brethren all whom she believed to be God's children, wherever she found them, or by whatever name they were called. Narrowness in religion she could not understand, nor ever sought to confine God to the purlieus of her own church.

Upon so firm a basis rested the domestic happiness of John Brown; and his children, though he sometimes chided

---

[1] Mr. Dwight Thacher, of Topeka, writes me (March 30, 1885) : "When the widow of John Brown made her first and only visit to Kansas, in November, 1882, she was for several days my guest. Reflected in her bearing, her words, her style of thought and expression, I fancied I could see unmistakable evidences of the lofty and rugged plane of life upon which the whole family had lived. She was the soul of truthfulness, of candor, — and had an unworldly air, as of one who had dwelt among high and eternal verities. John Brown's gravity and devotion to duty were admirably reflected in his widow."

their religious dissent, were worthy of such parents. His
quiver was full of those arrows which the wise king praises,
and he drew from it the means of attack upon wrong. But
for his sons, how different might have been his own fate !
They stood about him as guards and recruits, and died for
him as bravely as he would have died for them. Not often
in the divergent and estranging paths of modern life have
we seen a family so patriarchal in habit and in action.

Outside of his household the friends of John Brown were
found in every rank and condition of life, and those whom
he once attached were seldom estranged from him, though
they might not keep pace with him in his methods or purposes. Perhaps the best exemplification of this was given
by that generous and right-minded man, John A. Andrew,
afterward Governor of Massachusetts, and one of the most
helpful patriots in the Civil War. In the tumult of public opinion which followed Brown's foray in Virginia, Mr.
Andrew, then a leading lawyer and Republican politician
in Boston, said manfully, " Whatever may be thought of
John Brown's acts, *John Brown himself was right.*"

Foremost among the friends of John Brown in New England must be named Emerson, the poet-sage of Concord. In
1856 he had taken the same view of things in Kansas which
Mr. Andrew and Josiah Quincy expressed, — but he knew
how to utter his thought in more trenchant words. At
a Kansas aid meeting in Cambridge (Sept. 10, 1856), he
said : —

" In this country for the last few years the Government has been
the chief obstruction to the common weal. Who doubts that Kansas
would have been very well settled if the United States had let it alone ?
The Government armed and led the ruffians against the poor farmers.
. . . In the free States we give a snivelling support to slavery. The
judges give cowardly interpretations to the law, in direct opposition
to the known foundation of all law, — that every immoral statute is
void. And here, of Kansas, the President says, ' Let the complain-
ants go to the courts;' though he knows that when the poor plundered
farmer comes to the court, *he finds the ringleader who has robbed him
dismounting from his own horse, and unbuckling his knife to sit as
his judge.*"[1]

[1] Emerson's " Miscellanies," pp. 244–246.

Mr. Emerson's Diary for March, 1857, says : —

" Captain John Brown gave a good account of himself in the Town Hall last night to a meeting of citizens. One of his good points was the folly of the peace party in Kansas, who believed that their strength lay in the greatness of their wrongs, and so discountenanced resistance. He wished to know if their wrong was greater than the negro's, and what kind of strength that gave to the negro ? He believes, on his own experience, that one good, believing, strong-minded man is worth a hundred — nay, twenty thousand — men without character, for a settler in a new country, and that the right men will give a permanent direction to the fortunes of a State. For one of these bullying, drinking rowdies, he seemed to think cholera, small-pox, and consumption were as valuable recruits. The first man who went into Kansas from Missouri to interfere in the elections, he thought, ' had a perfect right to be shot.' He gave a circumstantial account of the battle of Black Jack, where twenty-three Missourians surrendered to nine Abolitionists. He had three thousand sheep in Ohio, and would instantly detect a strange sheep in his flock. A cow can tell its calf by secret signals, he thinks, by the eye, to run away, to lie down, and hide itself. He always makes friends with his horse or mule (or with the deer that visit his Ohio farm); and when he sleeps on his horse, as he does as readily as on his bed, his horse does not start or endanger him. Brown described the expensiveness of war in a country where everything that is to be eaten or worn by man or beast must be dragged a long distance on wheels. ' God protects us in winter,' he said ; ' no Missourian can be seen in the country until the grass comes up again.' "

Thus far the first Diary, as it now stands. But from time to time, as he saw Brown again, or heard of him from friends or from the newspapers, Emerson made other notes, which he has thus edited : —

" For himself, Brown is so transparent that all men see him through. He is a man to make friends wherever on earth courage and integrity are esteemed, — the rarest of heroes, a pure idealist, with no by-ends of his own. Many of us have seen him, and every one who has heard him speak has been impressed alike by his simple, artless goodness and his sublime courage. He joins that perfect Puritan faith which brought his ancestor to Plymouth Rock, with his grandfather's ardor in the Revolution. He believes in two articles —two instruments, shall I say ? — the Golden Rule and the Declaration of Independence ; and he used this expression in a conversation here concerning them: ' Better that a whole generation of men, women, and children should pass away by a violent death, than that one word of either should be violated in this country.' There is a Unionist, there is a strict constructionist for you! He believes in the Union of the States, and he conceives that the only obstruction to the Union is slavery; and for that reason, as a patriot, he works for its abolition.

. . . .

" He grew up a religious and manly person, in severe poverty; a fair specimen of the best stock of New England, having that force of thought and that sense of right which are the warp and woof of greatness. Our farmers were Orthodox Calvinists, mighty in the Scriptures; had learned that life was a preparation, a ' probation,' to use their word, for a higher world, and was to be spent in loving and serving mankind. Thus was formed a romantic character, absolutely without any vulgar trait; living to ideal ends, without any mixture of self-indulgence or compromise, such as lowers the value of benevolent and thoughtful men we know; abstemious, refusing luxuries, not sourly and reproachfully, but simply as unfit for his habit; quiet and gentle as a child, in the house. And as happens usually to men of romantic character, his fortunes were romantic. Walter Scott would have delighted to draw his picture and trace his adventurous career. A shepherd and herdsman, he learned the manners of animals, and knew the secret signals by which animals communicate. He made his hard bed on the mountains with them; he learned to drive his flock through thickets all but impassable; he had all the skill of a shepherd by choice of breed and by wise industry to obtain the best wool, and that for a course of years."

To the like purpose do the Diaries of Thoreau, during the years 1857–59, speak of Brown: —

" I should say that he is an old-fashioned man in his respect for the Constitution, and his faith in the permanence of this Union. Slavery he deems to be wholly opposed to these, and he is its determined foe. He is by descent and birth a New England farmer, a man of great common-sense, deliberate and practical as that class is, and tenfold more so, — like the best of those who stood at Concord Bridge once, on Lexington Common, and on Bunker Hill; only he was firmer and higher-principled than any that I have chanced to hear of as there. It was no Abolition lecturer that converted him. Ethan Allen and Stark, with whom he may in some respects be compared, were rangers in a lower and less important field. They could bravely face their country's foes, but he had the courage to face

his country herself when she was in the wrong. A Western writer
says, to account for his escape from so many perils, that he was concealed under a ‘rural exterior,’ — as if, in that prairie-land, a hero
should, by good rights, wear a citizen’s dress only.

. . . .

“He was never able to find more than a score or so of recruits
whom he would accept, and only about a dozen (among them his
own sons) in whom he had perfect faith. When he was here, he
showed me a little manuscript book, — his ‘orderly-book’ I think he
called it, — containing the names of his company in Kansas, and the
rules by which they bound themselves; and he stated that several
of them had already sealed the contract with their blood. When
some one remarked that with the addition of a chaplain it would
have been a perfect Cromwellian troop, he observed that he would
have been glad to add a chaplain to the list, if he could have found
one who could fill that office worthily. I believe that he had prayers
in his camp morning and evening, nevertheless. He is a man of
Spartan habits, and at sixty was scrupulous about his diet at your
table, excusing himself by saying that he must eat sparingly and fare
hard, as became a soldier, or one who was fitting himself for difficult
enterprises, a life of exposure. A man of rare common-sense and
directness of speech as of action, a transcendentalist, above all a man
of ideas and principles, — that is what distinguishes him. Not yielding to a whim or transient impulse, but carrying out the purpose of a
life. I noticed that he did not overstate anything, but spoke within
bounds. I remember particularly how, in his speech here, he referred
to what his family had suffered in Kansas, without ever giving the
least vent to his pent-up fire. It was a volcano with an ordinary
chimney-flue. Also referring to the deeds of certain Border Ruffians,
he said, rapidly paring away his speech, like an experienced soldier
keeping a reserve of force and meaning, ‘They had a perfect right to
be hung.’ He was not in the least a rhetorician, was not talking to
Buncome or his constituents anywhere, had no need to invent anything, but to tell the simple truth, and communicate his own resolution; therefore he appeared incomparably strong, and eloquence in
Congress and elsewhere seemed to me at a discount. It was like the
speeches of Cromwell compared with those of an ordinary king.

. . . .

“When I expressed surprise that he could live in Kansas at all
with a price set on his head, and so large a number, including the
authorities, exasperated against him, he accounted for it by saying,
‘It is perfectly well understood that I will not be taken.’ Much
of the time for some years he has had to skulk in swamps, suffering from poverty and from sickness which was the consequence of

exposure, befriended only by Indians and a few whites. But though it
might be known that he was lurking in a particular swamp, his foes
commonly did not care to go in after him. He could even come out
into a town where there were more Border Ruffians than Free-State
men, and transact business without delaying long, and yet not be
molested. ‘ For,’ said he, ‘ no little handful of men were willing to
undertake it, and a large body could not be got together in season.’

. . . .

“ Yet he did not foolishly attribute his success to his ‘ star,’ or to
any magic. He said truly, that the reason why such greatly superior
numbers quailed before him was, as one of his prisoners confessed,
because they ‘ lacked a cause,’ — a kind of armor which he and his
party never lacked. When the time came, few men were found
willing to lay down their lives in defence of what they knew to be
wrong ; they did not like that this should be their last act in this
world.”

Mr. Alcott’s record of the man is more methodical as to
days and events. He writes : —

OSAWATOMIE BROWN.

“ Concord, May 8, 1859. This evening I hear Captain Brown
speak at the town hall on Kansas affairs, and the part taken by him
in the late troubles there. He tells his story with surpassing simplicity and sense, impressing us all deeply by his courage and religious earnestness. Our best people listen to his words, — Emerson,
Thoreau, Judge Hoar, my wife ; and some of them contribute something in aid of his plans without asking particulars, such confidence
does he inspire in his integrity and abilities. I have a few words
with him after his speech, and find him superior to legal traditions,
and a disciple of the Right in ideality and the affairs of state. He
is Sanborn’s guest, and stays for a day only. A young man named
Anderson accompanies him. They go armed, I am told, and will
defend themselves, if necessary. I believe they are now on their
way to Connecticut and farther south ; but the Captain leaves us
much in the dark concerning his destination and designs for the
coming months. Yet he does not conceal his hatred of slavery, nor
his readiness to strike a blow for freedom at the proper moment. I
infer it is his intention to run off as many slaves as he can, and so
render that property insecure to the master. I think him equal to
anything he dares, — the man to do the deed, if it must be done, and
with the martyr’s temper and purpose. Nature obviously was
deeply intent in the making of him. He is of imposing appearance,

personally, — tall, with square shoulders and standing ; eyes of deep gray, and couchant, as if ready to spring at the least rustling, dauntless yet kindly ; his hair shooting backward from low down on his forehead ; nose trenchant and Romanesque ; set lips, his voice suppressed yet metallic, suggesting deep reserves ; decided mouth ; the countenance and frame charged with power throughout. Since here last he has added a flowing beard, which gives the soldierly air and the port of an apostle. Though sixty years old, he is agile and alert, and ready for any audacity, in any crisis. I think him about the manliest man I have ever seen, — the type and synonym of the Just. I wished to see and speak with him under circumstances permitting of large discourse. I am curious concerning his matured opinions on the great questions, — as of personal independence, the citizen's relation to the State, the right of resistance, slavery, the higher law, temperance, the pleas and reasons for freedom, and ideas generally. Houses and hospitalities were invented for the entertainment of such questions, — for the great guests of manliness and nobility thus entering and speaking face to face : —

> " ' Man is his own star ; and the soul that can
> Render an honest and a perfect man
> Commands all light, all influence, all fate.
> Nothing to him falls early or too late :
> Our acts our angels are, — or good or ill,
> Our fatal shadows, that walk by us still.' "

The days pass on, and Brown makes his foray in Virginia, the news of it reaching Concord on the 18th of October, 1859. For some days the dismal tidings find no entry in the daily journal at the Orchard House, since Mr. Alcott is busy harvesting his apples. But a week after the attack at Harper's Ferry this record appears, followed by many more : —

" *October* 23. Read with sympathy and a sense of the impossibility of any justice being done him by South or North, by partisans or people, — by the general mankind, — the newspaper accounts of Captain Brown's endeavor at Harper's Ferry, now coming to us and exciting politicians and everybody everywhere. This man I heard speak early in the season at our town hall, and had the pleasure of grasping his firm hand and of speaking with him after his lecture. This deed of his, so surprising, so mixed, so confounding to most persons, will give an impulse to freedom and humanity, whatever becomes of its victim and of the States that howl over it. There should be enough of courage and intrepidity in the North, — in Massachusetts men, — to steal South, since they cannot march openly there, rescue him from the slaveholders, the State and United States courts, and save him for the impending crisis. Captain Higginson would be good for that leadership, and No. 64 [1] will be ready to march with the rest. Captain Brown is of Puritan stock, and comes from Connecticut. He was born at Torrington, in Litchfield County, May 9, 1800, about fifteen miles from the place of my nativity.

"*Concord, Sunday, Oct.* 30, 1859. Thoreau reads a paper of his on John Brown, his virtues, spirit, and deeds, at the vestry this evening, and to the delight of his company, I am told, — the best that could be gathered on short notice, and among them Emerson. I am not informed in season, and have my meeting at the same time. I doubt not of its excellence and eloquence, and wish he may have opportunities of reading it elsewhere. [2]

"*Friday, Nov.* 4. Thoreau calls and reports about the reading of his lecture on Brown at Boston and Worcester. Thoreau has good right to speak fully his mind concerning Brown, and has been the first to speak and celebrate the hero's courage and magnanimity. It is these which he discerns and praises. The men have much in common, — the sturdy manliness, straightforwardness, and independence. It is well they met, and that Thoreau saw what he sets forth as none else can. Both are sons of Anak and dwellers in Nature, — Brown taking more to the human side, and driving straight at institutions, while Thoreau contents himself with railing at and letting them otherwise alone. He is the proper panegyrist of the virtues he owns himself so largely, and so comprehends in another.

"*Saturday, November* 5. Dine with Sanborn. He suggests that I should go to Virginia and get access to Brown if I can, and Governor Wise ; thinks I have some advantages to fit me for the adventure. I might ascertain whether Brown would accept a rescue from any company we might raise. Ricketson, from New Bedford, arrives. He and Thoreau take supper with us. Thoreau talks freely and

---

[1] Mr. Alcott himself.

[2] Thoreau's editor, Mr. Harrison Blake, has sent me this note from his friend : —

CONCORD, Oct. 31 [1859].

MR. BLAKE, — I spoke to my townsmen last evening, on "The Character of Captain Brown, now in the Clutches of the Slaveholder." I should like to speak to any company in Worcester who may wish to hear me ; and will come if only my expenses are paid. I think that we should express ourselves at once, while Brown is alive. The sooner, the better. Perhaps Higginson may like to have a meeting. Wednesday evening would be a good time. The people here are deeply interested in the matter. Let me have an answer as soon as may be.

HENRY D. THOREAU.

P. S. I may be engaged toward the end of the week.

enthusiastically about Brown, denouncing the Union, the President, the States, and Virginia particularly; wishes to publish his late speech, and has seen Boston publishers, but failed to find any to print it for him."

No list of Brown's friends could be complete without the names of those two practical idealists of Medford, — George and Mary Stearns, to whom he was more indebted for hos- pitalities and for liberal gifts of money and arms than to any, perhaps all, other persons.   Mr. Stearns was a merchant of Boston, of large income, but of larger heart, who was in- spired and seconded in all his patriotic efforts by his sensi- tive and clear-sighted wife, from whom no trait of character was hidden.   Mrs. Stearns saw at a glance across the whole field, and was critical in her judgments; but she accepted John Brown as a prophet and hero from the first.   Her husband, of slower speech and more deliberate temper, had misgivings now and then, but followed confidently the in- spiration of his wife.   Of him Emerson said, in a funeral address in 1867 : —

"We recall the all but exclusive devotion of this excellent man during the last twelve years to public and patriotic interests.   Known until that time in no very wide circle as a man of skill and persever- ance in his business, of pure life, of retiring and affectionate habits, happy in his domestic relations, his extreme interest in the national politics, then growing more anxious year by year, engaged him to scan the fortunes of freedom with keener attention.   He was an early laborer in the resistance to slavery.   This brought him into sympathy with the people of Kansas.   As early as 1855 the Emigrant Aid So- ciety was formed, and in 1856 he organized the Massachusetts State Kansas Committee, by means of which a large amount of money was obtained for the Free-State men at times of the greatest need.   He was the more engaged to this cause by making, in 1857, the ac- quaintance of Captain John Brown, who was not only an extraordi- nary man, but one who had a rare magnetism for men of character, and attached some of the best and noblest to him, on very short acquaintance, by lasting ties.   Mr. Stearns made himself at once necessary to Captain Brown as one who respected his inspirations, and had the magnanimity to trust him entirely, and to arm his hands with all needed help.   For the relief of Kansas in 1856–57 his own contributions were the largest and the first.   He never asked any one to give so much as he himself gave; and his interest was so manifestly pure and sincere that he easily obtained eager offerings in quarters where other petitioners failed. He did not hesitate to become the banker of his clients, and to furnish them money and arms in advance of the subscriptions which he obtained. His first donations were only entering wedges of his later; and, unlike other benefactors, he did not give money to excuse his entire preoccupation in his own pursuits, but as an earnest of the dedication of his heart and hand to the interests of the sufferers, a pledge kept until the success he wrought and prayed for was consummated."

But for the Stearnses and their gifts to Brown it is hard to see how he could have gone forward in his campaigns of the last two years, 1858–59; and how much he valued them we all knew who could read his heart. But the extent of their aid to him, and the length to which they were prepared to go, is not generally known, although Brown knew it well. At my request, Mrs. Stearns has furnished me an account of the origin of a most characteristic paper which Brown read to her in the first draft, and which is this: —

OLD BROWN'S FAREWELL

To the Plymouth Rocks, Bunker Hill Monuments, Charter Oaks, and Uncle Tom's Cabins.

He has left for Kansas; has been trying since he came out of the Territory to secure an outfit, or, in other words, the means of arming and thoroughly equipping his regular minute-men, who are mixed up with the people of Kansas. And he leaves the States with a feeling of deepest sadness, that after having exhausted his own small means, and with his family and his brave men suffered hunger, cold, nakedness, and some of them sickness, wounds, imprisonment in irons, with extreme cruel treatment, and others death; that after lying on the ground for months in the most sickly, unwholesome, and uncomfortable places, some of the time with sick and wounded, destitute of any shelter, hunted like wolves, and sustained in part by Indians; that after all this, in order to sustain a cause which every citizen of this "glorious republic" is under equal moral obligation to do, and for the neglect of which he will be held accountable by God, — a cause in which every man, woman, and child of the entire human family has a deep and awful interest, — that when no wages are asked or expected, he cannot secure, amid all the wealth, luxury.

and extravagance of this "heaven-exalted" people, even the necessary supplies of the common soldier. "How are the mighty
fallen!"

I am destitute of horses, baggage-wagons, tents, harness, saddles,
bridles, holsters, spurs, and belts; camp equipage, such as cooking
and eating utensils, blankets, knapsacks, intrenching-tools, axes,
shovels, spades, mattocks, crowbars; have not a supply of ammunition; have not money sufficient to pay freight and travelling expenses; and left my family poorly supplied with common necessaries.

BOSTON, April, 1857.

Mrs. Stearns writes me thus (April, 1885): —

"The newspaper reports of the Hon. Thomas Russell's address at
a John Brown commemoration in 1880, mentioning Mr. Stearns as
the generous friend of John Brown, contain a statement concerning
myself and the 'carriage and horses,' which must be my excuse for
relating the exact truth, both concerning the seven thousand dollars
offered by Mr. Stearns, and how John Brown came to write his
'Farewell to the Plymouth Rocks,' etc., which has appeared several
times in print, but without a word of explanation. As the address
states, Brown was keeping very quiet at Judge Russell's house in
Boston, partly on account of a warrant issued in Kansas for his arrest
for high treason, and partly because he was ill with fever and ague,
a chronic form of which had been induced by his exposures in Kansas. It was in April, 1857, and a chilling easterly storm had prevailed for many days. Mr. Stearns went frequently to visit him;
and on Saturday preceding the Sunday morning mentioned by Judge
Russell, Captain Brown expressed a wish that I should go to see
him, as he could not venture in such weather on a trip to Medford, —
emphasizing the request by saying that he wished to consult me about
a plan he had, and that I might come soon. Mr. Stearns gave me
his message at dinner, and I drove at once to Judge Russell's house.
As soon as my name was announced Brown appeared, and thanking
me for the promptness of my visit, proceeded to say that he had been
'amusing himself' by preparing a little address for Theodore Parker
to read to his congregation the next (Sunday) morning; and that he
would feel obliged to me for expressing my honest opinion about the
propriety of this. He then went upstairs, and returned with a paper,
which proved in the reading to be 'Old Brown's Farewell.' The
emphasis of his tone and manner I shall never forget, and wish I
could picture him as he sat and read, lifting his eyes to mine now
and then to see how it impressed me. When he finished he said:
'Well, now, what do you think? Shall I send it to Mr. Parker?'"

'Certainly; by all means send it. He will appreciate every word you have written, for it rings the metal he likes. But I have my doubts about reading it to his congregation. A few of them would understand its significance, but the majority, I fear, would not. Send it to Mr. Parker, and he will do what is best about it.' In reply he thanked me, and said I had confirmed his own judgment, had cleared his mind, and conferred the favor he desired. Then, I told him, he must give me a copy to preserve among my relics. He replied: 'I would give you this, but it is not fit. I had such an ague while writing that I could not keep my pen steady; but you shall have a fair copy.' In a few days he sent the copy I now have, by the hand of Mr. Stearns. It will be forwarded with other memorials to the Kansas Historical Society. The copy he gave Mr. Parker was found among his papers after Parker's death. I think it stimulated Mr. Parker to further exertions, for he collected quite a handsome sum from those parishioners who never failed to respond to his appeal.

"This matter being settled, Brown began talking upon the subject always uppermost in his thought, and, I may add, action also. Those who remember the power of his moral magnetism will understand how surely and readily he lifted his listener to the level of his own devotion; so that it suddenly seemed mean and unworthy — not to say wicked — to be living in luxury while such a man was struggling for a few thousands to carry out his cherished plan. 'Oh,' said he, 'if I could have the money that is *smoked away* during a single day in Boston, I could strike a blow which would make slavery totter from its foundations.' As he said these words, his look and manner left no doubt in my mind that he was quite capable of accomplishing his purpose. To-day all sane men everywhere acknowledge its truth. Well, I bade him adieu and drove home, thinking many thoughts, — of the power of a mighty purpose lodged in a deeply religious soul; of only one man with God on his side. The splendor of spring sunshine filled the room when I awoke the next morning; numberless birds, rejoicing in the returning warmth, filled all the air with melody; dandelions sparkled in the vivid grass; everything was so beautiful, that the wish rose warm in my heart to comfort and aid John Brown. It seemed not much to do to sell our estate and give the proceeds to him for his sublime purpose. What if another home were not as beautiful! When Mr. Stearns awoke I told him my morning thoughts. Reflecting awhile, he said: 'Perhaps it would not be just right to the children to do what you suggest; but I will do all I can in justice to them and you.' When breakfast was over, he drove to the residence of Judge Russell and handed Captain Brown his check for seven thousand dollars. But this fact was not known at that time, and only made public after the death of Mr. Stearns."

Brown's plan for Kansas was cordially approved by Theodore Parker, who, as Mrs. Stearns says, raised some money in aid of it, as he afterwards did for the Virginia enterprise. It was in connection with the latter that Brown made and showed to a few friends this draft of a letter introducing him to antislavery men, which I find among Brown's papers : —

JOHN BROWN'S DESCRIPTION OF HIMSELF (1858).

" This will introduce a friend who visits (Worcester) in order to secure means to sustain and further the cause of freedom in the United States and in all the world. In behalf of this cause he has so far exhausted his own limited means as to place his wife and three young daughters in circumstances of privation and of dependence upon the generosity of their friends, who have cared for them. He has contributed the entire services of two strong minor sons for two years, and of himself for more than three years, during which time they have all endured great hardships, exposure of health, and other privations. During much of the past three years he had with him in Kansas six sons and a son-in-law, who, together with himself, were all sick ; two were made prisoners, and subjected to most barbarous treatment ; two were severely wounded, and one murdered. During this time he figured with some success under the title of ' Old Brown,' often perilling his life in company with his sons and son-in-law, who all shared these trials with him. His object is commended to the best feelings of yourself and all who love liberty and equal rights in (Massachusetts), and himself indorsed as an earnest and steady-minded man, and a true descendant of Peter Brown, one of the ' Mayflower' Pilgrims."

Theodore Parker first met Brown at his Sunday congregation in the Boston Music Hall in January, 1857, unless he had briefly encountered him at Chicago two months earlier. They soon became warm friends, for Brown had heard Parker preach as early as 1853, and admired his deep piety, popular eloquence, and devotion to liberty, although they were far apart in theology. In April, 1857, when " Uncle Sam's hounds " were said to be on Brown's track, and he took refuge at the house of Judge Russell [1] in Boston, Parker wrote to Russell in these words : —

Sunday Morning.

MY DEAR JUDGE, — If John Brown falls into the hands of the marshal from Kansas, he is sure either of the gallows or of something yet worse.   If I were in his position, I should shoot dead any man who attempted to arrest me for those alleged crimes ; then I should be tried by a Massachusetts jury and be acquitted.

Yours truly,

T. P.

P. S.   I don't advise J. B. to do this, but it is what I should do.

Parker was one of the first in Boston to hear and entertain Brown's Virginia plans.   Plots in some degree similar were familiar to him, for other enthusiasts had brought their projects to be criticised or rejected by the clear judgment of the Boston radical.   Like others, Parker was deeply impressed with the sagacity of many parts of Brown's scheme and the wildness of the rest ; but he was willing to help it forward for Brown's sake, and raised money in aid of it. After it had culminated, he wrote from Rome the week following Brown's execution in these words concerning American, Italian, and universal affairs : —

---

[1] Judge Russell gives these anecdotes of Brown during this retirement at his house : " He used to take out his two revolvers and repeater every night before going to bed, to make sure of their loads, saying, ' Here are eighteen lives.'   To Mrs. Russell he once said, ' If you hear a noise at night, put the baby under the pillow.   I should hate to spoil these carpets, too, but you know I cannot be taken alive.'   Giving an account one day of his son Frederick's death, who was shot by Martin White, a Methodist preacher, Mrs. Russell broke out, ' If I were you, Mr. Brown, I would fight those ruffians as long as I lived.'   ' That,' he replied, ' is not a Christian spirit.   If I thought I had one bit of the spirit of revenge, I would never lift my hand ; I do not make war on slaveholders, even when I fight them, but on slavery.'   He would hold up Mrs. Russell's little girl, less than two years old, and tell her, ' When I am hung for treason, you can say that you used to stand on Captain Brown's hand ; ' and when he came to Boston two years after, in May, 1859, on his way to Harper's Ferry, he brought her some cakes of maple sugar from the Adirondac home."

Theodore Parker to R. W. Emerson.

Dec. 9, 1859.

MY DEAR EMERSON, — Mr. Apthorp leaves me a corner of his paper, which I am only too glad to fill with a word or two of greeting to you and yours. I rejoiced greatly at the brave things spoken by you at the Fraternity Lecture, and the hearty applause I knew it must meet with there. Wendell Phillips and you have said about all the brave words that have been spoken about our friend Captain Brown — No ! J. F. Clarke preached his best sermon on that brave man. Had I been at home, sound and well, I think this occasion would have either sent me out of the country — as it has Dr. Howe — or else have put me in a tight place. Surely I could not have been quite unconcerned and safe. It might not sound well that the minister of the Twenty-Eighth Congregational Church had "left for parts unknown," and that " between two days," and so could not fulfil his obligations to lecture or preach. Here to me " life is as tedious as a twice-told tale ; " it is only a strenuous idleness, — studying the remains of a dead people, and that too for no great purpose of helping such as are alive, or shall ever become so. I can do no better and no more. Here are pleasant Americans, — Mrs. Crawford, my friend Dr. Appleton, and above all the Storys, — most hospitable of people, and full of fire and wit. The Apthorps and Hunts are kind and wise as always, and full of noble sentiments. Of course, the great works of architecture, of sculpture and painting, are always here; but I confess I prefer the arts of use, which make the three millions of New England comfortable, intelligent, and moral, to the fine arts of beauty, which afford means of pleasure to a few emasculated dilettanti. None loves beauty more than I, of Nature or Art ; but I thank God that in the Revival of Letters our race — the world-conquering Teutons — turned off to Science, which seeks Truth and Industry, that conquers the forces of Nature and transfigures Matter into Man ; while the Italians took the Art of Beauty for their department. The Brownings are here, poet and poetess both, and their boy, the Only. Pleasant people are they both, with the greatest admiration for a certain person of Concord, to whom I also send my heartiest thanks and good wishes. To him and his long life and prosperity !

THEODORE PARKER.[1]

---

[1] Parker's letter to Francis Jackson on the deed and death of Brown was one of his last public utterances, — for he died and was buried in Florence, where Mrs. Browning was afterwards buried, in May, 1860.

I have spoken of the unstinted gifts of George and Mary Stearns, in aid of Brown and his work. Gerrit Smith, the baronial democrat of rural New York, was the counterpart of Stearns in generosity of giving. He did not finally bestow so much money on Brown's enterprises as Mr. Stearns, but he stood ready at all times to meet responsibility, and to contribute when appeals were made. He was early informed of the Virginia scheme, which he did not disapprove, and to aid which he gave hundreds of dollars, and would have given thousands if necessary. He saw fit after Brown's death to disguise in some ways his deep interest in the old hero; but this was from no disregard of Brown's great qualities, which he never ceased to praise. I will not enter now upon the reasons for this course of Smith, and I have set forth the facts in their proper place. To me he never denied his share in the enterprise of Brown; and he lived to see its grand results in the years directly following Brown's death. The part taken by Dr. Howe and Colonel Higginson in the enterprise has also been related, and need not be remarked upon further. Dr. Howe shrank at first from acknowledging his connection with Brown, and distressed some of his friends thereby; for he was overcome by the contemplation of results which he might have foreseen, but did not. Higginson desired even greater publicity for the truth than then seemed necessary, and the records which he has preserved are of material value in confirming any authentic account of the conspiracy.[1]

---

[1] Brown's secret committee kept no records, and its members generally destroyed their letters to each other after his capture, so that nobody should be injured by what had been written. Mrs. Gerrit Smith wrote to me in January, 1874, what I had heard from her son-in-law Charles Miller in November, 1859 : " Immediately after the Harper's Ferry affair Mr. Smith destroyed all the letters touching Brown's movements which he had received from persons in any degree privy to those movements ; and he took it for granted that his own similar letters to others had been destroyed." In replying (Jan. 16, 1874), I said : " My first proceeding upon hearing of the attack at Harper's Ferry, was to go over carefully all the papers and letters then in my hands, and destroy all that could implicate Mr. Smith or other persons. Two months later, when John A. Andrew placed in my hands my own letters to Brown (with a few from other persons) which Mr. Phillips had brought down from North Elba, after the funeral there, I

Although not specially a friend of John Brown before
then, the Boston sculptor Brackett was one of those profoundly impressed by his heroism at Harper's Ferry. He
had seen Brown once in a Boston street in 1857, and been
attracted by the dignity of his mien. The impression then
and afterwards made, kindled a glowing desire to perpetuate
in marble this remarkable man. The story of his bust of
Brown, as he told it at the time, runs thus : —

" I could hardly sleep or eat, so absorbing was the desire that took
possession of my mind. I had no money to make the journey to
Virginia, and I finally went, in turn, to Dr. Howe and Wendell
Phillips, requesting a loan for the purpose. Neither of them considered a marble bust of Brown really important, with so many other
things to be thought of. But I said there is one man who if he cannot help me will listen, and perhaps give me furtherance ; so I went
to Mr. Stearns. When I entered his counting-room he was just
leaving it for Medford. In a few moments, while walking along
with him, I explained in brief why I had come. He replied : ' You
are right : it ought to be done ; but just now I am fully occupied in
efforts to obtain funds for Brown's defence. I will mention the matter to Mrs. Stearns ; come to me to-morrow morning, and you shall
have her reply.' I did so ; when, putting the money needful into
my hand, he said : ' Mrs. Stearns says, " Take that, and start

went over these also carefully, before I left Boston that day, and destroyed
what would implicate others. But some of the correspondence of 1858-59
had lodged with Theodore Parker, and came back to me a year or two after
his death ; this I did not destroy. Colonel Higginson also had retained
some of the letters which passed through my hands, with copies of many
that he wrote to me or to Brown, and all these still exist. It is likely
Mrs. Stearns has documents touching the matter. I should doubt if Dr.
Howe had many ; but Vice-President Wilson told me, some weeks ago,
that he had recovered an important letter of his own, which in 1859-60
was supposed to be lost, when it went to Canada or somewhere, but has
now got home again. It cannot, therefore, be assumed that all written
evidence in the case is lost." In fact, I have since found several of the
notes which passed between members of the secret committee. Here is one
from Mr. Stearns, concerning a meeting at Theodore Parker's house, to
consult about raising money for Brown : —

BOSTON, Sept. 20, 1858.

MY DEAR FRIEND, — Yours of yesterday is at hand. I should prefer Saturday at
seven P. M., if that is agreeable to Mr. Parker and yourself. If you decide on that time,
please notify Mr. Parker and Dr. Howe. If you do not write me to change the time, I
shall be there without further notice.

immediately;" and these are her instructions: "John Brown will
refuse to have his bust taken; he will say, 'All nonsense; better give
the money to the poor!' And if Mr. Brackett replies that posterity
will want to know how he looked, he may also say, 'No consequence
to posterity how I looked; better give the money to the poor!' Then,
if every argument fails to convince him, let Mr. Brackett say that
he has come at the express wish and expense of Mrs. Stearns, and
that she will be deeply disappointed if he returns without the measurements."' The next morning I was on my way to Virginia, and
found on arriving at Charlestown that I had not come an hour too
soon. The excitement over the arrival of a stranger from the North
was intense and ridiculous. I was seized, and only escaped imprisonment by appealing to Mr. Griswold, whose services had been secured
for the defence. Through his efforts and influence the officials were
reassured, and I was allowed to accompany him to the prison, but
not to cross the threshold. Through the open door I saw the object
of my pilgrimage quietly reading, but heavily loaded with chains.
He was sitting in a chair, with both hands chained, and his feet
chained to the floor. Only those who saw him in that miserable
prison can have any adequate conception of the moral grandeur of
his presence! Everybody and everything was dwarfed in comparison. He looked up from his book, when addressed by his counsel,
and listened attentively to the request conveyed from me. Impressive
as the scene was, I could not restrain a smile when his reply repeated
the very words of Mrs. Stearns, — 'Nonsense! All nonsense! Better give the money to the poor!' When Mr. Griswold said he must
remember that he was becoming famous, and that posterity would
like to see how he looked, the prophecy was again fulfilled, and the
response came, even more emphatic, — 'No consequence to posterity
how I looked! Give the money to the poor!' For some time Mr.
Griswold labored to change his purpose, but finally returned to me
(still standing outside the door) and said: 'It is no use, he will not
yield one jot. I am sorry for your disappointment, but it is useless
arguing further.' The moment then had come for 'the last resort.'
'Please say to him that I have come at the express wish and pecuniary expense of Mrs. Stearns, and that she will be deeply disappointed
if I return without the measurements for a bust.' I watched his face
eagerly while Mr. Griswold repeated to him these words, on which
hung all my hopes. As he listened, I could see signs of interest,
mingled with surprise, in his face; then a grave thoughtfulness.
Presently his hands dropped at his sides, and he seemed lost in
thought. Then, lifting his head and straightening himself up, he
said, with emotion: 'Anything Mr. or Mrs. Stearns desire. Take
the measurements.'"

The measurements were thus secured, and the bust was made. It shows to what extent the artist was inspired by his subject, and faithfully represents the moral sublimity of the martyr. Charles Sumner exclaimed on seeing it, " There is nothing the sun shines upon so like Michael Angelo's Moses ! " and the art critic Jarves said : " If in some future age it should be dug up, men would ask, What old divinity is this ? " It is an idealized portrait of Brown, yet recalling the features of the man, as well as his grand air.

Mention must be omitted of the other friends of Brown ; nor need I dwell on my own friendship with him, which this volume sufficiently attests. My opinions were those of Brown, of Parker, of Emerson, Thoreau, Smith, and the older men who foresaw the catastrophe of American slavery. On the day of his death Brown penned this sentence, which he handed to one of his guards in the prison : —

CHARLESTOWN, VA., Dec. 2, 1859.

I, John Brown, am now quite certain that the crimes of this guilty land will never be purged away but with blood. I had, as I now think vainly, flattered myself that without very much bloodshed it might be done.

A week before, Parker had written from Rome to Francis Jackson in Boston : " A few years ago it did not seem difficult first to check slavery, and then to end it, without any bloodshed. I think this cannot be done now, nor ever in the future. All the great charters of humanity have been writ in blood. I once hoped that of American Democracy would be engrossed in less costly ink ; but it is plain now that our pilgrimage must lead through a Red Sea, wherein many a Pharaoh will go under and perish." So it happened ; and not only the Pharaohs, but the leaders of the people perished. Standing on the battle-field at Gettysburg, four years after Brown's execution (Nov. 19, 1863), Abraham Lincoln pronounced his eulogy on those who " gave their lives that the nation might live," calling on his hearers to resolve " that these dead shall not have died in vain ; that this nation, under God, shall have a new birth of freedom; and that government of the people, by the people and for the people, shall not perish from the earth," — thus echoing the very words of Parker, so often heard in prayer and sermon from his Boston pulpit.   Not long afterward Lincoln himself fell, the last great victim in the struggle, as John Brown had been its first great martyr. Henceforth their names are joined and their words remembered together, — the speech of the condemned convict at Charlestown and that of the successful statesman at Gettysburg going down to posterity as the highest range of eloquence in our time.   But those brave men whom Lincoln commemorated went forth to battle at the call of a great people; they were sustained by the resources and the ardor of millions.   I must daily remember my old friend, lonely, poor, persecuted, making a stand with his handful of followers on the outpost of Freedom, our own batteries trained upon him as the furious enemy swept him away in the storm of their vengeance; and then I see that history will exalt his fame with that of the liberators of mankind, who sealed their testament of benefactions with the blood of noble hearts.

CHAPTER XV.

THE FORAY IN VIRGINIA.

IT so happens that Brown left behind him a brief Diary, serving as a key to his correspondence from the time he reached Michigan with his freedmen in March, 1859, to the final arrangements for his campaign in October. Printed here with notes and comments, this Diary will make plain what might not be so clear from his letters alone, considering that most of Brown's own letters of this year were destroyed, either by those who received them or by members of the family who feared that they would compromise his friends.

JOHN BROWN'S LATEST DIARY.

From Detroit, March 10, 1859, to the Kennedy Farm, October 8.

March 10. Wrote Augustus Wattles to enclose to E. and A. King; also wrote Frederick Douglass at Detroit; also wrote W. Penn Clarke, Iowa City; also C. P. Tidd. Gave Kagi $1.25.

March 16. Wrote J. B. Grinnell. Wrote A. Hazlett, Indiana P. O., Indiana County, Pa.

March 25. Wrote wife and children to write me, care of American House, Troy, N. Y. Enclosed draft for $150. J. H. Kagi, Dr.: To cash for Carpenter, five dollars. Clinton Gilroy, Esq., New London, Conn.

[Between the dates March 25 and June 18, Brown was at Peterboro' (April 11–14), at Concord (May 7–9), at Boston (May 9–June 3), and at North Elba (June 6–9).]

West Andover, Ohio, June 18. Borrowed John's old compass, and left my own, together with Gunley's book, with him at West Andover; also borrowed his small Jacob staff; also gave him for expenses fifteen dollars; write him, under cover to Horace Lindsley, West Andover. Henry C. Carpenter.

June 21. Gave J. H. Kagi fifty dollars for expenses at Cleveland.

June 23. Wrote wife and children, and enclosed five dollars. Also wrote J. Henrie Kagi to inquire at Bedford for letters. If none found, he will wait.

June 27. Wrote J. Henrie that he will find a line at Chambersburg, or three Smiths and Anderson.

June 29. Wrote Horace Greeley & Co., enclosing three dollars for " New York Tribune." Gave Watson fifty dollars for P.

June 30. Wrote J. Henrie to write I. Smith & Sons at Harper's Ferry, if he needs to do so.

July 5. Wrote John and Jason about freight, etc.; also wife; also Charles Blair to forward freight; also to write I. Smith & Sons at Chambersburg. Gave Oliver for expenses $160. Gave Stephens for expenses, June 17, at West Andover, $25.

July 8. Wrote John, enclosing two fifty-dollar drafts. Gave John Henrie forty dollars for expenses.

July 12. Wrote John Henrie and J. Smith. Also Jacob Frery, Esq., about hogs.

July 22. Wrote John, enclosing draft for $100, with instructions. Also wrote Watson some instructions. Also John Henrie.

July 27. Wrote wife and children for Watson not to set out till we write him.

August 2. Wrote wife for Watson and Dauphin Thompson to come on; also wrote James N. Gloucester and J. Henrie.

August 6. Wrote J. Henrie.

August 8. Wrote same; also wife and children that friends had arrived, and about wintering stock. Date altered to August 11.

August 16. Wrote wife and John, Jr., for instructions, etc.

August 17. Wrote Jason for box, etc.

August 18. Wrote F. B. S[anborn] and other friends.[1]

August 24. Wrote Charles Blair.

September 9. Wrote wife, F. B. S[anborn], Frederick Douglass,

---

[1] This was about the time that Douglass visited Brown at Chambersburg. The purpose of Brown's letter to me was to raise three hundred dollars more, since he was delayed for want of money ; and I undertook to raise it. On the 4th of September I had sent him two hundred dollars, of which Dr. Howe gave fifty ; on the 14th I had all but thirty-five dollars of the remaining hundred, Colonel Higginson having sent me twenty dollars. I think the balance was paid by Mr. Stearns, who on the 8th of September had written thus to Higginson : "By reading Mr. Sanborn's note to me a second time, I see that the enclosed ought to have been sent to you with his note. Please read it and enclose again to him. I hope you will be able to get the fifty dollars. We have done all we could, and fall short another fifty as yet." The "enclosed" here was an urgent appeal from Chambersburg for money.

James N. Gloucester, J. W. L[oguen]; also came on the 20th of September.

October 1. Wrote wife and children on various matters, — wintering stock, money, etc. Also wrote (to J. B., Jr.) home, and at Cleveland. Also J. B. L. (September 30 and October 1).

October 8. Wrote wife and children about Bell and Martha, and to write John.

[To this paper was added the following.]

Names of Men to Call upon for Assistance.

Isaac J. White and William Burgess, Carlisle, Cumberland County, Pa.; Joseph A. Crowley, Elias Rouse, and John Fidler, Bedford, Pa.; E. D. Bassett, 718 Lombard Street, Philadelphia; John D. Scoville.

It will be seen that this Diary is incomplete, naming but a portion of the letters that Brown wrote in this period, and specifying less than half his expenses, which from March 10 to October 16 must have exceeded twenty-five hundred dollars. His sources of revenue have already been pointed out; but they may be more plainly indicated, now that it is no longer invidious to be known as the friend of John Brown. When he reached Canada from Kansas with his rescued fugitives, his exchequer was nearly exhausted, although he had supplied it to some extent in Kansas by collecting debts and property belonging to the defunct National Committee, as has been mentioned.[1]

---

[1] An evidence of this is found in the following notification to one of Mr. Whitman's Kansas agents, twelve months before the attack on Harper's Ferry : —

OTTUMWA, Oct. 7, 1858.

MR. JOHN T. COX.

SIR, — You are hereby notified that I hold claims against the National Kansas Committee which are good against them and all persons whatever; and that I have authority from said committee to take possession, as their agent, of any supplies belonging to said committee, wherever found. You will therefore retain in your hands all moneys, notes, or accounts you may now have in your custody, by direction of said committee or any of its agents, and hold them subject to my call or order, as I shall hold you responsible for them to me, as agent of said committee.

JOHN BROWN.
Agent National Kansas Committee.

Of the same date is the following receipt : —

Received as agent National Kansas Committee, of J. T. Cox, seven men's coarse cotton shirts, placed in his custody by E. B. Whitman, as agent of said committee, for sale or distribution.   JOHN BROWN,
Agt. Nat. Kan. Com.

The following letter from John Brown to Kagi gives his own report of the success he had in raising money at Gerrit Smith's, and of the arrangement proposed by Mr. Smith for the support of the Virginia campaign of 1859 : —

John Brown to Kagi.

DEAR SIR, — I am here, waiting a conveyance to take me home; have been quite prostrated almost the whole time since you left me at John's, with the difficulty in my head and ear, and with the ague in consequence. I am now some better. Had a good visit at Rochester, but did not effect much. Had a first-rate time at Peterboro'; got of Mr. Smith and others nearly one hundred and sixty dollars, and a note (which I think a good one) for two hundred and eighty-five dollars. Mr. S. wrote to Eastern friends to make up at least two thousand dollars, saying he was in for one fifth the amount. I feel encouraged to believe it will soon be done, and wish you to let our folks all round understand how the prospects are. Still, it will be some days (and it may be weeks) before I can get ready to return. I shall not be idle. If you have found my writing-case and papers, please forward them without delay, by express, to Henry Thompson, North Elba, Essex County, N. Y.

Your friend in truth,   B.

J. H. KAGI, ESQ.

Kagi replied to this on the 21st and 27th of April, while Brown was at North Elba; but no answer came from Brown until he had been a week in Boston, after his last visit to Concord, May 7–9, 1859. He then wrote as follows from the United States Hotel in Boston, where he was then lodging : —

John Brown to Kagi.

DEAR SIR, — I should have acknowledged the receipt of yours of April 21, to Henry Thompson, together with writing-case and papers (all safe, so far as I now see), and also yours of April 27 to me, but for being badly down with the ague, — so much so as to disqualify me for everything, nearly. I have been here going on two weeks, and am getting better for two days past; but am very weak. I wish you to say to our folks, all as soon as may be, that there is scarce a doubt but that all will be set right in a very few days more, so that I can be on my way back. They must none of them think I have been slack to try and urge forward a delicate and very difficult matter. I cannot now write you a long letter, being obliged to neglect replying to others, and also to put off some very important correspondence. My reception has been everywhere most cordial and cheering.   Your friend in truth,

JOHN BROWN.

J. H. KAGI, ESQ.

A brief note from Mr. Stearns, May 27, 1859, has this passage : " We are getting on slowly, — about fifty dollars per day ; and if Gerrit Smith accepts, will send the old man off early next week." This was done, and the "accept-ance " of Mr. Smith was shown by his sending Brown two hundred dollars early in June. I have accounts of seven hundred and fifty dollars given by Smith to Brown during 1859, while Mr. Stearns in that year gave him more than a thousand dollars. Out of a little more than four thousand dollars in money which passed through the hands of the secret committee in aid of his Virginia enterprise, or was known to them as contributed, at least thirty-eight hundred dollars were given with a clear knowledge of the use to which it would be put.

When the Boston visit was over, and Brown had again spent a few days at North Elba, he wrote thus : —

KEENE, N. Y., June 9, 1859.

DEAR SIR, — After being delayed with sickness and other hin-drances, I am so far on my way back, and hope to be in Ohio within the coming week. Will you please advise the friends all of the fact, and say to them that as soon as I do reach, I will let them know where I will be found. I have been middling successful in my business.   Yours in truth,

JOHN BROWN.

J. HENRIE, ESQ.

Before leaving Westport, June 10, Brown probably re-ceived a letter from Gerrit Smith, mentioned in the letter of June 4. which is given below with corrections from the copy published soon after Brown's capture, that first directed attention toward Mr. Smith as one of Brown's friends in his last campaign : —

PETERBORO', June 4, 1859.

CAPTAIN JOHN BROWN.

MY DEAR FRIEND, — I wrote you a week ago, directing my letter to the care of Mr. Stearns. He replied, informing me that he had forwarded it to Westport; but as Mr. Morton received last evening a letter from Mr. Sanborn, saying your address would be your son's home, — namely, West Andover, — I therefore write you without delay, and direct your letter to your son. I have done what I could thus far for Kansas, and what I could to keep you at your Kansas work. Losses by indorsement and otherwise have brought me under heavy embarrassment the last two years, but I must, nevertheless, continue to do, in order to keep you at your Kansas work. I send you herewith my draft for two hundred dollars. Let me hear from you on the receipt of this letter. You live in our hearts, and our prayer to God is that you may have strength to continue in your Kansas work. My wife joins me in affectionate regard to you, dear John, whom we both hold in very high esteem. I suppose you put the Whitman note into Mr. Stearns's hands. It will be a great shame if Mr. Whitman does not pay it. What a noble man is Mr. Stearns![1] How liberally he has contributed to keep you in your Kansas work!

Your friend,

GERRIT SMITH.

On the same day that Mr. Smith sent the letter last cited, I wrote to Higginson from Concord : —

June 4, 1859.

Brown has set out on his expedition, having got some eight hundred dollars from all sources except from Mr. Stearns, and from him

---

[1] To those who could read between the lines, this letter disclosed the whole method of the secret committee. No one of them might know at any given time where Brown was, but some other was sure to know, — and in this one note four persons are named who might be at any time in communication with Brown wherever he was, — George L. Stearns, Edwin Morton, F. B. Sanborn, and Mr. Smith himself. The phrase "Kansas work" misled none of these persons, who all knew that Brown had finally left Kansas and was to operate henceforth in the slave States. The hundred dollars given by Mr. Smith April 14, added to the two hundred named in this letter, and the note of E. B. Whitman, of Kansas, which Brown received from Mr. Smith, make up five hundred and eighty-five dollars, or more than one-fifth of the two thousand dollars which he told Brown he would help his "Eastern friends" raise. Those friends were Stearns, Howe, Higginson, and Sanborn, — for Parker was then in Europe, and unable to contribute.

the balance of two thousand dollars; Mr. S—— being a man who,
"having put his hand to the plow, turneth not back."   Brown left
Boston for Springfield and New York on Wednesday morning at 8.30,
and Mr. Stearns has probably gone to New York to-day, to make final
arrangements for him.   Brown means to be on the ground as soon
as he can, perhaps so as to begin by the 4th of July.   He could
not say where he should be for a few weeks, but letters are addressed
to him, under cover to his son John, Jr., at West Andover, Ohio.
This point is not far from where Brown will begin, and his son will
communicate with him.   Two of his sons will go with him.   He is
desirous of getting some one to go to Canada, and collect recruits for
him among the fugitives, — with Harriet Tubman or alone, as the
case may be.

This letter shows I had then no thought that the attack
would be made at Harper's Ferry ; nor had Mr. Stearns, to
whom I was in the habit of talking or writing about this
matter every few days.   I have no doubt he knew as much
as I did about the general plan, while Mr. Smith knew
more.   On the 6th of October — ten days before the attack
was made — I wrote to Higginson, "The three hundred
dollars desired has been made up and received.   Four or
five men will be on the ground next week, from these
regions and elsewhere."   These facts were all known to
Mr. Stearns, who within a fortnight of the outbreak was in
consultation with Mr. Lewis Hayden, and other colored men
of Boston, about forwarding recruits to Brown.   I think he
paid some of the expenses of these recruits, as Merriam
certainly did.

As Brown was setting forth for Virginia, he wrote
thus : —

John Brown to his Family.

UNITED STATES HOTEL, BOSTON, May 13, 1859.

DEAR WIFE AND CHILDREN, ALL, — I wrote you from Troy last
week, saying I had sent on the balance of articles I intended to buy,
and that it might be well to call on James A. Allen, Westport, for
them soon.   I would now say, if you are not in a strait for them
it may be as well to defer sending for a little, as I expect soon to be
at home again, and may in that case be able to save considerable
expense.   They are all directed to John Brown at Westport.   I feel
now very confident of ultimate success, but have to be patient, and I

have the ague to hinder me some lately. May God be the portion of you all !

Your affectionate husband and father,

JOHN BROWN.

BOSTON, MASS., May 19, 1859.

DEAR WIFE AND CHILDREN, ALL, — I intend to be with you again next week ; but as I may fail to bring it about, I now write to say to Watson and Oliver that I think it quite certain that I shall very soon be off for the southwest, so that they may (I think safely) calculate their business accordingly. I shall be glad to have my summer clothing put in order, so far as it can be done comfortably ; I have had no shake now for five days, and am getting quite smart again, and my hearing improves. You all may as well be still about my movements. God bless you all !

Your affectionate husband and father,

JOHN BROWN.

AKRON, OHIO, June 23, 1859.

DEAR WIFE AND CHILDREN, ALL, — My best wish for you all is that you may truly love God and his commandments. We found all well at West Andover, and all middling well here. I have the ague some yet. I sent a calf-skin from Troy by express, directed to Watson Brown, North Elba, to go by stage from Westport. I now enclose five dollars to help you further about getting up a good loom. We start for the Ohio River to-day. Write me under cover to John at West Andover, for the present. The frost has been far more destructive in Western New York and in Ohio than it was in Essex County. Farmers here are mowing the finest-looking wheat I ever saw, for fodder only. Jason has been quite a sufferer. May God abundantly bless and keep you all !

Your affectionate husband and father,

JOHN BROWN.

John Brown to J. H. Kagi.

CHAMBERSBURG, PENN., June 30, 1859.

JOHN HENRIE, ESQ.

DEAR SIR, — We leave here to-day for Harper's Ferry, *via* Hagerstown. When you get there you had best look on the hotel register for I. Smith & Sons, without making much inquiry. We shall be looking for cheap lands near the railroad in all probability. You can write I. Smith & Sons, at Harper's Ferry, should you need to do so.   Yours, in truth,

I. SMITH [JOHN BROWN].

The " three Smiths and Anderson," mentioned by Brown
in his diary for June 27, were himself (" Isaac Smith "), his
two sons, Owen (" Watson Smith "), and Oliver (" Oliver
Smith "), and his henchman, Jerry Anderson, who all appeared at Hagerstown June 30, and spent that night at a
tavern there. July 3, these four were at Harper's Ferry,
where Brown's lieutenant Cook had been living for some
months ; and on the 4th they strolled up the river road on
the Maryland side toward the house of J. C. Unseld, a
Maryland slaveholder, living on a mountain path a mile
northwest of the Ferry. Early that forenoon Unseld riding
down to the Ferry met them strolling along the edge of the
mountain which here overlooks the Potomac. " Well, gentlemen," said the planter, " I suppose you are out hunting
minerals, — gold and silver, perhaps ? " " No," said Brown,
" we want to buy land ; we have a little money, and want to
make it go as far as we can. How much is land worth an acre
here ? " Being told that it ranged from fifteen to thirty
dollars in that neighborhood, he said, " That is high ; I
thought I could buy for a dollar or two an acre." " No,"
said the Marylander, " not here ; if you expect to get land
for that price, you 'll have to go farther west, — to Kansas,
or some of those Territories where there is Congress land.
Where are you from ? " " The northern part of New York
State." " What have you followed there ? " " Farming,"
said Brown ; but the frost had been so heavy of late years
it had cut off their crops, they could not make anything
there, so he had sold out, and thought they would come
farther south and try it awhile.

Having thus satisfied a natural curiosity, Unseld rode on ;
but returning some hours afterward, he again met Smith
and his young men not far from the same place. " I have
been looking round your country up here," said he, " and it
is a very fine country, — a pleasant place, a fine view. The
land is much better than I expected to find it : your crops
are pretty good." As he said this he pointed to where the
men had been cutting grain, — some white men and some
negroes at work in the fields, as the custom is there ; for in
Washington County there were few slaves even then, and
most of the field work was done by whites or free-colored

men. Brown then asked if any farm in the neighborhood was for sale. "Yes, there is a farm four miles up the road here, toward Boonsborough, owned by the heirs of Dr. Booth Kennedy; you can buy that." "Can I rent it?" said Brown; then turning to his companions he said: "I think we had better rent awhile, until we get better acquainted, so that they cannot take advantage of us in the purchase of land." To this they appeared to assent, and Mr. Unseld then said: "Perhaps you can rent the Kennedy farm; it is for sale I know." Brown then turned to his sons and said: "Boys, as you are not very well, you had better go back and tell the landlord at Sandy Hook that Oliver and I shall not be there to dinner, but will go on up and see the Kennedy place. However, you can do as you please." Watson Brown looked at Anderson, and then said, "We will go with you." "Well," said the friendly Marylander, "if you will go on with me up to my house, I can then point you the road exactly." Arrived there he invited them to take dinner, for by this time it was nearly noon. They thanked him, but declined; nor would they accept an invitation to "drink something." "Well," said Unseld, "if you must go on, just follow up this road along the foot of the mountain; it is shady and pleasant, and you will come out at a church up here about three miles. Then you can see the Kennedy house by looking from that church up the road that leads to Boonsborough, or you can go right across and get into the county road, and follow that up." Brown sat and talked with Unseld for a while, who asked him "what he expected to follow, up yonder at Kennedy's?" adding that Brown "could not more than make a living there." "Well," said Brown, "my business has been buying up fat cattle and driving them on to the State of New York, and we expect to engage in that again." Three days later, Unseld, again jogging to or from the Ferry, again met the gray-bearded rustic, who said: "I think that place will suit me; now just give me a description where I can find the widow Kennedy and the administrator," which Unseld did. A few days after, he once more met the new-comer, and found Mr. Smith had rented the two houses on the Kennedy farm, — the farm-house, about three hundred yards from the public

road on the west side, where, as Unseld thought, " it makes
a very pretty show for a small house," and " the cabin,"
which stood about as far from the road on the east side,
" hidden by shrubbery in the summer season, pretty much."[1]
For the two houses, pasture for a cow and horse, and fire-
wood, from July till March, Brown paid thirty-five dollars,
as he took pains to tell Unseld, showing him the receipt of
the widow Kennedy.

How was it possible to mistrust a plain Yankee farmer
and cattle-drover who talked in that way, and had no con-
cealments, no tricks, and no airs ? Evidently the Marylander did not once mistrust him, though he rode up to the
Kennedy farm nearly every week from the middle of July
till the first of October. " I just went up to talk to the old
man," said he ; " but sometimes, at the request of others,
on business about selling him some horses or cows. He was
in my yard frequently, — perhaps four or five times. I
would always ask him in, but he would never go in, and of
course I would not go in his house. He often invited me
in ; indeed, nearly every time I went there he asked me to go
in, and remarked to me frequently, ' We have no chairs for
you to sit on, but we have trunks and boxes.' I declined
going in, but sat on my horse and chatted with him." Before the 20th of July he saw there " two females," who were
Martha, the wife of Oliver Brown, and Anne, the eldest unmarried sister of Oliver, then a girl of not quite sixteen
years. " Twice I went there," says Unseld, " and found
none of the men, but the two ladies ; and I sat there on my
horse, — there was a high porch on the house, and I could
sit there and chat with them ; and then I rode off and left
them. They told me there were none of the men at home,
but did not tell me where they were. One time I went
there and inquired for them, and one of the females answered me, ' They are across there at the cabin ; you had
better ride over and see them.' I replied it did not make

---

[1] It was at this cabin (since torn down) that Brown kept his boxes of
rifles and pistols, after they reached him from Ohio. The pikes from
Connecticut, a thousand in number, were stored in the loft or attic of the
farm-house, where Brown and his family lived.

any difference; I would not bother them; and I rode back home." [1]

John Brown to his Family.

CHAMBERSBURG, PENN., July 22, 1859.

DEAR FRIENDS, ALL, — Oliver, Martha, and Anne all got on safe on Saturday of the week they set out. If W. and D. set out in ten days or a week after getting this, they will be quite in time. All well. When you write, direct to I. Smith & Sons, Chambersburg, Penn.   Your friend,

ISAAC SMITH.

CHAMBERSBURG, PENN., July 27, 1859.

DEAR WIFE AND CHILDREN, ALL, — I write to say that we are all well, and that I think Watson and D. had not best set out until we write again, and not until sufficient hay has been secured to winter all the stock well. To be buying hay in the spring or last of the winter is ruinous, and there is no prospect of our getting our freight on so as to be ready to go to work under some time yet. We will give you timely notice. When you write, enclose first in a small envelope, put a stamp on it, seal it, and direct it to I. Smith & Sons, Harper's Ferry, Va.; then enclose it under a stamped envelope, which direct to John Henrie, Chambersburg, Penn. I need not say, do all your directing and sealing at home, and not at the post-office.

Your affectionate husband and father,

I. SMITH.

CHAMBERSBURG, PENN., Aug. 2, 1859.

DEAR WIFE AND CHILDREN, ALL, — If Watson and D. should set out soon after getting this, it may be well. They will avoid saying anything on the road about North Elba. It will be quite as well to say they are from Essex County; and need not say anything about it unless they are questioned, when they had better say as above. Persons who do not talk much are seldom questioned much. They should buy through tickets at Troy or at New York for Baltimore,

---

[1] This gossip pictures, as no description could, the quiet and drowsiness of this woodland, primitive, easy-going, hard-living population, amid the hills and mountains of Maryland, where John Brown spent the last three months of his free life, and gathered his forces for the battle in which he fell. It is a region of home-keeping, honest, dull country people; and so completely did Brown make himself one of its denizens, that he was accepted, as part and parcel of it, even when plotting his most audacious strokes.

where they will get tickets for Harper's Ferry; and there, by inquiring of Mr. Michael Ault, who keeps the toll-bridge over which they have to pass, they can find I. Smith on the Kennedy farm. Watson will be a son and D. his brother-in-law Thompson, if any inquiry is made at the bridge or elsewhere. They had better not bring trunks. We are all well. May God abundantly bless and keep you all!

Your affectionate husband and father.

Brown had not been living at the Kennedy farm many weeks when a touching incident occurred, which is thus related by his daughter Anne, who was then his housekeeper:

" One day, a short time after I went down there, father was sitting at the table writing, I was near by sewing (he and I being alone in the room), when two little wrens that had a nest under the porch came flying in at the door, fluttering and twittering; then flew back to their nest and again to us several times, seemingly trying to attract our attention. They appeared to be in great distress. I asked father what he thought was the matter with the little birds. He asked if I had ever seen them act so before; I told him no. 'Then let us go and see,' he said. We went out and found that a snake had crawled up the post and was just ready to devour the little ones in the nest. Father killed the snake; and then the old birds sat on the railing and sang as if they would burst. It seemed as if they were trying to express their joy and gratitude to him for saving their little ones. After we went back into the room, he said he thought it very strange the way the birds asked him to help them, and asked if I thought it an omen of his success. He seemed very much impressed with that idea. I do not think he was superstitious; but you know he always thought and felt that God called him to that work; and seemed to place himself, or rather to imagine himself, in the position of the figure in the old seal of Virginia, with the tyrant under her foot."

CHAMBERSBURG, PENN., Aug. 16, 1859.

DEAR WIFE AND CHILDREN, ALL, — I left all well at home yesterday but Martha, who was complaining a little. Am in hopes nothing serious is the matter. I will only now say I am getting along as well, perhaps, all things considered, as I ought to expect. We all want to hear from you; but we do not want you all to write, and you need only say all is well, or otherwise, as the case may be. When you write, enclose in a small envelope such as I now send, seal it, and write on it no other directions than I. Smith & Sons.

Enclose that in a stamped envelope and direct it to John Henrie, Esq., of Chambersburg, Franklin County, Penn., who will send it to us.   Affectionately yours,   I. S.

CHAMBERSBURG, PA., Sept. 8, 1859.

DEAR WIFE AND CHILDREN, ALL, — I write to say that we are all well, and are getting along as well as we could reasonably expect. It now appears likely that Martha and Anne will be on their way home in the course of this month, but they may be detained to a little later period. I do not know what to advise about fattening the old spotted cow, as much will depend on what you have to feed her with; whether your heifers will come in or not next spring; also upon her present condition. You must exercise the best judgment you have in the matter, as I know but little about your crops. I should like to know more as soon as I can. I am now in hopes of being able to send you something in the way of help before long. May God abundantly bless you all! Ellen, I want you to be very good.

Your affectionate husband and father,   I. S.

Sept. 9. Bell's letter of 30th August to Watson is received.

Sept. 20, 1859. All well. Girls will probably start for home soon.

Yours ever,   I. S.

CHAMBERSBURG, PA., Oct. 8, 1859.

DEAR WIFE AND CHILDREN, ALL, — Oliver returned safe on Wednesday of this week. I want Bell and Martha both to feel that they may have a home with you until we return. We shall do all in our power to provide for the wants of the whole as one family till that time. If Martha and Anne have any money left after getting home, I wish it to be used to make all as comfortable as may be for the present. All are in usually good health. I expect John will send you some assistance soon. Write him all you want to say to us. God bless you all!

Your affectionate husband and father.

From his rustic retreat Brown thus wrote to his comrades and his son : —

To Kagi, at Chambersburg.

(About July 12, 1859.)

"Look for letters directed to John Henrie at Chambersburg. Inquire for letters at Chambersburg for I. Smith & Sons, and write them at Harper's Ferry as soon as any does come.[1] See Mr. Henry

---

[1] See the Diary for July 12.

Watson at Chambersburg, and find out if the 'Tribune' comes on. Have Mr. Watson and his reliable friends get ready to receive company. Get Mr. Watson to make you acquainted with his reliable friends, but do not appear to be any wise thick with them, and do not often be seen with any such man. Get Mr. Watson, if he can, to find out a trusty man or men to stop with at Hagerstown (if any such there be), as Mr. Thomas Henry has gone from there. Write Tidd to come to Chambersburg, by Pittsburg and Harrisburg, at once. He can stop off the Pittsburg road at Hudson, and go to Jason's for his trunk. Write Carpenter and Hazlett that we are all well, right, and ready as soon as we can get our boarding-house fixed, when we will write them to come on, and by what route. I will pay Hazlett the money he advanced to Anderson for expenses travelling. Find yourself a comfortable, cheap boarding-house at once. Write I. Smith & Sons, at Harper's Ferry. Inquire after your four Cleveland friends, and have them come on to Chambersburg if they are on the way; if not on the road, have them wait till we are better prepared. Be careful what you write to all persons. Do not send or bring any more persons here until we advise you of our readiness to board them."

At this time Kagi was stationed at Chambersburg to receive and forward letters, arms, men, etc. He replied to the above letter, and to other messages of Brown, on Monday, July 18, and again July 22, enclosing letters from Charles Blair and from John Brown, Jr., who forwarded the rifles, etc., from West Andover, Ohio, on the 22d, 25th, and 27th of July, to "Isaac Smith & Sons," at Chambersburg. Kagi writes thus:—

July 18.

I wrote to Tidd one week ago to-day, several days before receiving your letter directing me to do so, and enclosing letter to H. Lindsley, which I forwarded by first mail. None of your things have yet arrived. The railroad from Harrisburg here does no freight business itself, that all being done by a number of forwarding houses, which run private freight cars. I have requested each of these (there are six or eight of them) to give me notice of the arrival of anything for you.

CHAMBERSBURG, Friday, July 22.

I received the within, and another for Oliver, to-day. I thought best not to send the other; it is from his wife. There are other reasons, which I need not name now. Have here no other letters from any one.   J. HENRIE.

" The within " was this note from John Brown, Jr., writing under the name of " John Smith," whose father was " Isaac " or " Squire " Smith : —

ASHTABULA, ASHTABULA COUNTY, OHIO, Monday, July 18, 1859.

DEAR FATHER, — Yours, dated at Chambersburg, Pennsylvania, July 5, and mailed at Troy, New York, July 7, and also yours of the 8th, with enclosed drafts for one hundred dollars, I received in due season; am here to-day to get drafts cashed. Have now got all my business so arranged that I can devote my time, for the present, entirely to any business you may see fit to intrust me; shall immediately ship your freight, as you directed, most probably by canal, from Hartstown (formerly Hart's Cross Roads, Crawford County), to the river at Rochester, Pennsylvania (formerly Beaver), thence by railroad *via* Pittsburg, etc., as you directed. Shall hold myself in readiness to go north on any business you choose to direct or confide in my hands. All well; have two or three letters from N. E., which I will forward to J. H. [Kagi].

In haste, your affectionate son,

JOHN SMITH.

" N. E." was New England, and the letters were from our secret committee, or some members of it.

In a note to John Brown, written August 27. Kagi says: " I to-day received the enclosed letter and check [fifty dollars]." This was the money sent on by Dr. Howe about August 25, and the letter was this : —

DEAR FRIEND, — I begin the investment with fifty dollars, and will try to do more through friends. Our friend from Concord called with your note.   DOCTOR.

I was the " friend from Concord," and on the 27th–30th August I wrote to Brown from Springfield, thus : —

DEAR FRIEND, — Yours of the 18th has been received and communicated. S. G. Howe has sent you fifty dollars in a draft on New York, and I am expecting to get more from other sources (perhaps some here), and will make up to you the three hundred dollars, if I can, as soon as I can; but I can give nothing myself just now, being already in debt. I hear with great pleasure what you say of the success of the business, and hope nothing will occur to thwart it. Your son John was in Boston a week or two since. I tried to find him, but did not; and being away from Concord, he did not come to see me. He saw S. G. Howe, George L. Stearns, Wendell Phillips, Francis Jackson, etc.; and everybody liked him. I am very sorry I could not see him. All your Boston friends are well. Theodore Parker is in Switzerland, much better, it is thought, than when he left home. Henry Sterns, of Springfield, is dead.

July 28.

I reached here yesterday and have seen few people as yet. Here I expect letters from those to whom I have written. I conclude that your operations will not be delayed if the money reaches you in course of the next fortnight, if you are sure of having it then. I cannot certainly promise that you will, but I think so. Harriet Tubman is probably in New Bedford, sick. She has stayed here in N. E. a long time, and been a kind of missionary. Your friends in C. are all well; I go back there in a week. God prosper you in all your works! I shall write again soon.

Yours ever,   F.

SPRINGFIELD, August 30, 1859.

DEAR FRIEND, — I enclose you a draft for fifty dollars on New York, bought with money sent by Mrs. Russell. Dr. Howe has already sent you fifty dollars, and G. S., of P.,[1] writes me has sent, or will send, one hundred dollars. The remainder will perhaps come more slowly; but I think it will come. I have sent your letter to Gerrit Smith. Please acknowledge the receipt of these sums.

Yours ever,   F.

John Brown to his son John.

CHAMBERSBURG, PA., August, 1859.

DEAR FRIEND, — I forgot to say yesterday that your shipments of freight are received all in apparent safety; but the bills are very high, and I begin to be apprehensive of getting into a tight spot for want of a little more funds, notwithstanding my anxiety to make my money hold out. As it will cost no more expense for you to solicit for me a little more assistance while attending to your other business, say two or three hundred dollars in New York, — drafts payable to the order of I. Smith & Sons, — will you not sound my Eastern or Western friends in regard to it? It was impossible for me to foresee the exact amount I should be obliged to pay out for everything. Now that arrangements are so nearly completed, I begin to feel almost certain that I can squeeze through with that amount. All my accounts

[1] Gerrit Smith, of Peterboro'.

are squared up to the present time; but how I can keep my little wheels in motion for a few days more I am beginning to feel at a loss. It is terribly humiliating to me to begin soliciting of friends again; but as the harvest opens before me with increasing encouragements, I may not allow a feeling of delicacy to deter me from asking the little further aid I expect to need. What I must have to carry me through I shall need within a very few days, if I am obliged to call direct for further help; so you will please expect something quite definite very soon. I have endeavored to economize in every possible way; and I will not ask for a dollar until I am driven to do so. I have a trifle over one hundred and eighty dollars on hand, but am afraid I cannot possible make it reach. I am highly gratified with all our arrangements up to the present time, and feel certain that no time has yet been lost. One freight is principally here, but will have to go a little further. Our hands, so far, are coming forward promptly, and better than I expected, as we have called on them. We have to move with all caution.

As will appear by the next series of letters, John Brown, Jr., undertook to organize forces in Canada after forwarding to his father the arms stored in Ohio: —

SYRACUSE, N. Y., Thursday, Aug. 11, 1859.

FRIEND J. HENRIE, — Day before yesterday I reached Rochester. Found our Rochester friend[1] absent at Niagara Falls. Yesterday he returned, and I spent remainder of day and evening with him and Mr. E. Morton, with whom friend Isaac [John Brown] is acquainted. The friend at Rochester will set out to make you a visit in a few days. He will be accompanied by that "other young man," and also, if it can be brought around, by the woman[1] that the Syracuse friend could tell me of. The son will probably remain back for awhile. I gave "Fred'k"[1] twenty-two dollars to defray expenses. If alive and well, you will see him ere long. I found him in rather low spirits; left him in high. Accidentally met at Rochester Mr. E. Morton. He was much pleased to hear from you; was anxious for a copy of that letter of instructions to show our friend at "Pr."[1] [Peterboro'], who, Mr. M. says, has his whole soul absorbed in this matter. I have just made him a copy and mailed him at R., where he expects to be for two or three weeks. He wished me to say to you that he had

---

[1] F. Douglass. The "woman" spoken of was Harriet Tubman, a Maryland Deborah. "Fred'k" is also Douglass. "Our friend at Pr." was Gerrit Smith, in whose family, it will be remembered, Edwin Morton was living; but he happened then to be visiting in Rochester.

reliable information that a certain noted colonel, whose name you are all acquainted with, is now in Italy. By the way, the impression prevails generally that a certain acquaintance of ours headed the party that visited St. J. in Missouri lately. Of course I don't try to deny that which bears *such* earmarks. Came on here this morning. Found Loguen gone to Boston, Mass., and also said woman. As T. does not know personally those persons in Canada to whom it is necessary to have letters of introduction, he thinks I had better get him to go with me there. I have made up my mind, notwithstanding the extra expense, to go on to Boston. Loguen is expecting to visit Canada soon, anyway, and his wife thinks would contrive to go immediately. I think for other reasons, also, I had better go on to Boston. Morton says our particular friend Mr. Sanborn, in that city, is especially anxious to hear from you; has his heart and hand both engaged in the cause. Shall try and find him. Our Rochester friend thinks the woman whom I shall see in Boston, " whose services might prove invaluable," had better be helped on. I leave this evening on the 11.35 train from here; shall return as soon as possible to make my visit at Chatham. Will write you often. So far, all is well. Keep me advised as far as consistent.

Fraternally yours,

JOHN SMITH.

SYRACUSE, N. Y., Thursday, Aug. 18, 1859.

FRIEND HENRIE, — I am here to-day, so far on my way back from Boston, whither I went on Friday last. Found our Syracuse friend there, but his engagements were such that he could not possibly leave until yesterday morning. We reached here about twelve o'clock last night. While in Boston I improved the time in making the acquaintance of those stanch friends of our friend Isaac. First called on Dr. Howe, who, though I had no letter of introduction, received me most cordially. He gave me a letter to the friend who does business on Milk Street [Mr. Stearns]. Went with him to his home in Medford, and took dinner. The last word he said to me was, " Tell friend Isaac that we have the fullest confidence in his endeavor, whatever may be the result." I have met no man on whom I think more implicit reliance may be placed. He views matters from the standpoints of reason and principle, and I think his firmness is unshakable. The friend at Concord [F. B. Sanborn] I did not see; he was absent from home. The others here will, however, communicate with him. They were all, in short, very much gratified, and have had their faith and hopes much strengthened. Found a number of earnest and warm friends, whose sympathies and theories do not exactly harmonize; but in spite of themselves their hearts will lead their heads. Our Boston friends thought it better that our old friend from Syracuse [J. W. Loguen] should accompany me in my journey northward. I shall leave in an hour or two for Rochester, where I will finish this letter. I am very glad I went to Boston, as all the friends were of the opinion that our friend Isaac was in another part of the world, if not in another sphere. Our cause is their cause, in the fullest sense of the word.

Going on to Rochester, the home of Douglass, John Brown, Jr., writes from there, Aug. 17, 1859, to Kagi, saying : —

"On my way up to our friend's [F. Douglass's] house, I met his son Lewis, who informs me that his father left here on Tuesday, August 16, *via* New York and Philadelphia, to make you a visit."

The exact date of Douglass's visit to Brown at Chambersburg seems to have been Friday, Saturday, and Sunday, August 19–21. He was at Mrs. Gloucester's in Brooklyn August 18, and carried to Brown from her the following letter : —

BROOKLYN, Aug. 18, 1859.

ESTEEMED FRIEND, — I gladly avail myself of the opportunity afforded by our friend Mr. F. Douglass, who has just called upon us previous to his visit to you, to enclose to you for the cause in which you are such a zealous laborer a small amount, which please accept with my most ardent wishes for its and your benefit. The visit of our mutual friend Douglass has somewhat revived my rather drooping spirits in the cause ; but seeing such ambition and enterprise in him, I am again encouraged. With best wishes for your welfare and prosperity, and the good of your cause, I subscribe myself

Your sincere friend,
MRS. E. A. GLOUCESTER.

What took place during the stay of Douglass and Brown in Chambersburg has thus been narrated by Douglass, omitting some particulars not essential to the story : —

JOHN BROWN IN CONFERENCE WITH DOUGLASS.

"At my house John Brown had made the acquaintance of a colored man, who called himself by different names, — sometimes 'Emperor,' at other times 'Shields Green,' — a fugitive slave who had made his escape from Charleston, S. C. He was a man of few words (and his language was singularly broken), but of courage and self-respect. Brown saw at once what stuff Green was made of, and confided to him his plans and purposes. Green easily believed in Brown, and promised to go with him whenever he should be ready to move. About nine weeks before the raid on Harper's Ferry, Brown wrote to me that a beginning would soon be made, and that before going forward he wanted to see me; he appointed an old stone-quarry near Chambersburg as our place of meeting. Mr. Kagi, his secretary, would be there, and they wished me to bring any money I could command and Shields Green along with me. He said that his 'mining-tools' and stores were then at Chambersburg, and that he would be there to remove them. I obeyed the summons, taking Shields; we passed through New York, where we called upon the Rev. James Gloucester and his wife, and told them where we were going, and that our old friend needed money. Mrs. Gloucester gave me ten dollars for John Brown, with her best wishes. When I reached Chambersburg surprise was expressed that I should come there unannounced; and I was pressed to make a speech, which I readily did. Meanwhile I called upon Mr. Henry Watson, a simple-minded and warm-hearted man, to whom Brown had imparted the secret of my visit, to show me the appointed rendezvous. Watson was busy in his barber's-shop, but he dropped all and put me on the right track. I approached the old quarry cautiously, for Brown was generally well armed and regarded strangers with suspicion. He was under the ban of the Government, and heavy rewards were offered for his arrest. He was passing under the name of Isaac Smith. As I came near, he regarded me suspiciously; but he soon recognized me, and received me cordially. He had in his hand a fishing-tackle, with which he had apparently been fishing in a stream hard by; but I saw no fish; fishing was simply a disguise, and certainly a good one. He looked every way like a man of the neighborhood, and as much at home as any of the farmers around there. His hat was old and storm-beaten, and his clothing about the color of the stone-quarry itself. His face wore an anxious expression, and he was much worn by thought and exposure. I felt that I was on a dangerous mission, and was as little desirous of discovery as himself.

"Captain Brown, Kagi, Shields Green, and myself sat down among the rocks, and talked over the enterprise about to be undertaken. The taking of Harper's Ferry, of which Brown had merely hinted before, was now declared his settled purpose, and he wanted to know what I thought of it. I at once opposed it with all the arguments at my command. To me, such a measure would be fatal to running off slaves (the original plan), and fatal to all engaged. It would be an attack on the Federal Government, and would array the whole country against us. Captain Brown did most of the talking on the other side. He did not at all object to rousing the nation; it seemed to him that something startling was needed. He had completely renounced his old plan, and thought that the capture of Harper's Ferry would serve as notice to the slaves that their friends had come, and as a trumpet to rally them to his standard. I was no match for him in such matters, but I told him that all his arguments, and all his descriptions of the place convinced me that he was going into a perfect steel-trap, and that once in, he would never get out alive; he would be surrounded at once, and escape would be impossible. He was not to be shaken, but treated my views respectfully, replying that even if surrounded, he would find means to cut his way out. But that would not be forced upon him; he should have the best citizens of the neighborhood as prisoners at the start, and holding them as hostages should be able to dictate terms of egress from the town. I told him that Virginia would blow him and his hostages sky-high rather than that he should hold Harper's Ferry an hour. Our talk was long and earnest; we spent the most of Saturday and a part of Sunday in this debate, — Brown for Harper's Ferry, and I against it; he for striking a blow which should instantly rouse the country, and I for the policy of gradually and unaccountably drawing off the slaves to the mountains, as at first suggested and proposed by him. When I found that he had fully made up his mind and could not be dissuaded, I turned to Green and told him he heard what Captain Brown had said; his old plan was changed, and I should return home, — if he wished to go with me he could do so. Captain Brown urged us both to go with him. In parting, he put his arms around me in a manner more than friendly, and said, 'Come with me, Douglass; I will defend you with my life. I want you for a special purpose. When I strike, the bees will begin to swarm, and I shall want you to help hive them.' When about to leave, I asked Green what he had decided to do, and was surprised by his saying, in his broken way, ' I b'lieve I 'll go wid de ole man.' " [1]

[1] Among the papers captured at the Kennedy farm was this copy of a letter to Douglass which was signed by colored citizens of Philadelphia, and received at Rochester in September : —

F. D., Esq.

Dear Sir, — The undersigned feel it to be of the utmost importance that our class be properly represented in a convention to come off right away (near) Chambersburg, in this State. We think you are the man of all others to represent us; and we severally pledge ourselves that in case you will come right on we will see your family well provided for during your absence, or until your safe return to them. Answer to us and to

Owen Brown

[1882.]

In regard to the opposition of his followers to Brown's plan of beginning the campaign at Harper's Ferry, Owen Brown makes this statement (May 5, 1885) : —

" In the early part of September, 1859, father and I went with the horse and covered wagon from the Kennedy farm to Chambersburg, — and at different times after in September and October, — to see if any *express packages* (colored volunteers) had arrived. We had many earnest discussions as to the feasibility of making the attack at Harper's Ferry, — which plan was not known to any of us until after our arrival at the Kennedy farm. All of our men, excepting Merriam, Kagi, Shields Green, and the colored men (the latter knowing nothing of Harper's Ferry), were opposed to striking the first blow there. During our talk on the road, I said to father : ' You know how it resulted with Napoleon when he rejected advice in regard to marching with his army to Moscow. I believe that in your anxiety to see that all is going on well at the three different points proposed to be taken (the Arsenal, the Rifle-works, and the Magazine), you will so expose yourself as to lose your life.' He said, finally, ' I feel so depressed on account of the opposition of the men, that at times I am

John Henrie, Esq., Chambersburg, Penn., at once. We are ready to make you a remittance, if you go. We have now quite a number of good but not very intelligent representatives collected. Some of our members are ready to go on with you.

Mr. Douglass writes me (April 15, 1885) : " You must be right about the time of my going to Chambersburg (Aug. 19, 1859). I took no note as to the exact time ; it was a night or two before Brown proposed to remove his arms to Harper's Ferry. This letter was sent to me from Philadelphia soon after I returned from meeting Captain Brown. It was signed by a number of colored men ; I never knew how they came to send it, but it now seems to have been prompted by Kagi, who was with Brown when I told him I would not go to Harper's Ferry. He probably thought I would reconsider my determination, if urged to do so by the parties who signed the letter." One of Brown's agents wrote thus to Kagi at the time of Douglass's visit : —

CLEVELAND, Aug. 22, 1859.

I wrote you immediately on receipt of your last letter ; then went up to Oberlin to see Leary. I saw Smith, Davis, and Mitchell ; they all promised, and that was all. Leary wants to provide for his family ; Mitchell to lay his crops by ; and all make such excuses, until I am disgusted with myself and the whole negro set. If you were here your influence would do something ; but the moment you are gone all my speaking don't amount to anything. I will speak to Smith to-day. I knew that Mitchell had n't got the money, and I tried to sell my farm and everything else to raise money, but have not raised a cent yet. Charlie Langston says " it is too bad," but what he will do, if anything, I don't know. I wish you would write to him, for I believe he can do more good than I. Please write to him immediately, and I will give up this thing to him. I think, however, nothing will inspire their confidence unless you come. I will do all I can.

almost willing to temporarily abandon the undertaking.' I replied, 'We have gone too far for that, — we must go ahead.' In the course of our talk he said to me, as he had many times to his men before, 'We have here only one life to live, and once to die; and if we lose our lives it will perhaps do more for the cause than our lives could be worth in any other way.' I agreed with him in this. As we found no *express packages* at Chambersburg, he remained there with Kagi, and I went back alone. In a day or two both returned to the Kennedy farm, and the next morning he called all his men together in the chamber of the Kennedy house, and said to them, ' I am not so strenuous about carrying out any of my particular plans as to do knowingly that which might probably result in an injury to the cause for which we are struggling;' and in the course of his remarks he repeated what he had said to me about our losing our lives. He then added, 'As you are all opposed to the plan of attacking here, I will resign; we will choose another leader, and I will faithfully obey, reserving to myself the privilege of giving counsel and advice where I think a better course could be adopted.' He did then resign. I first replied that I did not know of any one to choose as a leader in preference to him. In a short time, probably within five minutes, he was again chosen as the leader, and though we were not satisfied with the reasons he gave for making our first attack there, all controversy and opposition to the plan from that time was ended."

It must have been about the time of this journey of the father and son that Watson Brown wrote thus to his wife : —

Sept. 8, 1859.

DEAR BELLE, — You can guess how I long to see you only by knowing how you wish to see me. I think of you all day, and dream of you at night. I would gladly come home and stay with you always but for the cause which brought me here, — a desire to do something for others, and not live wholly for my own happiness. I am at home, five miles north of H. F., in an old house on the Kennedy farm, where we keep some things, and four of us sleep here. I came here to be alone; Oliver has just come in and disturbed me. I was at Chambersburg a few days ago, and wrote you a line from there. The reason I did not write sooner was that there are ten of us here, and all who know them think they are with father, and have an idea what he is at; so you see if each and every one writes, all his friends will know where we all are; if one writes (except on business) then all will have a right to. It is now dark, and I am in this old house all alone; but I have some good company, for I have just received your letter of August 30, and you may as well think I am glad to hear from you. You may kiss the baby a great many times a day for me ; I am thinking of you and him all the time.

Two events in no way connected with this visit of Douglass, but happening about that time, may be mentioned. The anonymous warning to the Government, from Cincinnati, that Brown was to strike at Harper's Ferry, was dated the Saturday that Douglass met Brown in Chambersburg, and mailed three days later. This was followed within a week by Gerrit Smith's letter to the colored men of Syracuse, in which he predicted almost exactly what happened at Harper's Ferry. The Cincinnati letter was as follows:

CINCINNATI, August 20.

SIR, — I have lately received information of a movement of so great importance, that I feel it my duty to impart it to you without delay. I have discovered the existence of a secret association, having for its object the liberation of the slaves at the South by a general insurrection. The leader of the movement is "old John Brown," late of Kansas. He has been in Canada during the winter, drilling the negroes there, and they are only waiting his word to start for the South to assist the slaves. They have one of their leading men (a white man) in an armory in Maryland, — where it is situated I have not been able to learn. As soon as everything is ready, those of their number who are in the Northern States and Canada are to come in small companies to their rendezvous, which is in the mountains in Virginia. They will pass down through Pennsylvania and Maryland, and enter Virginia at Harper's Ferry. Brown left the North about three or four weeks ago, and will arm the negroes and strike the blow in a few weeks ; so that whatever is done must be done at once. They have a large quantity of arms at their rendezvous, and are probably distributing them already. As I am not fully in their confidence, this is all the information I can give you. I dare not sign my name to this, but trust that you will not disregard the warning on that account.[1]

[1] The envelope is directed, "Hon. Mr. Floyd, Secretary of War, Washington," marked " private," and postmarked Cincinnati, August 23, 1859. Although the information sent to Floyd was very exact, and one would have supposed a Virginian specially sensitive to such intelligence, it does not appear that he gave the matter more than a passing thought. He received the letter at a Virginian watering-place, but did not read it twice,

This letter was not heeded; nor was the more public warning given by Gerrit Smith, who, writing August 27, said, among other things: —

"It is, perhaps, too late to bring slavery to an end by peaceable means, — too late to vote it down. For many years I have feared, and published my fears, that it must go out in blood. These fears have grown into belief. So debauched are the white people by slavery that there is not virtue enough left in them to put it down. If I do not misinterpret the words and looks of the most intelligent and noble of the black men who fall in my way, they have come to despair of the accomplishment of this work by the white people. The feeling among the blacks that they must deliver themselves gains strength with fearful rapidity. No wonder, then, is it that intelligent black men in the States *and in Canada* should see no hope for their race in the practice and policy of white men. . . . Whoever he may be that foretells the horrible end of American slavery is held both at the North and the South to be a lying prophet, — another Cassandra. The South would not respect her own Jefferson's prediction of servile insurrection; how then can it be hoped that she will respect another's? . . . And is it entirely certain that these insurrections will be put down promptly, and before they can have spread far? Will telegraphs and railroads be too swift for even the swiftest insurrections? Remember that telegraphs and railroads can be rendered useless in an hour. Remember too that many who would be glad to face the insurgents would be busy in transporting their wives and daughters to places where they would be safe from that worst fate which husbands and fathers can imagine for their wives and daughters. I admit that but for this embarrassment Southern men would laugh at the idea of an insurrection, and would quickly dispose of one. But trembling as they would for beloved ones, I know of no part of the world where, so much as in the South, men would be like, in a formidable insurrection, to lose the most important time, and be distracted and panic-stricken."

although he laid it away at first as a paper of some moment. It has never been ascertained who wrote it, but perhaps a young man then connected with a Cincinnati newspaper. This person had become acquainted with a Hungarian refugee, formerly in the suite of Kossuth, then living in Kansas, and who had fought on the side of the North, possibly under Brown, and had learned in some detail the plan of the Virginia campaign. This it is believed he communicated in an unguarded moment to the Cincinnati reporter, who could not contain the secret, but sat down at once and wrote to the Secretary of War. It is possible that the information came indirectly from Cook, who talked too freely. See p. 471.

Gerrit Smith's prediction passed unnoticed, although, as his biographer says, "this Cassandra spoke from certainty." He knew what Brown's purpose was ;[1] and his last contribution of money to Brown's camp-chest was sent about the time this Syracuse letter was written. Whether he also knew that Harper's Ferry was to be attacked is uncertain; for this was communicated only to a few persons except those actually under arms. Yet it was known by the Cincinnati correspondent of Secretary Floyd. Late in September Jeremiah Anderson, one of Brown's men who was killed at the side of his captain in the engine-house at Harper's Ferry, wrote to his brother in Iowa,—

"Our mining company will consist of between twenty-five and thirty well equipped with tools. You can tell Uncle Dan it will be impossible for me to visit him before next spring. If my life is spared, I will be tired of work by that time, and I shall visit my relatives and friends in Iowa, if I can get leave of absence. At present, I am bound by all that is honorable to continue in the course. We go in to win, at all hazards. So if you should hear of a failure, it will be after a desperate struggle, and loss of capital on both sides. But that is the last of our thoughts. Everything seems to work to our hands, and victory will surely perch upon our banner. The old man has had this operation in view for twenty years, and last winter was just a hint and trial of what could be done. This is not a large place,[2] but a precious one to Uncle Sam, as he has a great many tools here. I expect (when I start again travelling) to start at this place and go through the State of Virginia and on south, just as circumstances require; mining and prospecting, and carrying the ore with us. I suppose this is the last letter I shall write before there is something in the wind. Whether I shall have a chance of sending letters then I do not know, but when I have an opportunity, I shall improve it. But if you don't get any from me, don't take it for granted that I am *gone up* till you know it to be so. I consider my life about as safe in one place as another."

[1] This must also have been known to a writer in the "Anglo-African," a magazine for colored men, who said, in August, 1859 : —

"So profoundly are we opposed to the favorite doctrine of the Puritans and their co-workers the colonizationists, — *Ubi Libertas, ibi Patria*, — that we could almost beseech Divine Providence to reverse some past events, *and to fling back into the heart of Virginia and Maryland* their Sam Wards, Highland Garnets, J. W. Penningtons, *Frederick Douglasses, and the twenty thousand who now shout hosannas in Canada*, — and we would soon see some stirring in the direction of *Ubi Patria, ibi Libertas*."

[2] Harper's Ferry.

This letter shows the smallness of the force with which
Brown undertook his campaign. A few of those who were
expected to join him did not arrive, and his actual force
when he began was but twenty-two besides himself, perhaps only twenty-one, for there is some doubt concerning
the presence of John Anderson, the person last-numbered
in this list of Brown's band : —

1. John Brown, commander-in-chief; 2. John Henry Kagi, adju-
tant; 3. Aaron C. Stephens, captain; 4. Watson Brown, captain;
5. Oliver Brown, captain; 6. John E. Cook, captain; 7. Charles
Plummer Tidd,* captain; 8. William H. Leeman, lieutenant; 9.
Albert Hazlett, lieutenant; 10. Owen Brown,* captain; 11. Jeremiah G. Anderson, lieutenant; 12. Edwin Coppoc, lieutenant; 13.
William Thompson, lieutenant; 14. Dauphin Thompson, lieutenant; 15. *Shields Green;* [1] 16. *Dangerfield Newby;* 17. *John A.
Copeland;* 18. *Osborn P. Anderson;* * 19. *Lewis Leary;* 20. Stewart Taylor; 21. Barclay Coppoc;* 22. Francis Jackson Merriam;*
23. *John Anderson.* *

It will be seen that this company was but the skeleton
of an organization which it was intended to fill up with
recruits gathered from among the slaves and at the North;
hence the great disproportion of officers to privates. According to the general orders by Brown, dated at Harper's Ferry.
Oct. 10, 1859, his forces were to be divided into battalions
of four companies, which would contain, when full, seventy-
two officers and men in each company, or two hundred and
eighty-eight in the battalion. Provision was made for offi-
cering and arming the four companies of the first battalion,
which in the event of Brown's success would have been
filled up as quickly as possible. Each company was to be
divided into bands of seven men under a corporal, and every
two bands made a section of sixteen men, under a sergeant.
Until the companies were filled up, the commissioned officers were intended to act as corporals and sergeants in these
bands and sections, and they did so during the operations in
Maryland and Virginia.

Brown's youngest son wrote thus : —

[1] Those in italics were colored men ; those marked (*) escaped, but all
save Owen Brown are now dead. He was treasurer as well as captain.

Oliver Brown to his Family.

PARTS UNKNOWN, Sept. 9, 1859.

DEAR MOTHER, BROTHER, AND SISTERS, — Knowing that you all feel deeply interested in persons and matters here, I feel a wish to write all I can that is encouraging, feeling that we all need all the encouragement we can get while we are travelling on through eternity, of which every day is a part. I can only say that we are all well, and that our work is going on very slowly, but we think satisfactorily. I would here say that I think there is no good reason why any of us should be discouraged ; for if we have done but one good act, life is not a failure. I shall probably start home with Martha and Anna about the last of this month. Salmon, you may make any use of the sugar things you can next year. I hope you will all keep a stiff lip, a sound pluck, and believe that all will come out right in the end. Nell, I have not forgotten you, and I want you should remember me. Please, all write. Direct to John Henrie, Chambersburg, Pennsylvania.

Believe me your affectionate son and brother,

OLIVER SMITH.

How fully the Brown family were apprised of the details of the Virginia campaign it is hardly possible to infer from the letters extant; but so cautious was John Brown, and so irregular in his correspondence, that many points came late or not at all to the knowledge of individual members of the family. Thus John Brown, Jr., wrote to Kagi five weeks before the attack : —

WEST ANDOVER, Sept. 8, 1859.

FRIEND HENRIE, — I yesterday evening received yours of September 2, and I not only hasten to reply, but to lay its contents before those who are interested. . . . Through those associations which I formed in Canada, I am able to reach each individual member at the shortest notice by letter. I am devoting my whole time to our company business. Shall immediately go out organizing and raising funds. From what I even had understood, *I had supposed you would not think it best to commence opening the coal banks before spring,* unless circumstances should make it imperative. However, I suppose the reasons are satisfactory to you, and if so, those who own smaller shares ought not to object. I hope we shall be able to get on in season some of those old miners of whom I wrote you. Shall strain every nerve to accomplish this. You may be assured that what you say to me will reach those who may be benefited thereby, and those who would take stock, in the shortest possible time; so don't fail to keep me posted.

.   .   .   .

There is a general dearth of news in this region. By the way, I notice, through the "Cleveland Leader," that "Old Brown" is again figuring in Kansas. Well, every dog must have his day, and he will no doubt find the end of his tether. Did you ever know of such a high-handed piece of business? However, it is just like him. The Black Republicans, some of them, may wink at such things; but I tell you, friend Henrie, he is too salt a dose for many of them to swallow, and I can already see symptoms of division in their ranks. We are bound to roll up a good stiff majority for our side this fall. I will send you herewith the item referred to, which I clipped from the "Leader." Give regards to all, and believe me faithfully yours,   JOHN.

Other correspondence followed this, but little that need be cited. The five weeks intervening between this letter and the attack were busy ones; and, as usual, Brown was embarrassed for lack of money. I sent him through Kagi a draft for fifty dollars, August 30, and made a further remittance in September, amounting to one hundred and five dollars; this completed the sum I had agreed to raise, — nearly one third of which was given by Gerrit Smith. The last contribution which Brown received was about six hundred dollars in gold, carried to him by Francis Merriam [1]

---

[1] Young Merriam was a grandson and namesake of Francis Jackson, the Boston Abolitionist (well known as the friend of Garrison, Phillips, Parker, Quincy, and the other extreme Antislavery men), who had heard from Redpath and Hinton of Brown's general purpose, and in December, 1858, wrote to Brown, offering to join him "in any capacity you wish to place me, as far as my small capacities go." He had been in Kansas in 1857-58, with a letter from Wendell Phillips, but did not find Brown. In the spring of 1859, while Redpath and Merriam were in Hayti, Kagi had written to Hinton, asking the three to meet him in Boston; but this meeting never took place. In September, 1859, Merriam learned the details of the Virginia plan from Lewis Hayden, a Kentucky freedman, long resident in Boston, and came to me to renew the offer of his services. His father was dead, and he had inherited a small property which he was eager to devote to some practical enterprise for freeing the slaves. He was at this time twenty-two years old, enthusiastic and resolute, but with little judgment, and in feeble health.

from Boston the week before the attack was made at Harper's Ferry. Kagi's diary (October 10–15) records Merriam's arrival and movements : —

"*Monday, October* 10. — Mr. Merriam came ; went down with me to M——.

"*Tuesday.* — Dimas returned to Mrs. Ritner's. Wrote J. B., Jr. Saw Watson, and appointed meeting for Thursday eve. Saw Carlisle about purchases.

"*Wednesday.* — Wrote William Still. Wrote to S. Jones, sending men off. Leary and Copeland arrived.

"*Thursday.* — Received letter from Merriam, dated Baltimore.

"*Friday, October* 15. — Sent telegram to Merriam at Baltimore."

"Watson" was one of Brown's sons, from whose letters to his young wife during September and October a few sentences may be quoted : —

We have only two black men with us now ; one of these has a wife and seven children in slavery. I sometimes feel as though I could not make the sacrifice ; but what would I want others to do, were I in their place ? . . . Oh, Bell, I do want to see you and the little fellow [the young babe born in the father's absence] very much, but I must wait. There was a slave near here whose wife was sold off South the other day, and he was found in Thomas Kennedy's orchard, dead, the next morning. Cannot come home so long as such things are done here. . . . I sometimes think perhaps we shall not meet again. If we should not, you have an object to live for, — to be a mother to our little Fred. He is not quite a reality to me yet. We leave here this afternoon or to-morrow for the last time. You will probably hear from us very soon after getting this, if not before. We are all eager for the work, and confident of success. There was another murder committed near our place the other day, making in all five murders and one suicide within five miles of our place since we have lived there ; they were all slaves, too. . . . Give my regards to all the friends, and keep up good courage : there is a better day a-coming. I can but commend you to yourself and your friends if I should never see you again. Believe me yours wholly and forever in love.   Your husband,

WATSON BROWN.[1]

---

[1] Watson was just twenty-four, and had been married for three years to Isabel Thompson, whose brothers William and Dauphin Thompson, like her husband and brother-in-law, were killed at Harper's Ferry.

Brown himself wrote thus to his family : —

CHAMBERSBURG, PENN., Oct. 1, 1859.

DEAR WIFE AND CHILDREN, ALL, — I parted with Martha and Anne at Harrisburg, yesterday, in company with Oliver, on their way home. I trust before this reaches you the women will have arrived safe. I have encouragement of having fifty dollars or more sent you soon, to help you to get through the winter; and I shall certainly do all in my power for you, and try to commend you always to the God of my fathers.

Perhaps you can keep your animals in good condition through the winter on potatoes mostly, much cheaper than on any other feed. I think that would certainly be the case if the crop is good, and is secured well and in time.

I sent along four pairs blankets, with directions for Martha to have the first choice, and for Bell, Abbie, and Anne to cast lots for a choice in the three other pairs. My reason is that I think Martha fairly entitled to *particular* notice.[1]

To my other daughters I can only send my blessing just now. Anne, I want you, first of all, to become a sincere, humble, earnest, and consistent Christian ; and then acquire good and efficient business habits. Save this letter to remember your father by, Anne.

You must all send to John hereafter anything you want should get to us ; and you may be sure we shall all be very anxious to learn everything about your welfare. Read the "Tribune" carefully. It may not always be certainly true, however. Begin early to take good care of all your animals, and pinch them at the close of the winter, if you must at all.

God Almighty bless and save you all !

Your affectionate husband and father.

Harper's Ferry was named for Robert Harper, an English millwright, who obtained a grant of it in 1748 from Lord Fairfax, the friend of Washington. The first survey of this tract was made by Washington, who is said to have selected the Ferry, in 1794, as the site of a national armory. The scenery has been described by Jefferson in his " Notes on Virginia," written shortly before the death of Robert Harper in 1782, and presenting the view from Jefferson's rock,

---

[1] Martha was the wife of Oliver, and was to be confined in March. Bell was the wife of Watson, and the sister of William and Dauphin Thompson ; Abbie was the wife of Salmon Brown, who stayed at home with his mother.

above the village. "You stand on a very high point of land; on your right comes up the Shenandoah, having ranged along the foot of the mountain a hundred miles to find a vent; on your left approaches the Potomac, in quest of a passage also. In the moment of their junction they rush together against the mountain, rend it asunder, and pass off to the sea. The scene is worth a voyage across the Atlantic; . . . these monuments of a war between rivers and mountains which must have shaken the earth itself to its centre." Around this junction of the two rivers had grown up a village of three or four thousand inhabitants. North of the Potomac rise the Maryland Heights almost perpendicular to the river's bank, thirteen hundred feet above it. The Loudon Heights, across the Shenandoah, are lower, but both ridges overtop the hill between them, and make it untenable for an army, while this hill itself commands all below it, and makes the town indefensible against a force there. Therefore, when Brown captured Harper's Ferry, he placed himself in a trap where he was sure to be taken, unless he should quickly leave it. His first mistake (and he made many in this choice of his point of attack and his method of warfare) was to cross the Potomac at a place so near Washington and Baltimore, which are distant but sixty and eighty miles respectively from the bridge over which he marched his men. This bridge is used both by the Baltimore and Ohio railroad and by the travellers along the public highway; and the only approach to it from the Maryland side is by a narrow road under the steep cliff, or by the railroad itself. On the Virginia side there are roads leading up from the Shenandoah valley, and both up and down the Potomac. Harper's Ferry is indeed the Thermopylæ of Virginia. General Lee, the Hector of the Southern Troy, came here with soldiers of the national army to capture Brown in 1859; he came again and repeatedly as commander of the Southern armies during the next five years. His soldiers and their opponents of the Union army cannonaded, burned, pillaged, and abandoned the town, which has not yet recovered from the ruin of the war.

Before Brown's foray, one of his captains (Cook) had visited the house of Colonel Lewis Washington (great-grandson of George Washington's brother), and learned where to put his hand upon the sword of Frederick the Great and the pistols of Lafayette, presented by them to Washington, and by him to his brother's descendants. With that sense of historical association which led Brown to make his first attack upon slavery in Virginia and amid the scenes of Washington's early life, this liberator of the slaves had determined to appear at their head wielding Washington's own sword, and followed by freedmen who had owed service in the Washington family. He therefore assigned to Stephens and to Cook, as their first duty after Harper's Ferry should be taken, to proceed to Colonel Washington's plantation of Bellair, about four miles south of the Ferry, seize him, with his arms, set free his slaves, and bring him as a hostage to the captured town ; and he even directed that Osborn Anderson, a free black, should receive from Washington the historical weapons.[1]

Cook in his confession said : —

" There were some six or seven in Brown's party who did not know anything of our Constitution, and were also ignorant of the plan of operations until Sunday morning, October 16. Among this number were Edwin and Barclay Coppoc, Merriam, Shields Green, Copeland, and Leary. The Constitution was read to them by Stephens, and the oath afterward administered by Captain Brown. On Sunday evening Captain Brown made his final arrangements for the capture of Harper's Ferry, and gave to his men their orders. In closing, he said : ' And now, gentlemen, let me press this one thing on your minds. You all know how dear life is to you, and how dear your lives are to your friends; and in remembering that, consider that the lives of others are as dear to them as yours are to you. Do not, therefore, take the life of any one if you can possibly avoid it ; but if it is necessary to take life in order to save your own, then make sure work of it.' "

At the Kennedy farm-house, about eight o'clock on the evening of Sunday, — a cold and dark night, ending in rain, — Brown mustered his eighteen followers, saying, "Men,

---

[1] The Puritanic Quixotism and the prophetic symbolism of Brown's character united in this act, which will be remembered longer than many of his exploits that were more important in their results.

get on your arms; we will proceed to the Ferry." His horse
and wagon were brought to the door of the farmhouse, and
some pikes, a sledge-hammer, and a crowbar were placed in
the wagon. Brown " put on his old Kansas cap," mounted
the wagon, and said, " Come, boys! " at the same time driving his horse down the rude lane into the main road. His
men followed him on foot, two and two, Charles Plummer
Tidd, a Maine farmer who had joined him in Kansas, and
John E. Cook taking the lead. At a proper time they were
sent forward in advance of the wagon to tear down the telegraph wires on the Maryland side of the Potomac. The
other couples walked at some distance apart and in silence,
making no display of arms. Now and then some of them
rode beside Brown. When overtaken by any one, the rear
couple were to detain the stranger until the party had passed
on or concealed themselves, and the same order was given if
they were met by any one. The road was unfrequented
that night, and they passed down through the woods to the
bridge across the Potomac without delay or adventure.
Upon entering the covered bridge they halted and fastened
their cartridge-boxes, with forty rounds of ammunition, outside their coats, and brought their rifles into view. As they
approached the Virginia side, the watchman who patrolled
the bridge met them and was arrested by Kagi and Stephens, who took him to the armory gate, leaving Watson
Brown and Stewart Taylor to guard the bridge. The rest
of the company proceeded with Brown, in his wagon or on
foot, to the armory gate, which was but a few rods from the
Virginia end of the bridge. There they halted at about
half past ten o'clock, broke open the gate with the crowbar
in the wagon, rushed inside the armory yard, and seized one
of the two watchmen on duty. Brown himself with two
men then mounted guard at the armory gate, and the other
fourteen men were sent to different parts of the village.
Oliver Brown and William Thompson occupied the bridge
over the Shenandoah, and there arrested a few prisoners.
Kagi, with John Copeland, went up the Shenandoah a half-
mile or more to that part of the armory called "the rifle
works," where he captured the watchmen, sent them to
Brown, and occupied the buildings. Edwin Coppoc and

Albert Hazlett went across the street from the armory gate
and occupied the arsenal, which was not in the armory in-
closure. All this was done quietly and without the snapping
of a gun ; and before midnight the whole village was in the
possession of Brown and his men.   He then dispatched
Stephens, Cook, and others, six in all, on the turnpike
toward Charlestown to bring in Colonel Washington and
some of his neighbors, with their slaves.[1] This was done
before four in the morning ; and then some of the same party
went across into Maryland and brought in Terence Byrne,
a small slaveholder, at whose house they had expected to
find slaves, but did not. In the mean time, at 1.30 A. M.,
the railroad train from the west had come in, and a negro
porter, who was crossing the bridge to find the missing
watchman, was stopped by Watson Brown's guard.   Turn-

---

[1] The interview between Brown and Colonel Washington (who was one
of the military staff of the Governor of Virginia, and thence derived his
title) is thus described by Washington :   "We drove to the armory gate.
The person on the front seat of the carriage said : ' All 's well ;' and the
reply came from the sentinel at the gate, ' All 's well.' Then the gates
were opened, and I was driven in and was received by Old Brown. He did
not address me by name, but said : ' You will find a fire in here, sir ; it is
rather cool this morning.' Afterwards he came and said : ' I presume you
are Mr. Washington.   It is too dark to see to write at this time ; but when
it shall have cleared off a little and become lighter, if you have not pen
and ink I will furnish them, and shall require you to write to some of
your friends to send a stout, able-bodied negro.   I think, after a while,
possibly I shall be able to release you ; but only on condition of getting
your friends to send in a negro man as a ransom.   I shall be very atten-
tive to you, sir ; for I may get the worst of it in my first encounter, and if
so, your life is worth as much as mine.   My particular reason for taking
you first was, that as an aid to the Governor of Virginia I knew you
would endeavor to perform your duty ; and apart from that, I wanted
you particularly for the moral effect it would give our cause having one
of your name as a prisoner.'   I supposed at that time, from his actions,
that his force was a large one, — that he was very strong.   Shortly after
reaching the armory I found the sword of General Washington in Old
Brown's hand.   He said, ' I will take especial care of it, and shall endeavor to return it to you after you are released.'   Brown carried it in
his hand all day Monday ; when the attacking party came on, Tuesday
morning, he laid it on the fire-engine, and after the rescue I got it."
Colonel Washington survived the Civil War, in which he took no part.
His widow has sold this sword, with other mementos of Washington,
to the State of New York.

ing to run back and refusing to halt, he was shot and mortally wounded by one of the bridge guard, which was now increased to three. This was the first shot fired on either side, and was three hours after the entrance of Brown into the village. Shots were fired in return by some of the railroad men, and then no more firing took place until after sunrise. Before sunrise the train had been allowed to go forward, Brown and one of his men walking across the bridge with the conductor of the train to satisfy him that all was safe, and that the bridge was not broken down. The work of gathering up prisoners as hostages had also been pushed vigorously, and before noon Brown had more than twice the number of his own force imprisoned in the armory yard. None of his own men were killed or captured until ten or eleven o'clock on Monday morning, when Dangerfield Newby, the Virginia fugitive, was shot near the armory gate. Shortly afterward Stephens was wounded and captured, Watson Brown wounded, and William Thompson captured. For from nine o'clock (when the terrified citizens of Harper's Ferry found a few arms and mustered courage enough to use them) until night, the Virginians, armed and officered, had been surrounding Brown's position, and before noon had cut off his retreat into Maryland. During the four or five hours after daybreak when he might have escaped from the town, he was urged to do so by Kagi, by Stephens, and by others; but delayed until it was too late. For twelve hours he held the town at his mercy; after that he was firmly caught in the trap he had entered, and the defeat of his foray was only the question of a few hours' time. He drew back his shattered forces into the engine-house near the armory gate, soon after noon; but neither his men at the rifle works, nor those at the arsenal across the street, nor his son Owen, on the Maryland side of the Potomac, could join him. He fought bravely, and so did Kagi and his few men on the bank of the Shenandoah; but the latter were all killed or captured before the middle of the afternoon; and at evening, when Colonel Lee arrived from Washington with a company of United States marines, nothing was left of Brown's band except himself and six men, two of them wounded, in his weak fortress, and two unharmed and undiscovered men, Hazlett and Osborn Anderson, in the arsenal not far off. His enterprise had failed, and through his own fault.

Why, then, did Brown attack Harper's Ferry, or, having captured it, why did he not leave it at once and push on into the mountains of Virginia, according to his original plan? His explanation is characteristic: it was foreordained to be so. "All our actions," he said, "even all the follies that led to this disaster, were decreed to happen ages before the world was made." He declared that had he betaken himself to the mountains he could never have been captured, "for he and his men had studied the country carefully, and knew it a hundred times better than any of the inhabitants." He ascribed his ruin to his weakness in listening to the entreaties of his prisoners and delaying his departure from the captured town. "It was the first time," somebody reports him as saying, "that I ever lost command of myself; and now I am punished for it." But he soon began to see that this mistake was leading him to his most glorious success, — a victory such as he might never have won in his own way.

Among many accounts of the final scenes of tragedy at Harper's Ferry, one of the best is that of Captain Dangerfield, who at the time was a clerk in the armory, and was made prisoner early in the morning of October 17. He says: [1] —

" I walked towards my office, then just within the armory inclosure, and not more than a hundred yards from my house. As I proceeded, I saw a man come out of an alley, then another and another, all coming towards me. I inquired what all this meant; they said, 'Nothing, only they had taken possession of the Government works.' I told them they talked like crazy men. They answered, 'Not so crazy as you think, as you will soon see.' Up to this time I had not seen any arms. Presently, however, the men threw back the short cloaks they wore, and disclosed Sharp's rifles, pistols, and knives. Seeing these, and fearing something serious was going on, I told the men I believed I would return home. They at once cocked

---

[1] See the "Century Magazine" for June, 1885. I have abridged the narrative here and there.

their guns, and told me I was a prisoner. This surprised me, but I could do nothing, being unarmed. I talked with them some little time longer, and again essayed to go home; but one of the men stepped before me, presented his gun, and told me if I moved I would be shot down. I then asked what they intended to do with me. They said I was in no personal danger; they only wanted to carry me to their captain, John Smith. I asked them where Captain Smith was. They answered at the guard house, inside of the armory in-closure. I told them I would go there; that was the point for which I first started. (My office was there, and I felt uneasy lest the vault had been broken open.)

"Upon reaching the gate, I saw what indeed looked like war, — negroes armed with pikes, and sentinels with muskets all around. I was turned over to 'Captain Smith,' who called me by name, and asked if I knew Colonel Washington and others, mentioning familiar names. I said I did; and he then said, 'Sir, you will find them there,' motioning me towards the engine-room. We were not kept closely confined, but were allowed to converse with him. I asked him what his object was. He replied, 'To free the negroes of Virginia.' He added that he was prepared to do it, and by twelve o'clock would have fifteen hundred men with him, ready armed. Up to this time the citizens had hardly begun to move about, and knew nothing of the raid. When they learned what was going on, some came out with old shotguns, and were themselves shot by concealed men. All the stores, as well as the arsenal, were in the hands of Brown's men, and it was impossible to get either arms or ammunition, there being hardly any private weapons. At last, however, a few arms were obtained, and a body of citizens crossed the river and advanced from the Maryland side. They made a vigorous attack, and in a few minutes caused all the invaders who were not killed to retreat to Brown inside of the armory gate. Then he entered the engine-house, carrying his prisoners along, or rather part of them, for he made selections. After getting into the engine-house, he made this speech: 'Gentlemen, perhaps you wonder why I have selected you from the others. It is because I believe you to be more influential; and I have only to say now, that you will have to share precisely the same fate that your friends extend to my men.' He began at once to bar the doors and windows, and to cut portholes through the brick wall.

"Then commenced a terrible firing from without, at every point from which the windows could be seen, and in a few minutes every window was shattered, and hundreds of balls came through the doors. These shots were answered from within whenever the attacking party could be seen. This was kept up most of the day, and, strange to say, not a prisoner was hurt, though thousands of balls were imbedded in the walls, and holes shot in the doors almost large enough for a man to creep through. At night the firing ceased, for we were in total darkness, and nothing could be seen in the engine-house. During the day and night I talked much with Brown. I found him as brave as a man could be, and sensible upon all subjects except slavery. He believed it was his duty to free the slaves, even if in doing so he lost his own life. During a sharp fight one of Brown's sons was killed. He fell; then trying to raise himself, he said, 'It is all over with me,' and died instantly. Brown did not leave his post at the porthole; but when the fighting was over he walked to his son's body, straightened out his limbs, took off his trappings, and then, turning to me, said, 'This is the third son I have lost in this cause.' Another son had been shot in the morning, and was then dying, having been brought in from the street. Often during the affair in the engine-house, when his men would want to fire upon some one who might be seen passing, Brown would stop them, saying, 'Don't shoot; that man is unarmed.' The firing was kept up by our men all day and until late at night, and during that time several of his men were killed, but none of the prisoners were hurt, though in great danger. During the day and night many propositions, *pro* and *con*, were made, looking to Brown's surrender and the release of the prisoners, but without result.

"When Colonel Lee came with the Government troops in the night, he at once sent a flag of truce by his aid, J. E. B. Stuart, to notify Brown of his arrival, and in the name of the United States to demand his surrender, advising him to throw himself on the clemency of the Government. Brown declined to accept Colonel Lee's terms, and determined to await the attack. When Stuart was admitted and a light brought, he exclaimed, 'Why, are n't you old Osawatomie Brown of Kansas, whom I once had there as my prisoner?' 'Yes,' was the answer, 'but you did not keep me.' This was the first intimation we had of Brown's real name. When Colonel Lee advised Brown to trust to the clemency of the Government, Brown responded that he knew what that meant, — a rope for his men and himself; adding, 'I prefer to die just here.' Stuart told him he would return at early morning for his final reply, and left him. When he had gone, Brown at once proceeded to barricade the doors, windows, etc., endeavoring to make the place as strong as possible. All this time no one of Brown's men showed the slightest fear, but calmly awaited the attack, selecting the best situations to fire from, and arranging their guns and pistols so that a fresh one could be taken up as soon as one was discharged. During the night I had a long talk with Brown, and told him that he and his men were com-

mitting treason against the State and the United States. Two of his
men, hearing the conversation, said to their leader, ' Are we committing treason against our country by being here ? ' Brown answered,
' Certainly.' Both said, ' If that is so, we don't want to fight any
more ; we thought we came to liberate the slaves, and did not know
that was committing treason.' Both of these men were afterwards
killed in the attack on the engine-house. When Lieutenant Stuart
came in the morning for the final reply to the demand to surrender,
I got up and went to Brown's side to hear his answer. Stuart asked,
' Are you ready to surrender, and trust to the mercy of the Government ? ' Brown answered, ' No, I prefer to die here.' His manner
did not betray the least alarm. Stuart stepped aside and made a
signal for the attack, which was instantly begun with sledge-ham-
mers to break down the door. Finding it would not yield, the
soldiers seized a long ladder for a battering-ram, and commenced
beating the door with that, the party within firing incessantly. I
had assisted in the barricading, fixing the fastenings so that I could
remove them on the first effort to get in. But I was not at the door
when the battering began, and could not get to the fastenings till
the ladder was used. I then quickly removed the fastenings; and,
after two or three strokes of the ladder, the engine rolled partially
back, making a small aperture, through which Lieutenant Green of
the marines forced his way, jumped on top of the engine, and stood
a second, amidst a shower of balls, looking for John Brown. When
he saw Brown he sprang about twelve feet at him, giving an under
thrust of his sword, striking Brown about midway the body, and
raising him completely from the ground. Brown fell forward, with
his head between his knees, while Green struck him several times
over the head, and, as I then supposed, split his skull at every
stroke. I was not two feet from Brown at that time. Of course I
got out of the building as soon as possible, and did not know till
some time later that Brown was not killed. It seems that Green's
sword, in making the thrust, struck Brown's belt and did not penetrate the body. The sword was bent double. The reason that
Brown was not killed when struck on the head was, that Green was
holding his sword in the middle, striking with the hilt, and making
only scalp wounds.

" When Governor Wise came and was examining Brown, I heard
the questions and answers, and no lawyer could have used more careful reserve, while at the same time he showed no disrespect. Governor Wise was astonished at the answers he received from Brown.
After some controversy between the United States and the State of
Virginia, as to which had jurisdiction over the prisoners, Brown was
carried to the Charlestown jail, and after a fair trial was hanged. Of

course I was a witness at the trial; and I must say that I have never
seen any man display more courage and fortitude than John Brown
showed under the trying circumstances in which he was placed. I
could not go to see him hanged. He had made me a prisoner, but
had spared my life and that of other gentlemen in his power; and
when his sons were shot down beside him, almost any other man
similarly placed would at least have exacted life for life."

This Colonel Lee was the same officer who as General of
the Confederate Army afterwards maintained so bravely
the lost cause of slavery, and surrendered to General Grant
and the Army of the Potomac in April, 1865. He was in
1859 in high command, under General Scott, in the United
States Army, and then, as afterwards, a defender of slavery and slaveholding Virginia.[1] Both he and his subordinate, Major Russell, treated Brown, who was supposed to
be dying, with consideration. After his capture the crowd
gathered round Brown, who told them not to maltreat him,
— that he was dying, and would soon be beyond all injury.
Major Russell had him conveyed into a room, and kindly
ordered all attention to be paid him. Brown, recognizing
Russell, said, "You entered first. I could have killed
you, but I spared you." In reply to which the Major
bowed and said, "I thank you." Brown said:—

"My name is John Brown; I have been well known as Old
Brown of Kansas. Two of my sons were killed here to-day, and
I'm dying too. I came here to liberate slaves, and was to receive no
reward. I have acted from a sense of duty, and am content to
await my fate; but I think the crowd have treated me badly. I am
an old man. Yesterday I could have killed whom I chose; but I had
no desire to kill any person, and would not have killed a man had
they not tried to kill me and my men. I could have sacked and

---

[1] A year before General Lee's death he said to John Leyburn, at Baltimore, that he had never been an advocate of slavery, had emancipated
most of his slaves before the war, and rejoiced that slavery was abolished;
adding: "I would cheerfully have lost all I have lost by the war, and
have suffered all I have suffered, to have this object attained." I print
this in justice to a brave soldier; but his warfare was as much in defence
of slavery as Hector's in defence of Helen, though the great Trojan did not
approve of Paris as against Menelaus. General Lee's

"One best omen was *Virginia's* cause."

burned the town, but did not; I have treated the persons whom I took as hostages kindly, and I appeal to them for the truth of what I say. If I had succeeded in running off slaves this time, I could have raised twenty times as many men as I have now, for a similar expedition. But I have failed."

To the master of the armory, while a prisoner, Brown had said: —

" We are Abolitionists from the North, come to take and release your slaves ; our organization is large, and must succeed. I suffered much in Kansas, and expect to suffer here, in the cause of human freedom. Slaveholders I regard as robbers and murderers; and I have sworn to abolish slavery and liberate my fellow-men."

To a reporter he said : —

" A lenient feeling towards the citizens led me into a parley with them as to compromise ; and by prevarication on their part I was delayed until attacked, and then in self-defence was forced to intrench myself."

While Brown was thus undergoing questions from officers, reporters, citizens, and others, Colonel Lee said that he would exclude all visitors from the room if the wounded men were annoyed by them. Brown said that on the contrary he was glad to be able to make himself and his motives clearly understood. He conversed freely, fluently, and cheerfully, without fear or uneasiness, weighing well his words.

The "New York Herald " correspondent says : [1] —

---

[1] In a paper printed in the " Atlantic Monthly," July, 1874, I used this expression : "It was the everlasting reporter of the ' New York Herald ' who then and there [at Harper's Ferry, in October, 1859] noted down the undying words that might else have been lost, or distorted in the recital of the base men to whom they were spoken." In the last letter I ever received from Gerrit Smith, soon after my latest visit to him in the summer of 1874, he thus alluded to my remark : "By the way, I never before knew of the essential service of the ' New York Herald ' in preserving ' the undying words ' of John Brown. Remember that I was sick at that time. As Providence chose filthy ravens to feed Elijah, so did Providence choose this vile sheet to carry to mankind the precious truths which came from the lips of dear John Brown."

"When I arrived in the armory at Harper's Ferry, shortly after two o'clock in the afternoon of October 19, Brown was answering questions put to him by Senator Mason, who had just arrived from his residence at Winchester, thirty miles distant; Colonel Faulkner, member of Congress, who lives but a few miles off; Mr. Vallandigham, member of Congress from Ohio; and several other distinguished gentlemen. The following is a verbatim report of the conversation : —

BROWN'S INTERVIEW WITH MASON, VALLANDIGHAM, AND OTHERS.

Senator Mason. Can you tell us who furnished money for your expedition ?

John Brown. I furnished most of it myself ; I cannot implicate others. It is by my own folly that I have been taken. I could easily have saved myself from it, had I exercised my own better judgment rather than yielded to my feelings.

Mason. You mean if you had escaped immediately ?

Brown. No. I had the means to make myself secure without any escape ; but I allowed myself to be surrounded by a force by being too tardy. I should have gone away ; but I had thirty odd prisoners, whose wives and daughters were in tears for their safety, and I felt for them. Besides, I wanted to allay the fears of those who believed we came here to burn and kill. For this reason I allowed the train to cross the bridge, and gave them full liberty to pass on. I did it only to spare the feelings of those passengers and their families, and to allay the apprehensions that you had got here in your vicinity a band of men who had no regard for life and property, nor any feelings of humanity.

Mason. But you killed some people passing along the streets quietly.

Brown. Well, sir, if there was anything of that kind done, it was without my knowledge. Your own citizens who were my prisoners will tell you that every possible means was taken to prevent it. I did not allow my men to fire when there was danger of killing those we regarded as innocent persons, if I could help it. They will tell you that we allowed ourselves to be fired at repeatedly, and did not return it.

A Bystander. That is not so. You killed an unarmed man at the corner of the house over there at the water-tank, and another besides.

Brown. See here, my friend ; it is useless to dispute or contradict the report of your own neighbors who were my prisoners.

Mason. If you would tell us who sent you here, — who provided the means, — that would be information of some value.

Brown. I will answer freely and faithfully about what concerns myself, — I will answer anything I can with honor, — but not about others.

Mr. Vallandigham (who had just entered). Mr. Brown, who sent you here?

Brown. No man sent me here; it was my own prompting and that of my Maker, or that of the Devil, — whichever you please to ascribe it to. I acknowledge no master in human form.

Vallandigham. Did you get up the expedition yourself?

Brown. I did.

Vallandigham. Did you get up this document that is called a Constitution?

Brown. I did. They are a constitution and ordinances of my own contriving and getting up.

Vallandigham. How long have you been engaged in this business?

Brown. From the breaking out of the difficulties in Kansas. Four of my sons had gone there to settle, and they induced me to go. I did not go there to settle, but because of the difficulties.

Mason. How many are there engaged with you in this movement?

Brown. Any questions that I can honorably answer I will, — not otherwise. So far as I am myself concerned, I have told everything truthfully. I value my word, sir.

Mason. What was your object in coming?

Brown. We came to free the slaves, and only that.

A Volunteer. How many men, in all, had you?

Brown. I came to Virginia with eighteen men only, besides myself.

Volunteer. What in the world did you suppose you could do here in Virginia with that amount of men?

Brown. Young man, I do not wish to discuss that question here.

Volunteer. You could not do anything.

Brown. Well, perhaps your ideas and mine on military subjects would differ materially.

Mason. How do you justify your acts?

Brown. I think, my friend, you are guilty of a great wrong against God and humanity, — I say it without wishing to be offensive, — and it would be perfectly right for any one to interfere with you so far as to free those you wilfully and wickedly hold in bondage. I do not say this insultingly.

Mason. I understand that.

Brown. I think I did right, and that others will do right who interfere with you at any time and at all times. I hold that the Golden Rule, " Do unto others as ye would that others should do unto you," applies to all who would help others to gain their liberty.

Lieutenant Stuart. But don't you believe in the Bible?

Brown. Certainly I do.

.   .   .   .

Mason. Did you consider this a military organization in this Constitution? I have not yet read it.

Brown. I did, in some sense. I wish you would give that paper close attention.

Mason. You consider yourself the commander-in-chief of these " provisional " military forces?

Brown. I was chosen, agreeably to the ordinance of a certain document, commander-in-chief of that force.

Mason. What wages did you offer?

Brown. None.

Stuart. " The wages of sin is death."

Brown. I would not have made such a remark to you if you had been a prisoner, and wounded, in my hands.

A Bystander. Did you not promise a negro in Gettysburg twenty dollars a month?

Brown. I did not.

Mason. Does this talking annoy you?

Brown. Not in the least.

Vallandigham. Have you lived long in Ohio?

Brown. I went there in 1805. I lived in Summit County, which was then Portage County. My native place is Connecticut; my father lived there till 1805.

Vallandigham. Have you been in Portage County lately?

Brown. I was there in June last.

Vallandigham. When in Cleveland, did you attend the Fugitive Slave Law Convention there?

Brown. No. I was there about the time of the sitting of the court to try the Oberlin rescuers. I spoke there publicly on that subject; on the Fugitive Slave Law and my own rescue. Of course, so far as I had any influence at all, I was supposed to justify the Oberlin people for rescuing the slave, because I have myself forcibly taken slaves from bondage. I was concerned in taking eleven slaves from Missouri to Canada last winter. I think I spoke in Cleveland before the Convention. I do not know that I had conversation with any of the Oberlin rescuers. I was sick part of the time I was in Ohio with the ague, in Ashtabula County.

Vallandigham. Did you see anything of Joshua R. Giddings there?

Brown. I did meet him.

Vallandigham. Did you converse with him?

Brown. I did. I would not tell you, of course, anything that would implicate Mr. Giddings; but I certainly met with him and had conversations with him.

Vallandigham. About that rescue case?

Brown. Yes; I heard him express his opinions upon it very freely and frankly.

Vallandigham. Justifying it?

Brown. Yes, sir; I do not compromise him, certainly, in saying that.

Vallandigham. Will you answer this: Did you talk with Giddings about your expedition here?

Brown. No, I won't answer that; because a denial of it I would not make, and to make any affirmation of it I should be a great dunce.

Vallandigham. Have you had any correspondence with parties at the North on the subject of this movement?

Brown. I have had correspondence.

A Bystander. Do you consider this a religious movement?

Brown. It is, in my opinion, the greatest service man can render to God.

Bystander. Do you consider yourself an instrument in the hands of Providence?

Brown. I do.

Bystander. Upon what principle do you justify your acts?

Brown. Upon the Golden Rule. I pity the poor in bondage that have none to help them : that is why I am here; not to gratify any personal animosity, revenge, or vindictive spirit. It is my sympathy with the oppressed and the wronged, that are as good as you and as precious in the sight of God.

Bystander. Certainly. But why take the slaves against their will?

Brown. I never did.

Bystander. You did in one instance, at least.

Stephens, the other wounded prisoner, here said, "You are right. In one case I know the negro wanted to go back."

Bystander. Where did you come from?

Stephens. I lived in Ashtabula County, Ohio.

Vallandigham. How recently did you leave Ashtabula County?

Stephens. Some months ago. I never resided there any length of time; have been through there.

Vallandigham. How far did you live from Jefferson?

Brown. Be cautious, Stephens, about any answers that would commit any friend. I would not answer that.

[Stephens turned partially over with a groan of pain, and was silent.]

Vallandigham. Who are your advisers in this movement?

Brown. I cannot answer that. I have numerous sympathizers throughout the entire North.

Vallandigham. In northern Ohio?

Brown. No more there than anywhere else; in all the free States.

Vallandigham. But you are not personally acquainted in southern Ohio?

Brown. Not very much.

A Bystander. Did you ever live in Washington City?

Brown. I did not. I want you to understand, gentlemen, and [to the reporter of the "Herald"] you may report that, — I want you to understand that I respect the rights of the poorest and weakest of colored people, oppressed by the slave system, just as much as I do those of the most wealthy and powerful. That is the idea that has moved me, and that alone. We expected no reward except the satisfaction of endeavoring to do for those in distress and greatly oppressed as we would be done by. The cry of distress of the oppressed is my reason, and the only thing that prompted me to come here.

Bystander. Why did you do it secretly?

Brown. Because I thought that necessary to success; no other reason.

Bystander. Have you read Gerrit Smith's last letter?

Brown. What letter do you mean?

Bystander. The "New York Herald" of yesterday, in speaking of this affair, mentions a letter in this way: —

"Apropos of this exciting news, we recollect a very significant passage in one of Gerrit Smith's letters, published a month or two ago, in which he speaks of the folly of attempting to strike the shackles off the slaves by the force of moral suasion or legal agitation, and predicts that the next movement made in the direction of negro emancipation would be an insurrection in the South."

Brown. I have not seen the "New York Herald" for some days past; but I presume, from your remark about the gist of the letter, that I should concur with it. I agree with Mr. Smith that moral suasion is hopeless. I don't think the people of the slave States will ever consider the subject of slavery in its true light till some other argument is resorted to than moral suasion.

Vallandigham. Did you expect a general rising of the slaves in case of your success ?

Brown. No, sir ; nor did I wish it. I expected to gather them up from time to time, and set them free.

Vallandigham. Did you expect to hold possession here till then ?

Brown. Well, probably I had quite a different idea. I do not know that I ought to reveal my plans. I am here a prisoner and wounded, because I foolishly allowed myself to be so. You overrate your strength in supposing I could have been taken if I had not allowed it. I was too tardy after commencing the open attack — in delaying my movements through Monday night, and up to the time I was attacked by the Government troops. It was all occasioned by my desire to spare the feelings of my prisoners and their families and the community at large. I had no knowledge of the shooting of the negro Heywood.

Vallandigham. What time did you commence your organization in Canada ?

Brown. That occurred about two years ago ; in 1858.

Vallandigham. Who was the secretary ?

Brown. That I would not tell if I recollected ; but I do not recollect. I think the officers were elected in May, 1858. I may answer incorrectly, but not intentionally. My head is a little confused by wounds, and my memory obscure on dates, etc.

Dr. Biggs. Were you in the party at Dr. Kennedy's house ?

Brown. I was the head of that party. I occupied the house to mature my plans. I have not been in Baltimore to purchase caps.

Dr. Biggs. What was the number of men at Kennedy's ?

Brown. I decline to answer that.

Dr. Biggs. Who lanced that woman's neck on the hill ?

Brown. I did. I have sometimes practised in surgery when I thought it a matter of humanity and necessity, and there was no one else to do it ; but I have not studied surgery.

Dr. Biggs. It was done very well and scientifically. They have been very clever to the neighbors, I have been told, and we had no reason to suspect them, except that we could not understand their movements. They were represented as eight or nine persons ; on Friday there were thirteen.

Brown. There were more than that.

Q. Where did you get arms ? *A.* I bought them.

Q. In what State ? *A.* That I will not state.

Q. How many guns ? *A.* Two hundred Sharpe's rifles and two hundred revolvers, — what is called the Massachusetts Arms Company's revolvers, a little under navy size.

Q. Why did you not take that swivel you left in the house?
A. I had no occasion for it. It was given to me a year or two
ago.

Q. In Kansas? *A.* No. I had nothing given to me in Kansas.

Q. By whom, and in what State? *A.* I decline to answer. It
is not properly a swivel; it is a very large rifle with a pivot. The
ball is larger than a musket ball; it is intended for a slug.

Reporter. I do not wish to annoy you; but if you have anything
further you would like to say, I will report it.

Brown. I have nothing to say, only that I claim to be here in
carrying out a measure I believe perfectly justifiable, and not to act
the part of an incendiary or ruffian, but to aid those suffering great
wrong. I wish to say, furthermore, that you had better — all you
people at the South — prepare yourselves for a settlement of this
question, that must come up for settlement sooner than you are prepared for it. The sooner you are prepared the better. You may
dispose of me very easily, — I am nearly disposed of now; but this
question is still to be settled, — this negro question I mean; the end
of that is not yet. These wounds were inflicted upon me — both
sabre cuts on my head and bayonet stabs in different parts of my
body — some minutes after I had ceased fighting and had consented to
surrender, for the benefit of others, not for my own.[1] I believe the
Major would not have been alive; I could have killed him just as
easy as a mosquito when he came in, but I supposed he only came
in to receive our surrender. There had been loud and long calls
of "surrender" from us, — as loud as men could yell; but in the
confusion and excitement I suppose we were not heard. I do not
think the Major, or any one, meant to butcher us after we had
surrendered.

An Officer. Why did you not surrender before the attack?

Brown. I did not think it was my duty or interest to do so. We
assured the prisoners that we did not wish to harm them, and they
should be set at liberty. I exercised my best judgment, not believing the people would wantonly sacrifice their own fellow-citizens,
when we offered to let them go on condition of being allowed to
change our position about a quarter of a mile. The prisoners agreed
by a vote among themselves to pass across the bridge with us. We

---

[1] At the trial of Copeland the following evidence was given : —

Mr. Sennott. You say that when Brown was down you struck him in the face with
your sabre?

Lieutenant Green. Yes.

Q. This was after he was down? *A.* Yes; he was down.

Q. How many times, Lieutenant Green, did you strike Brown in the face with your
sabre after he was down? *A.* Why, sir, he was defending himself with his gun.

Mr. Hunter. *I hope the counsel for the defence will not press such questions as these.*

wanted them only as a sort of guarantee of our own safety, — that we should not be fired into. We took them, in the first place, as hostages and to keep them from doing any harm. We did kill some men in defending ourselves, but I saw no one fire except directly in self-defence. Our orders were strict not to harm any one not in arms against us.

Q. Brown, suppose you had every nigger in the United States, what would you do with them ?   *A.* Set them free.

Q. Your intention was to carry them off and free them ?   *A.* Not at all.

A Bystander.   To set them free would sacrifice the life of every man in this community.

Brown.   I do not think so.

Bystander.   I know it.   I think you are fanatical.

Brown.   And I think you are fanatical.   "Whom the gods would destroy they first make mad," and you are mad.

Q.   Was it your only object to free the negroes ?   *A.* Absolutely our only object.

Q.   But you demanded and took Colonel Washington's silver and watch ?   *A.* Yes ; we intended freely to appropriate the property of slaveholders to carry out our object.   It was for that, and only that, and with no design to enrich ourselves with any plunder whatever.

Bystander.   Did you know Sherrod in Kansas ?   I understand you killed him.

Brown.   I killed no man except in fair fight.   I fought at Black Jack Point and at Osawatomie ; and if I killed anybody, it was at one of these places.

There is no record so full as this of any conversation held with Brown after his capture.   We have notes and reports, more or less conflicting, of what took place in his conversation with Wise, the Governor of Virginia, a few hours after the engine-house was taken.   Wise had been a leading and turbulent Congressman from Virginia, had belonged to more than one political party, and was a man of force and courage, though infatuated, like most Virginians of his time, with slavery and Southern institutions.   A correspondent of " Harper's Weekly " (which was then supporting slavery as a pillar of the Union) has thus described Wise's interview with Brown : —

" The mid-day train (October 18) brought Governor Wise, accompanied by several hundred men from Richmond, Alexandria,

Baltimore, and elsewhere. Accompanied by Andrew Hunter, the Governor repaired to the guard-room where the two wounded prisoners lay, and had a conversation with Brown. The Governor treated the wounded man with a courtesy that evidently surprised him. Brown was lying upon the floor with his feet to the fire and his head propped upon pillows on the back of a chair. His hair was a mass of clotted gore, so that I could not distinguish the original color; his eye a pale blue or gray, nose Roman, and beard (originally sandy) white and blood-stained. His speech was frequently interrupted by deep groans, reminding me of the agonized growl of a ferocious beast. A few feet from the leader lay Stephens, a fine-looking fellow, quiet, not in pain apparently, and conversing in a voice as full and natural as if he were unhurt. However, his hands lay folded upon his breast in a child-like, helpless way, — a position that I observed was assumed by all those who had died or were dying of their wounds. Only those who were shot stone-dead lay as they fell.

"Brown was frank and communicative, answering all questions without reserve, except such as might implicate his associates. I append extracts from notes taken by Mr. Hunter : —

" ' Brown avers that the small pamphlet, many copies of which were found on the persons of the slain, and entitled Provisional Constitution and Ordinances for the People of the United States, was prepared principally by himself; under its provisions he was appointed Commander-in-Chief. His two sons and Stephens were each captains, and Coppoc a lieutenant ; they each had commissions, issued by himself. He avers that the whole number operating under this organization was but twenty-two, each of whom had taken the oath required by Article 48 ; but he confidently expected large reinforcements from Virginia, Kentucky, Maryland, North and South Carolina, and several other Slave States, besides the Free States, — taking it for granted that it was only necessary to seize the public arms and place them in the hands of the negroes and non-slaveholders to recruit his forces indefinitely. In this calculation he reluctantly and indirectly admitted that he had been disappointed.'

"When Governor Wise went away, some of us lingered, and the old man recurred again to his sons, of whom he had spoken several times, asking if we were sure they were both dead. He was assured that it was so. ' How many bodies did you take from the engine-house ?' he asked. He was told three. ' Then they are not both dead ; there were three dead bodies there last night. Gentlemen, my son is doubtless living and in your power. I will ask for him what I would not ask for myself; let him have kind treatment, for he is as pure and noble-hearted a youth as ever breathed the breath of life.' His prayer was vain. Both his boys lay stark and bloody by the Armory wall."

In this conversation, according to Governor Wise, Brown did not say a word which was personally offensive to him. Somebody in the crowd called Brown "robber," and Brown retorted, "You [the slaveholders] are the robbers." And in this connection he said, "If you have your opinions about me, I have my opinions about you." Wise then said: "Mr. Brown, the silver of your hair is reddened by the blood of crime, and you should eschew these hard words and think upon eternity. You are suffering from wounds, perhaps fatal; and should you escape death from these causes, you must submit to a trial which may involve death. Your confessions justify the presumption that you will be found guilty; and even now you are committing a felony under the laws of Virginia, by uttering sentiments like these. It is better you should turn your attention to your eternal future than be dealing in denunciations which can only injure you." Brown replied, "Governor, I have from all appearances not more than fifteen or twenty years the start of you in the journey to that eternity of which you kindly warn me; and whether my time here shall be fifteen months, or fifteen days, or fifteen hours, I am equally prepared to go. There is an eternity behind and an eternity before; and this little speck in the centre, however long, is but comparatively a minute. The difference between your tenure and mine is trifling, and I therefore tell you to be prepared. I am prepared. You all have a heavy responsibility, and it behooves you to prepare more than it does me."

In speaking of this conversation,[1] Wise said publicly:

"They are mistaken who take Brown to be a madman. He is a bundle of the best nerves I ever saw: cut and thrust and bleeding, and in bonds. He is a man of clear head, of courage, fortitude, and

---

[1] A Virginian gives me this addition to Brown's conversation with Wise:—

Jailer. I see in the papers that you told Governor Wise you had promises of aid from Virginia, Tennessee, and the Carolinas. Is that true, or did you make it up to "rile" the old Governor?

Brown. No; I did not tell Wise that.

Jailer. What did you tell him that could have made that impression on his mind?

Brown. Wise said something about fanaticism, and intimated that no man in full possession of his senses could have expected to overcome a State with such a handful

simple ingenuousness. He is cool, collected, and indomitable, and it is but just to him to say that he was humane to his prisoners, and he inspired me with great trust in his integrity as a man of truth. He is a fanatic, vain and garrulous, but firm, truthful, and intelligent. He professes to be a Christian in communion with the Congregational Church of the North, and openly preaches his purpose of universal emancipation; and the negroes themselves were to be the agents, by means of arms, led on by white commanders. . . . Colonel Washington says that he was the coolest and firmest man he ever saw in defying danger and death. With one son dead by his side, and another shot through, he felt the pulse of his dying son with one hand, held his rifle with the other, and commanded his men with the utmost composure, encouraging them to be firm, and to sell their lives as dearly as they could."

BROWN'S SPEECHES AT HIS TRIAL.

On the first day of his trial under indictment (October 25), in the court-house at Charlestown not far from Harper's Ferry, Brown and Coppoc were brought in manacled together. Brown appeared weak, haggard, and with eyes swollen from the effects of the wound in his head. The prisoners were severally charged with treason and murder. The Court asked if they had counsel, when Brown spoke as follows : —

" I did not ask for any quarter at the time I was taken; I did not ask to have my life spared. The Governor of the State of Virginia tendered me assurances that I should have a fair trial; but under no

of men as I had, backed only by struggling negroes ; and I replied that I had promises of ample assistance, and would have received it too if I could only have put the ball in motion. He then asked suddenly and in a harsh voice, as you 've seen lawyers snap up a witness : "Assistance ! From what State, sir ?" I was not thrown off my guard, and replied : "From more than you 'd believe if I should name them all ; but I *expected* more from Virginia, Tennessee, and the Carolinas than from any others."

Jailer. You "expected" it. You did not say it was promised from the States named ?

Brown. No ; I knew, of course, that the negroes would rally to my standard. If I had only got the thing fairly started, you Virginians would have seen sights that would have opened your eyes ; and I tell you if I was free this moment, and had five hundred negroes around me, I would put these irons on Wise himself before Saturday night.

Jailer. Then it was true about aid being promised ? What States promised it ?

Brown (with a laugh). Well, you are about as smart a man as Wise, and I 'll give you the same answer I gave him.

So far as the language goes, this is perhaps not very correctly reported, being from memory and at second hand.

circumstances whatever shall I be able to have a fair trial. If you seek my blood, you can have it at any moment, without this mockery of a trial. I have had no counsel. I have not been able to advise with any one. I know nothing about the feelings of my fellow-prisoners, and am utterly unable to attend in any way to my own defence. My memory does n't serve me; my health is insufficient although improving. There are mitigating circumstances that I would urge in our favor, if a fair trial is to be had; but if we are to be forced with a mere form, a trial for execution, you might spare yourselves that trouble. I am ready for my fate. I beg for no mockery of a trial, no insult, — nothing but that which conscience gives or cowardice drives you to practise. I ask again to be excused from the mockery of a trial. I do not even know what the special design of this examination is; I do not know what is to be the benefit of it to the Commonwealth. I have now little further to ask, other than that I may not be foolishly insulted, only as cowardly barbarians insult those who fall into their power."

As the trial went on, Brown again rose from the pallet on which he lay wounded, and said : —

"I do not intend to detain the Court, but barely wish to say, as I have been promised a fair trial, that I am not now in circumstances that enable me to attend to a trial, owing to the state of my health. I have a severe wound in the back, or rather in one kidney, which enfeebles me very much. But I am doing well, and I only ask for a short delay of my trial, and I think I may get able to listen to it; and I merely ask this, that, as the saying is, 'the devil may have his dues,' — no more. I wish to say, further, that my hearing is impaired and rendered indistinct, in consequence of wounds I have about my head. I cannot hear distinctly at all. I could not hear what the Court said this morning. I would be glad to hear what is said on my trial, and I am now doing better than I could expect to be under the circumstances. A very short delay would be all I would ask. I do not presume to ask more than a very short delay, so that I may in some degree recover, and be able at least to listen to my trial, and hear what questions are asked of the citizens, and what their answers are. If that could be allowed me, I should feel very much obliged."

The Court refused his requests, and a jury having been sworn, directed that the prisoner might forego the form of standing while arraigned, if he desired it. He therefore continued to lie prostrate on his cot-bed while the long indictment was read, — for conspiring with negroes to produce insurrection ; for treason to the Commonwealth, and for murder.

In the course of the first day's proceedings, Brown rose, evidently excited, and standing on his feet said : —

" *May it please the Court,* — I discover that, notwithstanding all the assertions I have received of a fair trial, nothing like a fair trial is to be given me, as it would seem.   I gave the names, as soon as I could get at them, of the persons I wished to have called as witnesses, and was assured that they would be subpœnaed.   I wrote down a memorandum to that effect, saying where those parties were, but it appears that they have not been subpœnaed, so far as I can learn. And now I ask if I am to have anything at all deserving the name and shadow of a fair trial, that this proceeding be deferred until to-morrow morning ; for I have no counsel, as I have before stated, in whom I feel that I can rely, but I am in hopes counsel may arrive who will see that I get the witnesses necessary for my defence.   I am myself unable to attend to it.   I have given all the attention I possibly could to it, but am unable to see or know about them, and can't even find out their names ; and I have nobody to do any errand, for my money was all taken from me when I was hacked and stabbed, and I have not a dime.   I had two hundred and fifty or sixty dollars in gold and silver taken from my pocket, and now I have no possible means of getting anybody to go any errands for me, and I have not had all the witnesses subpœnaed.   They are not within reach, and are not here.   I ask at least until to-morrow morning to have something done, if anything is designed.   If not, I am ready for anything that may come up."

Brown then lay down again, drew his blanket over him, closed his eyes, and appeared to sink in tranquil slumber. The day after, when insanity was pleaded in his defence, he desired his counsel to say that he did not put in the plea of insanity. This movement was made without his approbation or concurrence, and was unknown to him till then.   He then raised himself up in bed, and said : —

" I will add, if the Court will allow me, that I look upon it as a miserable artifice and pretext of those who ought to take a different course in regard to me, if they took any at all, and I view it with contempt more than otherwise.   As I remarked to Mr. Green, insane prisoners, so far as my experience goes, have but little ability to judge of their own sanity ; and if I am insane, of course I should think I knew more than all the rest of the world. But I do not think so. I am perfectly unconscious of insanity, and I reject, so far as I am capable, any attempts to interfere in my behalf on that score."

Brown was ably defended, among others, by a young Massachusetts attorney, George H. Hoyt, but of course was convicted. The prosecutor was Andrew Hunter, of Charlestown, who in his argument

" Contended that the code of Virginia defines citizens of Virginia as ' all those white persons born in any other State of this Union, who may become residents here ; ' and that evidence shows without a shadow of a question that when Brown went to Virginia, and planted his feet at Harper's Ferry, he came there to reside, and to hold the place permanently. True, he occupied a farm four or five miles off in Maryland, but not for the legitimate purpose of establishing his domicil there ; no, for the nefarious and hellish purpose of rallying forces into this Commonwealth, and establishing himself at Harper's Ferry, as the starting-point for a new government. Whatever it was, whether tragical, or farcical and ridiculous, as Brown's counsel had presented it, his conduct showed, if his declarations were insufficient, that it was not alone for the purpose of carrying off slaves that he came there. His ' Provisional Government ' was a real thing and no debating society, as his counsel would have us believe; and in holding office under it and exercising its functions, he was clearly guilty of treason. As to conspiring with slaves and rebels, the law says the prisoners are equally guilty, whether insurrection is made or not. Advice may be given by actions as well as words. When you put pikes in the hands of slaves, and have their master captive, that is advice to slaves to rebel, and is punishable with death."

During most of the arguments Brown lay on his back, with his eyes closed. When the verdict was read, " Guilty of treason, and of conspiring and advising with slaves and others to rebel, and of murder in the first degree," not the slightest sound was heard in the crowd present, who a moment before, outside the court, had joined in threats and imprecations. Brown himself said not a word, but as on any previous day turned to adjust his pallet, and then composedly stretched himself upon it. A motion for an arrest of judgment was put in, but counsel on both sides being too much exhausted to go on, Brown was removed unsentenced to prison.

CHAPTER XVI.

JOHN BROWN IN PRISON.

OF all the work done by this hero in behalf of the slave throughout a life almost wholly devoted to emancipation, none was so wonderful as that wrought by him in prison and on the scaffold. History seeks in vain for parallels to this achievement, — a defeated, dying old man, who had been praying and fighting, pleading and toiling, for years, to persuade a great people that their national life was all wrong, suddenly converting millions to his cause by the silent magnanimity or the spoken wisdom of his last days as a fettered prisoner. For Brown was not figuratively and rhetorically in chains during that period of frenzied terror which lay between his capture of Harper's Ferry, October 16, and his death at Charlestown, Dec. 2, 1859. He was loaded with chains, hand and foot; he was fastened to the floor of his cell, and watched day and night by armed men, whose instructions were to kill him if he should have any, the most remote, chance of escape. He was forced to rise from what was feared to be his dying bed, to hear the ferocious indictment against him recited; and during the most of his trial he lay on a pallet in the court-room. But that Divine Wisdom which he adored, and whose purposes he alone, of living or dying men, could best fulfil, was his guide and his guard; from the hand which had armed him with sword and rifle he now received that sword of the Spirit, heavenly in temper and in power, which won for him his final victory.

"For in all things, O Lord! Thou didst magnify Thy servant, and glorify him; neither didst Thou lightly regard him, but didst assist him in every time and place. When unrighteous men thought to oppress this righteous one in prison, they themselves, the prisoners of darkness, and fettered with the bonds of a long night, lay there exiled from the Eternal Providence. Yea, the tasting of death touched the righteous also; but then the blameless man made haste, and stood forth to defend them; and bringing the shield of his proper ministry, even prayer and propitiation, set himself against the wrath, and brought the calamity to an end. Declaring himself Thy servant, he overcame the destroyer, not with the strength of body or the force of arms; but with a word subdued he him that punished, alleging the oaths and covenants made with the fathers.

"This was he whom we had sometime in derision and a proverb of reproach; we, fools, accounted his life madness, and his end to be without honor. But how is he numbered among the children of God! His lot is among the saints. In the sight of the unwise he seemed to die; and his departure was taken for misery, his going from us to be utter destruction. But he is in peace. Though he be punished in the sight of men, yet is his hope full of immortality; and having been a little chastised, he shall be greatly rewarded.

"God proved him and found him worthy of Himself; he shall judge the nations, and have dominion over the people; and his Lord shall reign forever."

These words of an old Scripture, long disregarded, were found true of John Brown, — literally and exactly fulfilled, like the computations of the astronomer. And who shall doubt that there is an astronomy for the period of great souls, as for the stars in their courses, — a lore which the devout may learn, if they will but obey? To this John Brown had meekly schooled his imperious will; and nowhere in history do we find a more punctual submission to the Divine purpose, a more perfect resignation and composure, than this headstrong old warrior now displayed. Then appeared, what had before been but little regarded, the strange power and pathos of his unschooled words. His speech to the Court was the first great example of this, although his replies to Mason and Wise of Virginia had already taught the world to listen for every sentence he uttered. "What avail all your scholarly accomplishments and learning, compared with wisdom and manhood?" said Thoreau, speaking of John Brown. "To omit his other behavior, see what a work this comparatively unread and unlettered man wrote within six weeks! He wrote in prison, not

a 'History of the World,' like Raleigh, but an American
book which I think will live longer than that. What a variety of themes he touched on in that short space!" It is
the virtue of such writings that they continue to influence
mankind forever, so long as they continue to be read ; and
we may predict for these prison letters as long a life as for
the "Apology" of Socrates and the dying address to his
disciples. But what a work they have accomplished already, in the few brief years since John Brown was borne
from the scaffold in Charlestown to his resting-place beside
the great rock at North Elba, where the grave became his
stronghold, while "his soul went marching on!" Those
who mourned his death, now finding him risen and triumphant, may exclaim with Milton's Hebrews, after that
"last victory of Samson" which Brown had foretold for
himself : —

> " All is best, though we oft doubt
> What the unsearchable dispose
> Of highest wisdom brings about,
> And ever best found in the close.
> Oft He seems to hide His face,
> But unexpectedly returns,
> And to His faithful champion hath in place
> Borne witness gloriously ; whence Gaza mourns,
> And all that band them to resist
> His uncontrollable intent.
> His servants He, with new acquist
> Of true experience from this great event,
> With peace and consolation hath dismissed,
> And calm of mind, all passion spent."

PRISON LETTERS AND SPEECHES.

Letter to Judge Russell, of Boston.[1]

CHARLESTOWN, JEFFERSON COUNTY, VA., Oct. 21, 1859.
HON. THOMAS RUSSELL.

DEAR SIR, — I am here a prisoner, with several sabre-cuts in my
head and bayonet-stabs in my body. My object in writing to you is
to obtain able and faithful counsel for myself and fellow-prisoners

---

[1] A copy of this letter was also sent to Reuben A. Chapman, of Springfield, Mass., and a third to Daniel R. Tilden, of Ohio.

(five in all), as we have the faith of Virginia pledged through her Governor and numerous other prominent citizens to give us a fair trial. Without we can obtain such counsel from without the slave States, neither the facts in our case can come before the world, nor can we have the benefit of such facts as might be considered mitigating in the view of others upon our trial. I have money in hand here to the amount of two hundred and fifty dollars, and personal property sufficient to pay a most liberal fee to yourself, or to any suitable man who will undertake our defence, if I can be allowed the benefit of said property. Can you or some other good man come on immediately, for the sake of the young men prisoners at least? My wounds are doing well. Do not send an ultra Abolitionist.

Very respectfully yours,

JOHN BROWN.

Indorsed, " The trial is set for Wednesday next, the 25th inst. — J. W. Campbell, *Sheriff of Jefferson County.*"

To his Family.

CHARLESTOWN, JEFFERSON COUNTY, VA., Oct. 31, 1859.

MY DEAR WIFE AND CHILDREN, EVERY ONE, — I suppose you have learned before this by the newspapers that two weeks ago to-day we were fighting for our lives at Harper's Ferry; that during the fight Watson was mortally wounded, Oliver killed, William Thompson killed, and Dauphin slightly wounded; that on the following day I was taken prisoner, immediately after which I received several sabre-cuts on my head and bayonet-stabs in my body. As nearly as I can learn, Watson died of his wound on Wednesday, the second — or on Thursday, the third — day after I was taken. Dauphin was killed when I was taken, and Anderson I suppose also. I have since been tried, and found guilty of treason, etc., and of murder in the first degree. I have not yet received my sentence. No others of the company with whom you were acquainted were, so far as I can learn, either killed or taken. Under all these terrible calamities, I feel quite cheerful in the assurance that God reigns and will overrule all for his glory and the best possible good. I feel no consciousness of guilt in the matter, nor even mortification on account of my imprisonment and irons; and I feel perfectly sure that very soon no member of my family will feel any possible disposition to " blush on my account." Already dear friends at a distance, with kindest sympathy, are cheering me with the assurance that posterity, at least, will do me justice. I shall commend you all together, with my beloved but bereaved daughters-in-law, to their sympathies, which I do not doubt will soon reach you. I also commend you all to Him "whose mercy endureth forever," — to the God of my fathers, "whose I am, and whom I serve." "He will never leave you nor forsake you," unless you forsake Him. Finally, my dearly beloved, be of good comfort. Be sure to remember and follow my advice, and my example too, so far as it has been consistent with the holy religion of Jesus Christ, — in which I remain a most firm and humble believer. Never forget the poor, nor think anything you bestow on them to be lost to you, even though they may be black as Ebedmelech, the Ethiopian eunuch, who cared for Jeremiah in the pit of the dungeon; or as black as the one to whom Philip preached Christ. Be sure to entertain strangers, for thereby some have — "Remember them that are in bonds as bound with them."

I am in charge of a jailer like the one who took charge of Paul and Silas; and you may rest assured that both kind hearts and kind faces are more or less about me, while thousands are thirsting for my blood. "These light afflictions, which are but for a moment, shall work out for us a far more exceeding and eternal weight of glory." I hope to be able to write you again. Copy this, Ruth, and send it to your sorrow-stricken brothers to comfort them. Write me a few words in regard to the welfare of all. God Almighty bless you all, and make you "joyful in the midst of all your tribulations!" Write to John Brown, Charlestown, Jefferson County, Va., care of Captain John Avis.

Your affectionate husband and father,

JOHN BROWN.

Nov. 3, 1859.

P. S. Yesterday, November 2, I was sentenced to be hanged on December 2 next. Do not grieve on my account. I am still quite cheerful. God bless you!   Yours ever,

JOHN BROWN.

To Mrs. Child.

October 31.

MRS. L. MARIA CHILD.

MY DEAR FRIEND, — such you prove to be, though a stranger, — Your most kind letter has reached me, with the kind offer to come here and take care of me. Allow me to express my gratitude for your great sympathy, and at the same time to propose to you a different course, together with my reasons for wishing it. I should certainly be greatly pleased to become personally acquainted with one so gifted and so kind; but I cannot avoid seeing some objections to it under present circumstances. First, I am in charge of a most humane gentleman, who with his family have rendered me every possible attention I have desired or that could be of the least advantage; and I am so far recovered from my wounds as no longer to require nursing. Then, again, it would subject you to great personal inconvenience and heavy expense, without doing me any good. Allow me to name to you another channel through which you may reach me with your sympathies much more effectually. I have at home a wife and three young daughters, the youngest but little over five years old, the oldest nearly sixteen. I have also two daughters-in-law, whose husbands have both fallen near me here. There is also another widow, Mrs. Thompson, whose husband fell here. Whether she is a mother or not I cannot say. All these, my wife included, live at North Elba, Essex County, N. Y. I have a middle-aged son, who has been in some degree a cripple from his childhood, who would have as much as he could well do to earn a living. He was a most dreadful sufferer in Kansas, and lost all he had laid up. He has not enough to clothe himself for the winter comfortably. I have no living son or son-in-law who did not suffer terribly in Kansas.

Now, dear friend, would you not as soon contribute fifty cents now, and a like sum yearly, for the relief of those very poor and deeply afflicted persons, to enable them to supply themselves and their children with bread and very plain clothing, and to enable the children to receive a common English education? Will you also devote your own energies to induce others to join you in giving a like amount, to constitute a little fund for the purpose named?

I cannot see how your coming here can do me the least good; and I am quite certain you can do me immense good where you are. I am quite cheerful under all my afflicting circumstances and prospects; having, as I humbly trust, "the peace of God, which passeth all understanding," to rule in my heart. You may make such use of this as you see fit. God Almighty bless and reward you a thousand-fold!   Yours in sincerity and truth,

John Brown.

Letter from a Quaker Lady to John Brown.

Newport, R. I., Tenth Month, 27th, '59.

Captain John Brown.

Dear Friend, — Since thy arrest I have often thought of thee, and have wished that, like Elizabeth Fry toward her prison friends, so I might console thee in thy confinement. But that can never be; and so I can only write thee a few lines which, if they contain any comfort, may come to thee like some little ray of light.

* You can never know how very many dear Friends love thee with all their hearts for thy brave efforts in behalf of the poor oppressed; and though we, who are non-resistants, and religiously believe it better to reform by moral and not by carnal weapons, could not approve of bloodshed, yet we know thee was animated by the most generous and philanthropic motives. Very many thousands openly approve thy intentions, though most Friends would not think it right to take up arms. Thousands pray for thee every day; and oh, I do pray that God will be with thy soul. Posterity will do thee justice. If Moses led out the thousands of Jewish slaves from their bondage, and God destroyed the Egyptians in the sea because they went after the Israelites to bring them back to slavery, then surely, by the same reasoning, we may judge thee a deliverer who wished to release millions from a more cruel oppression. If the American people honor Washington for resisting with bloodshed for seven years an unjust tax, how much more ought thou to be honored for seeking to free the poor slaves.

Oh, I wish I could plead for thee as some of the other sex can plead, how I would seek to defend thee! If I had now the eloquence of Portia, how I would turn the scale in thy favor! But I can only pray "God bless thee!" God pardon thee, and through our Redeemer give thee safety and happiness now and always!

From thy friend,

E. B.

John Brown's Reply.

Charlestown, Jefferson County, Va., Nov. 1, 1859.

My dear Friend E. B. of R. I., — Your most cheering letter of the 27th of October is received; and may the Lord reward you a thousandfold for the kind feeling you express toward me; but more especially for your fidelity to the "poor that cry, and those that have no help." For this I am a prisoner in bonds. It is solely my own fault, in a military point of view, that we met with our disaster. I mean that I mingled with our prisoners and so far sympathized with them and their families that I neglected my duty in other respects. But God's will, not mine, be done.

You know that Christ once armed Peter. So also in my case I think he put a sword into my hand, and there continued it so long as he saw best, and then kindly took it from me. I mean when I first went to Kansas. I wish you could know with what cheerfulness I am now wielding the "sword of the Spirit" on the right hand and on the left. I bless God that it proves "mighty to the pulling down of strongholds." I always loved my Quaker friends, and I commend

to their kind regard my poor bereaved widowed wife and my daugh'-
ters and daughters-in-law, whose husbands fell at my side. One is
a mother and the other likely to become so soon. They, as well as
my own sorrow-stricken daughters, are left very poor, and have much
greater need of sympathy than I, who, through Infinite Grace and
the kindness of strangers, am "joyful in all my tribulations."

Dear sister, write them at North Elba, Essex County, N. Y., to
comfort their sad hearts. Direct to Mary A. Brown, wife of John
Brown. There is also another — a widow, wife of Thompson, who
fell with my poor boys in the affair at Harper's Ferry — at the same
place.

I do not feel conscious of guilt in taking up arms; and had it been
in behalf of the rich and powerful, the intelligent, the great (as men
count greatness), or those who form enactments to suit themselves
and corrupt others, or some of their friends, that I interfered, suffered,
sacrificed, and fell, it would have been doing very well. But enough
of this. These light afflictions, which endure for a moment, shall but
work for me " a far more exceeding and eternal weight of glory." I
would be very grateful for another letter from you. My wounds are
healing. Farewell. God will surely attend to his own cause in the
best possible way and time, and he will not forget the work of his
own hands.   Your friend,

                                        JOHN BROWN.

An Appeal.

CHARLESTOWN, JEFFERSON COUNTY, VA., Nov. 1, 1859.

TO MY FRIENDS IN NEW ENGLAND AND ELSEWHERE, — Aaron
D. Stephens, one of the prisoners now in confinement with me in
this place, is desirous of obtaining the assistance of George Sennott,
Esq., of Boston, Mass., in defending him on his trial to come off
before the United States Court. Anything you can do toward
securing the services of Mr. Sennott for the prisoner will add to the
many obligations of your humble servants.

                                        JOHN BROWN.

The above contains the expression of my own wishes.

                                        A. D. STEPHENS.

When brought into court, the day after his conviction,
to receive his sentence, Brown was taken by surprise at
being called on to say why sentence of death should not be
pronounced. He had expected some further delay, and
was unprepared at the moment. He rose, however, and in
a singularly mild and gentle manner made his famous plea,

in which we may recognize some of the phrases he had used in his letters: —

JOHN BROWN'S LAST SPEECH (NOV. 2).

" I have, may it please the Court, a few words to say.

" In the first place, I deny everything but what I have all along admitted, — the design on my part to free the slaves. I intended certainly to have made a clean thing of that matter, as I did last winter, when I went into Missouri and there took slaves without the snapping of a gun on either side, moved them through the country, and finally left them in Canada. I designed to have done the same thing again, on a larger scale.[1] That was all I intended. I never did intend murder, or treason, or the destruction of property, or to excite or incite slaves to rebellion, or to make insurrection.

" I have another objection: and that is, it is unjust that I should suffer such a penalty. Had I interfered in the manner which I admit, and which I admit has been fairly proved (for I admire the truthfulness and candor of the greater portion of the witnesses who have testified in this case), — had I so interfered in behalf of the rich, the powerful, the intelligent, the so-called great, or in behalf of any of their friends, — either father, mother, brother, sister, wife, or children, — or any of that class, — and suffered and sacrificed what I have in this interference, it would have been all right; and every man in this court would have deemed it an act worthy of reward rather than punishment.

---

[1] In explanation of this passage, Brown three weeks afterward handed to Mr. Hunter this letter: —

CHARLESTOWN, JEFFERSON COUNTY, VA., Nov. 22, 1859.

DEAR SIR, — I have just had my attention called to a seeming confliction between the statement I at first made to Governor Wise and that which I made at the time I received my sentence, regarding my intentions respecting the slaves we took about the Ferry. There need be no such confliction, and a few words of explanation will, I think, be quite sufficient. I had given Governor Wise a full and particular account of that; and when called in court to say whether I had anything further to urge, I was taken wholly by surprise, as I did not expect my sentence before the others. In the hurry of the moment I forgot much that I had before intended to say, and did not consider the full bearing of what I then said. I intended to convey this idea, — that it was my object to place the slaves in a condition to defend their liberties, if they would, without any bloodshed; but not that I intended to run them out of the slave States. I was not aware of any such apparent confliction until my attention was called to it, and I do not suppose that a man in my then circumstances should be superhuman in respect to the exact purport of every word he might utter. What I said to Governor Wise was spoken with all the deliberation I was master of, and was intended for truth; and what I said in court was equally intended for truth, but required a more full explanation than I then gave. Please make such use of this as you think calculated to correct any wrong impressions I may have given.   Very respectfully yours,

JOHN BROWN.

ANDREW HUNTER, ESQ., Present.

"This court acknowledges, as I suppose, the validity of the law of God. I see a book kissed here which I suppose to be the Bible, or at least the New Testament. That teaches me that all things whatsoever I would that men should do to me, I should do even so to them. It teaches me, further, to 'remember them that are in bonds, as bound with them.' I endeavored to act up to that instruction. I say, I am yet too young to understand that God is any respecter of persons. I believe that to have interfered as I have done — as I have always freely admitted I have done — in behalf of His despised poor, was not wrong, but right. Now, if it is deemed necessary that I should forfeit my life for the furtherance of the ends of justice, and mingle my blood further with the blood of my children and with the blood of millions in this slave country whose rights are disregarded by wicked, cruel, and unjust enactments, — I submit; so let it be done!

"Let me say one word further.

"I feel entirely satisfied with the treatment I have received on my trial. Considering all the circumstances, it has been more generous than I expected. But I feel no consciousness of guilt. I have stated from the first what was my intention, and what was not. I never had any design against the life of any person, nor any disposition to commit treason, or excite slaves to rebel, or make any general insurrection. I never encouraged any man to do so, but always discouraged any idea of that kind.

"Let me say, also, a word in regard to the statements made by some of those connected with me. I hear it has been stated by some of them that I have induced them to join me. But the contrary is true. I do not say this to injure them, but as regretting their weakness. There is not one of them but joined me of his own accord, and the greater part of them at their own expense. A number of them I never saw, and never had a word of conversation with, till the day they came to me; and that was for the purpose I have stated.

"Now I have done."

Brown was then taken from the court-room back to his prison, where he continued to recover from his wounds, but did not write many letters until a week after his conviction. He then wrote first to his family, as follows : —

CHARLESTOWN, JEFFERSON COUNTY, VA., Nov. 8, 1859.

DEAR WIFE AND CHILDREN, EVERY ONE, — I will begin by saying that I have in some degree recovered from my wounds, but that I am quite weak in my back and sore about my left kidney. My

appetite has been quite good for most of the time since I was hurt.
I am supplied with almost everything I could desire to make me
comfortable, and the little I do lack (some articles of clothing which
I lost) I may perhaps soon get again.   I am, besides, quite cheerful,
having (as I trust) "the peace of God, which passeth all understanding," to "rule in my heart," and the testimony (in some degree)
of a good conscience that I have not lived altogether in vain.   I can
trust God with both the time and the manner of my death, believing,
as I now do, that for me at this time to seal my testimony for God
and humanity with my blood will do vastly more toward advancing
the cause I have earnestly endeavored to promote, than all I have
done in my life before.   I beg of you all meekly and quietly to submit to this, not feeling yourselves in the least *degraded* on that
account.   Remember, dear wife and children all, that Jesus of Nazareth suffered a most excruciating death on the cross as a felon, under
the most aggravating circumstances.   Think also of the prophets and
apostles and Christians of former days, who went through greater
tribulations than you or I, and try to be reconciled.   May God
Almighty comfort all your hearts, and soon wipe away all tears from
your eyes!   To him be endless praise!   Think, too, of the crushed
millions who "have no comforter."   I charge you all never in your
trials to forget the griefs "of the poor that cry, and of those that
have none to help them."   I wrote most earnestly to my dear and
afflicted wife not to come on for the present, at any rate.   I will now
give her my reasons for doing so.   First, it would use up all the
scanty means she has, or is at all likely to have, to make herself and
children comfortable hereafter.   For let me tell you that the sympathy that is now aroused in your behalf may not always follow you.
There is but little more of the romantic about helping poor widows
and their children than there is about trying to relieve poor "niggers."   Again, the little comfort it might afford us to meet again
would be dearly bought by the pains of a final separation.   We must
part; and I feel assured for us to meet under such dreadful circumstances would only add to our distress.   If she comes on here, she
must be only a gazing-stock throughout the whole journey, to be remarked upon in every look, word, and action, and by all sorts of
creatures, and by all sorts of papers, throughout the whole country.
Again, it is my most decided judgment that in quietly and submis-
sively staying at home vastly more of generous sympathy will reach
her, without such dreadful sacrifice of feeling as she must put up
with if she comes on.   The visits of one or two female friends that
have come on here have produced great excitement, which is very
annoying; and they cannot possibly do me any good.   Oh, Mary!
do not come, but patiently wait for the meeting of those who love

God and their fellow-men, where no separation must follow. "They shall go no more out forever." I greatly long to hear from some one of you, and to learn anything that in any way affects your welfare. I sent you ten dollars the other day; did you get it? I have also endeavored to stir up Christian friends to visit and write to you in your deep affliction. I have no doubt that some of them, at least, will heed the call. Write to me, care of Captain John Avis, Charlestown, Jefferson County, Virginia.

"Finally, my beloved, be of good comfort." May all your names be "written in the Lamb's book of life!" — may you all have the purifying and sustaining influence of the Christian religion! — is the earnest prayer of

Your affectionate husband and father,

JOHN BROWN.

Nov. 9.

P. S.   I cannot remember a night so dark as to have hindered the coming day, nor a storm so furious or dreadful as to prevent the return of warm sunshine and a cloudless sky. But, beloved ones, do remember that this is not your rest, — that in this world you have no abiding place or continuing city. To God and his infinite mercy I always commend you.

J. B.

To Mrs. Spring.[1]

CHARLESTOWN, JEFFERSON COUNTY, VA., Nov. 8, 1859.

MRS. REBECCA B. SPRING.

MY DEAR FRIEND, — When you get home, please enclose this to Mrs. John Brown, North Elba, Essex County, N. Y. It will comfort her broken heart to know that I received it. Captain Avis will kindly let you see what I have written her. May the God of my fathers bless and reward you a thousandfold; and may all yours be partakers of his infinite grace!

Yours ever,

JOHN BROWN.

Nov. 9.

P. S.   Will try to write you at your home. I forgot to acknowledge the receipt of your bounty. It is hard for me to write, on account of my lameness.

Yours in truth,

J. B.

---

[1] "Written by John Brown on the back of a note sent by him to Mrs. Marcus Spring. This note and indorsement is now in my possession." — *James Freeman Clarke*, January, 1883.

To his Brother, Jeremiah Brown.

CHARLESTOWN, JEFFERSON COUNTY, VA., Nov. 12, 1859.

DEAR BROTHER JEREMIAH, — Your kind letter of the 9th inst. is received, and also one from Mr. Tilden; for both of which I am greatly obliged. You inquire, "Can I do anything for you or your family?" I would answer that my sons, as well as my wife and daughters, are all very poor; and that anything that may hereafter be due me from my father's estate I wish paid to them, as I will endeavor hereafter to describe, without legal formalities to consume it all. One of my boys has been so entirely used up as very likely to be in want of comfortable clothing for the winter. I have, through the kindness of friends, fifteen dollars to send him, which I will remit shortly. If you know where to reach him, please send him that amount at once, as I shall remit the same to you by a safe conveyance. If I had a plain statement from Mr. Thompson of the state of my accounts with the estate of my father, I should then better know what to say about that matter. As it is, I have not the least memorandum left me to refer to. If Mr. Thompson will make me a statement, and charge my dividend fully for his trouble, I would be greatly obliged to him. In that case you can send me any remarks of your own. I am gaining in health slowly, and am quite cheerful in view of my approaching end, — being fully persuaded that I am worth inconceivably more to hang than for any other purpose. God Almighty bless and save you all!

Your affectionate brother,   JOHN BROWN.

November 13.

P. S. Say to my poor boys never to grieve for one moment on my account; and should many of you live to see the time when you will not blush to own your relation to Old John Brown, it will not be more strange than many things that have happened. I feel a thousand times more on account of my sorrowing friends than on my own account. So far as I am concerned, I "count it all joy." "I have fought the good fight," and have, as I trust, "finished my course." Please show this to any of my family that you may see. My love to all; and may God, in his infinite mercy, for Christ's sake, bless and save you all!

Your affectionate brother,   J. BROWN.

To George Adams, Boston.

CHARLESTOWN, JEFFERSON COUNTY, VA., Nov. 15, 1859.

MY DEAR SIR, — Your kind mention of some things in my conduct here which you approve is very comforting, indeed, to my mind. Yet I am conscious that you do me no more than justice. I do certainly feel that through Divine grace I have endeavored to be "faithful in a few things," mingling with even these much of imperfection. I am certainly "unworthy even to suffer affliction with the people of God;" yet in infinite grace he has thus honored me. May the same grace enable me to serve him in a "new obedience" through my little remainder of this life, and to rejoice in him forever. I cannot feel that God will suffer even the poorest service we may any of us render him or his cause to be lost or in vain. I do feel, dear brother, that I am wonderfully "strengthened from on high." May I use that strength in "showing His strength unto this generation," and His power to every one that is to come! I am most grateful for your assurance that my poor, shattered, heart-broken family will not be forgotten. I have long tried to recommend them to "the God of my fathers." I have many opportunities for faithful plain-dealing with the more powerful, influential, and intelligent classes in this region, which I trust are not entirely misimproved. I humbly trust that I firmly believe that "God reigns," and I think I can truly say, "Let the earth rejoice!" May God take care of his own cause, and of his own great name, as well as of those who love their neighbors. Farewell!   Yours in truth,

JOHN BROWN.

To his Old Teacher.

CHARLESTOWN, JEFFERSON COUNTY, VA., Nov. 15, 1859.

REV. H. L. VAILL.

MY DEAR, STEADFAST FRIEND, — Your most kind and most welcome letter of the 8th inst. reached me in due time. I am very grateful for all the good feeling you express, and also for the kind counsels you give, together with your prayers in my behalf. Allow me here to say, notwithstanding "my soul is among lions," still I believe that "God in very deed is with me." You will not, therefore, feel surprised when I tell you that I am "joyful in all my tribulations;" that I do not feel condemned of Him whose judgment is just, nor of my own conscience. Nor do I feel degraded by my imprisonment, my chains, or prospect of the gallows. I have not only been (though utterly unworthy) permitted to "suffer affliction with God's people," but have also had a great many rare opportunities for "preaching righteousness in the great congregation." I trust it will not all be lost. The jailer (in whose charge I am) and his family and assistants have all been most kind; and notwithstanding he was one of the bravest of all who fought me, he is now being abused for his humanity. So far as my observation goes, none but brave men are likely to be humane to a fallen foe. "Cowards prove their courage by their ferocity." It may be done in that way with but little risk.

I wish I could write you about a few only of the interesting times I here experience with different classes of men, clergymen among others. Christ, the great captain of liberty as well as of salvation, and who began his mission, as foretold of him, by proclaiming it, saw fit to take from me a sword of steel after I had carried it for a time; but he has put another in my hand ("the sword of the Spirit"), and I pray God to make me a faithful soldier, wherever he may send me, not less on the scaffold than when surrounded by my warmest sympathizers.

My dear old friend, I do assure you I have not forgotten our last meeting, nor our retrospective look over the route by which God had then led us; and I bless his name that he has again enabled me to hear your words of cheering and comfort at a time when I, at least, am on the "brink of Jordan." (See Bunyan's "Pilgrim.") God in infinite mercy grant us soon another meeting on the opposite shore. I have often passed under the rod of him whom I call my Father, — and certainly no son ever needed it oftener; and yet I have enjoyed much of life, as I was enabled to discover the secret of this somewhat early. It has been in making the prosperity and happiness of others my own; so that really I have had a great deal of prosperity. I am very prosperous still; and looking forward to a time when "peace on earth and good-will to men" shall everywhere prevail, I have no murmuring thoughts or envious feelings to fret my mind. "I'll praise my Maker with my breath."

I am an unworthy nephew of Deacon John, and I loved him much; and in view of the many choice friends I have had here, I am led the more earnestly to pray, "gather not my soul with the unrighteous."

Your assurance of the earnest sympathy of the friends in my native land is very grateful to my feelings; and allow me to say a word of comfort to them.

As I believe most firmly that God reigns, I cannot believe that anything I have done, suffered, or may yet suffer will be lost to the cause of God or of humanity. And before I began my work at Harper's Ferry, I felt assured that in the worst event it would certainly pay. I often expressed that belief; and I can now see no possible cause to alter my mind. I am not as yet, in the main, at all disappointed. I have been a good deal disappointed as it regards myself in not keeping up to my own plans; but I now feel entirely reconciled to that, even, — for God's plan was infinitely better, no doubt, or I should have kept to my own. Had Samson kept to his determination of not telling Delilah wherein his great strength lay, he would probably have never overturned the house. I did not tell Delilah, but I was induced to act very contrary to my better judgment; and I have lost my two noble boys, and other friends, if not my two eyes.

But "God's will, not mine, be done." I feel a comfortable hope that, like that erring servant of whom I have just been writing, even I may (through infinite mercy in Christ Jesus) yet "die in faith." As to both the time and manner of my death, — I have but very little trouble on that score, and am able to be (as you exhort) "of good cheer."

I send, through you, my best wishes to Mrs. W.——[1] and her son George, and to all dear friends. May the God of the poor and oppressed be the God and Savior of you all!

Farewell, till we meet again.

Your friend in truth,

JOHN BROWN.

To his Wife.

CHARLESTOWN, JEFFERSON COUNTY, VA., Nov. 16, 1859.

MY DEAR WIFE, — I write you in answer to a most kind letter of November 13 from dear Mrs. Spring. I owe her ten thousand thanks for her kindness to you particularly, and more especially than for what she has done and is doing in a more direct way for me personally. Although I feel grateful for every expression of kindness or sympathy towards me, yet nothing can so effectually minister to my comfort as acts of kindness done to relieve the wants or mitigate the sufferings of my poor distressed family. May God Almighty and their own consciences be their eternal rewarders! I am exceedingly rejoiced to have you make the acquaintance and be surrounded by such choice friends, as I have long known by reputation some of those to be with whom you are staying. I

---

[1] The Rev. Leonard Woolsey Bacon, then of Litchfield, Conn., who first printed this letter, said in 1859 : "My aged friend, the Rev. H. L. Vaill, of this place, remembers John Brown as having been under his instruction in the year 1817, at Morris Academy. He was a godly youth, laboring to recover from his disadvantages of early education, in the hope of entering the ministry of the Gospel. Since then the teacher and pupil have met but once. But a short time since, Mr. Vaill wrote to Brown, in his prison, a letter of Christian friendship, to which he has received this heroic and sublime reply. I have copied it faithfully from the autograph that lies before me, without the change or omission of a word, except to omit the full name of the friends to whom he sends his message. The handwriting is clear and firm, but toward the end of the sheet seems to show that the sick old man's hand was growing weary. The very characters make an appeal to us for our sympathy and prayers. 'His salutation with his own hand. Remember his bonds.'"

am most glad to have you meet with one of a family (or I would rather say of two families) most beloved and never to be forgotten by me. I mean dear gentle ——. Many and many a time have she, her father, mother, brother, sisters, uncle, and aunt, like angels of mercy, ministered to the wants of myself and of my poor sons, both in sickness and health. Only last year I lay sick for quite a number of weeks with them, and was cared for by all as though I had been a most affectionate brother or father. Tell her that I ask God to bless and reward them all forever. "I was a stranger, and they took me in." It may possibly be that —— would like to copy this letter, and send it to her home. If so, by all means let her do so. I would write them if I had the power.

Now let me say a word about the effort to educate our daughters. I am no longer able to provide means to help towards that object, and it therefore becomes me not to dictate in the matter. I shall gratefully submit the direction of the whole thing to those whose generosity may lead them to undertake in their behalf, while I give anew a little expression of my own choice respecting it. You, my wife, perfectly well know that I have always expressed a decided preference for a very plain but perfectly practical education for both sons and daughters. I do not mean an education so very miserable as that you and I received in early life; nor as some of our children enjoyed. When I say plain but practical, I mean enough of the learning of the schools to enable them to transact the common business of life comfortably and respectably, together with that thorough training to good business habits which best prepares both men and women to be useful though poor, and to meet the stern realities of life with a good grace. You well know that I always claimed that the music of the broom, wash-tub, needle, spindle, loom, axe, scythe, hoe, flail, etc., should first be learned at all events, and that of the piano, etc., afterwards. I put them in that order as most conducive to health of body and mind; and for the obvious reason, that after a life of some experience and of much observation, I have found ten women as well as ten men who have made their mark in life right, whose early training was of that plain, practical kind, to one who had a more popular and fashionable early training. But enough of that.

Now, in regard to your coming here. If you feel sure that you can endure the trials and the shock which will be unavoidable (if you come), I should be most glad to see you once more; but when I think of your being insulted on the road, and perhaps while here, and of only seeing your wretchedness made complete, I shrink from it. Your composure and fortitude of mind may be quite equal to it all; but I am in dreadful doubt of it. If you do come, defer your journey till about the 27th or 28th of this month. The scenes which you will have to pass through on coming here will be anything but those you now pass, with tender, kind-hearted friends, and kind faces to meet you everywhere. Do consider the matter well before you make the plunge. I think I had better say no more on this most painful subject. My health improves a little; my mind is very tranquil, I may say joyous, and I continue to receive every kind attention that I have any possible need of. I wish you to send copies of all my letters to all our poor children. What I write to one must answer for all, till I have more strength. I get numerous kind letters from friends in almost all directions, to encourage me to "be of good cheer," and I still have, as I trust, "the peace of God to rule in my heart." May God, for Christ's sake, ever make his face to shine on you all!

Your affectionate husband,

JOHN BROWN.

To Thomas B. Musgrave.[1]

CHARLESTOWN, JEFFERSON COUNTY, VA., Nov. 17, 1859.

T. B. MUSGRAVE, ESQ.

MY DEAR YOUNG FRIEND, — I have just received your most kind and welcome letter of the 15th inst., but did not get any other from you. I am under many obligations to you and to your father for all the kindnesses you have shown me, especially since my disaster. May God and your own consciousness ever be your rewarders. Tell your father that I am quite cheerful; that I do not feel myself in the least degraded by my imprisonment, my chains, or the near prospect of the gallows. Men cannot imprison, or chain, or hang the soul. I go joyfully in behalf of millions that "have no rights" that this great and glorious, this Christian Republic "is bound to respect." Strange change in morals, political as well as Christian, since 1776! I look forward to other changes to take place in God's good time, fully believing that "the fashion of this world passeth away." I am unable now to tell you where my friend is, that you inquire after. Perhaps my wife, who I suppose is still with Mrs. Spring, may have some information of him. I think it quite uncertain, however.

Farewell. May God abundantly bless you all!

Your friend,

JOHN BROWN.

---

[1] The father of this gentleman was Mr. Musgrave, the English manufacturer at Northampton, mentioned in Chapter III.

To his Cousin, Rev. Mr. Humphrey.

CHARLESTOWN, JEFFERSON COUNTY, VA., Nov. 19, 1859.

REV. LUTHER HUMPHREY.

MY DEAR FRIEND, — Your kind letter of the 12th instant is now before me. So far as my knowledge goes as to our mutual kindred, I suppose I am the first since the landing of Peter Brown from the "Mayflower" that has either been sentenced to imprisonment or to the gallows. But, my dear old friend, let not that fact alone grieve you. You cannot have forgotten how and where our grandfather fell in 1776, and that he, too, might have perished on the scaffold had circumstances been but a very little different. The fact that a man dies under the hand of an executioner (or otherwise) has but little to do with his true character, as I suppose. John Rogers perished at the stake, a great and good man, as I suppose; but his doing so does not prove that any other man who has died in the same way was good or otherwise.

Whether I have any reason to "be of good cheer" or not in view of my end, I can assure you that I feel so; and I am totally blinded if I do not really experience that strengthening and consolation you so faithfully implore in my behalf: the God of our fathers reward your fidelity! I neither feel mortified, degraded, nor in the least ashamed of my imprisonment, my chains, or near prospect of death by hanging. I feel assured "that not one hair shall fall from my head without the will of my Heavenly Father." I also feel that I have long been endeavoring to hold exactly "such a fast as God has chosen." (See the passage in Isaiah which you have quoted.[1]) No part of my life has been more happily spent than that I have spent here; and I humbly trust that no part has been spent to better purpose. I would not say this boastingly, but thanks be unto God, who giveth us the victory through infinite grace.

---

[1] The reference here is to the familiar text in the fifty-eighth chapter of the prophet, who may be said to have foretold Brown as clearly as he predicted any event in Hebrew history : "Is not this the fast that I have chosen, — to loose the bands of wickedness, to undo the heavy burdens, and to let the oppressed go free, and that ye break every yoke ? Is it not to deal thy bread to the hungry, and that thou bring the poor that are cast out to thy house ? when thou seest the naked, that thou cover him: and that thou hide not thyself from thine own flesh ? . . . Then shalt thou call, and the Lord shall answer; thou shalt cry, and he shall say, Here I am. . . . Thou shalt raise up the foundations of many generations; and thou shalt be called the Repairer of the breach, the Restorer of paths to dwell in."

I should be sixty years old were I to live to May 9, 1860. I have enjoyed much of life as it is, and have been remarkably prosperous, having early learned to regard the welfare and prosperity of others as my own. I have never, since I can remember, required a great amount of sleep; so that I conclude that I have already enjoyed full an average number of working hours with those who reach their threescore years and ten. I have not yet been driven to the use of glasses, but can see to read and write quite comfortably. But more than that, I have generally enjoyed remarkably good health. I might go on to recount unnumbered and unmerited blessings, among which would be some very severe afflictions, and those the most needed blessings of all. And now, when I think how easily I might be left to spoil all I have done or suffered in the cause of freedom, I hardly dare wish another voyage, even if I had the opportunity.

It is a long time since we met; but we shall come together in our Father's house, I trust. Let us hold fast that we already have, remembering we shall reap in due time if we faint not. Thanks be unto God, who giveth us the victory through Jesus Christ our Lord. And now, my old, warm-hearted friend, good-by.

Your affectionate cousin,

JOHN BROWN.

To his Wife.

CHARLESTOWN, JEFFERSON COUNTY, VA., Nov. 21, 1859.

MY DEAR WIFE, — Your most welcome letter of the 13th instant I got yesterday. I am very glad to learn from yourself that you feel so much resigned to your circumstances, so much confidence in a wise and good Providence, and such composure of mind in the midst of all your deep afflictions. This is just as it should be; and let me still say, "Be of good cheer," for we shall soon "come out of all our great tribulations;" and very soon, if we trust in him, "God shall wipe away all tears from our eyes." Soon "we shall be satisfied when we are awake in His likeness." There is now here a source of much disquietude to me, — namely, the fires which are almost of daily and nightly occurrence in this immediate neighborhood. While I well know that no one of them is the work of our friends, I know at the same time that by more or less of the inhabitants we shall be charged with them, — the same as with the ominous and threatening letters to Governor Wise. In the existing state of public feeling I can easily see a further objection to your coming here at present; but I did not intend saying another word to you on that subject.

Why will you not say to me whether you had any crops mature this season? If so, what ones? Although I may nevermore intermeddle with your worldly affairs, I have not yet lost all interest in them. A little history of your success or of your failures I should very much prize; and I would gratify you and other friends some way were it in my power. I am still quite cheerful, and by no means cast down. I "remember that the time is short." The little trunk and all its contents, so far as I can judge, reached me safe. May God reward all the contributors! I wrote you under cover to our excellent friend Mrs. Spring on the 16th instant. I presume you have it before now. When you return, it is most likely the lake will not be open; so you must get your ticket at Troy for Moreau Station or Glens Falls (for Glens Falls, if you can get one), or get one for Vergennes in Vermont, and take your chance of crossing over on the ice to Westport. If you go soon, the route by Glens Falls to Elizabethtown will probably be the best.

I have just learned that our poor Watson lingered until Wednesday about noon of the 19th of October. Oliver died near my side in a few moments after he was shot. Dauphin died the next morning after Oliver and William were killed, — namely, Monday. He died almost instantly; was by my side. William was shot by several persons. Anderson was killed with Dauphin.

Keep this letter to refer to. God Almighty bless and keep you all!

Your affectionate husband,

JOHN BROWN.

DEAR MRS. SPRING, — I send this to your care, because I am at a loss where it will reach my wife.

Your friend in truth,

JOHN BROWN.

To his younger Children.

CHARLESTOWN, JEFFERSON COUNTY, VA., Nov. 22, 1859.

DEAR CHILDREN, ALL, — I address this letter to you, supposing that your mother is not yet with you. She has not yet come here, as I have requested her not to do at present, if at all. She may think it best for her not to come at all. She has (or will), I presume, written you before this. Annie's letter to us both, of the 9th, has but just reached me. I am very glad to get it, and to learn that you are in any measure cheerful. This is the greatest comfort I can have, except that it would be to know that you are all Christians. God in mercy grant you all may be so! That is what you all will certainly need. When and in what form death may come is but of small moment. I feel just as content to die for God's eternal truth and for suffering humanity on the scaffold as in any other way; and I do not say this from any disposition to "brave it out." No ; I would readily own my wrong were I in the least convinced of it. I have now been confined over a month, with a good opportunity to look the whole thing as "fair in the face" as I am capable of doing; and I now feel it most grateful that I am counted in the least possible degree worthy to suffer for the truth. I want you all to " be of good cheer." This life is intended as a season of training, chastisement, temptation, affliction, and trial; and the "righteous shall come out of" it all. Oh, my dear children, let me again entreat you all to "forsake the foolish, and live." What can you possibly lose by such a course ? " Godliness with contentment is great gain, having the promise of the life that now is, and of that which is to come." " Trust in the Lord and do good, so shalt thou dwell in the land ; and verily thou shalt be fed." I have enjoyed life much ; why should I complain on leaving it ? I want some of you to write me a little more particularly about all that concerns your welfare. I intend to write you as often as I can. " To God and the word of his grace I commend you all."　　　Your affectionate father,

JOHN BROWN.

To his older Children.

CHARLESTOWN, JEFFERSON COUNTY, VA., Nov. 22, 1859.

DEAR CHILDREN, — Your most welcome letters of the 16th inst. I have just received, and I bless God that he has enabled you to bear the heavy tidings of our disaster with so much seeming resignation and composure of mind. That is exactly the thing I have wished you all to do for me, — to be cheerful and perfectly resigned to the holy will of a wise and good God. I bless his most holy name that I am, I trust, in some good measure able to do the same. I am even "joyful in all my tribulations" ever since my confinement, and I humbly trust that " I know in whom I have trusted." A calm peace, perhaps like that which your own dear mother felt in view of her last change, seems to fill my mind by day and by night. Of this neither the powers of " earth or hell" can deprive me. Do not, my dear children, any of you grieve for a single moment on my account. As I trust my life has not been thrown away, so I also humbly trust that my death will not be in vain. God can make it to be a thousand times more valuable to his own cause than all the miserable service (at best) that I have rendered it during my life. When I was first taken, I was too feeble to write much; so I wrote what I could to North Elba, requesting Ruth and Anne to send you copies of all my letters to them. I hope they have done so, and that you, Ellen,[1] will

---

[1] Mrs. Jason Brown.

do the same with what I may send to you, as it is still quite a labor for me to write all that I need to. I want your brothers to know what I write, if you know where to reach them. I wrote Jeremiah a few days since to supply a trifling assistance, fifteen dollars, to such of you as might be most destitute. I got his letter, but do not know as he got mine. I hope to get another letter from him soon. I also asked him to show you my letter. I know of nothing you can any of you now do for me, unless it is to comfort your own hearts, and cheer and encourage each other to trust in God and Jesus Christ whom he hath sent. If you will keep his sayings, you shall certainly "know of his doctrine, whether it be of God or no." Nothing can be more grateful to me than your earnest sympathy, except it be to know that you are fully persuaded to be Christians. And now, dear children, farewell for this time. I hope to be able to write you again. The God of my fathers take you for his children.

Your affectionate father,

JOHN BROWN.

To the Rev. —— McFarland.

JAIL, CHARLESTOWN, Wednesday, Nov. 23, 1859.

THE REV. —— MCFARLAND.

DEAR FRIEND, — Although you write to me as a stranger, the spirit you show towards me and the cause for which I am in bonds makes me feel towards you as a dear friend. I would be glad to have you or any of my liberty-loving ministerial friends here, to talk and pray with me. I am not a stranger to the way of salvation by Christ. From my youth I have studied much on that subject, and at one time hoped to be a minister myself; but God had another work for me to do. To me it is given, in behalf of Christ, not only to believe on him, but also to suffer for his sake. But while I trust that I have some experimental and saving knowledge of religion, it would be a great pleasure to me to have some one better qualified than myself to lead my mind in prayer and meditation, now that my time is so near a close. You may wonder, are there no ministers of the gospel here? I answer, no. There are no ministers of Christ here. These ministers who profess to be Christian, and hold slaves or advocate slavery, I cannot abide them. My knees will not bend in prayer with them, while their hands are stained with the blood of souls. The subject you mention as having been preaching on the day before you wrote to me is one which I have often thought of since my imprisonment. I think I feel as happy as Paul did when he lay in prison. He knew if they killed him, it would greatly advance the cause of Christ; that was the reason he rejoiced so. On that same ground "I do rejoice, yea, and will rejoice." Let them hang me; I forgive them, and may God forgive them, for they know not what they do. I have no regret for the transaction for which I am condemned. I went against the laws of men, it is true, but "whether it be right to obey God or men, judge ye." Christ told me to remember them that were in bonds as bound with them, to do towards them as I would wish them to do towards me in similar circumstances. My conscience bade me do that. I tried to do it, but failed. Therefore I have no regret on that score. I have no sorrow either as to the result, only for my poor wife and children. They have suffered much, and it is hard to leave them uncared for. But God will be a husband to the widow and a father to the fatherless.

I have frequently been in Wooster, and if any of my old friends from about Akron are there, you can show them this letter. I have but a few more days, and I feel anxious to be away "where the wicked cease from troubling, and the weary are at rest." Farewell.

Your friend, and the friend of all friends of liberty,

JOHN BROWN.

To Mrs. Marcus Spring.

CHARLESTOWN, JEFFERSON COUNTY, VA., Nov. 24, 1859.

MY DEAR MRS. SPRING, — Your ever welcome letter of the 19th inst., together with the one now enclosed, were received by me last night too late for any reply. I am always grateful for anything you either do or write. I would most gladly express my gratitude to you and yours by something more than words; but it has come to that, I now have but little else to deal in, and sometimes they are not so kind as they should be. You have laid me and my family under many and great obligations. I hope they may not soon be forgotten. The same is also true of a vast many others, that I shall never be able even to thank. I feel disposed to leave the education of my dear children to their mother, and to those dear friends who bear the burden of it; only expressing my earnest hope that they may all become strong, intelligent, expert, industrious, Christian housekeepers. I would wish that, together with other studies, they may thoroughly study Dr. Franklin's "Poor Richard." I want them to become matter-of-fact women. Perhaps I have said too much about this already; I would not allude to this subject now but for the fact that you had most kindly expressed your generous feelings with regard to it.

I sent the letter to my wife to your care, because the address she sent me from Philadelphia was not sufficiently plain, and left me quite at a loss. I am still in the same predicament, and were I not ashamed to trouble you further, would ask you either to send this to her or a copy of it, in order that she may see something from me often.

I have very many interesting visits from proslavery persons almost daily, and I endeavor to improve them faithfully, plainly, and kindly. I do not think that I ever enjoyed life better than since my confinement here. For this I am indebted to Infinite Grace, and the kind letters of friends from different quarters. I wish I could only know that all my poor family were as much composed and as happy as I. I think that nothing but the Christian religion can ever make any one so much composed.

> " My willing soul would stay
> In such a frame as this."

There are objections to my writing many things while here that I might be disposed to write were I under different circumstances. I do not know that my wife yet understands that prison rules require that all I write or receive should first be examined by the sheriff or State's attorney, and that all company I see should be attended by the jailer or some of his assistants. Yet such is the case; and did she know this, it might influence her mind somewhat about the opportunity she would have on coming here. We cannot expect the jailer to devote very much time to us, as he has now a very hard task on his hands. I have just learned how to send letters to my wife near Philadelphia.

I have a son at Akron, Ohio, that I greatly desire to have located in such a neighborhood as yours; and you will pardon me for giving you some account of him, making all needful allowance for the source the account comes from. His name is Jason; he is about thirty-six years old; has a wife and one little boy. He is a very laborious, ingenious, temperate, honest, and truthful man. He is very expert as a gardener, vine-dresser, and manager of fruit-trees, but does not pride himself on account of his skill in anything; always has underrated himself; is bashful and retiring in his habits; is not (like his father) too much inclined to assume and dictate; is too conscientious in his dealings and too tender of people's feelings to get from them his just deserts, and is very poor. He suffered almost everything on the way to and while in Kansas but death, and returned to Ohio not a spoiled but next to a ruined man. He never quarrels, and yet I know that he is both morally and physically brave. He will not deny his principles to save his life, and he " turned not back in the day of battle." At the battle of Osawatomie he fought by my side. He is a most tender, loving, and steadfast friend, and on the right side of things in general, a practical Samaritan (if not Christian); and could I know that he was located with a population who were disposed to encourage him, without expecting him to pay too dearly in the end for it, I should feel greatly relieved. His wife is a very neat, industrious, prudent woman, who has undergone a severe trial in " the school of affliction."

You make one request of me that I shall not be able to comply with. Am sorry that I cannot at least explain. Your own account of my plans is very well. The son I mentioned has now a small stock of choice vines and fruit-trees, and in them consists his worldly store mostly. I would give you some account of others, but I suppose my wife may have done so.

Your friend,   JOHN BROWN.

To his Counsel.

CHARLESTOWN, JEFFERSON COUNTY, VA., Nov. 24, 1859.
GEORGE H. HOYT, ESQ.

DEAR SIR, — Your kind letter of the 22d instant is received. I exceedingly regret my inability to make you some other acknowledgment for all your efforts in my behalf than that which consists merely in words; but so it is. May God and a good conscience be your continual reward. I really do not see what you can do for me any further. I commend my poor family to the kind remembrance of all friends, but I well understand that they are not the only poor in our world. I ought to begin to leave off saying " our world." I have but very little idea of the charges made against Mr. Griswold, as I get to see but little of what is afloat. I am very sorry for any wrong that may be done him, but I have no means of contradicting any thing that may be said, not knowing what is said. I cannot see how it should be any more dishonorable for him to receive some compensation for his expenses and service than for Mr. Chilton, and I am not aware that any blame is attached to him on that score. I am getting more letters constantly than I well know how to answer. My kind friends appear to have very wrong ideas of my condition, as regards replying to all the kind communications I receive.

Your friend in truth,   JOHN BROWN.

In contrast with the letter of the good Quaker woman of Rhode Island, and as a key to the answer made by John Brown, I print next the expostulatory, not to say Pharisaical, letter of his aged cousin, the Rev. Dr. Heman Humphrey, of western Massachusetts, addressed to the martyr in his Virginia prison.

Dr. Humphrey to Captain Brown.

PITTSFIELD, MASS., Nov. 20, 1859.

MR. JOHN BROWN.

MY POOR WOUNDED AND DOOMED KINSMAN, — I should have written you before now if I had known what to say. That we all deeply feel for you in your present extraordinary circumstances you will not doubt. Most gladly would we fly to your relief, if the sentence under which you lie had not put you entirely beyond the reach of hope. All we can do is to pray for you. This we can do; and I am sure that prayer is offered without ceasing for you, that you may be prepared for that death from which I am persuaded nothing short of a miracle would save you. Oh, that we had known the amazing infatuation which was urging you on to certain destruction before it was too late! We should have felt bound to have laid hold upon and retained you by violence, if nothing short would have availed. You will not allow us to interpose the plea of insanity in your behalf; you insist that you were never more sane in your life, — and indeed, there was so much "method in your madness," that such a plea would be of no avail. I do not intend to use the word *madness* reproachfully. I am bound to believe that you were as conscientious as Saul of Tarsus was in going to Damascus; and I am sure it was in an infinitely better cause. But what you intended was an impossibility; and all your friends are amazed that you did not see it. They can never believe that if you had been John Brown of better days, — if you had been in your right mind, — you would ever have plunged headlong, as you did, into the lion's den, where you were certain to be devoured. Oh, that you would have been held back! But, alas! these are unavailing regrets; it is too late; it is done. The sentence is passed.

You have come almost to the foot of the scaffold, and I presume you have no hope of escape. All that remains is to prepare for the closing scene of the awful tragedy. Are you prepared? You have long been a professor of religion. I take it for granted that you will now anxiously examine yourself whether you are in the faith; whether you are a true child of God, and prepared to die and go to the judgment. I do not believe you had murder in your heart. Your object, as you say, was to liberate the slaves. You wanted to do it without killing anybody. It is astonishing you did not consider that it could not be done without wading in blood. The time has not come. It is not the right way, and never will be. It is right to pray, "O Lord, how long?" but not to run before and take the avenging sword into our own hands. You have nothing more to do in this world. You have done with the Border Ruffians, who hunted for your precious life. It becomes you prayerfully to inquire how far you will be answerable at the bar of God for the blood which was shed at Harper's Ferry, and for the fate of those who are to die with you. I judge you not; but there is One that judgeth, with whom is mercy and plentiful forgiveness to all who truly repent and savingly believe on him whose blood cleanseth from all sin. There is a great deal more danger that we shall think too little of our sins than too much. The time is now so short that it becomes you to spend it mostly in prayer and meditation over your Bible. Oh, how precious is every hour! I am sure you will welcome any pious friend who may visit you in prison; and I hope there is some godly minister who may come to you with his warmest sympathies and prayers. May God sustain you, my dying friend! Vain is the help of man.

Christ can stand by you and carry you through. Other help there is none. Oh, that there was a possibility that your life might be spared! But, no! there is nothing to hang a hope on. Farewell, my wounded and condemned friend. We shall not meet again in this world. Should I outlive you, it will not be long. I have passed my fourscore years. We trust that many of our kindred have gone to heaven. Oh, may we be prepared to meet, and to meet them there, washed in the Redeemer's blood!

From your affectionate and deeply affected kinsman,

H. HUMPHREY.

Captain Brown to Rev. Dr. Humphrey.

CHARLESTOWN, JEFFERSON COUNTY, VA., Nov. 25, 1859.
REV. HEMAN HUMPHREY, D.D.

MY DEAR AND HONORED KINSMAN, — Your very sorrowful, kind, and faithful letter of the 20th instant is now before me. I accept it with all kindness. I have honestly endeavored to profit by the faithful advice it contains. Indeed, such advice could never come amiss. You will allow me to say that I deeply sympathize with you and all my sorrowing friends in their grief and terrible mortification. I feel ten times more afflicted on their account than on account of my own circumstances. But I must say that I am neither conscious of being "infatuated" nor "mad." You will doubtless agree with me in this, — that neither imprisonment, irons, nor the gallows falling to one's lot are of themselves evidence of either guilt, "infatuation, or madness."

I discover that you labor under a mistaken impression as to some important facts, which my peculiar circumstances will in all probability prevent the possibility of my removing; and I do not propose to take up any argument to prove that any motion or act of my life is right. But I will here state that I know it to be wholly my own fault as a leader that caused our disaster. Of this you have no proper means of judging, not being on the ground, or a practical soldier. I will only add, that it was in yielding to my feelings of humanity (if I ever exercised such a feeling), in leaving my proper place and mingling with my prisoners to quiet their fears, that occasioned our being caught. I firmly believe that God reigns, and that he over-rules all things in the best possible manner; and in that view of the subject I try to be in some degree reconciled to my own weaknesses and follies even.

If you were here on the spot, and could be with me by day and by night, and know the facts and how my time is spent here, I think you would find much to reconcile your own mind to the ignominious death I am about to suffer, and to mitigate your sorrow. I am, to say the least, quite cheerful. " He shall begin to deliver Israel out of the hand of the Philistines." This was said of a poor erring ser-vant many years ago; and for many years I have felt a strong im-pression that God had given me powers and faculties, unworthy as I was, that he intended to use for a similar purpose. This most unmerited honor He has seen fit to bestow; and whether, like the same poor frail man to whom I allude, my death may not be of vastly more value than my life is, I think quite beyond all human foresight. I really have strong hopes that notwithstanding all my many sins, I too may yet die " in faith."

If you do not believe I had a murderous intention (while I *know* I had not), why grieve so terribly on my account? The scaffold has but few terrors for me. God has often covered my head in the day of battle, and granted me many times deliverances that were almost so miraculous that I can scarce realize their truth; and now, when it seems quite certain that he intends to use me in a different way, shall I not most cheerfully go? I may be deceived, but I humbly trust that he will not forsake me " till I have showed his favor to this generation and his strength to every one that is to come." Your letter is most faithfully and kindly written, and I mean to profit by it. I am certainly quite grateful for it. I feel that a great responsi-bility rests upon me as regards the lives of those who have fallen and may yet fall. I must in that view cast myself on the care of Him " whose mercy endureth forever." If the cause in which I engaged in any possible degree approximated to be " infinitely better " than the one which Saul of Tarsus undertook, I have no reason to be ashamed of it; and indeed I cannot now, after more than a month for reflection, find in my heart (before God in whose presence I expect to stand within another week) any cause for shame.

.   .   .   .

I got a long and most kind letter from your pure-hearted brother Luther, to which I replied at some length. The statement that seems to be going around in the newspapers that I told Governor Wise that I came on here to seek revenge for the wrongs of either myself or my family, is utterly false. I never intended to convey such an idea, and I bless God that I am able even now to say that I have never yet harbored such a feeling. See testimony of witnesses who were with me while I had one son lying dead by my side, and another mortally wounded and dying on my other side. I do not believe that Governor Wise so understood, and I think he ought to correct that impression. The impression that we intended a general insurrection is equally untrue.

Now, my much beloved and much respected kinsman, farewell. May the God of our fathers save and abundantly bless you and yours!

JOHN BROWN.

The following is an extract from the last letter received by Mrs. Brown before she started to go to Charlestown, bearing date Charlestown, Jefferson County, Va., Nov. 26, 1859, in which, after referring to his wife's being under Mrs. Mott's roof, he proceeds to say: —

. . . I remember the faithful old lady well, but presume she has no recollection of me. I once set myself to oppose a mob at Boston, where she was. After I interfered, the police immediately took up the matter, and soon put a stop to mob proceedings. The meeting was, I think, in Marlboro Street Church, or Hotel, perhaps. I am glad to have you make the acquaintance of such old pioneers in the cause. I have just received from Mr. John Jay, of New York, a draft for fifty dollars for the benefit of my family, and will enclose it made payable to your order. I have also fifteen dollars to send to our crippled and destitute unmarried son. When I can I intend to send you, by express, two or three little articles to carry home. Should you happen to meet with Mr. Jay, say to him that you fully appreciate his great kindness both to me and my family. God bless all such friends! It is out of my power to reply to all the kind and encouraging letters I get; I wish I could do so. I have been so much relieved from my lameness for the last three or four days as to be able to sit up to read and write pretty much all day, as well as part of the night; and I do assure you and all other friends that I am quite busy, and none the less happy on that account. The time passes quite pleasantly, and the near approach of my great change is not the occasion of any particular dread.

I trust that God, who has sustained me so long, will not forsake me when I most feel my need of Fatherly aid and support. Should he hide his face, my spirit will droop and die; but not otherwise, be assured. My only anxiety is to be properly assured of my fitness for the company of those who are "washed from all filthiness," and for the presence of Him who is infinitely pure. I certainly think I do have some "hunger and thirst after righteousness." If it be only genuine, I make no doubt I "shall be filled." Please let all our friends read my letters when you can; and ask them to accept of it as in part for them. I am inclined to think you will not be likely to succeed well about getting away the bodies of your family; but should that be so, do not let that grieve you. It can make but little difference what is done with them.

.   .   .   .

You can well remember the changes you have passed through. Life is made up of a series of changes, and let us try to meet them in the best manner possible. You will not wish to make yourself and children any more burdensome to friends than you are really compelled to do. I would not.

I will close this by saying that if you now feel that you are equal to the undertaking, do exactly as you feel disposed to do about coming to see me before I suffer. I am entirely willing.

Your affectionate husband,

JOHN BROWN.

CHARLESTOWN, JEFFERSON COUNTY, VA., Nov. 27, 1859.

THADDEUS HYATT, ESQ.

MY DEAR SIR, — Your very acceptable letter of the 24th instant has just been handed to me. I am certainly most obliged to you for it, and for all your efforts in behalf of my family and myself. I can form no idea of the objections to your mode of operating in their behalf, to which my friend Dr. Webb refers; and I suppose it is now too late for any explanations from him that would enlighten me. It (your effort) at any rate takes from my mind the greatest burden I have felt since my imprisonment, — to feel assured that in some way my shattered and broken-hearted wife and children would be so far relieved as to save them from great physical suffering. Others may have devised a better way of doing it. I had no advice in regard to it, and felt very grateful to know, while I was yet living, of almost any active measure being taken. I hope no offence is taken at yourself or me in the matter. I am beginning to familiarize my mind with new and very different scenes. Am very cheerful. Farewell, my friend.

JOHN BROWN.

To Miss Sterns, of Springfield.

CHARLESTOWN, JEFFERSON COUNTY, VA., Nov. 27, 1859.

MY DEAR MISS STERNS, — Your most kind and cheering letter of the 18th instant is received. Although I have not been at all low-spirited or cast down in feeling since being imprisoned and under sentence (which I am fully aware is soon to be carried out), it is exceedingly gratifying to learn from friends that there are not wanting in this generation some to sympathize with me and appreciate my motive, even now that I am whipped. Success is in general the standard of all merit. I have passed my time here quite cheerfully; still trusting that neither my life nor my death will prove a total loss. As regards both, however, I am liable to mistake. It affords me some satisfaction to feel conscious of having at least tried to better the condition of those who are always on the under-hill side, and am in hopes of being able to meet the consequences without a murmur. I am endeavoring to get ready for another field of action, where no defeat befalls the truly brave. That " God reigns," and most wisely, and controls all events, might, it would seem, reconcile those who believe it to much that appears to be very disastrous. I am one who has tried to believe that, and still keep trying. Those who die for the truth may prove to be courageous at last; so I continue " hoping on," till I shall find that the truth must finally prevail. I do not feel in the least degree despondent or degraded by my circumstances; and I entreat my friends not to grieve on my account. You will please excuse a very poor and short letter, as I get more than I can possibly answer. I send my best wishes to your kind mother, and to all the family, and to all the true friends of humanity. And now, dear friends, God be with you all, and ever guide and bless you!   Your friend,

JOHN BROWN.

To his sisters Mary and Martha.

CHARLESTOWN, JEFFERSON COUNTY, VA.,
Nov. 27, 1859 (Sabbath).

MY DEARLY BELOVED SISTERS MARY A. AND MARTHA, — I am obliged to occupy a part of what is probably my last Sabbath on earth in answering the very kind and comforting letters of sister Hand and son of the 23d inst., or I must fail to do so at all. I do not think it any violation of the day that God made for man. Nothing could be more grateful to my feelings than to learn that you do not feel dreadfully mortified, and even disgraced, on account of your relation to one who is to die on the scaffold. I have really suffered more, by tenfold, since my confinement here, on account of what I feared would be the terrible feelings of my kindred on my account, than from all other causes. I am most glad to learn from you that my fears on your own account were ill founded. I was afraid that a little seeming present prosperity might have carried you away from realities, so that "the honor that cometh from men" might lead you in some measure to undervalue that which "cometh from God." I bless God, who has most abundantly supported and comforted me all along, to find you are not ensnared. Dr. Heman Humphrey has just sent me a most doleful lamentation over my "infatuation and madness" (very kindly expressed), in which, I cannot doubt, he has given expression to the extreme grief of others of our kindred. I have endeavored to answer him kindly also, and at the same time to deal faithfully with my old friend. I think I will send you his letter; and if you deem it worth the trouble, you can probably get my reply, or a copy of it. Suffice it for me to say, "None of these things move me." Luther Humphrey wrote me a very comforting letter.

There are things, dear sisters, that God hides even from the wise and prudent. I feel astonished that one so exceedingly vile and unworthy as I am should even be suffered to have a place anyhow or anywhere among the very least of all who, when they come to die (as all must), were permitted to pay the debt of nature in defence of the right and of God's eternal and immutable truth. Oh, my dear friends, can you believe it possible that the scaffold has no terrors for your own poor old unworthy brother? I thank God, through Jesus Christ my Lord, it is even so. I am now shedding tears, but they are no longer tears of grief or sorrow; I trust I have nearly done with those. I am weeping for joy and gratitude that I can in no other way express. I get many very kind and comforting letters that I cannot possibly reply to; wish I had time and strength to answer all. I am obliged to ask those to whom I do write to let friends read what I send as much as they well can. Do write my deeply afflicted and affectionate wife. It will greatly comfort her to have you write her freely. She has borne up manfully under accumulated griefs. She will be most glad to know that she has not been entirely forgotten by my kindred. Say to all my friends that I am waiting cheerfully and patiently the days of my appointed time; fully believing that for me now to die will be to me an infinite gain and of untold benefit to the cause we love. Wherefore, "be of good cheer," and "let not your hearts be troubled." "To him that overcometh will I grant to sit with me in my throne, even as I also overcame and am set down with my Father in his throne." I wish my friends could know but a little of the rare opportunities I now get for

kind and faithful labor in God's cause.   I hope they have not been
entirely lost.

Now, dear friends, I have done.   May the God of peace bring
us all again from the dead!

Your affectionate brother,

JOHN BROWN.

CHARLESTOWN, JEFFERSON COUNTY, VA.,
Monday, Nov. 28, 1859.

HON. D. R. TILDEN.

MY DEAR SIR, — Your most kind and comforting letter of the 23d
inst. is received.   I have no language to express the feelings of gratitude and obligation I am under for your kind interest in my behalf
ever since my disaster.   The great bulk of mankind estimate each
other's actions and motives by the measure of success or otherwise
that attends them through life.   By that rule, I have been one of
the worst and one of the best of men.   I do not claim to have been
one of the latter, and I leave it to an impartial tribunal to decide
whether the world has been the worse or the better for my living
and dying in it.   My present great anxiety is to get as near in readiness for a different field of action as I well can, since being in a
good measure relieved from the fear that my poor broken-hearted
wife and children would come to immediate want.   May God reward
a thousandfold all the kind efforts made in their behalf!   I have enjoyed remarkable cheerfulness and composure of mind ever since my
confinement; and it is a great comfort to feel assured that I am permitted to die for a cause, — not merely to pay the debt of nature, as
all must.   I feel myself to be most unworthy of so great distinction.
The particular manner of dying assigned to me gives me but very
little uneasiness.   I wish I had the time and the ability to give you,
my dear friend, some little idea of what is daily, and I might almost
say hourly, passing within my prison walls; and could my friends
but witness only a few of these scenes, just as they occur, I think
they would feel very well reconciled to my being here, just what I
am, and just as I am.   My whole life before had not afforded me one
half the opportunity to plead for the right.   In this, also, I find much
to reconcile me to both my present condition and my immediate
prospect.   I may be very insane; and I am so, if insane at all.   But
if that be so, insanity is like a very pleasant dream to me.   I am not
in the least degree conscious of my ravings, of my fears, or of any
terrible visions whatever; but fancy myself entirely composed, and
that my sleep, in particular, is as sweet as that of a healthy, joyous
little infant.   I pray God that he will grant me a continuance of
the same calm but delightful dream, until I come to know of those

39

realities which eyes have not seen and which ears have not heard. I have scarce realized that I am in prison or in irons at all. I certainly think I was never more cheerful in my life.

I intend to take the liberty of sending by express to your care some trifling articles for those of my family who may be in Ohio, which you can hand to my brother Jeremiah when you may see him, together with fifteen dollars I have asked him to advance to them. Please excuse me so often troubling you with my letters or any of my matters. Please also remember me most kindly to Mr. Griswold, and to all others who love their neighbors. I write Jeremiah to your care.   Your friend in truth,

                                                        JOHN BROWN.

To Various Friends.

CHARLESTOWN, JEFFERSON COUNTY, VA., Nov. 29, 1859.

MY DEAR COVENANTER [Rev. A. M. Milligan], — Notwithstanding I now get daily more than three times the number of kind letters I can possibly answer, I cannot deny myself the satisfaction of saying a few words to a stranger, whose feelings and whose judgment so nearly coincide with my own. No letter, of a great number I have got to cheer, encourage, and advise me, has given more heartwarming satisfaction or better counsel than your own. I hope to profit by it; and I am greatly obliged for this your visit to my prison. It really seemed to impart new strength to my soul, notwithstanding I was very cheerful before. I trust, dear brother, that God, in infinite grace and mercy for Christ's sake, will neither leave me nor forsake me till I " have showed His power to this generation, and his strength to every one that is to come." I would most gladly commune further as we journey on; but I am so near the close of mine that I must break off, however reluctant.

Farewell, my faithful brother in Christ Jesus! Farewell!

                    Your friend,   JOHN BROWN.

CHARLESTOWN, JEFFERSON COUNTY, VA., Nov. 29, 1859.

MRS. GEORGE L. STEARNS, Boston, Mass.

MY DEAR FRIEND, — No letter I have received since my imprisonment here has given me more satisfaction or comfort than yours of the 8th instant. I am quite cheerful, and was never more happy. Have only time to write a word. May God forever reward you and all yours! My love to all who love their neighbors. I have asked to be spared from having any weak or hypocritical prayers made over me when I am publicly murdered, and that my only religious

Charlestown, Jefferson Co. Va. 29th Nov, 1859.

Mr. George L Stearns

Boston

Mass

My Dear friend

No letter I have
received since my imprisonment here, has given me more
satisfaction, or comfort, than yours of the 8th inst. I am
quite cheerful; & was never more happy. Have only
time write you a word. May God forever reward
you & all yours. My love to All who love their
Neighbours. I have asked to be spared from hav-
-ing any mock; or hypocritical prayers made over me, when
I am publicly murdered: & that my only religious attendants
be poor little, dirty, ragged, bare headed, & barefooted,
Slave Boys; & Girls; led by some old grey headed, Slave
Mother. Farewell, Farewell.

Your Friend

John Brown

Please

Mail This to her

attendants be poor little dirty, ragged, bareheaded, and barefooted slave boys and girls, led by some old gray-headed slave mother.

Farewell !   Farewell !

Your friend,   JOHN BROWN.

This is the copy of a letter that Mrs. Brown brought from Virginia, and sent to Mrs. Stearns, in a Bible.

CHARLESTOWN, JEFFERSON COUNTY PRISON, VA., Nov. 29, 1859.

J. Q. ANDERSON, ESQ.

MY DEAR SIR, — Your letter of the 23d instant is received ; but notwithstanding it would afford me the utmost pleasure to answer it at length, it is not in my power to write you but a few words. Jeremiah G. Anderson was fighting bravely by my side at Harper's Ferry up to the moment when I fell wounded, and I took no further notice of what passed for a little time.[1] I have since been told that

---

[1] At this point may be introduced the letter of an eye-witness of what happened during this "little time," when the hero had swooned from loss of blood and pain, and was believed to be dead. Mr. Tayleure, a South Carolinian, wrote thus to John Brown, Jr., six years ago : —

864 BROADWAY, NEW YORK, June 15, 1879.

DEAR SIR, — Duty took me to Harper's Ferry at the time of the raid in 1859 (I was then connected with the Baltimore Press), and by chance I was brought into close personal contact with both your father and your brother Watson. After the assault I assisted your father to rise, as he stumbled forward out of the historic engine-house ; and was able to administer to your brother, just before he died, some physical comfort, which won me his thanks. Subsequent to the capture of the party, I accompanied Captain J. E. B. Stuart and the battalion he commanded to the Kennedy farm ; and there, by another strange chance, I came into possession of a number of papers belonging to your father. These I afterwards delivered to Governor Wise, upon his requisition ; but there yet remains in my possession an old manifold letter-writer which belonged to your father. In this are several letters, in his handwriting, entitled "Sambo's Mistakes," written, apparently, for publication, and addressed "To the Editor of the 'Ramshorn.'" They contain a satirical summing up, related in the first person, of the mistakes and weaknesses common to the colored people. This book, together with a common carpet-bag, a red and white check blanket, a rifle, pistol, and pike, — all of which I found at the Kennedy house, — I kept, and yet have, I think, as mementos of that tragic affair. Two or three years ago I read in one of the magazines Owen Brown's relation of his escape from the Ferry, and was minded to supplement it with my narrative of the capture and its incidents, but the many demands upon my time prevented my doing so.

I am a South Carolinian, and at the time of the raid was very deeply imbued with the political prejudices of my State ; but the serenity, calm courage, and devotion to duty which your father and his followers then manifested impressed me very profoundly. It is impossible not to feel respect for men who offer up their lives in support of their convictions ; and the earnestness of my respect I put upon record in a Baltimore paper the day succeeding the event. I gave your brother a cup of water to quench his thirst (this was at about 7.30 on the morning of the capture), and improvised a couch for him out of a bench, with a pair of overalls for a pillow. I remember how he looked, — singularly handsome, even through the grime of his all-day struggles, and the

he was mortally wounded at the same moment, and died in a short time afterwards. I believe this information is correct; but I have no means of knowing from any acquaintances, not being allowed intercourse with other prisoners, except one. The same is true as to the death of one of my own sons. I have no doubt but both are dead.   Your friend,   JOHN BROWN.

CHARLESTOWN, JEFFERSON COUNTY, VA., Nov. 29, 1859.
S. E. SEWALL, ESQ., Boston.

MY DEAR SIR, — Your most kind letter of the 24th instant is received. It does indeed give me " pleasure " and the greatest encouragement to know of any efforts that have been made in behalf of my poor and deeply afflicted family. It takes from my mind the greatest cause of sadness I have experienced during my imprisonment here. I feel quite cheerful, and ready to die. I can only say, for want of time, May the God of the oppressed and the poor in great mercy remember all those to whom we are so deeply indebted !

Farewell !   Your friend,   JOHN BROWN.

CHARLESTOWN, VA., Nov. 30, 1859.
DR. THOS. H. WEBB, Boston.[1]

MY DEAR SIR, — I would most gladly comply with your request most kindly made in your letter of the 26th inst., but it came too late. It is out of my power. Farewell: God bless you !

                    Your friend,   JOHN BROWN.

intense suffering which he must have endured. He was very calm, and of a tone and look very gentle. The look with which he searched my very heart I can never forget. One sentence of our conversation will give you the key-note to the whole. I asked him, " What brought you here ? " He replied, very patiently, " Duty, sir." After a pause, I again asked : " Is it then your idea of duty to shoot men down upon their own hearth-stones for defending their rights ? " He answered : " I am dying ; I cannot discuss the question ; I did my duty, as I saw it." This conversation occurred in the compartment of the engine-house adjoining that in which the defence had been made, and was listened to by young Coppoc with perfect equanimity, and by Shields Green with uncontrollable terror.

I met at Pittsburg, some years ago, Mr. Richard Realf (if that is the name ; he was connected with the " Commercial " of that city) ; and on relating my experience, he not only expressed much interest in it, but said he thought the surviving members of John Brown's family would be gratified to hear what I had to tell. 'T is in remembrance of Colonel Realf that I obey the impulse to write you now. I do so with deep earnestness and with respect. The war, in which I took part on the Southern side, eradicated many errors of political opinion, and gave growth to many established truths not then recognized. I have, for my own part, no regrets for my humble share in the revolt ; but I have now to say, that I firmly believe the war was ordained of God for the extermination of slavery ; and that your father was an elected instrument for the commencement of that good work.   I am, sir, with respect.
                                        Yours truly,   C. W. TAYLEURE.

[1] This note refers to the publication of a photograph of Brown, for the benefit of his family, — the same mentioned in the letter to T. Hyatt.

John Brown's Last Letter to his Family.

CHARLESTOWN PRISON, JEFFERSON COUNTY, VA.,
Nov. 30, 1859.

MY DEARLY BELOVED WIFE, SONS, AND DAUGHTERS, EVERY
ONE, — As I now begin probably what is the last letter I shall ever
write to any of you, I conclude to write to all at the same time. I
will mention some little matters particularly applicable to little
property concerns in another place.

I recently received a letter from my wife, from near Philadelphia,
dated November 22, by which it would seem that she was about
giving up the idea of seeing me again. I had written her to come
on if she felt equal to the undertaking, but I do not know that she
will get my letter in time. It was on her own account, chiefly, that
I asked her to stay back. At first I had a most strong desire to see
her again, but there appeared to be very serious objections; and
should we never meet in this life, I trust that she will in the end be
satisfied it was for the best at least, if not most for her comfort.

I am waiting the hour of my public murder with great composure
of mind and cheerfulness; feeling the strong assurance that in no
other possible way could I be used to so much advantage to the
cause of God and of humanity, and that nothing that either I or all
my family have sacrificed or suffered will be lost. The reflection
that a wise and merciful as well as just and holy God rules not only
the affairs of this world but of all worlds, is a rock to set our feet
upon under all circumstances, — even those more severely trying ones
in which our own feelings and wrongs have placed us. I have now
no doubt but that our seeming disaster will ultimately result in the
most glorious success. So, my dear shattered and broken family, be
of good cheer, and believe and trust in God with all your heart
and with all your soul; for He doeth all things well. Do not feel
ashamed on my account, nor for one moment despair of the cause or
grow weary of well-doing. I bless God I never felt stronger confidence in the certain and near approach of a bright morning and glorious day than I have felt, and do now feel, since my confinement
here. I am endeavoring to return, like a poor prodigal as I am, to
my Father, against whom I have always sinned, in the hope that
he may kindly and forgivingly meet me, though a very great way
off.

Oh, my dear wife and children, would to God you could know
how I have been travailing in birth for you all, that no one of you
may fail of the grace of God through Jesus Christ; that no one of
you may be blind to the truth and glorious light of his Word, in

which life and immortality are brought to light. I beseech you, every one, to make the Bible your daily and nightly study, with a child-like, honest, candid, teachable spirit of love and respect for your husband and father. And I beseech the God of my fathers to open all your eyes to the discovery of the truth. You cannot imagine how much you may soon need the consolations of the Christian religion. Circumstances like my own for more than a month past have convinced me, beyond all doubt, of my own great need of some theories treasured up, when our prejudices are excited, our vanity worked up to the highest pitch. Oh, do not trust your eternal all upon the boisterous ocean, without even a helm or compass to aid you in steering! I do not ask of you to throw away your reason; I only ask you to make a candid, sober use of your reason.

My dear young children, will you listen to this last poor admonition of one who can only love you? Oh, be determined at once to give your whole heart to God, and let nothing shake or alter that resolution. You need have no fears of regretting it. Do not be vain and thoughtless, but sober-minded; and let me entreat you all to love the whole remnant of our once great family. Try and build up again your broken walls, and to make the utmost of every stone that is left. Nothing can so tend to make life a blessing as the consciousness that your life and example bless and leave others stronger. Still, it is ground of the utmost comfort to my mind to know that so many of you as have had the opportunity have given some proof of your fidelity to the great family of men. Be faithful unto death: from the exercise of habitual love to man it cannot be very hard to love his Maker.

I must yet insert the reason for my firm belief in the divine inspiration of the Bible, notwithstanding I am, perhaps, naturally sceptical, — certainly not credulous. I wish all to consider it most thoroughly when you read that blessed book, and see whether you cannot discover such evidence yourselves. It is the purity of heart, filling our minds as well as work and actions, which is everywhere insisted on, that distinguishes it from all the other teachings, that commends it to my conscience. Whether my heart be willing and obedient or not, the inducement that it holds out is another reason of my conviction of its truth and genuineness; but I do not here omit this my last argument on the Bible, that eternal life is what my soul is panting after this moment. I mention this as a reason for endeavoring to leave a valuable copy of the Bible, to be carefully preserved in remembrance of me, to so many of my posterity, instead of some other book at equal cost.

I beseech you all to live in habitual contentment with moderate circumstances and gains of worldly store, and earnestly to teach this to your children and children's children after you, by example as well as precept. Be determined to know by experience, as soon as may be, whether Bible instruction is of divine origin or not. Be sure to owe no man anything, but to love one another. John Rogers wrote to his children : " Abhor that arrant whore of Rome." John Brown writes to his children to abhor, with undying hatred also, that sum of all villanies, — slavery. Remember, " he that is slow to anger is better than the mighty," and " he that ruleth his spirit than he that taketh a city." Remember also that " they being wise shall shine, and they that turn many to righteousness, as the stars for ever and ever."

And now, dearly beloved family, to God and the work of his grace I commend you all.

Your affectionate husband and father,

JOHN BROWN.

CHARLESTOWN, JEFFERSON COUNTY, VA., Nov. 30, 1859.

MRS. MARY GALE (or the writer of the writing).[1]

DEAR FRIEND, — I have only time to give you the names of those that I know were killed of my company at Harper's Ferry, or that are said to have been killed ; namely, two Thompsons, two Browns, J. Anderson, J. H. Kagi, Stewart Taylor, A. Hazlett, W. H. Leman, and three colored men. Would most gladly give you further information had I the time and ability.

Your friend,

JOHN BROWN.

CHARLESTOWN PRISON, JEFFERSON COUNTY, VA.,
Dec. 1, 1859.

To MR. JAMES FOREMAN.[2]

MY DEAR FRIEND, — I have only time to say I got your kind letter of the 26th of November this evening. Am very grateful for all the good feelings expressed by yourself and wife. May God abundantly bless and save you all ! I am very cheerful, in hopes of entering on a better state of existence in a few hours, through infinite grace in Christ Jesus my Lord. Remember " the poor that cry," and " them that are in bonds as bound with them."

Your friend as ever,

JOHN BROWN.

---

[1] Written to the sister of Charles Plummer Tidd, one of those who escaped with Owen Brown.

[2] A former apprentice when Brown was a tanner in Pennsylvania.

On the day before his death, when with his wife, the conversation turned upon matters of business, which Brown desired to have arranged after his death. He gave his wife all the letters and papers needed for this purpose, and read to her the will which had been drawn up for him by Mr. Hunter, carefully explaining every portion of it.

JOHN BROWN'S WILL.

CHARLESTOWN, JEFFERSON COUNTY, VA., Dec. 1, 1859.

I give to my son John Brown, Jr., my surveyor's compass and other surveyor's articles, if found; also, my old granite monument, now at North Elba, N. Y., to receive upon its two sides a further inscription, as I will hereafter direct; said stone monument, however, to remain at North Elba so long as any of my children and my wife may remain there as residents.

I give to my son Jason Brown my silver watch, with my name engraved on inner case.

I give to my son Owen Brown my double-spring opera-glass, and my rifle-gun (if found), presented to me at Worcester, Mass. It is globe-sighted and new. I give, also, to the same son $50 in cash, to be paid him from the proceeds of my father's estate, in consideration of his terrible suffering in Kansas and his crippled condition from his childhood.

I give to my son Salmon Brown $50 in cash, to be paid him from my father's estate, as an offset to the first two cases above named.

I give to my daughter Ruth Thompson my large old Bible, containing the family record.

I give to each of my sons, and to each of my other daughters, my son-in-law, Henry Thompson, and to each of my daughters-in-law, as good a copy of the Bible as can be purchased at some bookstore in New York or Boston, at a cost of $5 each in cash, to be paid out of the proceeds of my father's estate.

I give to each of my grandchildren that may be living when my father's estate is settled, as good a copy of the Bible as can be purchased (as above) at a cost of $3 each.

All the Bibles to be purchased at one and the same time for cash, on the best terms.

I desire to have $50 each paid out of the final proceeds of my father's estate to the following named persons, to wit: To Allan Hammond, Esq., of Rockville, Tolland County, Conn., or to George Kellogg, Esq., former agent of the New England Company at that place, for the use and benefit of that company. Also, $50 to Silas

Havens, formerly of Lewisburg, Summit County, Ohio, if he can be found. Also, $50 to a man of Stark County, Ohio, at Canton, who sued my father in his lifetime, through Judge Humphrey and Mr. Upson of Akron, to be paid by J. R. Brown to the man in person, if he can be found; his name I cannot remember. My father made a compromise with the man by taking our house and lot at Munroville. I desire that any remaining balance that may become my due from my father's estate may be paid in equal amounts to my wife and to each of my children, and to the widows of Watson and Oliver Brown, by my brother.   JOHN BROWN.

JOHN AVIS, Witness.

CODICIL.

CHARLESTOWN, JEFFERSON COUNTY, VA., Dec. 2, 1859.

It is my desire that my wife have all my personal property not previously disposed of by me; and the entire use of all my landed property during her natural life; and that, after her death, the proceeds of such land be equally divided between all my then living children; and that what would be a child's share be given to the children of each of my two sons who fell at Harper's Ferry; and that a child's share be divided among the children of my now living children who may die before their mother (my present beloved wife). No formal will can be of use when my expressed wishes are made known to my dutiful and beloved family.   JOHN BROWN.

MY DEAR WIFE, — I have time to enclose the within and the above, which I forgot yesterday, and to bid you another farewell. "Be of good cheer," and God Almighty bless, save, comfort, guide, and keep you to the end!

                    Your affectionate husband,   JOHN BROWN.

This was undoubtedly the last work of the old hero with his pen. He had previously given directions for an inscription on his tombstone, and now sent his wife this paper, which was brought to Mrs. Brown after the execution: —

TO BE INSCRIBED ON THE OLD FAMILY MONUMENT AT NORTH ELBA.

OLIVER BROWN, born ——, 1839, was killed at Harper's Ferry, Va., Oct. 17, 1859.

WATSON BROWN, born ——, 1835, was wounded at Harper's Ferry, Oct. 17, and died Oct. 19, 1859.

(My wife can fill up the blank dates as above.)

JOHN BROWN, born May 9, 1800, was executed at Charlestown, Va., Dec. 2, 1859.

Brown's frequent mention in these letters of his opportunity to do good by preaching the truth to men who came
to see him out of curiosity, or to labor with him for his sins,
demands some explanation. Although fettered and guarded
as no man had ever been in Virginia since the capture of
John Smith by Powhatan and his Indians, John Brown was
visited by the sachems and priests of the tribe then domi-
nant in Powhatan's country, and by many good men who
were moved by his courage and fidelity. To such persons
Brown applied his touchstone of sincerity, and treated them
as their character deserved, whatever their opinions. He
was, of course, often visited by Virginia clergymen and
itinerant preachers, desirous of praying with him and of
converting him from his errors. One of these afterward
said that when he offered to pray with Brown the old man
asked if he was willing to fight, in case of need, for the freedom of the slaves. Receiving a negative reply, Brown said:
" I will thank you to leave me alone ; your prayers would
be an abomination to my God." To another he said that he
" would not insult God by bowing down in prayer with any
one who had the blood of the slave on his skirts." A Methodist preacher named March having argued to Brown in
his cell in favor of slavery as " a Christian institution," his
hearer grew impatient and replied : " My dear sir, you know
nothing about Christianity; you will have to learn its A,
B, C; I find you quite ignorant of what the word Christianity means." Seeing that his visitor was disconcerted by
such plain speaking, Brown added, " I respect you as a gentleman, of course ; but it is as a *heathen* gentleman." [1]   To

----

[1] This "heathen gentleman " seems to have left a successor at Charlestown, — the Presbyterian minister there in 1882, Abner C. Hopkins by
name, who in that year wrote to the English author Thomas Hughes, cor-
recting certain errors of fact concerning Brown, and then adding, *ex mero
motu*, and by way of certifying his own Christian spirit : —

" *We know*, and *records prove*, that John Brown, after full and fair trial before the
proper civil tribunal, was duly convicted of murders, including a negro slave's. . . .
The very copy of the Bible, owned and used by him in jail here, lies before me. Its
passages touching 'oppression,' etc., are heavily and frequently pencilled, but no *pencil
mark distinguishes or emphasizes a single passage that is distinctively Christian*. He was
religious, but not *Christian* ; religion was the crutch on which his fanaticism walked.
It was the 'higher law ' religion, under whose baleful influence many tears have been
wrung from the innocent, and the buttresses of governments have fairly crumbled, and

a lady who visited him in prison he said: "I do not believe
I shall deny my Lord and Master Jesus Christ, as I should
if I denied my principles against slavery. Why, I preach
against it all the time; Captain Avis knows I do;" whereat
his jailer smiled and said, "Yes." A citizen of Charlestown, named Blessing, had dressed Brown's wounds while
in prison, and had shown him other kind attentions, for
which Brown, who was very scrupulous about acknowledging and returning favors, desired to make him some acknowledgment. On one of the last days of November, therefore,
in the last week of his life, Brown sent for Mr. Blessing,
and asked him to accept his pocket Bible as a token of gratitude. In this book, which was a cheap edition in small
print, much worn by use, Brown had marked many hundred
passages bearing witness more or less directly against human slavery, by turning down the corner of a page and by
heavy pencillings in the margin. On the fly-leaf he had
written this: —

To JOHN F. BLESSING, of Charlestown, Va., with the best wishes
of the undersigned, and his sincere thanks for many acts of kindness
received. There is no commentary in the world so good, in order to
a right understanding of this blessed book, as an honest, childlike,
and teachable spirit.

                                                JOHN BROWN.

CHARLESTOWN, Nov. 29, 1859.

He had written his own name as owner of the book on
the opposite page, and immediately following it was this
inscription : —

the order and stability of society have been made to tremble on your continent and ours.
It has found further development in assassinations, — of the Czar in Russia, of the Emperor in Germany, of your own Lord Lieutenant and Secretary in Ireland, and of our
own President. There are many points of resemblance between the behavior of John
Brown and Guiteau; both claimed to be 'God's man,' to be doing God's work, to be
receiving strength from God; and Guiteau exceeded Brown in the resolution with
which he met death."

"New Presbyter is but old priest writ large." I will venture to call
this priest's attention to one or two passages "distinctively Christian."
"But the chief priests and elders persuaded the multitude that they
should ask Barabbas and destroy Jesus." — *Matt. xxvii.* 20. "Then cried
they all again, saying, Not this man, but Barabbas. Now Barabbas was a
robber." — *John xviii.* 40.

" The leaves were turned down by him while in prison at Charlestown. But a small part of those passages which in the most positive language condemn oppression and violence are marked."

Possibly the very last paper written by John Brown was this sentence, which he handed to one of his guards in the jail on the morning of his execution : —

CHARLESTOWN, VA., Dec. 2, 1859.

I, John Brown, am now quite *certain* that the crimes of this *guilty land* will never be purged away but with *blood*. I had, as I now think vainly, flattered myself that without very much bloodshed it might be done.

"Without the shedding of blood there is no remission of sins." This was John Brown's old-fashioned theology, which the nation was so soon to verify by a fierce but salutary civil war. In my earliest serious conversation with him, in January, 1857, when he assured me that Christ's Golden Rule and Jefferson's Declaration meant the same thing, he said further : "I have always been delighted with the doctrine that all men are created equal; and to my mind it is like the Saviour's command, 'Thou shalt love thy neighbor as thyself,' for how can we do that unless our neighbor is equal to ourself ? That is the doctrine, sir; and rather than have that fail in the world, or in these States, 't would be better for a whole generation to die a violent death. Better that heaven and earth pass away than that one jot or one tittle of this be not fulfilled." Such was the faith in which he died.

CHAPTER XVII.

THE DEATH AND CHARACTER OF JOHN BROWN.

THE prison-life of Brown may be inferred from his letters ; but there were sayings of his, during the month
between his sentence and its execution, which have been
reported by those who talked with him in his fetters.   To
Mrs. Spring, of New York, who obtained admission to his
cell November 6, he said : "I do not now reproach myself
for my failure ; I did what I could.   I think I cannot better
serve the cause I love so much than to die for it ; and in
my death I may do more than in my life.   The sentence
they have pronounced against me does not disturb me in the
least ; this is not the first time I have looked death in the
face.   I sleep as peacefully as an infant ; or if I am wake-
ful, glorious thoughts come to me, entertaining my mind.   I
do not believe I shall deny my Lord and Master Jesus
Christ, in this prison or on the scaffold ; but I should do so if
I denied my principles against slavery.   I have been trained
to hardships," added Brown, "but I have one unconquérable
weakness ; I have always been more afraid of going into an
evening party of ladies and gentlemen than of meeting a
company of men with guns."   An old Pennsylvania neighbor, Mr. Lowry, was permitted to see him in prison, and
asked him about his Kansas campaigns.   "Time and the
honest verdict of posterity," said Brown, "will approve
every act of mine to prevent slavery from being established
in Kansas.   I never shed the blood of a fellow-man, except
in self-defence, or in promotion of a righteous cause."   During this conversation Governor Wise was reviewing the Virginia militia near the prison, and the drums and trumpets
made a great noise.   His friend said : "Does this martial
music annoy you ? "   "Not in the least," said Brown, "it is

inspiring.[1] Tell my friends without that I am cheerful."[2]
A son of Governor Wise soon after accompanied a Virginia
colonel to Brown's cell, when the colonel asked him if he
desired the presence of a clergyman to give him "the consolations of religion." Brown repeated what he had said to
the Methodists, — that he did not recognize as Christians
any slaveholders or defenders of slavery, lay or clerical; adding that he would as soon be attended to the scaffold by
"blacklegs" or robbers of the worst kind as by slaveholding
ministers; if he had his choice he would rather be followed
to his "public murder," as he termed his execution, by
"barefooted, barelegged, ragged slave children and their
old gray-headed slave mother," than by such clergymen. "I
should feel much prouder of such an escort," he said, "and
I wish I could have it." From this saying of his, several
times repeated, no doubt arose the legend, that on his way
to the gallows he took up a little slave-child, kissed it, and
gave it back to its mother's arms.[3] On the same day with
this interview, Brown was again questioned concerning the
Pottawatomie executions, and said, as he uniformly had done
since that deed, "I did not kill any of those men, but I

[1] "Virginia," said Wendell Phillips at Brooklyn, while Brown lay in
prison, "is only another Algiers. The barbarous horde who gag each
other, imprison women for teaching children to read, prohibit the Bible,
sell men on the auction-block, abolish marriage, condemn half their women to prostitution, and devote themselves to the breeding of human
beings for sale, is only a larger and blacker Algiers. The only prayer of
a true man for such is, 'Gracious heaven! unless they repent, send soon
their Exmouth and Decatur.'" It was not long till Grant and Sheridan.

[2] "A music heard by thee alone
    To works as noble led thee on."
                                    EMERSON'S *Threnody.*

[3] It was physically impossible that this should have happened, for before
Brown left the jail his hands were fastened behind his back, as usual with
condemned criminals. His jailer, Avis, now dead, testified April 25, 1882,
thus: "Brown was between Sheriff Campbell and me, and a guard of soldiers surrounded him and allowed no person to come between them and the
prisoner, from the jail to the scaffold, except his escorts. . . . The only
thing that he said at or on the scaffold was to take leave of us, and then,
just about the time the noose was adjusted, he said, 'Be quick.' I did
not think his bearing on the scaffold was conspicuous for its heroism, — yet
not cowardly."

approved of their killing." He expressed pleasure that his body was ordered by Governor Wise to be delivered to his wife for burial at North Elba, and requested his jailer to assist Mrs. Brown, not only in this, but in getting together the remains of his sons and the other farmers of North Elba who had been slain at Harper's Ferry, for burial with him, — expressing the wish that their bodies should be burned, and the bones and ashes conveyed to his Adirondac home.[1] In regard to his own rescue from prison he had previously said : " I doubt if I ought to encourage any attempt to save my life. I may be wrong, but I think that my great object will be nearer its accomplishment by my death than by my life. I must give some thought to this." Having reflected on it, he said a few days before his death : " I am sure my sons cannot look forward to my fate without some effort to rescue me ; but this only in case I am allowed to remain in prison for some time with no more than ordinary precautions against escape. No such attempt will be made in view of the large military force now upon guard." In fact, he had intimated to his friends that he did not wish to be rescued,[2] and it soon became evident to all, as it was directly revealed to Brown, that his death, like Samson's, was to be his last and greatest victory.

[1] He did not make this suggestion in regard to his own remains, but only of those who had then been dead six weeks ; nor did he suggest it to Mrs. Brown at all, as she told me in 1882. She added that the published account of her interview with her husband the day before his death was incorrect.

[2] I was in daily communication with Brown's friends during November, and learned this with certainty. Mr. Emerson proposed that some gentlemen from the North should visit Governor Wise, and urge upon him the reprieve of Brown, and Mr. Alcott offered to go on this errand. On the 10th of November I answered Mr. Emerson's suggestion thus : —

" There is hope in every effort to save Brown, but not much, as it would seem, in the representations of a private gentleman to Governor Wise, who is in this matter the servant of others. It is the *Bellua multorum capitum* of Virginia that will execute the sentence if it is done ; and *that* is perhaps implacable. *Escape*, difficult as it seems, is probably Brown's best chance for life. If a reprieve, or an arrest of judgment for another month were possible, a rescue would not be so hard to manage. Brown's heroic character is having its influence on his keepers, as we learn; but at present he does not *wish* to escape."

> " Living or dying, thou hast fulfilled
>   The work for which thou wast foretold
>   To Israel, and now liest victorious
>   Among thy slain, self-killed, —
>   Not willingly, but tangled in the fold
>   Of dire necessity ; whose law in death conjoined
>   Thee with thy slaughtered foes, in number more
>   Than all thy life had slain before."

It was perhaps through the Russells, of Boston, the first of his personal friends to visit him, that we learned his intuition concerning a rescue. Judge Russell and his wife hastened from Boston as soon as it seemed expedient for any of his Antislavery associates to attempt the difficult task of an interview with Brown, — the former going to counsel with him as a lawyer in his defence, and Mrs. Russell, with a woman's instinct, joining in this journey. She took her needle with her, mended his torn and cut garments, sent the guard out of the room for a clothes-brush, and exchanged a few words privately with the martyr. Of this visit Judge Russell says : —

" I was just in time to hear the sentence of death pronounced on Brown, and to hear that magnificent speech in which, instead of assuming that his hearers were Christians, and arguing on that basis, he said : ' I see a book kissed here which I suppose to be the Bible, or at least the New Testament,' from which he inferred that Christianity was not quite unknown. I then went with Mrs. Russell to see him in the jail, and found him in the best of spirits. He said : ' I have no fault to find with the manner of my death ; the disgrace of hanging does not trouble me in the least. Indeed, I know that the very errors by which my scheme was marred were decreed before the world was made. I had no more to do with the course I pursued than a shot leaving a cannon has to do with the spot where it shall fall.' He was satisfied with what he had done."

I pass over the farewell between Brown and his wife the day before his death ; it was simple and heroic, in keeping with the character of both. They supped with the jailer in his own apartment ; and thus, perhaps for the first time, the condemned man was allowed to leave his cell, after sentence and before the day of execution. Upon that morning, Dec. 2, 1859, he was led from his cell to say farewell

to his companions. Copeland and Shields Green were confined together ; Cook and Coppoc were in another cell, and
Stephens by himself. To the two faithful colored men
Brown said: " Stand up like men, and do not betray your
friends ! " To Cook, who had made a confession, Brown
said: " You have made false statements, — that I sent you
to Harper's Ferry: you knew I protested against your coming." Cook demurred, but dropped his head, and replied at
last, " Captain Brown, you and I remember differently."
To Coppoc, Brown said: " You also made false statements,
but I am glad to hear you have contradicted them.   Stand
up like a man ! " He shook the hands of all, and gave to
each a small silver coin for remembrance. With Stephens
his interview was more intimate ; for he had greatly relied
on this stout soldier.   " Good by, Captain," said Stephens ;
" I know you are going to a better land."   " I know I am,"
was the reply ; " bear up, as you have done, and never betray your friends." Brown would not visit the sixth prisoner, Hazlett, — always persisting that he did not know
such a man.[1]

Meantime the soldiers of Virginia, more than two thousand in number, were mustered in the field where the gallows had been erected, with cannon and cavalry, and all the
pomp of war. At eleven o'clock Brown came forth from
his prison, walking firmly and cheerfully, and mounted the
wagon which was to carry him to the scaffold. He sat beside his jailer, and cast his eyes over the town, the soldiery,
the near fields, and the distant hills, behind which rose the
mountains of the Blue Ridge. He glanced at the sun and
sky, taking his leave of earth, and said to his companions:
" This is a beautiful country ; I have not cast my eyes over
it before, — that is, in this direction." Reaching the scaffold, he ascended the steps, and was the first to stand upon
it, — erect and calm, and with a smile on his face. With
his pinioned hands he took off his hat, cast it on the scaffold beside him, and thanked his jailer again for his kindness,

---

[1] One of Brown's prison guards says :   " He was a brave man, and had
the utmost contempt for a coward. He did not seem to care what became
of him after the capture, but his whole mind seemed to be bent on saving
the men who were taken with him ; and he pretended not to know them."

submitting quietly to be closer pinioned and to have the
cap drawn over his eyes and the rope adjusted to his neck.
" I can't see, gentlemen," said he ; "you must lead me ; "
and he was placed on the drop of the gallows. "I am ready
at any time, — do not keep me waiting," were his last reported words. No dying speech was permitted to him, nor
were the citizens allowed to approach the scaffold, which was
surrounded only by militia.[1] He desired to make no speech,
but only to endure his fate with dignity and in silence.
The ceremonies of his public murder were duly performed ;
and when his body had swung for nearly an hour on the
gibbet, in sight of earth and heaven, for a witness against
our nation, it was lowered to its coffin and delivered to his
widow, who received and accompanied it through shuddering cities to the forest hillside where it lies buried.
The most eloquent lips in America pronounced his funeral
eulogy beside this grave ; while in hundreds of cities and
villages his death was sadly commemorated. The Civil
War followed hard upon his execution ; and the place of his
capture and death became the frequent battle-ground of the
fratricidal armies. Not until freedom was declared, and
the slaves liberated as Brown had planned, — by force, —
was victory assured to the cause of the country.

I knew John Brown well. He was what all his speeches,
letters, and actions avouch him, — a simple, brave, heroic
person, incapable of anything selfish or base. But above
and beyond these personal qualities, he was what we may
best term a *historic* character ; that is, he had, like Cromwell,
a certain predestined relation to the political crisis of his
time, for which his character fitted him, and which, had he
striven against it, he could not avoid.   Like Cromwell and
all the great Calvinists, he was an unquestioning believer in
God's fore-ordination and the divine guidance of human

---

[1] Among the Virginia militia, pompously parading, who surrounded the
scaffold, was John Wilkes Booth (afterward the assassin of Abraham Lincoln), who was then an actor at Richmond, and left his theatre to join Company F from that city. This fact is given by the Virginia correspondent
of the "New York Tribune," Nov. 28, 1859. Booth assisted, therefore,
at the two chief murders of his time, — "Washington slaying Spartacus,"
as Victor Hugo said, and Sicarius slaying the second Washington.

affairs. Of course, he could not rank with Cromwell or with many inferior men in leadership; but in this God-appointed, inflexible devotion to his object in life he was inferior to no man; and he rose in fame far above more gifted persons because of this very fixedness and simplicity of character. His renown is secure.

A few words may be given to the personal traits of this hero. When I first saw him, he was in his fifty-seventh year, and though touched with age and its infirmities, was still vigorous and active, and of an aspect which would have made him distinguished anywhere among men who know how to recognize courage and greatness of mind. At that time he was close shaven, and no flowing beard, as in later years, softened the expression of his firm wide mouth and positive chin. That beard, long and gray, which nearly all his portraits now show, added a picturesque finish to a face that was in all its features severe and masculine, yet with a latent tenderness. His eyes were those of an eagle, — piercing blue-gray in color, not very large, looking out from under brows

"Of dauntless courage and considerate pride,"

and were alternately flashing with energy, or drooping and hooded like the eyes of an eagle. His hair was dark-brown, sprinkled with gray, short and bristling, and shooting back from a forehead of middle height and breadth; his nose was aquiline; his ears large; his frame angular; his voice deep and metallic; his walk positive and intrepid, though commonly slow. His manner was modest, and in a large company diffident; he was by no means fluent of speech, but his words were always to the point, and his observations original, direct, and shrewd. His mien was serious and patient rather than cheerful; it betokened the "sad wise valor" which Herbert praises; but though earnest and often anxious, it was never depressed. In short, he was then, to the eye of insight, what he afterward seemed to the world, — a brave and resolved man, conscious of a work laid upon him, and confident that he should accomplish it. His figure was tall, slender, and commanding; his bearing military; and his garb showed a singular blending of the

soldier and the deacon. He had laid aside in Chicago
the torn and faded summer garments which he wore
throughout his Kansas campaign, and I saw him at one
of those rare periods in his life when his clothes were
new. He wore a complete suit of brown broadcloth or ker-
seymere, cut in the fashion of a dozen years before, and
giving him the air of a respectable deacon in a rural parish.
But instead of a collar he had on a high stock of patent
leather, such as soldiers used to wear, a gray military over-
coat with a cape, and a fur cap. He was, in fact, a Puritan
soldier, such as were common in Cromwell's day, though not
often seen since. Yet his heart was averse to bloodshed,
gentle, tender, and devout.

Mr. Leonard, already quoted, who knew him at the age
of fifty, says : —

"It is almost impossible to convey by writing his appearance. I
can see it plainly, — that firm, decided set of the mouth, a certain
nervous twitch of the head ; but the flash of his eye, who can describe it ? It spoke the soul of the man, and carried conviction to
every one that he was in thorough earnest. In Redpath's 'Life'
there is a good engraving of the old man, when he had drawn himself up into his lofty look, which he sometimes did ; but generally
he carried his head pitched forward and a little down, and shoved his
right shoulder forward in walking. And he could look pleasant, —
as I have witnessed many a time, when I have been bantering him
about something."

Frederick Douglass says : —

"In person he was lean, strong, and sinewy ; of the best New
England mould, built for times of trouble, fitted to grapple with the
flintiest hardships. Clad in plain American woollen, shod in boots of
cowhide leather, and wearing a cravat of the same substantial material ; under six feet high, less than a hundred and fifty pounds in
weight, aged about fifty, — he presented a figure straight and sym-
metrical as a mountain pine. His bearing was singularly impressive. His head was not large, but compact and high. His hair was
coarse, strong, slightly gray, and closely trimmed, and grew low on
his forehead. His face was smoothly shaved, and revealed a strong
square mouth, supported by a broad and prominent chin. His eyes
were bluish gray, and in conversation they were full of light and
fire. When on the street, he moved with a long, springing, race-

horse step, absorbed by his own reflections, neither seeking nor shunning observation."

Such were his outward traits and belongings. The inward man was of singular faith and constancy. Of his last few months in life Mr. Wilder speaks thus : —

" Think of the slow movement to the Kennedy farm, the mystery, the anxiety about money, the opposition of Douglass, the resignation of his leadership by Brown, bad health, — in that most dispiriting of all diseases, the ague, — and yet the man goes forward ! What courage, what faith ! Common men live for years in despair, with only ordinary bad luck to contend with ; but here is a man absolutely alone, exiled from family, among hostile strangers, where barbarism is made popular by law and by fashion, — yet never in despair. Why this contrast ? He believed in God and justice, and in nothing else ; we believe in everything else, but not in God."

It is easy now to perceive the true mission of Brown, and to measure the force of the avalanche set in motion by him. But to the vision of genius and the illuminated moral sense this was equally perceptible in 1859–60 ; and it was declared, in words already cited, by Emerson, Alcott, and Thoreau. No less clearly and prophetically was it declared by Victor Hugo, and by the saintly pastor of Wayland, Edmond Sears. On the day of Brown's execution, and in the midst of the funeral services we were holding at Concord, Mr. Sears, who had made the opening prayer, wrote these lines in the Town Hall,[1] where Brown had twice addressed the sons of those yeomen who fought at Concord Bridge : —

> " Not any spot six feet by two
>   Will hold a man like thee ;
> John Brown will tramp the shaking earth
>   From Blue Ridge to the sea,
> Till the strong angel come at last
>   And opes each dungeon door,
> And God's Great Charter holds and waves
>   O'er all his humble poor.

[1] Mr. Alcott's Diary (Dec. 2, 1859) says : " Ellen Emerson sends me her fair copy of the Martyr Service. At 2 p. m. we meet at the Town Hall, our own townspeople present mostly, and many from the adjoining towns. Simon Brown is chairman ; the readings are by Thoreau, Emerson, C. Bowers, and Alcott ; and Sanborn's ' Dirge ' is sung by the company,

> "And then the humble poor will come
>   In that far-distant day,
> And from the felon's nameless grave
>   They 'll brush the leaves away ;
> And gray old men will point the spot
>   Beneath the pine-tree shade,
> As children ask with streaming eyes
>   Where Old John Brown is laid."

On the same day, from his place of exile in Guernsey, Victor Hugo thus addressed the American republic : —

"At the thought of the United States of America, a majestic form rises in the mind, — Washington. In this country of Washington what is now taking place ? There are slaves in the South; and this most monstrous of inconsistencies offends the logical conscience of the North. To free these black slaves, John Brown, a white man, a free man, began the work of their deliverance in Virginia. A Puritan, austerely religious, inspired by the evangel, ' Christ hath set us free,' he raised the cry of emancipation. But the slaves, unmanned by servitude, made no response; for slavery stops the ears of the soul. John Brown, thus left alone, began the contest. With a handful of heroic men he kept up the fight ; riddled with bullets, his two youngest sons, sacred martyrs, falling at his side, he was at last captured. His trial ? It took place, not in Turkey, but in America. Such things are not done with impunity under the eyes of the civilized world. The conscience of mankind is an open eye; let the court at Charlestown understand — Hunter and Parker, the slaveholding jurymen, the whole population of Virginia — that they are watched. This has not been done in a corner. John Brown, condemned to death, is to be hanged to-day. His hangman is not the attorney Hunter, nor the judge Parker, nor Governor Wise, nor the little State of Virginia, — his hangman (we shudder to think it and say it !) is the whole American republic. . . . Politically speaking, the murder of Brown will be an irrevocable mistake. It will deal the Union a concealed wound, which will finally sunder the States. Let America know and consider that there is one thing more shocking than Cain killing Abel, — it is Washington killing Spartacus."

standing. The bells are not rung. I think not more than one or two of Brown's friends wished them to be ; I did not. It was more fitting to signify our sorrow in the subdued way, and silently, than by any clamor of steeples or the awakening of angry feelings or any conflict, as needless as unamiable, between neighbors. The services are affecting and impressive, distinguished by modesty, simplicity, and earnestness, — worthy alike of the occasion and of the man."

A few months later (March 30, 1860) Victor Hugo wrote again : —

"Slavery in all its forms will disappear. What the South slew last December was not John Brown, but Slavery. Henceforth, no matter what President Buchanan may say in his shameful message, the American Union must be considered dissolved. Between the North and the South stands the gallows of Brown. Union is no longer possible : such a crime cannot be shared."

Again, upon the triumph of Garibaldi in Sicily, Victor Hugo said (June 18, 1860) : —

"Grand are the liberators of mankind! Let them hear the grateful applause of the nations, whatever their fortune! Yesterday we gave our tears; to-day our hosannas are heard. Providence deals in these compensations. John Brown failed in America, but Garibaldi has triumphed in Europe. Mankind, shuddering at the infamous gallows of Charlestown, takes courage once more at the flashing sword of Catalafimi." [1]

Although the course of events in America did not follow the exact line anticipated by the French republican, the general result was what he had foreseen, — that the achievement and death of John Brown made future compromises between slavery and freedom impossible. What he did in Kansas for a single State, he did in Virginia for the whole nation, — nay, for the whole world.

It has been sometimes asked in what way Brown performed this great work for the world, since he won no battle, headed no party, repealed no law, and could not even save his own life from an ignominious penalty. In this respect he resembled Socrates, whose position in the world's history is yet fairly established ; and the parallel runs even closer. When Brown's friends urged upon him the desperate possibilities of a rescue, he gave no final answer,

---

[1] Victor Hugo's "Actes et Paroles pendant l'Exil" (1859–60). In the *Édition Définitive* of his complete works, which was still going through the press at his death, in 1885, the author added this note to the passages cited above : "Victor Hugo avait, à propos de John Brown, prédit la guerre civile à l'Amérique, et, à propos de Garibaldi, prédit l'unité à l'Italie. Ces deux prédictions se réalisèrent." He had a right to claim this.

until at last came this reply, — that he "would not walk
out of the prison if the door was left open." He added, as
a personal reason for this choice, that his relations with
Captain Avis, his jailer, were such that he should hold it a
breach of trust to be rescued. There is an example even
higher than that of Socrates, which history will not fail to
hold up, — that Person of whom his slayers said: "He
saved others; himself he cannot save."

Here is touched the secret of Brown's character, — absolute reliance on the Divine, entire disregard of the present,
in view of the promised future.

> " For best befriended of the God
> He who in evil times,
> Warned by an inward voice,
> Heeds not the darkness and the dread,
> Biding by his rule and choice;
> Feeling only the fiery thread
> Leading over heroic ground
> (Walled with mortal terror round)
> To the aim which him allures, —
> And the sweet heaven his deed secures."

NOTE. — In Chapter XV., pp. 537 and 548, John Brown, Jr., speaks
of an affair at "St. J.," in Missouri, which was ascribed to his father.
John Brown had nothing to do with this gallant action of his old friend
Abbott, who had rescued Branson in 1855. Briefly, the facts were these :
"Dr. John Doy, imprisoned in St. Joseph, Mo., for abducting slaves from
that State, was released July 23, 1859, by Kansas men, led by Major
James B. Abbott, now living at De Soto, Johnson County. They entered
the jail at night, under pretence of wishing to confine a horse-thief. The
rescue was admirably managed, and its moral influence throughout Missouri and the whole South was very great."

In Chapter XVI., p. 576, the expression, "He was forced to rise from
what was feared to be his dying bed," does not refer to his attitude while
the indictment was read, but to his presence in the court-room.

INDEX.

ERRATA. The name of Dr. Samuel *Cabot* is misspelled "Cobb" on page 352, *note*.

There were two Stringfellows, whose initials were "B. F." and "J. H." They are not always distinguished from each other in these pages.

University Press: John Wilson & Son, Cambridge.

CPSIA information can be obtained
at www.ICGtesting.com
Printed in the USA
BVHW070224290621
610502BV00001B/15

9 789353 604417